Sacrament an Alter

1,000 Years of Cornish

Series Editors

Benjamin Bruch, Humanities Instructor, Pacific Buddhist Academy, Honolulu

D.H. Frost, Retired Principal of Holy Cross College
and University Centre, Bury, Lancs.

Andrew Hawke, Managing Editor and
Editor-in-Chief of *Geiriadur Prifysgol Cymru*

Ann Parry Owen, Professor, Centre for Advanced Welsh
and Celtic Studies, and Senior Editor of *Geiriadur Prifysgol Cymru*

Oliver Padel, Honorary Research Fellow, Department of
Anglo-Saxon, Norse, and Celtic, University of Cambridge

Matthew Spriggs, Robyn Doohan Visiting Fellow in
Celtic Studies, University of Sydney, and Emeritus Professor,
the Australian National University, Canberra

1,000 Years of Cornish aims to publish a complete series of critical editions of writings in or about the Cornish language during the period *c.*800–1800 CE. Many of the key manuscripts have never been published in any form and thus remain largely unavailable to scholars and others interested in the language, while some of the standard editions of Cornish texts were published over 150 years ago. We envisage an Occasional Series of such texts which would build up to form a complete set of writings from the period when Cornish was spoken as a native language.

Sacrament an Alter

THE SACRAMENT OF THE ALTAR:
A CRITICAL EDITION WITH TRANSLATION

D.H. Frost

UNIVERSITY
of
EXETER
PRESS

First published in 2023 by
University of Exeter Press
Reed Hall, Streatham Drive
Exeter EX4 4QR
UK
www.exeterpress.co.uk

© D.H. Frost 2023

The right of D.H. Frost to be identified as author of this work has been asserted by him in accordance with the Copyright, Designs and Patents Act 1988.

1,000 Years of Cornish

British Library Cataloguing in Publication Data
A catalogue record for this book is available from the British Library.

https://doi.org/10.47788/HBJR7915

ISBN 978-1-80413-030-8 Hbk
ISBN 978-1-80413-031-5 epub
ISBN 978-1-80413-032-2 pdf

Supported by the Marc Fitch Fund.

Cover design by Chris Bromley.

Cover image: Detail of a marginal drawing of a priest celebrating mass, from a Book of Hours, Sarum Use, c.1440–c.1450. (British Library, Harley 2915, f.84, used with permission)

Typeset in Gentium by BBR Design, Sheffield

Contents

Acknowledgements vii
List of Abbreviations ix

INTRODUCTION

1. The Tregear Manuscript 3
   1.1 Introduction to the Tregear Manuscript as a whole 3
   1.2 The palaeography and scribes of the manuscript 6
   1.3 The purpose of Bonner's homilies 9
   1.4 The printing of Bonner used by Tregear 10
   1.5 The Tregear Manuscript: increasingly significant for Cornish studies 11

2. *Sacrament an Alter* (SA) 13
   2.1 The specific nature of SA 13
   2.2 The scope of this critical edition of SA 15
   2.3 The authorship, form, date and language of SA 16
   2.4 The source of SA—Foxe's account of the 1554 Oxford Disputations 19
   2.5 The context of the Disputations 20
   2.6 The specific edition of Foxe used and date of SA 23
   2.7 How did the author compile and translate SA? 25
   2.8 Tregear and Stephyn in the wider orbit of Glasney 28

3. John Tregear—Translator of Bonner 31
   3.1 John Tregear, vicar of St Allen, 1544-1583 31
   3.2 Tregear and Lawrence Godfrey 34
   3.3 Tregear and John Tresteyn—clues to place of birth and ordination 35
   3.4 Tregear's 'church papism' 37

4. Thomas Stephyn—Compiler of *Sacrament an Alter* 41
   4.1 Thomas Stephyn, vicar of Newlyn East in 1557 41
   4.2 Thomas Stephyn, curate of Newlyn East in 1536 42

	4.3	The possible involvement of Stephyn in an illicit pilgrimage	45
	4.4	Distinguishing Stephyn from Cornwall, Stevyns from Devon	48
	4.5	Thomas Stephyn's 'recusancy'	49
	4.6	Thomas Stephyns elsewhere in the country	51
5.	Ralph Trelobys—the Link with Glasney College	55
	5.1	Ralph Trelobys, vicar of Crowan 1512–57 and Newlyn East 1518–57	55
	5.2	Trelobys and Glasney College	57
	5.3	Trelobys and 'Rad Ton'	59
6.	John Foxe and His Context	63
	6.1	Foxe's use of his sources	63
	6.2	The reception of Foxe and his vision of history	64
	6.3	Foxe and Stephyn in the light of current historiography	67
7.	Conclusions	71
	7.1	The end of the Marian years	71
	7.2	Tregear, Stephyn and the journey of the manuscript	72

EDITION

8.	Edition	77
9.	Commentary	147
10.	Notes	221

Appendix A. Thomas Stephyn's Contributions to TH	291
Appendix B. Images to Support Notes on 66r.1–9 and 66v.1–8	295

Glossary	297
Bibliography	319
Index	347

Acknowledgements

'A little learning is a dangerous thing', and it has proved so in my case. Some aspects of the complexity of the Tregear Manuscript—and especially of *Sacrament an Alter*—required a broad approach, encompassing ecclesiastical history, patristics and linguistics, including Celtic and classical languages. While almost everyone working in one or other of these fields was singularly better equipped, what landed me with the job was my very partial acquaintance with the whole range. For this text, someone with limited skill and experience in all the areas was perhaps at an advantage compared with those genuinely learned in one or two of the fields.

I therefore have a good number of people to thank, whose individual expertise has buttressed my limitations. In the Cornish aspects, the questions of Ray Edwards and Keith Syed got things started. Andrew Hawke shared the strong foundations of his own research and introduced me to Ben Bruch—my constant companion on the way. Richard Gendall offered advice and encouragement from the outset, while Oliver Padel and Nicholas Williams have been exceptionally generous with time, interest and expertise throughout. Many librarians have been of assistance, but Angela Broome and Angela Doughty were exceptionally supportive.

In the historical aspects, Fr David Myers reawakened my interest in the early modern period and Archbishop Peter Smith—by encouraging me to represent our diocese in the work of Gerallt Nash and his excellent team at St Fagan's— enabled me to sit at the feet of Madeleine Gray, John Morgan-Guy and John Harper. Philip Payton lifted my sights to the wider context, and Nicholas Orme and Alexandra Walsham helped me avoid a great many pitfalls and superficial judgements. Remaining errors and misjudgements are my own.

With regard to my 'small Latin and less Greek', a number of teachers and friends over the years would surely be surprised that their efforts to help me with classical and biblical languages eventually bore such unexpected fruit. My thanks are due to Philip Lambie, George Worthington, Rhona Lewis, Paul Joyce and Chris Hatcher.

In theology, I owe a great deal to the acuity of many teachers but especially Bishop Gordon Roe, Bishop David Wilcox, Geoffrey Cuming and Christopher Evans. For the opportunity to encounter the patristic faith as a living tradition, my time at the House of St Gregory and St Macrina, Oxford, was irreplaceable, and offered the inspiration of Nicolas Zernov and Metropolitan Kallistos of Diokleia. Profound thanks are also due to Gergely Juhász, Peter McGrail, Kenneth Newport and, above all, Gerald Pillay at Liverpool Hope University for faith, encouragement and inspiration. David Hawkins and the team at University of Exeter Press also deserve great thanks for unfailing editorial help, as do BBR Design for their exceptional typesetting. Above all, the patience and support of my wife Judy, and children Jago and Tamsin, have underpinned the whole endeavour.

Finally, the assistance of the Marc Fitch Fund in making publication possible is very gratefully acknowledged.

Abbreviations

Abbreviations for Cornish Language Texts

(For editions etc., see Printed and Online Source Editions and Printed Records/Cornish Language Texts in the Bibliography)

AB	*Archæologia Britannica*
ACB	*Archæologia Cornu-Britannica*
BK	*Beunans Ke/Bewnans Ke*
BM	*Beunans Meriasek*
Bodewryd	NLW Bodewryd MS 5
Boson	Cornish Writings of the Boson Family
CW	*Gwreans an Bys* (The Creation of the World)
JCH	*Jooan Chei a Horr (Jowan Chy an Horth)*
LLR	*Llyfr y Resolucion*
NG	*Nebbaz Gerriau dro tho Carnoack*
OM	*Origo Mundi* (first play of the *Ordinalia*)
PA	*Passyon agan Arluth* (Cornish Passion Poem/Mount Calvary)
PC	*Passio Christi* (second play of the *Ordinalia*)
RD	*Resurrectio Domini* (third play of the *Ordinalia*)
SA	*Sacrament an Alter*
TH	Tregear Homilies
VC	*Vocabularium Cornicum*/Old Cornish Vocabulary
WB	Letter of William Bodinar
WR	Cornish Writings of William Kerew/Rowe

General Abbreviations

BL	British Library
CCC	Catechism of the Catholic Church
CCSG	Corpus Christianorum Series Graeca
CCSL	Corpus Christianorum Series Latina
CPG	Clauis Patrum Graecorum

CRS	Catholic Record Society
CRO	Kresen Kernow, Redruth (formerly Cornwall Record Office, Truro)
CSEL	Corpus Scriptorum Ecclesiasticorum Latinorum
CUP	Cambridge University Press
D&C	Dean & Chapter Manuscripts, Exeter Cathedral Archive, Exeter
DCRS	Devon and Cornwall Record Society
DRO	Devon Record Office/Devon Heritage Centre, Exeter
GPC	*Geiriadur Prifysgol Cymru/A Dictionary of the Welsh Language*, Thomas et al., eds (Aberystwyth: University of Wales Press, 1967–2002)
HMSO	Her Majesty's Stationery Office
NLW	National Library of Wales/Llyfrgell Genedlaethol Cymru, Aberystwyth
NRSV	New Revised Standard Version (of the Bible)
OUP	Oxford University Press
PG	Patrologia Latina (Migne)
PL	Patrologia Graeca (Migne)
PRO	Public Record Office
RIC	Royal Institution of Cornwall
T&C	Townsend, George, and Cattley, Stephen Reed, ed., *The Acts and Monuments of John Foxe*, vol. 6 (London: Seeley and Birnside, 1838).
TAMO	*The Unabridged Acts and Monuments Online* or *TAMO* (The Digital Humanities Institute, Sheffield, 2011). Available from: https://www.dhi.ac.uk/foxe/ Accessed 30 June 2022.
TNA	The National Archives
UEP	University of Exeter Press
WRO	Wiltshire & Swindon Record Office, Salisbury

Abbreviations used in the Notes

N	Nance's first transcription (N1 and N2 where his two manuscript transcriptions conflict)
C	Nance and Smith's joint final typescript
T	Nance's manuscript translation[1]
B	Bice's cyclostyled reading[2]
S	Syed's electronic version of Bice's cyclostyled reading, where there is a significant difference[3]

---

1 Courtney Library, *Nance Bequest*, 7:22 (46) contains both N1 and N2, C and T. See note under Bibliography, Primary Sources, Courtney Library on P.A.S. Pool's renumbering of the folders.
2 Bice, *Homelyes xiij in cornysch* (see Privately Circulated/Unpublished Works).
3 Syed, *Homelyes xiij in cornysch* (see Privately Circulated/Unpublished Works).

ABBREVIATIONS xi

H	Hawke's transcription, originally for the Cornish Dictionary Project[4]
F	My earlier transcription[5]
E	The edited text below the diplomatic edition in this volume

Ideas and opinions from private communications with Nicholas Williams, Benjamin Bruch, Oliver Padel, Richard Gendall, Keith Syed, Ray Edwards and C.W.H. Hatcher are acknowledged as NW, BB, OP, RG, KS, RE and CH respectively.

---

4   Andrew Hawke, *Homelyes xiij in cornysche* (see Privately Circulated/Unpublished Works).
5   Frost, *Sacrament an Alter, 2009* (see Privately Circulated/Unpublished Works).

Introduction

CHAPTER ONE

The Tregear Manuscript

1.1 Introduction to the Tregear Manuscript as a whole

The Tregear Manuscript was first classified,[1] by the Royal Commission on Historical Manuscripts, as a series of homilies 'in Welsh ... nearly all ... transcribed or perhaps preached by John Tregear. The 12th and 13th are much tattered.'[2] This is curious, because they are headed *Homelyes xiij in cornisch*. Yet it was not until 1949 that the Gaelic scholar John Mackechnie confirmed the predominant language as Cornish, and initiated correspondence with Robert Morton Nance on the subject.[3]

The Puleston family, from whose library at Emral the manuscript came, claimed that a number of works in their possession were confiscated from a Catholic house during the course of their assiduous support of the Reformation,[4] although the family were also linked by marriage to the recusant Edwards family of Plas Newydd, Chirk,[5] and may possibly have acquired Catholic

---

1   BL Add. MS 46397. All references below for *Sacrament an Alter* (SA), are to this edition; for Tregear's Homilies (TH) to the yet unpublished edition by Benjamin Bruch, *The Tregear Homilies* [privately circulated, 2008]. In both, the numbering system described in note 11 is used. For an overview, see Brian Murdoch, *Cornish Literature* (Cambridge: D.S. Brewer, 1993), pp. 129-30; Talat Chaudhri, 'A Description of the Middle Cornish Tregear Manuscript', MA Thesis, 2001, Aberystwyth University.
2   *The Second Report of the Royal Commission on Historical Manuscripts* (London: Eyre & Spottiswoode, 1874), Appendix, p. 65.
3   See, all by Robert Morton Nance, 'The Tregear Manuscript', *Old Cornwall*, 4 (1950), pp. 429-34; 'More about the Tregear Manuscript', *Old Cornwall*, 5 (1951), pp. 21-7; 'Something New in Cornish', *Journal of the Royal Institution of Cornwall*, new series, 1 (1952), pp. 119-21; 'Cornish Words in the Tregear MS', *Zeitschrift für Celtische Philologie*, 24 (1954), pp. 1-5; and the correspondence between Nance, Mackechnie and others in Box 8 of the *Nance Bequest* in the Courtney Library, RIC, Truro.
4   See Geraint Bowen, *Welsh Recusant Writings* (Cardiff: University of Wales, 1999), p. 40, for a Puleston writing polemically in the 1580s.
5   Robert Thomas Jenkins, ed., *Dictionary of Welsh Biography (down to 1940)* (London: The Honourable Society of Cymmrodorion, 1959), p. 183, and Thomas Kennedy, 'The Edwards Family of Plas Newydd in Chirkland', *Trafodion Cymdeithas Hanes Sir Ddinbych/Denbighshire Historical Society Transactions*, 60: 41 (1992), pp. 71-85. Mrs K. Byrne of the Society (private communication) guided me to the link between the Puleston and Edwards families, although Donald Attwater

manuscripts from that source.[6] Whatever journeys the manuscript eventually made through Wales, however, it came originally from Cornwall and is unmistakably a document of the early years of the Counter-Reformation.

The work as we have it is a paper quarto, with two main sections. The first is a translation into the Cornish language of a book of homilies issued by Edmund Bonner, bishop of London in the reign of Mary I, as part of her programme to renew Catholicism in England through worship, preaching and catechesis.[7] This section of the manuscript is attributed in several places to *Johannes Tregear, clericus*, and is commonly referred to as the Tregear Homilies (TH). This priest was originally assumed to be the chaplain to a recusant family after the accession of Elizabeth,[8] but is now known to have been the vicar of St Allen in Cornwall from 1544 to 1583.[9]

(The original three authors of Bonner's twelve main homilies are well known, and their names are appended to the sections they wrote, even in the Cornish translation. They all held ecclesiastical office in Queen Mary's time: Bonner as bishop of London, John Harpsfield—who wrote the majority—as his archdeacon, and Henry Pendleton, one of his chaplains.)

The homilies are bound together with a second section, often misunderstood as a 'thirteenth homily', in a different hand. This section—the primary subject of this critical edition—has been shown to be a work of a quite different

---

mentioned it to Nance in a letter of 7 November 1951 (citing the *NLW Journal*, 6, pp. 324–5). The County Archivist of Flintshire, M. Bevans-Evans, also drew Nance's attention (in a letter of 27 August 1952) to Robert Davies of Gwysaney, 1658–1710, whose collection of manuscripts was divided between his heirs by weighing on a cheese-scale. For both letters see Box 8 of the *Nance Bequest* in the Courtney Library, RIC, Truro.

6 D.H. Frost, 'Sacrament an Alter—a Tudor Cornish Patristic *Catena* drawn from Foxe's Account of the Oxford Disputations of 1554', in Philip Payton, ed., *Cornish Studies*, 2nd series, 11 (Exeter: UEP, 2003), p. 305. I have drawn directly from this article at several places in this Introduction.

7 Edmund Bonner, ed. *Homelies sette forthe by the righte reuerende father in God, Edmunde Byshop of London [...]* (London: John Cawood, 1555); Gerald Bray, ed., *The Books of Homilies: A Critical Edition* (Cambridge: James Clarke & Co., 2016). For context: Eamon Duffy, *Fires of Faith: Catholic England under Mary Tudor* (New Haven and London: Yale University Press, 2009), pp. 64–8 and William Wizeman, SJ, *The Theology and Spirituality of Mary Tudor's Church* [Catholic Christendom 1300–1700] (Aldershot: Ashgate, 2006), pp. 19–23. See also 6.3.

8 This was, for example, the view of the Revd G.C. Sara and Nance (Courtney Library, *Nance Bequest*, 7: 22 (46)—at the foot of the typescript of 'Something New in Cornish'). See 3.1.

9 Matthew Spriggs, 'Where Cornish was Spoken and When: a Provisional Synthesis', and D.H. Frost, 'Glasney's Parish Clergy and the Tregear Manuscript', both in Philip Payton, ed., *Cornish Studies*, 2nd series, 15 (Exeter: UEP, 2007), pp. 248 and 31–34 respectively; and (both revised and updated) in Philip Payton, ed., *Cornwall in the Age of Rebellion, 1490–1690* (Exeter: UEP, 2021), pp. 73 and 167–70 respectively. Although in Cornish language texts the word for 'saint' is frequently omitted before the names of indigenous saints—see N.J.A. Williams, '*Saint* in Cornish', in Philip Payton, ed., *Cornish Studies*, 2nd series, 7 (Exeter: UEP, 1999), pp. 219–41—the widespread modern usage with Cornish place-names in English is followed here.

nature: a *catena* of patristic proof texts of Eucharistic doctrine, in both Cornish and Latin, compiled and added sometime after 1576. Its internal arrangement is curious, and offers clues to its ultimate source, which is not Bonner's homilies. It differs completely from Bonner's 'thirteenth homily' (in fact an *Aunswere to certayne common obiections*,[10] printed in editions of his *Homelies*), so it is properly distinguished from the first twelve 'Tregear Homilies' with the separate Cornish title found at the head of one of its folios, '*Sacrame[n]t an Alter*' (SA).[11] As will be discussed below, its texts—many already familiar from the liturgy (see 2.1)—were drawn, often in order, from the speeches of Catholic divines in the 1554 Eucharistic debates at Oxford, as recorded in John Foxe's *Actes and Monuments*.[12] Nonetheless, as Chaudhri hints, it is perhaps more than a coincidence that this title chimes with part of the English title of Bonner's 'thirteenth' homily.[13] It is in a different hand to TH (as are certain annotations and patristic references in the margins of homilies 11 and 12) and constitutes a separate gathering. Another name—that of *Thomas Stephyn, clericus*—is found at the end of some of these later annotations, in the same hand as SA. As with Tregear's name, it is unmentioned in any printed English edition of the homilies, so appears to be closely linked to the Cornish version.

While this edition will be focused on SA, its close interconnection with TH possibly reflects significant collaboration between those responsible. For this reason, and to establish clear dating, it is necessary to consider the manuscript as a whole, before turning specifically to SA.

10 Bonner, *Homelies*, f. 63ff.
11 SA 60v.1, although a different version of the title, *An sacrament an aulter*, is found at SA 61r.1. Traditionally, TH and SA were referenced using a convention in which the folio number was used for *recto*, and that number followed by lowercase *a* for *verso*—i.e. TH 14, SA 66a, etc. (with no line references). The system used here (which departs from Charles Penglase's in that Roman numerals are not assigned to titles) counts all full lines and title lines, using *r* and *v* to denote *recto* and *verso*, followed (after a point) by the line number (e.g. TH 14r.3, SA 66v.9). 'Marginal' notes are identified by *m* (e.g. SA 59r.2m) or, where written between lines, with additional letters (e.g. SA 61v.4a). See Charles Penglase, 'The Future Indicative in the Early Modern Cornish of Tregear', *Etudes Celtiques*, 34 (2000), p. 215.
12 Frost, 'Sacrament an Alter', pp. 291–307, especially pp. 296–8; John Foxe, *Actes and Monuments*—cited here from *The Unabridged Acts and Monuments Online* or *TAMO* (1576 edition and, where indicated, those of 1563, 1570 and 1580). Accessible at: https://www.dhi.ac.uk/foxe (The Digital Humanities Institute, Sheffield, 2011), accessed 1 December 2018. The John Foxe Book of Martyrs Project was a collaboration between the University of Sheffield, the British Academy and the Arts and Humanities Research Council, superseding the earlier printed edition of George Townsend and Stephen Reed Cattley, eds, *The Acts and Monuments of John Foxe* (London: Seeley and Birnside, 1841), and is used here with permission.
13 Chaudhri, 'A Description of the Middle Cornish Tregear Manuscript', p. 3.

1.2 The palaeography and scribes of the manuscript

There are two main hands in the Tregear Manuscript, each with two forms (although with a degree of overlap). The first hand uses a clear, italic script for Latin quotations (italic hand A) and a clear, elegant secretary hand of the sixteenth century for the Cornish text—which is the predominant portion (secretary hand A).

In the example given here, from TH 51v.1-6, the top three lines (a Hebrew/Latin title) are given in italic hand A: *Emanuel ... sacramento altaris et d[e] ... christi sub specie pan[is]...*

By contrast, the bottom three lines (where the text is in Cornish) are given in secretary hand A: **mabden unwith gra[ffys] ...... [v]irnans ha passion in ... duty ew the preparya ...**

From the way the single pen is used on the paper, the thickness of the line and other distinctive features, as well as the way the

© British Library Board
BL Add. MS 46397: f. 51v

work coheres, it seems likely that a single individual was responsible for both secretary hand A and italic hand A. Whether this hand belonged to the translator, or to a scribe, or to someone making a fair copy later, is difficult to determine from the textual evidence. There are few corrections in this hand on any given page, and it is responsible for the main text of the first twelve homilies. In a secretary hand, at the end of each of these homilies, the name John Tregear is written (as shown below from the foot of folio TH 16r). As has been noted, this name is usually followed by an abbreviation of the word *clericus*, 'clerk', effectively meaning 'priest' in this context.[14]

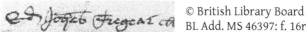

© British Library Board
BL Add. MS 46397: f. 16r

Taken together, these textual considerations suggest that John Tregear was connected in a particular way with the Cornish translation of these first twelve homilies. In fact, he is widely accepted to be responsible for the work of translation itself, although the characteristic sixteenth-century hand found throughout the first twelve homilies may or may not be his own. (The *Qd*—for *Quod*—before the name signifies attribution in manuscripts of this time and earlier, confirming the work is Tregear's, while leaving open the question of whether he was the scribe.)[15]

---

14 Given as *Johannes Tregear* in TH on ff. 11v, 16r, 26r, 54v, 58r and probably 51r (the page being slightly damaged), *Johannes Tregere* on f. 35r, *JT* on ff. 5v, 20r, 30r, 41r and 46r. In addition, there is a monogram doodle at the foot of f. 14r, which appears to involve the letter T.

15 This conventional use of *quod* appears to have originated from English *quoth* rather than the Latin relative pronoun (although later users may have confused the two—OP). The OED

The second important hand in the manuscript uses a different pen and more ink, and shows signs of considerable irregularity. In the (relatively clear) example given here, from SA 64r.16–21, most of the top three lines (part of a Latin quotation) are given in italic hand B: *pœna: tamen fit sat[isfactoria]... vel etiam offerentibus...pro tota pœna...*

© British Library Board
BL Add. MS 46397: f. 64r

Then the text changes to Cornish (with some borrowed English words) and secretary hand B: **hen[na] ... thetha gallus a sati[sfaction] ... in satisfaction, e the[w]... an quantite an ob[lation].**

Once again, the convention is loosely adopted of using an italic hand for Latin (italic hand B) and a secretary hand for Cornish (secretary hand B), with occasional confusion between the two. Both hands again exhibit features that strongly suggest they belong to the same person. The irregularity may be due to illness, age, or difficult writing conditions, but the work is confined to the latter parts of the manuscript, primarily the whole of the so-called thirteenth homily, *Sacrament an Alter* which, as a separate gathering, may have been added later. (Whether it replaced a now missing gathering or was an addition remains a matter for speculation.) The same (or a very similar) hand appears in various annotations and additional marginal notes in the eleventh and twelfth homilies of TH. The way in which these erratic annotations cross the original text or marginalia—but always refer to them—indicates that they were written later. At the foot of folios TH 54r and 58r there is what seems to be an autograph that also appears to be in secretary hand B: that of *Thomas Stephyn, clericus*:[16]

 © British Library Board
BL Add. MS 46397: f. 54r

Sacrament an Alter itself has no name at the end and may be unfinished (although it ends with a doxology), and is certainly heavily damaged, by mice or wear. It is in hand B throughout, exhibiting many features like the later annotations in TH. It therefore seems to be a reasonable hypothesis that these annotations and additional marginal notes in homilies 11 and 12 were made

---

Online (https://www.oed.com) gives (mostly Scottish) examples under *quoth*, I.1.c, but other instances occur, see Bart Besamusca, Gareth Griffith, Matthias Meyer, Hannah Morcos, 'Author Attributions in Medieval Text Collections: An Exploration', in *Amsterdamer Beiträge zur älteren Germanistik* 76 (Leiden: Brill, 2016), pp. 115, 117. The convention does not impinge on the question of whether a scribe may have read the English text to Tregear, suggested by forms such as *narracion* for 'an oration': cf. Ray Edwards and Keith Syed, *The Tregear Homilies with The Sacrament of the Altar* (Sutton Coldfield: Kernewek Dre Lyther, 2004), p. viii, and TH 45r.5.

16 The example here is from the foot of TH 54r.

by the Thomas Stephyn who appears to have appended his name in the same hand (secretary hand B) to those sections. Since *Sacrament an Alter* is in the same hand, a strong case can be made for attributing this to Stephyn also.[17]

That two separate authors were largely responsible for the Tregear Manuscript is no new discovery: it was suggested by Nance at the outset, and has for many years been the independent conclusion of most of those who have examined it.

(A view could be advanced, based on variations in style among the insertions at the very end of SA, that a third hand was involved with a small number of corrections, annotations and additional marginal notes—italic/secretary hand C.[18] In this case Tregear or his scribe used hand A, Stephyn or his scribe used hand B and a third writer corrected and supplemented material in both texts in hand C at a later point. On balance, however, there are as many arguments against this theory as for it. The relative neatness and smaller size of some of the final additions could simply be due to the greater limitations and concentration required for later insertion among other lines. There are also many places where hand B is very similar to this theoretical later hand C—for example, the early lines of SA 61r. The working hypothesis used here, therefore, is that the corrections, annotations and additional marginal notes in both TH and SA were written by the same scribe or author as SA, in hand B, but that the latter shows a good deal of variation in size and neatness.)

Interestingly, a third name appears, once only, in the upper left margin of TH 12v.8–12, written at right angles to the text in hand D. It may read Richard Logan (as Nance thought), or possibly Legan, and is followed by a word or words difficult to make out. The name and especially the following letters appear to be of a later period than either hand A or hand B.[19] Benjamin Bruch has argued convincingly that the whole reads *Richard Logan his writing*.[20] An image of this name on the manuscript is given here, with Bruch's proposed reconstruction:

© British Library Board BL Add. MS 46397: f. 51v

---

17 Frost, 'Sacrament an Alter', pp. 293–4. See also 4.2.
18 Compare *In cælum manum mittam*, SA 66v.9, with *Crede et edisti*, SA 66v.10.
19 It seems unlikely that the name might represent Logar or Legar (for modern Lodger or Ledger)—the *n* is clear.
20 Benjamin Bruch, 'Towards a Critical Edition of the Tregear Homilies', 27th Annual Harvard Celtic Colloquium, Barker Centre, Harvard University, 5 October 2007 (privately circulated, 2007.) The words following the name, which I first misread as *librarius* (Frost, 'Glasney's Parish Clergy', p. 29) have often been disregarded—although Nance noticed them. Having re-examined the original manuscript with Bruch, I am convinced that his reading is now the most likely.

It seems likely to represent someone with later access to the manuscript simply trying out his own handwriting although it remains possible that it is an earlier signature, subsequently endorsed (BB).

1.3 The purpose of Bonner's homilies

For many years, the Tregear Manuscript (and many other Cornish manuscripts) were presumed to have been written at Glasney College by its canons, but it is increasingly accepted that—while Glasney clergy may have commissioned or directed the programme of work—clergy in rural parishes executed it.[21] The commissioning of a Cornish translation of Bonner's homilies is likely to have fallen in Mary I's reign, and parallels other initiatives throughout England and Wales at this time. On Mary's accession, John Veysey of Exeter (like Day of Chichester, Bonner of London and Gardiner of Winchester) was restored to his see, but he was an extremely old man by this point, and reluctant to leave Sutton Coldfield.[22] He would have been required to ensure that homilies were issued in his diocese, but like his fellow bishops would have been impressed that Bonner had issued London's set so quickly. The obvious solution, as all soon realized, was to use these nationally.

Bonner's attempt appears to have been compiled under the influence of the success of the *First Book of Homilies* issued by Thomas Cranmer in 1547. (In fact, he had himself written the sixth of those homilies, which he recycled as the fifth in his own collection.)[23] Most of the others, as has been noted, were by John Harpsfield, archdeacon of London, except for the seventh and eighth by Henry Pendleton (or Pendilton, who is remembered for being fired at while preaching at St Paul's Cross in 1554).[24] The original 'thirteenth homily' might again have been by Bonner, or possibly by Harpsfield.[25] The bishop's aim was to reach the whole of society, and his homilies were accompanied by a range of other works, published between 1554 and 1556.[26] For clergy and literate laypeople he issued a revised and expanded version of the *King's Book*, setting out *A Profitable and Necessarye Doctryne*. For children and their teachers

---

21 Frost, 'Glasney's Parish Clergy', pp. 68–70, and in Payton, ed., *Cornwall in the Age of Rebellion*, pp. 210–11.
22 Thebridge, Stella, ed., *Holy Trinity, Sutton Coldfield: The Story of a Parish Church and its People, 1250-2020* (Cheltenham: The History Press, 2020), pp. 40–59.
23 Bray, ed., *The Books of Homilies*, pp. xiv–xvi.
24 Murdoch, *Cornish Literature*, p. 129. For a brief biography of Harpsfield see the footnotes to Quotation 60 in the Commentary.
25 Bray, ed., *The Books of Homilies*, pp. xiii–xvi.
26 Christopher Haigh, *English Reformations: Religion, Politics and Society under the Tudors* (Oxford: Clarendon Press, 1993), p. 216.

came *An Honest Godly Instruction*.[27] Throughout, he blended guidance on living the Christian life with corrective teaching on the Eucharist and the papacy, buttressed by the frequent quotation from biblical and patristic sources that is characteristic of Marian texts.[28] These educational efforts were complemented by careful visitations and enquiries.[29]

It is now widely accepted that the Marian Church's use of printing was both larger in scale and more effective than at first thought, and that Bonner's works (along with Watson's) were much to the fore in efforts made to re-catechize the population. Pole also achieved a great deal, and his synod planned to introduce its own new catechism, but until it was produced, Bonner's version was recommended. It is unsurprising, therefore, that Bonner's homilies were chosen to be the priority for translation into Cornish in Mary's reign.[30]

1.4 The printing of Bonner used by Tregear

The precise printing of Bonner's *Homelies* used by Tregear for his Cornish translation has been investigated by Bruch,[31] following earlier considerations by Andrew Hawke and Talat Chaudhri. With Hawke, Bruch underlines the remarkable consistency in general between the various printings and, with Chaudhri, he stresses that many of the surviving copies are pseudo-editions, containing slight inconsistencies and variations of type, compiled from various signatures and a range of printings.[32]

In general, each page contains the same text, with the same line divisions and the same word divisions in the case of hyphenation. There is, however, considerable variation in the running heads and textual citations in the

---

27 Edmund Bonner, *A Profitable and Necessarye Doctryne [...] for the instruction and enformation of the people beynge within his diocese of London [...]* (London: John Cawood, 1554); Edmund Bonner, *An Honest Godly Instruction, and information for the tradying, and bringinge up of Children, set furth by the Bishoppe of London [...]* (London: Cawood, 1556).
28 Wizeman, *Theology and Spirituality*, pp. 25–7.
29 E.g. Edmund Bonner, *Articles to be inquired of in the general visitation [...]* (London: John Cawood, 1554).
30 See David Loades, 'The Marian Episcopate', and Thomas F. Mayer, 'The Success of Cardinal Pole's Final Legation', both in Eamon Duffy and David Loades, eds, *The Church of Mary Tudor* (Aldershot and Burlington: Ashgate, 2006), pp. 33–56 and 149–75 respectively; also Alexandra Walsham, '"Domme preachers"? Post-Reformation English Catholicism and the Culture of Print', *Past and Present*, 168, 1 (August 2000), pp. 72–123, which opens by specifically drawing attention to the Marian use of printing in the context of Foxe's views.
31 Benjamin Bruch, 'Analysis and Classification of Twelve Copies of Bishop Edmund Bonner's Homilies (1555)', Canolfan Uwchefrydiau Cymreig a Cheltaidd Prifysgol Cymru [University of Wales Centre for Advanced Welsh and Celtic Studies], 29 June 2007 (report on work in progress, privately circulated, 2007).
32 Chaudhri, 'A Description of the Middle Cornish Tregear Manuscript', p. 1n.

margins (BB). Bruch's painstaking and detailed work, particularly focusing on the marginalia, eventually concludes that there is an extremely close match to what he calls the 'N' printing,[33] which can be shown to be relatively early. It is exemplified by the copy held by the British Library (STC 3285.4).

One of the most satisfying comparisons was of the marginal note at the top of TH f. 20r. Only a few printings cite the name Irenaeus in full, and only one of these then omits the second half of the reference (*gainſt Valen=tine, chap.4*). This is precisely the portion of the reference that Tregear omits. Taken with the other examples Bruch cites, the identification is a strong one, although, as he acknowledges, the book used by Tregear may have included one or two different signatures from the one now in the British Library.

1.5 The Tregear Manuscript: increasingly significant for Cornish studies

Although the Cornish translation of Bonner's *Homelies* was, as far as we know, never printed, someone clearly considered it worthwhile to produce a reasonably fair copy and may have originally imagined publication or at least wider dissemination.[34]

Presumably it was intended to support a Counter-Reformation programme of preaching, disputation or theological education in western Cornwall and is most likely to date from sometime between 1555 and 1558, although there is no incontestable internal evidence of this. Certainly, it was not made before 1555 when the *Homelies* were published, as it shows clear signs of being produced from a printed edition, as noted above in 1.4.[35] Perhaps there was an element of counterbalance to Cranmer's lack of diplomacy towards Cornish-speakers at the time of the 1549 Rising, in the reign of Edward VI.[36]

---

33 Bruch, 'Analysis and Classification', p. 7. The shelfmark of STC 3285.4 at the British Library is 1026.e.14.
34 There was a market at the time for scribal copies of forbidden or controversial texts: Bowen, *Welsh Recusant Writings*, p. 45.
35 Veysey's successor as bishop of Exeter, James Turberville, was appointed in 1555, no doubt with a commission to advance the Counter-Reformation agenda rapidly.
36 Cranmer had written, in response to the petitions of the rebels, 'I would gladly know the reason, why you Cornish men refuse utterly the new English, as you call it, because certain of you understand it not, and yet you will have the service in Latin, which almost none of you understand ...'. Henry Jenkyns, *The Remains of Thomas Cranmer, D.D., Archbishop of Canterbury* (Oxford: OUP, 1833), vol. 2, p. 231. For an interesting Cornish guild document, possibly of the same time, see Joanna Mattingly, 'The Helston Shoemakers' Guild and a Possible Connection with the 1549 Rebellion', in Philip Payton, ed., *Cornish Studies*, 2nd series, 6 (Exeter: UEP, 1998), pp. 23–45.

Eventually, in the twentieth century, Robert Morton Nance and A.S.D. Smith (following the rediscovery by Mackechnie of this longest surviving example of Cornish prose) laid the foundations for the study and interpretation of the manuscript. Christopher Bice's often-cited typed and cyclostyled reading for language students,[37] the only form in which the work was known by most scholars for many years, was drawn from Nance's work, which survives as accurate handwritten transcriptions (and an even better typescript version by Nance and Smith) in the Courtney Library at the Royal Institution of Cornwall. Had this latter ever been published in full, it would have advanced the study of Tregear's work (and the reputation of Nance) considerably.[38] All subsequent work on the first ten homilies is hugely indebted to it, directly or indirectly. Even Nance's largely accurate reading, however, has some omissions and defects within TH 11 and 12, and SA in particular.

Andrew Hawke, in his preliminary work towards a proposed dictionary of traditional Cornish,[39] revisited this early work of Nance and Smith, and carefully compared it with his own reading of the manuscript. He added huge value to our knowledge and established a very sound text for TH, although SA (and the marginalia of TH 11 and 12) still required further study when his focus had to move to the Welsh language.[40]

Given the paramount importance of BL Add. MS 46397 for the understanding of middle and early modern Cornish prose, the absence of a published critical edition of the entire manuscript remains a serious omission. Yet any such work requires a prior close study of SA and of the patristic quotations and comments made by its author in TH, to resolve the many uncertainties in Thomas Stephyn's contributions to the manuscript. It is the aim of this first critical edition to undertake this preliminary work, paving the way for a full edition of the whole manuscript.

---

37 Christopher Bice, ed., *Homelyes xiij in cornysch* (privately circulated, 1969), reprinted by Ray Edwards as Christopher Bice, ed., *The Tregear Homilies* (Sutton Coldfield: Kernewek Dre Lyther, 1994). Bice confirmed his source to Edwards.
38 The fair copy is in the Courtney Library, *Nance Bequest*, 7: 22 (46). A case could be made, even today, for the publication of all the MS transcriptions made by Nance (and Smith). The value of this body of meticulous scholarship has been insufficiently appreciated.
39 Andrew Hawke, *The Cornish Dictionary Project: First Progress Report* (Redruth: Institute of Cornish Studies, 1981), pp. 11–13.
40 Andrew Hawke, *Homelyes xiij in cornysche*, electronic file of unpublished reading [privately circulated, 1977–1998]. All recent work on the Tregear MS—including mine—is deeply indebted to Hawke's exceptional contribution to establishing the corpus of Cornish, generously shared. This work necessarily moved from centre stage when he took up his wider lexicographical role with the GPC, of which he eventually became managing editor.

CHAPTER TWO

Sacrament an Alter (SA)

2.1 The specific nature of SA

So far, we have considered the Tregear manuscript primarily as a whole and focused on the fact that its two main gatherings are taken up with a translation of Bonner's *Homilies*. Because of the title of the manuscript—*Homelyes xiij in cornysch*—we might have expected Bonner's 'thirteenth homily' to be appended, with its 'answer to objections made against this sacrament'. It is possible, of course, that Tregear did translate the *Aunswere*, and this portion of the manuscript has been lost, and replaced by the gathering containing *Sacrament an Alter*. Alternatively, Tregear may have stopped work at homily 12 for some reason and, eventually, Stephyn may have sought to repair the loss in a different way. Whatever is the case, the *catena* was appended to the *Homelies* much later—after 1576, as we shall see—and shows some features of development in language and spelling.

As already noted, longstanding textual problems arising from the heavily damaged later folios of SA meant that its source remained completely unidentified until 2003, when the link with Foxe was finally made.[1] Before this identification could be demonstrated, a fresh reading of the Cornish and Latin of SA was required, focusing on patristic sources and marginal references, since the Bice printing of Nance's reading was limited in its treatment of marginalia. In particular, the lack of identified sources had seriously hampered the reconstruction of words in the badly damaged last six folios.

Once this fresh reading was under way, it gradually became apparent that *Sacrament an Alter* was not a homily at all, but a collection of patristic quotations (from both the Greek and Latin Fathers of the early Church) on the subject of the Eucharist. This was a central doctrinal and devotional focus in the Marian Counter-Reformation and under the seminary priests, although the unity and inerrancy of the Church came a close second.[2] The task of identifying and correcting the damaged quotations was made easier by a measure of

---

1   Frost, 'Sacrament an Alter', p. 296.
2   Wizeman, *Theology and Spirituality*, pp. 162–72; John Coffey, *Persecution and Toleration in Protestant England, 1558–1689* (Harlow, Essex: Longman/Pearson, 2000), pp. 85–93.

overlap with other, contemporary collections of patristic texts. The tradition of *catenae* or 'chains' of such texts has a long and venerable history.[3] Scholastic debate, which placed great emphasis on the authors of Christian antiquity, drew heavily on such collections. Ivo of Chartres' *Decretum, Tripartita* and *Panormia* were among the sources of the *Decretum Gratiani*,[4] Gratian's widely used commentary on canon law that cited patristic references. Lombard's *Libri Quatuor Sententiarum* was a theological compendium commenting on biblical doctrine in a similar way.[5] The 'Sentences' in their turn were the foundation of many and extensive commentaries, such as those by Thomas Aquinas, William of Ockham, Bonaventure and Duns Scotus. Versions of many of the quotations in SA can be found in these sources. More still can be found in Reformation-era commentaries on Eucharistic texts, such as those of Cranmer or Tunstall, which will be discussed below (see 2.3). Nor should we forget that many of these quotations would have been familiar from the liturgy of the feast of Corpus Christi, particularly from the readings at Mattins throughout the Octave.

The pattern and arrangement of texts in SA, however, is very distinctive and not entirely logical, suggesting a specific source with a different purpose from which selective extracts have been made. Early research could not benefit from the online search facilities available now, but it eventually became clear what this particular arrangement of patristic quotations meant. It echoed the 1554 Disputations at Oxford staged under the aegis of the prolocutor of the Lower House of Convocation, Hugh Weston of Lincoln College, with Thomas Cranmer, Hugh Latimer and Nicholas Ridley (see 2.4). Some additional sections appear to be drawn from the doctoral examination of John Harpsfield, who wrote many of Bonner's homilies. (Weston invited Cranmer to take part in this.)

Furthermore, the author of SA had apparently gained his knowledge of these Disputations from an obvious source: the account of the proceedings in John Foxe's *Actes and Monuments*—commonly called 'Foxe's Book of Martyrs'.[6] Had Cornish been more widely known and studied when the Royal Commission was cataloguing the manuscript, this might have been noticed earlier, as Foxe's work was well known in many Victorian households. It was not until the work

---

3   Stephen J. Loughlin, of DeSales University, first introduced me (in a private communication) to the range and scope of medieval *catenae*.
4   See *Decretum Gratiani (Concordia discordantia canonum)* digital edition, http://geschichte. digitale-sammlungen.de/decretum-gratiani/online/angebot, Bayerische StaatsBibliothek (2009). Accessed 16 February 2015.
5   *Libri Quattuor Sententiarum*, digital transcription of Magistri Petri Lombardi [Peter Lombard], *Sententiae in IV libros distinctae*, Abbey of Grottaferrata, by the Hochschule Augsburg, Bibliotheca Augustana (Rome: Quaracchi, 1971), http://www.hs-augsburg.de/~harsch/ Chronologia/Lspost12/PetrusLombardus/pet_s000.html. Accessed 16 February 2015.
6   The best modern edition is *The Acts and Monuments Online* (TAMO). See Chapter 1, note 12 and Bibliography: Other Primary Sources and Records.

of Jenner and others at the beginning of the twentieth century,[7] however, that the language began to capture wide interest, and by the time Mackechnie and Nance began corresponding in the 1950s, Foxe was no longer such universal reading material. A lot of time could have been saved if familiarity with his martyrology had persisted, or if the evolution of the internet had proceeded more quickly.[8]

2.2 The scope of this critical edition of SA

The nature, scope and purpose of this first critical edition has required careful thought, with accuracy and completeness in representing the final part of the Tregear manuscript, *Sacrament an Alter*, being the chief goal. A first critical edition (by Nicholas Williams and Graham Thomas) of a recently rediscovered Cornish play establishes some useful yardsticks.[9] On the other hand, material that was not needed in their context could be desirable in this one: perhaps some sort of apparatus for comparing the manuscript version with previous attempts at transcription that have been in partial circulation, and a full commentary on the theological aspects of the text.

The overall aim of this edition is thus to provide the means of understanding *Sacrament an Alter* both for those who know Cornish (but have been put off by the theology) and for those who know theology (but have been put off by the Cornish). In addition, an attempt has been made to reconstruct—at least conjecturally—as many of the damaged sections as possible. Placing where the authors came from, and when they wrote, has also been important. Possible local usages of Tregear and Stephyn could be of great interest to scholars of Cornish, alongside dated evidence of the language developing (and changing rapidly) in its late phases.

The historical and theological material is also of great interest, not only for what it teaches us of the wider reception of Bonner's initiatives in London, but also as a specific (and unusual) example of the reception and use of Foxe, and of the role of patristic evidence in Eucharistic controversy at the time. An attempt is made, therefore, to trace, reference and set in context the entire patristic content of *Sacrament an Alter*, as well as to cross-reference passages

---

7 Henry Jenner, *A Handbook of the Cornish Language, chiefly in its later stages with some account of its history and literature* (London: David Nutt, 1904).
8 It was interesting to contribute in a limited way, at an early stage, to the John Foxe Book of Martyrs Project (which led to TAMO) through the identification of some of the patristic references in Foxe. Had TAMO been available a few years earlier, the contribution would certainly have been reversed.
9 Graham Thomas and Nicholas Williams, eds, *Bewnans Ke: The Life of St Kea. A Critical Edition with Translation*, Exeter Medieval Texts & Studies (Exeter: UEP/National Library of Wales, 2007).

that occur in Tregear (and therefore Bonner) or in Stephyn's annotations. Where discovered, an indication of the specific origin or authorship of a particular Latin translation (of the Greek) is sometimes useful. No systematic attempt has been made to go beyond this into investigating the known contents of libraries accessible to the protagonists in the Oxford Disputations or indeed to Foxe himself, although occasional illustrations can be given.

As mentioned above, there do appear to be several liturgical echoes in the text, though their significance should not be overestimated. Having previously encountered the liturgy of the period (in connection with the reconstruction of a medieval church at the National History Museum of Wales) it has been interesting to highlight some of these.[10]

As noted above, work on Homilies 1–10 already undertaken by Benjamin Bruch (and by me on Homilies 11 and 12) would ideally combine with the current work as part of a wider resurgence in the academic study of Cornish.[11]

2.3 The authorship, form, date and language of SA

As already explained, *Sacrament an Alter* is probably not by John Tregear. His name does not appear on it. Although now bound with his work, it is in a different hand, displays more features of later Cornish, makes use of slightly different grammatical and spelling conventions, and is certainly not a translation of Bonner. SA, in other words, is something additional, drawing from another source. Some of these differences from TH have been known from the outset but were difficult to resolve.[12]

---

10 See D.H. Frost, 'Interpreting a Medieval Church through Liturgy', Proceedings of the National History Museum of Wales Conference 'The Welsh Medieval Church and its Context' (15 Nov 2008), https://museum.wales/media/7059/DHFrost.pdf, accessed 30 June 2022, and Gerallt D. Nash, ed., *Saving St Teilo's: Bringing a Medieval Church to Life* (Cardiff: National Museum of Wales, 2009), pp. 20–4, 124–7. On resonances with the liturgy, see for example echoes of the *Agnus Dei* at SA 65v.3 (in Notes and Commentary) and the Corpus Christi office mentioned above.

11 A full series of critical editions of unpublished Cornish texts (and updated editions of those already published) is much needed, despite much excellent work in the past (see Bibliography: Printed and Online Editions and Records, Cornish Language Texts). There have been two significant developments in this direction recently: (1) Nicholas Williams has begun the *Corpus Textuum Cornicorum*, including introductory material, palaeographical transcriptions, facsimiles and revived Cornish versions of the major texts. The first volume is Nicholas Williams, Michael Everson and Alan M. Kent, eds, *The Charter Fragment* and *Pascon agan Arluth* (Dundee: Evertype, 2020). (2) Matthew Spriggs proposed the present series of volumes (first suggested by him at Tremough in 2008) entitled *1,000 Years of Cornish (Writing in and on the Cornish Language, c. 800–1800 ce)*, comprising full critical editions and companion works, including unpublished later material and secondary works alongside the major texts. The two series should thus be complementary.

12 Nance, 'More about the Tregear Manuscript', pp. 21–7.

In addition, as we have noted, the name Thomas Stephyn appears at the end of Tregear's homilies 11 and 12, both distinctive because of later marginal notes added in secretary hand B, characteristic of SA. It seems likely, therefore, that Stephyn was identifying himself as the author of these annotations by signing the homilies under Tregear. If so, Stephyn is almost certainly the author of SA too. Penglase has suggested this possibility in his work on verbal forms in the homilies.[13]

Until recently, the places of origin and ecclesiastical careers of John Tregear and Thomas Stephyn were largely unknown. Now we know that they were not canons at Glasney College but rural parish priests,[14] and we also know more about the levels of education and academic collaboration among non-graduate clergy. Some of them were certainly capable of projects such as TH and SA, perhaps coordinated by the college. It is possible, therefore, to consider the links between TH, SA and other key Cornish texts whose authors or scribes may similarly have worked in rural parishes, setting in context the whole endeavour of compiling and seeking to preserve them. Such investigations can make a valuable contribution to the understanding of what might be called a 'traditionalist' tendency among some clerics in Cornwall between 1530 and 1580, and possibly outside these dates.

By tracing the quotations in SA, it rapidly emerges that, apart from a few connecting phrases,[15] the work is largely made up of patristic (and occasionally biblical) proof texts of Eucharistic doctrine, given in Latin first, then in Cornish translation. Even where the Cornish seems to diverge from the Latin, it is still paraphrasing it or occasionally translating a little more of the original source. It also becomes clear that SA is not a wholesale translation of parts of well-known medieval *catenae*, such as the *Catena Aurea* on the Gospels compiled by Aquinas,[16] the theological collections of Gratian, Ivo of Chartres or Peter Lombard (see 2.1), or the Corpus Christi Mattins readings, although many quotations in SA are also found in all of these. Nor is it a direct translation of parts of controversial works on the Eucharist published in the sixteenth century—such as those by Cranmer and Tunstall.[17] Once again, however, there

---

13 Penglase, 'The Future Indicative in the Early Modern Cornish of Tregear', pp. 215–31.
14 Frost, 'Glasney's Parish Clergy', pp. 68–9, and in Payton, ed., *Cornwall in the Age of Rebellion*, pp. 210–11.
15 Such as *e ma S. Austen ow leverall* SA 64v.13, 'St Augustine says'.
16 The Latin text can be found in the online *Corpus Thomisticum* [Opera Omnia S. Thomae de Aquino], http://www.corpusthomisticum.org/iopera.html (Pamplona: Universidad de Navarra, 2000). Accessed 17 April 2015.
17 Thomas Cranmer, *A defence of the true and catholike doctrine of the sacrament of the body and bloud of our sauiour Christ [...] approued by ye consent of the moste auncient doctors of the Churche* (London: Reginald Wolfe, 1550), which Foxe translated, cf. Elizabeth Evenden and Thomas S. Freeman, *Religion and the Book in Early Modern England: The Making of Foxe's 'Book of Martyrs'* (Cambridge: CUP, 2011), p. 93; Cuthbert Tunstall, *De ueritate corporis et sanguinis domini nostri Jesu Christi in*

are many parallels and shared texts. Tunstall, bishop of Durham 1530–1552 and 1554–1559, used patristic sources well in controversy. So did Cranmer, ably assisted by his scholar-secretary Pierre Alexander. Although their works are also not the direct source, the great similarities begin to anchor the text in the public debate over Eucharistic doctrine, of which they were a part, in the mid- to late sixteenth century.

It has already been noted that SA is later than TH—as witnessed by the marginal notes added to the latter in the same hand. On linguistic grounds, also, it betrays several late features. (These are listed and discussed in detail in the General section of the Notes.) In other words, while TH appears to be from the reign of Mary, there is a greater likelihood of SA being a recusant document from the reign of Elizabeth. As Nance also noticed, with his developed palaeographical skills, the handwriting of SA argues for a later date than TH. Indeed, the poor condition of the manuscript may suggest it was repeatedly hidden or moved, at a less favourable date for such writings.

While later than TH, it should nonetheless be stressed that SA is intimately linked to it. Although its structure and order do not exactly marry with the order of quotations in homilies 11 and 12, the author did go over these, while compiling and translating SA, providing, in effect, Bonner's homilies with additional references. It appears he was entrusted with TH at some point and wished to anchor it even more fully to the great contemporary proof texts of Eucharistic doctrine.

All this suggests the rather determined survival of recusant thought in Cornish-speaking parts of Cornwall, which were after all very remote from London. Despite the shortage of the kind of 'protecting' great houses found in other regions, some did exist,[18] and (protected or not) the seminarian in Vallodolid who in 1600 gave an address in the language before Philip III— possibly Richard Pentreth—underlines the persistence of the recusant Cornish and their links with communities and scholars abroad.[19]

---

eucharistia, 2nd edn (Paris: Michel de Vascosan, 1554). Tunstall wrote and compiled this work in 1551 under house arrest, but by the time of its publication he was restored to his office as bishop of Durham.

18 P.A. Boyan, ed. 'Life of Francis Tregian, Written in the Seventeenth Century by Francis Plunkett, Cistercian Monk', in *Miscellanea*, Catholic Record Society, 32 (London: Catholic Record Society, 1932), pp. 1–44; Clare Talbot, ed., *Miscellanea: Recusant Records*, Catholic Record Society, 53 (London: Catholic Record Society, 1961), pp. 114–15, 154, 197; Charles Henderson, 'The 109 Ancient Parishes of the Four Western Hundreds of Cornwall', *Journal of the Royal Institution of Cornwall*, new series, 3, 2 (1958), p. 367; Philip Payton, *Cornwall: A History*, 2nd edn (Fowey: Cornwall Editions, 2004), pp. 126–7.

19 See Chapter 7, note 5 for references to Pentreth/Pentrey in seminary records, and Peter Berresford Ellis, *The Cornish Language and its Literature* (London: Routledge, Kegan & Paul, 1974), pp. 70–72 (citing Henry Jenner, 'A Cornish Oration in Spain in the Year 1600', *90th Annual Report of the Royal Cornwall Polytechnic Society*, 1923). The Welsh Catholics on the continent were also

2.4 The source of SA—Foxe's account of the 1554 Oxford Disputations

Where might the author of SA have found his source material? The arguments and patristic quotations put forward in the 1554 Eucharistic Disputations at Oxford have many texts in common. These were recorded by notaries at the time, then summarized for various interested parties (as well as being worked up into an official report). Several manuscripts survive.[20] The most cursory reading of some of them reveals that the patristic quotations in SA follow the same sequences (although there are occasional jumps from one Disputation to another, then back again). Indeed, SA includes very few passages that are not from the patristic age, and virtually all of the more recent quotations are found—again in sequence—in the contributions made by the disputants as they debated. What is more, almost all of the (seemingly 'original') remaining minor phrases—such things as 'St Augustine says' (*e ma S. Austen ow leverall*), 'upon these same words' (*whar an keth gerriow ma*) and 'that is to say' (*henna ew the leverall*)—are themselves translations of the very words used by the disputants in the same place.

Nonetheless, there is no need to believe the text of SA has been directly translated from any of the surviving annotated and abbreviated contemporaneous notes of the Disputations. A much closer match—down to the spelling of words, errors in citation and identical editorial choices—is found in the account of those Disputations set out in John Foxe's *Actes and Monuments*—commonly called 'Foxe's Book of Martyrs'.[21]

---

active in the production of literature to support those at home—a major theme in Bowen, *Welsh Recusant Writings*.

20 E.g. British Library, Harl. MSS 3642 (the official report from Weston to Bonner); Parker Library, Corpus Christi College, Cambridge, MS 340, 11, ff. 247-64 and 13, ff. 271-80 (short notes of the principal arguments); Cambridge University Library, MS Kk.5.14, ff. 13-29 (a longer document written in much greater haste, with many abbreviations—which therefore seems to be at least a candidate for something taken down at the time); British Library, Harl. MSS 422, art. 53, 60, 68 (Ridley's notes).

21 Foxe's English account should be compared with his precursor Latin ones: see Evenden and Freeman, *Religion and the Book*, p. 85. Foxe had finished his *Commentarii*, a first draft of the initial portion of the *Actes and Monuments*, before he left England in 1554. But for the Disputations more useful is John Foxe, *Rerum in Ecclesia Gestarum, quæ postremis & pericolis his temporibus euanerunt [...]* (Basle: Nicolaus Brylinger, 1559). Henry Christmas, ed., *The Works of Nicholas Ridley, DD, sometime Bishop of London* (Cambridge: CUP, 1841), contains, in Appendix 1, pp. 433-85, the part of Foxe's Latin text relevant to Ridley, revised using Parker Library MS 340 from Corpus Christi College, Cambridge. The usefulness of the comparison is clear from pp. 476-9, for example, if read alongside T&C vi, 497-500 (TAMO, 1576, Bk 10, pp. 1408-09 [1383-84]). See also Claire Cross, *Church and People 1450-1660: The Triumph of the Laity in the English Church* (London: Fontana Press, 1987), pp. 122-3.

We can assert this because on the whole the manuscripts are either solely in Latin or in summary, abbreviated form, while Foxe's English version—although it includes Latin (and sometimes Greek) extracts of the patristic passages—is worked up into a polished account of the whole debate in English, including texts and translations of the patristic passages. Furthermore, it soon becomes apparent that these English translations have often directly influenced those in Cornish, and the Latin passages have been copied verbatim from the English edition. Thomas Stephyn's translation has more of the beginnings of a 'late modern' flavour to its Cornish than that of John Tregear, whose style leans a little more towards the classical texts of Middle Cornish. At the same time, while he seems less inclined than Tregear to borrow an English word when a perfectly good Cornish one will do, he still resorts to English. It is significant, therefore, that when he does do so, he is echoing the words of Foxe closely: *doubtys* for 'doubts' (SA 61r.39; TAMO 1392); *remaynea* for 'remaine' (SA 63r.5; TAMO 1576, 1394); *verely* for 'verilye' (SA 61r.40; TAMO 1576, 1392); *touchia* for 'touchest' (SA 60v.7; TAMO 1576, 1389); *recevya* for 'receaue' (SA 59r.39; TAMO 1576, 1388)—all in exactly the same sentences as Foxe uses them.

One of the most telling examples summarizes the point. At SA 63r.6 Thomas Stephyn has: *Rag henna te a recevest an Sacrament: mas in very ded te a obtaynest grace han gallus a nature a Christ.* Foxe, reporting Weston, has: 'therfore in a similitude thou receiuest the sacrament: but in deede thou obtainest the grace and power of his nature'.[22]

While this is not an exact translation in every detail, it explains the anomalous verbal forms in the Cornish perfectly, along with the highly anglicized choice of vocabulary. When each passage of SA is laid beside the corresponding passage from Foxe—something offered for the first time in this edition—many such illuminating conjunctions occur. Careful comparison of the Cornish and Foxe's English editions makes it clear that the Latin edition of Foxe was not being used, but one of the English ones.

2.5 The context of the Disputations

Having identified the source of SA as Foxe's account of the 1554 Oxford Disputations, it may be helpful to look at the context of other Eucharistic

---

22 Cf. SA 63r.6-7 and TAMO, 1576, p. 1394 [1369]; (T&C vi, 465). When citing Foxe from TAMO, the relevant year of the edition is given, followed by the modern pagination in TAMO and Foxe's page number if different [the latter in square brackets]. Most relevant quotations are from Book 10 of the 1576 edition so, after some initial comparisons, the book number is only given if another book is involved. When a reference to Townsend and Cattley's edition of 1838 (T&C) is added, the volume number (in lower-case Roman numerals) and page are given, then the whole enclosed in round brackets.

debates at the time and explain briefly how they were conducted. Disputations had occurred throughout the medieval period, between different schools of thought and even between Christians and Jews. As the Reformation progressed, some of these precedents provided a methodology for exploring and challenging the growing differences. Disputations at Heidelberg and Leipzig (1518 and 1519) were followed by Zwingli's debates in Switzerland and others such as the Diet of Regensburg (1541). Initially, papal authority and justification were major areas of contention, but increasingly transubstantiation and Eucharistic doctrine came to the fore.

In May and June 1549, under Edward VI, four days of formal debate over Eucharistic theology took place in England, split between both universities. The reformers' case was led by the distinguished foreign theologian Peter Martyr (Vermigli). These were published, and the King himself took a great interest.[23] Both sides sought to demonstrate that they had the support of antiquity, using biblical and patristic quotations, but the conservatives were hampered in this initial encounter by a fear of citing sources that were too close to papal authority or the opponents of the former regime (such as Bishop John Fisher).[24]

The methodology in these debates was rhetorical and logical, according to the understanding of the times, and not dissimilar to the way in which doctoral candidates then 'disputed for their form'. (Indeed, one such disputation forms part of the source material for SA.)[25] They were entirely rooted in the medieval 'scholastic' method, which began with an *auctor* (author or authority) deemed to be reliable, then tested and explored through various *sententiae* (sentences), pitting one assertion against another through dialectical reasoning and logic. The most approved 'authors'—if the matter could not be resolved by biblical proof texts—were usually the early Church Fathers or first councils. Textbooks even existed (such as that by Philip II's chaplain, Fray Alfonso de Castro) on how to conduct such disputations. While these counselled against public displays, they often took place in a mix of private and public encounters.[26] At first the reformers accepted the traditional logical

---

23 Diarmaid MacCulloch, *Tudor Church Militant: Edward VI and the Protestant Reformation* (London: Allen Lane/Penguin, 1999), pp. 91–3. Peter Martyr's treatise and an account of proceedings appeared under the title *A discourse or traictise of Petur Martyr Vermilla Flore[n]tine, the publyque reader of diuinitee in the Vniuersitee of Oxford ... wherein he openly declared his whole and determinate iudgemente concernynge the sacrament of the Lordes supper in the sayde Vniuersitee* (London: Robert Stoughton [i.e. E. Whitchurch] for Nicholas Udall, 1550). For a modern edition see Joseph C. McLelland, tr. and ed., *Peter Martyr Vermigli: The Oxford Treatise and Disputation on the Eucharist, 1549* (Kirksville: Thomas Jefferson University Press, 1994). Chedsey (see Commentary, Quotation 1 and notes), who played a lead role in the 1554 Disputations, had been equally central in 1549, though in a less comfortable position.
24 MacCulloch, *Tudor Church Militant*, p. 119.
25 See Commentary, Quotations 60, 61, 66, 70, 71.
26 Duffy, *Fires of Faith*, pp. 103–07.

premises of their Catholic counterparts (indeed Foxe excelled at analysing these arguments), but increasingly they challenged the veracity of texts, the status of authors and the soundness of the logic.

The debates as we have them in Foxe are an account of the full-scale academic disputation conducted by theologians from both Oxford and Cambridge with the bishops Latimer, Ridley and Cranmer in April 1554. (These evolved into trials when, in September 1555, Ridley and Latimer were summoned before a legatine commission with power to deliver them to the secular arm.) While the aim in theory was to reason with the defendants until they accepted their errors and recanted, there was also an element of the public 'show trial', with hissing and booing from unsympathetic onlookers of both 'town and gown'. This was meant to demonstrate in a very public way that Protestantism had lost the argument as well as the positions of power.[27]

Why did Foxe then—almost immediately—seek to collate a narrative of Disputations that were meant to demonstrate the victory of Catholicism over Protestantism? Perhaps because he felt that he could use it to underline the sanctity and scholarship of the defendants, as well as to answer and undermine some of the main arguments advanced. It would be an integral part of his wider project of completely changing perceptions of the Catholic past. This was not easy. As early as the summer of 1555, Foxe complained to Peter Martyr of the challenges he faced.[28] (It is fascinating that Stephyn, in due course, attempted the difficult task of reversing the impact of Foxe's account again, by similar selectivity, as will be explored in the Commentary.)

The debates and disputations that had got into their stride under Edward VI and continued under Mary did not, of course, end under Elizabeth. Some of the disputants, such as Thomas Harding, continued—from the safe distance of Leuven (Louvain)—to engage with reformers such as Jewel. Once again, the crux of the matter often came down to which authorities were accepted by both sides, and how literally they were interpreted.[29] Leuven in the 1560s was an important centre for Catholic exiles, printing Nicholas Sander's *Supper of our Lord* as well as Harding's various contentions with Jewel.[30] (Pope Pius V gave both Harding and Sanders powers to issue faculties and rulings binding in England.)

---

27 Duffy, *Fires of Faith*, pp. 103, 97.
28 Evenden and Freeman, *Religion and the Book*, p. 73 (citing BL Harley MS 417, f. 115r–v); see 6.2.
29 For Harding's role in the Oxford Disputations and later see, for example, Commentary, Quotations 59 and 68 and notes.
30 Sander, Nicholas, *The Supper of our Lord set foorth according to the truth of the Gospel & Catholike faith ... by Nicolas Saunder, Doctor of Divinitie* (Leuven/Louvain: Joannes Foulerus, 1566).

2.6 The specific edition of Foxe used and date of SA

Once it is known that SA is a series of abstracts from the 1554 Disputations in Foxe, a further question arises: which edition of Foxe was the author working from? It is relatively easy to establish that SA was written no earlier than 1570, since it incorporates many changes made by Foxe after his first edition of 1563. Minor corrections in the Latin quotations in the English edition for 1570 provide an excellent way of illustrating this:

SA 59v.5 *sufficit*	TAMO 1563, Book 5, p. 1013, *sufficiet*;
	TAMO 1570, Book 10, p. 1636 [1598], *sufficit*.
SA 60r.27 *lectus aureus*	TAMO 1563, Book 5, p. 1013, *lectum aureum*;
	TAMO 1570, Book 10, p. 1636 [1598], *lectus aureus*.
SA 60v.15 *hominis*	TAMO 1563, Book 5, p. 1015, *nominis*;
	TAMO 1570, Book 10, p. 1637 [1599], *hominis*.

Other differences are more substantial, such as the omission of words:

SA 60v.21–2 *signatur*	TAMO 1563, Book 5, p. 1015, *caro signatur*;
	TAMO 1570, Book 10, p. 1637 [1599], *signatur*.

In places, whole passages are omitted. In the quotation from St Ambrose, *De Mysteriis, 1, 9, 52* which begins with *De tocius mundi* at SA 61v.3, Foxe's first edition (TAMO 1563, Book 5, p. 1020) continues only as far as *mutare naturas*.[31] His edition of 1570 goes on from *Sed quid argumentis* to *affectus sentiat* (TAMO 1570, Book 10, p. 1641 [1603]) and SA does exactly the same (at SA 61v.7-22). This makes it clear that the 1563 edition was not being used.

Foxe's work, from 1570 on, was supposed to be made available as a large, chained volume in every cathedral in the land and a number of larger churches. Such wide and free availability suggests the possibility that the Latin texts of SA may have been drawn from such a volume. John Craig has begun to look forensically at the small collections of books that grew up in parish churches in the early modern period. The Bible and Foxe were high on the list, but paraphrases (such as those of Erasmus) and theological works could also be included. Some of these volumes survive in a number of churches, but parish inventories, glebe terriers and churchwardens' accounts bear witness to others.[32] One could

---

31 See Quotation 22 in the Commentary.
32 John Craig, 'Erasmus or Calvin? The Politics of Book Purchase in the Early Modern English Parish', in *The Reception of Continental Reformation in Britain and Ireland*, edited by P. Collinson

imagine a priest being above suspicion, copying from a volume in church that even government 'watchers' trusted as a safe repository of Protestant martyrology. The fact that he might have been selectively transcribing arguments for transubstantiation, with supporting patristic quotations, could have passed unnoticed.

We also know that some Cornish parish priests had private collections of books and may have shared these with like-minded colleagues. They considered carefully who to leave them to on their death.[33] Although Foxe was very expensive, it is not impossible that Stephyn or one of his confrères had access to a private copy, perhaps through the collection of a wealthy family (such as the Arundells of Lanherne). Cross-confessional reading was not uncommon, as traditionalists sought to understand and challenge reformers, and vice-versa. Unfortunately, the churchwardens' accounts for neither Newlyn East nor St Allen survive, as they might have told us of relevant book purchases around the time.[34]

Whatever his source for Foxe, it is likely that Stephyn was working even later than 1570, and indeed after 1576. Although Foxe's edition of 1576 varies only very slightly from 1570 in the passages concerned, close comparison suggests the best match is with 1576. Examples of changes not made before that date include:

SA 61r.8 *crebro*	TAMO 1563, Book 5, p. 1015, *crebo*;
	TAMO 1570, Book 10, p. 1637 [1599], *crebo*;
	TAMO 1576, Book 10, p. 1389 [1364], *crebro*;
	TAMO 1583, Book 10, p. 1459 [1435], *crebro*.

and P. Ha, Proceedings of the British Academy 164 (Oxford: OUP for the British Academy, 2010), pp. 39–62.

33 See 3.2 for the interesting case of Lawrence Godfrey, who left Tregear his books. Other clergy owned and bequeathed the *Acts and Monuments* itself, as in the case of Henry Postlethwaite—see Claire Cross, 'Religion in Doncaster from the Reformation to the Civil War', in Patrick Collinson and John Craig, eds, *The Reformation in English Towns, 1500-1640* (Basingstoke: Macmillan, 1998), p. 58.

34 The designation Newlyn East—anciently Newlyn—was only introduced for this parish when Newlyn St Peter near Penzance was created from part of the ancient parish of Paul in 1851. I have not yet been able to consult the churchwardens' accounts for St Columb Major, a nearby parish, which was also a focus for traditional religion, although receipts do survive for 1586–1600 (CRO, DDP 36/8/1). Surviving accounts for other Cornish parishes (none particularly near to Newlyn East) are listed in Ronald Hutton, *The Rise and Fall of Merry England, the Ritual Year 1400-1700* (Oxford: OUP, 1994), pp. 266–7. John Hobson Matthews, *A History of the Parishes of Saint Ives, Lelant, Towednack and Zennor in the County of Cornwall* (London: Elliott Stock, 1892), transcribes St Ives accounts, but although they mention 'The works of Bishop Jewel against Harding' (p. 73), Foxe does not seem to feature.

SA 60r.25 *homele. 34*   TAMO 1563, Book 5, p. 1013, *Home. 24*;
                         TAMO 1570, Book 10, p. 1636 [1598], *Homel. 24*;
                         TAMO 1576, Book 10, p. 1388 [1363], *Homel. 34*;
                         TAMO 1583, Book 10, p. 1458 [1434], *Homil. 34*.

There are many more examples, but most decisive of all are the figures '[1]383' at the foot of folio 65v (65a). They follow the passage where we read: *ema tillar arall e mes Cucell an Nice. Nullus Apostolorum dixit, hæc est figura corporis Christi. Nullus venerabilium præsbyterorum dixit in cruentum altaris sacrificium figuram*. In the 1576 edition of Foxe—on p. 1383—the same arguments are rehearsed, and the same texts appear: 'I bring an other place out of the Coūcell of Nice. *Nullus Apostolorum dixit, hæc est figura corporis Christi. Nullus venerabilium præsbyterorum dixit incruentum altaris sacrificium figuram*'. The presence of this page reference is surely decisive. We are not dealing with a Latin edition of Foxe, or his sources, or his other editions. We are dealing with his English edition of 1576. The page numbers of this passage in the other editions of Foxe are 1045 (in 1563), 1621 (in 1570) and 1454 (in 1583).

It is for this range of reasons that we can date the Cornish of SA as being written no earlier than 1576, and conceivably somewhat later. This is clearly of the utmost importance to Cornish scholars. It is something of a vindication of Nance's view, expressed in notes on his translation and arrived at on linguistic and palaeographic grounds, that SA was probably written 'twenty years or more' after TH.[35]

2.7 How did the author compile and translate SA?

In 1554 the Oxford Disputations served their original purpose, asserting in public the return of the Church of England to traditional pre-Reformation teaching on the Eucharist, after it had been questioned under Edward VI. Shortly after the Disputations were concluded, a solemn procession with adoration of the Blessed Sacrament was held in the streets of Oxford. The official records of the Disputations might then have fallen into decent obscurity, but Foxe's work eventually gave them new life. In reconstructing the debates at some length, once Protestantism was restored, he inevitably made available some of the quotations advanced in support of traditional Catholic doctrine.

These then resurfaced in SA, which for the most part leaves alone the arguments themselves and concentrates on the patristic proof-texts chosen

---

35 Courtney Library, *Nance Bequest* 7: 22 (46). In none of the arguments above is it implied that the 1576 edition was as substantially different to 1570 as, say, 1570 was from 1563, or 1583 from 1576. (See Evenden and Freeman, *Religion and the Book*, pp. 262–71.) Nonetheless, small differences do enable us to pinpoint the use of 1576.

by the Catholic disputants. Where SA does use Cranmer's choice of texts—which it sometimes does—they are generally used against him. In addition, a substantial patristic quotation in the middle of a passage from Justin Martyr in SA (taken from Cranmer's Disputation) is given in a slightly different version, partly drawn from the corrected version used by Ward in the Disputation with Ridley.[36] This is significant, since virtually all the other quotations are given verbatim, and in context. It also shows that if an initial transcription was made from a chained 1576 edition of Foxe,[37] possibly in Exeter, Hereford or Cornwall itself, Stephyn had sufficient access and time to roam freely backwards and forwards through the pages of Foxe, or to make extensive notes. Using a private or library copy, he would have had more leisure.

In any case, what we have in SA is a translation—normally from the English of Foxe into the Cornish—though perhaps at times also influenced by the Latin source texts. It should therefore be remembered that there was a considerable interest in the art of translation in the early modern period, and works dealing directly with it, which may (directly or indirectly) have influenced both Stephyn and Tregear.

Roger Ascham, for example, distinguishes *translatio linguarum* ('the translation of languages') and *imitatio* ('imitation') in *The Scolemaster* (1570), but Lawrence Humphrey's *Interpretatio Linguarum* ('the interpretation of languages') in 1559 takes *interpretatio* to include both. In a context in which literary achievement can include both assimilation and originality, therefore, 'almost all texts' in the early modern period 'have to be understood as a dialogue with their sources'.[38] (This certainly seems to be the case with SA, where in many instances we have simplification or paraphrase rather than literal translation.)

Thinking theoretically about translation was also part of a wider European tradition, beginning with Cicero's *De Optimo genere oratorum* ('on the best kind of orator') and embracing the ideas of Erasmus, translators of the Bible and, no doubt, the experience of many educated people who had themselves wrestled as children with Latin translation and sometimes with Greek. Lucy Wooding has shown, in her work on Erasmus, how both religious conservatives and radicals made use of his ideas on translation. In a sense these ideas were themselves

---

36 St Justin, Martyr, *Apologiae 1, 66*—see Quotation 31 in the Commentary for detailed references and to compare TAMO 1576, Book 10, p. 1394 [1369]—Cranmer's Disputation with TAMO 1576, Book 10, p. 1404 [1379]—Ridley's Disputation.
37 Churches that had bought 1576 would have found it costly to 'update' in 1583, since the latter was a much 'improved' and considerably more expensive volume.
38 See Neil Rhodes, Gordon Kendal and Louise Wilson, eds, *English Renaissance Translation Theory* (London: Modern Humanities Research Association, 2013), pp. 1–4 (introduction by Neil Rhodes); Massimiliano Morini, *Tudor Translation in Theory and Practice* (London: Routledge, 2017), first published 2006, pp. vii–x, 3–34.

'translated' and, while claiming a common theoretical approach, were subtly adapted to suit conflicting perspectives.[39]

Translators at this time also often theorized about the specific circumstances of their own vernaculars.[40] This included those working with the other Celtic languages in the British Isles, which has obvious resonances for our understanding of Tregear and Stephyn as they translated English into the Celtic language of Cornwall. Versions of the scriptures in Celtic vernaculars were appearing almost contemporaneously: William Morgan's Welsh Bible appeared in 1588, and the Irish New Testament of Uilliam O'Domhnuill (William Daniel) in 1603.[41] At the same time, of course, there was a degree of official discouragement of those vernaculars. The use of English was being insisted upon in Welsh courts and promoted strongly in Irish and Scottish education. There was sometimes a perception that the native languages were 'barbarous' and English a more 'civil' tongue,[42] and, as we have seen, Cranmer himself insisted on the use of English in the liturgy in Cornwall. Motives were conflicting and complex.[43]

Another interesting development was the conscious attempt in other Celtic vernaculars to borrow terms appropriate to the new learning from Latin models.[44] This was resisted by those who argued that their native tongues were equal to the classical languages and as of great antiquity.[45] The discussion easily polarized, with some advocating a purification (including of English, as well as Celtic languages) from all foreign and classical vocabulary, while others introduced it copiously, both as an enrichment and in the name of maintaining fidelity to sacred originals.[46] In this context it is easy to see how translators

---

39 Lucy Wooding, 'Erasmus and the Politics of Translation in Tudor England', *Studies in Church History*, 53 (Cambridge: CUP, 2017), pp. 132–45.
40 Rhodes et al., eds, *English Renaissance Translation Theory*, p. 5.
41 Felicity Heal, 'Mediating the Word: Language and Dialects in the British and Irish Reformations', *Journal of Ecclesiastical History*, 56: 2 (Cambridge: CUP, April 2005), p. 263; Felicity Heal, *Reformation in Britain and Ireland* [Oxford History of the Christian Church] (Oxford: OUP, 2003), pp. 284–6.
42 Heal, 'Mediating the Word', pp. 263–8. Heal also comments (p. 280) on the use of Cornish in Cornwall and on Veysey's order that the Epistle, Gospel, Paternoster, Creed and Commandments should be explained and taught in the language. (Latin, and not the vernacular, was once the norm: Nicholas Orme, *Going to Church in Medieval England* (New Haven and London: Yale University Press, 2021), p. 356.) Gradually, the reformers overcame a desire for cultural and political conformity and adopted a similar recognition of the necessity of translation, as when the Irish canons of 1634/1635 allowed Irish if strictly necessary. See Marc Caball, 'Gaelic and Protestant: a case study in early modern self-fashioning, 1567–1608', *Proceedings of the Royal Irish Academy: Archaeology, Culture, History, Literature*, 110C (Dublin: Royal Irish Academy, 2010), pp. 194–5.
43 See Chapter 1, note 36, and Heal, *Reformation in Britain and Ireland*, pp. 279–86.
44 See, for example, Bowen, *Welsh Recusant Writings*, pp. 2–4.
45 Heal, 'Mediating the Word', pp. 269–75.
46 As was the case with Gregory Martin in his Catholic translation of the scriptures.

such as Tregear and Stephyn—quite legitimately and defensibly—might have introduced some English or Latin terms for theological concepts. (Admittedly, in their cases, English introductions are not so confined, raising questions for some about how habitual their use of Cornish was at this point.)

Equally of interest to us is the way that, once a written standard was established, some vernaculars were slow to make concessions to developing spoken usage.[47] Such a tendency is harder to argue for in Stephyn than in Tregear.

2.8 Tregear and Stephyn in the wider orbit of Glasney

As has been explained, it was formerly a common assumption among students of Middle and Tudor Cornish that most of the surviving religious texts in the language were collated and copied at the College of Our Lady and St Thomas of Canterbury, at Glasney in Penryn.[48] The college played a dominant role in mid-Cornish ecclesiastical life in the early sixteenth century, by which time it was responsible for the pastoral care of many local parishes and villages. It was a natural base for study, and its residential canons (technically 'prebendaries') and their vicars would have been influential.[49] These factors made it an obvious starting place for early researchers to look for Tregear and Stephyn, but the usual sources for Glasney canons in residence during the period did not yield their names.[50] For this reason they often assumed that Tregear and Stephyn were chantry priests at the college, or even private chaplains to wealthy families associated with it. Either way, the assumption remained that they were unrecorded members of the Glasney community.

The reality has proved somewhat different. Casting the net wider than Glasney itself, to include the dispersed parish clergy only loosely associated with the college—especially vicars and curates in parishes where Glasney had appropriated the rectorial tithes—the search yielded results. We find men with these names as ordinary secular priests under the wider influence of the

---

47 Anciently, however, oral tradition may have been valued more highly than written forms in the Celtic family of languages; S.A. Handford, tr., *Caesar: The Conquest of Gaul*, 1.1 (Harmondsworth: Penguin, 1951), p. 32.
48 Known after the Henrician reformation by the less politically contentious name of the College of Our Lady of Glasney. The fullest summary is still Thurstan C. Peter, *The History of Glasney Collegiate Church, Cornwall* (Camborne: Camborne Printing and Stationary Company, 1903). See also James Whetter, *The History of Glasney College* (Padstow: Tabb House, 1988) and John A.C. Vincent, trans., *Abstract of Glasney Cartulary, a Quarto MS ... in the Library of Jonathan Rashleigh, Esq. of Menabilly* (Truro: Lake & Lake, 1879).
49 A 'vicar' at this time was someone who undertook an ecclesiastical responsibility on behalf of another, more senior, cleric—often assuming a prolonged absence.
50 Despite suggestive local place-names such as Tregaire in St Gerrans near Penryn—see Peter, *The History of Glasney Collegiate Church*, p. 47 and note.

college, though not in its immediate area. Both appear to have been ordained before the Reformation, yet continued in various ways to function after it. As we shall see, Tregear, far from being a formal recusant, appears to have remained in his parish under Henry VIII, Edward VI, Mary I and Elizabeth I—however Catholic or 'church papist' his views may have been (see 3.4). If so, he was helped by the remoteness of his parish—it was a long way from London—and the fact that he died just as Elizabethan anti-Catholic measures stepped up in intensity following Campion's trial and the Throckmorton plot, and well before the Babington plot and the Armada. Cornwall was hardly in the vanguard of any new metropolitan movements—as the rebellion of 1549 shows—and the persistence of traditional religion in areas such as north Cornwall and Devon towards the end of the century underlines this.[51]

Tregear appears to have been closely linked with Stephyn, who—while he found preferment under Mary—is a figure much less rooted in the establishment, again as we will see (4.3, 4.5). He appears to have been a typical 'Marian priest',[52] though ordained long before, in Henry's time. The history of such clergy in the early years of Elizabeth is, in its nature, surrounded by a good deal of fog. (As a result, we know far more of the centrally ordered Jesuits from continental seminaries, who began their mission from 1576 onwards, than we do of the older local clergy who sought to bridge the gap in the years before those missionary priests began to arrive.) Only a small number of recusant Catholic gentry, as we have seen—such as the Arundells of Lanherne and the

---

51 See 3.4; note 52 below and Chapter 3, note 34; Eamon Duffy's work on the parish of Morebath in north Devon (and Mark Stoyle's on St Keverne and Manaccan) has raised the question of the extent to which normally law-abiding parishioners and traditionalist clergy may have been drawn into the 1549 'commotions'. See Eamon Duffy, *The Voices of Morebath: Reformation & Rebellion in an English Village* (New Haven and London: Yale University Press, 2001), pp. 118–41, esp. p. 135; Mark Stoyle, 'A Hanging at St Keverne: The Execution of Two Cornish Priests in 1549', *Devon and Cornwall Notes and Queries*, 42: 1 (2017), pp. 1–4; Mark Stoyle, 'Fully Bent to Fighte Oute the Matter: Reconsidering Cornwall's Role in the Western Rebellion of 1549', *The English Historical Review*, 129, 538 (Oxford: OUP, 2014), pp. 549–77; Frost, 'Glasney's Parish Clergy', pp. 56–7 and in Payton, ed., *Cornwall in the Age of Rebellion*, pp. 195–7. After completion but before publication of this edition, an important new study has been published: Mark Stoyle, *A Murderous Midsummer: The Western Rising of 1549* (New Haven, CT, and London: Yale University Press, 2022). Older studies include Rose-Troup, Frances, *The Western Rebellion of 1549: An Account of the Insurrections in Devonshire and Cornwall against Religious Innovations in the Reign of Edward VI* (London: Smith, Elder & Co., 1913) and Caraman, Philip, *The Western Rising, 1549* (Tiverton: Westcountry Books, 1994).

52 The term 'Marian priest' or 'old priest' usually refers not only to those ordained in Mary I's reign (and a few months after) but also to priests from earlier reigns, if they were ordained in the Catholic rite, welcomed the Marian restoration and perhaps even worked overtly to uphold traditional religion in the early years of Elizabeth I. Cf. Patrick McGrath and Joy Rowe, 'The Marian Priests under Elizabeth I', *Recusant History*, 17: 2 (October 1984), pp. 103–20.

Tregians of Golden—were able to maintain chaplains for their own needs and those of the local populace.

There is no need to assume a hard and fast division between the approaches of the two men. In Cornwall there were (often exaggerated) folk tales of the celebration of Mass 'in the tin mines' after the Reformation, in a way analogous to the celebrations at 'Mass stones' on the moors of Ireland or Lancashire. In practice, however, such celebrations were more likely to have been in the vicarage parlour.[53] Although ultimately the attempt to preserve traditional religion in the parishes failed, in the intriguing years between 1560 and 1580 the outcome often looked less sure. William Bradbridge sought to resign as bishop of Exeter diocese (which included Cornwall) in 1576, at least in part because his success had been so partial against defaulters from the Elizabethan settlement.[54]

To understand both elements of the Tregear Manuscript together, therefore, it is necessary to look in some detail at the parish careers of its two authors in rural western Cornwall. Both priests (and possibly others about whom Cornish language scholars have been curious) seem to have been based in ordinary local churches rather than in any college or religious community—although they may have been under the patronage of a particular canon before the dissolution.[55] After the dissolution, of course, it was only out in the parishes that efforts to preserve traditional religion through the medium of Cornish could be made.

---

53 Such as the Masses reported to have been said at St Columb Major as late as 1590: see 3.4, and Payton, *Cornwall, A History*, pp. 126-7 and, for the wider context, pp. 101-30.
54 R.J.E. Boggis, *A History of the Diocese of Exeter* (Exeter: William Pollard & Co., 1922), p. 377.
55 Considerably more detail, speculation and extensive further references for the next two chapters—on Tregear and Stephyn—may be found in the source from which they are partly drawn: Frost, 'Glasney's Parish Clergy', pp. 31-46, 52-65, 72-8 or, revised and updated, in Payton, ed., *Cornwall in the Age of Rebellion*, pp. 167-85, 191-205, 210-12.

CHAPTER THREE

John Tregear—Translator of Bonner

3.1 John Tregear, vicar of St Allen, 1544–1583

The Robert Morton Nance Bequest at the Courtney Library of the Royal Institution of Cornwall in Truro contains a number of notes gathered by Nance on the possible identity of Tregear, including the information that the Revd G.C. Sara had found an entry in the parish register of Newlyn East recording:

> John Tregear, clerk,
> bur[ied] the xxiv th day of march,
> the year [1583].[1]

Sara knew that Tregear was not the vicar or parish clerk of Newlyn East itself, as the names of these were known for the 1580s. Nor did he find Thomas Stephyn in this parish register. His suggestion was that Tregear and Stephyn held no benefices because of their Catholic views, and were perhaps private chaplains to a recusant household.[2]

Tregear's will might have resolved the question, but the records of the Exeter ecclesiastical courts were moved from the cathedral to the nearby Exeter Probate Registry before the Second World War, and it was bombed in 1942. A printed calendar of wills made at an earlier point records the will's existence:

> 1583, Tregear, John, vicar of St Alin. 384 W.[3]

---

1 Courtney Library, *Nance Bequest*, 7:22 (46)—in the opening notes placed with A.S.D. Smith's typescript (C) of Nance's transcription of Tregear. The year given is 1582, although Tregear died in March 1583: at that time the new year began with Lady Day—25 March—on the eve of which he was buried. (I have amended years to end on 31 December throughout, while retaining 'old style' for the dates.) The *Parish Registers of Newlyn East* are available on microfiche, along with transcripts, at the Archives and Cornish Studies Service, Kresen Kernow, in Redruth (formerly the CRO). The first volume contains baptisms from 1560 and marriages and burials from 1559.
2 Courtney Library, *Nance Bequest*, 7:22 (46) at the foot of the typescript of 'Something New in Cornish'.
3 Edward Alexander Fry, ed., *Calendar of Wills and Administrations relating to the Counties of Devon and Cornwall, proved in the Court of the Principal Registry of the Bishop of Exeter, 1559-1799 and, of*

The Episcopal Registers for the diocese have survived, and it is possible to confirm this. The second entry for 11 September 1583 in the Registers of Bishop Woolton describes the institution of Christopher Colmer:[4]

> *de vic. perpetu. Sti. Aluni Exon. Dioc.*
> [as vicar of St Allen in the diocese of Exeter]

There it is noted that the living had become vacant

> *per mortem Johannis Tregeare.*
> [by the death of John Tregear]

Slight errors of transcription in *Hennessy's Incumbents*, a manuscript study of institutions from the Episcopal Registers,[5] have in the past obscured Tregear's link with the parish. Hennessy lists the appointment of 'Xfer Colmo',[6] to St Allen, on the death of 'Jn Tregearn' [*sic*]. (Study of the entry in the Bishop's Register itself reveals that Hennessy should have recorded the spelling as 'Tregeare'.)

If Tregear's time at St Allen came to an end in 1583, when did it start? Hennessy records William Treruffe as Tregear's predecessor,[7] and the year he left office as 1544. It is therefore possible to return to the Registers—in this case those of John Veysey—and look for the institution of Tregear himself. There, in an entry for the 28 July 1544 we find the bishop granting

> *Johani Tregayre, presbitero*
> *vicariam p[er]petuam eccl[esi]e p[ar]ochialis de Alune in Cornub[ia].*[8]

Devon only, proved in the court of the Archdeaconry of Exeter 1540-1799, vol. I (Plymouth: British Record Society, 1908), p. xxi in the Preface, correcting the misreading 'of St Olave' on p. 2. This calendar (p. 183) also records the will of John Tresteyn, vicar of the adjacent parish of Newlyn East, who had died in 1581—cf. also CRO, *Parish Registers of Newlyn East*, vol. i, f. 86.

4 *Episcopal Registers of John Woolton*, DRO, Chanter 21, f. 11r. John Woolton was bishop of Exeter 1571–1593. Colmer may represent the modern name Colmore.

5 *Hennessy's Incumbents* (and a valuable copy, with indices) is deposited in the West Country Studies Library in Exeter (see DRO). Hennessy drew up his lists (of incumbents only) by working through inductions, collations and other appointments in the Exeter Episcopal Registers, omitting any references to unbeneficed clergy and the ordination registers. His work—although at times slightly inaccurate—is an invaluable partial index to the unpublished sixteenth-century registers.

6 *Hennessy's Incumbents*, list of incumbents for St Allen.

7 In some copies wrongly transcribed as William 'Trerusse'.

8 *Episcopal Registers of John Veysey*, DRO, Chanter 14, f. 113r. Tregear's appointment followed the resignation of William Treruffe (also sometimes recorded as 'Tyrruffe'), who may well have been a curate at Ewny Lelant in 1522 during the incumbency of James Gentle, later provost of Glasney, cf. *1522 Military Survey*, ed. Stoate (1987), p. 7.

> [John Tregear, priest,
> to be vicar of the parish church of St Allen in Cornwall.]

This indicates that while Tregear was effectively the parish priest, only the vicarial tithes would be his and not the great tithes of corn. As in a good number of parishes in central and western Cornwall—including Budock, Colan, St Enoder, Feock, St Goran, Gluvias, St Just in Penwith, Kea and Kenwyn, Manaccan, Mevagissey, Mylor, Sithney and Zennor—these had long been assigned to Glasney College, Penryn, as part of its considerable endowment, mostly accumulated between 1265 and 1288. (Mevagissey and St Just were added in the fourteenth century.)[9]

John Tregear was still vicar of St Allen three years after Queen Mary's death, in December 1561, when Bishop Alley (it is assumed) ordered a survey of all the clergy of the diocese for the records of Archbishop Parker. This survives among the manuscripts of the Parker Library at Corpus Christi College, Cambridge,[10] and contains a helpful entry for St Allen:

> Alene: Dominus Johannes Tregeyre, vic[arius],
> non grad[uatus],
> pres[byter] non coni[ugatus] nec conc[ubinarius],
> satis doctus,
> residet, hospitalis, ibid[em] degens,
> non pred[ica]t, nisi in prop[rio] ben[eficio] nullum aliud.
>
> [St Allen: Sir John Tregear,[11] vicar,
> non-graduate,
> unmarried priest, not co-habiting,
> sufficiently educated,
> resident, hospitable, living in the same place,
> non-preaching unless in his own parish, no other.]

---

9   At the time of Henry VIII's *Valor Ecclesiasticus*, the priest of St Allen would have received £8. 13s. 4d.—perhaps a little more in Tregear's time—see John Caley and Joseph Hunter, eds, *Valor Ecclesiasticus, tempore Regis Henrici Octavi* (London: British Record Commission, 1821), vol. 2, f. 398.

10   Parker Library MS 97, f. 177r. There is a transcript—probably made by A.J. Watson of the British Museum in 1927—in the DRO (Z19/10/1b: f. 54) along with photostats of the original (Z19/10/1a: f. 44). Alley's list for the diocese of Exeter, with an approximate date of Christmas 1561 from internal evidence, is the document fortunately preserved at Cambridge. See also *Devon & Cornwall Notes & Queries*, xv, 35, January 1928, pp. 38–41. Field argues for a slightly later date (19 July 1563) by the time the document was formally submitted: C.W. Field, *Exeter Diocese in 1563: Alley's Survey* (Robertsbridge, Sussex: privately published typescript, 1994), preface.

11   The Latin title *Dom* (for *Dominus*) was accorded at the time to any priest and translated into English as 'Sir' (with, of course, no implication of knighthood).

From this we learn that Tregear (1) was still vicar of St Allen; (2) had never been to university; (3) was still unmarried and genuinely celibate; (4) was reasonably well educated (and therefore had possibly gone to a grammar school, at Glasney or elsewhere, or had otherwise been taught to read and write Latin—and, we may add, Cornish);[12] (5) was not an absentee clergyman and was welcoming, hospitable and actually living in St Allen when the survey took place; (6) did not go about from parish to parish preaching, as some conservative clergy were reputed to do;[13] and (7) held no other living or church appointment.

3.2 Tregear and Lawrence Godfrey

Another clear reference to Tregear is as a witness to the will of neighbouring priest, Lawrence Godfrey, on 12 September 1563.[14] Godfrey describes himself as the vicar of 'Saincte Piran in zandes', that is, Perranzabuloe. There are some bequests to his godchildren, then he turns to John Tregear:

> Item: to Sir John Tregeare clarke Vicar of Alune
> one stone of my beste wooll my ffrocke and my cassok...
> ...and I doe ordaine the saide vicar of Alune to be my superviser
> vppon this my laste will and testament
> and he to sell my corne and devide the value thereof
> as muche as is drye amonge the poore
> and in workes of charitie for the healthe of my soule.
>
> Item my bookes, to be devided amonge prestes
> to the saide vicar of Alunis discrecion.

John Tregear was clearly held in high regard by Lawrence Godfrey, and there is a glimpse of some learning, and a valuing of it, among these Cornish country clergy.

---

12 For the extent of the language (and bilingualism) in Tregear's time see O.J. Padel, 'Where was Middle Cornish Spoken?' *Cambrian Medieval Celtic Studies (CMCS)*, 74 (Winter 2017) (Aberystwyth: CMCS, 2017), pp. 4–5, 14–15 and Spriggs, 'Where Cornish was Spoken and When'. (Also Julyan Holmes, 'On the Track of Cornish in a Bilingual Country', in Philip Payton, ed., *Cornish Studies*, 2nd series, 11 (Exeter: UEP, 2003), p. 71.)

13 Edward Scambler, bishop of Peterborough in 1564, complained of 'the stragling doctors and priestes who haue libertie to stray at there pleasures within this realme'. Mary Bateson, ed., 'A Collection of Original Letters from the Bishops to the Privy Council, 1564', *The Camden Miscellany*, 9 (London: Camden Society, 1893), p. 34 (and, for the particularly interesting situation in Herefordshire involving exiled Exeter clergy, pp. 19–21 and 4.4–5; for Cornwall pp. 69–70).

14 I am particularly indebted to Joanna Mattingly for drawing my attention to this will, preserved in The National Archives and available online, ref. TNA, PROB/11/47/298. For more on Godfrey see Frost, 'Glasney's Parish Clergy', pp. 36–8, and updated in Payton, ed., *Cornwall in the Age of Rebellion*, pp. 172–4.

3.3 Tregear and John Tresteyn— clues to place of birth and ordination

Because of the importance of his origins when considering the form of Cornish he uses in the manuscript, and his network of relationships with Stephyn, it would be helpful to have some indication of where Tregear was born. The form of the name in Cornish suggests a toponymic surname.[15] Camborne, Crowan, Sithney and Stithians all had families called Tregear, and there were others at Newlyn East, Cubert and elsewhere, but none can yet be conclusively linked with Tregear's family.[16]

Despite this uncertainty, an unproved but particularly intriguing possibility is that Tregear came from Crowan, where there was a noted family bearing the name. The Heraldic Visitation of 1620 traces a John Tregear (aged 9 in 1620) back through four generations to a John Tregear of Crowan who married Amy, the third daughter of John Owry—one of the Tregonwells).[17] Two John Tregears who make an appearance in the return for Crowan in the 1522 Military Survey are almost certainly of this family.[18] In the list for the Loan, rated at £10, John Tregear apparently has a son, John Tregear 'junior', listed with him. There is only one John Tregear noted, however, by the time of the later surveys of 1544 and 1562. It is therefore possible that a young Tregear could have been ordained soon after the 1522 Survey, or even have already been a priest at that point, serving as a chaplain informally in his home parish, and possibly an adjacent one.[19] In support of this idea, another priest, John Tresteyn,[20] appears in the same list as

---

15 It is not possible, without further evidence, to identify conclusively which of around ten occurrences of this place-name might have been the ultimate origin of Tregear's family. Even if we could do this, at this date it would no longer guarantee that Tregear himself had lived in that place. Toponymics were becoming fixed, and therefore portable.
16 *1522 Military Survey*, Camborne (p. 3), Crowan (pp. 25, 148), Sithney (p. 34, 154), Stithians (p. 151). See also Frost, 'Glasney's Parish Clergy', p. 82, nn. 140-4 or in Payton, ed., *Cornwall in the Age of Rebellion*, pp. 193, 230-1, nn. 145-9.
17 For the origins of the place-name Tregear at Crowan see O.J. Padel, Cornish Place-Name Elements, [English Place-Names Society (EPNS) vols 56-7] (Nottingham: EPNS, 1985), pp. 223-32; 50-4. For the visitation see J.L. Vivian, *The Visitations of Cornwall, comprising the Heralds' Visitations of 1530, 1573 & 1620* (Exeter: W. Pollard, 1887), pp. 469-70 (based on Harl. MS. 1162). Of course, there may be mistakes or omissions—deliberate or otherwise—in the pedigree given by the family, abstracted in Frost, 'Glasney's Parish Clergy', p. 53. Wills and other records could profitably be explored, and some may survive outside Cornwall.
18 *1522 Military Survey*, p. 25, spelt 'Tregere'.
19 It is interesting that, in the parish of Crowan, the Tregear homestead and farm appears to be a long-established settlement, lying adjacent to Tregear Round at SW 640343 (which typifies Padel's 'univallate curvilinear hillslope enclosures': Padel, *Cornish Place-Name Elements*, under **ker*, pp. 50-54).
20 He himself spells his name Tresteyn in the Subscriptions to the Renunciation of Papal Authority, TNA E 36/64, f. 40. His family name appears ultimately to derive from Trestain in

Tregear junior. It is possible that both were unbeneficed priests in or near Crowan at the time, adding another name to the group around Stephyn and Tregear.[21]

I have found no unambiguous John Tregear in any of the Exeter ordination registers of the right period (although many 'Johns' are ordained without surnames). The possibility of an ordination outside the diocese may resolve the impasse, and this is illustrated by the ecclesiastical careers of John Tresteyn and William Treruffe,[22] both mentioned above. Treruffe was one of Tregear's predecessors at St Allen (1531–1544) after which he moved to Cubert as a near neighbour.[23] Tresteyn was one of Stephyn's successors at Newlyn, also served at Manaccan and, as we have just noted, must have known Ralph Trelobys, the incumbent of Crowan and his assistant clergy.

Both men were therefore contemporaries of Tregear and Stephyn. Both were confirmed and made acolyte by Thomas Chard, bishop of Solubria, in the Lady Chapel of Exeter Cathedral on 22 December 1515. On the following 16 February both were made subdeacon by the same bishop in the same place.[24] It is therefore most interesting that when Chard moved on to conduct an ordination in the lady chapel of Wells Cathedral on 8 March 1516, these two went with him. There, among others—including many monks of Glastonbury—he deaconed Treruffe (with Launceston Priory as his title) and Tresteyn (with St John's Priory, Exeter as his title).[25] Finally, on 22 March—barely a fortnight later—he ordained both to the priesthood in his Priory of St Peter and St Paul at Montacute.[26]

Ruan Lanihorne, Roseland, across the water from Glasney, although we do not know whether Tresteyn himself came from there. For that place-name see Padel, *Cornish Place-Name Elements*, pp. 212, 223–32.

21 In the *1522 Military Survey*, also on p. 25 under Crowan, John 'Treger' and John 'Trestene' appear in the same valuation. Ralph Trelobys (here as 'Trelowbys') appears in this same list as vicar (see Chapter 5). On pp. 34–5, under Sithney, the neighbouring parish, John 'Tregeyr' and John 'Treleigne', clerk, are also both listed. 'Treleigne' looks like an error for 'Tristeigne' (which does occur in various clergy lists for Tresteyn, whereas no cleric with a name remotely like Treleigne otherwise appears). Perhaps the two men were serving both parishes in some way.

22 Hennessy sometimes reads the name as Trerusse, although it is clearly Treruffe in the registers and, in two places, Treruth.

23 *Episcopal Registers of John Veysey*, DRO, Chanter 14, f. 55r. Treruffe was appointed on 7 September 1531.

24 The confirmation (of 'Trystayne') took place in the Lady Chapel of Exeter Cathedral; *Episcopal Registers of Hugh Oldham*, DRO Chanter 13, f. 122v. For the subdeaconing (of 'Tristayn') in the same place see f. 123v.

25 *Episcopal Registers of Cardinal Hadrian de Castello*, bishop of Bath and Wells and cardinal priest of St Chrysostom, Somerset Record Office (SRO), D/D/breg/10, f. 157v. For the system of 'titles' see the useful summary in Tim Cooper, *The Last Generation of English Catholic Clergy: Parish Priests in the Diocese of Coventry and Lichfield in the Early Sixteenth Century* (Woodbridge: The Boydell Press, 1999), pp. 19–27.

26 *Episcopal Registers of Cardinal Hadrian de Castello*, SRO, D/D/breg/10, f. 158r. Treruffe is clearly spelled 'Treruffe' here, and Tresteyn as 'Tristeyne'. There was a short-lived attempt to restore

This surely gives quite a revealing picture of an aspect of Tudor church life not often appreciated. It also illustrates the difficulty of pinpointing Tregear's ordination, with so many portions of the episcopal records now being lost.[27]

3.4 Tregear's 'church papism'

There is evidence of Tregear's continuing ministry in his parish well into the Elizabethan era. Indeed, he and his parish may help us understand what has been called the 'church papist' position within the Church of England. The roots of this, especially in Cornwall, may be traced to dissatisfaction with religious policy under both Henry VIII and Edward VI, emerging more robustly under Elizabeth.[28] While the missionary priests increasingly challenged church papism, it continued in parallel with recusancy, with which it had a porous boundary.

Although Stephyn may have left the formal parochial structure, there is no reason to suppose that he and Tregear did not still work closely together. The terms 'recusant' and 'church papist' are not at all mutually exclusive at this point.[29] Indeed, as Walsham has argued, the relationship between those 'Catholics' living in partial conformity, those rejecting that conformity and between the various schools of thought on the subject among the missionary priests, is a complex and diverse picture. While the Jesuits, for example, maintained an overarching public resistance to conformity (not least for polemical reasons), their pastoral practice, particularly in reconciliation, was more lenient and nuanced.[30]

So, while it is hard to see how Tregear could have survived in the Church of England as long as he did, given his earlier inclinations, Duffy has shown how another conservative-minded priest in the diocese, Christopher Trychay,

---

Montacute under Mary I: see J.H. Betty, *Wessex from AD 1000: A Regional History of England* (London: Longman, 1986), p. 118.
27 Exeter ordination records between 1526 and 1547, for instance, are missing.
28 Walsham identifies George Gifford, in *A Dialogue between a Papist and a Protestant, applied to the capacitie of the unlearned* (London, 1582) f. 1v, as one of the first to use the term in print: cf. Alexandra Walsham, *Church Papists: Catholicism, Conformity and Confessional Polemic in Early Modern England* (Woodbridge: The Boydell Press, 1993) [reprinted 1999], p. 1.
29 Walsham, *Church Papists*, p. 73; see also pp. 73–9.
30 Cf. Alexandra Walsham, 'Yielding to the Extremity of the Time': Conformity, Orthodoxy and the Post-Reformation Catholic Community', in Peter Lake and Michael Questier, eds, *Conformity and Orthodoxy in the English Church, c. 1560–1660* [Studies in Modern British Religious History] (Woodbridge: The Boydell Press, 2000), pp. 211–36; Alexandra Walsham, *Catholic Reformation in Protestant Britain* [Catholic Christendom 1300–1700] (Aldershot: Ashgate, 2014), pp. 87–94; and Walsham, *Church Papists*, pp. xi–xvi.

stayed in office at Morebath for many years after the Reformation.[31] We have evidence from Wales of devout Catholic families still attending the parish church on Sunday as late as the 1570s. The elderly and much-respected Welsh exiles in Rome accepted this blending of loyalties, where the local vicar said Mass quietly and behind closed doors once the state-imposed service was performed.[32]

In Cornwall, there is scattered evidence that it was possible to resist conformity more comprehensively and for far longer than in many other areas. Such incidents as the vicar of Kilkhampton brazenly declaring in 1584 that he had 'never heard' of the new Prayer Book, and the reports of Mass still being said at St Columb Major as late as 1590, underline this.[33] It is true that Cornwall was short of wealthy families willing and able to help the laity resist unwelcome reforms by bearing the burden of fines and supporting priests who celebrated clandestine liturgies. But there were exceptions. Sir John Arundell of Lanherne was dispatched to the tower for protecting and perpetuating the old religion in 1584, and Sir Francis Tregian provided sanctuary to the first Jesuits, including the Catholic martyr now canonized as St Cuthbert Mayne.[34]

In April 1578, a 'Humphridus Hendye' was included on a list of recusants for daring to say that there was still 'holy brede, holy water, masse and mattens in Cornwall and that ytt shalbe every where shortlye', along with the hope that ere long 'the Quene should be no bodye'.[35] In 1586, not long after Tregear's death, a list was made by the puritans of around twenty of Veysey's or Turberville's priests still in Cornish parishes considered to be working against the new

---

31   Duffy, *The Voices of Morebath*, pp. 180–1, 190.
32   Daniel J. Mullins, 'St Francis Xavier College': unpublished lecture given to the Wales and Marches Catholic History Society in June 2006. I am grateful to Bishop Mullins for lending me his notes for this lecture. The evidence for this practice comes from, among other sources, a long letter written by Robert Gwyn of Bangor diocese. Gwyn entered Douai College in 1571, was ordained in 1575, and argues in this letter to his family that they should not attend the services of the established Church in future (alongside hearing Mass in private) as they had done hitherto.
33   Payton, *Cornwall, A History*, pp. 126–7.
34   See P.A. Boyan and G.R. Lamb, *Francis Tregian: Cornish Recusant* (London: Sheed & Ward, 1955), p. 47 for a list of others implicated with Cuthbert Mayne including Nicholas Roscarrock of St Endellion. The main historic sources for Tregian's life are: Oscott MS 545 (1593) printed in J. Morris, *The Troubles of our Catholic Forefathers, related by themselves* (London: Burns & Oates, 1877) and Francis Plunket, *Heroum Speculum: De vita DD. Francisci Tregeon cuius corpus septendecim post annos in aede D. Rochi integrum inentum est [...]* (Lisbon: Officina Craesbeeckiana, 1655), printed in *Miscellanea, 15*, Catholic Record Society 32 (London: Catholic Record Society, 1932). (Boyan & Lamb, *Francis Tregian*, also cite BL Add MS 24489, ff. 296; 21, 203; Cotton MSS, Titus B.7, f. 46; John Roche Dasent, ed., *Acts of the Privy Council*, new series, vol. 9, 1575–1577, p. 390 and vol. 10, p. 29.) See also A.L. Rowse, *Tudor Cornwall* (London: Jonathan Cape, 1941), pp. 344–75 for a less sympathetic view.
35   Talbot, *Miscellanea*, pp. 114–15. This is a transcript from the Cecil Papers, 9/112.

religion to a greater or lesser extent.³⁶ In this context, it is possible to imagine Tregear remaining in his parish without abandoning all his former beliefs. The undoubted compromises of such a position may have been balanced by a hefty degree of non-compliance. Had he lived much longer, of course, it would have been more difficult. As it is, he died before the storm gathered its full strength.

---

36 Albert Peel, ed., *The Seconde Parte of a Register, being a calendar of Manuscripts under that title intended for publication by the Puritans about 1593, and now in Dr Williams' Library, London* (Cambridge: CUP, 1915), vol. 2, pp. 98–110. The suspect priests, or 'Mass-men', were often harshly judged simply because they were ordained under the old rite: usually their integrity was criticized.

CHAPTER FOUR

Thomas Stephyn—Compiler of *Sacrament an Alter*

4.1 Thomas Stephyn, vicar of Newlyn East in 1557

Thomas Stephyn, the suggested compiler of *Sacrament an Alter*, has a much more common name than his collaborator Tregear, so his footprint is harder to trace. It is sometimes difficult to be sure we have the right man. Many Thomas Stephyns lived in Exeter diocese at this time, including more than one priest with the same or a similar name. Fixed surnames were becoming established as we have noted, but people did still change their names, sometimes being drawn from the traditional model based on patronymics to toponymics (with some occupational names and nicknames). The legacy of this pattern remains among the Cornish to this day.[1]

Fortunately, we have both a *terminus post quem* and a *terminus ante quem* for Stephyn's literary work, and some of the other Thomas Stephyns are insufficiently close to Tregear in age, location, clerical status or faith to fit. Nor is it likely that a stranger would have been entrusted with so important and dangerous a manuscript, with all the risks this could involve for individuals, families and their reputations. In addition, it is important to consider the areas where Cornish was still spoken at least bilingually at the time.[2] The Thomas Stephyn we are looking for has a reasonable knowledge of the language, albeit with many 'late' features and some interesting lapses into English usage. It is hard to prove conclusively either way whether his was a native knowledge, making accommodations to late usage and theological vocabulary in a context of bilingualism, or whether he learned the language at a later stage.

In the light of all this, it looks increasingly likely that the Thomas Stephyn appointed in 1557 as vicar of Newlyn East—the adjacent parish to St Allen—is the

---

1 See O.J. Padel, 'Cornish Surnames in 1327', *Nomina*, 9 (1985), pp. 81–7, and H.S.A Fox and O.J. Padel, eds (2000), *The Cornish Lands of the Arundells of Lanherne, Fourteenth to Sixteenth Centuries*, Devon and Cornwall Record Society (DCRS), new series, 21 (Exeter: Devon and Cornwall Record Society, 2000), pp. cxxiv–cxxxvii; see also Bernard Deacon, *The Surnames of Cornwall* (Redruth: CoSerg, 2019).
2 See Chapter 3, note 12.

man we are looking for.[3] He appears not to have been an incumbent before and is unlikely to have been a committed Protestant, being appointed vicar under James Turberville, Veysey's successor as bishop of Exeter under Queen Mary. When he was instituted on 5 March 1557—St Piran's Day—his job would have been to restore Catholic practice according to the typical pattern of the Marian Counter-Reformation, with Masses, processions and even, perhaps, sermons and joint pilgrimages with nearby parishes. He may not have continued long in the parish after the accession of Elizabeth, as his successor Richard Martyn was replaced himself in 1573.[4]

Fortunately, we have an almost contemporary account of a procession of relics to the chapel of St Nectan in this very parish at Rogationtide during the Marian years. Rogation processions were very popular, and although banned under Edward, they were restored under Mary and even tolerated under Elizabeth. The account is included in Nicholas Roscarrock's *Lives of the Saints*:

> Ther was a chapple in the parishe of Sct Newlan in Cornwall called Sct Neghtons of the saint to which it was dedicated, which chapple had a yard belonginge vnto it in which ther were four stones on a little mount or hill at the Northwest corner wher the crosses and reliques of Sct Piran, Sct Crantocke, Sct Cuthbert, Sct Newlan were wont to bee placed in rogation weeke, at which time they vsed to meete ther [and had a] sermond made to the people, and the last was preached by persone Crane in Queene Maries tyme, as I haue bene credibly informed by a priest who had bene an eye witnesse.[5]

4.2 Thomas Stephyn, curate of Newlyn East in 1536

Even if this procession took place before Stephyn became the incumbent, there are very good reasons for thinking he might well have been there (and was possibly even the eyewitness from whom Roscarrock heard the account). This is because, in addition to his spell as vicar, he seems to have been an assistant curate in the parish for a considerable period beforehand, trusted to run it during the incumbent's periods of residence elsewhere. This underlines what may have been a long association with the area (and with Tregear). For evidence of this

---

3   *Episcopal Registers of James Turberville*, DRO, Chanter 18, f. 15r.
4   See note 29 below.
5   Nicholas Orme, ed., *Nicholas Roscarrock's Lives of the Saints, Cornwall and Devon* (Exeter: Devon and Cornwall Record Society, 1992), p. 94, with useful notes on pp. 159-60. The original is at Cambridge University Library, MS Add. 3041 (C), although the first and last sections are missing, and the manuscript title—*A Briefe Regester or Alphabeticall Catalogue [...]*—may in fact be merely a subtitle of one section. Henry Crane was the rector of Withiel and, in Orme's view, 'probably a moderate conservative'.

curacy at Newlyn we can turn to a valuable manuscript in the archives of the Dean and Chapter of Exeter, sometimes known as 'Bishop Veysey's *Valor*' (D&C 3688). It takes the form of a paper book, torn, with the covering page missing, around 9 × 12 in and with thirty-six folios. It is a sort of clerical subsidy for the diocese of Exeter, listing all the cathedral dignitaries and personnel, as well as the rectors, vicars and—most useful of all—curates throughout the whole diocese by name, with the amount of their assessed contributions.[6]

On 3 November 1534, parliament had passed the Act awarding to Henry VIII the first fruits (i.e. the first year's income) of all ecclesiastical offices and an annual pension of 10 per cent of all church incomes.[7] The bishops, having accepted Henry's earlier criticisms and demands, had only whetted his appetite for more, and fines for clerical *praemunire* and other 'misdemeanours' followed. The dating of the Exeter subsidy is, however, complex. It was formerly based on the names of two archdeacons: George Carew, not collated to the archdeaconry of Totnes until April 1534, and Rowland Lee, elevated to the see of Lichfield in the same month—therefore early 1534 seemed a reasonably safe conjectural date.[8] However, Ralph Oldon was not appointed to Perranzabuloe until 1535, and the same is true of John Kenall's appointment to Wendron;[9] and both are in place by the time of the manuscript. More telling is the fact that it places John Rose at Maker and John Taylor at St Erme,[10] and they were both appointed in 1536. This brings us closer to the time of the official return from the diocese under the Act—made in early 1536, but not at first considered sufficiently detailed. A further return was required of Bishop Veysey and was sent by him to the Crown on 3 November 1536, making it possible that D&C 3688 was a draft of the more detailed information collected for this purpose, or even a revision compiled slightly later.[11] It may represent the last of three instalments of the fine that the clergy agreed to pay to Henry VIII for their

---

6   Exeter Cathedral Archive, D&C Exeter MS 3688. The information for the Archdeaconry of Cornwall begins on f. 26. I am particularly indebted to Nicholas Orme for drawing my attention to this MS. (Cf. also DRO, Chanter 15, ff. 86r–99v.)
7   *Letters and Papers, Foreign & Domestic, Henry VIII, Volume 7, 1534*, ed. James Gairdner (London: HMSO, 1883), pp. 523–7 (nos 1377–1385).
8   John Le Neve, *Fasti Ecclesiae Anglicanae 1300–1541, IX, Exeter Diocese*, compiled and revised by Joyce M. Horn (London: Athlone Press, University of London Institute of Historical Research, 1964), p. 17. While Thomas Bedyll was collated to the archdeaconry on 2 March and installed (by proxy) on 11 June 1535, he was dead by 1537 and Thomas Wynter was installed on 10 October 1537. Bedyll's short term may account for some of the confusion over the archdeaconry.
9   Kenall was ordained priest on the vigil of Trinity, 22 May 1535.
10 Exeter Cathedral Archive, D&C Exeter MS 3688, f. 30r.
11 Peter, *The History of Glasney Collegiate Church*, p. 99. For example, Robert Swimmer is shown (Exeter Cathedral Archive, D&C Exeter MS 3688, f. 35r) at Minster, where Hennessy notes he went on 30 October 1537. Perhaps the document is based on information gathered over a range of dates.

'breach of *praemunire*'. It is unlikely to have been compiled after 1537, as Simon Butler of St Clement (Moresk) died in that year, and such deaths were generally noted if they occurred before the document was finalized.

In any case, the manuscript clearly places Thomas Stephyn as the curate of Newlyn in the mid-1530s. Under the Deanery of Pydar we find:

> Newlyn   Mr Radulphus Trelobys Vic
>   d Thomas Stephyn cur[12]
>
> [Newlyn East Master Ralph Trelobys, vicar
>   Sir Thomas Stephyn, curate]

The use of 'Mr' (for *magister*) suggests that Ralph Trelobys, the vicar, held a degree and was of a certain social standing (the title 'Mr' not being used indiscriminately for incumbents in this document.) The *d* (for *dominus*) in the case of Thomas Stephyn tells us no more than that he was a priest—and Trelobys's curate. It seems very likely that this is the same man who, after the death of the vicar, was appointed as incumbent himself.

The final and decisive piece of evidence establishing the link between this Thomas Stephyn of Newlyn East with *Sacrament an Alter* is an autograph signature. We have already seen the signature of a Thomas Stephyn in the Tregear Manuscript itself. Can this be compared with a known signature of the curate of Newlyn East? In fact, comprehensive collections of the signatures of individual clergy were made by the Tudor state between 1534 and 1535 in the months following the Act of Supremacy, to ensure that all clergy accepted the Act and its consequences. These lists still survive, bound into a volume (TNA E 36/64) at The National Archives, of 'Subscriptions to renunciation of papal supremacy (Province of Canterbury) with signatures' confirming the formal 'renunciation of the Pope's supremacy by the clergy in divers dioceses & archdeaconries'. There is an excellent match between the *Sacrament an Alter* signatures and an Exeter Diocese, Archdeaconry of Cornwall signature reading:

> dominus Thomas Stephyn curatus de Nulyn[13]
>
> [Sir Thomas Stephyn curate of Newlyn East].

---

12 Exeter Cathedral Archive, D&C Exeter MS 3688, f. 33r.
13 TNA E 36/64, p. 42. For a brief description of the context of these signatures see Nicholas Orme, *Cornwall and the Cross: Christianity 500-1560* (Chichester: Phillimore & Victoria County History, 2007), pp. 134–5. The *d* in D&C 3688 and the *dns* in E 36/64 both abbreviate *dominus* as indicated above, which would have been 'Sir' in the vernacular usage of the time—see Chapter 3, note 11. The name below is Tregona, not Tregear. In the opinion of Frederick Devon, Assistant Keeper in 1846, not all signatures are autographs as some names at the

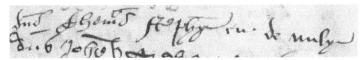

© The National Archives (TNA E 36/64 p. 42) reproduced with kind permission.

This is surely conclusive, and allows us to state with certainty that the curate (and Marian incumbent) of Newlyn East is the same Thomas Stephyn who signed *Sacrament an Alter*. It also tells us that, at the outset of the Reformation, he complied with the demand to assent to the Act of Supremacy, whatever reservations he may have had. It is only later that we find indications that he may have rejected this requirement of clerical service when it was reimposed by Elizabeth.

4.3 The possible involvement of Stephyn in an illicit pilgrimage

Another reference to a 'Sir Thomas', 'parish priest of St Newlyn', occurs around this time, in 1537.[14] Alexander Carvanell, a deputy to Peter Grisling a 'searcher' (a customs official, effectively a government spy) of Truro, wrote to the Council (i.e. to Cromwell) to record the occurrence of an unauthorized 'pope-holy' pilgrimage to Brittany. Carvanell and Grisling were on the lookout for illicit sea crossings. The ship concerned was the *Magdalen* of Truro, and the allegation was that, through the connivance of three priests, it had set out to take people on pilgrimage to a Breton pardon at *Lantregar* (probably Tréguier) and had refused cooperation with the port authorities who wished to search it:

> that is to saye, that the M^r of a certain Ship of the said poort of Trewrew called the Maudelyn ... thorough the Counsaill of thre preste[s], faynyng a poope holly pilgrymage to a p[ar]donne in Brytayn, denyed not oonly the said deputie sercheor to s[e]rche the said ship, but also my deputie of thadmyraltie in those partes to doo his Office and duetie.[15]

---

end of each list are added in the same handwriting. *Reports from Commissioners etc. 1846: Seventh Report of the Deputy Keeper of the Public Records* (London: William Clowes/HMSO, 1846), p. 279. A belt and braces approach appears to have been adopted, and where a priest did not appear at a particular session (because he had signed at another one) his name was added. Nonetheless, Stephyn's signature, like the vast majority, gives every indication of being a genuine autograph—see p. 7.

14 *Letters and Papers*, vol. 12, pt. 2 (1891), p. 124 (no. 301) and p. 476 (no. 1325). I am grateful to Nicholas Orme for pointing me to this reference. I have, however, worked principally from microfilms of the original documents. (PRO/TNA, SP (Hen. VIII) 1/123, pp. 40–1. And SP 1/127, p. 183—not 193 as in the PRO calendar.)

15 TNA Hen. VIII SP 1/123/41.

We already know from several sources (such as the Military Surveys) of the considerable number of Bretons (including some priests) living in Cornish parishes at the period. It is unsurprising that journeys in the other direction were undertaken (including for religious reasons) as here. The greatest interest of this incident, however, lies in the identity of the priests who were behind it. The ringleader is described as 'parish priest of St Newlyn', and his name is given as Sir Thomas 'Trebilcok'. There is a long list of others involved:

> These are the namys of the ry[t]tous p[er]sons hereafter following.
> Ffyrst Sr Thomas Trebilcok p[ar]yshe pryste of Saynt Newlyn.
> Sir Phillip [...] p[ar]ishe preste of Saynt Annys
> John Michell junior of Trewrew Captayn[16]
> Rychard Barrett m[er]chawnt of Trewrew.
> Pascawe Trehar of Newlyn.
> Richard Otes of Ffoweok[17] of the said ship.
> John Tradrack breton als spycer the masters mate.
> John Loo brewton
> John Hoskyn of Trewrew
> John Hewitt brewton
> Wyll[ya]m Mathewe
> Wyll[ya]m Salpyn
> Wyll[ya]m Carselyk w[i]t[h] other to the number of l p[er]sons.[18]

It is fairly clear that the names here are confused and even mangled. The priests and crew were far from cooperative, so may well have given false names; the list also appears to be partly conjectural and may be second or third hand.[19] The name of the first priest, Thomas 'Trebilcok', could be a misremembering or conflation, taking elements from the names of both Thomas Stephyn and Ralph Trelobys, as three priests are mentioned and only two names given. Another possibility is that Thomas Stephyn was known by a nickname or an alternative name—ultimately derived from the place-name Trebilcock in Roche. (At the period in question, however, there were also Trebilcocks

---

16   Michell was a merchant engaged in seagoing trade—of various degrees of legality—and later became MP for Truro: see N.M. Fuidge, *Michell, John (d. c. 1588), of Truro, Cornw.*, in the History of Parliament Online, http://historyofparliamentonline.org/volume/1558-1603/member/michell-john-1588. Accessed 25 May 2016. This is the online version of P.W. Hasler, *The History of Parliament: The House of Commons, 1558–1603*, 3 vols (London: The Stationery Office/Boydell & Brewer, 1981).

17   Feock, further down the ria.

18   TNA Hen. VIII SP 1/127/183. Note there were 50 (l) persons not formally listed.

19   In the case of Trebilcock, even if the priest gave it falsely or in a jocular fashion, the name ultimately derived from Trebilcock in Roche parish, although, as noted in the text, some of the family had moved to Stithians and elsewhere and at this date we cannot be sure from a toponymic where the holder was born.

at Stithians,[20] a more likely origin for the priest, taking together his career, his clerical contacts, any possible early association with Glasney and his knowledge of Cornish.)

With regard to the second priest explicitly mentioned, it may be tempting to identify St Anne with St Allen. This would, however, presuppose a considerable mangling of the intelligence, and the priest's name is given as Sir Phillip, not Sir William.[21] The more obvious identification is with St Agnes, often known at this time as St Anne's (although this was also true of Advent).[22] St Agnes was a chapel of ease within Perranzabuloe parish (until 1846, when it became a parish in its own right), and we have already noted the link between the priests of Perranzabuloe and St Allen at a later date, through Lawrence Godfrey's will. The identification of 'Saynt Annys' with St Agnes seems most likely, therefore, and is reinforced by the fact that a Sir Philip Tonkyn or Tomkyn was chaplain of St Agnes in 1559, when he witnessed the wills of a number of St Agnes men.[23]

Who the third priest was is not clear, but the ship certainly gave Carvanell a run for his money.[24] He had attempted to board with two other men, Alexander Cock and John Bartholomew, but was thrown overboard. Catching up with the vessel at St Mawes, he managed to arrest Richard Otes with four of his mariners, but in the end the crew would not let the ship be searched and carried Carvanell and his men out to sea. They put Cock and Bartholomew into a small boat about 5 miles beyond Falmouth, and cast them adrift, but Carvanell was carried all the way to Brittany, threatened continually with being cast over the side or towed at the stern. Once in Tréguier similar rough sport continued, with the crew encouraging the Bretons to pick quarrels with him, 'shuldryng and buffeting him as though he had bene a turke or a Sarzin'. Eventually he got home in another ship and filed his report. The case was to be examined by Godolphin, but any surviving record of this remains to be found and explored.

20 Cf. T.L. Stoate, ed., *Cornwall Subsidies in the Reign of Henry VIII, 1524 and 1543 and the Benevolence of 1545* (Bristol: T.L. Stoate, 1985), pp. 20–1; see also *1522 Military Survey*, p. 151 (Stithians) and 158 (Perranzabuloe). That alternative surnames existed at the period is witnessed by the Thomas Stephyns (also known as Thomas Penick) who died at Grade on the Lizard peninsula, a strongly Cornish-speaking area, in 1586, although his is not a convincing example of a toponymic surname (OP).
21 William Treruffe was the vicar of St Allen at that time.
22 Oliver Padel has drawn my attention to 'Saynct Anne's hille' (= St Agnes Beacon) in Leland, I, 317, and for Advent see Nicholas Orme, *English Church Dedications*, Exeter (Exeter: University of Exeter, 1996), p. 67.
23 Henderson, 'The 109 Ancient Parishes' (1955), p. 5.
24 Cf. TNA Hen. VIII SP 1/123/41.

4.4 Distinguishing Stephyn from Cornwall, Stevyns from Devon

Simply to avoid confusion for later researchers, it is perhaps worth distinguishing more carefully the two priests called Thomas Stephyn serving the diocese at this time. They occur in the same sources, with one exercising a ministry in Cornish-speaking Cornwall, the other in English-speaking Devon. The first (who is easiest to identify with the Thomas Stephyn of Newlyn East) was a curate of Mylor in 1522. The second, 'Devon' man—whose name was more often spelled with a *v*—was only ordained in 1530, although it is impossible to be completely sure beyond all doubt which is which in all the subsequent references.

When the 'Cornish' man began his ministry in Mylor (a Glasney parish), John Tregythyowe was the vicar. Since he lived in Exeter, much fell upon his curates, 'Thomas Stephyn, chaplain', curate of Mylor and 'John Sampson, chaplain, curate of Lavabe' (Mabe). There is further information in the 1522 Military Survey:

> Thomas Stephyn, chaplain, curate there
> has in stipend £5.6.8, in goods £3.[25]

Stephyn was effectively the parish priest, and such a young but experienced pastor would then have been an ideal appointment for Newlyn, given the fact that the vicar, Trelobys, also resided elsewhere, like the vicar of Mylor. Trelobys may even have known Stephyn from Glasney, if Stephyn had been schooled there.

Of course, it may be objected that this curate of Mylor must have been born too early to have written *Sacrament an Alter* as he would have been a very old man by 1576. Yet others had a similarly long ecclesiastical career at the time. Ordained in 1516, John Tresteyn[26] appears to have been a curate at Crowan in 1522 (also under Ralph Trelobys, who served both Crowan and Newlyn).[27] He may be—allowing for misspelling—the 'd[om] Joh^{es} Tresene' who was curate in charge at Perranarworthal in the mid-1530s.[28] Later in life, Tresteyn was one of Stephyn's successors at Newlyn (replacing Richard Martyn in 1573).[29] He died

---

25 *1522 Military Survey*, p. 34. John Sampson is also noted as owning some land in Wendron and Gluvias parishes (pp. 29, 36). Mylor and Mabe are both near Glasney.
26 See Chapter 3, notes 20–21, 24–26.
27 *1522 Military Survey*, p. 25. He may also—if there has been a slight misreading of the MS Survey—have been the John 'Treleigne' who held some land in Sithney parish at the same time (p. 32).
28 Exeter Cathedral Archive, D&C Exeter MS 3688, f. 30v.
29 *Episcopal Registers of William Bradbridge*, DRO, Chanter 20, f. 15v. Tresteyn was appointed on 23 August 1573—he was also vicar of Manaccan from 1572. Tresteyn's immediate predecessor at Newlyn, Richard Martyn, resigned at this point, but it is not known when he himself was appointed.

in December 1581, not long before John Tregear.[30] It was not impossible, then, for a rural parish priest—albeit in a modest way—to follow in the footsteps of a bishop such as Veysey, who lived and worked into his nineties.[31] If Stephyn lived as long, and was the curate of Mylor, SA could have been written any time between 1576 and 1590—although the death of Tregear in 1583 seems a particularly likely time for his papers to have come into Stephyn's possession.

The second, 'Devonian' Thomas Stephyn (or Stevyns) did not begin his ministry until some eight years later than the curate of Mylor. On 11 June 1530, in the parish church of Colyton, the auxiliary bishop Thomas Chard,[32] mentioned above, confirmed a Thomas Stevyns.[33] At the next ordination on 19 September in the Lady Chapel of the Cathedral, a Thomas Stephyns is recorded as having been made subdeacon by Thomas Vyvyan, titular bishop of Megara.[34] After a very short interval for prayer and reflection, on 17 December 1530, this Thomas Stevyns was made deacon—again by Vyvyan, in his priory church at Bodmin.[35] In the next likely reference to this man, D&C 3688 records a Thomas Stevyn as one of several clergy at the prebendal church of Cullompton around late 1536, at the same time as the 'Cornish' Thomas Stephyn was already at Newlyn.

4.5 Thomas Stephyn's 'recusancy'

The 'Cornish' Stephyn seems to disappear from church life in the area after the accession of Queen Elizabeth. Did he jump or was he pushed? There were many other deprivations and departures in the diocese, including those of James Turberville the bishop, Thomas Reynolds the dean, Thomas Nutcombe the sub-dean, John Blaxton the treasurer, eleven cathedral prebendaries (almost

---

30   CRO, *The Parish Registers of Newlyn East*, 1581, f. 86.
31   *Episcopal Registers of John Veysey*, DRO, Chanter 16, f. 31v. See also Thebridge, ed., *Holy Trinity, Sutton Coldfield*, pp. 54–8 for his death at Sutton Coldfield, where his impressive tomb still survives.
32   The term 'auxiliary' has been preferred here to avoid confusion with modern uses of the word 'suffragan' and the possible implication that these bishops served in one diocese only. Thomas Chard, titular bishop of Solubria, was active as an auxiliary bishop in both Exeter and Bath and Wells dioceses. His will may be found at TNO PROB 11/30/240; he died in 1544. Cf. William Stubbs, ed., *Registrum Sacrum Anglicanum*, 2nd edn (Oxford: OUP, 1897), p. 201.
33   *Episcopal Registers of John Veysey*, DRO, Chanter 14, f. 171v. (The folios of Veysey's registers are not numbered and have not been published; this pagination is my own.)
34   *Episcopal Registers of John Veysey*, DRO, Chanter 14, f. 172v.
35   *Episcopal Registers of John Veysey*, DRO, Chanter 14, f. 173r. On the same occasion, the bishop subdeaconed Gerens John under the title of Glasney College. I have not been successful in finding the ordination of Thomas Stephyn of Newlyn in the Exeter Registers, although both a Henry Stephyn and a John Stephyn were made deacon at the paschal vigil, 7 April 1520.

half the total) and around thirty incumbents, including some resignations.[36] These departures—not least among the senior diocesan staff—suggest that the Elizabethan Settlement was far from being a smooth transition in the diocese, and that clergy (like Stephyn) who had affirmed the Act of Supremacy in 1535 were no longer prepared to do so having seen where it all led.

John Rokeby, for example, Stephyn's neighbour at St Erme, who (like Stephyn) had been instituted in Mary's time, was soon ejected under Elizabeth. Manaccan, Creed, Roche and St Columb Major also lost their priests, but they were exceptional since most deprivations were in the more eastern parts of Cornwall. The western clergy seem generally to have escaped censure at this point, and may have been too remote for immediate action. Western Cornwall was very distant from the centres of power: even Exeter (the regional ecclesiastical centre) was a considerable travelling distance from St Allen and Newlyn East, and London was a different world. It remained possible for some time to delay compliance in remote areas. Even those who lived near regional centres of power could move to other regions to continue their resistance. Of those diocesan clergy who did leave, some had outstanding recusant careers: Blaxton went on to be a thorn in the side of the bishop of Hereford, helping to establish a robust Catholic enclave in the Welsh borders, with clergy and laity moving in from elsewhere.[37]

It is possible, of course, that Stephyn, although less well known to history, may have joined Blaxton across the Severn estuary. No evidence has yet been found for his own deprivation, ejection or resignation, however. He may have fled abroad for a time—like John Smart of Maker (one of the cathedral prebends) and Robert Yendall (of Menheniot) who boarded a boat and escaped to Brittany.[38]

No incumbent at all at Newlyn is recorded in Alley's 1563 survey, nor is any other Thomas Stephyn recorded as an incumbent anywhere else in the diocese at that time.[39] Intriguingly, the formal parish registers seem to have been well ordered from 1559 onwards—if not by Stephyn himself, then under the direction of an immediate successor whose name has been lost,[40] or of a neighbouring priest such as Tregear. What we know of his later views, however,

---

36 C.W. Field, *The Province of Canterbury and the Elizabethan Settlement of Religion* (Robertsbridge, Sussex: privately published typescript, 1972), pp. 102–6, 108–9, 113–14.
37 Field, *The Province of Canterbury*, pp. 106–7; Mary Ann Everett Green, ed., *Calendar of State Papers Domestic Series, of the reign of Elizabeth* [I], vol. 6, 1601–1603 with Addenda, 1547–1565 (London: HMSO, 1870), p. 522, and Chapter 3, note 13. Bonner's own chaplains were 'wandering about seditiously', particularly one 'Morren' (or Morwyn) in Lancashire (p. 524).
38 Field, *The Province of Canterbury*, p. 109. It is also a possibility that, assuming Stephyn took Tregear's work with him, he may have researched and written *Sacrament an Alter* entirely outside Cornwall. Indeed, he may not have been able to return, and his Cornish catena may never have been seen there (OP).
39 Cf. Corpus Christi College, Cambridge, MS 97 and transcription (Z19/10/1b) at the DRO.
40 Unless Richard Martyn began his ministry there as soon as Stephyn left.

might suggest that Stephyn was an unlikely candidate to remain in office under Elizabeth. Inasmuch as we can judge from his editorial work, he appears to be completely 'Marian' in his approach.[41]

4.6 Thomas Stephyns elsewhere in the country

If we cast the net wider and look outside the diocese of Exeter for Marian priests in trouble with the government over religion in Elizabethan times, a considerable number of Thomas Stephyns crop up. None of these are necessarily anything to do with the author of *Sacrament an Alter*, and this time we have no further signatures to confirm identity in the context of such a common patronymic. I will nonetheless summarize what we know of one or two of them because they shed some light on what other priests of 'suspect' views were doing at this stage of the Reformation.[42]

First of all, things changed very markedly and rapidly after Elizabeth's accession. Already on 19 January 1559, it was clear that traditional religion was under attack. The bishop of Winchester was under house arrest for 'such offenses as he committed in his sermon at the funeralles of the late Quene',[43] and by 3 April 1559, the bishops of Chester, Carlisle and Coventry & Lichfield—and Doctors Cole, Harpsfield and Chedsey—were required to report to the Privy Council daily.[44] Soon they were in prison. It is therefore of interest that in the Pardon Rolls of 1559, in the year after Elizabeth came to the throne, there is a decree for 'Pardon for all treasons, felonies and other offences...' The roll includes

> Thomas Stephens, clerk, of
> Wood Bevington, co. Warwick,
> Alias of Baddisley Clynton, co. Warwick,
> Alias of Glawdestre, co. Radnor.[45]

---

41 See Lucy Wooding, 'The Marian Restoration and the Mass', in Eamon Duffy and David Loades, eds, *The Church of Mary Tudor* (Aldershot: Ashgate, 2006), pp. 227–57.

42 As noted above, more detail on these Stephyns (and others) may be found in Frost, 'Glasney's Parish Clergy' (in this case at pp. 39–46, 59–65, 72–8), and updated in Payton, ed., *Cornwall in the Age of Rebellion*, pp. 182–5, 195–7, 200–5.

43 John Roche Dasent, ed., *Acts of the Privy Council of England, vol. 7, 1558–1570* (London: HMSO, 1893). British History Online. http://www.british-history.ac.uk/acts-privy-council/vol7. Accessed 13 May 2016.

44 Dasent, ed., *Acts of the Privy Council of England, vol. 7*, p. 79.

45 TNA C 67/68 *Letters Patent for Pardon (Pardon Rolls)*, 1 Elizabeth (1559), part 2 (Supplementary Patent Roll 68), MS f. 19. See also *Calendar of Patent Rolls, Elizabeth I, vol. 1* (London: HMSO, 1939), p. 217.

Baddesley Clinton is a well-known recusant house, now in the care of the National Trust. It appears to have been a Catholic centre throughout the religious changes and harbours a number of priest-holes. Wood Bevington is less well known, but almost as interesting. The manor house is 6 miles north of Evesham and is a fourteenth century timber-framed building, with a chapel.[46] There were links by marriage with Baddesley Clinton, and evidence later of defaulting on the rent.[47] The suggestion is that it was very much a Catholic house, at least by the mid-seventeenth century and possibly earlier. There is a detailed inventory of 1578, which includes details of the 'chapel chamber',[48] and mentions a 'picture of Mary Magdalen, 12d'.[49]

Since Baddesley Clinton and Wood Bevington can be shown to have been Catholic centres in penal times, it would seem likely that there was another safe house at Gladestry of much the same kind.[50] Such a centre would fit neatly into a chain of recusancy from Monmouth right along the Welsh borders up through Chirk to Holywell, approximately along the line of Offa's Dyke. The eventual appearance of the Tregear Manuscript near Wrexham might mean that at some point its custodian made similar journeys.

The Privy Council was also very interested in apprehending and personally interviewing a Thomas Stephens from Cornwall in 1564. From St James's Palace, on 4 November 1564, they sent:

---

46 The village is now little more than a row of houses, along a single track at SP 056538.
47 Philip Styles, ed., *A History of the County of Warwick, Volume 3: Barlichway Hundred* (London: Victoria County History, 1945), p. 160. Michael Hodgetts (who has made a comprehensive study of the recusant houses of the Midlands) has raised the question as to whether the lease or the surrender was a legal dodge to avoid sequestration.
48 H.S. Gunn, *History of the Old Manor House of Wood Bevington* (1911), pp. v–xvi.
49 The whole of this paragraph is based firmly on research undertaken by Michael Hodgetts, and generously shared with me (personal communication). More detail may be found in Frost, 'Glasney's Parish Clergy', pp. 62–3, or in Payton, ed., *Cornwall in the Age of Rebellion*, p. 203 and notes.
50 Gladestry (in Welsh, Llanfair Llethonw) had an ancient house known as the Cwrt, which at one time belonged to Sir Gelly Meyrick (Gelli Meurig) who, in Elizabeth's time, was attainted for high treason, condemned and executed. See N.M. Fuidge, *Meyrick (Merrick) Gelly (c. 1556–1601), of Gellyswick, Hascard, Pemb.; Wigmore Castle, Herefs; Gladestry, Rad. And Essex House, London*. History of Parliament Online, http://historyofparliamentonline.org/volume/1558-1603/member/meyrick-(merrick)-gelly-1556-1601. Accessed 25 May 2016. Despite his rebellious end, Gelly Meyrick was the son of the protestant bishop of Bangor, Rowland Meyrick (himself the second son of Meurig ap Llywelyn). He may have been more political than religious in his interests and alliances, although these did eventually lead him into involvement with the second earl of Essex, Robert Devereux, and downfall as a result of the Essex rebellion. For the nature and coherence of Offa's Dyke see Chris Peers, *Offa and the Mercian Wars* (Barnsley: Pen & Sword, 2017), pp. 136–40.

A letter to the Sheryf of Cornewall to take order that Thomas Stephens, Thomas Jenkins and John Coken, thonger, may be aprehended and good bandes be taken of them to appere before the Lords of the Queen's Majesties Pryvey Councell within such short tyme as they may convenientlye travaill hyther; and to use the like order with John Williams, Henry Otes, Rychard Boswall, Pyres Mychell and John Coken, thelder, remayninge in his warde.[51]

Earlier, on 30 September 1564, Sir Peter Carew was ordered to apprehend a 'Stevins' of Falmouth among others for the 'victuallyng of pyrattes'.[52] This may explain the subsequent letter, without any connection to the priest of Newlyn, though it is possible that the term 'pyrattes' was sometimes used not only for those seeking commercial gain, but also for those with Catholic reasons for sailing to Brittany.

Much later on, another interesting 'Stephens' is the associate of Edmund Campion reported in the Acts of the Privy Council for 4 August 1581. We hear of Campion that

> he delivered a copie of his challenge to one Norice, a priest, commonlie remaining about London, and that he delivered it to one Pounde, then prisoner in the Marshallsey, who is thought to have dispersed the same abroade, and that one Stephens brought the said Pound to speak with Campion at Throgmorton House in London.[53]

Even if all these possible leads fail to afford us any solid proof of Stephyn's own recusancy, there remains the circumstantial evidence that Newlyn parish rapidly became a stronghold for such views. The Borlases of Treluddra certainly remained Catholics—unlike other branches of the family—rivalling the Arundells of Lanherne in their loyalty. The last of the line, Humphrey Borlase, was strongly supportive of King James II and was raised to the peerage by him (after the king's exile, so it was never recognized by the authorities in England).[54] Henderson records, from a 1706 list of 'Popish Recusants' in Newlyn:

> John Burlase [Borlase], John his son,
> James Lincolne & his wife, Nicholas James & his wife,
> Simon Trescowthick, Philip Oliver & his wife, and Alice Rowe.

---

51 Dasent, ed., *Acts of the Privy Council*, vol. 7, p. 156. The appearance of another Otes and Mychell in such a context is intriguing: see 4.3.
52 Dasent, ed., *Acts of the Privy Council*, vol. 7, p. 153.
53 John Roche Dasent, ed., *Acts of the Privy Council of England, 1581-2*, vol. 13 (London: HMSO, 1896), p. 153.
54 Charles Henderson, *Materials for a History of the Parish of Newlyn*, MSS in the Courtney Library, Royal Institution of Cornwall (at the Royal Cornwall Museum, Truro), the second part, on subsidies (dated approximately 1924).

Again, under a slightly later date, he notes:

> As at Mawgan there was a colony of Catholics in this parish centred upon Treluddra and they doubtless had a place of assembly in the mansion. In 1745 there were still 5 Catholic families (13 souls) in Newlyn.[55]

Among documents and wills of the Borlase family there may yet be references to be found connecting them with Thomas Stephyn.

---

55   Henderson, 'The 109 Ancient Parishes' (1958), p. 367.

CHAPTER FIVE

Ralph Trelobys—the Link with Glasney College

5.1 Ralph Trelobys, vicar of Crowan 1512–57 and Newlyn East 1518–57

Ralph Trelobys was officially Tregear's neighbour at Newlyn East,[1] and in his time employed both John Tresteyn (Tregear's successor) and Thomas Stephyn as curates. When he died, Trelobys was typical of a successful Tudor clergyman in rural Cornwall, and—until Glasney's dissolution—had been a long-serving canon there, with many links to its wider orbit of parishes.[2]

Trelobys is a much rarer surname than either Stephyn or Tregear. There is only one place-name in the whole of Cornwall that coincides with its historical distribution. His birth (probably around 1488) may not have been at Trelubbas, just north of Helston, as by this date many toponymic surnames were being inherited. Nonetheless, his family must originally have come from the close vicinity, at that time a strongly Cornish-speaking area.[3]

As with Tregear and Stephyn, we have no record of Trelobys's formal education. He was always described as *magister* by contemporaries, however,

---

1   Ralph Trelobys spells his own name Trelobys (in the Glasney signatures of assent to the royal supremacy in TNA E 25/58/3) but contemporary documents also give forms like Trelabys, Trelebs, Trelobbes, Trelobes, Treloubes, Trelowbys and even Treloves. In modern times it is usually Trelubbas or Trelubbis. (See, in this chapter, notes 11, 12 and 17.)
2   As noted above, technically a prebendary, but canon was the common use.
3   Trelubbas Wartha (Upper Trelubbas) lies at SW 667296 near Coverack Bridges, and the boundary between the old Wendron and Sithney parishes. Trelubbas Wolas (Lower Trelubbas) also existed in the sixteenth century. Ralph Trelobys was certainly linked to the parish of Wendron in which Trelubbas lies. In the 1520s to 1540s, the only parish where a surname derived from that place-name appeared, anywhere in Cornwall, was in Wendron, its parish of origin—apart from Ralph Trelobys in the adjacent parish of Crowan. The 1522 Military Survey gives both John and Thomas 'Trelobbys' in Wendron parish in 1522 (p. 30) and (printed at p. 153 in the printed edition of the 1522 Military Survey) the 1535 Tinners Muster lists a Ralph Trelobys under Wendron, most likely because the vicar of Crowan still had property in the parish or, if not, family. He was clearly serving very close to his original home (OP).

including in lists where this term is otherwise reserved for graduates.[4] This suggests he studied at university, presumably Oxford, though clear evidence has not yet been found. On 15 February 1505, he was ordained priest in Exeter Cathedral by Thomas Cornish, titular bishop of Tenos, an auxiliary who worked in Bath & Wells, Exeter and throughout the South West.[5] Within eight years he was appointed, on 1 December 1512, as vicar of Crowan.[6] While not formally a Glasney parish, it lay between Sithney (which was) and Camborne (which had strong links with several provosts of Glasney).

A few years later, on 16 April 1518, Trelobys was made, in addition, vicar of Newlyn East,[7] which lay sandwiched between the Glasney churches of St Allen, St Colan and St Enoder. Both his livings, therefore, may have helped the college to conveniently 'link up' areas where it already had a degree of control. Trelobys appears to have held both parishes in plurality until his death, probably residing more in Crowan than Newlyn. The particular significance of Trelobys for SA is that Thomas Stephyn appears to have worked as curate for this important local priest and canon of Glasney. According to the *Valor Ecclesiasticus*, Trelobys received £16 13s. 4d. per annum for his work as vicar of Newlyn, and £11 9s. ½d. for Crowan.[8] To this should be added his income as a canon of Glasney (around £11 per annum at the dissolution),[9] giving a total of around £39. This was a good level of income.[10]

---

4   Such as 'Bishop Veysey's *Valor*', Exeter Cathedral Archive, D&C Exeter MS 3688, f. 33r. However, his name is not among the surviving lists of Oxford and Cambridge alumni in the reference works such as A.B. Emden, *A Biographical Register of the University of Oxford, A.D. 1501 to 1540* (Oxford: Clarendon Press, 1970) nor in the comprehensive recent list by Nicholas Orme, 'The Cornish at Oxford, 1180–1540', *Journal of the Royal Institution of Cornwall* (2010), pp. 43–82, although inevitably many records have been lost.

5   *Episcopal Registers of Hugh Oldham*, DRO, Chanter 13, f. 83r. Cornish succeeded the Augustinian canon John Valens as bishop of Tenos from 1486 until his death in 1513. See Hamilton A. Thompson, *The English Clergy (Ford Lectures for 1933)* (Oxford: OUP, 1947), p. 49n) and Rowse, *Tudor Cornwall* (1969 edition), p. 152.

6   *Episcopal Registers of Hugh Oldham*, DRO, Chanter 13, f. 48r. (Transcribed as 'Trelovys' in Hennessey's *Incumbents* but Trelobys in the original.) He succeeded to the parish of Crowan on the death of Richard Hooper.

7   *Episcopal Registers of Hugh Oldham*, DRO, Chanter 13, f. 75v. (Transcribed as 'Treloves' in Hennessey's *Incumbents*, but Trelobes in the original.) He succeeded to the parish of Newlyn on the resignation of Robert Strangeways.

8   Caley & Hunter, eds, *Valor Ecclesiasticus*, vol. 2, f. 400 (Newlyn) and f. 395 (Crowan).

9   Lawrence S. Snell, *Documents towards a History of the Reformation in Cornwall: 1. The Chantry Certificates for Cornwall* (Exeter: James Townsend & Sons, 1953), pp. 36–40.

10 Around 10 marks (£6 13s. 4d.) was considered the fitting stipend of a vicar not in possession of the rectorial tithes and until Henry VIII clerical incomes below this level were rarely taxed.

5.2 Trelobys and Glasney College

Ralph Trelobys was certainly a canon of Glasney by 1534, since he subscribed to the king's supremacy on 17 August in that year under Provost James Gentle.[11] Almost all the bishops and clergy did so at this point (with, of course, some notable exceptions). According to Bishop Veysey's *Valor*, Trelobys was still in post at Glasney in 1536, as well as continuing his work at Crowan and Newlyn. Being a college of secular priests and to a large extent a chantry foundation, Glasney escaped the dissolution of the minor religious houses in 1536 as well as the final surrender of the greater houses in 1539. We have already noted Trelobys's appearances in Bishop Alley's survey, and his possible involvement with the 1537 'pope-holy pilgrimage'.

(There are in existence two interesting conveyances, preserved at the Courtney Library at Truro, which show Trelobys in his social context and give us an indication of the wider community involvement of Glasney canons at this period. The first dates from 1541, and the second follows the dissolution.[12] In the first, his name is variously spelt as Rd° Trelowbys, Rad^{us} Trelowbys, Ralph Trelobes and even Richard Trelobes, which may be helpful in another context.)[13]

The dissolution of Glasney came in 1548, when Edward VI abolished the chantries.[14] Regrettably, the school was not saved,[15] and almost nothing survives of the church above ground, though its outline is marked out in brick in College Field. Penryn at that time was counted as having at least 400 communicants (in some sources many more) and, as one of the Chantry Certificates makes plain, a provost and twelve prebendaries, seven additional assistant

---

11   The name *Radulphus Trelobys Canonicus* (probably his own signature) appears on Glasney's subscription to the supremacy, TNA E 25/58/3. See also Peter, *The History of Glasney Collegiate Church*, p. 80. *Reports from Commissioners etc. 1846: Seventh Report of the Deputy Keeper of the Public Records* (London: Clowes/HMSO, 1846), p. 297.

12   Courtney Library, RIC, Truro, St Aubyn Collection, HA/14/7 (Hend. Cal. 16 p. 106, no. 225), and Courtney Library, RIC, Truro, Bassett Collection, HB/1/1 (Hend. Cal. 5 p. 145, no. 587). Angela Broome was most helpful in identifying Trelobys documents in the library's collections. For transcriptions of the conveyances, see Frost, 'Glasney's Parish Clergy', pp. 49–52, 64–8, summarised in Payton, ed., *Cornwall in the Age of Rebellion*, pp. 188–90.

13   There are also a few rare instances in the Bishops' Registers where 'Rad' alternates with Ric^{us} as an abbreviation for Richard, although it usually stands for Ralph (Radulphus). See 5.3 with respect to Rad/Richard Ton.

14   Although some colleges seem to have escaped notice at that time, including St Buryan and Crantock.

15   Throughout the country, the promised potential for education of the dissolution of the chantries fell short of early expectations. Only after 1550 did increasing complaints lead to the foundation of the 'free grammar schools of King Edward VI', cf. Nicholas Orme, *Medieval Schools, from Roman Britain to Renaissance England* (New Haven and London: Yale University Press, 2006), pp. 324–7.

priests known as the vicars, and several others, such as three chantry priests and four boy choristers:

> The Towne of Peryn wherin ar[e] howselyng people cccc. The Colledge of Seynt Thomas of Glasney, standing in the said Towne, being the p[ar]ishe churche off the foundacon of Walter Goode sometyme Bisshoppe of Exceter to fynde a Provost & xij p[re]bendaryes wherof the said provost and vij of the said prebendaryes be now Resident and v not residente, vij vicars, a Chapell Clerke, a Bellrynger, iiij querysters and iij chantry prestes to celebrate in the said colledge.[16]

Trelobys was 70 when the college was dissolved: it must have been a considerable wrench for him.[17] The reinforcing of the residency requirement for canons of Glasney may have reduced the time Trelobys could spend in Crowan, and the college had probably become his main home. His status there is mentioned several times in the Chantry Certificates:

> Rauff Trelobbes of thage of lxx yeres hathe for his sallary in the said Colledge xij^{li} besides his promocions in other places vj^{li}.[18]

Elsewhere his salary at Penryn is now recorded as being just over £10 and his pension, to which he was entitled following the dissolution, somewhat less than this:

> Raufe Trelobbes Prebendarye for his salary clere x^{li} ij^s ij^d.
> Pen. vj^{li} xiij^s iiij^d.[19]

As well as financial loss, there were spiritual depredations across the diocese, including decrees against Palm Sunday processions, images of the saints, requiems, votive candles, rood screens, Easter sepulchres and parish guilds. Simon Heynes, the notorious reforming dean of Exeter—at odds with most of the people and clergy of the diocese—demolished statues in the cathedral in

---

16 Chantry Certificate 9/1, printed in Snell, *The Chantry Certificates for Cornwall*, p. 36. 'Peryn' = Penryn; 'howselyng' = houselling [i.e. communicant] people; Walter [Bronescombe, the] Good, Bishop of Exeter.
17 And for others. In addition to 'Ralf Trelobys' (70), the certificates also list Mr John Libby, Provost; John Harrys LLB (80); Mr Thomas Vivian (70); Mathew Newcombe (60), Matthew Broke (45); Gerens John (46) and Nicholas Nicholls (45). Non-resident were Henry Kyllyfree, Thomas/John Molesworthy and Rauf/Philip Couch.
18 This gives another summary of his income at the age of 70—£12 from the college and £6 from other appointments. Snell, *The Chantry Certificates for Cornwall*, p. 37.
19 In this case a salary of £10 2s. 2d. and pension of £6 13s. 4d. Chantry Certificate 10/1, Snell, *The Chantry Certificates for Cornwall*, p. 39.

front of his helpless canons. Another leading reformer, Miles Coverdale, was brought in as bishop, and Veysey was put out to grass.

Trelobys lived just long enough, however, to see a partial and temporary restoration of traditional practice under Mary. Coverdale was deprived and Vesey got his old see back (although he spent most of his time after his restoration in the Midlands, developing his charitable foundations). The bishop was very old by this stage, and unable to travel long distances easily. Able assistants served him in Cornwall until, as the Registers record:

> *Vicesimo tertio die mensis Octobris anno d[o]m[in]i mill[es]imo*
> *qui[n]gentesimo qui[n]quagesimo quarto In manerio suo*
> *de More place infra p[ar]ochiam de Sutton collfylld*
> *in Com[itatu] Warwik d[omi]n[u]s ab hac luce migravit. Cuius*
> *anime p[ro]piciet[ur] deus. Amen.*

> [On the twenty third day of the month of October in the year of our Lord one thousand five hundred and fifty-four, in his manor of Moor Place within the parish of Sutton Coldfield, in the County of Warwick, the Lord [Bishop] departed this life. On whose soul may God have mercy. Amen.][20]

He was in his 90s. Not long afterwards, Ralph Trelobys also died. His will was proved in the court of the principal registry of the bishop of Exeter in 1557, as that of 'Raff Trelobys, clerk, Crowen'.[21]

5.3 Trelobys and 'Rad Ton'

We ought perhaps to end with one of the most elusive Cornish writer-priests of the period, and ask whether he too was, like Tregear and Stephyn, connected with Glasney through Trelobys. At the end of *Beunans Meriasek*, one of two surviving medieval saint's plays in the Cornish language,[22] appear the words:

---

20 *Episcopal Registers of John Veysey*, DRO, Chanter 16, f. 31v, and George Oliver, *Lives of the Bishops of Exeter* (Exeter: William Roberts, 1861), pp. 124–5. This transcription has been corrected from that given in Frost, 'Glasney's Parish Clergy, p. 51, the notable change being from 13 October to 23 October. For a revised version of this passage see Payton, ed., *Cornwall in the Age of Rebellion*, pp. 190–1, and for Veysey's charitable foundations see Thebridge, ed., *Holy Trinity, Sutton Coldfield*, pp. 45–54.
21 Edward Alexander Fry, ed., *Calendar of Wills and Administrations relating to the Counties of Devon and Cornwall, proved in the Consistory Court of the Bishop of Exeter, 1532–1800*, vol. 2 (Plymouth: British Record Society, 1914), p. 206.
22 National Library of Wales/Llyfrgell Genedlaethol Cymru, Aberystwyth, Peniarth MS 105B— *Beunans Meriasek*, 'The Life of St Meriasek/Meriadoc'; see Myrna Combellack, 'A Critical Edition of *Beunans Meriasek*' (PhD dissertation, 1985, University of Exeter); see also Whitley Stokes, ed.,

*Finit[ur] p[er] d[omi]n[u]m Rad Ton
ann[o] d[omi]ni m ^{l} v $^{c[en]t}$ iiij*²³

[finished by Sir Ralph Ton
in the year of our Lord 1504]

They appear to be written with the same implement, ink and style as the majority of the text (i.e. all except the first ten folios—the first part of the manuscript has been restored later in another, quite different hand). This mysterious 'Rad Ton' has been variously read and identified since the discovery of the play. Early suggestions failed to take account of *dominum/dompnum* usually requiring a Christian name, so Dominus Hadton or even Dominus Nadton were offered, but Combellack and most modern scholars accept that Charles Thomas was right in reading Rad as representing a Christian name (e.g. Latin 'Radulphus', English 'Ralph', or possibly 'Richard').²⁴ The date of 1504 seems correct.²⁵

As Thomas observes, Ton is not unknown as a Cornish surname, but it is rare.²⁶ There appear to be no Tons among the parish clergy of the time to match the name appended to *Beunans Meriasek*, with one glaring exception. In around

---

Beunans Meriasek: The Life of St Meriasek, Bishop and Confessor, A Cornish Drama (London: Trübner & Co., 1872). I am grateful to the NLW for allowing me to examine the manuscript itself. Digital images are available on the NLW website (see following note). For the possible political dimension of the play see Olson, Lynette, 'Tyranny in *Beunans Meriasek*', in Philip Payton, ed., *Cornish Studies: Five* (Exeter: UEP, 2002), pp. 52–9, updated as '*Beunans Meriasek*—A Political Play?', in Philip Payton, ed. *Cornwall in the Age of Rebellion, 1490-1690* (Exeter: UEP, 2021), pp. 118–34.

23 An excellent digital image of this page (accessed 20 Nov. 2018) may be viewed at: *Beunans Meriasek (The Life of St Meriasek)* https://www.library.wales/discover/digital-gallery/manuscripts/the-middle-ages/beunans-meriasek/ National Library of Wales, Aberystwyth (2018)—select p. 186 of 211 (which directs to f. 92r). In abbreviating his name to Rad, it seems possible that Richard Ton was influenced by Ralph Trelobys. Nonetheless, the latter's autograph (examined from the Glasney subscriptions to the royal supremacy, TNA E 25/58/3) is quite different, and lacks Ton's distinctive *R*.

24 Charles Thomas, *The Christian Antiquities of Camborne* (St Austell: Warne, 1967), p. 25; Combellack, 'A Critical Edition of *Beunans Meriasek*', pp. 12–14.

25 When studying the manuscript itself, at first it appeared that an extremely faint 'x' before the 'iiij' (and possibly an even fainter 'v' after the 'x') could mean we would have to revise the date upwards, at least to 1514 and possibly 1518 or 1519, which might have accorded even better with Ton being part of Trelobys's project. However, Maredudd ap Huw, the Manuscript Librarian, re-examined it under ultraviolet light and believes 1504 is still the best interpretation: the suggestions of 'x' and 'v' are probably colour variations in the paper. See the discussion on dating in Combellack, 'A Critical Edition of *Beunans Meriasek*', pp. 14–20.

26 Thomas, *Christian Antiquities*, p. 23. The Ton family was, however, established nearby around this time according to the *1522 Military Survey*. There is a William Tonne in Sithney (p. 33) and a Peter Ton in Mabe (p. 33), both near Glasney. Also Stoate, ed., *Cornwall Subsidies in the Reign of Henry VIII*, p. 23 (Mabe) and p. 41 (Sithney) reports some Tons, though none of these sources mention a Ralph or Richard.

1536, according to D&C 3688, where we have already found Thomas Stephyn working for Ralph Trelobys, we find the following entry for Crowan:

> Crowen   Mr Radullphus Trelobys Vic
> d Ricus Ton cur[27]
>
> [Crowan   Master Ralph Trelobys, vicar
> Sir Richard Ton, curate]

Because of the significance of Trelobys for Stephyn (and possibly for Tregear), this is exciting. If some of those seeking to preserve Cornish Catholic heritage through the medium of the language shortly afterwards were not at Glasney, but were possibly influenced by a Glasney priest out in the parishes, could the same be true of Ton? We have already seen that the abbreviation Rad was occasionally confused (if incorrectly) with Ricardus—as in the case of Trelobys. While it is difficult for us to accept that a priest transcribing a document in 1504 could have been a curate thirty years later, we have also seen that Thomas Stephyn was likely to have been a curate from before 1522 and did not become an incumbent until 1557. Nance considered the possibility and mentions it in several places among his papers. Thomas also discusses it and provides a fascinating reference for the death of 'Sir Ric. Tone, prest', buried at Camborne in 1547.[28] This firmly links Ton with Camborne, where *Beunans Meriasek* was presumably performed. The common factor of the possible involvement of Trelobys with all three Cornish clerical writers adds weight to the supposition.

---

27 Exeter Cathedral Archive, D&C Exeter MS 3688, f. 33r. Combellack has a useful list of other Tons/Tones/Tonnes in the area and discusses Nance's view of the possible link with Richard Ton of Crowan: Combellack, 'A Critical Edition of *Beunans Meriasek*', pp. 13–14.

28 Thomas, *Christian Antiquities*, p. 23, quoting Tapley-Soper in S.E. Gay, H. Fox, S. Fox and H. Tapley-Soper, eds, *The Register of Marriages, Baptisms and Burials of the Parish of Camborne, Co. Cornwall, A.D. 1538 to 1837* (Exeter: Devon and Cornwall Record Society, 1945), vol. 1, p. 78.

CHAPTER SIX

John Foxe and His Context

6.1 Foxe's use of his sources

It seems appropriate to end this Introduction with John Foxe himself, Stephyn's primary source. In writing his account of the Disputations, Foxe used some manuscripts already mentioned, such as the notaries' reports,[1] and additional letters and papers of the disputants, especially Ridley's notes.[2] He also raided official records, registers and court books, sometimes removing them from government repositories or even cutting out pages to add to his collection.[3] Several of these sources were highly abbreviated and required expansion for complete understanding. They also differed from each other—Ridley's notes omitted or rephrased some passages or references found in the notaries' accounts, and vice versa. This led to many paraphrases, as comparing Ridley's Latin notes with Foxe's English edition makes clear.[4]

Foxe therefore had choices and used them to his advantage. Even in unpacking the economy of the Latin he could colour his descriptions. So, Smith's *Tergiversaris* becomes 'You make delayes for the nonce', or Ridley's *Bona verba. Auditores sunt eriditi: intelligunt utrumque nostrum* 'Say not so, I pray you. Those that heare vs, be learned: they can tel both what you oppose, and what I aunswere well enough, I warrant you.'[5] Foxe—and his contemporaries Miles Coverdale and Henry Bull—were telling the story of the Reformation from their own perspective, and naturally differed from each other in their approach to sources. Wabuda has shown that their use of the surviving manuscripts relating to the Oxford 'martyrs' was particularly selective. Bull omitted personal information from letters, and deleted evidence of how disunited the reformers were. Foxe chose to omit any embarrassing or extreme unorthodox views, as

---

1 E.g. Cambridge University Library, Kk.5.14, ff. 13–29.
2 Parker Library, Corpus Christi College, Cambridge, MS 340, 11, ff. 247–64 and MS 340, 13, ff. 271–80.
3 Duffy, *Fires of Faith*, pp. 102–3.
4 E.g. Christmas, ed., *The Works of Nicholas Ridley*, comparing, for example, pp. 476–9, with T&C vi, 497–500 (TAMO, 1576, Bk 10, pp. 1408–9 [1383–4]).
5 Christmas, ed., *The Works of Nicholas Ridley*, p. 457, and T&C vi, 484 (TAMO, 1576, Bk 10, p. 1402 [1377]).

Catholic critics pointed out.[6] He disliked showing reformers faltering in the face of persecution and omitted letters that showed them in a less heroic light. He could also be credulous in the stories of divine retribution for those who resisted the reforms.[7]

In addition, the *Actes and Monuments* used illustration and juxtaposition to great effect. When discussing the preacher Bilney, to whom Latimer attributed his evangelical conversion, Foxe presents no evidence demonstrating that friars were responsible for pulling Bilney from the pulpit. But the adjacent illustration clearly shows this happening.[8] Certainly the role of John Day, Foxe's printer, can hardly be over-emphasized in the achievement of some of these effects.[9] Overall, however, there was a genuine aspiration towards accuracy and integrity and, as Duffy has suggested, although Foxe is often our only source, the fact that we can even attempt to reconstruct what might actually have happened says a great deal for him.[10]

6.2 The reception of Foxe and his vision of history

How Foxe was used, understood and received by his own contemporaries—and indeed after his time—is an important and fascinating area of study, if largely beyond the scope of this edition. Clearly the way he was used in SA is

---

6   Evenden and Freeman, *Religion and the Book*, pp. 137-42; Brad S. Gregory, *Salvation at Stake: Christian Martyrdom in Early Modern Europe* (Cambridge, MA: Harvard University Press, 1999), pp. 23-4, 185-7 and Susan Wabuda, 'Henry Bull, Miles Coverdale, and the Making of Foxe's Book of Martyrs', in Diana Wood, ed., *Martyrs and Martyrologies*, Studies in Church History, 30 (Oxford: Blackwell, 1993), pp. 255-6 (and, in the same work, the valuable studies by Euan Cameron, 'Medieval heretics as Protestant Martyrs' and David Loades, 'John Foxe and the Traitors: the Politics of the Marian Persecution'). See also Patrick Collinson, 'Truth and Legend: The Veracity of John Foxe's Book of Martyrs', in *Elizabethans* (London and New York: A&C Black, 2003), pp. 151-69; Thomas Freeman, 'Notes on a Source for John Foxe's Account of the Marian Persecution in Kent and Sussex', *Historical Research*, 67 (1994), 206-7; Thomas S. Freeman, 'Fate, Faction, and Fiction in Foxe's Book of Martyrs', *Historical Journal*, 43.3 (2000), pp. 602-23; I have not been able to consult, but am aware of the importance of, Thomas S. Freeman, '*Great searching out of bookes and autors*; John Foxe as an Ecclesiastical Historian', PhD dissertation, 1995, Rutgers University. See also Christopher Highley and John N. King, eds, *John Foxe and his World* (Oxford: Routledge, 2017) [first published in 2002]; David Loades, ed., *John Foxe: An Historical Perspective* (Aldershot: Ashgate, 1999).
7   Alexandra Walsham, *Charitable Hatred: Tolerance and Intolerance in England, 1500-1700* (Manchester and New York: Manchester University Press, 2006), pp. 195-6. Gregory, *Salvation at Stake*, pp. 181-2; and, for a survey of the whole territory, James Frederic Mozley, *John Foxe and his Book* (London: SPCK, 1940).
8   Susan Wabuda, *Preaching During the English Reformation* (Cambridge: Cambridge University Press, 2002), pp. 124-5.
9   Evenden and Freeman, *Religion and the Book*, pp. 1-2.
10 Duffy, *Fires of Faith*, p. 103.

an extraordinary example of the way his carefully constructed polemic could be deconstructed, reconstructed and reused for completely different purposes. But SA did not reach a wide audience whereas Foxe's mainstream impact was very considerable. Although not universally recognized in his own day, his work gained prominence over time and was by the nineteenth century quite pivotal—not only for historiography of the reformation era, but also for its mythology.

The old criticism that Protestantism could not be true Christianity—because it had only appeared in earnest one and a half millennia after Christ—badly needed answering, and Foxe (eventually) understood this, learning from Rabus and van Haemstede.[11] The Oxford disputants, for example, brought quotation after quotation from the early Fathers showing the antiquity of traditional Eucharistic belief, and plainly elements of that belief had been widespread for over a thousand years. The Church had been founded by Christ, who promised he would send the Holy Spirit to guide it 'into all the truth'.[12] If Protestantism was the fulness of that truth, why did it not appear earlier than the Tudor period?[13]

Foxe's ingenious answer to this was that it did. The *Actes and Monuments* seeks to recast history, attempting to show that Protestantism did indeed have a long lineage, in the 'heretical' and unorthodox minorities that throughout history had been opposed, excluded and sometimes persecuted by Catholics. Some of those who had been condemned as heretics hitherto should now be viewed, Foxe argues, as proto-Protestants and even proto-martyrs. By contrast, some of the 'orthodox' saints of old were in fact crypto-papists, who had harboured errors and even led people astray.[14] His book sought to 'reveal the hidden shape of history' at the same time as making large historical claims—to be based on true copies, letters, archives and registers.[15]

Of course, who was and who was not a 'martyr' in the Christian past was open to debate. While some historians (such as Crespin and van Haemstede) would be careful not to include iconoclasts, or those with unorthodox understandings

---

11 Gregory, *Salvation at Stake*, p. 171; Evenden and Freeman, *Religion and the Book*, pp. 139–40.
12 Jn 16:13 NRSV.
13 This question also stood alongside questions about the destiny of generations of Christian ancestors: were they in heaven, despite their unreformed Catholic faith? If so, was that faith as defective as claimed? See Alexandra Walsham, 'History, Memory and the English Reformation', *The Historical Journal*, 55, 4 (Cambridge: Cambridge University Press, December 2012), pp. 909–14.
14 Walsham, 'History, Memory and the English Reformation', pp. 903–5; Walsham, *Charitable Hatred*, pp. 172–3.
15 Eamon Duffy, *Reformation Divided: Catholics, Protestants and the Conversion of England* (London: Bloomsbury, 2007), p. 311.

of the Trinity, among their 'heroes' of the past, others were less scrupulous, including Foxe.

Although he was hugely influential on later generations in England, in his own time Foxe was possibly eclipsed in Europe by the rival accounts of Nicholas Harpsfield (John's brother) whose *Dialogi Sex* was published in 1566, and Robert Persons' *De Persecutione Anglicana* which ran to eleven editions following its publication in 1581. Sander's *De Origine ac Progressu Schismatis Anglicani* was published in 1585 and translated into German and French, becoming the basis of other similar accounts in many languages.[16] Persons' *Three Conversions of England* also addresses itself to Foxe's claims,[17] refusing to accept many of his premises. It is clear that the modern debate around Foxe has had many antecedents.

Nonetheless, John Foxe was certainly a historian as much as he was a storyteller—for in his day the growth of the discipline of history from Ciceronian and Eusebian roots was well under way.[18] Just because he does not conform fully to our contemporary idea of dispassionate, liberal, evidential narrative does not mean he was not evidential in his own way. His compilation of original documents was large scale, but fused with a scriptural vision, in which his contemporary 'martyrs' were painted in the colours of the Bible and the early Church. Elements of the account of Ridley's and Latimer's deaths were drawn directly from Eusebius and the martyrdom of Polycarp, fused with other elements from first-hand eyewitness accounts.[19] To a certain extent his evidential approach nonetheless anticipated modern methods, although an overarching, revisionist zeal drove everything he did.

Whatever is said of him as a historian, however, it is to Foxe's credit that, as a man, he was never easily impressed with arguments that heretics should be persecuted and killed—despite the precedents for this and the practical and theological arguments behind it. Perhaps this was because of early experiences in Oxford under Henry, perhaps because of later ones under Mary. Either way, he himself clearly felt that clemency and persuasion were better ways forward.[20] This is evident in his reporting of the Oxford Disputations, and the occasional glimpses of human kindness there, transcending the divisions.

---

16 Duffy, *Reformation Divided*, p. 287; Evenden and Freeman, *Religion and the Book*, pp. 137–9.
17 Robert Parsons, *A Treatise of Three Conversions of England from Paganism to Christian Religion* (London: Henry Hills, 1603) [reprinted 1688].
18 Patrick Collinson, 'John Foxe as Historian'—Essay 3 in the introductory material for TAMO—(Sheffield: HRI Online Publications, 2011), https://www.johnfoxe.org/index.php?realm=more&gototype=&type=essay&book=essay3, accessed 10 June 2014.
19 Collinson, 'John Foxe as Historian', section III.
20 Coffey, *Persecution and Toleration*, pp. 100, 210–11.

6.3 Foxe and Stephyn in the light of current historiography

While disputed in his own day, it is undeniable that Foxe and his 'Book of Martyrs' eventually played an enormous part in forming later perceptions of the Marian period and its theological preoccupations. What was portrayed as the self-defeating cruelty of the regime, trapped in insularity and tradition, came to dominate narratives. In modern times the English response to the Reformation was long believed to lack many of the positive features of the Counter-Reformation. Historians followed the lead of A.G. Dickens in seeing the reign as essentially a failure on its own terms, albeit not always because of the direct fault of Mary.[21]

Bossy, however, accepting a radical discontinuity between medieval 'observance-based' Catholicism, and a more vigorous Tridentine 'devotional' and 'confessional' approach, reopened interest in the positive aspects of the Marian period, while still displaying 'tell-tale marks of a denominational paradigm inherited from the past'.[22] Duffy, Haigh and others have subsequently argued powerfully that there was widespread support for the Marian project, not simply on account of Mary's regal claims, but also because of a strong attachment to traditional religion and a desire to see it restored and reformed by its own lights.[23] An absence of work on the Marian period has gradually been filled, not least by important and detailed local studies that have revealed not only an attachment to the pre-Reformation faith and the initial weakness of Protestantism, Haigh's 'sickly child',[24] but also the valuable contribution of 'Marian' priests.

Not all scholars accept this 'revisionist' judgement wholeheartedly, however. Wooding seeks to judge the Marian Church less by its traditionalism

---

21 A.G. Dickens, *The English Reformation*, revised edn (London: Fontana, 1967), pp. 355–85; David Loades, *Mary Tudor: A Life* (Oxford: Blackwell, 1992), pp. 338–45, but see also David Loades, *Mary Tudor: The Tragical History of the First Queen of England* (Kew: The National Archives, 2006), pp. 212–19 and Wizeman, *Theology and Spirituality*, pp. 6–7.
22 Walsham, *Catholic Reformation*, p. 8; cf. John Bossy, *The English Catholic Community, 1570-1850* (London: Dalton, Longman & Todd, 1975).
23 Duffy, *Stripping of the Altars*, pp. 527–43; Duffy, *Fires of Faith*, pp. 1–28; Haigh, *English Reformations*, pp. 205–6; Christopher Haigh, 'The Continuity of Catholicism in the English Reformation', *Past and Present*, 93, 1 (November 1981), pp. 33–69. Christopher Haigh, 'Catholicism in Early Modern England and Beyond' (review article), *The Historical Journal*, 45, 2 (Cambridge: Cambridge University Press, 2002), pp. 481–94. For an overview of the Cornish dimension see Mark Stoyle, 'Rediscovering Difference: The Recent Historiography of Early Modern Cornwall' [2002], in Philip Payton, ed., *Cornish Studies: Ten* (Exeter: UEP, 2002), pp. 104–15 and reprinted in Philip Payton, ed., *Cornwall in the Age of Rebellion, 1490-1690* (Exeter: UEP, 2021), pp. 377–90.
24 Christopher Haigh, 'The English Reformation: A Premature Birth, A Difficult Labour and a Sickly Child', *The Historical Journal*, 33, 2 (1990), pp. 449–59.

and more by 'its adaptability, and its capacity for regeneration'.[25] She sees its roots in Catholic humanism rather than a simple response to Protestantism and would question the automatic right of later Catholic generations to see an unbroken continuity in tradition from medieval times. With MacCulloch, she would also argue that the claims of the Oxford Movement to similar continuity were exaggerated and far from demonstrable.[26] In practice, while the Marian restoration of Catholicism was welcomed by many with respect to the Mass, it proved harder to re-engage the population with papal obedience, and in some cases an almost Henrician appeal to statute was required.[27]

Duffy's work in particular, however, has highlighted the proactive and energetic engagement with the Counter-Reformation that was exemplified in the efforts by Bonner, Watson and others to embrace publication as a missionary strategy under Mary.[28] They often did a better job—for example with Bonner's *Homilies*—than the original Protestant material they built on or responded to.[29] It can therefore still be argued that there was indeed a 'capacity for regeneration' in the Marian Church, which was certainly Counter-Reformation in nature.[30] Its efforts at reform can be securely placed in the context of wider international initiatives for the rejuvenation of the Catholic faith. (This would include the efforts in other nations to recover 'territories and peoples temporarily lost to the forces of heresy' as well, perhaps the efforts to spread the faith in Asia and the Americas.)[31]

In this context, then, what was Stephyn's contribution? Of course, the 1554 Disputations themselves—and Foxe's account of them—show different sides of a very polarized struggle. But it is intriguing, to say the least, to find a traditionally minded priest in the 1570s, using a Protestant account of the Disputations to provide the spine of his *catena* of patristic proof texts of transubstantiation and the sacrifice of the Mass. Of course, Foxe was one of the few accessible sources available to Stephyn, but it is still possible to perceive in the latter's work a purposeful engagement with the Counter-Reformation project that Tregear and others had been involved with. As Walsham has argued convincingly, the line between missionary recusant activity and traditional leanings within the established Church is not easy to draw. Post-Reformation English society was pluralistic, and the boundary between confessional positions was porous and

---

25 Lucy E.C. Wooding, *Rethinking Catholicism in Reformation England* (Oxford: Clarendon Press, 2000), p. 269; Wizeman, *Theology and Spirituality*, pp. 7–8.
26 Wooding, *Rethinking Catholicism*, p. 270; Diarmuid MacCulloch, 'The Myth of the English Reformation', *Journal of British Studies*, 30, 1 (Jan. 1991), pp. 1–19.
27 Wooding, *Rethinking Catholicism*, pp. 134–6.
28 Duffy, *Fires of Faith*, pp. 64–70.
29 Duffy, *Stripping of the Altars*, pp. 534–7.
30 Wizeman, *Theology and Spirituality*, pp. 251–4.
31 Walsham, *Catholic Reformation*, p. 5.

susceptible to political and practical imperatives. As Wizeman notes, it was beginning to harden, but perhaps this was less so in distant Cornwall than in some other places.³² We have seen that Tregear, despite his initial employment in the Marian Counter-Reformation project, remained in his parish until his death. Stephyn may have left his but appears to have been working on Tregear's manuscript in old age, using Foxe as a window back to the debates of the Marian years. Even a cautious reading of these facts suggests that, right into the 1570s and 1580s, traditionally minded clergy did not feel 'everything was over' and therefore saw a value in marshalling the old arguments in new ways.

Indeed, the appearance of Campion's *Rationes Decem*, printed at Stonor Park in 1581 and distributed surreptitiously at Oxford, placed a renewed emphasis on patristic proofs for Catholic doctrine, fuelling an upsurge of interest in the Fathers as important in the controversy between Protestants and Catholics. It would not be surprising if this emphasis in contemporary debate was one factor in Stephyn seeking out patristic texts at almost exactly the same time.³³

---

32 See 3.4 and Walsham, *Church Papists*, pp. 73–9; Walsham, *Catholic Reformation*, pp. 87–94, but also Wizeman, *Theology and Spirituality*, pp. 4–5. For wider context, see Mark Stoyle, *West Britons: Cornish Identities and the Early Modern British State* (Exeter: UEP, 2002). In his annotations to TH, Stephyn also makes use of the Geneva Bible: *The Bible and Holy Scriptvres, conteyned in the Olde and Newe Testament ...* (Geneva: Rowland Hall, 1560, distributed from 1576 in England). This was the first English Bible he would have seen that included biblical chapters and verses, which he uses extensively, even paraphrasing some of the textual notes, though Protestant scholars had compiled them (see Appendix A).

33 Edmund Campion, *Ten Reasons [Rationes Decem]* (London: Manresa Press, 1914), Latin Text pp. 30–87, English Translation pp. 89–145, especially, in relation to the Fathers, pp. 61–5; 109–18. A copy of the original 1581 clandestine printing is held at Stonyhurst. In his choice of patristic texts and references from the Geneva Bible (see previous note) in the margins of TH, Stephyn seems to be equipping himself for a dialogue with Protestants, and not just the clandestine education of Catholics.

CHAPTER SEVEN

Conclusions

7.1 The end of the Marian years

With the passing of the Supremacy laws soon after Elizabeth's coronation, the prospect of the technical reversal of all that the disputants had reasserted came into view. Although Heath, the archbishop of York, led a united party of bishops in the House of Lords against further religious changes, and supported fresh disputations, these were inconclusive. Within a few months, most of the bishops were deprived and, in due course, almost every Oxford head of house joined them.[1]

Safer in exile, some of the disputants (such as Harding and Smyth) continued to have distinguished academic careers and to contend at arm's length with Protestants, as has been noted. Others, who remained in England rather than fleeing to Leuven or Douai, perforce had to keep a lower profile, often because of imprisonment or house arrest.[2] Sympathetic clergy such as Tregear and Stephyn had a number of options, from church papism to an itinerant educational ministry.

Initially the government seemed to believe that the old religion would wither on the vine with the change in state sponsorship. Prosecution for non-attendance was patchy, although parliament was more proactive.[3] Gradually the authorities became more apprehensive, after the arrival of Mary Queen of Scots in 1568, the Northern Rebellion of 1569, and the publication of the papal bull *Regnans in Excelsis* that excommunicated Elizabeth in 1570. As has already been described, the climate in which Tregear or Stephyn could continue to promote the views they held under Mary with reasonable safety in Cornwall slowly came to an end.

---

1   David Loades, *Mary Tudor: The Tragical History of the First Queen of England* (Kew: The National Archives, 2006), p. 209; Duffy, *Fires of Faith*, pp. 200–2.
2   Duffy, *Reformation Divided*, pp. 136–44.
3   Coffey, *Persecution and Toleration*, p. 85.

7.2 Tregear, Stephyn and the journey of the manuscript

It remains to summarize what has been learned about Tregear, Stephyn and their colleagues in a few paragraphs. They seem to have come from the borders of northern Kerrier and eastern Penwith, around Camborne, Crowan, Helston, Sithney and Wendron, although their area of operation extended beyond Glasney to Mylor, Truro, St Allen and Newlyn East. Perhaps their writing projects were inspired by one of the Glasney canons, Ralph Trelobys, although the evidence for this is circumstantial.

Whoever inspired the work, Tregear's possible links with Crowan—as well as his incumbency of the parish next to Newlyn, and Stephyn's role as curate of Newlyn in 1537—underline the importance of Ralph Trelobys in the story. As well as being a canon of Glasney, he had been vicar of both parishes as well as Richard Ton's incumbent. He knew all three men, suggesting a possible link between three key texts in Cornish that bear witness to the pre-Reformation heritage of the region. Trelobys also embodies the link between these literate, parochial clergy and Glasney.

Tregear certainly remained in St Allen ministering to his people until his death in 1583. At some point—possibly in that very year—his manuscript passed to Thomas Stephyn, who had been vicar of neighbouring Newlyn East in Queen Mary's time, but had stepped down between the beginning of Elizabeth's reign and the arrival of Richard Martyn at some date before his resignation in 1573.[4] We know that Stephyn did not add *Sacrament an Alter* to Tregear's manuscript before 1576, and he probably did so a few years later.

It is impossible to be sure how far the final, completed manuscript may have travelled before eventually settling in Flint. Cornishmen such as Richard Pentreth and Michael Penkevill—had made their way to the seminaries of the continent, including the Iberian peninsula.[5] Brittany and Ireland were of course much closer than that.

In the end, however, or even directly, the manuscript's journey led to Wales. Whether undertaken personally by Stephyn or by later priests, such crossings were far from unusual. There was a bustling trade between Fowey and St Ives on the one hand and Neath and Milford Haven on the other throughout the period.[6] Both Newport and Chepstow also had considerable ports by this

---

4 See Chapter 4, note 29: we know when John Tresteyn replaced Martyn—1573—but we do not yet know when Martyn began his ministry at Newlyn East.
5 See Chapter 2, note 19; Edwin Henson, ed. *Registers of the English College at Vallodolid, 1589–1862*, Catholic Record Society, 30 (London: CRS, 1930), p. 59 (n. 166), and Edwin D. Burton, and Thomas L. Williams, *The Douay College Diaries, third, fourth and fifth, 1598–1654, with the Rheims Report 1579–80* (vol. 1), Catholic Record Society, 10 (London: CRS, 1911), pp. 33, 38.
6 Cf. E.A. Lewis, ed., *Welsh Port Books, 1550–1603: with an Analysis of the Customs Revenue Accounts of Wales for the Same Period*, Cymmrodorion Record Series XII (London: The Honourable Society of Cymmrodorion, 1927).

time, the latter with many international links. From South Wales a network of Catholic houses stretched up through the Marches to traditionalist Flint, where the manuscript came to rest. Eventually, as with all the important Cornish manuscripts in Wales, the details of provenance were forgotten. What came to be seen as 'thirteen homilies in Welsh' ended up a long way from St Allen and Newlyn East, where they had their origin.[7]

Yet the manuscript survived and gives testimony to a limited degree of Cornish Catholic continuity under Elizabeth. Distant from the centres of power, Tregear continued his ministry, however modified. In due course, wherever he was, Stephyn augmented the manuscript, apparently with ideas of its future usefulness. Its very survival is a witness, therefore, to another survival: clandestine, reflective and perhaps compromised, but nonetheless real.

---

7   Frost, 'Glasney's Parish Clergy', p. 70, and in Payton, ed., *Cornwall in the Age of Rebellion*, p. 212.

Edition

CHAPTER EIGHT

Edition

Editorial Method

Diplomatic Edition

The edition is planned in double-page sections. First, at the top of the 'left-hand' page as printed, the diplomatic edition. This offers a complete, uncorrected text of the manuscript, reproducing as many of the interesting features of the original as accurately as possible.

Capitalization and word division are as in the manuscript and deletions, alterations and anomalies are indicated or—where this is impossible for practical reasons—commented on in the Notes. (Sometimes an arbitrary decision needs to be made on capitalization, as Stephyn can use large lower-case letters for upper case.) Superscript is used for obvious later insertions (but ye simply represents *y* with *e* written above, a contraction for *the*). Regular type is used for Stephyn's secretary hand (secretary hand B) and italic for his italic hand (italic hand B). Original punctuation is given, though this is often arbitrary, and intruded lines, brackets and so on are included. Customary contractions and abbreviations of the period are, however, expanded. In passages of regular type they are distinguished by showing them in italic (and vice versa).

Where the manuscript is damaged, square brackets and points indicate missing or partly unreadable letters of the text. (It is by no means certain that this folio damage all took place after writing.) If a few letters of damaged text are at least partially visible and are confirmed to some extent by Foxe, they are suggested in the square brackets, in both Cornish and Latin transcriptions. Where the identity of a whole Latin word, difficult to read but still partially visible, is absolutely certain from the source, it is also completed in square brackets. Portions of irreparably damaged MS or completely missing Latin words are never restored in the diplomatic edition, however certain, but are suggested in the edited text. In the case of whole Cornish words that cannot be read or are missing (where the spelling is far less certain than is the case with Latin), they are all left blank, and possible reconstructions are suggested in the Notes and the edited text. (In the case of marginal references, because they are not repeated in the edited text, a slightly different practice is followed. Isolated missing letters and numerals—where reasonably certain as parts of whole names or titles—are suggested in square brackets to facilitate understanding. Whole words are never restored, but the Commentary gives the full references for each passage, which can differ from those given in SA.)

In cases of doubt, or of unusual forms, reference is made in the Notes. Catchwords are shown and the layout of the manuscript is followed as faithfully as possible. Marginalia, however, are shown in type smaller than the main text, to enable them to be located at the correct places alongside it. Overwriting and correction, whether by a second hand or the same hand at a later point, is indicated with superscript and by placing the original letters, struck through, before or after the overwritten letters, as best reflects the original. The final reading is given in the edited text, the Notes making reference to any unusual features.

The folios have, at some point, been numbered in pencil continuously with the Tregear Manuscript. Little comment is made on these numbers, after 59r.1. Line numbers are editorial, and on the right of the text. References to the marginal notes add the letter *m*.

Nicholas Williams, Oliver Padel and Benjamin Bruch have been generous throughout in offering many helpful suggestions on the diplomatic edition in a series of private communications. Important specific contributions are acknowledged by the initials NW, OP and BB respectively. Similarly helpful suggestions from Ray Edwards, Keith Syed, Richard Gendall, and C.W.H. Hatcher are acknowledged by RE, KS, RG and CH respectively. At the outset, free online discussion with Ray Edwards and Keith Syed illuminated many wider aspects of the work, so a general acknowledgement is also due.

Corrected, Edited Text

Below the diplomatic edition, a corrected, edited text (E) is offered. While this is not usually necessary in an English (or indeed Cornish) edition of the same period (although Graham Thomas and Nicholas Williams include one in their edition of *Bewnans Ke*),[1] it will help some readers with this complex text. Other editions in the *1,000 Years of Cornish* series will not necessarily follow suit, opting instead for a minimally edited diplomatic edition, with word division and punctuation adjusted for clarity. In the case of SA, however, never edited before and drawing from its source in unpredictable ways, extra aids to interpretation could assist the general reader. It also facilitates complete fidelity in the diplomatic edition, by adding a version dividing words and punctuating conventionally.[2] To remind readers of SA's essential nature, the edited text is shown as continuous prose (as far as matching with the translation allows).

1 Cf. Thomas and Williams, *Bewnans Ke*, pp. lxxix–lxxxi.
2 So, for example, at 59r.12, the *me agispys* of the MS and diplomatic edition is written as *me a'gis pys* in the edited text, distinguishing more clearly the verbal particle *a*, infixed 2 pl. (possess.) pron. *'gis* as object, and 3 sg. *pys* from *pysy*, 'to pray, ask'.

The edited text still adheres closely to manuscript spelling and adaptions are only made where clear scribal errors or ambiguity in the original require them. Inserted corrections or reconstructions are clearly identified by square brackets and explained in the Notes. Where occasionally letters are supplied to improve clarity in the division of words, these are also shown in square brackets. If initial letters are removed for the same reason—usually because of a duplication at the beginning of a word of the final *n* of the definite article *an*—this is not shown, but is clear in the diplomatic edition and referenced in the Notes. Words requiring deletion from a particular place in E, because they belong elsewhere, or are erroneous, are enclosed in curly brackets—e.g. {ema}—but left in place.

Suggested reconstructions of missing whole words, phrases or sentences are sometimes offered (in square brackets with additional italics to distinguish them clearly) in the edited text, but never in the diplomatic edition. While they may be of use to some users who are interested in exploring Stephyn's adaption of the overall meaning of a passage, there is no intention to suggest that they are a reliable guide to the now missing portions of the original text. Where given, however, they are supplied on the basis of existing, attested vocabulary and grammar from SA, TH or closely related texts.

Source Material from Foxe

On the following, 'right-hand' page, the relevant extracts from Foxe's *Actes and Monuments* are set out, using (with permission) the transcription of the 1576 edition found in TAMO—*The Acts and Monuments Online* (see Bibliography under 'Printed & Online Source Editions & Printed Records'). In citing Foxe from TAMO, the relevant year of the edition is given and both the pagination in TAMO and Foxe's own page number if different (the latter in square brackets—following the practice of TAMO). As almost all quotations are from Book 10, the book number is not given (except where very occasionally another book is used.)

Alongside this, in round brackets, references to the 1838 edition of Townsend and Cattley (T&C) are also given.[3] (Although T&C has been superseded by TAMO as a scholarly tool, it may still be of use to readers wishing to follow the underlying theological debates quickly, in modern spelling.) SA does not always follow its sources line by line, but an attempt has been made, in setting out the extracts, to align them as helpfully as possible with the MS reading. Material omitted for reasons of space is shown by '…'.

---

3   Townsend and Cattley, *Acts & Monuments*, vol. 6, op. cit., cited in notes as T&C vi, with the page number following, e.g. T&C vi, 455.

Translation

This final section, at the bottom of the 'right hand' page as printed, attempts to be an idiomatic, modern English translation of the Cornish and Latin originals, as these (and particularly the former) sometimes differ from the source text. It may be useful for those without Cornish who nonetheless wish to study the reception and use of Foxe in the peninsular context of the time. No attempt is made in this translation to reproduce the eccentric punctuation or minor errors of the original: these are normalized. The translation allows for direct comparison between the sense of the manuscript reading and the original source material, identified as far as possible in the section above it.

Notes (& Apparatus)

In the Notes that follow the Commentary, an attempt is made to elucidate particularly interesting (or partially damaged) features of the Cornish (and a bare minimum of similar passages in the Latin), giving explanations of the suggested reconstructions in the case of damaged passages.

Every 'new' reading of Tregear and SA stands on the shoulders of all earlier work, gratefully acknowledged here. 'Such a wealth of material, much of it unpublished and literally fading from existence on the page' often lies in pencilled notes in boxes at the Royal Institution of Cornwall, as Myrna Combellack has observed. Had it been published, our understanding of the texts (and our appreciation of the work of Nance and Smith) would have been greatly enhanced.[4] The RIC is to be commended for recent efforts to preserve these annotations, particularly in the dictionaries Nance kept close to hand.

As a result of the quality of this earlier work, common readings (largely passed over in silence in the Apparatus integrated into the Notes) vastly outnumber differences, which are shown primarily to assist those working to adapt electronic files of previous readings. It will be realized by attentive readers how rare they are for the vast majority of the text. This is in itself a tribute to the quality of early work on this manuscript and underlines the continuity of this edition with that work. Where differences do occur, citation is as follows:

First for the 'Nance' family of readings: N for Nance's first work (or N1 and N2 where his two first manuscript transcriptions conflict); C for Nance and Smith's joint final typescript and T for Nance's manuscript translation;[5] B for Bice's cyclostyled version of Nance's work and S for Keith Syed's electronic

---

4   Combellack, 'A Critical Edition of *Beunans Meriasek*', pp. ii; 76 (note 3). See also Introduction 1.5, and Chapter 1, note 38.
5   Courtney Library, *Nance Bequest*, 7:22 (46). Box 7 and Folder 22 (renumbered by Peter Pool as Folder 46) contains both N1 and N2, T and C.

version of this (although S is only cited where a rare significant difference is found).⁶

Andrew Hawke's preliminary work towards the Cornish Dictionary Project was the second major foundation of my work,⁷ and was of the highest value in beginning the edition. It is cited as H and deserves to share equally with Nance's work a good deal of the credit for our contemporary understanding of SA. Once again, while it is in the nature of the Apparatus to show the relatively few differences in readings, I would not like this to obscure the immense accuracy of this piece of work as a whole, or my indebtedness to it.

F is used in the Apparatus for my own earlier transcription of SA,⁸ which was the basis of Ray Edwards' version for Cornish revivalists (as he generously acknowledged).⁹ For this reason, I have not included references to both in the Apparatus, although I have noted the very few instances where Edwards disagreed with my reading.

---

6 Bice, *Homelyes xiij in cornysch*; an electronic copy of this, identified here as S, was made by R. Keith R. Syed, *Homelyes xiij in cornysch* (privately circulated, 2003).
7 Hawke, *Homelyes xiij in cornysche*; Hawke, *The Cornish Dictionary Project*, pp. 11–13.
8 Frost, *Sacrament an Alter*, 2003.
9 Ray Edwards, ed., *The Tregear Homilies with The Sacrament of the Altar [converted to Kernewek Kemmyn by Keith Syed]* (Sutton Coldfield: Kernewek Dre Lyther, 2004), pp. iv–vi; x–xii. As Ray explains there, it was his own gentle questioning about possible patristic sources in SA that launched my journey towards a full critical edition.

Folio 59r [59]

	Crist ny rug vsya trope k[..............] 59
[Augus]tinus	dewetha, kepare del vg[e] S. A[ust]
[D]e Vnitate	I ma .S. Austen ow leverall in y lever entituled: *De Vnitate*
[Ec]clesie. x	*ecclesiæ.* in y .x. chapter: *Quid hoc est rogo? Cum verba nouissi[ma]*
Dist.	*hominis morientis audiantur, ituri ad inferos, nemo eum dicit* 5
	esse mentitum, et illius non iudicatur, hæres qui forte ea contemp
	serat. Quomodo ergo effugiemus iram dei, si vel non credentes,
	vel contemnentes, expulerimus verba nouissima et vnici filij dei
	et domini nostri, saluatoris, et ituri in cœlum et inde prospectu
	ri quis ea negligat, quis non obseruet, et inde venturi vt 10
	de omnibus iudicet? henew ye leverall. 59
	me agispys panadra ew hemma? pan vo an dewetha gyrr^{y}ow
	clowis a onen a vo in ^{e}y ^{g}wely marnance: ha paris ye verwall
	den veith ny lavar a vos gow gansa: na negew ef compti[s]
	ye heare, neb^{p}ne theffa regardya, an keth gyrr^{y}ow ma: 15
	fatla wrere^{ne} ny a voyday[a] anger a thew; rag ne geran
	cregy nanyle regardia gerryow dew ha only mab dew,
	agyn arluth han saviour, ew ascendis then nef ha y
	weth ow gwelas pew vge ow despisea, h^a gwetha, y
Chrisostom	errow beg^{n}egas ef, ha ef a vyn Dos ye Iudgia oll an bobell. 20

Crist ny rug usya trope [*kepare e gerryow*] dewetha, kepare del uge S. Austen…

Ima S. Austen ow leverall in y lever entituled *De Unitate Ecclesiae*, in y 10 chapter: *Quid hoc est rogo? Cum verba novissima hominis morientis audiantur, ituri ad inferos, nemo eum dicit esse mentitum, et illius non iudicatur haeres qui forte ea contempserat. Quomodo ergo effugiemus iram Dei, si vel non credentes, vel contemnentes, expulerimus verba novissima et unici Filii Dei et Domini nostri, Salvatoris, et ituri in caelum et inde prospecturi quis ea negligat, quis [non][10] observet, et inde venturi ut de omnibus iudicet?* Hen ew the leverall, 'Me a'gis pys, panadra ew hemma? Pan vo an dewetha gyrryow clowis a onen a vo in e gwely marnance, ha paris the verwall, den veith ny lavar a vos gow gansa; na neg ew ef comptis e heare nep ne theffa regardya an keth gyrryow-ma. Fatla wrene ny avoydaya anger a Thew? Rag neg eran cregy nanyle regardia gerryow Dew ha only Mab Dew, agyn Arluth ha'n Saviour— ew ascendis the'n nef ha yweth ow gwelas pew uge ow despisea ha gwetha y errow benegas ef—ha ef a vyn dos the judgia oll an bobell.'

---

10   *non*: in Foxe, but not in all editions.

Foxe, TAMO, 1576, p. 1387 [1362]; (T&C vi, 450)—Cranmer's Disputation

Oglethorpe: No man of purpose doth vse tropes in his testament...

Weston: Austine in hys booke entituled, *De vnitate Ecclesiæ*. the x. chap. hath
these wordes following: *Quid hoc est rogo? Cum verba nouissima
hominis morientis audiantur ituri ad inferos, nemo eum dicit
esse mentitum; & illius non iudicatur hæres, qui fortè ea contempserat.
Quomodo ergo effugiemus iram die, si vel non credentes,
vel contemnentes, expulerimus verba nouissima, et vnici filij dei
& domini nostri salvatoris, & ituri in cœlum, et inde prospecturi
quis ea negligat, quis non obseruet; & inde venturi, vt
de omnibus iudicet?* That is to say.
What a thing is this I pray you? when the last words
of one lying on his death bed are heard: which is ready to go to his graue,
no man saith that he hath made a lye: and he is not accompted
his heire, which regardeth not those wordes.
How shall we then escape gods wrath if either not
beleuyng or not regardyng, we shall reiect the last woordes both of the only
sonne of god and also of our lord and sauiour, both ascending into heauen,
and beholding from thence who despiseth and who obserueth then not, and
shall come from thence to iudge men?

Christ did not use a figure of speech [as his] last [words], as St A[ugustine]

St Augustine says, in his book entitled *Of the Unity of the Church*, in his 10th chapter: *What is this, I ask? When the last words of a dying man are heard, on his way to the next world, no one calls him a liar: he would not be counted his heir, who so treated them with contempt. How, then, will we escape God's anger, if by unbelief or out of contempt we reject the last words of the only Son of God, our Lord and Saviour, on his way to heaven—who from there is able to see who neglects and who fails to keep them—and who will come from there as judge of all?* That is to say, 'I pray you, what is this? When the last words are heard of one who is on his death-bed, and ready to die, no one says he is lying; nor is he considered his heir, who does not respect these same words. How, then, shall we avoid the anger of God? For we neither believe nor respect the words of God and the only Son of God, our Lord and Saviour— who has ascended into heaven, and sees, too, who despises and who keeps his holy words —and he will come to judge all the people.'

Folio 59r [59]

home.83
Jr 26.
Jf math.

Christ a ruge ry then an keith kigge na, a ruge ef keme
ras vrth an worthias marya. rag e ma Chrisostome
ow leverall: *Veniat tibi in mentem quo sis honore hon[o]*
ratus, qua mensa fruaris. Ea namque re nos alimur, qu[a]m
angeli. etc. henna ew ye leverall: gas ve ye remmembra, 25
fatla arave inta, tha honora, ha pana tabell esta
owsetha: rag e thony megys, gans an kethsam tra, vgy
an elath ow gwelas ha ow trembla, rag negyns abell y^e
welas, hebb mere a own, rag an golowder, vse ow tos
tha worta: rag y thony gwres ovn kigg gans agen ar[lu] 30
th Christ. Pew a lavar an gallus agen arluth dew, [y^e]
dclarya^{11} e honour ef? pana bug[e]ll a ruge bithquat[h]
maga e thevas, gans e members e honyn? Lowarth
mamb wore e flehis the benenas erall, ye vaga [...]
agan arluth Christ na vennas gwell in della, mas ef aga[n] 35
magas ny gans e gorf e honyn, han Ivnyas ny th[e]
theffe e honyn b^{k}eg^{p}are a ra an mam maga e flogh gans
e leath: Indella e may christ, ^{w}orth agyn maga ny, gans e
[gor]f ^{ay} gos[e]f; gans agen ganow, e gorfe ny a rys recevya
dell vgy Chrisostom affirmya. 40

Christ a ruge ry then an keith kigge-na, a ruge ef kemeras urth an Worthias Marya. Rag ema Chrisostome ow leverall: *Veniat tibi in mentem quo sis honore honoratus, qua mensa fruaris, ea namque re nos alimur, quam angeli, etc.* Henna ew the leverall, 'Gas ve the remmembra fatla a ra' ve in ta tha honora, ha pana tabell esta ow setha: rag eth o[n] ny megys gans an kethsam tra ugy an elath ow gwelas ha ow trembla, rag neg yns abell th'e welas hebb mere a own, rag an golowder use ow tos thaworta. Rag yth o[n] ny gwres un kigg gans agen Arluth Christ. 'Pew a lavar an gallus a'gen Arluth Dew, the d[e]clarya e honour ef?' Pana bugell a ruge bithquath maga e thevas gans e members e honyn? Lowar mamb wore e flehis the benenas erall the vaga, [bus] agan arluth Christ na vennas gwell indella, mas ef agan magas ny gans e Gorf e honyn, han junyas ny theth'effe e honyn. Kepare [<begar?] a ra an mam maga e flogh gans e leath, indella em[a] Christ worth agyn maga ny, gans e [Gor]f [h]a'y Gos ef.' 'Gans agen ganow, e Gorfe ny a rys recevya', dell ugy Chrisostom affirmya.

---

11 dclarya [*sic*].

Foxe, TAMO, 1576, p. 1388 [1363]; (T&C vi, 452]—Cranmer's Disputation

Weston: He gaue vs the same flesh which he tooke
of the Virgin ... Chrisostome is against you ... where he
sayth: *Veniat tibi in mentem quo sis honore honoratus,
qua mensa fruaris. Ea namque re nos alimur, quam
angeli. &c.* That is. Let it come into thy remembraunce
with what honour thou art honoured, and what table thou
sittest at: for wyth the same thing we are nourished, which
the angels do behold and tremble at: neither are they able to
behold it without great feare for the brightnes which commeth
therof: and we be brought and compact into one heape or masse with him,
beyng together one body of Christ, and one flesh with him. Who shall speake
the powers of the Lord, and shall declare forth al his prayses? What Pastor
hath euer nourished his shepe with hys owne members? Many
mothers haue put forth their infantes after their birth, to other Nurses:
which he would not do, but
feedeth vs with his owne body, and conioyneth and vniteth vs
to hymselfe. Like as mothers nurse their children with
milke: so Christ nourished vs with his body ...
[we should receaue] the body by the mouth ...
I proue it out of Chrysostome....

Christ gave to us that same flesh, which he took from the Virgin Mary.
For Chrysostom says: *Call to mind what sort of honour you are honoured with, what
table you enjoy, for we are indeed fed with what angels, etc.* That is to say, 'Let me
remind you how I honour you well, and what sort of table you are sitting at: for
we are fed by that selfsame substance which the angels see and tremble over, since
they are not able to see it without great awe, because of the brightness coming from it. For
we are made one flesh with our Lord Christ. 'Who shall speak of the power of our
Lord God, to declare his honour?' What shepherd ever fed his sheep with
parts of his own body? Many a mother entrusts her children to other women
for nursing, [yet] Christ our Lord would not do so, but would rather feed us
with his own Body, and join us to his very self. Just as the mother feeds her
child with her milk, so Christ feeds us, with his [Body]
and his Blood.' 'With our mouth we should receive his Body', as Chrysostom
affirms.

Folio 59v [59a]

	[Erubesc]it fieri nutrix, quæ facta est [m]ater.	
	Christus autem non ita ipse nutritor est noster: ideo pro	
[Chr]isostom	cibo carne propria nos pascit, et pro potu suum sanguinem	
[in] psalm.50	nobis propinabit. Item in cap. Mathæi, homel. 83. Non e[ni]m	
[i]tem. Hom.83	sufficit ipsi hominem fieri, flagellis interim cædi: sed nos	5
26. ca: mt	secum in Vnam vt ita dicam, massam reducit: neque id	
	re ipsa nos corpus suum efficit? henna ew yᵉ leverall	
	An mam, agemar meth treweythow rag boos mammath	
	mas Christ, an mammath nyy, ne gesee, o gwell in della	
	genan. Insted rag henna a boos, e ma ef agyn maga	10
	gans e kegg e honyn, ha e weth, in sted a thewas,	
	e may vrth agen maga gans e woos. Indella e	
Chrisost.	weth, in 26, chapter [a] mathew, an 83. homeli. o levera[..]	
homil.	rag ne gew lowr rag Christ the vose mab dene,	
83. in	ha the voese whippys: mas thagyn dry ny, tha	15
26. cap	voese onyn gans ef, ha gvle ny e gorf ef, [n]ot	
mat.	der faith only, mas e weth in very deed.	
gans	ema Chrisostom o leverall gans ganow. 2.Cor.13 homili.29.	
ganow	rema ew e irrow: Non vulgarem honorem consequutum est,	
Christost	os nostrum, accipiens corpus dominicum .i. nyn gew nebas	20

Erubescit fieri nutrix, quae facta est mater. Christus autem non ita ipse nutritor est noster: ideo pro cibo carne propria nos pascit, et pro potu suum sanguinem nobis propina[v]it. Item in cap. Mathaei, homel. 83. Non enim sufficit ipsi hominem fieri, flagellis interim caedi: sed nos secum in unam ut ita dicam, massam reducit.
Neque id [fide solum, sed]¹² *re ipsa nos corpus suum efficit?* Henna ew the leverall, 'An mam a gemar meth treweythow rag boos mammath, mas Christ, an Mammath nyy, neg esee o gwell indella genan. Insted rag henna a boos, ema ef agyn maga gans e kegg e honyn, ha eweth, insted a thewas, ema [e] urth agen maga gans e Woos.' Indella eweth, in 26 chapter [a] Mathew, an 83 homeli, o levera[ll] 'Rag neg ew lowr rag Christ the vose mabdene, ha the voese whippys, mas th'agyn dry ny tha voese onyn gans ef, ha gule ny e Gorf ef, not der faith only, mas eweth in very deed.' Ema Chrisostom o leverall 'gans ganow' (2 Cor. 13, Homilia [30]), [An] re-ma ew e irrow: *Non vulgarem honorem consequutum est, os nostrum, accipiens Corpus dominicum*: i.e. 'Nyng ew nebas...

---

12 In Foxe, but omitted from SA.

Foxe, TAMO, 1576, p. 1388 [1363]; (T&C vi, 452–3)—Cranmer's Disputation

Weston: *Erubescit fieri nutrix, quæ facta est mater.*
Christus autem non ita ipse nutritor est noster: ideo pro
cibo carne propria nos pascit, & pro potu suum sanguinem
nobis propinauit. Item in. 26. cap. Mathæi, Homel. 83. Non enim
sufficit ipsi hominem fieri, flagellis interim cædi: sed nos
ecum in vnam vt ita dicam, massam reducit: neque id fide solum, sed
reipsa nos corpus suum efficit? That is.
Shee that is a mother, shameth sometime to play the Nourse.
But Christ our Nurse doth not so play
with vs. Therfore in steede of meate he feedeth vs
with his owne flesh, and in steede of drinke
he feedeth vs wyth hys owne bloud. Likewise
vpon the. 26. chap. of Mathew, the. 83. homely he saith:
For it shall not be enough for hym to become man, and in the meane whyle
to be whipped: but he doth bring vs into one masse or lumpe with him selfe
(as I may so call it) and makyth vs hys body, not
by fayth alone, but also in very deede.
Weston: *Chrisost. 2. Cor. cap. 13. Homel. 29.*
hath these wordes: *Non vulgarem honorem consequutum estos*
nostrum, accipiens corpus dominicum. i. No litle…

She who becomes a mother may blush to nurse her child, but Christ, in nourishing us, does not do so. Rather, for food he feeds us with his own flesh and, for drink, it is his own blood that he offers to us.' Likewise in Homily 83 on the 26th chapter of Matthew: 'It is not enough for him to be made man and scourged with whips, but he brings us to be one with himself, so that, I may say, we become a whole: not by [faith alone, but] in actual fact, he makes us his body. That is to say, 'The mother gets embarrassed sometimes to be nursing, but Christ, our Nurse,
does not act like that with us. Therefore instead of food, he nourishes us with his own flesh and, what is more, instead of drink he nourishes us with his Blood.' So also in the 26th chapter of Matthew, the 83rd homily, he says 'For it is not enough for Christ to be [made] man and to be whipped, but to bring us to be one with him, and make us his Body, not through faith only, but also in very deed.' Chrysostom says 'by mouth' (2 Cor. 13, Homily [30])—these are his words: *It is no ordinary honour that has befallen our mouth receiving the Body of the Lord.* That is, 'It is not slight…

Folio 59v [59a]

home:	an honour ew reys tha gen ganow, the recevy[a]
29. in	recevya corf agyn arluth. agen ganow e
epist	ma o mos in Corf agen arluth Christ, rag dout
[C]or. 13	den veith tha vostya, an corf na a rugg
	entra in Corf agen arluth Christ: I ma 25
	lowarth onyn, o bostia, fatla vgy faith an tasow coth
[C]hristost	a vam egglys in an sy: but decevis ens sy, rag
hom.	Chrisostom^{em[a]} in [k]eth keth poyntma ow leverall,
pop.	homil.2. ad populum Antiochenum. *Tanquam maximam*
[An]tio	*hereditatem Elisæus melotem suscepit. Etenim veré* 30
	maxima fuit hæreditas omni auro prætiosior
	vt erat duplex: Helias ille: et erat sursum Helias
	et deorsum Helias. Noui quód iustum illum beatum putatis et

[vel]letis quisque esse vt ille. Quid igitur, si vobis demonstrauero qui[d]
[a]liud, quod illo multo maius omnes sacris misteriis imbuti recipimu[s]
[H]elias quidem melotem discipulo reliquit: Filius autem De[i] ascendens
[su]am nobis carnem demis[it]. Sed Helias
[qu]idem exvt[us: C]hristus autem

---

an honour ew reys th'agen ganow, the recevya Corf agyn Arluth.' Agen ganow ema o mos
in Corf agen Arluth Christ: rag dout den veith tha vostya, an [*ganow*]-na a rug entra in
Corf agen Arluth Christ.' Ima lowar onyn o bostia, fatla ugy faith an tasow coth
a Vam Egglys inans y: but decevis ens y, rag [ema] Chrysostom i'n keth
point-ma ow leverall: *Homilia 2, Ad Populum Antiochenum: Tanquam maximam hereditatem*
Elisæus melotem suscepit. Etenim vere maxima fuit hæreditas, omni auro praetiosior, ut erat
duplex Helias ille: et erat 'sursum Helias' et 'deorsum Helias'. Novi quod
iustum illum beatum putatis, et velletis quisque esse ut ille. Quid igitur, si vobis demonstravero
quid aliud quod illo multo maius, omnes sacris misteriis imbuti recipimus? Helias quidem meloten
discipulo reliquit; Filius autem Dei, ascendens, suam nobis carnem demisit. Sed Helias quidem
exutus ... Christus autem..

Foxe, TAMO, 1576, p. 1388 [1363]; (T&C vi, 452-3)—Cranmer's Disputation

Weston: ...honor is geuen to our mouth,
receiuing the body of the Lord...
Cranmer: With our mouth we receaue *the* body of Christ...

Foxe, TAMO, 1576, p. 1402 [1377]; (T&C vi, 485)—Ridley's Disputation

Smith: Now where as you boast that your fayth is *the* very fayth of the
auncient Church: I will shew here that is not so...
I wyll bring in Chrysostome for this poynt.
*Hom.2. ad populum Antiochenum. Tanquam maximam
hæreditatem Elisæus melotem suscepit. Etenim verè
maxima fuit hæreditas, omni auro prætiosor:
& erat duplex Helias ille: & erat sursum Helias,
& deorsum Helias. Noui quòd iustum illum beatum putatis, &
et velletis quisque esse vt ille. Quid igitur, si vobis demonstrauero quid
aliud, quod illo multo maius omnes sacris mysterijs imbuti recipimus.
Helias quidem melotem discipulo reliquit; Filius autem dei ascendens,
suam nobis carnem dimisit. Sed Helias
quidem exutus...*

---

the honour that is given to our mouth, to receive the body of our Lord.' Our mouth goes into the Body of Christ our Lord, for no one hesitates to boast that that [mouth] entered into the Body of Christ our Lord. There are many who boast that the faith of the ancient fathers of Mother Church is in them, but they are deceived, for Chrysostom says on this same point: *Homily 2, To the People of Antioch: As his greatest inheritance*
Elisha received the sheepskin cloak. It was a truly great inheritance, more precious than any gold, that double presence of Elijah: for he was the 'Elijah above' and the 'Elijah below'. I know you count that just man to be blessed, and each of you would want to be like him. What then, if I show you that we all receive something far greater, who receive the holy mysteries? For Elijah left only a cloak to his disciple; but the Son of God, ascending, left us his own flesh. And Elijah, indeed, cast it off before he went up ... but Christ...

Folio 60r [60]

60

Chrisost.	*Christus autem et nobis carnem reliquit, et ipsam habens ascendit*
homil.2.	henna ew ye leverall. Eliseus a rug recevia e mantall
[a]d popu	kepare e lell, ha meer inheritance. rag e tho e gwryonath
[l]um Antio	ha moy presius, agis owr veith. e thesa ^ii deow helias:
chum:	onyn a wartha, ha helias awolas. me a wor inta, why 5

tha bedery tha vos maga benegas agis & dean gwyrryan Elias
pan drevynnough leverall, mar tema disquethas theugh, certy[n]
tacclow arall, mere moy agis helma, pan vo ny, oll, endewis
gans an mysteris benegas ma? Helias asas e mantall in ded gans
e scholar. Mab Dew ascendias then neff, hef a sas vmma, e kig   10
the ny, ha e weth, ef a woras e kig gansa, the gwlas neff. 60

Chrisost.	Chrisostom, e ma o leverall, in e lyver. 3. han. 3.chapter. *de*
de dignita	*dignitate Sacerdotij: O miraculum, O dei beneuolentiam.*
te Sacerdo	*qui sursum sedet, tempore sacrificij, hominum manibus*
tij . li. 3. cap	*continetur; ac ipse tradit volentibus ipsum accipere et* 15
3	*complecti. Fit autem id ill nullis præstigii, sed apertis et*

circumspicientibus circumstantium omnium oculis. henna ew ye leverall.
O markell, ha blonogath da a thew, disquethis the ny, vgy
setha in gwlas neff, vgy ^intyr dowla tvse & beis, in tirmyn
an sacrifice, tha Canevar den gwyrrian a vo desyrius e gowis: 20

Christus autem et nobis carnem reliquit, et ipsam habens ascendit. Henna ew the leverall,
'Eliseus a rug recevia e mantall kepare e lell ha meer inheritance, rag eth o e gwryonath ha
moy presius agis owr veith. Eth esa deow (2) Helias: onyn 'awartha', ha Helias 'awolas'.
Me a wor in ta, why tha bedery tha vos maga benegas agis an dean gwyrryan Elias.
Pandre vynnough leverall, mar tema disquethas theugh certyn tacclow arall, mere moy
agis helma, pan vo ny oll endewis gans an mysteris benegas-ma? Helias [a] asas e mantall
in ded gans e scholar. Mab Dew ascendias the'n neff; hef a [a]sas umma e kig
the' ny, ha eweth, ef a woras e kig gansa, the gwlas neff.' Chrisostom ema o leverall,
in e Lyver 3 ha'n 3 Chapter, *De Dignitate Sacerdotii: O miraculum! O Dei benevolentiam! Qui
sursum sedet, tempore Sacrificii, hominum manibus continetur;*
ac ipse tradit volentibus ipsum accipere et complecti. Fit autem id nullis
praestigiis sed apertis et circumspicientibus circumstantium omnium oculis. Henna ew the
leverall: 'O markell, ha blonogath da a Thew disquethis the' ny, ugy setha in gwlas
neff, ugy intyr dowla tuse an beis in tirmyn an sacrifice, tha canevar den gwyrrian a vo
desyrius e gowis:

Foxe, TAMO, 1576, p. 1402 [1377]; (T&C vi, 485)—Ridley's Disputation

Smith: *...Christus autem & nobis reliquit, et ipsam habens ascendit.*
That is: *Eliseus* receyued the mantell
as a right great inheritaunce. For it was in deede a right excellent inheritance,
and more precious then any gold beside. And the same *Helias* was a double
Helias: He was both *Helias* aboue, and *Helias* beneath. I know well you thinke
that iust man to be happy, and you would gladly be euery one of you as he is.
What will you then say, if I shall declare to you a certayne
other thyng, which all we that are indued with these holy mysteries, do
receiue, much more then that? *Helias* in dede left hys mantell to
his scholer. But the sonne of God ascendyng, dyd leaue here his flesh
vnto vs .... & ascended also to heauen hauing it with him.

Foxe, TAMO, 1576, p. 1388 [1363]; (T&C vi, 453)—Cranmer's Disputation

Cranmer: Chrysostome in his booke *de dignitate Sacerdotij lib. 3. cap. 3.* sayth:
*O miraculum, O Dei beneuolentiam. Qui sursum sedet, tempore sacrificij, hominum
manibus continetur ... ac seipse tradit volentibus ipsum accipere & complecti. Fit
autem id nullis præstigijs, sed apertis & circumspicientibus circumstantium
omnium oculis.* That is: O myracle, O the good wil of God towardes vs, which
sitteth aboue at the right hand of the father, & is holden in mens handes at the
sacrifice tyme, and is geuen to feed vpon, to them th[a]t are desirous of him.

---

but Christ both left his flesh for us here, and yet ascended with it. That is to say,
'Elisha received his mantle as his true and great inheritance, for it was so in truth and
more precious than any gold. There were two Elijahs: one 'above', and an Elijah 'below'.
I know well, that your thoughts are to be as happy as the righteous man Elijah.
What will you say, then, if I show you certain other things, much greater
than these, when we are all filled with these holy mysteries? Elijah truly left his mantle
with his disciple. The Son of God ascended to heaven; and left his flesh here
for us, yet also took his flesh with him, into the kingdom of heaven.' Chrysostom says, in
his Book 3 and 3rd Chapter of *On the Dignity of the Priesthood: O miracle! O loving kindness of
God! He who sits on high is, at the time of the Sacrifice, contained in human hands
and he gives himself over to those willing to receive and embrace him. This is done, however, not
secretly, but openly and before the eyes of all who stand near to see.* That is to
say, 'O miracle, and goodwill of God revealed to us! He who sits in the kingdom of
heaven, is held in human hands at the time of the Sacrifice, for every righteous man who
desires to have him:

Folio 60r [60]

Christ ew devethis, not dir subtelnath, bus openly tha keneve[.]
a whelha, ha vo o sevall rebta. Vmma why a glow Christ
ew gwelys pub deth vmma war^e an ^{nore} b^{v}ys, eff ew touchis,
eff ew squardis gans dens, a gan tavas ew ruth gans
e gos. E ma Chrisostom o leverall in e. homele. 34. *Quod summo*   25
christost | *honore dignum est. Id tibi in terra ostendo. Nam quemadmo*
homele. | *dum in regiis non parietes, non lectus aureus, sed regum^{13} corpus*
.34. | *in throno sedens omnium præstantissimum est: ita quoque in cælis*
              regium corpus, quod nunc in terra proponitur. Non Angel[os,]
non Archangelos, non cælos cælorum, sed ipsum horum omnium Dominum tibi   30
ostendo. Animaduertis quonam pacto quod omnium maximum est atque
præcipium in terra, non conspicaris tantum sed tangis, neque
solum tangis, sed comedis, atque eo accepto domum redis. Absterg[e]
igitur ab omni sorde animam tuam: henna ew ye leverall,
[.] thesa ve o disquethas these, vmma waren nore, ew worthy   35
[..] vos an moygha honoris, kepare ha mytearne, o setha
dan queth a stat, a pub tra ew an moigha
[.]xcellent: indella ew corf agen arluth
dew in gwlas neff, ew sittis [......]
deragan in nore vise: 40

Christ ew devethis, not dir subtelnath, bus openly tha kenever a whelha ha vo o sevall
rebta. Umma why a glow Christ ew 'gwelys pub deth umma ware an norevys, eff ew
touchis, eff ew squardis gans dens, agan tavas ew ruth gans e gos'. Ema Chrisostom o
leverall in e Homele 34, *Quod summo honore dignum est, id tibi in terra ostendo.*
Nam quemadmodum in regiis non parietes, non lectus aureus, sed regium corpus in throno sedens
omnium praestantissimum est: ita quoque in caelis regium corpus, quod nunc in terra proponitur.
Non Angelos, non Archangelos, non caelos caelorum, sed ipsum horum omnium Dominum tibi
ostendo. Animadvertis quonam pacto quod omnium maximum est atque praecipium in
terra, non conspicaris tantum sed tangis, neque solum tangis, sed comedis, atque eo accepto
domum redis. Absterge igitur ab omni sorde animam tuam. Henna ew the leverall: '[E]th esa' ve
o disquethas these, umma war en nore, ew worthy [the] vos an moygha honoris. Kepare
ha mytearne, o setha dan queth a stat, a pub tra ew an moigha [e]xcellent. Indella ew Corf
agen Arluth Dew in gwlas neff, ew sittis [*lemmyn*] deragan i'n norevise...

---

13   *regum* [sic] for *regium*.

Foxe, TAMO, 1576, p. 1388–9 [1363–4]; (T&C vi, 453)—Cranmer's Disputation

Cranmer: And that is brought to passe by no subtiltie or craft, but with the open and beholdyng eyes of all the standers by ... Thus ye heare Christ is seene here in earth euery day, is touched,
is torne with the teeth, that our toung is red with his bloud...
Weston: But harken what Chrisostome sayth. Homel. 34. *Quod summo honore dignum est, id tibi in terra ostendo. Nam quemadmodum
in regijs non parietes, non lectus aureus, sed regum [sic] corpus
in throno sedens omnium præstantissimum est: ita quoque in cælis
regium corpus, quod nunc in terra proponitur. Non Angelos,
non Archangelos, non cælos cælorum, sed ipsum horum omnium Dominium tibi ostendo. Animaduertis quonam pacto quod omnium maximum est atque
præcipium in terra, non conspicaris tantum sed tangis, neque
solum tangis, sed comedis, atque eo accepto domum redis. Absterge
igitur ab omni sorde animam tuam:* that is to say.
I shew forth that thing on earth vnto the which is worthy
the greatest honor. For lyke as in the Palace of kynges, neither the walles nor the sumptuous bed but the body of kynges sittyng vnder the cloth of estate and royall seate of Maiestie, is of all thinges els the most excellent: so is in lyke maner the kynges body in heauen, which is now set
before vs on earth...

Christ has come, not in a hidden way, but openly to all who would see, and stand by him. Thus you hear that Christ is 'seen every day here upon earth, he is touched, he is torn by teeth, our tongue is red with his blood.' Chrysostom
says in his Homily 34: *What is worthy of the greatest honour, that I show you—here on earth. For, as at court, it is not the walls, nor the golden couch—but the royal body that sits on the throne, that is the most glorious thing. So in heaven with the King's body, now set before us here on earth. It is not Angels, nor Archangels, nor the heavens of heavens, but the Lord himself of all of these, that I show you. Do you see, therefore, how it is the greatest thing of all and most outstanding on earth, that you not only see but touch, not only touch but eat, and receiving him
return home? Make your soul clean, therefore, from every stain.* That is to say, 'I will show you, here on earth, what is worthy to be the most highly honoured; like
a king, sitting under a cloth of state, who is of all things the most excellent. So is the Body of our Lord God in the kingdom of heaven, which is set [now] before us in the world...

Folio 60v [60a]

Sacrame[n]t an alter.

[Ch]risost In della ew corf age*n* arluth dew in ᵍˡgwlas neff, ew sittis
[H]omele. 34. lemmy*n* derage*n* in nore ves. ne gesa ow desquethas
theugh, elath, nanyle Arth elath, mas an very corf,
age*n* master ha pe*n*sevike oll. Tee a ill *p*ercevia, pavanar, 5
a sort, esta o qvelas age*n* saviour christ, bus e dochya, not only
[.] touchia, bus e thibbry, an moygha tra a pub tra oll, vs war[e]
[.]n nor, ew agen saviour Iesus Christ, ha pa*n* vova recevis
[.]enas, kee thath tre; ha gwra golhe theth enaff, thaworth
[.]ll mvstethas a pehosow: kepar dell wruck; S.Thomas 10
iohn .20. touchia corfe Christ; indella ny ara touchia christ in
sacrame*n*t. rag Christ ew yᵉ vos touchis, rag e vos eff
keveris Dew ha deane. Rag ema Tertullia*n*, *De carnis*
[T]ertullian *resurrectione*, o leverall: *Videamus de propria*
[D]e resur *christiani hominis forma, quanta huic substantiæ frivolæ* 15
[r]ectione *et sordidæ apud deum prærogatiua sit. Et si sufficeret*
[c]arnis *illi quod nulla omnino anima salutem possit adipisci,*
nisi dum est in carne, crederit[14]: *adeó caro salutis,*
[ca]*rdo est, de qua cum anima deo alligatur, ipsa est quæ effici[t]*
[u]*t anima alligari possit: sed et caro abluitur, vt anima* 20

Sacrament an Alter. Indella ew corf agen Arluth Dew in gwlas neff,
ew sittis lemmyn deragen i'n noreves. Neg esa' ow desquethas theugh elath, nanyle
arthelath, mas an very corf agen Master ha Pensevike oll. Tee a ill percevia pa vanar
a sort esta o quelas agen Saviour Christ, bus e dochya; not only e touchia,
bus e thibbry. An moygha tra a pub tra oll us ware an nor ew agen Saviour Jesus
Christ, ha pan vo va recevis genas, kee tha'th tre: ha gwra golhe the'th enaff thaworth
oll mustethas a pehosow'. Kepar dell wruck S. Thomas touchia Corfe Christ, indella ny a ra
touchia Christ i'n sacrament, rag Christ ew the vos touchis, rag e vos eff keveris Dew ha
deane. Rag ema Tertullian, *De carnis resurrectione*, o leverall: *Videamus de propria Christiani
hominis forma, quanta huic substantiae frivolae et sordidae apud Deum praerogativa sit. Etsi
sufficeret illi, quod nulla omnino anima salutem possit adipisci nisi dum est in carne cred[id]erit:
adeo caro salutis cardo est, de qua cum anima Deo alligatur, ipsa est quæ efficit ut anima alligari
possit. Sed et caro abluitur, ut anima...*

---

14   *crederit* [*sic*] for *crediderit*.

Foxe, TAMO, 1576, p. 1389 [1364]; (T&C vi, 453–5)—Cranmer's Disputation

Weston: ...so is in lyke maner the kynges body in heauen, which is now set before vs on earth. I shewe the[e] neither
Aungels, nor Archaungels, nor the heauens of heauens, but the very Lord
& maister of all these thinges. Thou perceauest after what
sorte thou doest not onely behold, but touchest, and not onely
touchest but eatest that which on the earth is the greatest and chiefest thing
of all other, and when thou hast receaued the same,
thou goest home: Wherfore clense thy soule from
all vncleannes.
Foxe: As Thomas touched the body of Christ, so we touch it in the sacrament.
Chedsey: This is because of the vnion: so that God is sayd to be touched,
when Christ which is both God and man is touched. Tertullian *De carnis resurrectione* sayeth: *Videamus de propria
Christiani hom[in]is forma, quanta huic substantiæ friuolæ
& sordidæ apud deum prærogatiua sit. Etsi sufficeret
illi quod nulla omnino anima salutem posset adipisci
nisi dum est in carne, crediderit: adeo caro salutis,
cardo est, de qua cum anima deo alligatur, ipsa est quæ efficit
vt anima alligari possit: sed & caro abluitur, vt anima...*

The Sacrament of the Altar. So is the body of our Lord God in the kingdom of heaven, which is set now before us in the world. I show you neither angels, nor
archangels, but the very body of our Master and Prince of all. You can perceive how and
in what manner you [not only] see our Saviour Christ, but touch him, not only touch him,
but eat him. The greatest thing of all the things that are upon earth is our Saviour Jesus
Christ, and when you receive him, go home: and cleanse your soul from
all foulness of sin'. Just as St Thomas touched Christ's Body, so do we
touch Christ in the sacrament, for Christ is to be touched, because he is both God and
man. For Tertullian, in *On the Resurrection of the Body*, says: *Let us see [now] the true nature of
a Christian, and how this paltry and base substance is so highly honoured by God. Since
it is clear that no soul can arrive at salvation unless it believes while it is in the flesh,
then flesh is the hinge of salvation and, when the soul is linked to God, the flesh itself makes it
possible for the soul to be so joined. But the flesh is also washed, that the soul...*

Folio 60v [60a]

[e]maculetur: caro inugitur, vt anima consecretur: sig
[n]atur, vt anima muniatur: caro manus impositione
[a]dumbratur, vt anima spiritu illuminetur: caro corpore
[e]t sanguine Christi vescitur, vt anima de Deo saginetur.
[h]enna ew tha leverall, pana haker ew, agen substance ny   25
derag dew & neff, an ena mab den neffra sawis; mase
dir criggyans da, dirr vo an enaf in kigg mab deane.
an kigg yma causya an ena tha vos Ivnys ye dew & neff:
pan vo & kigg gulhis, an nenaf a veth glanhis: an
kigg ew anoyntis, may halla an nenaf bos consecratis   30
an kigg ew selis, may halla an nenaf bos defendis
[.]n kigg ew touchis gans dowla, rag malla an nenaf,
[..]s golowis gans & spiris sans: & kigg e ma ow tibbry
[.]orf ha eva gose agen arluth Iesus christ rag ma[.]
halla an nenaf bos mekys worth Dew golosake hae   35
vab ras agen saviour Iesus Christ.

An sac

---

emaculetur; caro inu[n]gitur, ut anima consecretur; [caro] signatur, ut anima
muniatur; caro manus impositione adumbratur, ut anima Spiritu illuminetur;
caro Corpore et Sanguine Christi vescitur, ut anima de Deo saginetur. Henna ew tha leverall,
'Pana haker ew agen substance ny derag Dew an neff! An ena
mabden neffra [o] sawis, mase dir criggyans da, dirr vo an enaf in kigg mabdeane.
An kigg yma causya an ena tha vos junys the Dew an neff. Pan vo an kigg gulhis, an
enaf a veth glanhis; an kigg ew anoyntis, may halla an enaf bos consecratis; an kigg ew
selis, may halla an enaf bos defendis; an kigg ew touchis gans dowla, rag malla
an enaf [bos] golowis gans an Spiris Sans; an kigg ema ow tibbry Corf ha eva Gose
agen Arluth Jesus Christ, rag may halla an enaf bos mekys worth Dew Golosake ha'e
Vab Ras agen Saviour Jesus Christ'.

Foxe, TAMO, 1576, p. 1389 [1364]; (T&C vi, 455)—Cranmer's Disputation

Chedsey: ...*emaculetur: caro inungitur, vt anima consecretur: signatur, vt anima muniatur: caro manus impositione adumbratur, vt anima spiritu illuminetur: caro corpore & sanguine Christi vescitur, vt anima de deo saginetur.* Let vs consider...what great prerogatiue this vayne and foule substance of ours hath with God... no soule could euer get saluation vnlesse it beleue while it is in the flesh...that where as the soul so is linked vnto God, it is the sayd flesh that causeth the soul to be linked: yet the flesh moreouer is washed, that the soule may be clensed: the flesh is annointed that the soule may be consecrated, the flesh is signed that the soule may be defended, the flesh is shadowed by the imposition of handes, that the soule may be illuminated with the spirite: the flesh doth eate the body and bloud of Christ, that the soule may be fed of God.

---

may be cleansed; the flesh is anointed, that the soul may be consecrated; signed, that the soul may be strengthened; the flesh by the imposition of hands is overshadowed, that the soul may be enlightened with the Spirit; the flesh is nourished with Body and Blood of Christ, that the soul may feast upon God. Which is to say, 'How disfigured is our nature before the God of heaven! The soul of mankind [was] never saved except through good faith, while the soul is in human flesh. The flesh causes the soul to be joined to the God of heaven. When the flesh is washed, the soul will be cleansed; the flesh is anointed, in order that the soul be consecrated; the flesh is sealed, in order that the soul be protected; the flesh is touched with hands, in order that the soul be enlightened by the Holy Spirit; the flesh eats the Body and drinks the Blood of our Lord Jesus Christ in order that the soul be nourished by Almighty God and his beloved Son, our Saviour Jesus Christ'.

Folio 61r [61]

Phoceus	**An Sacrament an aulter**
[i]. corinth	Corf Christ ew dibbris gans ganaw mab dean, Phoceus
[c]hap. 11.	e ma ow leverall, whar an keth gyrreow ma. *Reus erit*
Reus erit	*Quod ait, reus corporis et sanguinis, istud declarat quod*
[co]rporis	*sicut Iudas ipsum quidem tradidit, Iudæi contumeliosé in ipsum* 5
[et san]guinis	*insaniebant: sic ipsum inhonorant qui sanctissimum ipsius corpus*
Christi etc.	*corpus impuris manibus suscipiunt, tanquam Iudæi ipsi tenen[t]*
t.	*tenent et execrabili ore recipiunt. Quód crebro mentio*

[n]em: facit corporis et sanguinis Domini, manifestat quod non sit simplex
simplex homo qui sacrificatur, sed ipse Dominus omnium factor, 10
tanquam per hæc quidem ipsos perterrefaciens. henna ye leverall
pan rug age*n* saviour Christ leverall: ef ew gilty an Corf
han gos age*n* arluth Christ, indelma e ma ef o tisquethas,
kepar a rug Iudas betraya e arluth dew, an nethewan
a ve spitfull war byn age*n* arluth Christ: In della e movns 15
hⁱy. dishonora Christ, pan vonsy y recevia ef hae corf bene
gas ef ga*n*s dowla mustethas, ha pecar a ruk an nethewan,
e sensy, ha e recevia ef lymmyn, gans mustethas ganaw.
magapell dall vge a keth deane ma Phoceus, lowarth gwyeth
o gwyell me*n*tion an Corf, han gos agen arluth Dew, e ma, 20

An Sacrament a'n aulter. Corf Christ ew dibbris gans ganaw mab dean. Phoceus e ma ow leverall, whar an keth gyrreow-ma 'Reus erit'. Quod ait, 'reus corporis et sanguinis', istud declarat quod sicut Iudas ipsum quidem tradidit, Iudaei contumeliose in ipsum insaniebant, sic ipsum inhonorant qui sanctissimum ipsius corpus impuris manibus suscipiunt. Tanquam Iudaei ipsi tenent et execrabili ore recipiunt. Quod crebro mentionem facit
corporis et sanguinis Domini, manifestat quod non sit simplex homo qui sacrificatur, sed ipse Dominus omnium factor, tanquam per haec quidem ipsos perterrefaciens. Henna [ew] the leverall: 'Pan rug agen Saviour Christ leverall 'ef ew gilty a'n Corf ha'n Gos agen Arluth Christ', indelma ema ef o tisquethas, kepar a rug Judas betraya e Arluth Dew [h]a'n Ethewan a ve spitfull warbyn agen Arluth Christ, indella emouns [y] dishonora Christ, pan vons y y recevia ef ha'e Corf benegas ef gans dowla mustethas (ha pecar a ruk an Ethewan e sensy) ha'e recevia ef lymmyn, gans mustethas ganaw. Maga pell dall uge a' keth deane-ma, Phoceus, lowar gwyeth o gwyell mention a'n Corf ha'n Gos agen Arluth Dew, ema…

*Foxe, TAMO, 1576, pp. 1389–90 [1364–5]; (T&C vi, 455–6)—
Cranmer's Disputation*

Chedsey: *Ergo* the body of Christ is eaten with the mouth. *Item Phoceus 1. ad
Corinth. Capit. 11.* vpon these words: *Reus erit corporis & sanguinis. &c.
Quod ait, reus corporis & sanguinis, istud declarat quod
sicut Iudas ipsum quidem tradidit, Iudæi contumeliosè in ipsum
insaniebant: sic ipsum in honorant qui sanctissimum ipsius corpus
impuris manibus suscipiunt, tanquam Iudæi ipsi tenent
& execrabili ore recipiunt. Quod crebro mentionem
facit corporis & sanguinis Domini, manifestat quod non sit simplex
homo qui sacrificatur, sed ipse Dominus omnium factor,
tanquam per hæc quidem ipsos perterrefaciens.*
Where as he saith: Is gilty of the body
and bloud: this he declareth,
that lyke as Iudas betrayed him, & the Iews
were fierce & spiteful against him: so do they
dishonour him which receyue his holy body
with their impure hands, and as the Iewes did
hold him then, do now receiue hym with vnpure mouthes.
And where as he often
maketh mention of the body and bloud of the Lord, he…

The Sacrament of the Altar. The Body of Christ is eaten by the human mouth. Photius
says, on these same words 'He will be guilty. In saying, 'Guilty of the body and blood', he
declares that just as Judas betrayed him, and some Jews insanely abused him, so
they dishonour him, who take his most holy body into their impure hands and (just as some Jews
held him [captive] once) with an impure mouth receive him. By making frequent mention of the
Body and Blood of the Lord, he shows that it is not simply a man who is sacrificed, but the
Lord himself, the maker of all things, in this way thoroughly frightening them.' That [is] to
say: 'When our Saviour Christ said 'he is guilty of the Body and the Blood of Christ our
Lord', he showed that just as Judas betrayed his Lord God, and the Jews
were spiteful against Christ our Lord, so they dishonour Christ when they
receive him and his holy body with unclean hands (just as the Jews
held him) and receive him now with unclean mouth. In so far as this same man,
Photius, many times mentions the Body and Blood of our Lord God, he…

Folio 61r [61]

ef o tisquethas, n*y*n go ef only deane ew^{vo} sacrificed, mas
age*n* arluth christ e honyn. an gwrerer a pub tra oll.

Tertulian	:*Corpus vescitur vt anima saginetur*, .i. an corf o ma tibbry,
De resurr	rag malla an enaf bos megys. Phoceus. 1. Cor. ca. 11.
[e]ctione car	Phoceus e ma o leverall: neb vge o recivia corf 25
nis	dew, gans dowla mustethas, e thew ef, gilty an
Phoseus	gos agen arluth dew, kepar a ve Iudas. Tertullian
. Cor .	e ma o leverall: *Non possunt ergo seperari in mercede, quos*
cap . 11 .	*opera coniungit* .i. Na illansy bos seperatis in a ge gobe[.]
Tertullian	pan vonsy o gwiell an ober warbarth. John.17.21. & 14.10.11 30
Hillar .	Christ a gemeras kigg ha ve genys worth an worthias
. 8 . De	maria, ha e weth, e thesan ny, o recivia, dan a*n* lell
trinita *te*	mystery, kigg ay corf benegas, dîr he*n*na e thony
John . 6 .	onyn in ef: rag Christ a gowsys: ow kyg ew verel[.]
.55.	bos. ha ow gois ew verely dewas. neb a theffa dib[...] 35
	ow kig, ha eva ow dewas, e ma ef ow trega innaff
	ve, ha me in eff. concernya an gweranath an kig h[..]
	gois age*n* arluth Christ, n*y*n gvs gesis tella veth the
	doubtys: rag lym*m*en dir distvny age*n* arluth Christ

ha e weth dir faith da ny, e thew verely | Christ   40
kyg ha verely gois [ag]e*n* arl[.]th Ies[..]

---

ef o tisquethas, nyng o ef only deane e vo sacrificed, mas agen Arluth Christ e honyn, an gwrerer a pub tra oll. *Corpus vescitur ut anima saginetur*—i.e. 'An corf oma [o] tibbry, rag malla an enaf bos megys'. (Phoceus. 1. Cor. ca. 11) Phoceus ema o leverall: 'Neb uge o recivia corf Dew, gans dowla mustethas, eth ew ef gilty an gos agen Arluth Dew, kepar a ve Judas'. Tertullian ema o leverall: *Non possunt ergo separari in mercede, quos opera coniungit*—i.e. 'Na illans y bos seperatis in age gobe[r], pan vons y o gwiell an ober warbarth'. (John 17:21; 14:10-11.) Christ a gemeras kigg ha ve genys worth an Worthias Maria, ha eweth, eth esan ny o recivia, dan an lell mystery, kigg a'y Corf benegas, dir henna eth o' ny onyn in ef. Rag Christ a gowsys: 'Ow kyg ew verel[y] bos, ha ow Gois ew verely dewas: neb a theffa dib[bry] ow kig, ha eva ow dewas, ema ef ow trega innaff ve, ha me in eff'. Concernya an gweranath a'n kig ha'n Gois agen Arluth Christ, nyng us gesis tella[r] veth the doubtys, rag lymmen—dir distuny agen Arluth Christ ha eweth dir faith da ny—eth ew verely kyg ha verely Gois agen Arluth Jesus Christ.

Foxe, TAMO, 1576, pp. 1390–2 [1365–7]; (T&C vi, 456–7; 460–1)—
Cranmer's Disputation

Chedsey: ...declareth that it is not simply man that is sacrificed, but euen the Lord hymselfe, beyng the maker of all thinges, hereby... making them afraid.
Weston: ...*Corpus vescitur vt anima saginetur. i.* The body eateth
that the soule may be fed...
Chedsey: What say ye to *Phoceus* saying: They which receiue the body
with impure handes, are gilty of the
Lords bloud, as Iudas was.
Weston: That which foloweth in Tertullian doth take away your shift, where as he saith: *Non possunt ergo separari in mercede, quos*
opera coniungit. i. They cannot be separated in reward,
whom one worke ioyneth together.
Chedsey: If Christ haue taken verely the flesh of our body, & the man that was verely borne of the virgin Mary is Christ, and also we receaue vnder the true mystery the flesh of his body, by meanes wherof we shall be
one ... For he sayth: My flesh is meat in dede,
and my bloud is drynke in deede. He that eateth
my flesh & drinketh my bloud, abydeth in me
and I in hym. As touching the veritie of his flesh
and bloud, there is left no place of
doubt: or now, both by the testimony of the Lord,
and also by our fayth, it is verilye
flesh, and verily bloud.

---

shows it was not only a man who was sacrificed, but Christ our Lord himself, the maker of all things.' *The body feeds that the soul may feast:* i.e. 'The body eats, that the soul may be nourished'. (Photius, 1 Cor. chapter 11) Photius says: 'Whoever receives the Body of God with unclean hands is guilty of the Blood of our Lord God, just as Judas was'. Tertullian says: *They cannot therefore be separated in reward, who are joined together in work*: i.e. 'They cannot be separated in their reward when they do the work together'. (John 17:21 & 14:10–11) Christ took flesh and was born from the Virgin Mary and also we receive, under the true mystery, the flesh of his holy Body, through which we are one in him. For Christ said: 'My flesh is true food, and my Blood is true drink: whoever eats my flesh, and drinks my drink, he dwells in me, and I in him'. Concerning the truth of the flesh and the Blood of Christ our Lord, there is no more room for doubt now, for—through the testimony of Christ our Lord and also through our good faith—it is truly the flesh and Blood of our Lord Jesus Christ.

Folio 61v [61a]

an Sacrament a Corf & gois agen savior Iesus.

[A]mbros. De | De iis, qui initiantur sacris, cap.9. Ambros o leverall:
[ii]s qui ini | De tocius mundi operibus legisti, <u>quia ipse dixit et facta</u>
[tian]tur etc. | <u>sunt, ipse mandauit et creata sunt</u>. Sermo Christi qui po
cap.9 Psalm:105 | tuit ex nihilo facere quod non erat, non potest ea qu[æ]
31-34 | sunt in id mutare quæ non erant? Non enim minus est nou[as]
nouas res dare, quam mutare naturas: Sed quid argumentis vtim[ur?]
suis vtamur exemplis, incarnationisque exemplo astruamus mysterii
veritatem. Nunquid naturæ vsus præcessit cum Dominus Iesus ex
Maria nasceretur? Si ordinem quærimus, Viro mixta fœmina
generare consueuit, Liquet igitur quod præter naturæ ordinem
Virgo generauit: et hoc quod conficimus corpus ex Virgine est.
Quid hic quæris naturæ ordinem in Christi Corpore, cum præ
ter naturam sit ipse Dominus Iesus partus ex Virgine? Vera
vtique caro Christi quæ Crucifixa est, quæ sepulta est: veré
ergó illius Sacramentum est. Clamat Dominus Iesus: Hoc est
corpus meum. Ante benedictionem verborum cælestium alia specie[s]
nominatur, post consecrationem corpus significatur. Ipse dic[it]
sanguinem suum. Ante consecrationem aliud dicitur: post consecrat[io]
nem sanguis nuncupatur. Et tu dicis, Amen: hoc est, verum est.

An Sacrament a Corf ha Gois agen Savior Jesus. *De iis, qui initiantur sacris, cap. 9*—Ambros o leverall: *De totius mundi operibus legisti, 'Quia ipse dixit et facta sunt, ipse mandavit et creata sunt'. Sermo Christi qui potuit ex nihilo facere quod non erat—non potest ea quae sunt in id mutare quae non erant? Non enim minus est novas res dare, quam mutare naturas. Sed quid argumentis utimur? Suis utamur exemplis: incarnationisque exemplo astruamus mysterii veritatem. Nunquid naturae usus praecessit cum Dominus Jesus ex Maria nasceretur? Si ordinem quaerimus, viro mixta femina generare consuevit. Liquet igitur quod praeter naturae ordinem Virgo generavit—et hoc quod conficimus Corpus ex Virgine est. Quid hic quaeris naturae ordinem in Christi Corpore, cum praeter naturam sit ipse Dominus Jesus partus ex Virgine? Vera utique caro Christi quae crucifixa est, quae sepulta est: vere ergo illius Sacramentum est. Clamat Dominus Iesus: 'Hoc est corpus meum'. Ante benedictionem verborum caelestium alia species nominatur, post consecrationem Corpus significatur. Ipse dicit Sanguinem suum. Ante consecrationem aliud dicitur: post consecrationem Sanguis nuncupatur. Et tu dicis, 'Amen'—hoc est, 'Verum est'.*

Foxe, TAMO, 1576, p. 1393 [1368]; (T&C vi, 463)—Cranmer's Disputation

Young: Ambros. *De ijs qui initiantur sacris, cap. 9.* sayeth:
*De totius mundi operibus legisti, quia ipse dixit & facta
sunt, ipse, mandauit & creata sunt. Sermo Christi qui potuit
ex nihilo facere quod non erat, non potest ea quæ
sunt in id mutare quæ non erant? Non enim minus est nouas
res dare, quam mutare naturas: Sed quid argumentis vtimur?
suis vtamur exemplis, incarnationisque exemplo astruamus mysterij
veritatem. Nunquid naturæ vsus præcessit cum Dominus Iesus ex
Maria nasceretur? Si ordinem quærimus, viro mixta fœmina
generare consueuit, Liquet igitur quod præter naturæ ordinem
virgo generauit: & hoc quod conficimus corpus ex virgine est.
Quid hic quæris naturæ ordinem in Christi corpore, cum præter
naturam sit ipse Dominus Iesus partus ex virgine? vera
vtique caro Christi quæ Crucifixa est, quæ sepulta est: verè
ergò illius Sacramentum est. Clamat Dominus Iesus: Hoc est
corpus meum. Ante benedictionem verborum cælestium alia species
nominatur, post consecrationem corpus significatur. Ipse dicit
sanguinem suum. Ante consecrationem aliud dicitur: post consecrationem
sanguis nuncupatur. Et tu dicis, Amen: hoc est, verum est.*

The Sacrament of the Body and Blood of our Saviour Jesus. 'On those Initiated into the Sacred Mysteries', Chap. 9—Ambrose says: *Concerning the works of the whole world you have read, 'He spoke and they were made, he commanded and they were created'. If Christ's word can make out of nothing what did not exist—can it not change things which already are into what they were not? For it is not a smaller matter to create a new thing, than to change a thing's nature. But why use arguments? Let us use his own examples and, by the example of the incarnation, prove the truth of the mystery. Did the ordinary course of nature prevail when the Lord Jesus was born of Mary? If we look at the usual order, the union of a man and a woman produces conception. But it is clear that in a way beyond the order of nature the Virgin gave birth—and this Body which we consecrate is [that born] of the Virgin. So why do you seek the natural order in the case of the Body of Christ, since in ways beyond the natural order the Lord Jesus was born of the Virgin? It was certainly the true flesh of Christ which was crucified and buried: truly, therefore, this is the Sacrament of [of the same]. The Lord Jesus proclaims: 'This is my Body'. Before the blessing of the heavenly words another outward form is named, but after the consecration the Body is signified. He himself speaks of his Blood. Before the consecration something else was said: after the consecration it is named as Blood. And you say: 'Amen'—that is, 'It is true'.*

Folio 61v [61a]

Quod os loquitur, mens interna fateatur: quod Sermo sonat,
affectus sentiat. henna ew: Te a redias, oll an oberow an norvys.
Dew a cowsas an ger, ha hy a ve gwris: ha Christ a commandias
ha y a ve creatis. Gear Christ ill changia, takclennow, y^e
nappith, na ve travith derag dorn? Na esyn vsya Argumentys 25
  mas vsya exampels Christ, ha e negegath, agen arluth Iesus
    Christ a ve genis vrth an Worthias Maria. an lell
      kig agen arluth Christ a ve goris in grows, marow ha
        inclithis: rag henna, e thew an lell Sacrament ay corf ha
        e gois benegas. An arluth Iesus e honyn a cryas: hemma 30
        ew ow corf ve. kyns an girryow benegas the vos
^(leveris)benegis kyn tra e tho hynvis: bus osa an consecration
      e tho gwris corf agen arluth Christ, han hynwis e gois.
      ha te a worryb Amen: henna ew gwryonath. gas an
      mynd confessia da achy, an pith a whrella an ganow cows. 35
    gas an golan percyvia da, an geer a vo soundis.

Ambro	.S.Ambros in e .iiii. lever an Sacrament, han .iiii. chpter
[s l]ib.⁴ . De	o leverall in delma: *Panis iste, panis est ante verba Sacramen*
[S]acramentis	*torum: Vbi accesserit consecratio, de pane fit caro Christi. Hoc*
[c]ap. 4 .	*igitur astruamus: quomodo potest, qui panis est, corpus* 40
	esse Christi consecratione? consecratio igitur quibus verbis
	est, et cuius sermonibus? Domi[ni] Iesu.

Quod os loquitur, mens interna fateatur: quod Sermo sonat, affectus sentiat. Henna ew: 'Te a
redias oll an oberow a'n norvys, "Dew a cowsas an ger, ha [y] a ve
gwris; ha Christ a commandias ha y a ve creatis". Gear Christ, [na] ill changia
takclennow the nappith, na ve travith derag dorn? Na esyn usya argumentys mas usya
exampels Christ, ha'e enegegath. Agen Arluth Jesus Christ a ve genis urth an Worthias
Maria, an lell kig agen Arluth Christ a ve goris i'n grows, marow ha inclithis. Rag henna,
eth ew an lell Sacrament a'y Corf ha'e Gois benegas. An Arluth Jesus e honyn a cryas:
"Hemma ew ow Corf ve". Kyns an girryow benegas the vos leveris kyn tra eth o hyn[w]is;
bus osa an consecration eth o gwris Corf agen Arluth Christ ... a'n hynwis e
Gois, ha te a worryb "Amen", henna ew, "Gwryonath". Gas an mynd confessia da achy, an
pith a whrella an ganow cows; gas an golan percyvia da, an geer a vo soundis'. [*Ema*] S.
Ambros in e 4 Lever a'n Sacrament[ys], ha'n 4 Chapter, o leverall indelma: *Panis iste, panis*
est, ante verba Sacramentorum. Ubi accesserit consecratio, de pane fit caro
Christi. Hoc igitur astruamus: quomodo potest, qui panis est, Corpus esse Christi?
Consecratione. Consecratio, igitur, quibus verbis est, et cuius sermonibus?
Domini Iesu.

Foxe, TAMO, 1576, p. 1393 [1368]; (T&C vi, 463-4)—Cranmer's Disputation

Young: *...Quod os loquitur, mens interna fateatur: quod Sermo sonat, affectus sentiat.* That is. Thou hast red of the workes of all the world, that he spake the worde and they were made: he commaunded and they were created. Can not the word of Christ ... chaunge those thynges that are, into that they were not? ... But what vse we Argumentes? let vs vse hys owne examples ... of his incarnation ... the Lord Iesus was conceiued of a Virgine? It was the true flesh of Christ which was crucified and whiche was buried: therfore it is truly the sacrament of hym. The lorde Iesus hymselfe crieth: This is my body. Before the blessing of the heauenly wordes, it is named an other kynd: but after the consecration the body of Christ is signified. He calleth it hys bloud ... and thou sayest Amen: that is, it is true. That the mouth speaketh, let the inward mynd confesse: that the word soundeth, let the hart perceiue. The same Ambrose in hys 4. booke of sacraments the 4. chap. sayth thus: *Panis iste, panis est ante verba Sacramentorum: vbi accesserit consecratio, de pane fit caro Christi. Hoc igitur astruamus: quomodo potest, qui panis est, corpus esse Christi consecratione? consecratio igitur quibus verbis est, & cuius sermonibus? Domini Iesu.*

What the mouth speaks, let the mind within acknowledge: what the Word utters, let the heart feel. That is: 'You have read of all the works of the world, "God spoke the word, and they were made; and Christ commanded, and they were created." Can the word of Christ [not] change things to something, that were nothing beforehand? Let us not use arguments but use the examples of Christ, and his birth. Our Lord Jesus Christ was born of the Virgin Mary; the true flesh of Christ our Lord was crucified, dead and buried. Therefore, it is the true Sacrament of his holy Body and Blood. The Lord Jesus himself proclaimed: "This is my Body". Before those holy words were said, it was called something else; but after the consecration it was made the Body of Christ our Lord, and [he] called it his Blood, and [to that] you answer "Amen", that is, "Truth". Let the mind within confess well what the mouth says; let the heart understand well the word that is uttered'. St Ambrose in his 4th book 'On the Sacraments', and the 4th chapter, says thus: *This bread is bread—before the Sacramental words. Once consecrated, from being bread it becomes the flesh of Christ. This, then, let us confirm: how can what is bread become the Body of Christ? By consecration. By what words, then, is consecration made, and by whose expressions? [By those of] the Lord Jesus.*

Folio 62r [62]

[....] ha gwyn d[i]r girreow dew: trilys [y^e] corf ha [....]

Ambros
[l]ib . 4 . De
Sacramen
tis . cap . 4
exodi 20 .11.

Consecratio igitur quibus verbis est, et cuius sermonibus? **y thew**
Domini Iesu. Nam ad reliqua omnia quædicuntur, laus Deo [defer]
tur, oratione petitur pro populo, pro regibus, pro cæ[teris,]
vbi venitur vt conficiatur venerabile Sacramentum, [iam non] 5
suis sermonibus Sacerdos vtitur, sed sermonibus Christi
Ergo sermo Christi hoc conficit Sacramentum. Quis sermo? nimpe
[i]s quo facta sunt ommia. Iussit Dominus et fac-tum est cælum:
iussit Dominus et facta est terra: iussit dominus, et fac-ta sunt
maria. et c. vides ergo quam operationem operatorius sit sermo Christi. 10
Si ergo tanta vis est in sermone Domini, vt inciperent esse quæ non
erant, quanto magis operatorius est, vt sint quæ erant et in aliud
commutentur. henna ew, An keth bara ma ew bara, kyns an girreow
an Sacramentys y^e ^vos cowsis, pan O an girreow an consecration devethis
then bara, & bara ew gwres kig agen arluth Christ. Rag henna 15
gesen confirnia hemma: fatla ew an bara Corf Christ, dir consecra
tion & girreow? Consecration ew gwris? dir girreow agen arluth
Iesus. Rag oll girreow erall a vo leveris, ew ger^pe peiadow
rag an bopell, rag meternath, ha rag an remnant. pan vo
an geir devethis rag gwiell an reverent Sacrament, nena ne 20
ra an pronter vsya girreow e honyn, mas girreow Christ:
rag henna gere Christ, e ma gwiell an keth Sacrament

[Bara] ha gwyn, dir girreow Dew, trilys [the] Corf ha [Gois] yth ew.
[Consecratio ... Iesu—as before] Nam ad reliqua omnia quae dicuntur [in superioribus, a sacerdote dicuntur[15]] laus Deo defertur, oratione petitur pro populo, pro regibus, pro ceteris, ubi venitur ut conficiatur venerabile Sacramentum, iam non suis sermonibus sacerdos utitur, sed sermonibus Christi. Ergo sermo Christi hoc conficit Sacramentum. Quis sermo? Nempe is quo facta sunt [omnia]. Iussit Dominus et factum est caelum; iussit Dominus et facta est terra; iussit Dominus, et facta sunt maria, etc. Vides ergo quam operatorius sit sermo Christi. Si ergo tanta vis est in sermone Domini, ut inciperent esse quae non erant, quanto magis operatorius est, ut sint quae erant et in aliud commutentur. Henna ew, 'An keth bara-ma ew bara, kyns an girreow a'n Sacramentys the vos cowsis. Pan [v]o an girreow a'n consecration devethis the'n bara, an bara ew gwres kig agen Arluth Christ. Rag henna gesen confir[m]ia hemma: fatla ew an bara Corf Christ—dir consecration an girreow? Consecration ew gwris? Dir girreow agen Arluth Jesus. Rag oll girreow erall a vo leveris ew pejadow rag an bopell, rag meternath, ha rag an remnant. Pan vo an geir devethis rag gwiell an reverent Sacrament, nena ne ra an pronter usya girreow e honyn, mas girreow Christ: rag henna gere Christ ema gwiell an keth Sacrament-ma.

15   Omitted in Foxe and SA.

Foxe, TAMO, 1576, p. 1393 [1368]; (T&C vi, 463–4)—Cranmer's Disputation

Young: ... *consecratio igitur quibus verbis est, & cuius sermonibus?*
Domini Iesu. Nam ad reliqua omnia quæ dicuntur, laus Deo defertur,
oratione petitur pro populo, pro regibus, pro cæteris:
vbi venitur vt conficiatur venerabile Sacramentum, iam non
suis sermonibus Sacerdos vtitur, sed sermonibus Christi.
Ergò sermo Christi hoc conficit Sacramentum. Quis sermo? nempe
is quo facta sunt omnia. Iussit Dominus & factum est cœlum:
iussit Dominus & facta est terra: iussit dominus & facta sunt
maria. &c. Vides ergo quam operatorius sit sermo Christi.
Si ergo tanta vis est in sermone Domini, vt inciperent esse quæ non
erant, quanto magis operatorius est, vt sint quæ erant & in aliud
commutentur. That is to say. This bread is bread before the wordes of
the Sacraments. When the consecration commeth to it,
of bread it is made the flesh of Christ. Let vs confirm this therfore: how can
that which is breade, by consecration be the bodye of Christ? by what wordes
then is the consecration made, & by whose wordes? by the wordes of our
Lord Iesus. For touchyng all other thinges that are sayd, prayse is geuen to
God, prayer is made for the people, for kinges, and for the rest. When it
commeth, that the reuerend Sacrament must be made, then the
Priest vseth not his owne wordes, but the wordes of Christ:
therfore the word of Christ maketh this Sacrament.

Bread and wine, through God's words, are changed to (his) Body and [Blood]
[*consecration...Jesus*—as before] *For in all the rest that is said [before this, by the priest], God's praise is offered, and prayer is asked for the people, for kings, and for the rest. But when it comes to the consecration of the Most Holy Sacrament, then the priest does not use his own expressions, but those of Christ. Therefore the word of Christ consecrates this sacrament. What word? Surely that by which all things were made. The Lord gave the order, and heaven was made; the Lord gave the order, and the earth was made; the Lord gave the order, and the seas were made, etc. You see there how effective the word of Christ is. If, then, there is such power in the word of the Lord, that things begin to exist which did not exist before, how much more effective it will be at changing things that exist into something else.* That is, 'This same bread is bread, before the sacramental words are spoken. [But] when the words of consecration come upon the bread, the bread is made the flesh of Christ our Lord. Therefore let us confirm this: how is the bread the Body of Christ—through the consecration of the words? [How] is the consecration made? Through the words of our Lord Jesus. For all the other words that are said are prayers for the people, for kings, and for the rest. When it comes to the word that makes the Most Holy Sacrament, then the priest does not use his own words, but the words of Christ: therefore the word of Christ is what makes this same Sacrament.

Folio 62r [62]

ma: pub tra oll a ve gwreis dir geir dew. an arluth a
    commandias, ha nef a ve gwreis: & arluth a commandias, an nore
    a vegwreis: an arluth a commandias, han more a ve gwreis: 25
    & arluth a commandias, ha pub creature a ve gwreis. lemmen
te a wele an g Crefder a gere Christ o conys, the changia,
pith ny ve derag dorn. *S.Ambros.* in e *liber. 4. cap. 5.* e ma o

Ambros.	gweill, an keth sentence ma, playn, *Cælum non erat, mare*
[D]e Sacra	*non erat, terra non erat. Sed audi dicentem: ipse dixit et* 30
mentis. lib.	*facta sunt, ipse mandauit et creata sunt. Ergo tibi respondeam,*
4. cap. 5.	*non erat Corpus Christi ante consecrationem, sed post*

consecrationem dico tibi quod iam Corpus Christi est: henna ew.
    Nefna ve ~~gwreis~~, more na ve ~~gwreis~~, nore na ve.
    mas gwra clowas dew o cowse; ef causis an geir   35
    ha y a ve gwreis: ef a commandias, y a ve creatis.
Rag henna, tha orybe gee, nyn ᵍᵒ Corf Christ kyns ef thavos
consecratis, bus osa the vos consecratis, me a laver the gee,
e thew lymmen Corf agen arluth Iesus Christ

[Am]bros.	*Antequam consecretur, panis est: vbi autem verba Christi* 40
[l]ib [4] ca.	*accesserint, Corpus est Christi. i.* kyns an bara yᵉ vos
5.	consecrᵃetis, ith thew bara: mas pan ruge girreow

agen saviour Christ dos warnotha, e thew [co]rf
agen arluth Iesus Christ

Pub tra-oll a ve gwreis dir geir Dew. An Arluth a commandias, ha'n nef a ve gwreis; an
Arluth a commandias, ha'n nore a ve gwreis; an Arluth a commandias, ha'n more a ve
gwreis; an Arluth a commandias, ha pub creature a ve gwreis. Lemmen te a wele an
crefder a gere Christ, o conys the changia pith ny ve derag dorn'.
S. Ambros—in e *Liber 4, Cap. 5.*—ema o gweill an keth sentence-ma playn: *Caelum non erat,*
mare non erat, terra non erat. Sed audi dicentem: 'Ipse dixit et facta sunt, ipse
mandavit et creata sunt.' Ergo tibi [ut] respondeam, non erat Corpus Christi ante
consecrationem, sed post consecrationem dico tibi quod iam Corpus Christi est. Henna ew:
'Nef na ve, more na ve, [an] nore na ve. Mas gwra clowas Dew o cowse: "Ef [a] causis an
geir ha y a ve gwreis; ef a commandias, y a ve creatis". Rag henna, tha orybe gee, nyng o
Corf Christ kyns ef tha vos consecratis, bus osa the vos consecratis, me a laver the gee, eth
ew lymmen Corf agen Arluth Jesus Christ.' *Antequam consecretur, panis est: ubi autem*
verba Christi accesserint, Corpus est Christi—i.e. 'Kyns an bara the vos
consecratis, ith ew bara: mas pan ruge girreow agen Saviour Christ dos warnotha, eth ew
Corf agen Arluth Jesus Christ.'

Foxe, TAMO, 1576, p. 1393 [1368]; (T&C vi, 463–4)—Cranmer's Disputation

Young: ...That word, by which all things were made. The Lorde
commaunded, and heauen was made: the Lord commaunded and the earth
was made: the lord commaunded, and the seas were made:
the lord comaunded, and all creatures were made. Doest thou not
see then how strong in workyng the worde of Christ is? ... that those things
should begin to be which were not before...
Weston: ...wordes that follow, which maketh the sense of Ambrose playne...
Young: *Cælum non erat, mare non erat, terra non erat. Sed audi dicentem: Ipse
dixit & facta sunt, ipse mandauit & creata sunt. Ergo tibi vt respondeam,
non erat corpus Christi ante consecrationem, sed post
consecrationem dico tibi quòd iam corpus Christi est.*
Heauen was not, the sea was not, the earth was not,
but heare hym that sayd: he spake the word
and they were made: he commaunded, and they were created.
Therfore to answer thee, it was not the body of Christ before
consecration, but after the consecration I say to thee, that
now it is the body of Christ.
*Antequam consecretur, panis est: vbi autem verba Christi
accesserint, corpus est Christi. i.* Before it be
consecrated, it is bread: but when the words of
Christ come to it, it is the body
of Christ.

Everything was made by the Word of God. The Lord commanded, and heaven was made; the Lord commanded [&] the earth was made; the Lord commanded, and the sea was made; the Lord commanded, and every created thing was made. Now you see the strength of the word of Christ, working to change what was not [there] before'.
S. Ambrose—in his *Book 4, Chapter 5*—makes this same sentence plain: *The heaven was not, the sea was not, the earth was not. But hear what he says: 'He spoke and they were made; he commanded and they were created.' So, to answer you, there was no Body of Christ before the consecration but, after the consecration, I tell you that now it is the Body of Christ.* That is: 'Heaven was not, sea was not, earth was not. But hear God speaking: "He spoke the word and they were made; he commanded, they were created". Therefore, to answer you, it was not the Body of Christ before it was consecrated but, after being consecrated, I say to you, it is now the Body of our Lord Jesus Christ.' *Before it is consecrated, it is bread: but when Christ's words have been added, it is the Body of Christ*—i.e. 'Before the bread is consecrated, it is bread: but when the words of our Saviour Christ come upon it, it is the Body of our Lord Jesus Christ.'

Folio 62v [62a]

cap.	[....] han gwyn dir geir dew, ew trylis ye corf ha
	whath moy, e ma. S. Ambros o leverall: **gois Chris[.]**
	Accipite, edite, hoc est Corpus meum: Kemerogh, debbrog[.]
	hem ew ow corff ve. *Ante verba Christi calix est*
	vini et aquæ plenus: Vbi verba Christi operata fu[erint] 5
	ibi sanguis efficitur, qui redemit plebem. henna ew:

kyns an girreow Christ tha vos leveris, an chalys ew len[...]
a gwyn ha dowr, pan vo girreow Christ cowsys, en[a]
e ma gwrys gois agen arluth Christ. pandra ill bos, moy
playn? pelha e ma S Ambros ow leverall: *Vides*   10
quam operatorius sit sermo Christi. Si ergo tant[a]
vis in sermone domini: et vt supra. henna ew:
why a welle an gallus a geir Christ, fatla vgy
ow conys. Rag henna mar see^i s mar ver gallus in
geir agen arluth Christ, tha gwiel pith nyn go derag   15
dorne, paseil moy gallus, tha gonys, ha changya
an pith na go derag dorne? kep*ar* del ve, leveris kyn[.]

Ambros.	Gosoweth pan drvge .S. Ambros, ow leverall i[n]
lib. 6.	e vi lever han. 1. chapter.
cap. 1.	*Forte dicas, quomodo vera? qui similitudinem video, non* 20

[Bara] ha'n gwyn, dir geir Dew, ew trylis the Corf ha Gois Christ ... Whath moy ema
S. Ambros o leverall: *Accipite, edite, hoc est Corpus meum*. 'Kemerogh, debbrogh, hem ew ow
Corff ve.' *Ante verba Christi calix est vini et aquæ plenus; ubi verba Christi*
operata fuerint, ibi sanguis efficitur, qui redemit plebem. Henna ew:
'Kyns an girreow Christ tha vos leveris, an chalys ew [lenwis] a gwyn ha dowr; pan vo
girreow Christ cowsys, ena ema gwrys Gois agen Arluth Christ.' Pandra ill bos
moy playn? Pelha, ema S. Ambros ow leverall: *Vides quam operatorius sit sermo Christi. Si*
ergo tanta vis in sermone domini (et ut supra). Henna ew: 'Why a welle an gallus a
geir Christ, fatla ugy ow conys. Rag henna, mars ees mar ver gallus in geir agen Arluth
Christ, tha gwiel pith nyng o derag dorne, pa seil moy gallus, tha gonys ha
changya an pith {nag} o derag dorne?' (kepar del ve leveris kyns). Gosoweth pandr'uge
S. Ambros ow leverall in e 6 lever ha'n 1 chapter: *Forte dicas, quomodo vera? Qui similitudinem*
video, non...

Foxe, TAMO, 1576, pp. 1393–4 [1368–9]; (T&C vi, 464–5)—
Cranmer's Disputation

Young: But heare what he sayth more:
Accipite, edite, hoc est corpus meum: Take ye, eate ye,
this is my body. *Ante verba Christi calix est*
vini & aquæ plenus: vbi verba Christi operata fuerint,
ibi sanguis efficitur, qui redemit plebem. That is.
Before the wordes of Christ, the cuppe is full
of wyne and water: when the wordes of Christ haue wrought, there
is made the bloud of Christ... What could be more playne?
Young: [earlier] ... Heare what Ambrose saith *Vides*
quam operatorius sit sermo Christi. Si ergo tanta
vis in sermone domini. &c. vt supra. That is.
You see what a workyng power the word of Christ hath.
Therfore if there be so great power in the
lordes worde, that those thinges which were not, begin to bee,
how much more of strength is it to worke that those thinges that were,
should be chaunged into an other thyng?
Weston: Heare what Ambrose saith in
the 6. Booke and 1. Chap.
Forte dicas, quomodo vera? Qui similitudinem video, non...

Bread and wine, through the word of God, are changed to the Body and Blood of Christ.
S. Ambrose says still more: *Take, eat, this is my Body.* 'Take, eat, this is my
Body.' *Before the words of Christ, the chalice is full of wine and water; when the words of Christ*
have done their work, there the Blood is made really present, which redeems the people. That is:
'Before the words of Christ are said, the chalice is full of wine and water; when the
words of Christ are spoken, there it is made the blood of Christ our Lord.' What could be
plainer? Furthermore, S. Ambrose says: *You see how effective the word of Christ is. If,*
then, there is such power in the word of the Lord (etc., as above). That is, 'You see the power of
Christ's word, how it works. Therefore, if there is so great a power in the word of Christ
our Lord, to bring into being what did not exist before, how much more power to effect
a change to what was {not} there before?' (as was said previously). Listen to what
S. Ambrose says in his 6th book and the 1st chapter. *Perhaps you say, 'In what sense true?' I see a*
symbol, I do not

Folio 62v [62a]

De Sacra	*video sanguinis veritatem. Primum omnium dixi tibi de*
mentis.	*sermone Christi qui operatur, vt possit mutare et*
operari:	*conuertere genera instituta naturæ. Deinde vbi*
Mutare.	*non tulerunt sermonem discipuli eius, sed audientes,*
conuertere.	*quod carnem suam dedit manducaturi, et sanguinem* 25
	suum dedit bibendum, recedebant. Solus tamen Petrus
Johan. 6.	*dixit: Verba vitæ æternæ habes, et ego a te quo*
	recedam? Ne igitur plures hoc dicerent, veluti
	quidam esset horror cruoris, sed maneret gratia
	redemtionis, ideo in similitudinem quidem accipis 30
	Sacramentum, sed vere naturæ gratiam virtutemque
	consequeris. henna ew ye leverall. Martesyn, te a

lavar, fattellans bos gwyer? e vosama ow gwel[.. ..]
shap, an not an gwyer gois age*n* arluth Christ. An ky[n]s[a]
oll me a leveris thees, a geyr Christ, vge changia an   35
kyndes ew ordaynes a nature: An discipels nyn go abe[.]
perthy gyrreow, age arluth Christ, pan rvga ry e corf th[.]
[v]oes dibbrys, ha e gois tha vos evys, y a departias. [..]
[...]wort[h] age arluth Christ. **Bara han gw[yn]**

---

video sanguinis veritatem. Primum omnium dixi tibi de sermone Christi qui operatur, ut possit mutare et convertere genera instituta naturae. Deinde ubi non tulerunt sermonem discipuli eius, sed audientes, quod carnem suam dedit manducari, et sanguinem suum dedit bibendum, recedebant. (Solus tamen Petrus dixit: 'Verba vitae aeternae habes, et ego a te quo recedam?') Ne igitur plures hoc dicerent, veluti quidam esset horror cruoris— sed maneret gratia redemptionis—ideo in similitudinem quidem accipis Sacramentum, sed vere naturae gratiam virtutemque consequeris. Henna ew the leverall: 'Martesyn, te a lavar, "Fatt'ellans bos gwyer? E vosama ow gwelas an shap, *and not* an gwyer Gois agen Arluth Christ." An kynsa oll me a leveris thees a geyr Christ, uge changia an kyndes ew ordaynes a nature. An discipels nyng o abel perthy gyrreow age Arluth Christ, pan ruga ry e Corf th[a] voes dibbrys ha e Gois tha vos evys. Y a departias [tha]worth age arluth Christ. **Bara han gw[yn]**

Foxe, TAMO, 1576, p. 1394 [1369]; (T&C vi, 465)—Cranmer's Disputation

Weston: *...video sanguinis veritatem. Primum omnium dixi tibi de sermone Christi qui operatur, vt possit mutare & conuertere genera instituta naturæ. Deinde vbi non tulerunt sermonem discipuli eius, sed audientes, quod carnem suam dedit manducari, & sanguinem suum dedit bibendum, recedebant. Solus tamen Petrus dixit: verba vitæ æternæ habes, & ego a te quo recedam? Ne igitur plures hoc dicerent, veluti quidam esset horror cruoris, sed maneret gratia redemptionis, ideò in similitudinem quidem accipis sacramentum, sed verè naturæ gratiam virtutemque consequeris.* That is to say, Peraduenture thou wilt say, how be they true? I which see the similitude, do not see the truth of the bloud. First of all I told thee of the word of Christ, which so worketh, that it can chaunge and turne kyndes ordeyned of nature. Afterwarde, when the Disciples could not abide the wordes of Christ, but hearyng that he gaue hys flesh to eate, and hys bloud to drinke, they departed:

---

see the reality of blood.' First of all I have told you of the words of Christ which can work to change and alter the established laws of nature. Then, [I told you] of when his disciples did not tolerate the words, but hearing that he gave his flesh to eat, and his blood to drink, they drew back. (Peter alone, however, said: 'You have the words of eternal life, and where shall I go from you?') So, therefore, that no others might speak as they did, through some dread of 'drinking blood'—but so that grace might endure for redemption—as a 'likeness' you outwardly receive the Sacrament although in truth the grace and power of its nature are what you obtain. That is to say: 'Perhaps you say, "How can those things be true? I see the outward form [of wine], and not the true Blood of Christ our Lord." First of all I told you of Christ's word which [can] change original natural forms. The disciples were not able to bear the words of Christ their Lord, when he gave his Body to be eaten, and his Blood to be drunk. They went away from Christ their Lord. **Bread and wine**

Folio 63r [63]

Bara han gwyn dir geir Dew, ew gwris corf ha [....] Christ

Ambo. De | Only Peder a leveris, e ma genas ge girreow bewn[a]n[s]
sacramen | heb dewath: pe tha ve mos, tha worthas? kepare
lib. 6. | a vo ceartaine abhorria worth gois agen arluth Christ
[c]ap. 1. | wath dir grace christ, e ma remaynea ye redemya: a redemtion.   5
[R]ag henna te a recevest an Sacrament: mas in ded, te a obtaynest
grace han gallus a nature a Christ. Gosough pan dresy S. Ambros

Ambros. | *Si operar̃tus est sermo cœlestis in aliis rebus, non operatur*
De Sacra | *in sacramentis cœlestibus? Ergo didicisti quod e pane corpus*
mentis. lib. | *fiat Christi, et quod vinum et aqua in calicem mittitur, sed fit*   10
4. | *sanguiˢnis consecratione verbi cœlestis. Sed forte dices,*
speciem sanguinis non videri. Sed habet similitudinem, Sicut
enim mortis similitudinem sumsisti, ita etiam similitudinem presiosi
sanguinis bibis, vt nullus horror cruoris sit, et pretium   63
tamen operetur redemptionis. Didicisti ergo, quia quod   15
accipis, Corpus est Christi. henna ew ye leverall.

Mar crvg, an geir an tas an nef, gonis in taglenno erall,
mer voy e ma gonys in Sacramentes benegas? Rag henna te
a thoskas, an bara ew gwrys cosʳf agen arluth Christ: han
gwyn han dowr ew goris in Chalis: dir consecration an geir [...]   20

[An] bara ha'n gwyn dir geir Dew: ew gwris Corf ha [Gois] Christ.
(Only Peder a leveris "Ema genas ge gyrreow bewnans heb dewath: peth a' ve mos
thaworthas?") Kepare a vo ceartaine abhorria worth Gois agen Arluth Christ,
wath, dir grace Christ, ema remaynea [the redemya] a' redemtion. Rag henna te a recevest
an Sacrament, mas inded te a obtaynest grace ha'n gallus a['n] nature a Christ'. Gosough
pandr'esy S. Ambros [o leverall]: *Si operatus est sermo caelestis in aliis rebus, non operator in
sacramentis caelestibus? Ergo didicisti quod e pane corpus fiat Christi, et quod vinum
et aqua in calicem mittitur, sed fit sanguis consecratione verbi caelestis. Sed forte
dices, 'speciem sanguinis non videri'. Sed habet similitudinem. Sicut enim
mortis similitudinem sumpsisti, ita etiam similitudinem pretiosi sanguinis bibis, ut nullus horror
cruoris sit, et pretium tamen operetur redemptionis. Didicisti ergo, quia
quod accipis, Corpus est Christi.* Henna ew the leverall: 'Mar crug an geir a'n Tas a nef
gonis in taglenno erall, mer voy ema gonis in Sacramentes benegas. Rag henna
te a thoskas, an bara ew gwrys Corf agen Arluth Christ. Ha'n gwyn ha'n dowr ew goris
i'n chalis: dir consecration an geir...

Foxe, TAMO, 1576, p. 1394 [1369]; (T&C vi, 465)—Cranmer's Disputation

Weston: ... Only Peter said, thou hast the wordes of eternall life: whether should I go from thee? ...as though there should be a certaine horror of bloud, and yet the grace of redemption should remayne: therfore in a similitude thou receiuest the sacrament: but in deede thou obtainest the grace and power of his nature.
Chedsey: Heare what Ambrose saith, *lib. 4. De sacrament. Si operatus est sermo cœlestis in alijs rebus, non operatur in sacramentis cœlestibus? Ergo didicisti quod e pane corpus fiat Christi, & quod vinum & aqua in calicem mittitur, sed fit sanguis consecratione verbi cœlestis. Sed forte dices, speciem sanguinis non videri. Sed habet similitudinem. Sicut enim mortis similitudinem sumpsisti, ita etiam similitudinem preciosi sanguinis bibis, vt nullus horror cruoris sit, & pretium tamen operetur redemptionis. Didicisti ergo, quia quod accipis, corpus est Christi.* That is to say.
If the heauenly worde did worke in other things, doth it not worke in the heauenly sacramentes? Therfore thou hast learned, that of bread is made the body of Christ: & that wyne and water is put into that cup: but by consecration of the heauenly word...

Bread and wine, through God's word, are made the Body and [Blood] of Christ.
(Only Peter said, "You have the words of life eternal: where shall I go from you?") As if there might be a certain recoiling from the blood of Christ our Lord, yet, through Christ's grace, the redemption remains. Therefore you received the Sacrament, but in truth you obtained the grace and power of the nature of Christ'. Hear what S. Ambrose [says]: *If the heavenly word does its work in other matters, does it not do so in the heavenly sacraments? So you learnt that the Body of Christ is made from bread, and that wine and water put in the chalice are made Blood by the consecration of the heavenly Word. But perhaps you say, 'I do not see the outward appearance of blood.' No, it has a sacramental form. Just as you took on the form of death, so you drink the sacramental form of the precious Blood, that there may be no repugnance at it, and yet the Price of Redemption is still at work. Therefore you have learnt that what you receive is the Body of Christ.* That is to say, 'If the word of the heavenly Father worked in other things, how much more does it work in the holy Sacraments? Therefore, you have learnt, the bread is made the Body of Christ our Lord. And wine and water is put into the chalice: through consecration by the holy word...

Folio 63r [63]

	benegas, e thew gwris gois. Matesyn whath te a vyn
	leverall, shap a gois nyn gew gwelis, te a recevias an
	shap a myrnans Christ, indella e thesta eva, e presivs gois.
	dir henna nyn gew gois Christ abhorris, ha what e ma
	ef ow conys an prys tha redemya ny. Dir henna e thos 25
	diskys, te ye recevia pith ew Corf Christ. henna ew
Iustinus.	girrew Iustin. *Quemadmodum per Verbum Dei caro factus*
Apolog. 2.	*Iesus Christus Saluator noster, carnem habuit et sanguinem*
	pro salute nostra: sic et cibum illum consecratum per sermonem
	precationis ab ipso institutæ, quo sanguis carnesque 30
Mutacio	*nostræ per communionem nutriuntur, eiusdem Iesu*
nem:	*qui caro factus est, carnem et sanguinem esse*
	accepimus. henna ew the leverall. Dir geir
	Dew, hagen saviour Iesus Christ, ew greis gwreis kigg
	ha gois, rag sawya ny; indella e thew disquethis thyn[y] 35
	[..] bois ye vos consecratis, dir geir a peIadow, ha appoyntis
	tha vois, kigg ha gois agen saviour Iesus Christ

...benegas, eth ew gwris gois. Matesyn, whath te a vyn leverall, "Shap a gois nyng ew gwelis." Te a recevias an shap a myrnans Christ: indella eth esta eva e Presius Gois. Dir henna, nyng ew Gois Christ abhorris, ha [whath] ema ef ow conys an prys tha redemya ny. Dir henna, eth os diskys te the recevia pith ew Corf Christ.'
Henna ew girrew Justin: *Quemadmodum per Verbum Dei caro factus Iesus Christus Salvator noster, carnem habuit et sanguinem pro salute nostra: sic et cibum illum consecratum per sermonem precationis ab ipso institutae, quo sanguis carnesque nostrae per communionem nutriuntur, eiusdem Iesu qui caro factus est, carnem et sanguinem esse accepimus.* Henna ew the leverall, 'Dir geir Dew, agen Saviour Jesus Christ ew gwreis kigg ha gois rag sawya ny; indella eth ew disquethis thyn [ny], [an] bois the vos consecratis, dir geir a pejadow, ha appoyntis tha vois kigg ha gois agen Saviour Jesus Christ.'

Foxe, TAMO, 1576, p. 1394 [1369]; (T&C vi, 465–6)—Cranmer's Disputation

Chedsey: ...it is made bloud. But thou wilt say peraduenture,
that the lykenes of bloud is not seene. But it hath a similitude. For as thou
hast receiued the similitude of his death so also thou drinkest the similitude
of his precious bloud, so that there is no horror of bloud, & yet
it worketh the price of redemption. Therfore thou hast
learned, that that which thou receiuest, is the body of Christ.
Chedsey: The wordes of Iustine... *Quemadmodum per verbum Dei caro factus
Iesus Christus Saluator noster, carnem habuit & sanguinem
pro salute nostra: sic & cibum illum consecratum per sermonem
precationis ab ipso institutæ, quo sanguis carnesque
nostræ per communionem nutriuntur, eiusdem Iesu
qui caro factus est, carnem & sanguinem esse
accepimus.* That is to say. As by the worde of
God, Iesus Christ our sauior beyng made flesh, had both flesh
and bloud for our saluation: so we are taught, that
the meate consecrated by the worde of prayer, instituted of hym...
is the flesh and bloud of the same Iesus, which was made flesh' etc.

...it is made Blood. Perhaps, you will still say, "The likeness of blood is not
seen". You have received the likeness of Christ's death: in a similar way you drink his
Precious Blood. In that way the Blood of Christ is not recoiled from, and it still pays the
price to redeem us. Therefore you are taught that what you receive is the Body of Christ'.
That is, [in] the words of Justin: *Just as, being made flesh by the word of God, Jesus Christ our
Saviour had both flesh and blood for our salvation: so the food consecrated by the
word of prayer, as he ordered, (and by which our own flesh and blood are nourished in Communion)
is the flesh and blood of the very same Jesus who was made flesh, as we all accept.* That is to say,
'Through the word of God, our Saviour Jesus Christ was made flesh and blood to save us;
so likewise it is revealed to us [that the] food is consecrated, through the word of (the) prayer, and
instituted to be the flesh and blood of Jesus Christ our Saviour.'

Folio 63v [63a]

         Bar[.] ha gwyn [...] g[..]reow dew, corf ha gois Christ
                                                    gwris e thew.

[I]ustinus	*Neque ver[o, hæc] pro pane potuue communi sumimus:*
[M]artyr.	*Imo quemadmodum verbo Dei Iesus Christus, Seruator*
Apolog. 2.	*noster incarnatus, habuit pro salute nostra carnem [et]*
	sanguinem: ita per orationem illius verbi consecratu[m] 5
	hoc alimentum, quo sanguis et carnes nostræ per
	mutacionem etriuntur eiusdem incarnati carnem et
	sanguinem esse sumus edocti. henna ew ye leverall.

Ne geranny ow kemeras hemma, rag common bara ha dewas,
mas kigg ha gois agen Saviour Iesus Christ, thaken   10
sawya ny: pan vova consecratis. Irenæus e ma ow lever[...]

	:Eum calicem qui est cretura, suum corpus confirmauit,
Irenæus.	*ex quo nostra auget corpora. Quando et mixtus calix*
	et fractus panis percipit verbum Dei, fit Eucharest[ia]
	sanguinis et corporis Christi, ex quibis augetur e[t] 15
	consistit carnis nostræ substantia. henna ew

An keith chalys ma ew creature a thew, Christ a rug e confirmia
ye vos e corf ef, rag cressya agen corfow ny. pan vo

Bara ha gwyn [dir] g[ir]reow Dew, Corf ha Gois Christ gwris eth ew. *Neque vero hæc pro pane potuve communi sumimus. Imo, quemadmodum verbo Dei Iesus Christus, Servator noster incarnatus, habuit pro salute nostra carnem et sanguinem: ita—per orationem illius verbi—consecratum hoc alimentum, quo sanguis et carnes nostræ per [im]mutationem e[nu]triuntur, eiusdem incarnati carnem et sanguinem esse, sumus edocti.* Henna ew the leverall: 'Neg eran ny ow kemeras hemma rag common bara ha dewas, mas kigg ha gois agen Saviour Jesus Christ th'aken sawya ny, pan vo va consecratis.' Irenæus ema ow leverall: *Eum calicem qui est creatura, [suum sanguinem qui effusus est, ex quo auget nostrum sanguinem; et eum panem, qui est a creatura*[16]*] suum corpus confirmavit, ex quo nostra auget corpora. Quando et mistus calix et factus panis percipit verbum Dei, fit Eucharistia sanguinis et corporis Christi, ex quibis augetur et consistit carnis nostræ substantia.* Henna ew 'An keith chalys-ma ew creature a Thew: Christ a rug e confirmia the vos e Corf ef, rag cressya agen corfow ny. Pan vo...

---

16 Omitted in Foxe and SA.

Foxe, TAMO, 1576, p. 1404 [1379]; (T&C vi, 489–90)—Ridley's Disputation

Ward: *Neque vero hæc pro pane potuue communi sumimus:*
Imo quemadmodum verbo dei Iesus Christus, Seruator
noster in carnatus, habuit pro salute nostra carnem &
sanguinem: ita per orationem illius verbi consecratum
hoc alimentum, quo sanguis & carnes nostræ per
immutationem enutriuntur, eiusdem incarnati carnem &
sanguinem esse sumus edocti.
For we do not take this for common bread & drincke, but like as Iesus Christ
our Sauiour... had fleshe and bloud for our saluation: ... when it
is consecrated by the prayer of his word, to be the flesh and bloud of the same
Iesus incarnate.

Foxe, TAMO, 1576, p. 1394 [1369]; (T&C vi, 466–7)—Cranmer's Disputation

Weston: Heare then what Irenæus sayth: *Eum calicem qui est creatura, suum*
corpus confirmauit, ex quo nostra auget corpora. Quando & mixtus calix,
& Fractus panis percipit verbum Dei, fit Eucharistia
sanguinis & corporis Christi, ex quibus augetur &
consistit carnis nostræ substantia. This is.
The same cup whiche is a creature, hee confirmed
to be his body, by which he encreaseth our bodyes. When both...

Bread and wine through God's words, the Body and Blood of Christ are made. *Neither do we take this for common bread and drink. Rather, just as by the Word of God, Jesus Christ our Saviour was incarnate, and has taken for our salvation flesh and blood: even so—by the prayer of the word—this consecrated food, through which our blood and flesh by transformation are nourished, is the flesh and blood of the same incarnate [Lord], as we have been taught.* That is to say, 'We do not take this for common bread and drink, but as the flesh and blood of our Saviour Jesus Christ to save us—when it is consecrated'. Irenaeus says: *[He has confirmed] the cup, a created thing, [as his blood which was poured out, giving life to our blood, and this bread, a created thing,] he has confirmed as his body, by which our bodies are given increase. When both the mingled cup and the broken bread receive the word of God, it becomes the Eucharist of the Body and Blood of Christ, which makes the substance of our flesh grow and maintain existence.* That is, 'This same chalice, which is a creature of God: Christ confirmed as his Body, to give increase to our bodies. When

Folio 63v [63a]

an chalys han bara Ivnis warbarth, dir geir dew,
e thew ef gwryes an Sacrament a Corf ha gois agyn 20
saviour Iesus Christ, tha creffe agen corfow. Irenæus
pelha ow levera. *Quomodo carnem negant capacem esse*
Irenæus	*donationis Dei quæ est vita æterna, quæ sangui*
lib. 5.	*ne et corpore Christi nutritur? lib.5. post*
	duo folia a principio. henna ew: fatla vgy an 25

bobell ow leverall, an kigg na ill recevia gifte dew,
henna ew bewnans heb dewath, ew megis gans corf
ha gois agen saviour Christ: henna ew tha vos
redys, in. v. lever a Iremæus, ij folen tha worth an dallath
An Greciens[kys] e ma kelwall Eucharistia. henna ew, grasce ye D[..]. 30
De consecra	:Emissenus: *Mirare cum reuerendum altare cibi [s ....]*
tione. Distin.	*tualibus saciandus ascendis: sacrum Dei tui corp[us]*
.2. Quia.	*et sanguinem fide respice, honorem mirare, merito*
Emissenus.	*continge.et c.* henna ew. gwra marvgian pan vosta

davethis imban then reverent alter the vos megis gans an spirituall 35
bois: kemer faith da, then corf han gois benegas ath Dew: **:Bara**
[.]wra marvgian ay honor: ha gwra worthel[y e Do.....ia]

...an chalys ha'n bara junis warbarth, dir geir Dew, eth ew ef gwryes
an Sacrament a Corf ha Gois agyn Saviour Jesus Christ, tha creffé agen
corfow'. [*Ema*] Irenæus pelha ow levera': *Quomodo carnem negant capacem esse
donationis Dei quae est vita aeterna, quae sanguine et corpore nutritur?* (*Lib. 5,
post duo folia a principio.*) Henna ew: 'Fatla ugy an bobell ow leverall an kigg na ill recevia
gifte Dew—henna ew bewnans heb dewath—ew megis gans Corf ha Gois agen Saviour
Christ?' (Henna ew tha vos redys in 5 lever a Irenæus, 2 folen thaworth an dallath.) An
Grekys ema kelwall Eucharistia—henna ew "Grasce the Dew".
Emissenus: *Mirare cum reverendum altare cibis spiritualibus satiandus ascendis:
sacrum Dei tui corpus et sanguinem fide respice, honorem mirare,
merito continge, etc.* Henna ew: 'Gwra marugian pan vosta davethis im ban then reverent
alter the vos megis gans an spirituall bois. Kemer faith da the'n Corf ha'n Gois benegas
a'th Dew: gwra marugian a'y honor ha gwra worthely e [*douchia*]'. **Bara...**

Foxe, TAMO, 1576, pp. 1394–5 [1369–70]; (T&C vi, 466–7)—
Cranmer's Disputation

Weston: ...the cup mixed, and the bread broken hath ioyned to it the worde of God, it is made the sacrament of the body & bloud of
Christ of which the substaunce of our fleshe is increased, and consisteth.
Weston: Looke what he sayth more. *Quomodo carnem negant capacem esse donationis Dei quæ est vita æterna, quæ sanguine*
& corpore Christi nutritur? Lib. 5. post
duo folia a principio. That is. How do they
say, that the flesh can not receyue the gift of God
that is eternal lyfe, which is nourished with the bloud
and body of Christ? This is in the
5. booke two leaues from the beginnyng.
Chedsey: ...called of the Greekes *Eucharistia*, that is, Thankes geuyng....
Weston: ...another place of Emissenus... *Mirare cum reuerendum altare cibis spiritualibus satiandus ascendis: sacrum Dei tui corpus*
& sanguinem fide respice, honorem mirare, merito
continge. &c. That is. Maruell thou when thou
commest vp to the reuerend alter to be filled with spirituall
meates: looke in fayth to the holy body and bloud of thy God:
maruell at his honour: worthely touch him.

...the chalice and the bread are joined together, through the word of God is made the Sacrament of the Body and Blood of our Saviour Jesus Christ, to strengthen our bodies'. Irenaeus says further: *How can they deny that the flesh is capable of receiving God's gift, which is eternal life, when it is nourished by the Blood and Body of Christ? (Book 5, two pages after the beginning.)* That is: 'How do people say that the flesh cannot receive the gift of God—which is everlasting life—when it is fed by the Body and Blood of Christ our Saviour?' (That can be read in the 5th book of Irenaeus, 2 pages from the beginning.) The Greeks call [it] Eucharist—that is, "Thanksgiving to God"'.
Emissenus: *Be filled with wonder when you go up to the sacred altar to be nourished by that spiritual food. Gaze upon the holy Body and Blood of your God with faith: marvel at the honour, worthily take hold, etc.* That is, 'Be amazed when you come up to the sacred
altar to be fed with the spiritual food. Take good faith in the holy Body and Blood of your God: marvel at his honour and worthily [touch him]'. **Bread...**

Folio 64r [64]

Bara ha gwyn [...]   gyrriow dew, Corf ha gois C[.................] ⁶⁴

Emissenus	*honora Corpus Dei tui* henna ew, Gwra honora, Co[..]
Emissenus	thith Dew: *Et si quæras quare voluit Ecclesia eligere*
	istum intellectum ita difficilem huius articuli, cum verba
	Scripturæ possint saluari secundum intellectum facil[e]m 5
	et veriorem, secundum apparentiam, de hoc articulo. et cæt[era].

henna ew, Mar tewhy demandea, praga a ruke an ⁶⁴ egglo[s]
dewys mar galys Vnderstandyng, an keth Arickell ma
girryow an scripture ^a yll bos eaisy vnderstandis (kepare
dell vgy apperia), owrth an artickell ma. *et cætera.*   10

Thomas	*:In quantum vero est sacrificium habet vim satisfactiu[a]m*
Aquinas.	*Sed in satisfactione attenditur magis affectio offerentis*
	quam quantitas oblationis. Vnde Dominus dicit apud
Lucæ.	*lucam de Vidua quæ obtulit duo æra, quod pluS omnibus*
21.	*misit. Quamuis ergo hæc oblatio ex sui quantitate sufficiet* 15
vers. 2.	*ad satifaciendum pro omni pœna: tamen fit satisfactoriaillis*
	pro quibus offertur, vel etiam offerentibus secundum quantitatem
	suæ deuotionis, et non pro tota pœna. henna ew: magapel[.]

dell ewa sacrafice, e ma thetha gallus a satisfaction. neb
a vge offra an affection in satisfaction, e thew moy, the   20

Bara ha gwyn dir gyrriow Dew, Corf ha Gois C[hrist gwris eth ew]. *Honora Corpus Dei tui.* Henna ew: 'Gwra honora Corf thi'th Dew'. *Et si quæras quare voluit Ecclesia eligere istum intellectum ita difficilem huius articuli, cum verba Scripturæ possint salvari secundum intellectum facilem et veriorem, secundum apparentiam, de hoc articulo, etc.* Henna ew: 'Mar te' why demandea, praga a ruke an Egglos dewys mar galys understandyng an keth ar[t]ickell-ma, girryow an Scripture a yll bos eaisy understandis (kepare dell ugy apperia) owrth an artickell-ma, etc.'

In quantum vero est sacrificium habet vim satisfactivam. Sed in satisfactione attenditur magis affectio offerentis quam quantitas oblationis. Unde Dominus dicit apud Lucam de vidua quae obtulit duo aera, quod 'plus omnibus misit'. Quamvis ergo haec oblatio ex sui quantitate sufficiat ad satisfaciendum pro omni poena: tamen fit satisfactoria illis pro quibus offertur (vel etiam offerentibus) secundum quantitatem suae devotionis, et non pro tota poena. Henna ew: 'Maga pell dell ewa sacrafice, ema thetha gallus a satisfaction. Neb a uge offra an affection in satisfaction, eth ew moy the...

Foxe, TAMO, 1576, p. 1395 [1370]; (T&C vi, 467–8)—Cranmer's Disputation

Weston: ...*Honora corpus Dei tui. i.* Honour the body of thy God....
Weston: *Et si quæras quare voluit Ecclesia eligere*
istum intellectum ita difficilem huius articuli, cum verba
Scripturæ possint saluari secundum intellectum facilem
& veriorem, secundum apparentiam, de hoc articulo. &c.
That is. And if you demaund why the church did
chuse this so hard an vnderstanding of this Article, where as
the words of scripture may be salued after an easie and true vnderstanding (as
appeareth) of this article, &c.
Weston: *In quantum vero est sacrificium habet vim satisfactiuam.*
Sed in satisfactione attenditur magis affectio offerentis,
quam quantitas oblationis. Vnde Dominus dicit apud
Lucam de vidua quæ obtulit duo æra, quòd plus omnibus
misit. Quamuis ergo hæc oblatio ex sui quantitate sufficiet
ad satisfaciendum pro omni pœna: tamen fit satisfactoria illis
pro quibus offertur, vel etiam offerentibus secundum quantitatem
suæ deuotionis, & non pro tota pœna. That is. In as much
as it is a sacrifice, it hath the power of satisfaction. But
in satisfaction the affection of the offerer is more to...

Bread & wine through God's words, are made the Body and Blood of Christ
Honour the Body of your God. That is: 'Honour the Body of your God'. And if you ask why the
Church opted for such a difficult understanding of this point, when the words of Scripture would
support an—apparently—easier and truer interpretation of this article, etc. That is:
'If you should ask why the Church chose so difficult an
understanding of this same article, the words of Scripture can be easily understood
(as is made plain) from this article', etc.
In so far as it is a sacrifice, it has a satisfactory power. Yet, in regard to satisfaction, the feelings of
the donor are more relevant than the quantity of the offering. So the Lord says, in [the Gospel of]
Luke, of the widow who offered the two mites, that 'more than all of them she put in'. Therefore,
although this offering is enough in itself to satisfy for all the penalty due: yet it also is made
sufficient for those for whom it is offered (or the donors) according to the measure
of their devotion, rather than for the whole penalty. That is: 'As far as it is a sacrifice, it has
[the] power of satisfaction. Whoever offers from the heart in satisfaction, is more to...

Folio 64r [64]

vose consideris, dell ew an quantite an oblation. Rag
henna, an arluth Dew ow leverall, e ma, in nawaile a
lucæ 21 .S.Luke: rag an wethvas a ruke offrennia ij mittes,
vers.   hy a dowlas in offeringys ^{a Dew} moy agis y oll. Rag henna,
.2.   an quantite an oblation ma, ew sufficient, rag oll
      an payn. whath e thew gwrys satisfaction, the
      thans rag neb a vo offrys, accordyng then
      quantyte age devotion & not rag oll an payn
Onyn an sans egglos, ew gilwis Vigilius a martyr, ef ave disky[s]
[...]th an Abostolath a Christ, than keth tyrmyn ma. dir
girryow an tasow a vam egglos. e thesa ve ow menya, a Iustine,
Irenæ; Tertullian; Origene, Eusebius, Emisene, Athanasius.C[yr]ill
Epiphanius; Hierom, Chrisostom, Augustine; [.]i[.]ilius, Fulgentius [.......]
lowarth onyn erall an tasaw coeth.

...vose consideris dell ew an quantite a'n oblation. Rag henna, [*ema*] an Arluth Dew ow leverall {*ema*}, i'n Awaile a S. Luke: 'Rag an wethvas a ruke offrennia 2 mittes, hy a dowlas in offeringys a Dew moy agis y oll. Rag henna, an quantite an oblation-ma ew sufficient rag oll an payn. Whath eth ew gwrys satisfaction thethans rag neb a vo offrys, accordyng the'n quantyte age devotion *and not* rag oll an payn'. Onyn an sans Egglos ew gilwis Vigilius a' martyr; ef a ve diskys [wor]th an Abostolath a Christ, tha'n keth tyrmyn-ma. Dir girryow an Tasow a Vam Egglos, eth esa' ve ow menya, a Justine, Irenae, Tertullian, Origene, Eusebius Emisene, Athanasius, Cyrill, Epiphanius, Hierome, Chrisostom, Augustine, [Vig]ilius, Fulgentius, [*Bertram ha*] lowar onyn erall an Tasaw coeth.

Foxe, TAMO, 1576, p. 1395 [1370]; (T&C vi, 468)—Cranmer's Disputation

Weston: ...bee weyed then the quantity of the oblation.
Wherfore the Lord sayd in Lukes Gospell
of the wydow which offered two mites,
that shee cast in more then they all. Therfore,
although this oblation of the quantity of it selfe will suffice to satisfy for all
payne, yet it is made satisfactorye to them,
for whome it is offered, or to the offerers, accordinge to the
quantitye of theyr Deuotion, and not for all the payne.

Foxe, TAMO, 1576, p. 1398 [1373]; (T&C vi, 474)—Ridley's Disputation

Ridley: ...which *Vigilius* a Martyr and graue wryter sayth was taught
of the Apostles ... vntyll hys tyme. By the sayinges of the fathers, I mean of
Iustine, Irenee, Tertullian, Origene, Eusebius, Emisene, Athanasius, Cyrill,
Epiphanius, Hierome, Chrysostom, Augustine, Vigilius, Fulgentius, Bertram,
and others most auncient fathers.

...be taken account of, than the quantity of the offering. Therefore the Lord God
says, in the Gospel of S. Luke, of the widow who offered 2 mites, [that] she cast in more
divine offerings than all of them. So the measure of this oblation is sufficient for
all the pain, yet it becomes a satisfaction, to those for whom it is offered, according to the
measure of their devotion—and not for all the pain'. One of the Holy Church is called
Vigilius, a martyr; he was taught by the Apostles of Christ, at this very time, through the
words of the Fathers of Mother Church. I mean, by Justin, Irenaeus, Tertullian, Origen,
Eusebius Emissenus, Athanasius, Cyril, Epiphanius, Jerome, Chrysostom, Augustine,
Vigilius, Fulgentius, [Bertram and] many another one of the ancient Fathers.

Folio 64v [64a]

[................] gyrryow dew, Corf ha gois Christ gwris e thew.

[Te]rtullian contra Martion libr 4	*Desiderio desideraui hoc pascha manducare vobiscum.* henna ew. ow thesyre ew gans oll ow holan, yᵉ dibbry an pask onn ma genogh. e ma Tertullian ow leverall, pana pask onn, ow Christ wensys tha thibbry gans e apostelath. *Tertullian. libr. 4: Contra Martionem: Professus itaque se concupiscentia concupiscere edere pascha suum (indignum enim vt alienum concupisceret Deus) acceptum panem et distribut[um] discipulis, suum corpus illum fecit: Hoc est corpus meum, dicendo. et c. i.* ef rag henna, a ruge protestia, myᵉr a	5 10

thesyre yᵉ thybbry e bask, me a laver e bask e honyn (rag nyn
go met, ef yᵉ deserya, mas e bask e honyn) Christ a gemeras
bara, ha e ruk ₑ distributia, the e Discipels, ha ef a ruk e corf
ha leveris. Hemma ew ow corf ve. e ma. S.Austen ow lever[...]

August. in psalm. .98. + 3. reg. .8.	in psalm. 96. *Adorate scabellum pedum eius .i.* gwregh ho~~nar~~ⁿᵒr[a] scavall e dryˢes, et c. *Quæro, inquit, quid sit scabellum p[e] dum eius. Et dicit michi Scriptura. Terra scabellum pedum ~~eius~~ meorum: Fluctuans conuerto me ad Christum, quia ipsum quæro hic, et inuenio, quomodo sine impietate adore tur scabellum pedum eius. Suscepit enim terram de terra, quia*	15 20

[Bara ha gwyn dir] gyrryow Dew, Corf ha Gois Christ gwris e thew.
Desiderio desideraui hoc pascha manducare vobiscum. Henna ew: 'Ow thesyre ew, gans oll ow
holan, the dibbry an Pask Onn-ma genogh'. Ema Tertullian ow leverall: 'Pana
Pask Onn [o], Christ wensys tha thibbry gans e Apostelath?' *Tertullian. libr. 4, Contra
Marcionem: Professus itaque se concupiscentia concupiscere edere pascha suum (indignum enim
ut alienum concupisceret Deus) acceptum panem et distributum
discipulis, suum corpus illum fecit: Hoc est corpus meum, dicendo. etc., id est:* 'Ef, rag henna, a
ruge protestia mer a thesyre the thybbry e Bask. Me a laver, e Bask e honyn (rag nyng o
met ef the deserya mas e Bask e honyn). Christ a gemeras bara, ha [a] ruk e distributia the
e discipels, ha ef a ruk [e] e Corf ha leveris: "Hemma ew ow Corf ve"'. Ema S. Austen ow
leverall in Psalm [98]: *Adorate scabellum pedum eius. Id est,* 'Gwregh [honora] scavall e
drys', etc. *Quæro inquit, quid sit scabellum pedum eius? Et dicit mihi Scriptura: 'Terra scabellum
pedum meorum'. Fluctuans converto me ad Christum, quia ipsum quæro hic, et invenio, quomodo
sine impietate adoretur* [terra, sine impietate adoretur] *scabellum pedum eius. Suscepit enim terram
de terra, quia...*

Foxe, TAMO, 1576, p. 1405 [1380]; (T&C vi, 490–1)—Ridley's Disputation

Ward: *Desiderio desideraui hoc pascha manducare vobiscum. i.*
I haue desired with my hartie desire to eate this Paschall
with you. What Paschall I pray you
desired he to eate? If you stand in doubt you have
Tertullian Lib. 4. Contra Martionem: Professus itaque
se concupiscentia concupiscere edere pascha suum (indignum
enim vt alienum concupisceret Deus) acceptum panem & distributum
discipulis, suum corpus illum fecit: Hoc est corpus meum,
dicendo. &c. i. He therfore protestyng a great
desire to eate his Paschall, his owne Paschall I say (for it was not
meete that he should desire any other then his owne) takyng
bread and distributyng it to his Disciples, made it his body,
saying: This is my body. Augustine in the Psalme. 96. Wryting vpon
these wordes: *Adorare scabellum pedum eius. i.* Worshyppe
his footestole. &c.. *Quæro, inquit, quid sit scabellum pedum*
eius. Et dicit mihi Scriptura, Terra scabellum pedum
meorum: Fluctuans conuerto me ad Christum, quia
ipsum quæro hic, & inuenio quomodo sine impietate adoretur
scabellum pedum eius. Suscepit enim de terra terram, quia...

Bread & wine through God's words, are made the Body and Blood of Christ
With what longing have I longed to eat this Passover with you! That is,
'My desire, with all my heart, is to eat this Passover with you'. Tertullian says, 'What sort
of Passover was it, that Christ desired to eat with his Apostles?' *Tertullian, Book 4, 'Against*
Marcian': And therefore having expressed with what longing he longed to eat his Passover (it
would have been unworthy for God to long for another Passover) taking bread he gave it to the
disciples, making it his own body, saying: 'This is my Body' etc. That is, 'He, therefore,
expressed much longing to eat his Passover. I say his own Passover (for it was not
fitting for him to desire any Passover but his own.) Christ took bread, and shared it out to
his disciples, and he made [it] his Body and said: "This is my Body"'. St Augustine
says, on Psalm 96: *'Worship his footstool'*, that is, *'Worship his footstool,*
etc. I ask, what is his footstool? And Scripture tells me: 'The earth is my footstool.'
Wavering, I turn to Christ, because I seek him here, and I then find how, without
impiety, [both earth and] his footstool may be worshipped. For he took on earth from
earth;

Folio 64v [64a]

[2] para.	caro de terra est, et de carne Mariæ carnem accepit,
6	et quia in ipsa carne hic ambulauit, et ipsam carnem nobis
[ve]rs 6	manducandam ad salutem dedit: nemo autem illam carnem
.1.	manducat nisi prius adorauerit. Inuentum est, quomodo 25
psal.	tale scabellum pedum Domini adoretur, Vt non solum non
Act. 7.40	peccemus adorando, sed peccemus non adorando ipsum et c .i.

E thesa ve ow covyn (mith ef) pandrew an skavall e drys eff,
& Scripture e ma ow leverall thym: an grond ew an skavall
ow thrys ve, ha dir sarchia & scripture, e thesa ow trylya
[.]w honyn tho Arluth Christ, ha e whelas ef vmma war a [....]   30
rag honora scavall e drys: rag ef a kemeras dore a thore, ha
dir henna e thew ef kigg & nore, ha kemeras kigg worth an
worthias Marya, ha ef a walkias in kigg na: omma war a nore.
ef a ros then, an kethsam kigg na, then yᵉ thibbry. Nyn gvs
[d..] vith ow tybbry an kigg na, arr ne theffa   .**Bara.**   35
[.................]

...caro de terra est, et de carne Mariæ carnem accepit; et quia in ipsa carne hic ambulavit,
et ipsam carnem nobis manducandam ad salutem dedit. Nemo autem illam carnem manducat
nisi prius adoraverit. Inventum est, quomodo tale scabellum pedum Domini
adoretur: ut non solum non peccemus adorando, sed peccemus non adorando ipsum etc.
id est: 'Eth esa' ve ow covyn (mith ef) pandr'ew an skavall e drys eff? [ha'n] Scripture ema
ow leverall thym: 'An grond ew an skavall ow thrys ve', ha dir sarchia an Scripture, eth
esa' ow trylya ow honyn tho['n] Arluth Christ, ha e whelas ef umma war a' [nore] rag honora
scavall e drys. Rag ef a kemeras dore a thore, ha dir henna eth ew ef kigg a'n nore, ha
kemeras kigg worth an Worthias Marya, ha ef a walkias i'n kigg-na omma war a' nore. Ef
a ros then an kethsam kigg-na, then the thibbry. Nyng us [den]vith ow tybbry an kigg-na,
arrne theffa [honora derag dorn...] **Bara...**

Foxe, TAMO, 1576, p. 1405 [1380]; (T&C vi, 491)—Ridley's Disputation

Ward: *...caro de terra est, & de carne Mariæ carnem accepit,
& quia in ipsa carne hic ambulauit, & ipsam carnem nobis
manducandam ad salutem dedit: nemo autem illam carnem
manducat nisi prius adorauerit. Inuentum est, quo modo
tale scabellum pedum domini adoretur, vt non solum non
peccemus adorando, sed peccemus non adorando ipsum. &c.*
I aske (sayth he) what is the footestole of his feete,
and the Scripture telleth me: The earth is the footestoole
of my feete. And so in searchyng therof I turne
my selfe to Christ, because I seeke hym here in the earth, and I finde how,
without impietie, the footestole of hys feete may be worshypped: for he tooke
earth of earth, in that he is flesh of the earth, and of the fleshe of Mary he
tooke fleshe, and because that in the same flesh here he walked
and also he gaue the same fleshe to vs, to be eaten vnto saluation. But
no man eateth that flesh except he... [haue worshypped before.]

[And so it is founde, how such a footestole of the feete of the Lord is to be
worshypped, so that, not onely we sinne not in worshyppyng, but also do
sinne in not worshyppying the same.]

---

*since flesh is from the earth, and he received flesh from the flesh of Mary; and because he walked
here in that same flesh, and gave us that same flesh to eat for our salvation. But no one eats of that
flesh unless he has first worshipped. So it is revealed in what sense such a 'footstool' of the Lord
may be adored. For not only do we not sin by adoring it, but rather we sin if we do not adore it, etc.
That is:* 'I ask (he says) what is his footstool? and Scripture
tells me: 'The earth is my footstool', and by searching the Scripture I
turn myself towards Christ the Lord, and seek him here upon earth
to honour his footstool. For he took earth from earth, and because of that he is flesh of the
earth; and he took flesh from the Virgin Mary, and he walked here upon the
earth in that flesh. He gives us that selfsame flesh, for us to eat. No one eats
that flesh, until he has [first worshipped...] **Bread...**

Folio 65r [65]

[.]ara ha gwyn dir gyrryow dew, C[........................]

August. contra	*Austen* contra *Favstum. lib. 20. ca[....................]*
fastum. lib 20.	*Panem et calicem, Cererem [................................]*
cap. 13.	*et c .i.* e ma ran ow pedery fatla e[...y........]
	ha gwyne, honora ⌐ dew a bara, ha Dew a [g..n]e 5
[Ch]risostom	Gosowhog, pandregy Chrisostom ow leverall, whar an
.Cor. 10	keth place na. *Panis quem frangimus, nonne communicatio*
[ve]rs. 16.	*corporis christi est? Quare non dixit participatio?*
	Quia amplius, quid significare voluit, et multam inter
+	*hæc conuenientiam ostendere. Non enim participatio[n]e tantum* 10
	et acceptione, sed vnitate communicamus. Quemadmodum enim
	corpus illud vnitum est Christo, ita et nos per hunc panem
	vnione coniungimur. henna ew: an bara erany ow 65

tyrry, ne gew an Communication a corf Christ? ha rag henna, na
ruk Christ gylwall parti^{ci}pation? rag malla ef signifia brossa   15
mater, ha e weth brassa coniunction in trethans. Rag kepare
ew an Corf na Iunys thagan saviour Christ, indella e thony
Ivnis thagan Saviour Christ, dir an keth bara na.

Bara ha gwyn dir gyrryow Dew, C[orf ha Gois Christ gwris yth ew]. Austen contra
*Faustum. lib. 20. ca[p. 13. Non nulli propter] Panem et Calicem, Cererem
[& Bacchum nos colere existimabant] etc. Id est:* 'Ema ran ow pedery fatla [eran ny insted
a bara] ha gwyne, honora dew a bara, ha dew a [gwyne]'. Gosowhog pandr'egy Chrisostom
ow leverall, whar an keth place-na: *Panis quem frangimus, nonne 'communicatio' Corporis
Christi est? Quare non dixit 'participatio'? Quia amplius, quid significare voluit, et multam inter
haec convenientiam ostendere. Non enim 'participatione' tantum et acceptione, sed 'unitate'
communicamus. Quemadmodum enim Corpus illud*
unitum est Christo, ita et nos per hunc Panem unione conjungimur. Henna ew: 'An Bara era' ny
ow tyrry, neg ew an communication a Corf Christ? Ha rag henna, na ruk Christ [e]
gylwall participation? Rag malla ef signifia brossa mater, ha eweth
brassa conjunction intrethans. Rag kepare [dell] ew an Corf-na junys th'agan Saviour
Christ, indella eth o' ny junis th'agan Saviour Christ dir an keth Bara-na.'

Foxe, TAMO, 1576, p. 1405 [1380]; (T&C vi, 492)—Ridley's Disputation

Glyn: Austen *Contra Faustum. Lib. 20. cap. 13 Non nulli propter panem & calicem, Cererem & Bacchum nos colere existimabant. &c.* Some there were which thought vs in stede of bread and of the cup, to worshyp Ceres & Bacchus.

Foxe, TAMO, 1576, p. 1407 [1382]; (T&C vi, 495)—Ridley's Disputation

Watson: Harken what Chrisostome sayth vpon that place: *Panis quem frangimus, nonne communicatio corporis Christi est? Quare non dixit participatio? Quia amplius quid significare voluit, & multam inter hæc conuenientiam ostendere. Non enim participatione tantum & acceptione, sed vnitate communicamus. Quemadmodum enim corpus illud vnitum est Christo, ita & nos per hunc panem vnione coniungimur.* That is. The bread which we breake, is it not the Communication of Christes body? Wherfore dyd he not say participation? because he would sygnifie some greater matter, and that hee would declare a great conuenience and coniunction betwixt the same. For we doe not communicate by participation onely & receauyng, but also by counytyng. For likewise as that body is covnited to Christ, so also we by the same bread are conioyned and are vnited to hym.

Bread & wine through God's words, are made the Body and Blood of Christ. Augustine, *Against Faustus, Book 20, Cha[p. 13: Some have thought that] in the Bread and the Cup, Ceres [& Bacchus are our objects of worship] etc.* That is, 'There are some who thought that [we, in the bread] and wine, honour a god of bread, and a god of [wine]'. Listen to what Chrysostom says, upon that same place: *'The Bread which we break, is it not a 'communion' with the Body of Christ?' Why does he not say a 'participation'? Because he wished to express something greater, and to show a greater harmony in these things. That is, it is not only by 'participating' and receiving, but by a deeper 'unity', that we communicate. For just as that Body is united to Christ, so by this Bread are we joined together in union with him.* That is: 'The bread that we break, is it not a communion with the Body of Christ?' And therefore Christ did not call [it] participation, in order that he could suggest something greater, and also a deeper union amongst them. For just as that Body is joined to Christ our Saviour, so are we joined to Christ our Saviour, through that same Bread'.

Folio 65r [65]

August.	Me a thro vmma Augustine *in psalm. 33. Concio. 1.*
[in] psalm.	expoundyng an gyrryow ma: *Ferebatur in manibus suis.*
33. Concio	ef a ve degys inter e thowla *.i. regum.*
.1.	*Hoc quomodo possit fieri in homine, quis intelligat? Manibus*
	enim suis nemo portator, sed alienis. Quomodo i[n]telligat[ur]
	d Dauid secundum literam, non inuenimus: de Christo aut[e]m
	inuenimus. Ferebatur enim Christus in manibu[s.....]
	cum diceret: Hoc est corpus meum. Ferebat enim [.....]
	Corpus in manibus suis. et c. henna ew. fat[......]

hemma bos vnderstandis yᵉ vos gwrys [i..d..................]
veith nyn gew [.....................................]
cafas, fatla ill [...........................]
an prophet be[.................]
tha worth [......................]
[.] honyn [....................]
rag [.......................................]
[..]
[..]

Me a thro umma Augustine *In Psalm 33. Contio. 1*, expoundyng an gyrryow ma: *Ferebatur in manibus suis.* 'Ef a ve degys inter e thowla'. *1 Regum. Hoc quomodo possit fieri in homine, quis intelligat? Manibus enim suis nemo portator, sed alienis. Quomodo intelligatur [de] David secundum literam, non invenimus: de Christo autem invenimus. Ferebatur enim Christus in manibus suis cum diceret: 'Hoc est Corpus meum'. Ferebat enim illud Corpus in manibus suis. etc.* Henna ew: '[Fatla ill] hemma bos understandis the vos gwrys [in deane? Rag denveith] nyng ew [degys inter e thowla e honyn. Ne wrene ny] cafas, fatla ill [hemma bos understandis] a'n prophet [benegas David] tha worth [an lether. Mas a Christ e] honyn [eth eran ny e gafas.] Rag...

[...Christ o degys inter e thowla e honyn pan ruk e leverall 'Hem ew ow Corff ve', rag eff a ruke degy an kethsam Corff inter e thowla e honyn' etc.]

Foxe, TAMO, 1576, p. 1407 [1382]; (T&C vi, 496)—Ridley's Disputation

Smith: I bring here Augustine *in Psal. 33. Conc. I.*
expounding these wordes: *Ferebatur in manibus suis,*
he was caried in his own handes. *1. Regum.*
Hoc quomodo possit fieri in homine, quis intelligat? Manibus
enim suis nemo portatur, sed alienis. Quomodo intelligatur
de Dauid secundum literam, non inuenimus: de Christo autem
inuenimus. Ferebatur enim Christus in manibus suis
cum diceret: Hoc est corpus meum. Ferebat enim illud
corpus in manibus suis. &c. That is. How may
this bee vnderstanded to be done in man? For
no man is caryed in his owne handes, but in the handes of other.
How this may be vnderstanded
of Dauid
after the letter, we do not finde. Of Christ
we finde it.
For...
[...Christ was borne in hys own hands when he sayth: This is my body, for he
caryed that same body in hys owne handes. &c.]

Here I will bring in Augustine *On Psalm 33 (Oration 1)* expounding these words: *He was carried in his hands.* 'He was carried in his hands'. 1 Kings. How can this be understood to happen to a man? For in his own hands no one is carried, but [only] by others. How to understand [this] of David literally, we cannot work out: of Christ himself [though] we can work [it] out. For Christ was carried in his own hands when he said: 'This is my Body'. For then indeed he carried his [own] Body in his hands, et c. That is, 'How can this be understood to be done [to a man? For] no one is [carried in his own hands. We do not] find, how [this] can [be understood of] the [holy] prophet [David] from [the letter—but of Christ] [him]self [we find it]. For ...

[...Christ was carried in his own hands when he said 'This is my Body', for he carried that same Body in his own hands etc.]

Folio 65v [65a]

[...........................]yow dew Corf ha gois Christ ew

[................................C]orf Christ ew, ᵉma warre an alter 14
[........................]Austen *lib.5. contra Donatistas Capi.* 8: luk 22
          Joan. 13   *13. vers. 26*   .21. .18. Ioan

    [................] *buccellam Dominus tradidit non malum accip[.....]*
    [.........*acci*]*piendo Pec*[*c*]*auit. et c.* Kepare a ruk [.....] 5
      [....]ysya e arluth Dew, [not] ef yᵉ recevia pith ew badd, [...]
[....26 21...] [..........] recevias Corf dew warlerth badd maner. et c. e[..]
S. Austen ow cowse nebas moy. *Quia aliquis non ad salutem manduc*[*at*]
non ideo non est corpus .i. e ma ran, nyn gegy, ow tybbry Corf
Christ, thaga sawya, ha rag henna, nyn gew thethans Corf Dew. 10

Theophelact.	e ma ow leverall, Iudas a ruke tastia Corf an arluth.
	Ostendit dominus crudelitatem Iudæ, qui cum argueretur
	non intellexit, et gustauit carnem domini, et c .i. An arluth

a thisquethas an cruelte a Iudas, pan rvg an arluth Dew e
rebukya, whath na ruk Iudas e vnderstandya, ef a tastyas 15
kigg an arluth Dew. hemma ew ᵍⁱʳʳʸᵒʷ kvsell an Nice *humiliter spec*[*te*]

Cusell an	*mus propositum panem et potum, sed exaltata mente fidelite*[*r*]
Nice	*credam*us *iacere in illa sacra mensa agnum dei, tollentem*
	peccata mundi, a sacerdotibus sacrificatum. Na esyn ny

[Bara ha gwyn dir girr]yow Dew Corf ha gois Christ ew [gwris].
[*Rag henna an gwyr ha naturall* C]orf Christ ew ema warre an alter. [*Me a bref henna thaworth*
S.] Austen *liber 5, Contra Donatistas, capitulum 8:* [*Sicut enim Judas cui*] *buccellam Dominus*
tradidit non malum accip[*iendo, sed male acci*]*piendo peccavit, etc.* 'Kepare a ruk
[*Judas despysya*] e Arluth Dew, [not] ef the recevia pith ew badd, [*mas ef a*] recevias Corf
Dew warlerth badd maner', etc. [*Ema*] S. Austen ow cowse nebas moy: *Quia aliquis non ad*
salutem manducat, non ideo non est corpus. Id est: 'Ema ran nyng egy ow tybbry Corf Christ
th'aga sawya, ha rag henna, {nyng} ew thethans Corf Dew'. Theophelact ema ow leverall,
Judas a ruke tastia Corf an Arluth: *Ostendit Dominus crudelitatem Judae qui, cum argueretur,*
non intellexit, et gustavit carnem Domini, etc. Id est: 'An Arluth a thisquethas an cruelte a
Judas, pan rug an Arluth Dew e rebukya, whath na ruk Judas e understandya:
ef a tastyas kigg an Arluth Dew'. Hemma ew girryow Kusell a Nice: [*Ne*] *humiliter*
spectemus propositum panem et potum, sed exaltata mente fideliter credamus iacere in illa sacra
mensa Agnum Dei, tollentem peccata mundi, a sacerdotibus sacrificatum.
Na esyn ny...

Foxe, TAMO, 1576, p. 1408 [1383]; (T&C vi, 497–8)—Ridley's Disputation

Tresham: *Ergo* the true and naturall body of Christe is on the aultar...

Tresham: I proue the contrary by S. Austen, *Lib. 5. contra Donatistas Cap. 8.*

Sicut enim Iudas cui buccellulam Dominus tradidit, non malum accipiendo, sed male accipiendo peccauit. &c. Lyke as Iudas, to whom the Lorde gaue the morsel, dyd offend, not in takyng a thyng that was euyl, but in receiuyng it after an euyll maner. &c.
And a litle after, *Quia aliquis non ad salutem manducat, non ideo non est corpus. i.* Because some do not eate vnto saluation, it foloweth not therfore that it is not his body.
Weston: Theophilacte...saith, that Iudas did taste the bodie of the Lord. *Ostendit Dominus crudelitatem Iudæ, qui cum argueretur, non intellexit, et gustauit carnem domini.* &c. *i.* The Lord did shewe the crueltie of Iudas, which, when he was rebuked, did not vnderstand, and tasted the Lordes flesh. &c.
Watson: What say you then to the Councell of Nice? The wordes of the Councel be these: *Ne humiliter spectemus propositum panem et potum, sed exaltata mēte fideliter credamus iacere in illa sacra mēsa agnum dei, tollentem peccata mundi, a sacerdotibus sacrificatum.* Let vs not...

[Bread & wine through] God's words, are [made] the Body and Blood of Christ. [Therefore the true and natural] Body of Christ is here upon the altar: [I prove that from St] Augustine, Book 5, 'Against the Donatists' Chapter 8: [*Just as Judas, to whom*] *the Lord gave a morsel, not by taking something evil* [*but by the evil way*] *he took* [*it*] *sinned, etc.* 'Just as [Judas despised] his Lord God, [not] that he received what is bad, [but that he] received the Body of God in a bad manner', etc. St Augustine says a little more: *Just because someone does not eat it 'to salvation' does not mean that it is not the Body.* That is: 'There are some who do not eat the Body of Christ to their salvation, and so it is {not} the Body of God to them'. Theophilact says Judas tasted the Body of the Lord: *The Lord showed the cruelty of Judas who, when challenged, did not understand, yet tasted the Lord's flesh, etc.* That is, 'The Lord showed the cruelty of Judas, when the Lord God rebuked him, yet Judas did not understand it, he tasted the Lord God's flesh'. These are the Nicene Council's words: *Humbly let us* [*not*] *look on the Bread and Drink set forth but, with uplifted mind, let us faithfully believe the Lamb of God lies on that holy table, to take away the sins of the world, in the priestly sacrifice.* Let us not...

Folio 65v [65a]

meras war an bara ^{han} dewas ew sittys deragen, mas derevall 20
agen mynd ha colan da, mas cregy faithfully, fatla ew sittis onne
dew war an alter benegas, vge ow kemeras e ker pegh an
bobell, an pith ew benegys gans prontyrryan. *Exaltata*
mente. i. gans mynd hewwall tha thew, *Agnus Dei iacet in mensa:*
Onne athew ew sittis war an alter. ema tillar arall e mes 25
Cucell an Nice. *Nullus Apostolorum dixit, hæc est figura corpo*
          ris Christi. Nullus venerabilium præsbyterorum
          dixit incruentum altaris sacrificium figuram: .i.
     [......s] onyn an apostelath a lev[..........] ew figur ow
     [..]leveris 30
     [...o]rf ef.
                    [1]383.

---

meras war an Bara ha'n Dewas ew sittys deragen, mas derevall agen mynd ha colan da, [ow] cregy faithfully, fatla ew sittis Onne Dew war an alter benegas, uge ow kemeras e ker pegh an bobell: an pith ew benegys gans prontyrryan'. *Exaltata mente. Id est:* 'Gans mynd hewwall tha Thew'. *Agnus Dei iacet in mensa:* 'Onne a Thew ew sittis war an alter'. Ema tillar arall e mes Cucell a Nice: *Nullus Apostolorum dixit, haec est figura Corporis Christi. Nullus venerabilium presbyterorum dixit incruentum altaris sacrificium figuram. Id est:* ['Nyng us] onyn an apostelath a lev[eris, hemma] ew figur ow [Arluth Jesus Christ. Nyng us onyn an reverent prontyrryan a] leveris [sacrafice an alter tha vos figur e go]rf ef'.
[1383].

Foxe, TAMO, 1576, p. 1408 [1383]; (T&C vi, 497–8)—Ridley's Disputation

Watson: ...looke alowe by the grounde vppon the bread & the drinke set before vs, but lyfting vp our mind, let vs faithfully beleue, there vpō the holy table to lie the lambe of God taking away the sinnes of the worlde, being sacrificed of the priestes.
Watson: (*Exaltata mente*) with a minde exalted... *Agnus dei iacet in mensa:* the Lambe of God lieth on the table, saith the Councel.
Smith: I bring an other place out of the Councell of Nice. *Nullus Apostolorum dixit, hæc est figura corporis Christi. Nullus venerabilium præsbyterorum dixit incruentem altaris sacrificium figuram: Ergo, &c.* That is:
None of the Apostles said, this is a figure of
the body of Christ: None of the reuerend Elders said,
the vnbloudy sacrifice of the altar to be a figure.

[ref. to f. 1383 of Foxe, 1576.]

---

look [simply] on the Bread and the Drink that is set before us, but raise up our mind and a good heart; believing faithfully that the Lamb of God is set on the holy altar, who takes away the sin of the people: which is what is consecrated by the priests'. *With uplifted mind. That is:* 'With a mind high towards God'. *The Lamb of God lies on the altar:* 'The Lamb of God is set upon the altar'. There is another place out of the Council of Nicaea: *None of the Apostles said, this is a 'figure' of the Body of Christ. None of the venerable elders said the unbloody sacrifice of the altar was a 'figure'. That is,* ['Not] one of the Apostles said, [this] is a figure of my [Lord Jesus Christ. Not one of the reverend priests] said [the sacrifice of the altar was a figure of] his Body'.
[1383].

Folio 66r [66]

[...]a ha gwyn dir ger[..]

[C]hrisostom	Chrisostom ema ow leverall, N[.. ....]
De incompre	tvs only angwra. CeChrisostom [.........................]
[hen]sibile Dei	9. chapter an Acts Apostelath: Qu[.................]
[n]atu[r]a .	manibus sacerdotis. et c. Pan[...] [l]avirta ge[.....] host 66 5
3 .	benegas e ma inter dowla an pronter. [......] e ma
[...]ust	Chrisostom ow leverall in tillar arall. Non temeré ab Apostolis
[..... 3]8.	est institutum. nyn gew dir hastenab apoyntis ye worth
[Ch]risostom	an Apostelath. pelha, e ma Chrisostom, ow scrifa thanphilippians
[Ad] populum	A remembrance, a vea res thotha bos, in keth sacrament na 10
[An]tiochum	rag an marow. Ema. S. Austen ow leverall, in e E[.....]id[.o]n
69	& 110 chapter: Non est negandum defunctorum animos pietate suorum
[Au]gust	viuentiumm releuari, quum pro illis sacrificium mediatoris affer=
[ ] 98	tur. henna ew. na illen denaha, an nenevow, tha vos

[.]elevis dir an devotion aga hvnthmans ew bew, pan vo offrys   15
[.]n sacrafice a Corf Christ, ha pege rag an nene^{w}vow, An keth
[.]usten ma a leveris a feran rag e vam Monaca.

[Bar]a ha gwyn dir ger[ryow Dew Corf ha Gois Christ gwris e thew]. Chrisostom ema
ow leverall, N[on solum homines, etc. Id est: 'Nyng ew] tus only a'n gwra'. Chrisostom,
[yweth, whar an] 9 chapter an Acts Apostelath: Qu[id dicis? Hostia in]
manibus sacerdotis, etc. 'Pan[dra] lavirta ge[? An] host benegas ema inter
dowla an pronter', [etc. Ha] ema Chrisostom ow leverall in tillar arall: Non temere ab
Apostolis est institutum. 'Nyng [o] dir hastenab apoyntis theworth an Apostelath'. Pelha,
ema Chrisostom ow scrifa [war] Philippians a remembrance, a vea res thotha bos i'n
keth sacrament-na rag an marow. Ema. S. Austen ow leverall, in e Enchiridion, an 110
chapter: Non est negandum defunctorum animos pietate suorum viventium relevari,
quum pro illis sacrificium mediatoris offertur. Henna ew: 'Na illen denaha an
Enevow tha vos relevis dir an devotion aga hunthmans ew bew, pan vo offrys
an sacrafice [a'n Mean ragthans'. Omma ema ef ow prevy an gweronath] a Corf Christ ha
pege rag an Enewow. An keth Austen-ma a leveris Aferan rag e vam Monaca.

Foxe, TAMO, 1576, p. 1413 [1388]; (T&C vi, 509)—Latimer's Disputation

Weston: Augustine in the. 38. Psal. & Chrysostome, concerning the incomprehensible nature of God, *Tom. 3.* say: *Non solum homines. &c.*
Weston: You shall heare Chrysostome againe, vpon the.
ix. chap. of the Actes. *Quid dicis? Hostia
in manibus sacerdotis. &c.* He doth not call it a cup of wyne.
Weston: You shal heare it to be so: and I bring an other place of Chrysostome out of the same treatise: *Non temerè ab Apostolis
est institutum. &c.*
Weston: Here in an other place of Chrysostome to the people of Antioch, Homil. 69. and also *ad Philippenses* he saith, *There should be a memorie and sacrifice for the dead.*
Weston: Augustine in his Enchiridion the. 110. chap. saith: *Non est negandum defunctorum animos pietate suorum viuentium releuari, quum pro illis sacrificium Mediatoris offertur:* that is: We must not denye, that the soules of the dead are relieued by the deuotion of their frends which are liuyng, when the sacrifice of the Mediator is offered for them. Where he proueth the verity of Christes body, and praying for the dead. And it is saide, that the same Austine sayde masse for his mother.

[Br]ead & wine through [God's words are made Christ's Body & Blood] Chrysostom says, [*It is not only men, etc. That is:* 'It is not] only men that make it'. Chrysostom [again, on the] 9 chapter of the Acts of the Apostles: *What [do you say? The host is]
in the hands of the priest, etc.* 'What do you say? [The] Blessed Host is in the hands of the priest', [etc. And] Chrysostom says in another place: *It was not by the Apostles rashly instituted.* 'It was not rashly instituted by the Apostles'. Furthermore,
Chrysostom writes, [on] Philippians, about remembrance, that it should be [made] in that same sacrament, for the dead. St Augustine says, in his Enchiridion, the 110th chapter: *It is undeniable that the souls of the departed are aided by the devotion of their living friends, when the Mediator's Sacrifice is offered for them.* That is: 'We cannot deny that the [Holy] Souls are relieved through the devotion of their living friends, when we offer the Sacrifice [of the Mediator for them'. Here he is proving the truth] of the Body of Christ and praying for the [Holy] Souls. This same Augustine said Mass for his mother Monica.

Folio 66r [66]

[Cyr]ill	e ma Cyrill. ow leverall: *Per communionem corporis Christi, h[......]*
	in nobis Christus corporaliter. henna ew, dir an Commun[...]
	a Corf Christ, e ma Christ Corporally ow trega in[...] 20
	ema. S. Ambros ow leverall. *Videmus principem sacerd[otem]*
[De]	*ad nos venientem, et offerentem sanguinem. et c.* henna e[w]
appara	ny a welas an pensevik pronter, ow tose then [.....]
[ti]one ad	offra gois agan arluth Christ, ema an doctors [.........]
Missam	nyn gegy cowse vith a deow habblys, arna theffe[...] 25
[..]e^{a}n keth geyr ma, *Panis, quem dabo caro mea est* [......]
[A]ugustin	An bara a theffan ry, ew ow kigg ve. Rag [............]
[ ] 11.	di^{e}bbry worthely kigg agen saviour Christ, ye theff [.......]
[C]hrisost	bewnans heb dewath, mith. S. Austen, ha. S. paule. 1. cor. 11.
1.Cor	*Calex est vini noui testamenti: est sanguis qui effunditur* 30
home.	*in remissione tocius mundi. Quod vinum est et aqua in*
[ ] .Cap.	*calicem, non speciems sanguinis sui, sed est præciosum corpus*
&	*et sanguis Christi, qui effunditur pro nobis .i.*
[Am]bros	An chalys a Testament nowth: ew an gois ew skvllys, ha
	e thew an presivs Corf han gois a gyn saviour 35
	Christ, a ve skvlliys ragan [..] popell an beys

Ema Cyrill ow leverall: *Per communionem Corporis Christi, h[abitat] in nobis Christus corporaliter.* Henna ew: 'Dir an Commun[yon] a Corf Christ, ema Christ corporally ow trega [innan ny'.] Ema S. Ambros ow leverall: *Vid[i]mus Principem Sacerd[otem] ad nos venientem, et offerentem Sanguinem, etc.* Henna e[w]: 'Ny a welas an Pensevik Pronter, ow tose then [ny, ha] offra Gois agan Arluth Christ'. Ema an Doctors [ow hagrya] nyng egy cowse vith a De [Y]ow Habblys, arna [theffens y tha'n] keth geyr-ma, *Panis quem dabo, caro mea est[. Id est:]* 'An bara a theffan ry, ew ow kigg ve'. 'Rag [eff neb uge o] dibbry worthely kigg agen Saviour Christ, theth'eff [a ra dos] bewnans heb dewath', mith S. Austen. Ha S. Paule, 1 Cor. 11: *Calix est, vini Novi Testamenti: est Sanguis qui effunditur in remissione totius mundi. Quod vinum est et aqua in calicem? Non species sanguinis sui, sed est pretiosus Corpus et Sanguis Christi, qui effunditur pro nobis. Id est:* 'An chalys [a'n] Testament Nowith ew an Gois ew skullys, ha eth ew an Presius Corf ha'n Gois agyn Saviour Christ, a ve skulliys ragan [ny,] popell an beys'.

Foxe, TAMO, 1576, pp. 1412–13 [1387–8]; (T&C vi, 509)—Latimer's Disputation

Smith: *Per communionem corporis Christi, habitat in nobis Christus corporaliter.* that is, By the communicating of the body of [Christ], Christ dwelleth in vs corporally.
Weston: I will recite vnto you a place of S. Ambrose, *De apparatione ad Missam*, where he saith: *Videmus principem sacerdotem ad nos venientem, & offerentem sanguinem. &c.* That is, We see the chiefe prieste commyng vnto vs, and offeryng bloud. &c.

*Foxe, TAMO, 1576, p. 1416 [1391]; (T&C vi, 517–18)—
Harpsfield's Doctoral Disputation*

Harpsfield: The fathers do agree that there is not entreatie made of the supper of the Lord, before they come vnto, *Panis quem dabo vobis, caro mea est, etc.* ... .S. Augustine meaneth, that he who eateth Christ's fleshe. &c. after a certaine manner ... should liue for euer.

[Precise sources unestablished: see Quotations 62 & 63 in the Commentary]

...*calix Sanguinis mei, novi et eterni Testamenti ... qui pro vobis et pro multis effundetur in remissionem peccatorum...* (cf. Roman Canon).

...*et quod vinum et aqua in calicem mittitur ... speciem sanguinis non videri ... ita etiam similitudinem Pretiosi Sanguinis bibis...* (cf. De Sacramentis 4, 4, 19).

Cyril says: *Through the Communion of the Body of Christ, Christ lives in us in a bodily way.* That is: 'Through the Communion of the Body of Christ, Christ dwells in us corporally'. St Ambrose says: *We have seen the High Priest coming towards us, offering [his] blood, etc.* That is, 'We saw the Prince-Priest coming to us [and] offering the Blood of Christ our Lord'. The theologians [agree] there is no mention of the Lord's Supper until [they] come [to] these same words, *The Bread which I shall give is my flesh. [That is:]* 'The Bread which I shall give is my flesh'. 'For [him who] eats the flesh of our saviour Christ worthily, for him [is]life eternal', says St Augustine; and St Paul, 1 Cor. 11: *'It is the cup of the New Covenant's wine: it is the Blood, poured out for the forgiveness of the whole world. What is the wine and water in the Cup? Not the outward form of his blood—but the precious Body and Blood of Christ, which was poured out for us.* That is, 'It is the Chalice of the New Testament: the Blood that is shed, and it is the precious Body and Blood of our Saviour Christ, which was poured out for us, the people of the world'.

Folio 66v [66a]

        [....................] panis. Corpus quia dicitur Corpus
        [....................]mone de Tempore dicit.
        [............o]mnia infidelitatis suspicio, et tum non te
        [....]iuet quomodo sunt accidentia atque substantia
        [....] substantia absque accidentibus. Henna ew   5
    Panis ew henwis bara, Corpus ew henwis Cor[f]
[g]as oll thiscrygians, mith S.Austen, ha nona navethi[..]
troublis gans Accidens na substans v[e]tholl.
.✠. infra. In cœlum manum mittam, vt Christum teneamus. et [c.]
        Crede et edisti [........] Crig ge, ha e thesta [......]   10

Hillarius.	Panis trans elementatur. Quoniam infirmi sumus
in psalm. 118.	et horremus crudas carnes commedere, maxim[e]
Theophelac.	huius carnem: ideo Panis quidem apparet,
in mat. 26.	sed caro est. hennaew. Bara ew trylis, ye worth [...]
[v]ers. 26	elyment, the gela. Rag an vosan ny mar gwa[n....] 15
[....] xxi.	kemeras skrvth tha thybbry kygg kref[f.....]
[....] 14.	chieffly kygg an keth dean ma, rag henn[a.....]

        [h]e^{f}velap a bara, mas e thew kygg, agen arluth Iesu Ch[rist]

[Panis, quia dicitur] panis. Corpus, quia dicitur Corpus. [S. Augustinus in Ser]mone de
Tempore dicit. [............o]mnia infidelitatis suspicio, et tum non te [....]ivet quomodo
sunt accidentia atque substantia [....] substantia absque accidentibus. Henna ew:
'Panis ew henwis bara, Corpus ew henwis Corf.' [Gas] oll thiscrygians, mith S. Austen, ha
nona navethi[th] troublis gans accidens na substans veth-oll.
[✠ Infra – In cœlum manum mittam, ut Christum teneamus, etc.] Crede et
edisti. [Henna ew:] 'Crig ge, ha eth esta [tibbry.'] 'Panis transelementatur'. Quoniam infirmi
sumus et horremus crudas carnes comedere—maxime hominis carnem—ideo
panis quidem apparet. Sed caro est. Henna ew: 'Bara ew trylis theworth [an eyl] elyment, th'e
gela'. 'Rag an vosan ny mar [gwan, ha ow] kemeras skruth tha thybbry kygg kreff, [ha]
chieffly kygg an keth dean-ma. Rag henna [eth ew in] [h]efelap a bara, mas eth ew kygg
agen Arluth Jesu Christ'...

EDITION 143

[Precise sources unestablished: see Quotations 64 & 65 in the Commentary]

> *[?Panis quia dicitur] panis. Corpus quia dicitur corpus...*
>
> *[............o]mnia infidelitatis suspicio, et tum non te [...]ivet quomodo sunt accidentia atque substantia [....] substantia absque accidentibus*
>
> *In caelum manum mittam...* (cf. Quotation 70, 66v.11-14).

Foxe, TAMO, 1576, p. 1412 [1387]; (T&C vi, 507)—Latimer's Disputation

Latimer: ...for the same s. Augustine saith: *Crede, et manducasti. i.* Beleue, and thou hast eaten.

Foxe, TAMO, 1576, p. 1404 [1379]; (T&C vi, 489)—Ridley's Disputation

Harding: For the wordes in Greke are, μεταστοιχειται, which is in Latin, *transelementatur*, that is, turned from one element into an other.
Harding: *Quoniam infirmi sumus, & horremus; crudas carnes comedere, maximè hominis carnem: ideo panis quidem apparet, sed caro est.* That is: Because we are infirme, and abhorre to eate raw flesh, especially the flesh of man: therefore it appeareth bread, but it is flesh...

[Because bread is called] bread. Because Body is called Body. [St Augustine in a Ser]mon on the Church Year says. [Eschew] every trace of unfaithfulness, and then it does not [concern] you how there are accidents but at the same time substance [and then] substance without accidents. That is, *Panis* is called 'bread', *Corpus* is called 'Body'.[Therefore leave] all unbelief, says St Augustine, and then you will not be troubled by any 'accidents or substance' at all. See ✠ below—'I reach with my hand into heaven, to hold fast to Christ' etc. Believe and you have eaten. [That is:] 'Believe, and you [eat'.] 'The elements of the bread are changed'. Because we are so weak, and tremble with horror at eating 'raw flesh'—especially human flesh—for that reason it does appear to be bread. But it is flesh. That is: 'Bread is turned from [one] element to the other'. 'For we are so weak, trembling with horror at eating 'raw flesh', [and] especially that man's flesh. For that reason [it is in the] likeness of bread, but it is the flesh of our Lord Jesus Christ.'

Folio 66v [66a]

Theophelac.	Panis qui non est figura, sed transformatur in
[ ] Iohn.	Corpus Christi ipsa est caro Christi, Secundum 20
[ ].35.	benedictionem spiritus sancti. henna ew yᵉ lever[...]
	Bara nyngew figure, mas transfvrmys the
	Corf Christ, ha henna ew kygg Christ, [...]
[ew][17]	beniiicter an spvrissans. thotheff rebo oll
	honor ha glory in gwlas heb deweth. Ame[n] 25

[V]erba sequentia scribantur hoc signa .✠. supra.
An gyrryow ma scryfys a vea Res bos a laha in keth
signma .✠.

Vigilius.   In cælum manum mittam, vt Christum teneamus,
mitte fidem et tenuisti, Iudei tenebant veram car[ne]m   30
nos maiestatem in corde. Tenere Christum significat grat[iam]
vt habemus visibiliter in sacramento.
Theophelactus Liber [....] Secundum maiestatem Christum tenemus
[firmiter...] dir faith e thesan s[.......]
[................................]

Panis, qui non est figura, sed transformatur in Corpus Christi, ipsa est caro
Christi, secundum benedictionem Spiritus Sancti. Henna ew the leverall, 'Bara nyng ew
figure, mas transfurmys the Corf Christ, ha henna ew kygg Christ, [dir]
benijicter an Spuris Sans'. Thoth'eff re bo oll honor ha glory i'n gwlas heb deweth. Amen.

Verba sequentia scribantur hoc signa ✠ supra.
An gyrryow-ma scryfys a vea res bos a-laha in keth sign-ma ✠

*In cælum manum mittam, ut Christum teneam; mitte fidem et
tenuisti. Iudei tenebant veram carnem; nos maiestatem in corde. Tenere Christum significat
gratiam ut habemus visibiliter in Sacramento. Theophelactus Liber [....]:
Secundum maiestatem Christum tenemus* [firmiter, per fidem.] Dir faith, eth esan [sensy
fast Christ herwyth e majesty...]

---

17   ew/ow wrongly attached from 66v.15/17. See Notes.

Foxe, TAMO, 1576, p. 1404 [1379]; (T&C vi, 488–9)—Ridley's Disputation

Oglethorpe: That place of Theophilact maketh openly agaynst you. For he sayth in that place, that Christ sayd not: This is a figure of my body, but my body.
Ridley: ...It is transformed sayth Theophilactus, in the same place, by a mysticall benediction, and by the accession or commyng of the holy Ghost vnto the flesh of Christ...

Foxe, TAMO, 1576, p. 1414 [1389]; (T&C vi, 512–13)— Harpsfield's Doctoral Disputation

Weston: I wyll ouerthrow S. Augustine with S. Augustine: who saith this also: *Quomodo quis possit tenere Christum? fidem mitte & tenuisti.* that is, How may a man hold Christ? send thy fayth, and thou holdest hym.
Weston: S. Augustine saith, that these words *Ego ero etc.* I wyl be with you, euen to the ende of the worlde, are accompanied *secundum maiestatem,* Accordyng to hys maiesty: But *secundum præsentiam carnis, non est hic,* By the presence of his flesh he is not here. The Church hath hym not in fleshe, but by beliefe.

The Bread which is not a figure, but is transformed into the Body of Christ, is the actual flesh of Christ after the consecration of the Holy Spirit. That is to say, 'Bread is not a figure, but transformed into the Body of Christ, and that it is the flesh of Christ, [through] the blessing of the Holy Spirit.' To him be all honour and glory in the eternal land. Amen.

Let the following words be written by this sign ✠ *above.*
These words should be written [before?/by rights?] at this same sign ✠.

I reach with my hand into heaven, to hold fast to Christ. Reach with your faith and you have taken hold. The Jews held the true flesh, we the majesty in our hearts. To hold Christ means the grace that we have visibly in the Sacrament. Theophylact in Book [ ]:
We hold Christ, according to his majesty, [firmly through faith........]. Through faith we [hold Christ firmly according to his majesty...]

CHAPTER NINE

Commentary

The focus of the Commentary is on the theology and structure of SA, while that of the following Notes is primarily on the language. Thomas Stephyn is referred to throughout as the author/scribe of SA, as discussed in the Introduction (4.2), although this is not intended as an assertion that he worked completely alone.

Hermeneutical Method

First of all, references are given for the patristic passages. Critical editions are cited wherever available,[1] although references to Migne are also given in square brackets,[2] for those with more limited access to libraries. (It is not implied that Migne's editions are considered equivalent.) After the key words that identify the beginning and end of each quotation (in ***italic bold***) the subject of the argument (not a translation) is given in brackets.

The method is first to comment briefly on authorship and, where appropriate, any interesting features of the text, such as the version used. A necessarily very brief allusion to the patristic context follows, the first time an author or work appears, or where it casts light on a difficult passage. Brief comment is similarly made on biblical references where significant, but it is generally assumed that readers will look elsewhere for expert commentary on the biblical and patristic texts and their authors. (Some passages are only comments from the disputants, and commentary for these begins as below.)

Some consideration is then given to the use of the quotation in the Oxford Disputations with Cranmer, Ridley and Latimer, or Harpsfield's doctoral disputation (all as reported by Foxe). Again, it is assumed that specialist works will

---

1 Particularly from the *Corpus Scriptorum Ecclesiasticorum Latinorum* (CSEL) (Vienna/Salzburg: Tempsky/De Gruyter, 1866–present) and the *Corpus Christianorum, Series Latina* (CCSL) and *Series Graeca* (CCSG) (Turnhout: Brepols, 1953–present).
2 Jacques-Paul Migne, *Patrologiae Cursus Completus*, Latin series (*Patrologia Latina* [PL], 221 vols, Paris: Imprimerie Catholique, 1844–1855) and Greek series (*Patrologia Graeca* [PG], 165 vols, 1856–1858).

be consulted for wider context.³ Finally a brief comment is usually made on the apparent purpose of the quotation within SA.

Some of the theological arguments behind the favoured quotations of the day now melt away in the light of later scholarship, not least because of reattribution or reinterpretation of sources, or the discovery of earlier sources.

An elephant in the room is that throughout TH 11 and 12 there are also patristic references added in Stephyn's hand. His motivation in compiling SA may have included a desire to amplify or edit Tregear's earlier work, although the sequence in Tregear does not govern that in SA. Comment here has been confined to identifying the passages Stephyn inserts in the text or margins of TH 11 and 12, and their overlap with SA. (They are noted in the headings and his patristic references in TH are summarized in Appendix A.)

In the Commentary, quotations from Stephyn's Cornish are given with the word division and expansions of E, to aid rapid understanding of the arguments.

---

3 For the context in Foxe, the references at the head of each Quotation are deemed sufficient, unless adjacent pages are involved, when these are briefly noted from T&C (to facilitate following the arguments quickly in conventional spelling). For a summary of Cranmer's (and his colleagues') views on the Eucharist see Brian Douglas, *A Companion to Anglican Eucharistic Theology, Volume 1: The Reformation to the 19th Century* (Leiden/Boston: Brill, 2012) and, on Cranmer in particular, Diarmaid MacCulloch, *Thomas Cranmer: A Life* (New Haven and London: Yale, 1996), pp. 397-407, 562-69, 614-66 (also MacCulloch, *Tudor Church Militant*, pp. 67-70, 172-73). Two differing wider earlier studies are C.W. Dugmore, *The Mass and the English Reformers* (London: Macmillan, 1958) and Francis Clark, *Eucharistic Sacrifice and the Reformation* (Chulmleigh, Devon: Augustine Publishing Company, 1980). A more recent review of the debate is Amanda Wrenn Allen, *The Eucharistic Debate in Tudor England: Thomas Cranmer, Stephen Gardner and the English Reformation* (London and New York: Lexington, 2018).

Quotation 1. SA 59r.1–2 (Cornish only)

Oglethorpe[4]
Christ ny rug usya trope ... kepare del uge S. Austen
(Christ's words have a more than figurative meaning)
[Foxe, TAMO, p. 1387 [1362]; (T&C vi, 450); Cranmer's Disputation.]

The word *trope* was used from the 1530s for a 'figure' in the sense of 'figurative language',[5] a concept central to SA. Cranmer asserts that he does not believe the 'substance' of the bread or wine changes in the Eucharist: the true 'giving' of the Saviour's body was done upon the cross. Pressed by Chedsey,[6] however, he agrees that the body of Christ is in some sense 'given' in the Eucharist, but only 'spiritually',[7] since he believes the bread must remain bread, to preserve 'the nature of a sacrament'.

His opponents see this as a denial of the plain meaning of Christ's words: 'This is my body'. Chedsey argues that this was 'no fantastical, no feigned, no spiritual body, nor body in faith; but the substance of the body'.[8] Oglethorpe adds that, approaching death, Christ would speak plainly and clearly, as a man 'making his will or testament'. For Cranmer, such an argument is not scriptural, but 'drawn out of the affairs of men'.

Stephyn appears to have inserted this phrase as a possible introduction to the main text if read aloud. 'St Augustine says ...' (*Ima S. Austin ow leverall*) could then become 'Christ did not use a 'figure' for his last words, as St Augustine

---

4   Owen Oglethorpe (c. 1502/3–1559), of Newton Kyme near Tadcaster in Yorkshire, later bishop of Carlisle. He crowned Elizabeth, but ignored her request not to elevate the host at the Coronation Mass and was removed from all his offices shortly before he died in 1559. Cf. Margaret Clark, 'Owen Oglethorpe (1502/3–1559)', in *Oxford Dictionary of National Biography* online, https://doi.org/10.1093/ref:odnb/20617. Accessed 20 October 2018.
5   Or of 'a figure of speech which consists in the use of a word or phrase in a sense other than that which is proper to it', C.T. Onions, ed., *The Shorter Oxford English Dictionary*, 3rd edn (Oxford: Clarendon, 1965), p. 2252 under *trope*.
6   William Chedsey (c. 1510/11–1577?) was a Somerset man and one of Bonner's chaplains. Held in custody by Edward VI but released by Mary, he was deprived by Elizabeth of his office as archdeacon of Middlesex and committed to the Fleet. Cf. Luke MacMahon, 'William Chedsey (1510/11–1577), Roman Catholic priest', in *Oxford Dictionary of National Biography* online, https://doi.org/10.1093/ref:odnb/5204. Accessed 20 October 2018.
7   T&C vi, 449.
8   Much of the debate was linked to Aristotelian understandings of 'substance' now interpreted less narrowly by all sides. See Pope Paul VI in *Mysterium Fidei*, tr. Rev. A. Garvey (London: Catholic Truth Society, 1965), p. 21 and in *The 'Credo' of the People of God* (London: Catholic Truth Society, 1968), p. 13, where he speaks of 'the order of reality which exists independently of the human mind'. Even in Stephyn's time apologists such as Harding, while defending transubstantiation, accepted it was beyond human understanding: Wooding, *Rethinking Catholicism*, pp. 206-07.

says ...' (In the reconstructed text, *Christ ny rug usya trope kepare e gerryow dewetha, kepar del uge S. Austin ow leverall ...*)

In many ways the whole argument of SA is summed up in these opening words. Stephyn intends throughout to select material that presents the case that Christ's words about his body and blood in the Eucharistic mystery are not metaphorical or figurative. They describe a reality.

Quotation 2. SA 59r.3–11 (Latin) 12–20 (Cornish)

St Augustine of Hippo, *Epistola ad Catholicos fratres contra Donatistas (De Unitate Ecclesiae)* 1, 11, 28.[9]
Quid hoc est rogo? ... et inde venturi ut de omnibus iudicet.
(Near death, Christ would speak plainly and clearly)
[Foxe, TAMO, 1576, p. 1387 [1362]; (T&C vi, 450)—Cranmer's Disputation]

Augustine (354–430), bishop of Hippo Regius (now Annaba in Algeria), was an articulate defender of Catholic Christianity against a range of heretical beliefs, as well as an original philosopher and theologian who greatly influenced the development of Western Christianity.[10]

Here he is asking, which is the true Catholic Church? That which is found all over the world, or the Donatist community that arose during the Diocletian persecution and is confined to a particular geographical area and culture?

If the scriptural passages suggesting the former are merely figurative and inapplicable to a visible church, then what of other foundational texts, such as Luke 24:46 (on the passion and resurrection)? The passage beginning 'I ask you, what is this? (*Quid hoc est rogo?*)—originally a reference to Christ's words about Jerusalem—reinforces this argument.

Weston applies the passage somewhat out of context,[11] to Christ's words the night before his crucifixion. Cranmer counters this, and then—when challenged for 'disagreeing with all the churches'—he says that he only disagrees 'with the

---

9   Cf. Michael Petschenig, ed. *S. Aureli Augustini: Contra litteras Petiliani, Epistula ad catholicos de secta Donatistarum, Contra Cresconium grammaticum et Donatistam*, Corpus Scriptorum Ecclesiasticorum Latinorum (CSEL 52) (Vienna: Tempsky, 1909), pp. 263–64 [PL 43, 410]. The *[non]* in the edited text and Foxe is not present in all sources. Note that Weston, like SA, gives this as Chapter 10 not 11.

10 For St Augustine's background and context see Henry Chadwick, *The Early Church* (London: Pelican, 1967) [reprinted by Penguin, 1990], pp. 216–36.

11 Hugh Weston (c. 1510–1558), of Burton Overy, Leicestershire, was an Oxford academic who became archdeacon of Cornwall in 1547. He was imprisoned under Edward VI but on the accession of Mary I became successively dean of Westminster, archdeacon of Colchester and dean of Windsor. Accused of adultery, he sought to appeal to Rome but was detained in the Tower, eventually being released on account of sickness just before dying in 1558. Cf.

papistical church'.[12] Just after, he is cornered into asserting that the sacrament 'is not [Christ's] body', except in a figurative way.

The implication from Stephyn is that those who argue for a merely figurative interpretation of Christ's words are, like the Donatists, denying scriptural texts their plain meaning. Such debates are often revealing beyond the formal logic of positions, because they can reveal Tudor authors' 'true ideas about translation, despite their formal protestations'.[13]

Quotation 3. SA 59r.21–2 (Cornish only)

Weston—cf. also St Hilary of Poitiers, *De Trinitate*, 8, 13.[14]
Christ a ruge ry then an keith kigge-na a ruge ef kemeras urth an Worthias Marya
(Christ gave us the same flesh which he took of the Virgin)
[Foxe, TAMO, 1576, p. 1388 [1363]; (T&C vi, 452]—Cranmer's Disputation]

Hilary (*c.* 310–*c.* 367) was bishop of Poitiers and wrote against the Arian heresy while also completing commentaries, doctrinal works and histories. *De Trinitate* was composed largely during exile (356-360) and finished around the time he returned.

Weston seems to be alluding to Hilary's statement that 'the man that was born of the Virgin Mary was truly Christ, and we truly receive—under a mystery—the flesh of his body' (see Quotation 21). He makes a threefold rhetorical argument: (1) he gave us the same flesh that he took of the Virgin; (2) he took flesh of the Virgin truly, not figuratively; (3) therefore he gave us his true flesh.

Stephyn takes this phrase of Weston, which appears in Foxe just a few lines before the following quotation from Chrystostom, as a suitable reinforcement of the idea that Christ's presence is not merely 'spiritual'. It is a bridge into the graphic imagery that follows.

  C.S. Knighton, 'Hugh Weston (1510–1558), dean of Windsor', in *Oxford Dictionary of National Biography* online, https://doi.org/10.1093/ref:odnb/29122. Accessed 20 October 2018.
12 T&C vi, 450–51.
13 Morini, *Tudor Translation in Theory and Practice*, pp. viii and, more widely, 35–64.
14 P. Smulders, ed., *Sancti Hilarii Pictaviensis Episcopi: De Trinitate, Libri VIII–XII* [CCSL 62A] (Turnhout: Brepols, 1980), pp. 325–26 [PL 10, 246B].

Quotation 4. SA 59r.23–25 (Latin, part only), 25–39 (Cornish)

St John Chrysostom, *Homiliae in Matthæum*, 82, 5.[15]
Veniat tibi in mentem ... Ea namque re nos alimur, quam angeli etc.
(We are honoured to be nourished by Christ himself)
[Foxe, TAMO, 1576, p. 1388 [1363]; (T&C vi, 452]—Cranmer's Disputation]

John Chrysostom (349–407), archbishop of Constantinople, worked tirelessly to promote unity and justice. The epithet Χρυσόστομος, 'golden-mouthed', refers to the eloquence of his preaching. An advocate for the poor, unpopular with the civil authorities, he was banished twice and died in exile. (For notes on dating his works, see Quotations 54 and 55.)

Here he is commenting on Matthew 26:26–28, the 'institution narrative' of the Eucharist.[16] With its twofold emphasis on Bread and Cup, the passage echoes other Matthaean double parables,[17] and hints at the notion of sacrifice through the separation of the body and the blood.[18] In any case, Jesus clearly connects the bread which is broken with his body soon to be offered up on the cross.[19]

Chrysostom's words are striking: 'feeding us himself with his own blood, and by every possible means joining himself intimately with us'. Elsewhere in the same passage he speaks of 'lips being reddened by that most awful blood'. Priests should take immense care that they do not admit to the mysteries those who might consume the sacrament 'without discerning the body' and consequently 'eat or drink judgement against themselves'.[20]

Weston argues from Chrisostom that, if we are nourished as a mother feeds her baby, then this is not a 'merely' spiritual feeding, indeed Christ has 'suffered us to fasten our teeth in his flesh'.[21] Cranmer grants that Christ does give his real flesh for us—on the Cross—but claims that, in the sacrament, we only feed on him spiritually: 'We receive with the mouth the sacrament; but the thing

---

15 Frederick Field, ed., *Joannis Chrysostomi homiliae in Matthaeum*, vol. 2 (Cambridge: Cambridge University Press, 1839), p. 469C, beginning Ἐνόησον ποίαν ἐτιμήθης τιμήν [PG 58, 743]. See also Quotation 7, which just precedes it. Foxe 1576 and 1583 have 'nourished'; 1563 and 1570 have 'nourisheth' (cf. 59r.39). The psalm verse is Ps 106:2 (105:2 Vulgate).
16 The translation is by George Trapezontius (but omitting: 'And why speak only of shepherds?' before 'Many mothers etc. ...') See, for example, *Opervm Divi Ioannis Chrysostomi Archiepiscopi Constantinopoli etc.* (Basle: Ex Officina Hervagiana, 1539), vol. 2, f. 450. This is identical to Foxe and SA, except that they both have *tibi* preceding *in mentem*. The passage is from Homily 82, not 83.
17 E.g. Mt 7:24–27 and Mt 13:44–46.
18 John C. Fenton, *Saint Matthew*, Pelican New Testament Commentaries (Harmondsworth: Penguin, 1963), p. 417.
19 Fenton, *Saint Matthew*, p. 418.
20 1 Cor 11:29 NRSV.
21 T&C vi, 451.

and matter of the sacrament we receive by faith.' Weston then insists: 'Nay, the body by the mouth' and Cranmer comes back: 'That I deny.'²²

This is clearly a pivotal debate for Stephyn, who continues the nursing (and 'by mouth') theme throughout Quotations 4 to 6. This passage thus fits neatly between Augustine's challenge of merely figurative explanations of scripture, and the quotations soon to be introduced, that stress we receive Christ's flesh and blood 'by the mouth'.

Quotation 5. SA 59r.39–40 (Cornish only)

Weston
Kepare a ra an mam maga e flogh ... gans agen ganow e Gorfe ny a rys recevya
(We partake of Christ with our mouths)
[Foxe, TAMO, 1576, p. 1388 [1363]; (T&C vi, 452)—Cranmer's Disputation]

Stephyn from time to time includes—alongside the main diet of patristic quotations—some of the incidental dialogue, as at Quotations 1 and 3, and here. Weston, building on Chrysostom, insists that 'Like as mothers nurse their children with milk, so Christ nourished us with his body.'

The repeated emphasis on the reception 'by [our] mouth' (*gans [agen] ganow*) in SA (see also 59v.18ff) is interesting. It seems to echo Weston's phrase 'the body by the mouth'. But it may also reflect a common marginal reference used in *catenae* of the period to identify Quotation 6 or be a kind of contemporary shorthand for this doctrine. Alternatively, it may simply reflect the strength of Stephyn's feeling that this is the crux of the matter.

Quotation 6. SA 59v.1–4 (Latin)
8–12 (Cornish) [and TH 54v.10–17m]

'St John Chrysostom', *Expositio in Psalmos*, 50, 1, 6.²³
Erubescit fieri nutrix ... et pro potu suum sanguinem nobis propinavit
(Christ nourishes us, as a mother nurses her child)
[Foxe, TAMO, 1576, p. 1388 [1363]; (T&C vi, 452)—Cranmer's Disputation]

This passage (now often judged to be Pseudo-Chrysostom) comments very obliquely on Ps 51 (Ps 50 in the Vulgate/LXX) and is hardly a direct exposition

---

22 T&C vi, 453.
23 Lacking a modern, critical edition this is from Migne, beginning Αἰσχύνεται γὰρ γενέσθαι τροφὸς [PG 55, 572]. See also Henry Savile, ed., *S. Ioannis Chrysostomi Opera Graeci* (Eton: John Norton, 1612), 8 vols, and the translation of Robert Charles Hill, *St John Chrystostom:*

of scripture. The Latin translation is almost identical to Hervet's.²⁴

The *propinavit*, with its overtones of raising the cup of Sacrifice, reminded the late Ray Edwards of the parallelism of Christ being offered the sponge soaked in vinegar: 'Behold, I have it ready / gall and vinegar mingled / wassail! if anyone thirsts.' (*Ottense gynef parys / bystel, eysel kymyskys / wassel marsus seghes bras* PC 2976–8.)

Cranmer continues to contrast receiving 'the sacrament' by mouth but 'the body' by faith—seeing a baptismal parallel, with its outward sign of water and inward grace.²⁵ Weston argues that the two sacraments differ, as the Gospels refer explicitly to Christ's body being taken and eaten.

Stephyn, by contrast, seems to be selecting passages that most graphically emphasize that Christ 'feeds us with his own flesh' (*agan maga gans e kegg e honyn*).

Quotation 7. SA 59v.4–7 (Latin) 14–17 (Cornish)

St John Chrysostom, *Homiliae in Matthæum*, 82, 5.²⁶
Non enim sufficit ipsi hominem fieri ... nos corpus suum efficit
(Christ became one with us, to make us one with him)
[Foxe, TAMO, 1576, p. 1388 [1363]; (T&C vi, 452]—Cranmer's Disputation]

This passage comes a little before Quotation 4 in Chrysostom's original. He is arguing for purity in approaching the sacrament, given the spiritual 'fire' in Christ's Body and Blood.

Between the two passages comes a direct reference to Christ's flesh being 'torn with the teeth' and the tongue being 'reddened with his blood'.²⁷ Both Weston and Cranmer knew this, so Cranmer will quote it first at Quotations 9 and 13, knowing that Weston would otherwise have done so. But the main emphasis here is that Christ did not merely become man to share our sorrows. His intention was to bring us into one body—'one mass or lump'—with himself, not only in terms of faith but in reality. Cranmer grants this sharing of the nature of Christ: his dispute is about the 'mechanism' by which it is achieved.

Commentary on the Psalms (Brookline: Holy Cross Orthodox Press, 1998), 2 vols. For the work of Mayer and her collaborators towards new editions of Chrysostom, see Quotations 54 or 55.
24 Cf. Gentian Hervet, *D. Ioannis Chrysostomi Archiepiscopi Constantinopolitani Opera etc.* (Venice: Ad Signum Spei, 1549), vol. 1, f. 214v—except that the central clause here is *ideo & pro cibo propria nos carne pascit*.
25 T&C vi, 452.
26 Field, ed., *Joannis Chrysostomi homiliae in Matthaeum*, vol. 2, p. 469B, beginning Οὐδὲ γὰρ ἤρκεσεν αὐτῷ [PG 58, 743].
27 T&C vi, 453. See Quotation 13.

Stephyn, by his selection, endorses the main thrust of Weston's argument—that the partaking of Christ's body is ordered towards the sharing of his nature. That is, the incarnation is not simply a matter of example or teaching. It is a real union.

Quotation 8. SA 59v.18–20 (Latin) 20–22 (Cornish)

St John Chrysostom, *Homiliae in secundum ad Corinthios*, 30, 2.[28]
Non vulgarem honorem consequuutum est ... accipiens corpus dominicum
(It is a great honour to receive the body of Christ with our mouths)
[Foxe, TAMO, 1576, p. 1388 [1363]; (T&C vi, 453)—Cranmer's Disputation]

This passage was well known in controversy and appeared in contemporary *catenae* on the Eucharist with regularity.[29] Originally, Chrysostom was commenting on the phrase 'Greet one another with a holy kiss' (2 Cor 13:12 NRSV). Unlike the kiss of Judas, the Christian kiss of peace honours the other as a temple, for 'through these gates and doors Christ ... entered into us and does enter'.

Weston, responding to Cranmer's 'with the mouth, I deny', points out that Chrysostom's argument in fact rests on Christ entering through our mouth. Stephyn is evidently very interested in this exchange. It seems to intrigue him that it is not only Weston who cites Chrysostom on this point, but that Cranmer himself identifies a text even stronger in this direction, in Quotation 9 and 13.

Quotation 9. SA 59v.22–5 (Cornish only)

Cranmer
Agen ganow ema o mos ... in Corf agen Arluth Christ
(We receive the body of Christ with our mouth)
[Foxe, TAMO, 1576, p. 1388 [1363]; (T&C vi, 453)—Cranmer's Disputation]

In Foxe, Cranmer says at this point that 'With our mouth we receive the body of Christ, and tear it with our teeth, that is to say, the sacrament of the body

---

28 Frederick Field, ed., *Sancti Patris Nostri Joannis Chrysostomi Archiepiscopi Constantinopolitani Interpretatio Omnium Epistolarum Paulinarum ...*, tom. 3 [*Homiliae in Divi Pauli Epistolam ad Corinthios Posteriorem*] (Oxford: J.H. Parker, 1845–1847), p. 311, beginning Καὶ γὰρ οὐχ ὡς ἔτυχε [PG 61, 607].
29 E.g. Tunstall, *De ueritate corporis et sanguinis*, f. 70v, and Jean Garet of Leuven (Johannes Garetius Louaniensis), *Omnium Ætatum Nationum ac Provinciarum in Veritate Corporis Christi in Eucharistia*, 3rd edn (Antwerp: Philip Nutius, 1569), f. 28v, Google Books, Accessed 1 August 2018. (The 1st edn, *De vera præsentia corporis Christi in sacramento Eucharistiæ*, was published in 1561.)

of Christ.' He is paraphrasing a passage that falls directly between the two extracts already considered in Quotation 7. It will reappear at Quotation 13.

The words 'with our mouth' (see Quotation 5) again catch Stephyn's eye. He emphasizes them in the margin (and in the added clause in the text), writing 'our mouth goes into the body of Christ'. He puts *corf*, 'body' for *ganow*, 'mouth' in the second instance at 59v.24 (though see Seton's version at Foxe, TAMO, 1576, p. 1416 [1391]. See Quotation 62 for Seton himself).

Quotation 10. SA 59v.25–7 (Cornish only)

Smith[30]
Ima lowar onyn o bostia ... but decevis ens sy
(Many who say they are following the Fathers are doing quite the opposite)
[Foxe, TAMO, 1576, p. 1402 [1377]; (T&C vi, 485)—Ridley's Disputation]

The narrative in SA now moves to Ridley's Disputation, partly perhaps because of the reference to boasting, which may have reminded Stephyn of this later passage. Smith has been speaking of the *Quo Vadis* legend, as 'evidence' that Christ was able to act on earth after his ascension. (The reformers were often accused of placing Christ 'in fetters', by saying he could no longer do so.)

Ridley understands the point and makes it clear he wished to place no such restrictions on Christ (although he personally doubted the authority and antiquity of the *Quo Vadis* story). However, although Christ, 'according to his divine pleasure', can do whatever he wills, 'it is contrary to the nature of ... his body that he should be ... at one instant both in heaven and on earth'.

This is reminiscent of the so-called Black Rubric, which says that 'the naturall Body and Blood of our sauiour Christ ... are in heauen and not here. For it is agaynst the trueth of Christes true natural bodye, to be in moe places then in one, at one tyme.'[31]

---

30 Richard Smith (or Smyth) (c. 1499/1500–1563) of Worcestershire was the first Regius Professor of Divinity at Oxford in 1536. He may have conformed initially under Edward VI but then fled to Leuven. He returned under Mary I but was deprived under Elizabeth I, escaping to Douai, where Philip II appointed him dean of St Peter's and, in 1563, chancellor of the university. He died later that year. Cf. J. Andreas Löwe, 'Richard Smyth [Smith] (1499/1500 1563)', in *Oxford Dictionary of National Biography* online, https://doi.org/10.1093/ref:odnb/25885. Accessed 20 October 2018.

31 Douglas Harrison, ed., *The First and Second Prayer Books of Edward VI* (London: Dent, 1968), p. 393. While the Forty-Two Articles of 1552 opposed reservation, processions, elevation or worship of the Blessed Sacrament, the Scottish reformer John Knox argued that kneeling to receive Holy Communion still implied adoration. Cranmer therefore persuaded the Privy Council to include a riposte in the 1552 Prayer Book, clarifying that no adoration was intended. This 'Black Rubric' (originally on a separate leaf, in black ink) was omitted in the 1559 revision

Stephyn probably sees this as a human argument, neither scriptural nor patristic, agreeing with Smith that some theologians who boast their faith is 'the very faith of the ancient church ... directly strive against the faith of the old fathers', by interpreting them in a sense other than that held by the Universal Church.

Quotation 11. SA 59v.28–60r.1 (Latin) 60r.2–11 (Cornish) [and TH 55r.17–20m]

St John Chrysostom, *Homiliae ad populum Antiocheum (De Statuis)* 2, 26.[32]
Tanquam maximam hereditatem ... et ipsam habens ascendit
(Elijah left Elisha his cloak—Christ left us his flesh)
[Foxe, TAMO, 1576, p. 1402 [1377]; (T&C vi, 485)—Ridley's Disputation]

Bernardo Brixiano's translation of *De Statuis* (On the Statues) agrees reasonably well with the text given here.[33] The second part of the passage is also found in Tunstall.[34] *Christus autem* (at 59v.38) are catchwords for the next page—the usual practice in SA.

This homily seems to have been preached when Chrysostom was still a priest in Antioch. Following the imposition of a new tax, statues of the emperor and his family were attacked. Chrysostom laments the disorder and explores the relationship between material troubles and Christian duty.[35] Citing 1 Tim 6:17 from the day's lectionary, with 2 Kings 8–15 in mind, he extols the value of heavenly gifts, such as the cloak Elijah left with Elisha,[36] or the sacraments Christ left to his Church. (Elijah, at the end of his ministry, was 'taken up into heaven'. Elisha continued his ministry as an 'Elijah below', assisted by the spiritual power of the 'Elijah above', symbolized and mediated by the bequest of this cloak.)

---

but reintroduced in 1662 at the request of the puritans. For Weston's view, see Foxe, TAMO, 1576, p. 1413 [1388]; (T&C vi, 510).
32 Unable to access a modern, critical edition of *De Statuis* (CPG 4330) I have used Migne, beginning at Ἐδέξατο καθάπερ μεγίστην κληρονομίαν [PG 49, 46].
33 Hervet, ed., *D. Ioannis Chrysostomi ... Opera*, vol. iv, f. 117r.
34 Tunstall, *De ueritate Corporis et Sanguinis*, f. 73r.
35 Wendy Mayer, 'The Biography of John Chrysostom and the Chronology of his Works', proceedings of the conference Chrysostomika II, Augustinianum, Rome, 2007; https://www.academia.edu/6448810/The_Biography_of_John_Chrysostom_and_the_Chronology_of_his_Works, updated 2014 and accessed 1 November 2018, p. 18.
36 For the full account see 2 Kings 1–18. The word for a sheepskin cloak, *pallium* (4 Kings 2:13, Vulgate), is *melotem* here, reflecting Greek μηλωτή (4 Kings 2:13, LXX), a sheepskin cloak or mantle.

Smith claims that, although Ridley avows respect for antiquity and tradition, in fact he 'doth directly strive against' it,[37] since Chrysostom clearly states that, as well as having his flesh with him on his ascension into heaven, Christ also left it to us here on earth. Ridley accepts this, but only in the sense that Christ took his 'corporal substance' to heaven and left his flesh on earth 'in mystery', as a 'spiritual communication', including 'by hearing the gospel, and by faith'.

Stephyn evidently feels, with Smith, that Chrysostom's text directly addresses the reformers' assertion that Christ's 'natural' body cannot be 'in more places than one'. Elijah was great, and worked many miracles, but none as great as we ourselves experience, when we are 'endued with the holy mysteries'.

Quotation 12. SA 60r.13–17 (Latin) 18–22 (Cornish)

St John Chrysostom, *De Sacerdotio*, 3, 4.[38]
O miraculum, O Dei benevolentiam ... circumstantium omnium oculis
(Christ sits at the right hand of the Father, but is also held in men's hands)
[Foxe, TAMO, 1576, p. 1388 [1363]; (T&C vi, 453)—Cranmer's Disputation]

We return to Cranmer's Disputation. The Latin translation of the passage given in Foxe and SA is similar to that found in Tunstall.[39]

Like the *De Fuga* of Gregory Nazianzen or the *Regula Pastoralis* of Gregory the Great, Chrysostom's *De Sacerdotio* was written about the episcopal ministry,[40] possibly before AD 386 and certainly before 392, when Jerome mentions it.[41] Chrysostom's devotion is clear throughout: 'When you see the Lord sacrificed and lying before you, and the High Priest standing over the sacrifice and praying, and all who partake being tinctured with that precious blood, can

---

37 T&C vi, 453.
38 J. Arbuthnot Nairn, ed., Περὶ Ἱερωσύνης *(De Sacerdotio) of St John Chrysostom* (Cambridge: Cambridge University Press, 1906), III, 4; p. 52, beginning ὦ τοῦ θαύματος· ὦ τῆς τοῦ Θεοῦ φιλανθρωπίας [PG 48, 642]. (Note III, 4 and not III, 3 as in Foxe and SA.)
39 Tunstall, *De ueritate Corporis et Sanguinis*, f. 75r, but with *omnium manibus* for *hominum manibus*. See also Hervet, ed., *D. Ioannis Chrysostomi ... Opera*, vol. 5, f. 8v, beginning *O miraculum, ô Dei benignitatem*.
40 Nairn, ed., Περὶ Ἱερωσύνης, pp. xii–xvii. See also Mayer, 'The Biography of John Chrysostom', p. 17, and, more generally, Wendy Mayer, *The Homilies of St John Chrysostom—Provenance: Reshaping the Foundations*, Orientalia Christiana Analecta 273 (Rome: Pontificio Istituto Orientale, 2005).
41 Graham Neville, tr., *Saint John Chrysostom: Six Books on the Priesthood* (London: SPCK, 1977), pp. 20–4.

you think that you are still among men and still standing on the earth? Do you not rather feel transported straightway into heaven?'[42]

There is a sense of Cranmer wishing to 'get there first' in his use of the passage to 'neutralize' it—especially when it continues by saying the one 'who sits above with the Father is at that moment held in our hands'. His bold argument is that Chrysostom's language is simply so graphic, that 'no man having any judgement' could possibly take it as 'spoken without trope or figure'. (This, of course, is neither an argument from scripture nor from the Fathers.)

One has the sense that, for all his scholarship, Cranmer is at his weakest in this exchange. When Weston concludes that 'the body of Christ is showed us upon the earth', he retorts 'What! Upon the earth? No man seeth Christ upon the earth.' Yet he has just quoted Chrysostom's 'by no subtilty or craft, but with the open and beholding eyes of all the standers-by'.

Stephyn's version is even more direct, with a hint of a moral imperative: *tha kenever a whelha, ha vo o sevall rebta*, 'for all who see, and stand by him'. It can be argued that some of the distortions and simplifications in Stephyn's translations are attributable to clumsiness, poor skill in translation or failure to understand the source texts. Nonetheless a counter-argument is possible in several instances—and this is one—that these simplifications and changes are quite deliberate.

Quotation 13. SA 60r.22-5 (Cornish only)

Cranmer, quoting St John Chrysostom, *Homiliae in Matthæum*, 82, 5 (see Quotations 4 and 7) and *Homiliae in Johannem*, 46, 3.[43]
Umma why a glow Christ ew gwelys pub deth ... agan tavas ew ruth gans e gos
(Christ is touched and broken, his blood reddens our tongue)
[Foxe, TAMO, 1576, p. 1388 [1363]; (T&C vi, 453)—Cranmer's Disputation]

As noted under Quotation 7, Chrysostom's *Homilies on the Gospel of Matthew* speak of our tongue being reddened with Christ's blood. His *Homilies on the Gospel of John* also argue that Christ gave to those who long for him the ability to touch and eat, and 'fix their teeth in his flesh'—so 'embracing' him mystically and satisfying all their love.

---

42 Neville, *Six Books on the Priesthood*, p. 70; Bettenson, *The Later Christian Fathers*, p. 175.
43 Field, ed., *Joannis Chrysostomi homiliae in Matthaeum*, 46, 3, vol. 2, p. 469B–C, beginning Τίνος οὖν οὐκ [PG 58, 743]. Then *Homiliae in Johannem*, 46, 3—on Jn 6: 52—beginning ἀλλὰ καὶ ἅψασθαι, καὶ φαγεῖν. This ends with a long section on Christ's blood, beginning Τοῦτο τὸ αἷμα τὴν εἰκόνα. Migne's text (from Montfaucon, but taking Savile into account) is used here, in the absence of a modern critical edition [PG 59, 260–1].

Once again, Cranmer seeks out these most graphic passages, his point being that such vivid language cannot be intended literally. It is perhaps surprising that none of the disputants cite Aquinas here to develop their perspectives.[44]

Stephyn, however, by removing the context of the debate, and Cranmer's exposition of the point, restores the force of Chrysostom's original.

Quotation 14. SA 60r.25–34 (Latin) 60r.35–60v.10 (Cornish)

St John Chrysostom, *Homiliae in primum ad Corinthios*, 24, 8.[45]
Quod summo honore dignum est … Absterge igitur ab omne sorde animam tuam
(We touch and eat the greatest thing on earth or in heaven—the King's body) [Foxe, TAMO, 1576, p. 1388–9 [1363–4]; (T&C vi, 453)—Cranmer's Disputation]

The correct homily number, 24, was misprinted as 34 in 1576 (as at 60r.25) which underlines the edition of Foxe used in SA. The Latin translation is similar to that in a number of contemporary works.[46] The fact that *tectum*, 'roof', has become *lectus*, 'couch' 60r.27 (perhaps originally by slip of pen to *lectum*, grammatically regularized later) is also confirmatory of a later edition of Foxe.[47]

Chrysostom sympathized with St Paul among the Corinthians. His own ministry at Constantinople brought him into contact (and at times conflict) with the luxury of the imperial court. Writing at the height of his powers and before his exile, he points beyond material to spiritual treasures. 'As in royal courts the most glorious thing is … the king's own body sitting on the throne, so … likewise in heaven with the body of our King. Yet you are permitted to see this upon earth … Do you grasp … how what is more precious than all other things is seen by you on earth? And not only seen but touched, not only touched, but also eaten.'[48]

---

44 Cf. *Summa Theologica*, III, Q. 77, Art. 7, 3ff. *Corpus Thomisticum*, Accessed 10 October 2018. St Thomas's *Catena Aurea* was also a widely available source of eucharistic quotations; cf. John Henry Newman, ed., *Catena Aurea: Commentary on the Four Gospels collected out of the Works of the Fathers by St Thomas Aquinas*, 4 vols (Oxford: John Henry Parker, 1841). Reprinted in facsimile (London: St Austin Press, 1997).
45 Field, ed., *Ioannis Chrysostomi … Omnium Epistolarum Paulinarum …*, tom. 2 [*Homiliae in epistolam ad Corinthios priorem*], p. 296, beginning Τὸ γὰρ πάντων ἐκεῖ τιμιώτερον [PG 61, 205].
46 E.g. Jean Tavernier, *De veritate corporis et sanguinis Christi in sacramento altaris* (Paris: Vivant Gaultherot, 1548), 2nd edn (Paris: Claude Fremy, 1556), f. 47v. Google Books, accessed 1 October 2018.
47 In 1563 the intermediate stage *lectum aureum* is found, emended to *lectus aureus* in 1570, 1576 and 1583.
48 Adapted from the translation by Hubert Cornish and John Medley in John Keble, ed., *The Homilies of St John Chrysostom, Archbishop of Constantinople, on the First Epistle of St Paul the Apostle to the Corinthians*, Part I, Homilies i–xxiv (Oxford: John Henry Parker, 1839), p. 335 (on 1 Cor 10:24).

Weston feels this refutes Cranmer's contention that Chrysostom does not imply any literal presence. But Cranmer remains unmoved, as he holds axiomatically that Christ's body cannot be at the same time in heaven and on the earth.

Stephyn, of course, omits all references to any difficulty about taking the words literally, while repeating the most challenging of them. We are told that Christ 'is touched and torn by teeth' (*eff ew touchis, eff ew squardis gans dens*, SA 60r.23-4), that he is 'set before us in the world' (*sittis deragan in nore vyse*, SA 60r.39-40) and that we 'not only touch him but eat him' (*not only [e] touchia bus e thibbry*, SA 60v.7).

Quotation 15. SA 60v.10-13 (Cornish)

Chedsey, rephrased by Foxe
Kepar del wruck S. Thomas touchia Corfe Christ ... keveris Dew ha deane
(Christ is to be touched—as Thomas touched him—because he is both God and man)
[Foxe, TAMO, 1576, p. 1389 [1364]; (T&C vi, 455)—Cranmer's Disputation]

Stephyn now jumps to an argument of Chedsey's further on, based on St Thomas touching the body of Christ after the resurrection.[49]

The point is rooted in the incarnation: we must be touching God in the Eucharist, since we are touching Christ there, who is both God and man. A parallel point, from the seventh ecumenical council, occurs in the liturgy for the first Sunday in Lent (the Sunday of Orthodoxy) in the Byzantine Rite: 'The uncircumscribed Word of the Father became circumscribed, taking flesh ... This our salvation we confess in deed and word.'[50] Although this derives from another debate (about the legitimacy of icons) the central point is the same. If God in Christ appeared to our eyes, he may (and perhaps even should) be depicted, as testimony to his incarnation; and perhaps something analogous can be said about touching him sacramentally with our hands.

Stephyn, in shortening the extract, particularly emphasizes the *availability* of Christ to be touched in this way. He takes his version of the phrase from Foxe's slight reordering of the original, and his choice should be seen in the context of the Quotations which frame it, 14 and 16.

---

49 Cf. Jn 20:26-28.
50 Mother Mary and Archimandrite Kallistos Ware, tr., *The Lenten Triodion* (London: Faber & Faber, 1978), p. 306.

Quotation 16. SA 60v.14–24 (Latin) 60v.25–36 (Cornish) [and TH 57v.14–18m]

Tertullian, *De Resurrectione Mortuorum [De Resurrectione Carnis]*, 8, 2.[51]
Videamus de propria christiani hominis forma ... ut anima de Deo saginetur
(Our flesh is nourished with the body and blood of Christ)
[Foxe, TAMO, 1576, p. 1389 [1364]; (T&C vi, 455)—Cranmer's Disputation]

Tertullian (c. 150/160, fl. 190–216), a Berber from Carthage (now part of Tunis in Tunisia), was one of the first Christian apologists and an opponent of Gnosticism and other significant heresies (see Quotation 42). His sympathy for Montanism meant he was never canonized, but his writings were highly valued, not least because of their early date.[52] Here, he is arguing in favour of the resurrection of the body, against the Gnostics.[53] Far from being an obstacle, he asserts, the flesh is now the 'hinge' of salvation, because of the incarnation. The text is deeply sacramental, with allusions to the liturgy throughout (the form *iungitur* representing *ungitur/inungitur*, the anointing of either confirmation or ordination) to affirm that 'by every possible means' Christ unites us 'intimately to himself'.[54]

Cranmer asserts that it is simply not 'sound doctrine to affirm that God is touched'.[55] Chedsey replies that, on the contrary, because of the incarnation we can speak of 'touching' God.[56] In fact, the flesh is central: 'it is the said flesh that causeth the soul to be linked' to God. Cranmer makes his usual response that Tertullian cannot possibly intend a literal meaning of such words. He could accept, however, that the soul is fed by Christ, *at the same time as* the body is fed by the sacrament. Chedsey reiterates with Tertullian: 'the flesh doth eat the body'.

Clearly, for Stephyn too, to touch and eat the sacrament is to approach God through the incarnation of 'his beloved Son, our Saviour Jesus Christ'. He concludes by summarizing: 'the body of Christ is eaten by human mouth' (*Corf Christ ew dibbris gans ganaw mab dean*).

---

51 Ernest Evans, ed., *Q. Septimii Florentis Tertulliani De Resurrectione Carnis Liber/Tertullian's Treatise on the Resurrection* (London: SPCK, 1972), p. 24, lines 3–12, beginning *Videamus nunc de propria*. This work is now available online at http://tertullian.org/articles/evans_res/evans_res_01title.htm. Accessed 18 October 2018. [Following the discovery of the Codex Trecensis 523, which has *Mortuorum* in its title, the work has been renamed; see also A. Gerlo, et al., eds, *Tertulliani Opera II: Opera montanistica* (CCSL 2) [19, J.G.P. Borleffs, ed., *De resurrectione mortuorum*] p. 931 (Turnhout: Brepols, 1954), reprinted 1996 [PL 2/2 [1844], 806A.]
52 Chadwick, *The Early Church*, pp. 89–93.
53 Cf. Gergely M. Juhász, *Translating Resurrection: The Debate between William Tyndale and George Joye in its Historical and Theological Context* (Leiden: Brill, 2014), pp. 89–90.
54 Some sources had *nominis* for *hominis*. It is clearly *hominis* in SA but in Foxe it varies: 1563 *nominis*; 1570 *hominis*; 1576 *homis*; 1583 *hominis*. While this is a point against 1576 as Stephyn's source, it seems likely he simply corrected the *hom[in]is*.
55 T&C vi, 455.
56 See Quotation 15.

Quotation 17. SA 61r.3–11 (Latin) 61r.12–22 (Cornish) [and TH 51v.9–14; 53v.20–4m]

'Oecumenius of Tricca', *Commentarius in Epistolam I ad Corinthios*, on 1 Cor 11:27[57]
'Reus erit': Quod ait, reus corporis ... per haec quidem ipsos perterrefaciens
(To dishonour Christ in the sacrament is a betrayal as real as that of Judas)
[Foxe, TAMO, 1576, pp. 1389–90 [1364–5]; (T&C vi, 455–6)—Cranmer's Disputation]

This passage is common in *catenae*, in Greek and in translation.[58] (The Cornish has 'When our Saviour Christ said' prefixed. It was, of course, St Paul who said this, in 1 Cor 11:27–9, not Christ in the Gospels.)

Although some sources attribute the passage to Photius I (St Photios the Great), c. 810/20–893, archbishop of Constantinople,[59] its origin appears to be from a *catena* attributed to Oecumenius, a sixth-/seventh-century writer from Asia Minor (long believed to be the tenth-century bishop of Tricca in Thessaly). For the title and marginal reference *Reus erit*, 'will be liable, answerable', see 1 Cor 11:27.[60] The same phrase occurs in the Gospel of Matthew, translating ἔνοχος ἔσται τῇ κρίσει (Vulgate: *reus erit judicio*): 'will be liable to judgement' (Mt 5:22 NRSV).

The liability and guilt referred to applies to receiving the body of the Christ unworthily, with the aim of 'thoroughly frightening' (CH) those who treat it lightly. The incidental reference to the Jews in the passage is open to misuse: similar language has often fuelled anti-semitism in the past. It has therefore been loosely translated 'some Jews' and should be understood with reference

---

57 E.g. *Expositiones antiquae ac valde utiles brevitatem ... ab Oecumenio & Aretha collectae ...* (Verona: 1532), p. 454, beginning Ἔνοχος ἔσται. Τὸ ἔνοχος τοῦ σώματος [PG 118, 807–8C]. This is a *catena* of works by Oecumenius, Photius and others. It reappears with a Latin translation by Hententius (1547) in *Oecumenii Commentaria* (Paris: apud Carolum Morellum, 1630), vol. 1, p. 532, beginning *Reus erit*, and thence to Migne. No modern, critical edition is available (but both of the above are on Google Books). I am grateful to C.W.H. Hatcher for his help with this passage.
58 Foxe agrees with Verona 1532 (see previous note), but he lacks αὐτὸν οἱ τὸ πανάγιον αὐτοῦ σῶμα χερσὶν (referring to receiving 'his holy body' in their hands) between ἀτιμάζουσι and ἀκαθάρτοις δεξόμενοι.
59 Photius occupied in the ninth century the see that John Chrysostom did in the fifth. The passage we have here does not appear to come from his *Bibliotheca* (or *Myriobiblos*), nor his *Amphilochium*, although there are passages in the *Amphilochium* that are reminiscent, eg. Photius, *Ad Amphilochium, Q.73 (sometimes 72)*—PG 101,451–456, especially 455B and 455D).
60 'Whoever, therefore, eats the bread or drinks the cup of the Lord in an unworthy manner <u>will be answerable</u> for the body and blood of the Lord' NRSV; *Itaque quicumque manducaverit panem hunc, vel biberit calicem Domini indigne, <u>reus erit</u> corporis et sanguinis Domini*, Vulgate. (Unless specified, the Vulgate is quoted from Roger Gryson et al. (after Robert Weber), eds, *Biblia Sacra iuxta Vulgatam versionem [Biblia Sacra Vulgata]* (Stuttgart: Deutsche Bibelgesellschaft, 1994), here from p. 1781.)

to a small number of individuals in a concrete historical situation, and not of a whole people.

Since this passage follows on quickly from that of Tertullian (as Cranmer complains) it is never really answered, as both Chedsey and Weston continue to press home the arguments from Tertullian, and this distracts Cranmer.

In SA it serves to reinforce the point that the body of Christ can be taken in human hands—indeed in impure hands and received by an impure mouth (although to condemnation). In other words, Christ is not merely present in the sacrament to those of good faith and conscience, but in an objective way.

Quotation 18. SA 61r.23 (Latin) 61r.23-4 (Cornish)

Weston quoting Tertullian, *De Resurrectione Mortuorum*, 8, 2.[61]
Corpus vescitur ut anima saginetur
(The body feeds [on the body of Christ] that the soul may feast [on God])
[Foxe, TAMO, 1576, p. 1390 [1365]; (T&C vi, 456)—Cranmer's Disputation

Weston and Chedsey press home their point: Tertullian claims that we, mere creatures of flesh, feed on the body and blood of Christ, and thereby feast (lit. 'are fattened') on God.[62] Cranmer reintroduces his customary distinction: Tertullian must surely be saying that the body feeds on the sacrament, while the soul feeds on God simultaneously. He cannot possibly be speaking in a 'literal' way.

Stephyn incorporates this pithy redaction by Chedsey as a summary of his convictions about the physical and spiritual feeding that take place in the sacrament. Unlike Cranmer, he has no difficulty in seeing their essential unity.

Quotation 19. SA 61r.25-7 (Cornish only)

Chedsey paraphrasing Oecumenius, *in Epistolam I ad Corinthios*, on 1 Cor 11:27.[63]
Neb uge o recivia Corf Dew gans dowla mustethas ... kepar a ve Judas
(Those who receive the body with impure hands, are guilty of the Lord's blood)
[Foxe, TAMO, 1576, p. 1390 [1365]; (T&C vi, 457)—Cranmer's Disputation]

Chedsey paraphrases the earlier quotation from 'Photius' (Oecumenius), but again it receives little attention, as Weston follows immediately with more

---

61 Evans, ed., *Tertulliani: De Resurrectione Carnis*, p. 24, lines 3-12 [PL 2/2 [1844], 806A]. See Quotation 16.
62 Bettenson, *The Early Christian Fathers*, p. 148; Weston's phrase is a contraction of Tertullian's fuller one: *Caro corpore et sanguine vescitur, ut et anima Deo saginetur*.
63 [Oecumenius], *Expositiones antiquae*, p. 454. See Quotation 17.

from Tertullian. (All the disputants may have felt on uncertain ground with Quotation 17, its attribution and authenticity.)

Nonetheless, Stephyn adds Chedsey's reinforcement to his *catena*. Generally, he moves straight to the next patristic quotation in Latin, but from time to time he approves of one of the Disputants' interventions sufficiently to include it.

He clearly thinks the objective presence of Christ in the sacrament is underlined if St Paul can discuss unworthy reception. The comparison is to Judas, who ate at the Last Supper, knowing he was going to betray Christ (Mt 26:20–25).

Quotation 20. SA 61r.28–9 (Latin) 61r. 29–30 (Cornish)

Weston quoting Tertullian, *De Resurrectione Mortuorum*, 8, 2.[64]
Non possunt ergo separari in mercede, quos opera coniungit
(Partaking of the sacrament feeds both body and soul)
[Foxe, TAMO, 1576, p. 1390 [1365]; (T&C vi, 457)—Cranmer's Disputation]

The argument returns to Tertullian, although his point here is a very general one: flesh and soul work together in this life and reach the end of life together. It is therefore fitting that they are together in the resurrection. As Cranmer puts it: 'the flesh shall rise again, because it is joined in one work with the soul'. It is difficult to argue (with Weston) that 'work' here refers to eating, or 'manducation'. His 'expounding' of Tertullian, *una opera coniungit, sed non idem operandi modus*, is not in itself a quotation. But he uses it to assert that, just as body and soul are inseparably linked, so are spiritual and sacramental realities. If God choses to work through visible signs and sacraments, and we treat them irreverently or lightly, we are rejecting what God considers important for our human nature.

This emphasis appears to have struck a chord with the editor of SA, who had lived through the Edwardine rejection of so much outward symbolism, its restoration under Mary, then the loss of a good deal of it once again under Elizabeth.

---

64 Evans, ed., *Tertulliani: De Resurrectione Carnis*, p. 24, lines 3–12 [PL 2/2 [1844], 806A]. See Quotation 16.

Quotation 21. SA 61r.31–41 (Cornish only)

Chedsey quoting St Hilary of Poitiers, *De Trinitate*, 8, 13–14.[65]
Christ a gemeras kigg ha ve genys ... eth ew verely kyg ha verely gois
(We receive truly, under a mystery, the flesh of Christ's body)
[Foxe, TAMO, 1576, p. 1392 [1367]; (T&C vi, 460–61)—Cranmer's Disputation]

This is the second of two simplified extracts from *De Trinitate* (the first was at Quotation 3). Part of the argument concerns a textual difference: whether Hilary said 'we receive truly, under a mystery, the flesh of his body' or 'we receive, under a true mystery, the flesh of his body'. The former is correct.[66]

Hilary's exile, in an Arian-dominated region of modern Turkey, reinforced for him the definitions of the Council of Nicaea and baptism in the name of 'the Father and of the Son and of the Holy Spirit' (Mt 28:19 NRSV). Equally, he sees the Eucharist as reflecting the incarnation: 'he has mingled the nature of his flesh with the nature of eternity under the sacrament of the flesh which is communicated to us'.[67]

Chedsey accuses Cranmer of misrepresenting the text of *De Trinitate* in his book on the Eucharist.[68] More seriously, however, Cranmer resists the idea that Christ assumed our 'existing' flesh at his incarnation. He argues that a new creation of humanity flows from Christ's nativity. Weston scents heresy here, and bids the notaries to 'Write, sirs', but Cranmer, strangely confident, urges them 'Yea, write.'

Once again, the substance of the passage from Hilary is not discussed in detail. Stephyn, in choosing it, shows that his mind remains focused on the parallels between incarnational and sacramental theology. Christ takes on our flesh in his incarnation, and we receive his flesh in the Eucharist. For him, as for Chedsey, 'there is left no place of doubt'.

---

65 Smulders, ed., *Hilarii: De Trinitate* [CCSL 62A], pp. 325–6 [PL 10, 246B]. See Quotation 3.
66 *De Trinitate* 8, 13, reads: *Si vere igitur carnem corporis nostri Christus assumpsit, et vere homo ille, qui ex Maria natus fuit, Christus est, nosque vere sub mysterio carnem corporis sui sumimus, et per hoc unum erimus*, continuing (after a quotation from Jn 6:55) at 8, 14 with: *De veritate carnis et sanguinis non est relictus ambigendi locus. Nunc enim et ipsius Domini professione, et fide nostra vere caro est, et vere sanguis est.* For a similar version see Tunstall, *De ueritate Corporis et Sanguinis*, ff. 63v, 64.
67 Henry Bettenson, ed. and tr., *The Later Christian Fathers* (Oxford: Oxford University Press, 1974), p. 57; Chadwick, *The Early Church*, p. 213.
68 Thomas Cranmer, *A defence of the true and catholike doctrine of the sacrament of the body and bloud of our sauiour Christ [...] approued by ye consent of the moste auncient doctors of the Churche* (London: Reginald Wolfe, 1550). Cranmer acknowledges in the Disputation he may have previously misquoted Hilary (with *vero* rather than *vere*) but attributes the mistake to one of his sources (perhaps Gardiner, although a small number of manuscripts also give this variant).

Quotation 22. SA 61v.3–22 (Latin)
61v.22–36 (Cornish) [and TH 58r.1–6m]

St Ambrose, *De Mysteriis*, 1, 9, 52.[69]
De totius mundi operibus legisti ... quod Sermo sonat, affectus sentiat
(The word of Christ can change the nature of things)
[Foxe, TAMO, 1576, p. 1393 [1368]; (T&C vi, 463)—Cranmer's Disputation]

Ambrose (Ambrosius Aurelianus), c. 340–397, was Roman governor of Liguria and Emilia before being made bishop of Mediolanum (Milan) by popular acclaim in 374.[70] An opponent of Arianism, his sacramental teaching was deeply rooted in the incarnation. Such teaching was reserved for the baptized and protected by the *disciplina arcani*, 'the discipline of the secret' which, although less evident in the first centuries, was well established by Ambrose's time. As the neophytes journeyed through Lent, the deeper meaning of the Scriptures was explained to them until they received the Creed on Palm Sunday. Then, through Holy Week and Easter Week, alongside the direct experience of Christian initiation, came teaching on the Lord's Prayer and the sacraments, including the mystery of the Eucharist. The value of *De Mysteriis* is that it appears to derive from 'shorthand' notes for such instruction, preached around the year 387.[71] This may explain its 'unliterary' nature, and why phrases are included that appear to be mere subheadings: as notes they were never polished.

There was little dispute about the authorship of this work until the sixteenth century, when inconsistencies in style and the biblical text used were stressed. By the nineteenth century, however, these were challenged in turn,[72] and, while agreement is not universal, the modern consensus is that *De Mysteriis* is indeed by Ambrose, on account of similarities with themes in his other works.[73]

---

69   Josef Schmitz, ed. *De Sacramentis. De Mysteriis/Über die Sakramente. Über die Mysterien* [Fontes Christiani] (Freiburg: Herder, 1990), pp. 246 (line 17)–248 (line 17). This takes full account of Otto Faller, *Ambrosius: Explanatio symboli, De sacramentis, De mysteriis, De paenitentia, De excessu fratris Satyri, De obitu Valentiniani, De obitu Theodosii* (CSEL 73) (Vienna: Hoelder-Pichler-Tempsky, 1955). [PL 16, 406C]. SA/Foxe differs from Schmitz's text in only a few minor respects.
70   Chadwick, *The Early Church*, pp. 167–68; 240–41; 268–69.
71   Cf. Schmitz, *De Sacramentis*, pp. 15–63; Roy J. Deferrari, *St Ambrose: Theological and Dogmatic Works* (Washington: Catholic University of America, 1963), pp. 265–67. *De Mysteriis* was also titled *De iis, qui initiantur mysteriis*, as at 61v.2–4m.
72   See the Introduction in Dom Bernard Botte, *Ambroise de Milan, Des Sacrements, Des Mystères, Explication du Symbole*, Sources Chrétiennes 25bis (Paris: Editions du Cerf, 1994) and Roy J. Deferrari, *St Ambrose: Theological and Dogmatic Works* (Washington: Catholic University of America, 1963), pp. 265–67.
73   For example, his characteristic 'eastern' use of the Song of Songs in initiation, the value he places on the 'foot-washing' and parallels with his book *On Abraham*. See T. Thompson and

If so, it is a remarkable survival, and a window into the most profound elements of Christianity in the fourth century. Young may well have been working from an edition,[74] rather than a *catena*.[75] 61v.3–4 is a direct quotation of Ps 148:5 Vulgate, *Quia ipse dixit et facta sunt, ipse mandavit et creata sunt* (see Ps 148:5 NRSV: 'he commanded and they were created', reflecting the shorter version in the Masoretic text).[76] The marginal reference is to Ps 105: 31–34 (Vulgate 104: 31–34) where the Lord again 'speaks' and his will is immediately executed by the natural world.

Cranmer appears to accept the attribution to Ambrose, and is clearly rattled by Young, whom he accuses of 'sophistical cavillation', 'subtleness' and 'crafty fetches'.[77] The argument is once again about the words 'This is my Body'.[78] Young and Weston argue they should be taken at their face value and must surely have 'wrought somewhat'. Cranmer retorts that this idea is contrary to 'all the old writers'. Young then cites Ambrose's teaching on the Eucharistic consecration. Avoiding a response, Cranmer exclaims 'O glorious words! You are too full of words' and simply restates his opposition to the idea of any real change in the sacrament, saying that 'God worketh in his faithful, not in the sacraments.'[79]

By selecting these quotations and omitting some of the surrounding debate, Stephyn focuses on the action of the Word of God: 'Let the heart perceive well the word that is sounded' (*gas an golan percyvia da, an geer a vo soundis*). Why else would Ambrose be arguing that Christ has the power to change the nature of things, in the context of the words 'This is my Body', if he does not believe a real change to take place?[80]

J.H. Srawley, eds, *St Ambrose on the Mysteries and the Treatise on The Sacraments by an unknown author*, Translations of Christian Literature, Series III, Liturgical Texts (London: SPCK, 1919) pp. xiv–xvi.

74 John Young (1514-1580) was born in Yorkshire and took part in Disputations from an early date. He came before the Privy Council in 1551 for opposing Edward's reforms, but was rehabilitated under Mary, becoming Regius Professor at Cambridge. On the accession of Elizabeth, he was deprived and imprisoned successively in the Counter, the Marshalsea and Wisbech Castle, where he died. Cf. Judith Ford, 'John Young, 1514–1581/2', in *Oxford Dictionary of National Biography* online, https://doi.org/10.1093/ref:odnb/30267. Accessed 20 October 2018.

75 The text in Foxe is similar but not identical to the (shorter) extracts in Tunstall, *De ueritate Corporis et Sanguinis*, f. 77r; Tavernier, *De veritate Corporis et Sanguinis*, f. 37v.

76 Gryson et al., eds, *Biblia Sacra Vulgata*, p. 952.

77 T&C vi, 462.

78 1 Cor 11:24, Mk 14:22, Mt 26:26, Lk 22:19.

79 T&C vi, 464.

80 61v.39–41; T&C vi, 461.

Quotation 23. SA 61v.38–62r.13 (Latin) 62r.13–28 (Cornish) [and TH 55r.8–16m; 57r.1–5]

'St Ambrose', *De Sacramentis*, 4, 4, 14.[81]
Panis iste, panis est, ante verba Sacramentorum ... et in aliud commutentur
(The word of Christ makes this sacrament the flesh of Christ)
[Foxe, TAMO, 1576, p. 1393 [1368]; (T&C vi, 463–4)—Cranmer's Disputation]

De Sacramentis ('On the Sacraments'), by contrast with *De Mysteriis*, is less securely attributed to Ambrose in its current form, although it quotes from a pre-Gelasian Canon and refers to Arianism.[82] It quotes *De Mysteriis* itself, however, and has a similar link to Easter homilies preached to neophytes. A northern Italian provenance is likely, within Rome's influence yet touched by Milan's distinctive traditions. The reformers, while questioning its attribution, probably welcomed what they may have seen as its less 'carnal' approach to the Eucharist than *De Mysteriis*. Phrases such as *in similitudinem*, 'in a likeness', echo earlier Western language and seem to moderate other phrases in Ambrose.[83]

Like Foxe and SA, Tunstall omits *in superioribus, a sacerdote dicuntur* (a confusion arising from two occurrences of *dicuntur* in the original, perhaps mediated by Erasmus).[84] The original meaning is that in prayers of petition the priest may use his own words, but for the consecration he must use the words of Christ.[85] The passage (clearly borrowing from Quotation 22) reiterates that the bread becomes 'the flesh of Christ' by the word of Christ. Weston urges Young to continue to the next section (Quotation 24 below), which ends: 'it was not the body of Christ before consecration ... but ... now it is the Body of Christ'. Cranmer concedes that such language is common in the Fathers, accepting now that 'God doth chiefly work in the sacraments'. Despite this concession, however, he remains unwilling to accept any change in the elements of bread and wine themselves—only 'in the faithful'.

While following the order of the Disputation here, Stephyn contributes typical simplifications and perhaps some liturgical resonances. 'Was born of

---

81 Schmitz, *De Sacramentis*, pp. 142–4. [PL 16, 439B]. This is substantially the same text as in Foxe/SA, except for the omission noted above and the absence of *Consecratione* and *operationem* (the latter also being omitted from Foxe).
82 Thompson and Srawley, eds, *St Ambrose on the Mysteries*, pp. xvi–xx. There is a seventh century manuscript, however: St Gallen MS 188.
83 Thompson and Srawley, *St Ambrose on the Mysteries and the Treatise on The Sacraments*, p. xxxvii.
84 Tunstall, *De ueritate Corporis et Sanguinis*, f. 77v.
85 The correct *de pane fit caro Christi*, as at 61v.38, corresponds with Foxe 1563. This *fit* became *sit* in 1570 but was corrected back to *fit* in 1576. No edition of Foxe appears to have the *operationem* found at 62r.10.

the Virgin Mary', *a ve genis urth an Worthias Maria* 61v.27 and, below it, 'Was crucified, dead and buried', *a ve goris in crows, marow ha inclethis* 61v.28-9, echo phrases from the Apostles' Creed. Permission was granted to teach this in Cornish in certain parishes, and perhaps Stephyn was drawing from such a version as he departs slightly from Young.[86] (The other liturgical phrase found in this passage: 'This is my Body', *hemma ew ow Corf ve*, 61v.30-1, would have been said in Latin in the liturgy, rather than Cornish. See Notes on 65v.21-2 for a further example.)

Quotation 24. SA 62r.29-33 (Latin) 62r.34-9 (Cornish)

'St Ambrose', *De Sacramentis*, 4, 4, 14.[87]
Cælum non erat ... post consecrationem dico tibi iam Corpus Christi est
(After the consecration ... it is the Body of Christ)
[Foxe, TAMO, 1576, p. 1393 [1368]; (T&C vi, 464)—Cranmer's Disputation]

This is a continuation of Quotation 23. Although, as noted above, *De Sacramentis* asserts the real presence less strongly than *De Mysteriis*, here it goes the other way—hence Weston's urging its use. The phrase from *De Mysteriis* 'after the consecration the Body is signified' (*post consecrationem corpus significatur*) becomes 'after the consecration, I tell you that now the Body of Christ is there' (*post consecrationem dico tibi quod jam corpus Christi est*).

Cranmer chooses to divert the argument to wider questions (such as the change in the faithful wrought in baptism) claiming the change meant here is a change in the believing community.

As expected, Stephyn omits Cranmer's responses and simply uses the passage as Weston intended, to strengthen and clarify what has gone before.

---

86 As, for example, in Veysey's instructions following his May 1538 visitation: James Gairdner, ed., *Letters and Papers, Foreign & Domestic, Henry VIII* (London: HMSO, 1892), vol. 13, pt. 1, January–July 1538 (30 Henry VIII), vol. 1, p. 403, no. 1106.
87 Schmitz, ed., *De Sacramentis*, p. 144. [PL 16, 439B]. Again, there are only minor differences from the text as in Foxe/SA. Note that it is still from *De Sacramentis* 4, 4 and not from 4, 5 as SA cites. See Quotation 23.

Quotation 25. SA 62r.40–41 (Latin) 62r.41–4 (Cornish) [and TH 56v.1–5m]

'St Ambrose', *De Sacramentis*, 4, 5, 23.[88]
Antequam consecretur, panis est ... Corpus est Christi
(When the words of Christ come upon it, it is the Body of Christ)
[Foxe, TAMO, 1576, p. 1393 [1368]; (T&C vi, 464)—Cranmer's Disputation]

This is a further continuation of *De Sacramentis*, as above. The text as we have it was often quoted. St Thomas Aquinas makes the same theological point,[89] but quoting *De Mysteriis*, 9, 3.

Young, perhaps uneasy with some of the earlier exchanges on 'likeness', introduces this passage, which is unambiguous: 'when the words of Christ come to it, it is the Body of Christ'. Cranmer first tries to argue that this refers to the 'strength' of Christ at work in the sacramental action, rather than any real presence in the sacrament itself. When Pie returns to the words 'there is made the blood',[90] Cranmer concedes at least that the 'sacrament of the blood' is 'made'. Interpreted narrowly, he could be suggesting a 'sacramental' (even if not substantial) presence under the signs of bread and wine; interpreted broadly he could simply mean the whole sacramental action brings the Blood of Christ close to the believer. Indeed, he continues, 'not that the blood is in the cup, but in the receiver'. (Although Cranmer was influenced away from simple receptionism by Ridley, at times he still comes close to it.)

Stephyn omits the exchanges between Young, Weston and Cranmer and moves directly to the next quotation. His focus remains on Christ's words, and the change they work in making 'the blood of Christ which redeemed the people' really present.

---

88 Schmitz, ed., *De Sacramentis*, pp. 148–50, the same text as Foxe/SA. [PL 16, 444A]. See Quotation 23.
89 *Summa Theologica*, III, Q. 75, Art 3. See also Art 7. *Corpus Thomisticum*, Accessed 10 October 2018.
90 William Pie (or Pye) (*c.* 1500–1557), was principal of St Mary's Hall, Oxford and archdeacon of Berkshire under Henry, then canon of Lichfield under Edward. Mary made him dean of Chichester, canon of Westminster and, shortly before he died, canon of St George's Chapel, Windsor. Cf. Claire Cross, 'The English Universities, 1553–58' and Thomas F. Mayer, 'The Success of Cardinal Pole's Final Legation', both in Duffy and Loades, eds, *The Church of Mary Tudor*, pp. 65, 170; also S.L. Ollard, *Fasti Wyndesorienses* (Windsor: Dean and Canons of St George's Chapel, May 1950) and W.D. Peckham, *The Acts of the Dean and Chapter of the Cathedral Church of Chichester, 1545-1642* (Cambridge: Sussex Record Society, 1959), Nos. 523, 525, 567.

Quotation 26. SA 62v.3–6 (Latin) 62v.3–4, 7–9 (Cornish)

'St Ambrose', *De Sacramentis*, 4, 5, 23.[91]
Accipite, edite, hoc est Corpus meum ... ibi sanguis efficitur, qui redemit plebem
(When the words of Christ are spoken, it is made the Blood of Christ)
[Foxe, TAMO, 1576, p. 1393 [1368]; (T&C vi, 464)—Cranmer's Disputation]

Again, this passage follows on almost immediately from the previous ones in *De Sacramentis*. The scriptural quotation at the beginning 'Take, eat, this is my Body' (*Accipite, edite, hoc est Corpus meum*), is close to the Vulgate version of Mt 26: 26 (*Accipite et comedite hoc est corpus meum*).[92] Some versions of *De Sacramentis* have *Accipite, et edite ex eo omnes; hoc est enim corpus meum*, which is closer to the form in the Roman Canon (*Accipite et manducate ex hoc omnes: hoc est enim corpus meum*). The edition used by Young (or Foxe) may have been more deliberately 'biblical'.

The passage continues: 'before the words of Christ, the cup is full of wine and water: when the words of Christ are wrought, there is made the blood of Christ'. This relatively straightforward language still does not bring Cranmer to accept any transformation of the elements. He is convinced that any patristic quotations of this nature simply cannot be intended in a literal sense.

Stephyn slightly separates Christ's words from those from *De Sacramentis*, by translating the former before moving on to the latter. Once again, the passage is well grouped with others that assert the ability of Christ to work any change he wishes.

Quotation 27. SA 62v.9–10 (Cornish only)

Young
Pandra ill bos moy playn?
(What can be more plain?)
[Foxe, TAMO, 1576, p. 1393 [1368]; (T&C vi, 464)—Cranmer's Disputation]

In fairness to Young, the previous passage (Quotation 26) is fairly plain, but Cranmer replies boldly: 'Nay, what can be less to the purpose?' He repeatedly indicates that such passages will always be 'figurative' for him, since 'no man having any judgement' could contemplate the alternative.[93] The frustration

---

91 Schmitz, ed., *De Sacramentis*, p. 150. The biblical passage has been slightly changed in Foxe/SA, as described above, and *plebem* and *redemit* are also inverted in the following patristic passage. [PL 16, 444A]. See Quotation 23.
92 Gryson et al., eds, *Biblia Sacra Vulgata*, p. 1568.
93 T&C vi, 453 and commentary on Quotation 12.

COMMENTARY

of his opponents with this stance is palpable. On the one hand, he insists he is guided by Scripture and the writers of the early Church: on the other, he imposes his private judgement over what their texts can be allowed to say.

It is always interesting, however, when Stephyn includes a phrase that has not attracted his attention merely because it is one of the chain of Latin quotations in Foxe. He must feel, with Young, that *De Sacramentis* could hardly be clearer.

Quotation 28. SA 62v.10–12 (Latin) 62v.13–17 (Cornish)

'St Ambrose', *De Sacramentis*, 4, 4, 15.[94]
Vides quam operatorius sit sermo Christi ... Si ergo tanta vis in sermone Domini
(The word of Christ is effective)
[Foxe, TAMO, 1576, p. 1393 [1368]; (T&C vi, 464)—Cranmer's Disputation]

See Quotation 23 above, from which this is a partial extract, repeated by Young, as the words *et ut supra*, *kepar del ve leveris kyns* and 'as was said before' all indicate.

Stephyn follows Young in reintroducing a quotation whose value he must feel keenly. If the world came into being through the Word, then that same Word surely has the power to work a miraculous change. For Stephyn, as for Young, this is not difficult to believe, and Cranmer's rebuttal remains unsatisfactory.

Quotation 29. SA 62v.20–32 (Latin) 62v.32–63r.7 (Cornish) [and TH 52v.11–14m; 55v.7–20m]

'St Ambrose', *De Sacramentis*, 6, 1, 1.[95]
Forte dicas, quomodo vera? ... sed vere naturae gratiam virtutemque consequeris
(The truth of the Blood lies beneath the 'similitude')
[Foxe, TAMO, 1576, p. 1394 [1369]; (T&C vi, 465)—Cranmer's Disputation]

This text was often found in patristic *catenae*, as in Gratian's *Decrees*,[96] or Tavernier,[97] and contains an early translation or paraphrase of Jn 6:68, where

---

[94] Schmitz, *De Sacramentis*, pp. 142–4. [PL 16, 440B].
[95] Schmitz, *De Sacramentis*, p. 180. [PL 16, 454C]. See Quotation 23.
[96] *Decretum Gratiani*, digital edition, Accessed 1 October 2018. Pars 3, *De Consecratione*, Dist. II, C. XLIII. [PL 187, 1751A].
[97] Tavernier, *De veritate Corporis et Sanguinis*, f. 39v.

Peter expresses his trust in the Christ's words about eating his flesh and drinking his blood.⁹⁸

Cranmer now seizes on the word 'similitude'. Weston replies that this cannot mean that the sacrament is a mere 'likeness', but that 'it is ministered under another likeness', since the passage also says the 'blood which redeemed the people' is 'made'. He quotes from *De Sacramentis* 6, 1, where 'similitude' clearly refers to the outward sign under which 'the truth of the blood' subsists, to protect us from a 'certain horror of blood' (*horror cruoris*) that might otherwise occur.⁹⁹ Indeed, the passage recalls that some disciples, horrified at Christ's words about eating his Body and drinking his Blood, departed from him. Only Peter fully trusted these 'words of eternal life'. Cranmer simply sticks to his guns. If it is accepted that we receive *under* a 'similitude', then we should be able to assert that the whole sacrament *is* a 'similitude', even in its nature.

Stephyn uses the passage to underline the effectiveness of Christ's word, 'which so worketh, that it can change and turn kinds ordained by nature'. He retains the section which about the potential objection to 'eating and drinking' the Body and Blood of Christ. No doubt he encountered similar objections, given the time at which he was working. The passage accepts that, while we receive the true grace and power of Christ's own 'nature' in the sacrament, we need to do so under signs congenial to the human mind. Leaving aside Cranmer's reply, Stephyn then moves directly to the next passage from *De Sacramentis*.

Quotation 30. SA 63r.8–16 (Latin)
63r.17–26 (Cornish) [and TH 57v.27+ (28–30)]

'St Ambrose', *De Sacramentis*, 4, 4, 19.¹⁰⁰
Si operatus est sermo cœlestis in aliis rebus ... Corpus est Christi
(What you receive is the Body of Christ)
[Foxe, TAMO, 1576, p. 1394 [1369]; (T&C vi, 465)—Cranmer's Disputation]

The need for an 'outward sacramental form', to avoid any 'horror' at the idea of eating flesh and drinking blood, is now reinforced.¹⁰¹ ('Species' is the technical term in Catholic theology for this outward form. The concept is rooted in a belief that 'what is seen [τὸ βλεπόμενον] was made from things that are not visible', or 'was not made out of visible things [μὴ ἐκ φαινομένων]', but rather

---

98 'Lord to whom can we go? You have the words of eternal life' (NRSV). Compare Jn 6:69 Vulgate *Domine, ad quem ibimus: verba vitae aeternae habes*, Gryson et al., eds, *Biblia Sacra Vulgata*, p. 1670.
99 Schmitz, *De Sacramentis*, p. 180. [PL 16, 455A].
100 Schmitz, *De Sacramentis*, pp. 146–8. [PL 16, 442B–443A]. See Quotation 23.
101 Aquinas adds two other reasons: avoiding the misunderstanding of unbelievers and fostering faith: *Summa Theologica*, III, Q. 75, Art. 5, 4. *Corpus Thomisticum*, Accessed 10 October 2018.

from underlying realities, ultimately deriving from the word and mind of God himself.)[102]

Chedsey focuses on the phrase 'wine and water is put into that cup ... by consecration ... it is made blood.' This is, of course, a difficult passage for Cranmer. He argues cleverly that the author is using language itself in a sacramental way: 'he useth the signs for the things signified'. Conceding that, in this author, 'bread is not called bread, but his body', he maintains that this is done to underline the 'excellency and dignity' of the sacrament. He even goes so far as to acknowledge that we 'receive the mystical cup of his blood'—but only in a 'type or figure'.

Stephyn makes subtle changes in the Cornish version that go beyond the English and Latin originals. The most striking of these is the phrase 'so you drink his Precious Blood' (*indella eth esta eva e precius gois* 63r.23), whereas Foxe has 'thou drinkest the similitude of his precious bloud'. For Stephyn, there is no need for the word 'similitude'.

Quotation 31. SA 63r.27–33 (Latin)
63r.33–7 (Cornish) [and TH 56r.26+ (27–9)]

St Justin, Martyr, *Apologiae*, 1, 66.[103]
Quemadmodum per verbum Dei ... carnem et sanguinem esse accepimus
(The food consecrated by the word of prayer is the flesh and blood of Jesus)
[Foxe, TAMO, 1576, p. 1394 [1369]; (T&C vi, 466)—Cranmer's Disputation]

Justin Martyr (*c.* 100–*c.* 165) was born in the Greek-speaking town of Flavia Neapolis (ancient Shechem, now Nablus under the Palestinian Authority). Initially a student of Pythagoras and the Stoics, he was deeply impressed by Christians he knew and embraced their faith. His *First Apology* was probably written in around 155–157, possibly as a response to the martyrdom of Polycarp.[104] He has great importance because of his very early date: his Greek

---

102 Cf. Heb 11:3 NRSV and note; also note 8 in this Commentary. The phrase *mortis similitudinem sumsisti* 63r.13 ('you took on the form of death') is a reference to baptism, since St Paul likens the symbolic immersion to being buried (Rom 6:4).
103 Cf. Charles Munier, ed. *Saint Justin: Apologie pour le Chretiens* [Sources Chrétiennes 507] (Paris: Éditions du Cerf, 2006), p. 306, beginning ἀλλ' ὃν τρόπον διὰ λόγου θεοῦ σαρκοποιηθεὶς [PG 6, 427C]; Basil Lanneau Gildersleeve, ed. *The Apologies of Justin Martyr, to which is appended the Epistle to Diagnotus* (New York: Harper & Brothers, 1877), pp. 62-3. (Despite the marginal note—*Apolog. 2*—in SA, in modern editions this extract is found in the *First Apology*, chapter 66.)
104 For more background see Chadwick, *The Early Church*, pp. 74-81.

original is given by Chedsey and reported in Foxe.[105] It is, however, susceptible to different interpretations.[106]

Justin points out that the persecutors of the Christians are hypocrites, guilty of the very immorality and human sacrifice they wrongly attribute to their victims. He demonstrates that doctrines such as those concerning the Eucharist are far from 'carnal' and surpass in profundity all the pagan philosophy he has studied. Humanity is now nourished by the incarnate Christ, who took on human nature.

Chedsey reinforces this link with the incarnation. Quoting Justin, he asserts that 'As ... Jesus Christ ... had both flesh and blood for our salvation ... so ... our blood and flesh are nourished by communion', which is 'the flesh and blood of the same Jesus.' The quotation is very telling. Cranmer cannot deny that Justin speaks of being nourished by the Body of Christ, but wishes to maintain a distinction between the (sacramental) bread nourishing the body, and the (heavenly) Body of Christ nourishing the soul.[107]

Stephyn, after including the passage from Justin, chooses once again to move from Cranmer's Disputation to Ridley's for a fuller version of the text. Perhaps to his satisfaction, it occurs in the context of claims that Cranmer had expanded and explained the original version in such a way as to change its meaning.

Quotation 32. SA 63v.2–8 (Latin) 63v.9–11 (Cornish)

St Justin, Martyr, *Apologiae*, 1, 66.[108]
Neque vero hæc pro pane potuve communi sumimus ... esse sumus edocti
(We do not take this for common bread and drink)
[Foxe, TAMO, 1576, p. 1404 [1379]; (T&C vi, 489–90)—Ridley's Disputation]

This is the same passage as Quotation 32 but beginning earlier, and in a slightly different translation. In Ridley's Disputation it forms part of a debate as to whether the meaning of the words 'This is my Body' are figurative or not. Ward

---

105 [ἀλλ'] ὃν τρόπον διὰ λόγου θεοῦ σαρκοποιηθεὶς Ἰησοῦς Χριστὸς ὁ σωτὴρ ἡμῶν καὶ σάρκα καὶ αἷμα ὑπὲρ σωτηρίας ἡμῶν ἔσχεν: οὕτως καὶ τὴν δι' εὐχῆς λόγου τοῦ παρ' αὐτοῦ εὐχαριστηθεῖσαν τροφήν, ἐξ ἧς αἷμα καὶ σάρκες κατὰ μεταβολὴν τρέφονται ἡμῶν, ἐκείνου τοῦ σαρκοποιηθέντος Ἰησοῦ καὶ σάρκα καὶ αἷμα ἐδιδάχθημεν εἶναι.

106 Bettenson, *The Early Christian Fathers*, p. 62, suggests δι' εὐχῆς λόγου, 'through word of prayer' could also represent 'the prayer of the word' or even 'the prayer of the Word who came from him'.

107 Weston challenges this at Quotation 33 (q.v., with the notes for Quotation 50).

108 Munier, ed., *Saint Justin: Apologie*, p. 306, beginning Οὐ γὰρ ὡς κοινὸν ἄρτον οὐδὲ κοινὸν πόμα ταῦτα λαμβάνομεν, Gildersleeve, ed., *Apologies of Justin*, p. 62 [PG 6, 427C]. See Quotation 31.

implies that Cranmer has translated Justin wrongly (although the passage in Cranmer is more of an exposition than a translation).

Stephyn has deliberately departed from the sequence of Cranmer's Disputation to include this second, fuller translation of Justin, including the words *Neque vero haec pro pane potuve communi sumimus* ('Neither do we take this for common bread and drink'). Indeed, this is the portion Stephyn translates into Cornish, not repeating the whole.[109] Once again, he stresses his belief that the elements, 'when ... consecrated', become the 'flesh and blood of our Saviour Jesus Christ'.

Quotation 33. SA 63v.12–16 (Latin) 63v.17–21 (Cornish)

St Irenaeus, *Adversus Haereses*, 5, 2, 2–3.[110]
Eum calicem qui est creatura ... augetur et consistit carnis nostræ substantia
(Our flesh is strengthened by the sacrament of the body and blood of Christ)
[Foxe, TAMO, 1576, p. 1394 [1369]; (T&C vi, 466)—Cranmer's Disputation]

Irenaeus (130–202) was born in Greek-speaking Smyrna (modern Izmir in Turkey) but served as a bishop in Lugdunum (Lyon in France). Like Justin, he was valued for his early date and the survival of early manuscripts.[111] In his *Adversus Haereses*, chiefly against Gnosticism, he speaks of the moment 'when ... the cup that is mixed, and the bread that is made, takes on the word of God'.[112] Affirming the resurrection of the body against the Gnostics, he turns to St Paul's First Letter to the Corinthians. The chalice is a new covenant in the blood of Christ; the bread which we break is Christ's body.[113] In other words, far from rejecting the body, God takes the created cup of wine and makes it his own blood. A 'spiritual' Christ did not come to an alien 'material' world, but to his own creation—which he uses, by his incarnation, in his work of salvation.

---

109 He also writes *per mutacionem etriuntur* for Foxe's *per immutacionem enutriuntur*, probably a copying error.
110 Adelin Rousseau et al., eds, *Irénée de Lyon, Contre les hérésies: Dénonciation et refutation de la gnose au nom menteur*, nouvelle edition (Paris: Éditions du Cerf, 2001), pp. 573–74 [PG 7/1, 1125–6].
111 Eg. Cambridge University Library MS 4113, Papyrus Oxyrhyncus 505, dated between 174 and 189. The full and original title was 'The Detection and Overthrow of the So-Called Gnosis' (ἔλεγχος καὶ ἀνατροπὴ τῆς ψευδωνύμου γνώσεως). A Latin translation survives, and Greek quotations in other authors, with partially surviving Syriac and Armenian versions. For further context see Chadwick, *The Early Church*, pp. 79–84.
112 Ὁπότε οὖν καὶ τὸ κεκραμένον ποτήριον, καὶ ὁ γεγονὼς ἄρτος ἐπιδέχεται τὸν λόγον τοῦ Θεοῦ. Weston's (or Foxe's) *fractus* (63v.14) derives from a misreading of *factus* (γεγονὼς) in a Latin translation.
113 1 Cor 12:24–25.

The strange phrase (in Weston) that 'the same cup which is a creature, he confirmed to be his body' is explained by a copying omission, owing to the double occurrence of *creatura*. The omitted portions are underlined: 'He has confirmed the cup (which is a created thing) <u>to be his own blood, from which he gives life to our blood; and the bread (also a created thing)</u> to be his own body', etc.[114]

Cranmer is clear that, for him, there can be no confusion between the soul's food and the body's food. While the sacrament nourishes our bodies, Christ's Body—which is in heaven and no longer on earth—separately nourishes our souls. Chedsey, Cole and Weston believe something rather different: that the whole Christ—body, soul and divinity—is present in the sacrament and feeds the whole human person, body and soul. Weston cites Irenaeus to confirm that the substance of our flesh is increased by the 'sacrament of the body and blood of Christ' itself. Cranmer fastens on the distinction between 'sacrament' and 'body and blood', claiming support from Tertullian. His paraphrase departs from the original, however,[115] and Weston comes back with another passage from the same writer that undermines it.

Neither deny that the body of Christ can act on our human bodies. In the Prayer of Humble Access, Cranmer prays 'that our synfull bodyes may bee made cleane by his body'.[116] But he does not believe the sacrament to *be* the body of Christ; rather it is a *pledge*, that the body of Christ is acting on the faithful from heaven.

The message from Stephyn, however, is clear: we are nourished in every way by the sacrament, which is truly the body and blood of Christ—underlining Chedsey's point. Omitting Cranmer's riposte (perhaps because he is aware it is not a direct quotation from Tertullian), he stays with Irenaeus.

---

114 *Eum calicem, qui est creatura, <u>suum sanguinem qui effusus est, ex quo auget nostrum sanguinem; et eum panem, qui est a creatura,</u> suum corpus confirmavit, etc.* Catholic theologians do not refer to the blood of Christ as 'wine', preferring 'cup' or 'chalice' instead. The word 'Bread' (appropriately qualified) is treated slightly differently, since 'Bread of Life' is one of Christ's Johannine titles.

115 Tertullian, in *De Resurrectione Mortuorum*, 8, 2 follows his claim that 'the flesh is the hinge of salvation' (*adeo caro salutis est cardo*) by saying 'the flesh feeds on the body and blood of Christ, that the soul may feast on God' (*caro corpore et sanguine Christi vescitur, vt anima de Deo saginetur*—cf. 60v.23-4.) The point is summarized by Chedsey's paraphrase: 'the body eateth that the soul may be fed' (*corpus vescitur ut anima saginetur*, cf. 61r.23-24). Cranmer, too, is paraphrasing when he says 'our flesh is nourished with symbolical or sacramental bread; but our soul is nourished with the body of Christ' (*nutritur corpus pane symbolico, anima corpore Christi*). This is not found in Tertullian himself.

116 Douglas Harrison, ed., *The First and Second Prayer Books* (London: Dent, 1968), p. 225; Robert Van de Weyer, *The First English Prayer Book* (Winchester: John Hunt, 2008), p. 32.

COMMENTARY

Quotation 34. SA 63v.22–4 (Latin) 63v.25–8 (Cornish)

St Irenaeus, *Adversus Haereses*, 5, 2, 3.[117]
Quomodo carnem negant capacem ... quae sanguine et corpore Christi nutritur
(The flesh ... which is nourished with the body and blood of Christ)
[Foxe, TAMO, 1576, p. 1394 [1369]; (T&C vi, 467)—Cranmer's Disputation]

To address Cranmer's repeated assertions that the Fathers only refer to the 'body and blood of Christ' in a 'symbolical or sacramental' way, Weston turns again to *Adversus Haereses*. 'How then can they allege that flesh is incapable of the gift of God, which is eternal life, seeing that the flesh is fed on the flesh and blood of the Lord and is a member of him?'[118]

In response, Cranmer comes as near as he may to Weston, acknowledging that the believer's body is both 'nourished with the sacrament, and with the body of Christ. With the sacrament to a temporal life; with the body of Christ to eternal life.' But, for him, the two are not the same.

Stephyn may have chosen these quotations because he had encountered similar arguments, even locally. His use of the Geneva Bible (and Foxe) for his annotations in TH hints at a world in which Catholic and Protestant clergy, arguments and sources are somewhat jumbled together. Once again, he is drawn to Irenaeus's vision of the 'community and unity of flesh and spirit'. With Cranmer giving some (limited) ground on this point, Stephyn now moves on to other aspects of the Eucharist. (That Foxe is still his source is underlined by his reference to the 5th book of Irenaeus, *ij folen thaworth an dallath*, directly translating Weston's '2 leaves from the beginning'.)

Quotation 35. SA 63v.30 (Cornish only)

Chedsey, referring to St Justin, Martyr, *Apologiae*, 1, 66.[119]
An Grekys ema kelwall Eucharistia, henna ew, grasce the Dew
(And this food is called among us Εὐχαριστία)
[Foxe, TAMO, 1576, p. 1394 [1369]; (T&C vi, 467)—Cranmer's Disputation]

Chedsey is probably thinking of the phrase 'And this food is called among us Εὐχαριστία' in St Justin, Apology 1, 66, a little before the passage used in Quotation 32. (Chedsey no doubt had access to fuller texts and editions, not merely *catenae*.)

---

117 Rousseau, et al., eds, *Irénée de Lyon, Contre les hérésies*, p. 574 [PG 7/1, 1126]. See Quotation 33.
118 St Irenaeus, *Adversus Haereses*, 5, 2, 2, tr. Bettenson, *Early Christian Fathers*, p. 97.
119 Munier, *Saint Justin: Apologie*, p. 306; Gildersleeve, ed., *Apologies of Justin*, p. 62. [PG 6, 427C]. See Quotations 31 and 32.

Stephyn chooses this small sentence, including the name 'Eucharist' (which means 'thanksgiving'), to introduce a section of SA that focuses more on the spiritual meaning of the Mass than the material questions hitherto considered. He ignores the wider point in Chedsey's intervention, perhaps considering it already established.

Quotation 36. SA 63v.31–4 (Latin) 63v.34–7 (Cornish) [and TH 56r.14–19m; 57r. 25+ (26–8); 58r.20]

Eusebius 'Gallicanus', *Collectio Homilarum*, 17 (De Pascha, 6), 3.[120]
Mirare cum reverendum altare ... fide respice, honorem mirare, merito continge
(Marvel when you approach the altar to be fed with the holy body and blood)
[Foxe, TAMO, 1576, p. 1395 [1370]; (T&C vi, 467)—Cranmer's Disputation]

Only very few genuine writings of Eusebius of Emesa ('Emissenus') survive, and this is not one of them. Later works attributed to him and quoted by both sides in the Reformation era include this *Homilia de corpore et sanguine Christi*. Its unknown author is given the title Eusebius 'Gallicanus' for convenience.[121] The seventy-six sermons in the collection are from the mid- to late fifth century, with the collection itself being made in the sixth century. The author of this particular homily is unknown, as is the precise context in which it was originally preached. Nonetheless, Lisa Bailey has gone a considerable way towards elucidating its *sitz im leben*.[122]

Mirare—'be amazed'—appears to be the 'working title' of this passage in *catenae* and contemporary theological discourse: 'When you go up to the sacred altar to be fed, look upon the holy body and blood of your God: give due honour, be amazed, hold fast with your mind'.[123]

---

120 F. Glorie, ed. (after J. Leroy), *Eusebius 'Gallicanus', Collectio Homilarum*, vol. 1 (CCSL 101) (Turnhout: Brepols, 1970), Homily XVII, *De corpore et sanguine Christi* (De Pascha, 6), 3, lines 53–5, p. 198 [Pseudo-Jerome, *Epistolae, 38*—PL 30, 272D]. I am grateful to Roger Norris whose photocopies of Durham University Library MS Cosin V.IV.2, ff. 161r–165r, set me on the road to understanding 'Eusebius Emissenus'.
121 Glorie, ed., *Eusebius 'Gallicanus'* (CCSL, vol. 101), Prologue, p. ix.
122 Lisa Kaaren Bailey, *Christianity's Quiet Success: The Eusebius Gallicanus Sermon Collection and the Power of the Church in Late Antique Gaul* (Notre Dame: University of Notre Dame Press, 2010). See also Lisa Bailey, 'Monks and Lay Communities in Late Antique Gaul: The Evidence of the Eusebius Gallicanus Sermons', *Journal of Medieval History*, 32, 4 (December 2006), pp. 315–32.
123 The marginal note refers to *De Consecratione 2, Emissenus*, 'Quia'—cf. *Decretum Gratiani*, digital edition, Pars 3, *De Consecratione*, Dist. II, C. XXXV: *et cum reuerendum altare cibis spiritualibus satiandus ascendis, sacrum Dei tui corpus et sanguinem fide respice, honora, mirare, mente continge ...* [PL 187, 1746B].

The discussion starts with the accusation that Cranmer has falsified the text in his works. He defends himself by explaining that the phrase he used—*cibis satiandus spiritualibus*—came from the Decrees (of Gratian). Certainly, the word *spiritualibus* does appear in most later versions, including the one shortly to be quoted by Weston. Cranmer also disputes the *merito continge*, 'worthily touch him', perhaps knowing that some early texts give *mente continge*, 'touch him with your mind'.

Stephyn is less interested in misquotations than in moving to more devotional ground. He goes straight to the word *Mirare*, which he translates 'marvel' or 'be amazed' (*Gwra marugian*—see Notes on 63v.34, 37), alluding to the wonder due as the altar is approached (echoing the thanksgiving of the previous Quotation.)

Quotation 37. SA 64r.2 (Latin)
64r.2–3 (Cornish) [and TH 56r.14–19m]

Weston, summarizing Eusebius 'Gallicanus', 17, 3.[124]
honora Corpus Dei tui ... Gwra honora Co[rf] thith Dew
(Honour the body of your God)
[Foxe, TAMO, 1576, p. 1395 [1370]; (T&C vi, 467)—Cranmer's Disputation]

Quotation 36 is reduced to its essence by Weston here as 'honour the body of your God' (*honora Corpus Dei tui*). Cranmer admits he has differently paraphrased the original as 'honour him which is thy God' (*honora eum qui est Deus tuus*), arguing that this was a justifiable change, for 'a weighty cause'—to avoid the 'error of the Anthropomorphites'.

Audianism was hardly the most prevalent of heresies in Tudor England; but Cranmer may genuinely have felt that traditional spirituality came close to it, given its veneration of images (including of the Holy Trinity) and phrases such as 'Mother of God' and 'Body of God'. While these are justifiable theologically, as upholding the incarnation, they inevitably encouraged devotion in directions he found uncomfortable.

For Stephyn, the passage is a simple reiteration, reduced to essentials and seen very much as an imperative. He writes *Corpus Dei* with slightly larger letters, in a bold italic hand. We perhaps catch a glimpse of the resolution with which he is undertaking this task, and the faith behind it.

---

124 Glorie, ed., *Eusebius 'Gallicanus'* (CCSL 101), Homily XVII, 3, lines 53–5 [PL 30, 272D]. See Quotation 36.

Quotation 38. SA 64r.3–6 (Latin) 64r.7–10 (Cornish)

Blessed John Duns Scotus, *In Sententiarum*, Bk 4, Dist. 11, Q. 3, 15.[125]
Et si quaeras quare voluit Ecclesia ... secundum apparentiam, de hoc articulo
(Scripture only 'apparently' supports an easier interpretation)
[Foxe, TAMO, 1576, p. 1395 [1370]; (T&C vi, 468)—Cranmer's Disputation]

Despite the marginal reference in SA, this is not from Eusebius 'Gallicanus', but from John Duns Scotus (1265-1308). A Scot, probably born in Duns, Berwickshire, he became a Franciscan in Dumfries, moving steadily south to Northamptonshire, Oxford, then France. He was lecturing in the University of Paris by 1302, though he transferred to Cologne towards the end of his life and is buried there.[126] The quotation comes from his lectures on Lombard's *Four Books of Sentences*, as the text and margin in Foxe indicate.

While recognizing potential objections to the doctrine of transubstantiation, Duns ultimately rejects them on the grounds of the certainty of God's word. While rational arguments are valuable in elucidating and supporting revelation, we should not use them to overthrow it, he says, given what we know about their inconclusive nature. Of course, we should not lightly accept interpretations of scripture that are difficult to believe, but *apparently* difficult interpretations may be embraced when we know them to be true from revelation.[127] While neither the Bible nor the earliest fathers refer to transubstantiation explicitly, the Fourth Lateran Council seems to have settled the matter for Duns. In choosing this interpretation, 'the Church was guided by the same Spirit through which the Scriptures were written and handed down'.[128]

Cranmer reverses the perspective: some things that scripture *apparently* says are surely not intended in a literal sense. Duns himself says that 'the words of scripture might be expounded more easily and more plainly without

---

125 John Duns Scotus, *Reportata super ... (primum-quartum) ... Sententiarum*, bk 4, d.11, q.3 (Paris: Jean Granion, 1517–1518), p. 618, Google Books, accessed 23 October 2018. An online critical edition of Duns Scotus is under way, but not yet completed.
126 In his own day Duns was considered innovative but nonetheless orthodox and of international importance. The inscription on his tomb in Cologne reads: *Scotia me genuit. Anglia me suscepit. Gallia me docuit. Colonia me tenet.* Philosophically, he is remembered for his ideas on the unity of essence and existence (the 'univocity of being') and on the intrinsic nature of things (later 'haecceity'). Theologically, he is known for his arguments for the existence of God and the Immaculate Conception.
127 Cf. David Burr, 'Eucharistic Presence and Conversion in Late Thirteenth-Century Franciscan Thought', in *Transactions of the American Philosophical Society*, 74, 3 (Philadelphia: American Philosophical Society, 1984), pp. 92–3. Google Books, accessed 18 October 2018. I am grateful to C.W.H. Hatcher for his help with this passage.
128 Burr, 'Eucharistic Presence and Conversion', p. 93.

transubstantiation'.¹²⁹ So, says Cranmer, Duns has only embraced it out of loyalty to the church of Rome. Weston challenges this, chiding Cranmer for failing to translate Duns's *secundum apparentiam* adequately and indeed for wrongly translating *ecclesia catholica* as 'the church of Rome'. Cranmer's answer is admittedly thin,¹³⁰ although once again the substance is sidestepped, to focus on inaccuracies and errors. This suggests that Weston understood the power of Cranmer's scholarship and detailed memory (evidenced even in the Disputations, though he was weak with imprisonment), and was as concerned to undermine his reputation as to engage with his beliefs.

We should remember that Stephyn is not simply compiling a précis of Foxe. He moves from 'honour the Body of your God' straight to this passage, ignoring the personal exchange between Weston and Cranmer. He wishes to extract as many Latin proof texts from Foxe as he can, perhaps under pressure of time. Nonetheless he is still following ideas, possibly with the intention of reordering and expanding the material later. From Duns he takes the idea that any apparent complexity required to reconcile transubstantiation with scripture is just that—'apparent' only.

Quotation 39. SA 64r.11–18 (Latin) 64r.18–28 (Cornish)

St Thomas Aquinas, *Summa Theologica*, III, Q. 79, Art. 5.¹³¹
In quantum vero est sacrificium ... et non pro tota poena
(The sacrifice applies satisfactory power, according to the devotion of the offerers)
[Foxe, TAMO, 1576, p. 1395 [1370]; (T&C vi, 468)—Cranmer's Disputation]

Thomas Aquinas (1225-1274), from Aquino, between Rome and Naples, was pre-eminent in the development of classical, 'scholastic' Catholic theology and Eucharistic spirituality. Though educated at Monte Cassino, he became a Dominican and moved to Paris then Cologne, where he wrote his early theological commentaries. In due course returning to Naples and Orvieto, he wrote the *Summa Contra Gentiles*, his *Catena Aurea* on the Gospels and some material for the new feast of Corpus Christi.¹³² Called to Rome by Clement IV, he undertook his most famous work, the *Summa Theologica*. Both orthodox

---

129 As Cranmer argued in his *Aunswere* to Stephyn Gardiner. Cf. John Edmund Cox, ed., *The Writings and Disputations of Thomas Cranmer ... Relative to the Sacrament of the Lord's Supper*, Parker Society (Cambridge: Cambridge University Press, 1844), p. 302 (and p. 34 in the appended Latin translation).
130 'Yea, but he meant the Romish church', T&C vi, 468.
131 Sancti Thomae de Aquino, *Summa Theologiae* (Roma: Editiones Paolinae, 1962), p. 2296; St Thomas Aquinas, *Summa Theologica*, III, Q. 79, Art. 5, *Corpus Thomisticum*, accessed 18 October 2018.
132 Miri Rubin, *Corpus Christi: The Eucharist in Late Medieval Culture* (Cambridge: Cambridge University Press, 1991), pp. 185–96.

and speculative in nature, it brought together scripture, reason, classical philosophy and all that was then known of nature in a rational synthesis.[133]

For Thomas, the sacrifice of the Mass is not an *additional sacrifice* to the sacrifice of Calvary, but rather it is the *same sacrifice* as Calvary, represented and made sacramentally present so that its benefits can be applied to us. While Christ's sacrifice is certainly sufficient to forgive the sins of the whole world, individuals, as in the story of the Widow's Mite,[134] encounter it in different ways according to their own faith and devotion. The more faith we put into the treasury of Christ's sacrifice, the more we will experience its 'satisfactory power'.

Weston remarks that Cranmer has 'depraved' this passage, altering *sacrificium*, 'sacrifice' to *sacrificium sacerdotis*, 'sacrifice of the priest', as well as excising some words from the end.[135] More interested in exposing Cranmer's subtlety than debating the theological point, he declares that 'The truth may be pressed' (by 'the craft and deceit of heretics') but 'it cannot be oppressed'. His colleagues then cry out *Vincit veritas*, 'the truth overcometh', and Cranmer's Disputation comes to an end.

For Stephyn, subtleties in Cranmer's scholarship are irrelevant. Perhaps drawn by the words *vero est sacrificium*, 'it is a true sacrifice', taken at face value, he includes St Thomas' point about the importance of faith and devotion in relation to the satisfactory power of the sacrifice, then returns to Ridley's Disputation.

Quotation 40. SA 64r.29–34 (Cornish only) [and TH 54v.18–28m]

Ridley
Onyn an sans Egglos ew gilwis Vigilius ... lowar[th] onyn erall an Tasow coeth
(A list of some of the Fathers of the Church)
[Foxe, TAMO, 1576, p. 1398 [1373]; (T&C vi, 474)—Ridley's Disputation]

Lists of supporting Fathers often appeared in disputations and *catenae*.[136] In Ridley's list most are well known but, in both Stephyn and Foxe, the names

---

133 He himself considered it a mere introduction, to help beginners. In any case, returning to Naples towards the end of his life, he had a number of mystical experiences that led him to consider all his writings as mere straw.
134 Lk 21:2.
135 Cox, ed., *The Writings and Disputations of Thomas Cranmer*, pp. 84–5. At p. 423, Cox notes that—in the MS transcript—Cranmer confesses he 'would not write all that long treatise'. Weston also alleges that Cranmer has 'chopped in' here the word *sacerdotis*, 'of the priest', whereas the only place he employs the word 'priest' when rendering the whole New Testament is 'where Christ is put to death'.
136 E.g. Tunstall, *De ueritate Corporis et Sanguinis*, f. 117v.

Eusebius and Emisene are separated by a comma. The church historian Eusebius of Caesarea is probably not intended, but rather Eusebius 'Gallicanus' (then called 'Emissenus').

While Ridley refuses transubstantiation, he is comfortable with other affirmations of the Eucharistic presence in patristic sources, as this preliminary material shows. He accepts the 'grace of Christ's body' (with Cyprian), the 'virtue of the very flesh of Christ' (with Cyril) and that 'we eat life and drink life' (with Augustine). He believes we 'receive the mystical advent and coming of Christ' (with Basil) and 'the sacrament of his very flesh' (with Ambrose), the 'body by grace' (with Epiphanius) and the 'grace of the Spirit' (with Chrysostom). He is not of the opinion that we receive simply and only 'a figure of the body of Christ'.[137] Indeed, Ridley is much happier than Cranmer to make affirmations such as 'Christ's body is in the sacrament' and to be understood in a partially conservative sense. Like Cranmer, nonetheless, he subtly exploits the different meanings of the word 'sacrament', to say of the whole rite things he might not want to say of the sacramental species alone.

It is interesting that Stephyn chose to copy out all the authorities that Ridley felt were against transubstantiation and concomitance (the acceptability of communion under one kind), though he leaves out Fulgentius from his list in TH. No doubt he disagreed with Ridley, but their inclusion at this point seems a digression, unless a personal addition to amplify Quotation 10.

Quotation 41. SA 64v.2 (Latin) 64v.3–4 (Cornish)

Ward, quoting Lk 22:15, after Tertullian, *Adversus Marcionem*, 4, 40.[138]
Desiderio desideravi hoc pascha manducare vobiscum
('I have longed to eat this Passover with you')
[Foxe, TAMO, 1576, p. 1405 [1380]; (T&C vi, 490)—Ridley's Disputation]

These words come a little before the passage at Quotation 42 (q.v.) They are from Luke 22:15 in the Vulgate, where the phrase above is completed with the words *antequam patiar* ('before I suffer').[139] Christ is with his disciples in the Upper Room, just prior to the institution of the Eucharist, the night before his crucifixion.

---

137 T&C vi, 475.
138 Ernest Evans, ed., *Tertullian: Adversus Marcionem* (Oxford, Oxford University Press, 1972), p. 492, online at http://www.tertullian.org/articles/evans_marc/evans_marc_00index.htm. Accessed 18 October 2018. [PL2/2, 460B].
139 The arguments around the Passover context are surveyed by Joachim Jeremias, *The Eucharistic Words of Jesus* (London: SCM, 1966), pp. 42–84.

Tertullian quotes the passage in the context of arguing that Christ, far from being a 'destroyer of the Law', in fact fulfils the Law's commands, although it was not the lamb of the supper that Christ desired, but to 'accomplish the figure of his saving blood' (*figuram sanguinis sui*).[140] Ward explains this as Christ longing not for the Jewish Passover (the 'Judaicall Lambe') but his own new Passover, continuing with the following Quotation, which Stephyn also gives.

Quotation 42. SA 64v.6–10 (Latin) 64v.10–14 (Cornish)

Tertullian, *Adversus Marcionem*, 4, 40.[141]
Professus itaque se concupiscentia ... est corpus meum dicendo.
(Taking bread, he gave it to the disciples, making it his own body)
[Foxe, TAMO, 1576, p. 1405 [1380]; (T&C vi, 490)—Ridley's Disputation]

Marcion (c. 85–160) came from Sinape (modern Sinop, in Turkey). Although his father was a bishop, he came to share Cerdo's view that the God of the Old Testament was different from the all-forgiving Christian God. This led him to reject the entire Hebrew Bible, retain only a heavily pruned version of the New Testament and embrace elements of Gnosticism while rejecting the incarnation. Tertullian was naturally eager, then, to remind him of Christ's bodily nature. The first version of *Adversus Marcionem* may date from as early as 197,[142] although it was finalized in the early years of the next century. Citing that longing to eat the Passover, and the Church's teaching on the real presence, Tertullian makes clear that Christ was not merely 'spiritual'. 'When establishing the covenant sealed with his own blood, he affirmed the reality of his body: for there can be no blood except from a body which is flesh.'[143]

Ridley again affirms that we are fed with the true flesh of Christ, 'for he is the very and true meat of the soul', but denies that 'the substance of his flesh taken in the womb of the Virgin Mary' is involved. This leads Ward to Tertullian's view that the Passover that Christ was longing for was his own action: his sacrificial death and—linked with it—the taking of bread and 'making it his body'. Ridley finally concedes that 'Tertullian may here dally in sense analogical'.[144] (This is a term used by the reformers when they believe an author is saying something apparently contrary to their doctrine and should therefore be interpreted as speaking mystically. Foxe comments that 'Analogical sense

---

140 Evans, ed., *Tertullian: Adversus Marcionem*, pp. 492–3.
141 Evans, ed., *Tertullian: Adversus Marcionem*, p. 492. See Quotation 41. [PL2/2, 460B].
142 Evans, ed., *Tertullian: Adversus Marcionem*, p. xviii.
143 Evans, ed., *Tertullian: Adversus Marcionem*, p. 495.
144 T&C vi, 491.

is that which hath a high and mystical understanding, that lieth abstruse and profound under the external letter.')

Interestingly, neither Ward nor Ridley explores in detail Tertullian's use of the word *figura*, although Tertullian's sense here is very specific to the context.[145]

Stephyn focuses on Tertullian's claim that Christ took bread but 'made it his body' (*corpus illum fecit*). For him, the text underlines further the transformation of the bread into the body of Christ.[146]

Quotation 43. SA 64v.15–26 (Latin) 64v.15, 27–35 (Cornish) [and TH 55v.25+ (26–32); 58r.14–19m]

St Augustine of Hippo, *Enarrationes in Psalmos*, 98, 9, on Ps 99:5.[147]
Adorate scabellum pedum eius ... Quæro inquit ... sed peccemus non adorando ipsum
(No one eats of that flesh unless he has first adored)
[Foxe, TAMO, 1576, p. 1405 [1380]; (T&C vi, 491)—Ridley's Disputation]

The *Enarrationes* display the creative allegory and breadth of interpretation for which Augustine's exegetical works are known. Here, he argues that to 'worship God's footstool' (in the Latin version he is using) reminds us that Christ took 'flesh of the earth'. He may be worshipped in the flesh since, by his incarnation, he united our flesh with the Godhead. This incarnational perspective is buttressed by Eucharistic doctrine. Christ 'gave the same flesh to us, to be eaten unto salvation' and—just after—'no man eateth that flesh except he have worshipped before'.

Unfortunately, the text as we have it here hosts many confusions. First, because of the repetition of *adoretur*, several words have been omitted (here underlined): 'I turn to Christ ... and I understand how, without impiety, we may worship <u>the earth; without impiety</u> we may worship his footstool (*quomodo sine*

---

145 Evans notes that here '*figura* does not indicate anything merely figurative, but a visible objective shape'—Evans, ed., *Tertullian: Adversus Marcionem*, p. 493.
146 For an overview of Marian views of the Eucharistic presence see Wizeman, *Theology and Spirituality*, pp. 162–9.
147 Eligius Dekkers, Johannes Fraipont, eds, *Sancti Aurelii Augustini: Enarrationes in Psalmos LI-C* [CCSL 39] (Turnhout: Brepols, 1956), p. 1385. The editors (2nd edn, 1990, p. ix) acknowledge their debt to the Benedictines of St Maur, as at [PL 37, 1264]. The CSEL (93–4) critical editions under way (by C. Weidmann, F. Gori, H. Müller), make greater use of the families of MSS but do not yet encompass Pss 61–100. For Augustine himself see Quotation 2. (NB the 96 in Foxe 1570/1576 is strange, as it is 98 in 1563/1583—see Note on 64v.15.) Stephyn has 96 in the text, 98 in the margin (and 99 in his marginalia at TH 55v.25m, perhaps reflecting his use of the Geneva Bible).

impietate adoretur terra, sine impietate adoretur scabellum pedum eius)—for he took upon himself earth from earth.'

The straightforward meaning of the original passage has also been lost in translation. Modern Bibles have 'Worship at his footstool' (Ps 99:5 NRSV),[148] reflecting the Hebrew (לַהֲדֹם) of the Masoretic text and the dative of the Septuagint (Ps 98:5 προσκυνεῖτε τῷ ὑποποδίῳ), but the Vulgate has 'adore his footstool' (Ps 98:5 *adorate scabillum*). None of this, however, will prevent Ward from giving us a window into Augustine's Eucharistic belief (and that of the early Church), sometimes elusive because of the *disciplina arcani* (see Quotation 22).

So neither Ward nor Ridley challenge Augustine's interpretation of the psalm: both accept that Christ gave us his flesh to be eaten, a flesh originally taken from earthly matter. Ward argues, however, that the 'only' place where Christ clearly gives his flesh is at the last supper and concludes that 'in the Eucharist he gave us his flesh'. Ridley wishes to broaden the concept of feeding upon Christ's 'flesh' to his wider self-giving, 'in the word, as also upon the cross'. When Smith interjects that he can show from Augustine that Christ did not merely give only a 'figure' of his body, but 'his own very flesh', Ridley does not deny this. Once again, he is clear that he accepts that Christ 'gave his own body verily', but he did so by a 'spiritual communication', which was nonetheless 'real and effectual'.[149]

Stephyn corrects Foxe's *Adorare*,[150] of 1576 (see Note on 64v.15), to *Adorate* (which Foxe also gives as *Adorate* when Cartwright quotes the passage in Latimer's Disputation).[151] The imperative to adore is important to him, and he

---

148 Cf. J.W. Rogerson and J.W. McKay, *Psalms 51-100* (Cambridge: Cambridge University Press, 1977), p. 229. Reference to God's 'footstool' is made in several contexts in the Hebrew Bible: it can mean the earth (Isa 66:1), the temple at Jerusalem (Lam 2:1), the tabernacle (Ps 32:7) or the ark (1 Chr 28:2). with perhaps an additional implication here of turning towards, and bowing before, the ark.

149 Jewel, in his reply to Harding's *Answer*, gives an exposition that sheds light on how Ridley and other Reformers may have understood this passage. 'We must adore the flesh of Christ. We grant; we believe it; it is our faith ... no man eateth that flesh but first he adoreth it ... he deadly offendeth God, and is wicked ... that adoreth it not.' But, for Jewel, both the 'eating' and the 'adoring' take place by reaching into heaven, by faith: 'There we see Christ's body; there we approach unto it; there we touch it; there we taste it; there we eat it; there we adore it'—not here on earth. When Ambrose says that 'we adore Christ's flesh in the mysteries', Jewel interprets this as meaning 'in the ministration of the mysteries', i.e. during the course of the rite, but not within the Eucharistic elements. John Ayre, ed., *The Works of John Jewel, Bishop of Salisbury* (Cambridge: Cambridge University Press and Parker Society, 1848), part 3, p. 542.

150 Probably written because he had seen Augustine's *rursum timeo non adorare scabellum pedum eius* in another edition, but cf. Ps 98: 5 Vulgate: *Adorate scabillum pedum eius*, Gryson et al., eds, *Biblia Sacra Vulgata*, p. 894.

151 TAMO 1576, p. 1412 [1387]; T&C vi, 508, as it is in the psalm.

may have selected the marginal references to the Temple himself.[152] The body of Christ is the new Temple, the church.[153]

The last of the marginal references tells us something of Stephyn's ability to consider contrary texts in reaching a scriptural synthesis. Acts 7.40-3 recalls the folly of idol worship in ancient Israel, and Stephyn clearly contrasts this to worship of the Blessed Sacrament.[154] For him this is no idol or mere image but the true presence of Christ and, as Augustine says in the passage Stephyn quotes, we 'sin if we do not adore it' (*peccemus non adorando ipsum*).

Quotation 44. SA 65r.2-3 (Latin) 65r.4-5 (Cornish)

St Augustine of Hippo, *Contra Faustum Manichaeum*, 20, 13.[155]
Panem et calicem, Cererem ...
(We do not worship Ceres and Bacchus)
[Foxe, TAMO, 1576, p. 1405 [1380]; (T&C vi, 492)—Ridley's Disputation][156]

The folio is badly damaged, but is possible to reconstruct the quotation as *Austen contra Faustum. lib. 20. ca[p.13. Non nulli qui nos propter] Panem et calicem, Cererem [& Bacchum colere existimant]*.[157]

Faustus, from Milevum (now Mila in Algeria), embraced Manichaeism and Marcionism (see Quotation 42). Some Manichaeans believed God came to them in everything they ate. Augustine explains the Christian position: bread and wine are not worshipped in their natural forms but, when consecrated, become sacred. It is absurd to maintain that Christ is equally present in all we consume: Faustus is equating true religion with error. 'This is more foolish than to say, as some do, that we worship Ceres and Bacchus in the bread and cup.'

Ridley says he does 'worship Christ in the sacrament' but not because he is 'included in the sacrament'. In the same way, he worships Christ in the

---

152 The reference at 64v.19-20m to *3 reg 8*, is to the Temple, God's appointed 'meeting-place' with mankind, celebrated in the prayer of King Solomon at its consecration (3 Kings 8:27-30 Vulgate; 1 Kings 8:27-30 NRSV). The reference at 64v.21m to *[2] para 6*, is also to the Temple, and how God's name will be enshrined among his people in the ark (2 Paralipomena 6:1-20 Vulgate; 2 Chr 6:1-20 NRSV).
153 Cf. Jn 2:19, Mt 26:61, Mk 14:58. Col 1:24 equates the church with Christ's body.
154 The verse number is given: see Appendix A for Stephyn's use of the Geneva Bible.
155 Josef Zycha, ed., *S. Aureli Augustini Operum 6: De utilitate credendi, De duabus animabus, Contra Fortunatum Manichaeum, Contra Adimantum, Contra epistulam fundamenti, Contra Faustum Manichaeum* [CSEL 25/1] (Vienna: Tempsky, 1891), p. 553 [PL 42, 379].
156 This folio in Foxe 1576 is wrongly headed 'Disputation of M. Latimer at Oxford'.
157 Cf. Foxe, *Rerum in Ecclesia Gestarum*, p. 679, and Philip Schaff, ed., *St Augustine: the Writings against the Manichaeans, and Against the Donatists*, Nicene and Post-Nicene Fathers, First Series (originally published 1887) (New York: Cosimo, 2007), p. 259.

Scriptures, but does not believe they literally or physically contain him. Glyn then cites *Contra Faustum*,[158] to show that even in Augustine's time Christians were criticized for their Eucharistic worship. Could something of such antiquity and persistence be wrong if—as both he and Ridley believed—the Church 'is taught of the Holy Ghost'? Ridley partly concedes, accepting 'worship' of the 'symbols',[159] if that means to handle them with reverence because of what they represent, but he cannot accept 'transubstantiation'.

Stephyn does not explain Glyn's argument, but seems to have approved it: the Church has always 'worshipped the flesh of Christ in the Eucharist', and since it is the 'pillar and stay of the truth', this cannot be idolatrous. It is curious, however, that Stephyn should have been slipshod in his terminology at 65r.5, writing 'wine' (*gwyne*) instead of 'chalice' (*chalys*) or 'cup' (*haneth*).[160]

Quotation 45. SA 65r.7–13 (Latin) 65r.13–18 (Cornish) [TH 57v.27+ (31–33)]

St John Chrysostom, *Homiliae in primum Corinthios*, 24, 4 [on 1 Cor 10:16].[161]
Panis quam frangimus ... Quare non dixit participatio? ... unione conjungimur
(It is not by merely receiving, but by a deeper unity that we communicate)
[Foxe, TAMO, 1576, p. 1407 [1382]; (T&C vi, 495)—Ridley's Disputation]

Chrysostom's point is that 'communion' is something far deeper than merely 'participation' or receiving.[162] Just as Christ is joined to 'that body', we too, 'by the same bread', are 'conjoined to him'.

---

158 William Glyn (or Glynn) (1504-1558), of Heneglwys near Llangefni in Ynys Môn (Anglesey), was pragmatic at Cambridge under Henry VIII, but increasingly disaffected under Edward VI, resigning his chair. Under Mary he became vice chancellor of the university and bishop of Bangor but died in 1558. Cf. Glyn Roberts (2004), 'William Glyn (1504–1558), bishop' in the National Library of Wales' *Y Bywgraffiadur Cymreig/Dictionary of Welsh Biography* online, https://biography.wales/article/s-GLYN-WIL-1504. Accessed 3 November 2018. See also Glanmor Williams, *Wales and the Reformation* (Cardiff: University of Wales Press, 1999), pp. 164, 210–12, 339–46.
159 Worship in the sense of acknowledge the 'worth'—he rejects the word *adoremus*, 'we adore'.
160 Cf. *chalys* SA 63v.19 and *haneth* TH 22v.22, *hanath* AB 33, 45, earlier *hanaf* VC 875.
161 Field, ed., *Ioannis Chrysostomi ... Omnium Epistolarum Paulinarum ...*, tom. 2, p. 288, beginning Ὁ ἄρτος ὃν κλῶμεν [PG 61, 200].
162 The Vulgate has <u>communicatio</u> for the cup, but goes on to say *Panis quem frangimus nonne <u>participatio</u> corporis Domini est*. In both cases the Greek is κοινωνία, however, and more recent versions use *communicatio* for both. (Cf. Gryson et al., eds, *Biblia Sacra Vulgata*, p. 1780; *Nova Vulgata: Bibliorum Sacrorum Editio*, edition iuxta editionem typicam alteram (Vatican City: Libreria Editrice Vaticana, 1998), p. 1707.)

Watson is responding to Ridley's citation of 1 Cor 10:16: 'the bread which we break, is it not a communication of the body of Christ?'.[163] He explores the meaning of 'bread' here, using Chrysostom to suggest it is the body of Christ, since it unites us to him. Ridley puts this down merely to Chrysostom's 'manner of speaking', but Watson goes on a little further in the same homily where Chrysostom says more clearly that what is received is the body of Christ. The discussion runs into the sand, however, when the focus shifts to the detail of the wording.

Stephyn appears to value Chrysostom's distinction between 'communication' and 'participation'. The former is a 'greater matter' (*brossa mater*), involving being 'conjoined' (*junys*) to our Saviour Christ.[164]

Quotation 46. SA 65r.20–27 (Latin) 65r.21, 30–36 (Cornish) [and TH 58r.1+]

St Augustine of Hippo, *Enarrationes in Psalmos*, 33, 1, 10 [on 1 Sam 21:13/14][165]
Ferebatur in manibus suis ... Hoc quomodo possit ... Corpus in manibus suis
(Christ was 'carried in his own hands' when he said 'This is my body')
[Foxe, TAMO, 1576, p. 1407 [1382]; (T&C vi, 496)—Ridley's Disputation][166]

It should be said at the outset that Augustine's whole discussion, and that of the disputants, rests upon a misunderstanding of an early reading of 1 Sam 21:13-14 unsupported by the Masoretic text. The passage is from *Concio/Contio 1*, which introduces Augustine's exposition of Ps 33, as the marginal reference indicates.[167]

---

163 Thomas Watson (1513–1584), born in Nunstainton, Co. Durham (north-east of modern Newton Aycliffe) helped introduce Greek scholarship at Cambridge. Imprisoned for his opposition under Edward VI but restored to favour under Mary I, he became Dean of Durham, then Bishop of Lincoln. Under Elizabeth I he was deprived, imprisoned and committed to Wisbech Castle. He died in 1584. Cf. Kenneth Carleton, 'Thomas Watson (1513–1584)', in *Oxford Dictionary of National Biography* online, https://doi.org/10.1093/ref:odnb/28865. Accessed 21 October 2018. See also William Wizeman, 'The Theology and Spirituality of a Marian Bishop: the Pastoral and Polemical Sermons of Thomas Watson' in Duffy and Loades, eds, *The Church of Mary Tudor*, pp. 258-80.
164 Of course, at 65r.15 Stephyn should speak of Paul, not of Christ.
165 Eligius Dekkers, Jean Fraipont et al., eds, *Sancti Aurelii Augustini: Enarrationes in Psalmos I-L* [CCSL 38] (Turnhout: Brepols, 1956), p. 280. [PL 36, 306]. The reference at 65r.21 to *1:regum* is because 1 Sam is titled 1 Kings in some editions of the Vulgate.
166 See also TAMO, 1576, Book 8, 1031 [1006]; TAMO, 1576, Book 11, 1799 [1773].
167 This is the first of two *contiones*, see [Sister] Maria Boulding [OSB], tr., *Expositions of the Psalms, vol. 2, 33-50* [The Works of St Augustine: A translation for the 21st century] (New York: New City Press, 2000) pp. 13-22. Google Books, accessed 26 October 2018.

In 1 Samuel 21, David is on the run from Saul and, coming into the presence of Achish of Gath and his servants (who suspect his real identity), he changes his behaviour and 'feigns madness in their hands' (וַיִּתְהֹלֵל בְּיָדָם).[168] The Vulgate has David 'swooning (*collabebatur/conlabebatur*) into their hands',[169] while the Septuagint has him getting 'carried away with his hands' (παρεφέρετο ἐν ταῖς χερσὶν αὐτοῦ); that is, waving them about wildly.[170] One can see how, translated over-literally as 'he was carried in his hands' (*ferebatur in manibus suis*), this was misunderstood.[171]

Augustine begins his exposition by reflecting on the psalm's title:[172] 'Of David, when he feigned madness before Abimelech'.[173] While his meanings of the names are no longer accepted—David ('strong of hand'), Abimelech ('My father's kingdom') and Achish ('How can this be?')—they remind him of the humility of Christ, expressed in his sacrifice on the cross and self-giving in the Eucharist. 'Think of the humility of it', he says, 'humans have eaten the bread of angels'.[174] He then links the supposed 'How can this be?' with Jn 6:53–56, where some of the disciples baulked at Christ's teaching about eating his flesh and drinking his blood. Although it seems insane to the world (like the behaviour of David), Augustine argues it is intelligible to the eyes of faith. Then, of the phrase 'he was carried in his own hands', he says: 'We have no way of knowing what it literally means in David's case, but we can make sense of it with regard to Christ. Christ was being carried in his own hands when he handed over his body, saying "This is my body"; for he was holding that very body in his hands when he spoke.'[175]

Ridley is aware that the biblical text has been 'otherwise read of other men, after the verity of the Hebrew text, and it is also otherwise to be expounded'.[176] but esteems Augustine highly and will 'go not from him'. He therefore grants

---

168 Karl Elliger, Willhelm Rudolph et al., eds, *Biblia Hebraica Stuttgartensia*, editio funditus renovata (Stuttgart: Deutsche Bibelstiftung, 1977), p. 486 [at 1 Sam 21:14]; Peter R. Acroyd, *The First Book of Samuel* (Cambridge: Cambridge University Press, 1971), pp. 172–3.

169 Gryson et al., eds, *Biblia Sacra Vulgata*, p. 401 [at 1 Sam 21:13]; Ronald A. Knox, tr., *The Holy Bible: a translation from the Latin Vulgate in the light of the Hebrew and Greek originals* (London: Burns & Oates, 1961), OT, p. 248 [at 1 Kings 21:13].

170 Alfred Rahlfs, ed. *Septuaginta*, vol. 1 (Stuttgart: Deutsche Bibelstiftung, 1935), vol. 1, p. 545 [at 1 Kings 21:14 LXX].

171 Between *quis intelligat* and *manibus enim* a phrase of Augustine's original appears to be missing from Smith's version: *Quis enim portatur in manibus suis? Manibus aliorum potest portari homo.* Compare Foxe, *Rerum in Ecclesia Gestarum*, p. 692 with Tunstall, *De ueritate Corporis et Sanguinis*, f. 99r, for instance.

172 See Quotations 2 and 43.

173 Ps 34, title, NRSV.

174 Boulding, *Exposition of the Psalms, 33–50*, p. 17.

175 Boulding, *Exposition of the Psalms, 33–50*, p. 21.

176 Henry VIII's Great Bible had 'fayned him self madd in theyr handes' for the passage in question, cf. *The Byble in Englyshe that is to saye the content of al the holy scripture ...* (London: Edward Whytchurche, 1540), f. 33. The Geneva Bible kept the same: 'fained him selfe mad in

that 'Christ did bear himself in his own hands', *quodam modo*, 'after a certain manner'—but not 'carnally', only spiritually and sacramentally. Smith takes this as a victory, saying to Ridley: 'You are holden fast, neither are you able to escape out of this labyrinth.'

Much of Stephyn's translation is lost, but he appears to have valued part of the argument sufficiently to have included it.

Quotation 47. SA 65v.2 (Cornish only)

Tresham[177]
[C]orf Christ ew ema warre an alter
(The body of Christ is present on the altar)
[Foxe, TAMO, 1576, p. 1408 [1383]; (T&C vi, 497)—Ridley's Disputation]

These words are built on Tresham's argument from the council of the Lateran, concerning transubstantiation.[178] The council was a relatively recent one, and Tresham suspects Ridley of not accepting it, which Ridley confirms. Tresham cries out to the scribes, *Scribite, scribite*,[179] which provokes an even clearer response: 'No sir, I receive not that council; *scribite, et rescribite*.'[180]

The argument then turns on whether evil men eat the body of Christ in the sacrament, or whether it is only present to the believer. Tresham argues that they do so eat (albeit to their condemnation),[181] therefore 'the true and natural body of Christ is on the altar'. Ridley concedes that evil men 'do eat the very true and natural body of Christ sacramentally', but 'no further'.

Because of the damage to the folio we cannot be sure, but it seems likely that Stephyn has appreciated the clarity of Tresham's phrase 'the true and natural body of Christ is on the altar' and incorporated it into SA. Only the final part survives.

---

their hands', cf. *The Bible and Holy Scriptvres, conteyned in the Olde and Newe Testament* (Geneva: Rowland Hall, 1560), f. 131r.
177 William Tresham (c. 1500-1569), of Oakley Magna, Northamptonshire, was vice chancellor of Oxford several times. Assisting Henry VIII in his theological innovations, he was imprisoned under Edward VI but rehabilitated under Mary I. On the accession of Elizabeth, he offered the congratulations of the university but would not take the oath of supremacy. Deprived of most positions, he was allowed to retire to Northamptonshire. Cf. Gary G. Gibbs, 'William Tresham (1495-1567), priest' in *Oxford Dictionary of National Biography* online, https://doi.org/10.1093/ref:odnb/27714. Accessed 20 October 2018.
178 Lateran IV, convoked by Innocent III in 1213, convened in Rome in 1215. With such ample notice a great many bishops attended, as Tresham points out.
179 'Write, write'.
180 'Write and write again'.
181 Cf. 1 Cor 11:27-29.

Quotation 48. SA 65v.4–5, 8–9 (Latin)
65v.5–7, 9–10 (Cornish)

St Augustine of Hippo, *De Baptismo (contra Donatistas)*, 5, 8 (9).[182]
buccellam Dominus tradidit ... [acci]piendo pec[c]avit ... Qui aliquis ... non est corpus
(Because someone does not eat it 'to salvation', does not mean it is not the body)
[Foxe, TAMO, 1576, p. 1408 [1383]; (T&C vi, 498)—Ridley's Disputation]

The biblical references in SA just prior to this passage may be reconstructed. Mk 14:17–21 corresponds with Jn 13:26–27, where Jesus dips a morsel (*buccella*) of bread into a dish at the Passover supper, and gives it to Judas.[183] Lk 22:21 refers to Judas's hand being on the Passover table with the Lord. Jn 18:3 recounts the betrayal by Judas in the Garden of Gethsemane. All four, therefore, have a direct bearing on the passage itself, from *Contra Donatistas*.

Augustine is writing here—around the year 400—against the Donatists, who were rebaptizing converts. He uses Cyprian to support his contention that baptism still has efficacy even if the recipient is not in full Catholic unity. Then he draws an analogy with Judas, 'who did not receive what is bad, but received it badly', saying: 'it was nonetheless the body and blood of the Lord, even for those to whom the Apostle said: he who eats unworthily, eats and drinks damnation to himself'.[184]

Tresham uses the text to show that the unworthiness of the recipient does not change the objective reality of the sacrament.[185] It is a clear challenge to 'receptionism'—which holds that the body of Christ is present only to those who receive with faith and good intentions. Ridley accepts that the unworthy receive the body—that is, the *sacrament* of the body—making his (and Cranmer's) customary distinction, but he draws attention to another place in Augustine. There, he says, a distinction is made between *panem Domini* and *panem Dominum*. The point is obscure, and Tresham does not pick it up. (In fact, in that place, Augustine is saying that 'they [the apostles] ate the bread of the Lord; he [Judas] ate the Lord's bread against the Lord: they ate life, he punishment', which, if anything, supports Tresham's argument.)[186]

---

182 Michael Petschenig, ed., *S. Aureli Augustini Operi 7: Psalmus contra partem Donati, Contra epistulam Parmeniani, De baptismo* [CSEL 51/1] (Vienna: Tempsky, 1908), p. 270 [PL 43, 181].
183 There is no connection with the *scabellum*, 'footstool' of 64v.15—a possibility suggested by Nance).
184 *Corpus enim Domini, et sanguis Domini nihilominus erat, etiam illis quibus dicebat Apostolus: 'Qui manducat & bibit indignè, iudicium sibi manducat & bibit'*.
185 Tunstall, *De ueritate Corporis et Sanguinis*, ff. 37v, 38r & 98v, has *locum in se diabolo præbuit* rather than *peccavit*. Tresham paraphrases the second phrase.
186 Cf. Radbod Willems, ed., *Sancti Aurelii Augustini: In Iohannis evangelium tractatus CXXIV*, 59, 1 [CCSL 36] (Turnhout: Brepols, 1954), p. 476. [PL 35, 1796].

Stephyn shares Tresham's view but mistranslates him spectacularly. The original double negative 'Because some do not eat unto salvation, it followeth not therefore that it is not his body' becomes in Cornish 'There are some who do not eat the Body of Christ to their salvation, and so it is not the Body of God to them' (*e ma ran nyng egy ow tybbry Corf Christ th'aga sawya, ha rag henna, nyng ew thethans Corf Dew*). Stephyn may mean, 'Those who receive unworthily, do so in a way that will not help their salvation, for they do not recognize the Body.' If so, that is perfectly orthodox. All the same, he should have written something like 'but it is still the Body of God to them' (*bus whath eth ew thethans Corf Dew*). Straining at gnats while swallowing camels he does, however, correct the diminutive *buccellulam* ('little morsel') in Foxe to the Vulgate's *buccellam* ('morsel').

Quotation 49. SA 65v.12-13 (Latin) 65v.13-16 (Cornish)

St Theophylact of Ohrid, *Enarratio in Evangelium Matthaei*, 26:20-25.[187]
Ostendit Dominus crudelitatem Judae … et gustavit carnem Domini
(Judas behaved harshly and failed in understanding, but still tasted the Lord's flesh)
[Foxe, TAMO, 1576, p. 1408 [1383]; (T&C vi, 498)—Ridley's Disputation]

The word 'Theophelact' appears to have been started as a marginal reference, but then incorporated it into the narrative. The text we have—*ostendit Dominus crudelitatem Iudae … qui cum argueretur non intellexit, et gustauit carnem Domini* differs from some widely available contemporary versions,[188] explained by variant translations of the Greek original.

Born in Chalcis, Euboea (modern Khalkida, Evia) just off the Greek mainland, Theophylact (c. 1055-1107+) moved to Constantinople, where he taught the imperial heir before becoming archbishop of Ohrid.[189] He wrote his commentary on the Gospel of Matthew in around 1100. Though much later, he still had to contend with Gnostic and Manichaean ideas, as had Augustine and Tertullian. Like them, he turned to the incarnational and the sacramental

---

187 A modern, critical edition is unavailable, but see *Theophylacti Archiepiscopi Bulgariæ in Quatuor Domini Nostri Iesu Christi Euangelia …* (Paris: Charles Guillard, 1546), ff. 81r-81v, Google Books, Accessed 18 October 2018. (Migne makes use of the same translation, via an intermediary edition [PG 123, 443B].)
188 For example: *Apposuit autem vescentibus, ut ostenderet crudelitatem Iudæ, [quia in mensa et communione ciborum illius, quando si & fera fuisset, mansuetiorem se exhibuisset:] tunc neque quum argueretur, intellexit, sed & corpus illius gustans non pœnituit*, in *Theophylacti Archiepiscopi Bulgariae In Quatuor … Euangelia* (op. cit.), ff. 81r-81v.
189 Historically Bulgarian in culture, this city was part of the Byzantine Empire and is now in North Macedonia.

aspects of apologetics. (Aquinas quoted him in his *Catena Aurea*,[190] which gave him greater prominence in the West, and in the 1540s editions of his commentaries were printed.)

Here he is commenting on the 'harshness' of Judas in betraying Jesus immediately after the last supper, even though he had just 'tasted the Lord's flesh'.[191] While the quotation makes this point clearly, Weston does not point out that there are other places where Theophylact remarks that there is not universal agreement on it.[192] Nonetheless, he does add: 'For he did not say, this is a figure, but this is my body.'[193]

In response, Ridley claims that Judas tasted the Lord's flesh 'insensibly', quickly clarifying that by 'flesh' he means 'the sacrament of the Lord's flesh'. Weston replies by quoting Chrysostom, who says that the punishment due to those who receive the body of the Lord unworthily is the same as that due to those who crucified him. Ridley accepts that evil men 'defile the Lord's body', in the sense that they 'eat the body of Christ sacramentally'. One senses here the possibility of a meaningful discussion, had both sides been more open. As it happens, Watson takes the debate in another direction.

Stephyn reinforces one of his central points, that the 'flesh of the Lord God' (*kigg an Arluth Dew* 65v.16) is truly present on the altar. The next two quotations continue in the same vein.

Quotation 50. SA 65v.16–19 (Latin) 65v.19–23 (Cornish)

'Gelasius' of Cyzicus, *Commentarius Actorum Concilii Nicæni*, 2, 30.[194]
Humiliter spectemus propositum panem et potum ... a sacerdotibus sacrificatum
(Let us faithfully believe the Lamb of God lies on that holy table)
[Foxe, TAMO, 1576, p. 1408 [1383]; (T&C vi, 498)—Ridley's Disputation]

Cussel a Nice refers to the Council of Nicaea (İznik in modern Turkey, not Nice in modern France). The passage was cited in Convocation in 1553 under

---

190 Although not directly in his collection of quotations on Mt 26:20–25. Cf. Newman, ed., *Catena Aurea*, vol. 1, pp. 284–5 on Mk 14:22–25; vol. 3, pp. 708–11, on Lk 22:24–30; and particularly vol. 4, pp. 241–5 on Jn 6:52–59, which gives the whole passage.
191 I am grateful to C.W.H. Hatcher for invaluable advice on aspects of this passage.
192 Newman, ed., *Catena Aurea*, vol. 1, p. 287.
193 See Quotations 68–69.
194 Cf. Günther Christian Hansen, ed., *Anonyme Kirchengeschichte (Gelasius Cyzicenus, CPG 6034)* (Berlin: Walter de Gruyter, 2002), 2, 31, 6, p. 89, line 25, beginning Ἐπὶ τῆς θείας τραπέζης. [PG 85, 1317–18B]. This can also be found in Philippe Labbé and Gabriel Cossart, eds, *Sacrosancta Concilia ad Regiam Editionem Exacta ...* (Paris: Societas Typographica Librorum Ecclesiasticorum, 1671), vol. 2, col. 232D (in some printings 234D). The translation in Labbé and Cossart appears to be earlier than that found in Tunstall, *De ueritate Corporis et Sanguinis*, f. 40r. Interestingly,

Mary I, when transubstantiation was reaffirmed as the doctrine of the Church of England.[195]

The first ecumenical Council of Nicaea took place in 325 and the second in 787. While Nicaea I does contain material relevant to the Disputations and Bonner's Homilies,[196] the quotation at first sight seems to have a later flavour (though Nicaea II was little discussed in the time of SA).[197] It turns out, however, that it comes from a history of Nicaea I, written around the year 475 (that is, some 150 years after it), by an unknown priest of Cyzicus, later given the name 'Gelasius' by Photius I. This work was known and trusted by both Ridley and his opponents, and in recent years has been restored to credibility as a primary historical source. Gelasius wished to show that the council had not taken a Monophysite position, so he highlights the real presence, in the context of the incarnation. He invites us not to look downwards, but to 'lift up the mind' with 'a good heart'—implying a moral dimension to orthodoxy—and 'believe faithfully' that the Lamb of God is truly present 'upon the holy table ... taking away the sins of the world, in the priestly sacrifice'.

Ridley acknowledges this account as 'a great authority' and accepts it. He points out however, that it refers to *bread* being set before us, and 'having our minds lifted up' considering him 'which *is in heaven*'. While, in a sense, the Lamb of God is present 'on the table', this is 'by a spiritual presence, by grace, not after the corporal substance of his flesh taken of the Virgin Mary'. This is an important explanation of Ridley's position, which increasingly influenced Cranmer's. It is far from being a purely receptionist one, and Zwingli would not have agreed with it.[198]

For Stephyn, however, this is exactly the sort of passage he is looking for. In his eyes, it states clearly that 'the Lamb of God is set upon the altar' and that this is 'what the priests consecrate' (*an pith ew benygys gans prontyrryan*).

---

the version he gives in his discussion—seemingly made by Oecolampadius, the reformer (cf. ff. 40v–41v)—is closer to SA.)
195 Dugmore, *The Mass and the English Reformers*, p. 196.
196 Cf. P. Prodi, ed., *Conciliorum Oecumenicorum Decreta* (Bologna: Herder, 1962), p. 8.
197 Bellarmine, for example, points out that it seemed unknown even to St Thomas Aquinas (St Robert Bellarmine, *De Imaginibus Sanctorum, 2, 22*, in Vitus Erbermann, ed., *Disputationum Roberti Bellarmini Politiani S.J., S.R.E. Cardinalis De Controversiis Christianæ Fidei ...* vol. 2 (Venice: Malachinus, 1721), f. 409E. Google Books, accessed 18 October 2018). But see note 204 below.
198 Nor would Luther, for other reasons. For a summary of the context and historiography see Allen, *The Eucharistic Debate in Tudor England*, pp. 1–12; for arguments for elements of orthodoxy and historical continuity within Cranmer's and Ridley's teachings see Dugmore, *The Mass and the English Reformers*, pp. 127–31, 176–201; for a critique of their positions see Clark, *Eucharistic Sacrifice and the Reformation*, pp. 127–76.

Quotation 51. SA 65v.23–4 (Latin) 65v.24–5 (Cornish)

Watson, quoting 'Gelasius', *Commentarius Actorum Concilii Nicæni*, 2, 30.[199]
Exaltata mente ... Agnus Dei jacet in mensa
(If we lift up our minds, we will recognize the Lamb of God upon the altar)
[Foxe, TAMO, 1576, p. 1408 [1383]; (T&C vi, 498)—Ridley's Disputation]

When Watson reminds him again of the direct quotation from Gelasius, Ridley claims it is 'figurative speech'. Watson presses his point, citing the Greek, that the Lamb of God himself 'lies' (κεῖται) on the altar—it is not his 'operation' (as Ridley says) that lies there. This forces Ridley to reaffirm that 'the heavenly Lamb is ... on the table' with a 'spiritual presence', but he questions whether either side really thinks Christ lies there 'prostrate with his members spread upon the table'.[200]

Stephyn appears to be sensitive to the translation of *mensa* as 'table' in this context, perhaps looking back to the Edwardine desecrations of the stone *mensae*, where some were put to secular purposes or even placed near church entrances, to be walked upon. He translates the word as *alter*.

Quotation 52. SA 65v.26–8 (Latin) 65v.29–32 (Cornish)

Smith, quoting Nicaea II, *Acta* 6, 3.[201]
Nullus apostolorum dixit haec est figura ... incruentum altaris sacrificium figura
(None of the apostles or elders said the unbloody sacrifice of his Body was a 'figure')
[Foxe, TAMO, 1576, p. 1408 [1383]; (T&C vi, 499)—Ridley's Disputation]

The figures [1]383 at the damaged foot of this folio almost certainly refer to folio 1383 of the 1576 edition of Foxe, where the relevant passage is found. This is a decisive piece of evidence in establishing the edition of Foxe used by Stephyn.

Ridley observes: 'This canon is not in the council of Nice; for I have read over this council many times.' He is correct if he means Nicaea I, but the passage is indeed found among the *Acta* of Nicaea II, the seventh ecumenical council, which

---

199 Hansen, ed., *Anonyme Kirchengeschichte*, p. 89, line 25, Labbé and Cossart, eds, *Sacrosancta Concilia*, vol. 2, col. 232D [PG 85, 1317–18B]. See Quotation 50.
200 According to Foxe. This final sentence does not appear in Ridley's Latin notes.
201 Cf. Giovanni Domenico Mansi, *Sacrorum Conciliorum Nova et Amplissima Collectio* (Florence: Antonio Zatta, 1768), vol. 13, 263–4E. (The Latin translation differs here from the one found in SA and Foxe.) Documenta Catholica Omnia online, http://www.documentacatholicaomnia. eu/04z/z_1692-1769__Mansi_JD__Sacrorum_Conciliorum_Nova_Amplissima_Collectio_Vol_013__LT.pdf.html. Accessed 15 November 2018.

defended orthodox teaching on the use of icons.²⁰² Even in this context, the council avoided suggesting that Christ's Eucharistic presence was symbolic or iconic.

The passage in question comes from the refutation of a false council during the Sixth Session (6 October 787), read by the deacon Epiphanios.²⁰³ He points out that 'none of those clarions of the Spirit, the saints, apostles or illustrious fathers, ever spoke of the icon of his body (εἰκόνα τοῦ σώματος αὐτοῦ) in connection with our unbloody sacrifice (ἀναίμακτον ἡμῶν θυσίαν) which is made in commemoration of Christ, according to his explicit command', and neither did Christ himself say 'take, eat the image of my body'. Indeed, 'although the figure of the bread and wine can still be seen, after the consecration the [elements] are believed to be nothing else than the body and blood of Christ'.²⁰⁴

Smith's introduction of this passage clearly has an impact on Ridley, even though he doubts its source. By speaking of the figure of bread, rather than the figure of the body, it upturns the discussion. Although Ridley sometimes resorts to 'figurative' arguments,²⁰⁵ he is also 'far ... from that opinion ... that the godly and faithful ... receive nothing ... but a figure of the body of Christ'.²⁰⁶ Before things can go further, however, there is another interjection, this time about the Council of Florence.²⁰⁷ While Ridley responds by claiming there was 'nothing agreed concerning transubstantiation' at that council, the whole exchange nudges him to concede that the 'unbloody sacrifice of the body of Christ' is indeed 'offered' in the Eucharist, providing these terms are 'rightly' understood.

This is one of the few passages in SA (and indeed in the Tregear Manuscript as a whole) where there is a clear allusion to the *incruentum sacrificium*, the 'unbloody sacrifice' of the Mass.²⁰⁸ Despite his focus on Christ's real presence, we see that the Mass as sacrifice is also important to Stephyn, who notes the page number in Foxe.

---

202 See note 197 just above.
203 Cf. Mansi, *Sacrorum Conciliorum*, vol. 13, 265–6D.
204 A similar text is found in Aquinas (via Gratian), wrongly attributed to Ambrose: *Licet figura panis et vini videatur, nihil tamen aliud quam caro Christi et sanguis post consecrationem credenda sunt*: St Thomas Aquinas, e.g. *Summa Theologica*, III, Q. 75, Art. 2 (*Corpus Thomisticum*, Accessed 10 October 2018); *Decretum Gratiani*, Pars 3, *De Consecratione*, Dist II, C. LXXV. (See Quotation 29 for a related point.)
205 Cf. Quotation 51 and T&C vi, 498.
206 T&C vi, 475.
207 This council, which sought reconciliation between East and West, concluded in 1447, but by the Fall of Constantinople in 1453 hopes of ending the Great Schism had receded.
208 The term 'unbloody sacrifice' is often linked with the Council of Trent (Session 22, chap I, cf. Giuseppe Alberigo, ed., *Conciliorum Oecumenicorum Decreta*, 3rd ed. (Bologna: Istituto per le Scienze Religiose, 1973), pp. 732f), but it has a long history and *De Sacramentis*, 4, 6, 27, quoting an early form of the Roman Canon, speaks of the *incruentam hostiam*. (Schmitz, *De Sacramentis*, p. 152.) It remains important in Catholicism today, as in John Paul II, *Dominicae Cenae* (24 Feb. 1980), II, 9.

Quotation 53. SA 66r.2 (Latin) 66r.3 (Cornish)

St John Chrysostom, *De incomprehensibili Dei natura (seu contra Anomœos)* 3, 40.[209]
N[on solum homines &c.]
(It is not only men who are praying ... Angels, too, fall down in adoration)
[Foxe, TAMO, 1576, p. 1413 [1388]; (T&C vi, 509)—Latimer's Disputation]

Stephyn jumps to Latimer's Disputation. Although only the initial 'N' of *Non solum homines &c.* survives, the Cornish 'It is not only men that make it' (*[Nyng ew] tus only a'n gwra*) is more complete, and the passage is confirmed in Foxe.[210]

This treatise was written to challenge the Anomoean (Eunomian) Arians, who asserted the inequality of the Son and claimed to know God as he knows himself, which incensed Chrysostom. In a series of homilies, he stressed the mystery and transcendence of God.[211] Once again he draws from the liturgy: 'It is not only men who are making their voices heard in that prayer, a prayer which is filled with the holiest fear and dread. Angels, too, fall down in adoration before their Lord, archangels beg his favour. They have that sacred moment to fight for them as their ally: they have the Sacrifice to lend them aid.'[212] Prayer and the Mass are intertwined.

Bombarded by such quotations, Latimer, like Ridley, concedes that we do 'worship' Christ 'in the sacrament'. While rejecting transubstantiation and what he calls the 'massing worship', he accepts that the 'true blood' of Christ is tasted (although 'spiritually') and that a 'sacrifice memorative' is indeed offered. Weston seeks to build on this, citing *Non solum homines* after Quotation 59 (q.v.). Latimer is unfamiliar with it, commenting that Chrysostom often speaks in a 'figurative' way.

As noted above, Stephyn has purposely chosen to reposition this passage here and, unlike Foxe, he translates it. Clearly, he shares something of its mystical vision.

---

209 Cf. Jean Daniélou, Anne-Marie Malingrey, Robert Flacelière, eds, *Jean Chrysostome: Sur l'incompréhensibilité de Dieu* [Sources Chrétiennes 28 bis, CPG 4318] (Paris: Editions du Cerf, 1970), III, 450, p. 224, line 451, beginning Οὐκ ἄνθρωποι μόνοι, cf. also Introduction, pp. 58–60 [PG 48, 726]. For Chrysostom in general, see Quotations 4, 6 and 12.
210 See Textual Notes and Appendix B for this and adjacent passages: some small fragments have been wrongly repositioned in the conserved MS.
211 The homilies were thought to have been preached in 386–7, but Mayer suggests a date of 398 at Constantinople—cf. Mayer, 'The Biography of John Chrysostom', p. 18.
212 Paul W. Harkins, tr., *On the Incomprehensible Nature of God by St John Chrysostom* (Washington: Catholic University of America, 1982), p. 113.

Quotation 54. SA 66r.4–5 (Latin) 66r.5–6 (Cornish) [and TH 56r.4–7m][213]

St John Chrysostom, *Homiliae in Acta Apostolorum*, 21, 4.[214]
Qu[id dicis? Hostia in] manibus sacerdotis &c.
(What do you say to this? The host is held in the hands [of the priest])
[Foxe, TAMO, 1576, p. 1413 [1388]; (T&C vi, 509)—Latimer's Disputation]

The attention here is on the Eucharistic host being held in the hands. (Weston adds the word *sacerdotis*, 'of the priest', but he hardly needs to.) Foxe again chooses not to translate or continue this quotation.

Chrysostom moves from the miraculous raising of the dead (Acts 9:32–43; Mk 5:21–24, 35–43) to works of charity and prayer for the departed. Citing the deacon's prayers in the liturgy for those who have fallen asleep, he writes the following (possibly edited) passages:[215] 'What do you say to this? The Sacrifice is held in the hands,[216] and all things necessary are set out and well prepared. Angels are there, and Archangels; the Son of God is there; all stand with such awe, silent and yet crying out ...';[217] 'his Death, that awesome Sacrifice, that unutterable mystery, is being celebrated'.

Latimer, feeling frail and already subjected to a barrage of what he calls Chrysostom's 'emphatical locutions', claims that the saint never suggests Mass can be offered 'for the quick and the dead'. Weston comes straight back with this passage from *Homiliae in Acta Apostolorum*. Set firmly in the context of liturgical prayer for the departed, it is a thoroughgoing vision of the power and majesty of the sacrifice of the Mass. Weston wryly observes: 'he doth not call it a cup of wine'. Latimer shifts his ground, saying that at least Chrysostom does not call it a *'propitiatory* sacrifice'.

It is clear which way the argument is now going. Like Weston, Stephyn now focuses on the Mass as 'the sacrifice of the Body of Christ', offered for the dead as well as the living, through which the Holy Souls are 'relieved'.

---

213 Incorrectly cited in TH as from *De incomprehensibili Dei natura*, 3: cf. Quotation 53.
214 In the absence of a modern, critical edition of this text I have used Migne [PG 60, 170], beginning Τί λέγεις; Ἐν χερσὶν ἡ θυσία / *Quid dicis? Hostia in manibus.*
215 Mayer, 'The Biography of John Chrysostom', p. 14 (after Francis T. Gignac, 'Evidence for deliberate scribal revision in Chrysostom's *Homilies on the Acts of the Apostles*' in John Petruccione, ed., *Nova & Vetera. Patristic Studies in Honor of Thomas Patrick Halton* (Washington, DC, 1998), pp. 209–25) suggests two distinct recensions.
216 Or 'sacrificial victim' (θυσία/hostia).
217 *Quid dicis? In manibus est hostia, & omnia proposita sunt bene ordinata, adsunt angeli, adsunt archangeli, adest filius Dei, cum tanto horrore adstant omnes, adstant illi clamantes omnibus silentibus*—Tunstall, *De ueritate Corporis et Sanguinis*, f. 66r.

Quotation 55. SA 66r.7–8 (Latin) 66r.8–11 (Cornish)

St John Chrysostom, *In epistolam ad Philippenses commentarius*, 4 (3).[218]
Non temere ab Apostolis est institutum
(The Apostles ordered the commemoration of the departed at the Eucharist)
[Foxe, TAMO, 1576, p. 1413 [1388]; (T&C vi, 509)—Latimer's Disputation]

The loose fragments containing *temere ab Apostolis* were affixed during conservation well above their proper place—but are now restored in this edition (see Textual Notes and Appendix B). Judging from N, either Nance suspected this, or the fragments had not yet detached when he was working. Weston's initial reference (repeated in the margin of both Foxe and SA) to *De Statuis*—see Quotation 11—appears to be incorrect. There is no homily '69' in that sequence.[219] His second reference is to Chrysostom writing 'to the Philippians', meaning his Homilies on St Paul's letter to the Philippians, which is indeed where this is found. The dating of *Ad Philippenses* is far from certain,[220] nor were the homilies necessarily delivered in sequence.[221] Allen argues that some date from Antioch, some from Constantinople.[222]

Chrysostom, starting from the passage 'For me, living is Christ, and dying is gain' (Phil 1:21 NRSV) discusses pastorally and theologically appropriate ways to commemorate the departed, including memorial offerings and prayer during the Eucharist: 'Not in vain did the Apostles arrange that remembrance should be made in those wondrous Mysteries for the dead. They knew that great gains would result from it, great benefit. For at that moment when everyone stands with uplifted hands, with all the priests, and that most awe-inspiring Sacrifice is revealed, how should God not be pleased to answer such prayers?'

Foxe has Weston quoting only the opening words of this passage, passing over it quickly with neither translation nor expansion. Yet it has considerable bearing on what Christians of Chrysostom's time thought of prayer for the dead. Latimer is not particularly deferential to patristic testimony, however. He considers any idea of the 'sacrifice of the Mass' to be a kind of 're-offering',

---

218 Field, ed., *Ioannis Chrysostomi ... Omnium Epistolarum Paulinarum ...*, tom. 5 [*Homiliae in epistolam ad Philippenses*] (Oxford: J.H. Parker, 1847), p. 37, beginning Πῶς και τίνι τρόπῳ [PG 62, 204]; Pauline Allen, tr., *John Chrysostom, Homilies on Paul's Letter to the Philippians* (Atlanta: Society of Biblical Literature, 2013), pp. 72–5. The passage is taken from Homily 4 (in some editions, Homily 3) on Phil 1:18–22.
219 Although, in Homily 6, 19, Chrysostom speaks of the 'prayers of the holy fathers' helping us as we depart this life [PG 49, 91].
220 See Quotation 54 and Mayer, 'The Biography of St John Chrysostom', p. 13.
221 Pauline Allen and Wendy Mayer, 'Chrysostom and the Preaching of Homilies in Series: A Re-Examination of the Fifteen Homilies *In Epistulam Ad Philippenses* (CPG 4432), *Vigiliae Christianae* (Leiden: Brill, 1995), vol. 49, issue 3, pp. 270–89.
222 Allen, ed., *John Chrysostom, Homilies on ... Philippians*, p. xviii.

rather than a 're-presentation' and simply does not accept that Christ can be offered in this way: 'He is too precious a thing for us to offer, he offereth himself.' (Of course, the disputants also believed that Christ offered himself, but understood that sacrificial offering to be made present in the celebration of Mass.)

In this series of quotations Stephyn is listing briefly some of his main patristic sources for prayer for the departed at Mass, and it may reasonably be assumed that he had had access to fuller versions or remembered more than he set down. These references made sense to him and were perhaps his proof texts. Unlike Foxe, he translates the portion he gives.

Quotation 56. SA 66r.12–14 (Latin) 66r.14–16 (Cornish)

St Augustine of Hippo, *Enchiridion de Fide, Spe et Charitate*, 29, 110.[223]
Non est negandum defunctorum ... sacrificium mediatoris affertur
(The souls of the departed are aided by their friends when the Sacrifice is offered)
[Foxe, TAMO, 1576, p. 1413 [1388]; (T&C vi, 509)—Latimer's Disputation]

The *Enchiridion* was written in the later years of Augustine's life (c. 420) and sums up Christian worship in the context of a life of faith, hope and love. It is a sort of catechism or handbook, written in response to a certain Laurentius, and has inspired many later catechisms with its focus on the Lord's Prayer and the Apostles' Creed.

Augustine acknowledges that very holy Christians are hardly in need of prayer when they die but feels that others could indeed be helped by it. A little after the passage quoted here, he explains that the 'sacrifice of the altar' (or loving works undertaken in Christ, such as 'almsgiving') can be offered up for the Christian dead. When applied to the good and holy, this has the nature of thanksgiving; when applied to those who have sinned (but not grievously), it may help them overcome the consequences of their sins. Even in the case of the very bad, such offerings at least console those left behind.

Since Latimer is now accepting the Mass as in some sense a sacrifice, Weston presses him on whether that sacrifice can be offered for the departed. While

---

223 M.P.J. van den Hout, M. Evans et al., eds, *Sancti Aurelii Augustini: De fide rerum invisibilium; Enchiridion ad Laurentium de fide et spe et caritate etc.* [CCSL 46] (Turnhout: Brepols, 1969), p. 108 [PL 40, 283]. The passage is also found in *De octo dulcitii quaestionibus*, Q.2, 4, e.g. [PL 40, 158]. Cf. Tunstall, *De ueritate Corporis et Sanguis*, f. 95, with the reference '*Augustinus in Enchiridio, cap.* 110': *Neque negandum est defunctorum animas pietate suorum uiuentium releuari, cum pro illis sacrificium mediatoris offertur, uel eleemosynæ in Ecclesiis fiunt*. Note the minor differences from this and Foxe in the SA text, particularly *viventiumm* and *affertur*.

some reformers treated prayer for the departed as unnecessary (as they did not believe in an 'intermediate state' between death and either heaven or hell), others accepted it, partly because of passages like this in Augustine (or Chrysostom).[224] Whatever they thought of such prayer in theory, however, most agreed in opposing masses for the dead in practice, arguing that, in popular devotion, the purpose of the Eucharist had been largely subverted into a vast *cultus* of prayer for the departed.

Hence Weston's question, and Latimer's dismissive reply: 'it needeth not, and it booteth not'. Weston then brings the quotation from the *Enchiridion*, but Latimer feels no duty to trust Augustine unless he considers his teachings 'manifest in scripture'. This shows how far back he thought 'error' had crept into Christian belief.

The Cornish translation omits part of the original, indicated here in square brackets: 'when the sacrifice [of the Mediator] is offered [for them. Where he proveth the verity] of Christ's body and praying for the dead.' A conjectural reconstruction of this is offered in the edited text (see Notes).

Quotation 57. SA 66r.16–17 (Cornish only)

Weston, alluding to St Augustine of Hippo, *Confessiones*, 9, 12, 32.[225]
... an keth Austin ma a leveris aferan rag e vam Monaca ...
(This same Augustine said Mass for his mother Monica)
[Foxe, TAMO, 1576, p. 1413 [1388]; (T&C vi, 509)—Latimer's Disputation]

The reference in SA is a simple translation of Weston's brief allusion to this passage from Augustine's 'Confessions'.[226] These were written towards the end of the fourth century, during Augustine's first years as a bishop, and include his mother Monica's funeral. 'When the body was carried to the grave, we went, we returned—without tears. Nor [did I weep] during those prayers which we

---

224 E.g. St John Chrysostom, *Homiliae in primum ad Corinthios*, 41, 5. Field, ed., *Ioannis Chrysostomi ... Omnium Epistolarum Paulinarum ...*, tom. 2 [*Homiliae in epistolam ad Corinthios priorem*], pp. 525–66 [PG 61, 361C] 'Let us help and commemorate them. If Job's sons were purified by their father's sacrifice, why should we doubt that our offerings for the dead bring them some consolation? Let us not hesitate to help those who have died and to offer our prayers for them.' (Quoted in the *Catechism of the Catholic Church* [CCC] (London: Catholic Truth Society, 2016), revised edition, 2, 3 art.12, III, n. 1032 (p. 242).
225 Lucas Verheijen, *Sancti Augustini: Confessionum libri XIII* [CCSL 27] (Turnhout: Brepols, 1981), p. 151. [PL 32, 775]. Cf. also Pius Knöll, ed., *S. Aureli Augustini: Confessionum libri XIII* [CSEL 33] (Vienna: Tempsky, 1896), pp. 221–2.
226 Confirming the expression 'to say Mass' in Cornish. See Notes on 66r.17.

poured out before Thee, when the sacrifice of our redemption was offered for her, as the corpse was placed beside the grave before being buried.'²²⁷

Although it is clear that Augustine thought the sacrifice of the Mass could be offered for the benefit of departed souls,²²⁸ Latimer argues the saint's understanding of this must have been very different to the Catholic one, saying 'that mass was not like yours'. Weston retorts that Augustine clearly accepted it as a sacrifice, made upon an altar. Latimer concedes further ground, agreeing it 'may be called an altar', but again insists there is 'no propitiatory sacrifice, only Christ'.²²⁹

In continuing to follow the argument in Foxe, Stephyn perhaps shows how important this area is to him personally. (The suppression of the chantries and offerings for the dead under Edward VI would have had a huge impact on the minor clergy in Cornwall.)

Quotation 58. SA 66r.18–19 (Latin) 66r.19–20 (Cornish) [and TH 57r.11–15m]

St Cyril of Alexandria, *In Joannis Evangelium* 10, 2 [on Jn 6:56-7]²³⁰
Per communionem corporis Christi, habitat in nobis Christus corporaliter
(Through the communion of the Body of Christ, Christ dwells in us bodily)
[Foxe, TAMO, 1576, p. 1412 [1387]; (T&C vi, 509)—Latimer's Disputation]

Cyril of Alexandria (*c.* 370–444) was Patriarch of that city from 412 to 444 and contended with forms of both Arianism and Gnosticism, addressing many related issues in his biblical commentaries. Hardly a man of eirenic spirit, his zeal against heresy knew no bounds. He was a prime mover (with Pope Celestine I) at the Council of Ephesus in 431, defending the Blessed Virgin's

---

227 Vernon J. Bourke, trans., *Saint Augustine: Confessions*, The Fathers of the Church, 21 (New York, Catholic University of America, 1953), p. 257.
228 Latimer could also have been aware of other passages ascribed to Augustine, such as *Sermones, 172,2* (or *de Verbis Apostolis 32*) [PL38, 936]: *Orationibus vero sanctae Ecclesiae, et sacrificio salutari, et eleemosynis, quae pro eorum spiritibus erogantur, non est dubitandum mortuos adiuvari.* ('There is no doubt that the dead are helped by the prayers of holy Church, by the saving sacrifice, and by alms offered for their souls.')
229 Later on, he even concedes that the Eucharist can be called a 'propitation' in the limited sense that it is 'a sacrament of the propitation' (T&C vi, 510).
230 Cf. Philip Edward Pusey, ed., *Sancti Patris Nostri Cyrilli Archiepiscopi Alexandrini in D. Joannis Evangelium* (Oxford: Clarendon, 1872), vol. 2, pp. 542, line 8, beginning ἆρ' οὐχὶ καὶ σωματικῶς [PG 74, 342B]. See also *Nonne corporaliter quoque facit communicatione carnis Christi, Christum in nobis habitare* in *Divi Cyrilli Archiepiscopi Alexandrini Opera Omnium ... Tomus Primus* [vol. 1] (Cologne: Melchior Novesian, 1546), lib. 10, cap. 13, f. 283v. Google Books, accessed 29 December 2018.

title of Theotokos,[231] as well as the hypostatic union of the two natures of Christ, against Nestorius. Both sides of the Reformation controversy quoted him in their defence, although what exactly he meant by the word σωματικῶς (translated as *corporaliter* or 'corporally') was contested.

In the passage concerned, Cyril is commenting on Jn 6:56–57 in the context of 1 Cor 10:17. He argues that these texts cannot be explained without reference to the power of the 'mystical host':[232] 'for why do we take it into ourselves? Is it not so that Christ may dwell in us, even corporally, by our participation and communion in his holy flesh?' (He goes on to argue that 'as when we melt wax upon wax, we form one body of two, so by sharing in the body and blood of Christ, he is united to us and we are joined to him'.) Like other Fathers, he uses liturgical spirituality to defend and explain the incarnation.[233]

Latimer also takes an incarnational line (following Cranmer as usual): Christ does dwell in us corporally, but only 'by taking our flesh upon him'. Weston interjects, accusing Latimer of not thinking for himself, saying such learning is 'let out to farm, and shut up in my Lord of Canterbury's book'.

Stephyn has moved on from his quotations defending the offering of Mass for the departed and now returns to the real presence. By taking the English word 'corporally' directly into the Cornish, he sidesteps some of the controversy.

---

231 Θεοτόκος, *Dei Genetrix*, 'Mother of God'—see Chadwick, *The Early Church*, pp. 194–211. For Cyril's Second Letter to Nestorius, setting out his theological position, see J. Stephenson, ed., *Creeds, Councils and Controversies* (London: SPCK, 1973), pp. 276–9. For his purist stance on the Nicene Creed see J.N.D. Kelly, *Early Christian Creeds*, 3rd edn (London: Longman, 1972), pp. 309–12.
232 The words *eulogia mystica* (from Cyril's phrase τῆς μυστικῆς εὐλογίας) refer to the Eucharistic species in this context. The later use in the East of εὐλογία, for the distinct 'blessed bread' shared at the end of the Divine Liturgy, is not intended here.
233 J.N.D. Kelly, *Early Christian Doctrines*, 5th edn (London: Adam & Charles Black, 1977), pp. 444–5.

Quotation 59. SA 66r.21–2 (Latin) 66r.23–4 (Cornish)

St Ambrose, *Ennarationes in 12 Psalmos Davidicos*, 38, 25 [on Ps 39:6][234]
Videmus principem sacerdotem ad nos venientem, et offerentem sanguinem[235]
(The High Priest comes to us, offering the Blood of our Lord)
[Foxe, TAMO, 1576, p. 1413 [1388]; (T&C vi, 509)—Latimer's Disputation]

The citation *[De] apparatione ad Missam* in both Foxe and SA is interesting. Perhaps this authentic quotation from St Ambrose on *Twelve Psalms of David* did form part of the preparation of the priest before Mass in some missals. More likely, Weston (or Foxe) has confused its reference to the High Priest with the prayer *Summe Sacerdos et vere Pontifex, Iesu Christe* (edited by the Benedictine spiritual writer Jean de Fécamp in the twelfth century), still used in this context.

Either way, the quotation appears genuine and embodies a vision of the Mass going back to at least the fourth century. Ambrose explains how the 'water from the rock' and other Old Testament types foreshadow the sacramental mystery. He goes on: 'We see the chief priest coming unto us and offering blood. We follow, inasmuch as we are able, being priests; and we offer the sacrifice on behalf of the people.'

Later reformers questioned whether such language should be taken at its face value. Jewel, in his controversy with Harding,[236] argues from words such as 'We have seen him ... and have thrust our fingers into the dents of his nails' that much was *self-evidently* purely figurative.[237] Weston nonetheless wishes to remind Latimer that such words were once part of his own daily practice, in the very different theological landscape 'forty years ago'. Latimer, without his books (and, as he admits, especially Cranmer's book), can no longer keep up, saying: 'I am not ashamed to acknowledge mine ignorance: these testimonies are more than I can bear away.'

---

234 Michael Petschenig, ed. (editio altera, Michaela Zelzer), *Sancti Ambrosi Opera 6: Explanatio psalmorum XII* [CSEL 64] (Vienna: Verlag der Österreichischen Akademie der Wissenschaften, 1999), p. 203 [PL 14, 1051D]—Ps 38:7 in Ambrose's version.
235 Some sources (but not Foxe) have *principem sacerdotum* (Prince of priests) instead of *principem sacerdotem* (Prince-Priest).
236 Thomas Harding (1516–1572)—from Barnstaple and not to be confused with the Buckinghamshire Protestant—was a humanist and scholar loyal to Henry VIII and even friendly with Lady Jane Grey. He disapproved of the changes under Edward VI but returned to favour under Mary. When Elizabeth came to the throne he was deprived and imprisoned, fleeing to Leuven for a second career as a controversialist, particularly against John Jewel. Cf. L.E.C. Wooding, 'Thomas Harding (1516–1572), theologian and religious controversialist', in *Oxford Dictionary of National Biography* online, https://doi.org/10.1093/ref:odnb/12264. Accessed 27 October 2018.
237 Ayre, ed., *The Works of John Jewel*, pt. 2, p. 730, quoting St Ambrose.

To a traditional sensibility such as Stephyn's, what separates these different perspectives is perhaps their attitude to mystical theology. (When Christians sing 'We have seen the true light, we have received the heavenly Spirit',[238] their words are not merely figurative, but proclaim a spiritual 'reality' which involves both body and soul.) He continues to collect quickly and briefly the 'meat' of the arguments, expressed in the patristic quotations, concerning presence, priesthood and sacrifice.

Quotation 60. SA 66r.26 (Latin) 66r.24–7 (Cornish, with Jn 6:51 in Latin)

Harpsfield, on Jn 6:26–69.
Ema an doctors ... Panis quem dabo ... An bara a theffan ry ew ow kigg ve
(The Fathers' understanding of the Eucharist from John 6)
[Foxe, TAMO, 1576, p. 1416 [1391]; (T&C vi, 517)—Harpsfield's Disputation]

Harpsfield is here 'disputing for his form',[239] or, as we might now say, undergoing the *viva* for his doctorate. Cranmer's scholarship is sufficiently respected that— despite his perceived heresies—he is asked to take part. The difference between the two men concerns the 'objective' presence of Christ in the sacrament. For Cranmer, 'the wicked do not eat his flesh, or drink his blood'. For Harpsfield, they do—albeit to their condemnation. (He is wrong, however, to imply that there is no patristic testimony for linking the earlier parts of this passage to the Eucharist.)[240]

---

238 Cf. Athenagoras Kokkinakis [Archbishop of Thyateira and Great Britain], *Η Λειτουργία της Ορθοδόξου Εκκλησίας / The Liturgy of the Orthodox Church* (London and Oxford: Mowbrays, 1979), pp. 11–12, 132. See also Vladimir Lossky, *The Mystical Theology of the Eastern Church* (Cambridge and London: James Clark & Co., 1957) reprinted 1973, pp. 180–2, 217–20, esp. p. 220 and Timothy Ware [Metropolitan Kallistos of Diokleia], *The Orthodox Church* (Harmondsworth: Penguin Books, 1963) reprinted 1978, pp. 290–4.

239 John Harpsfield (1516–1578) born in Old Fish Street, London, was the first Regius Professor of Greek at Oxford, archdeacon of London in 1554 and dean of Norwich in 1558. (His younger brother Nicholas was archdeacon of Canterbury.) John wrote nine of Bonner's homilies (having written one of Cranmer's). On Elizabeth's accession he was deprived of all his offices and committed to the Fleet, but eventually released to safe custody on health grounds (unlike his brother, who remained in the Tower). (Cf. William Wizeman, 'John Harpsfield (1516–1578), religious writer and Roman Catholic priest', in *Oxford Dictionary of National Biography* online, https://doi.org/10.1093/ref:odnb/12368. Accessed 21 October 2018.)

240 See, for example, Newman, ed., *Catena Aurea*, vol. 4, pp. 233–9 on Jn 6:41–51.

COMMENTARY

It is hard to say why Stephyn has included this sentence: it adds little to his arguments.²⁴¹ Even if he was working quickly, moving from one Latin phrase to the next, he would have known that this was a simple reference to Jn 6:51.²⁴²

Quotation 61. SA 66r.27–9 (Cornish only)

Harpsfield, conflating various passages from St Augustine.²⁴³
Rag [...] dibbry worthily kigg agen Saviour Christ ... bewnans heb dewath
(He who eats the flesh of Christ worthily inherits eternal life)
[Foxe, TAMO, 1576, p. 1416 [1391]; (T&C vi, 518)—Harpsfield's Disputation]

The Quotations now become less precise and more general. Harpsfield summarizes from Augustine that he who eateth Christ's flesh ... after a certain manner ... should live for ever', and Stephyn paraphrases him. The phrase 'after a certain manner' is pivotal to the argument. It alludes to Augustine's *est quidam modus manducandi*, 'there is a certain way of eating', from *Sermo* 71, 11 (not from *Ad Fratres in Eremo* as Weston says shortly after.²⁴⁴ That text is later, part of a 'Myth of Augustine' that sought to assert his familiarity with the eremitical life,²⁴⁵ just as collections of Augustine's sermons such as Jordan of Quedlingberg's *Collectanea Sancti Augustini* were continually augmented with additional, later material.)²⁴⁶ Harpsfield is also perhaps alluding to Augustine's *In Joannis evangelium tractatus* 26, 11–20.

The issue remains whether someone who eats the sacrament 'unworthily' (failing to 'discern the body') in any sense 'takes' the Body of Christ. Cranmer has already asserted: 'I am sure that evil men do not eat the flesh and drink the

---

241 But for the interesting Cornish translation of 'the supper of the Lord' here—*De [Y]ow Habblys* (Maundy Thursday)—see Notes on 66r.25.
242 The bread that I will give [for the life of the world] is my flesh ...' Jn 6:51 NRSV. (*Panis, quem dabo caro mea est [pro mundi vita]*, Vulgate Jn 5:52.)
243 Harpsfield's arguments here appear to rely on St Augustine of Hippo, *In Joannis evangelium tractatus* 26, 11–20 [PL 35, 1611–15], perhaps also influenced by passages cited under Quotation 48, as well as by *Sermo* 71, 11 (*De Verbis Evangelii Matthaei*, XII, 32) [PL 38, 453]. The Pseudo-Augustinian *Ad Fratres in Eremo Commorantes*, 28 (sometimes 29), *De Cena Domini* [PL 40, 1282–7] is less important. For a near-contemporary edition of some of these texts see *D[ivi] Aurelii Augustini Hipponensis Episcopi Operum*, vol. 10 (Paris: Cum Privilegio [Regis], 1586): cf. ff. 18C and 727–8.
244 The confusion may be due to a succession of clauses with *Nunquid* in both sources.
245 For an account of the editions (developing significantly the dating by Rano and Walsh) see Eric Leland Saak, *Creating Augustine: Interpreting Augustine and Augustinianism in the Later Middle Ages* (Oxford: Oxford University Press, 2012), Chapter 3, particularly pp. 81–101. Saak shows that *De Cena Domini* was not part of the main group that persisted across many editions.
246 Saak, *Creating Augustine*, p. 82n, citing the research of Karl Gersbach.

blood'.²⁴⁷ Harpsfield believes they do, at least in the sense of taking it into their mouths, though they do not gain eternal life by it; on the contrary, they are condemned.²⁴⁸ Both parties are agreed, however, that the unworthy recipient cannot be one with Christ and therefore—in that sense—'have' him. As Foxe notes, Harpsfield has already said 'we have him in receiving of him worthily, otherwise not'.²⁴⁹

Part of Stephyn's translation is lost, but the link between 'eating the flesh of our Saviour Christ worthily' (*dibbry worthely kigg agan Saviour*) and attaining eternal life (*bewnans heb dewath*) is not.

Quotation 62. SA 66r.30–31 (Latin), 66r.34, 36 (Cornish)

Stephyn? paraphrasing the Roman Canon (and Chrysostom on 1 Cor 10:16)
Calix est ... Novi Testamenti ... Sanguis ... qui effunditur in remissione totius mundi.
(The chalice of the New Covenant, the blood poured out to forgive the world)
[cf. Foxe, TAMO, 1576, Book 8, p. 1136 [1135]; (T&C v, 269)—On the Six Articles]

Stephyn, already paraphrasing a conflation from Harpsfield in the last Quotation, now departs completely from his usual practice. This quotation does not appear to derive directly from Foxe's account of the Oxford Disputations at all. Instead, it echoes the words at the consecration of the chalice. (These differed slightly depending on the exact source. The scriptural accounts slightly differ,²⁵⁰ as do other early sources such as Hippolytus,²⁵¹ and *De Sacramentis*.)²⁵² Although the marginal reference to Chrysostom, *Homiliae in primum ad Corinthios* (presumably Homily 24, 3, on 1 Cor 10:16) also has relevance, it is not the direct source. Chrysostom speaks of the blood 'which flowed from his side', an unspeakable gift, 'poured out' and 'given to us all'. 'If you desire blood,' he imagines Christ

---

247 T&C vi, 517, perhaps thinking of *In Joannis evangelium tractatus* 26, 18 (note 243 above).
248 T&C vi, 519.
249 T&C vi, 513.
250 In the Vulgate these are: Mt 26:26–8: *hic est enim sanguis meus novi testamenti qui pro multis effunditur in remissionem peccatorum*; Mk 14:23–4: *hic est sanguis meus novi testamenti qui pro multis effunditur*; Lk 22:20: *hic est calix novum testamentum in sanguine meo quod pro vobis funditur*; 1 Cor 11:25: *hic calix novum testamentum est in meo sanguine hoc facite quotienscumque bibetis in meam commemorationem*. (Gryson et al., eds, *Biblia Sacra Vulgata*, pp. 1568, 1600, 1651, 1781.)
251 *Hic est sanguis meus qui pro vobis effunditur*, cf. Joseph A. Jungmann, *The Mass of the Roman Rite: its Origins and Development* (New York: Benziger, 1951), vol. 1, p. 51.
252 *Accipte et bibite ex hoc omnes, hic est enim sanguis meis*, cf. Schmitz, *De Sacramentis*, p. 148 (4, 5, 22).

saying, 'redden not the idols' altars by the slaughter of animals, but my altar with my blood.'[253]

There are also some limited similarities with a passage in Book 8 of Foxe, related to the Six Articles of Henry VIII.[254] (Cranmer later averred that, had Henry not intervened personally in parliament, these articles, which reflected the king's rather traditional understanding, might not have passed.)[255]

A far more direct source than any of these, however, is surely the Roman Canon, which Stephyn used constantly when celebrating Mass: 'This is the chalice of my blood, of the new and eternal Covenant, the mystery of faith: which will be poured out for you and for many for the forgiveness of sins.'[256] Even so, it is very much paraphrased (and misspelt). In choosing it, Stephyn may have been influenced by Latimer's quotation of *Bibite ex hoc omnes* just before Quotation 64 (q.v.), in his disputation with Seton.[257] It is intriguing that, in this significant departure from his normal methodology, he turns first to the liturgy.

---

253 St John Chrysostom, *Homiliae in primum ad Corinthios*, 24, 3. Cf. Field, ed., *Ioannis Chrysostomi ... Omnium Epistolarum Paulinarum ...*, tom. 2, p. 288 [PG 61, 200].
254 Foxe, TAMO 1576, p. 1136 [1135]; T&C v, 269, quoting Fulgentius: 'This cup is the new testament; that is, this cup which I deliver unto you, signifieth the new testament'. For the Six Articles see MacCulloch, *Thomas Cranmer*, pp. 237–58 and G.W. Bernard, *The King's Reformation* (New Haven and London: Yale University Press, 2005), pp. 498–505.
255 Cf. John Edmund Cox, ed., *Miscellaneous Writings and Letters of Thomas Cranmer, Archbishop of Canterbury*, Parker Society (Cambridge: Cambridge University Press, 1846), vol. 2, p. 168.
256 *Hic est enim calix Sanguinis mei, novi et eterni Testamenti, Mysterium fidei: qui pro vobis et pro multis effundetur in remissionem peccatorum*, Nick Sandon, ed., *The Use of Salisbury: The Ordinary of the Mass*, 2nd edn (Newton Abbot, Antico Church Music, 1990), p. 30. Cf. also St Thomas Aquinas, *Summa Theologica*, III, Q. 78, Art. 3. *Corpus Thomisticum*, accessed 10 October 2018.
257 TAMO, 1576, p. 1412 [1387]; (T&C vi, 507). John Seton (c. 1498–1567) was an advocate of the new learning, author of a book of logic and a chaplain of John Fisher, whom he attended in the Tower. Moving to serve Stephen Gardiner, he remained 'settled in papistry' when Elizabeth came to the throne. After a time of imprisonment he went to Rome, where he died in 1567 and was buried in the chapel of the Venerable English College, near the altar. Cf. Glyn Redworth, 'John Seton (1508/9–1572), Roman Catholic priest and writer on logic', in *Oxford Dictionary of National Biography* online, https://doi.org/10.1093/ref:odnb/25124. Accessed 21 October 2018. See also Redworth, *In Defence of the Church Catholic*, p. 272.

Quotation 63. SA 66r.31–3 (Latin), 66r.34–6 (Cornish)

Stephyn? paraphrasing 'St Ambrose', *De Sacramentis*, 4, 4, 19 or 4, 5, 23.[258]
Quod vinum est et aqua in calicem ... qui effunditur pro nobis.
(The wine and water in the chalice become the precious body and blood of Christ)
[cf. Foxe, TAMO, 1576, pp. 1393–4 [1368–9]; (T&C vi, 464–5)—Cranmer's Disputation]

This quotation appears to be a reduction and simplification of a passage from either Quotation 30 or 25 (q.v.), or a combination of both, that Stephyn has already used both in SA and in his marginalia in TH:

> 4, 4, 19: 'So you have learned ... that wine and water are put in the chalice [*quod vinum & aqua in calicem mittitur*] and are made his blood ... But perhaps you say, I do not see any outward appearance of blood [*speciem sanguinis non videri*].'

> 4, 5, 23: 'Before the words of Christ the chalice is full of wine and water [*calix est vini et aquae plenus*]. When the words of Christ have acted upon it, then it is made to be [his] blood which redeemed the people [*sanguis efficitur qui plebem redemit*]'.

Once again, Stephyn appears to have departed from literal following of the Disputations to sum up, in his own slightly defective paraphrase, the whole discussion. (It remains possible that there is another, exact source for these quotations, so far unidentified.)

Quotation 64. SA 66v.1–2 (Latin), 66v.6 (Cornish)

St Augustine of Hippo/Pseudo-Augustine, *Sermone de Tempore?*
[Panis quia dicitur] panis. Corpus quia dicitur Corpus.
(Bread because bread is said; the body because the body is said)
[cf. Foxe, TAMO, p. 1387 [1362]; (T&C vi, 450);—Cranmer's Disputation.]

A definitive identification has not yet been made of the remains of this quotation, in the most damaged part of the MS (see Appendix B, Quotation 53 and the Notes on 66r.3–7 and 66v.1–6). The fragment *Panis ew* (once thought to read *Panis A*) is conserved at 66v.3 but belongs below at 66v.6 (as can be shown from the recto equivalents at Quotation 53). This gives *Panis ew henwis*

---

258 Schmitz, *De Sacramentis*, p. 146 or p. 150 [PL 16, 442B–443A or 444A] respectively.

bara, *Corpus ew henwis Cor[f]*, 'Bread is called *Panis*, Body is called *Corpus*', in the Cornish translation, which suggested *[Panis quia dicitur] panis, Corpus quia dicitur Corpus* in the conjectural reconstruction.

It should be noted that many patristic quotations attributed to Augustine in the late Middle Ages and even the Early Modern period were not by him. Of the early printings of Augustine, almost two-thirds are really Pseudo-Augustine.[259]

Fascinatingly, however, Cranmer uses a few of the same words (*Itaque panis non dicitur panis, sed corpus* ... 'and therefore the bread is not called bread, but his body ...') in his Disputation, although it is far from an exact match.[260] With such fragmentary evidence, however, it is hard to say more.

Quotation 65. SA 66v.3–5 (Latin), 66v.7–8 (Cornish)

St Augustine of Hippo/Pseudo-Augustine, *Sermone de Tempore?*
[o]mnia infidelitatis suspicio ... substantia absque accidentibus.
([Eschew] all unfaithfulness, and you will not worry about substance and accidents)
[cf. Foxe, TAMO, 1576, pp. 1397–8 [1372–3]; (T&C vi, 474)—Ridley's Disputation]

Again, this quotation—which may simply be a continuation of the previous one—has not yet been identified and does not appear to come from Foxe.[261] The words 'accidents' and 'substance' are sometimes found among Augustinian material,[262] but not in this context. Nor does it seem to come from contemporary model sermons such as might have been used by Stephyn in the parish.[263] These in many ways were practical and devotional, rather than doctrinal.[264] Once again, until a satisfactory source is identified, it is difficult even to guess at the meaning.

---

259 Cf. Arnoud S.Q. Visser, *Reading Augustine in the Reformation* (Oxford: Oxford University Press, 2011), p. 15. I am grateful to Eric Saak for guiding me to Visser's important study.
260 Only the English is in 1576 (cf. Foxe, TAMO, 1576, p. 1394 [1369]; (T&C vi, 465), but the Latin is in Foxe, *Rerum in Ecclesia Gestarum*, p. 656 of the 1559 edition.
261 Although substance and accidents are discussed: cf. Foxe, *Rerum in Ecclesia Gestarum*, p. 664; Foxe, TAMO, 1576, pp. 1397–8 [1372–3]; (T&C vi, 474). See also Cox, ed., *The Writings and Disputations of Thomas Cranmer*, p. 43 in the Latin appendix, again raising the question as to whether Stephyn had one of Cranmer's or Gardiner's books.
262 E.g. Sermon 131, *Corporis et sanguinis Christi sacramentum*, St Augustine of Hippo, *Sermones* [PL 38, 729–30].
263 E.g. Sermon for Corpus Christi in Mirk's *Festial*—see Erbe, Theodor, ed., *Mirk's Festial: A Collection of Homilies by Johannes Mirkus (John Mirk), edited from Bodl. MS. Gough Eccl. Top. 4, with variant readings from other MSS.* (London: Kegan, Paul, Trench, Trübner & Co. for the Early English Texts Society, 1905). Internet Archive, https://archive.org/details/mirksfestialcoll01mirkuoft/page/n1. Accessed 23 December 2018.
264 Rubin, *Corpus Christi*, pp. 213–32.

Quotation 66. SA 66v.9 (Latin only)

St Augustine of Hippo, *In Joannis evangelium tractatus* 50, 4.[265]
In cœlum manum mittam, ut Christum teneamus.
(We reach the hand [of faith] towards heaven, that we may hold Christ)
[cf. Foxe, TAMO, 1576, p. 1414 [1389]; (T&C vi, 512–13)—Harpsfield's Disputation]

A clear 'sign of the cross' here refers to an insertion at the foot of the folio—similarly marked—which gives the full text. The line—although it is numbered in the ordinary sequence in the edition—has been inserted later by Stephyn, rather in the style of his marginal notes in the last two homilies of TH. Only the beginning of the quotation is given here, but it is continued below at SA 66a.26, Quotation 70, where full references and commentary are provided.

Quotation 67. SA 66v.10 (Latin) 66v.10 (Cornish)

St Augustine of Hippo, *In Joannis evangelium tractatus* 25, 12.[266]
Crede et edisti
(Believe and you have eaten)
[Foxe, TAMO, 1576, p. 1412 [1387]; (T&C vi, 507)—Latimer's Disputation]

Foxe has here *Crede et manducasti*, 'Beleue, and thou hast eaten', easily accommodated with the proposed reconstruction of the Cornish (*Crig ge, ha e thesta [tibbry]*),[267] and according with most editions of Augustine.[268] Stephyn, interestingly, has *Crede et edisti*: the intended meaning is the same, so perhaps he baulked at the overtones (of physically chewing) in *manducasti*, or—as in some of the other later quotations in SA—was remembering imperfectly. There is a stylistic and theological echo of Quotation 70: *Mitte fidem et tenuisti*, 'Reach out with faith and you have taken hold.'

Augustine says 'This, then, is how to eat the food which does not perish, but endures for eternal life ... why prepare teeth or stomach? Believe, and you have eaten already.' The context is an exposition of faith and justification, based on Romans 3:28 and 10:4—which would have strongly appealed to the

---

265 Willems, ed., *In Iohannis evangelium tractatus* [CCSL 36], p. 434 [PL 35, 1759-60].
266 Willems, ed., *In Iohannis evangelium tractatus* [CCSL 36], p. 254 [PL 35, 1602].
267 Nance in T gives: 'Believe thou, and ~~do thou~~ declare it'—but this would require *edidisti* rather than *edisti*.
268 Tunstall, *De ueritate Corporis et Sanguinis*, f. 100r, has *Hoc est opus Dei ut credatis in eum quem misit ille. Hoc est ergo manducare cibum non qui perit, sed qui permanet in uitam æternam: ut quid paras dentes & uentrem? crede & manducasti.*

reformers—and he ends, 'faith is not to be contrasted with works, but faith itself is true work, and works by love' (Gal 5:6).

Latimer sets Augustine's *Crede et manducasti*, 'Believe and you have eaten' against the same author's 'drink boldly the blood ... poured out', cited by Weston. Weston, Tresham and Pie all come back to him with nuances but Latimer insists: 'I grant it is blood drunk in the New Testament, but we receive it spiritually.'[269]

Stephyn, perhaps misunderstanding, sees 'Believe, and you have eaten' as complementary to the 'leave all disbelief' of Quotation 66. He is clearly concluding his work, collecting the final few links of the chain.

Quotation 68. SA 66v.11–14 (Latin) 66v.14–18 (Cornish)

St Theophilact of Ohrid, *Enarratio in Evangelium Matthaei*, 26:26.[270]
Panis trans-elementatur ... ideo panis quidem apparet. Sed caro est.
(The outward appearance is of bread, because we are so weak: but it is flesh)
[Foxe, TAMO, 1576, p. 1404 [1379]; (T&C vi, 489)—Ridley's Disputation]

For Theophylact, see Quotation 49 above. The marginal note referencing St Hilary of Poitiers on Ps 118 is not to either the previous or the current quotation, but to a passage quoted just before in the Disputation to underline the truth of Christ's words at the Last Supper: 'All God's words or sayings are true, and neither idly placed, nor unprofitably, but fiery, and wonderful fiery without all doubtfulness of superfluous vanity, that there may be nothing thought to be there, which is not absolute and proper.'[271]

The words *panis transelementatur* do not appear together in Foxe. Stephyn is going further than Harding, or Theophylact who says: 'It is transformed (μεταποιεῖται) by a mysterious, indescribable action ... it does appear to be bread, but it is really flesh (σὰρξ δὲ τῷ ὄντι ἐστί.).'[272] Stephyn unpacks this in

---

269 T&C vi, 508.
270 Quoted here (as by the disputants and Foxe) in Philip Montano's translation, published 1546: *quoniam infirmi sumus, et abhorremus crudas carnes comedere, maximè hominis carnem: & ideo panis quidem apparet, sed caro reuera est.* [Theophylact], *Theophylacti Archiepiscopi Bulgariæ In Quatuor ... Euangelia*, ff. 81v, F, beginning *Non enim dixit, hoc est figura*. (This is almost identical to Tunstall, *De ueritate Corporis et Sanguinis*, f. 112v.) [PG 123, 443–4D].
271 *Vera omnia sunt, & neque ociose, neque inutiliter constituta dei verba, sed extra omnem ambiguitatem superfluae inanitatis, ignita, & ignita vehementer, ne quid illic esse quod non perfectum ac proprium sit, existimetur.* [Foxe, TAMO, 1576, p. 1378; (T&C vi, 488)]. Cf. St Hilary of Poitiers, *Tractatus super Psalmos*, PL 9, 622D, on section 18, ꙗ.
272 We do find the word *transelementatur* [μεταστοιχειούμενος] in Theophylact, for example in a passage just after Quotation 69 (f. 324v D) when discussing our own transformation into the body of Christ (as Ridley suggests), and Harding cites μετάστοιχεῖται in Foxe. In connection

Cornish as 'changed from one element into the other' (*trylis theworth [an eyl] elyment th'e gela*). He focuses the natural tendency to 'tremble with horror' (*kemeras skruth*) at the thought of eating human flesh still further, on the horror of eating 'this man's flesh' (*kygg an keth dean-ma*). Nonetheless, he concludes, 'it is the flesh of our Lord Jesus Christ' (*eth ew kygg agan Arluth Jesu Ch[rist]*).

Quotation 69. SA 66v.19–21 (Latin) 66v.22–4 (Cornish)

Ridley, quoting St Theophylact of Ohrid, *Enarratio in Evangelium Joannis*, 6: 48–52.[273]

Panis qui non est figura ... transformatur ... secundum benedictionem Spiritus Sancti
(The bread is not a figure but is the body of Christ, through the Holy Spirit)
[Foxe, TAMO, 1576, p. 1404 [1379]; (T&C vi, 488–9)—Ridley's Disputation]

The explicit mention of the Holy Spirit—*secundum benedictionem Spiritus Sancti*—points to Theophylact on John, cited in the margin (rather than the similar passage in Matthew we have already encountered).[274] The new passage reads: 'He does not say "The bread that I give you is a figure of flesh", but "is my flesh". That bread is transformed by the sacred words, and the mystical blessing and the coming down of the Holy Spirit, into the flesh of the Lord.'[275] Harding is paraphrasing slightly with *Panis non est figura*, although the rest of his quotation is close to the Greek.

Ridley then displays his 'moderate realism' at its clearest.[276] He allows that the bread is truly 'converted or turned into the flesh of Christ'—but by a 'sacramental conversion or turning' and not by 'transubstantiation'. With Theophylact he can say that the bread is 'transformed', but without any 'expulsion or driving away' of its substance. Nonetheless, Christ is truly present: at no time doth the Divine Majesty 'absent himself from the divine

---

with the Eucharist it is also used by St Gregory of Nyssa [as μεταστοιχειώσας]: James Herbert Srawley, ed., *The Catechetical Oration of Gregory of Nyssa* (Cambridge: Cambridge University Press, 1903), p. 152, lines 7–8 [PL 45, 97–8B].

273 [Theophylact], *Theophylacti Archiepiscopi Bulgariæ In Quatuor ... Euangelia*, ff. 323v C–323v D, beginning *Non enim dixit, panis quem ego dabo, figura est carnis*; [PG 123, 1307–8C], beginning Οὐ γὰρ εἶπεν.

274 See Quotation 68.

275 [Theophylact], *Theophylacti Archiepiscopi Bulgariæ In Quatuor ... Euangelia ...* (op. cit.), ff. 323r–323v, in Montano's translation of 1546: *Non enim dixit, Panis quem ego dabo, figura est carnis, sed caro mea est. Transformatur enim arcanis uerbis panis ille, per mysticam benedictionem et accessionem sancti spiritus, in carnem domini* (again, almost identical to Tunstall, *De ueritate Corporis et Sanguinis*, f. 113r).

276 See the very helpful summary in Douglas, *Companion to Anglican Eucharistic Theology*, pp. 97–101.

mysteries'.²⁷⁷ Weston, intrigued by Ridley's willingness to go so far, recalls that Peter Martyr would not do so, but preferred to deny the authenticity of the passage from Theophylact. Foxe, indeed, is clearly uncomfortable that Ridley has accepted as much as he has.²⁷⁸

Interestingly, Stephyn gives the full quotation in Latin, although it is not in Foxe 1576 or *Rerum Gestarum*.²⁷⁹ This underlines the question as to whether he was using another source for these final extracts or paraphrasing from memory. Either way, he clearly believes the quotation speaks for itself. At this point, he may originally have intended to end his work, closing with a doxology: 'To him be all honour and glory, world without end' (*thotheff re bo oll honor ha glory in gwlas heb deweth*).²⁸⁰

Quotation 70. SA 66v.11–14 (Latin) 66v.14–18 (Cornish)

Stephyn, paraphrasing St Augustine of Hippo, *In Joannis evangelium tractatus* 50, 4.²⁸¹

In cælum manum mittam ... ut habemus visibiliter in sacramento.
(Reach out with faith and take hold of Christ in the sacrament)
[Foxe, TAMO, 1576, p. 1414 [1389]; (T&C vi, 512–13)—Harpsfield's Disputation]

Vigilius (fl. 484), bishop of Thapsus (near Bakalta in modern Tunisia), wrote his *Adversus Eutychem*, or *Contra Eutychetem libri quinque*),²⁸² to affirm the Chalcedonian position against Arian and Sabellian views. Nonetheless, this passage does not appear to be from him, but from Augustine's homilies on the Gospel of John. Perhaps in the immediate source of the quotation the two were in close proximity, as in the dialogues between Cranmer and Gardiner, or (later) Harding and Jewel.²⁸³

---

277 T&C vi, 489. Cf. Bucer (perhaps quoting Cyprian) in Cox, ed. *The Writings and Disputations of Thomas Cranmer*, p. 223.
278 Foxe, TAMO, 1576, p. 1404 [1379]; (T&C vi, 489n).
279 Foxe, *Rerum in Ecclesia Gestarum*, pp. 676–77.
280 Translation from T: see Notes on 66v.25.
281 Willems, ed., *In Iohannis evangelium tractatus* [CCSL 36], p. 434 [PL 35, 1759–60]. C.W.H. Hatcher gave valuable assistance with this passage.
282 Cf. Vigilius of Thapsus, *Contra Eutychetem*, 4, 14 [PL 62, 0126C] and following footnote.
283 For example, in John Jewel's reply (1565) to Thomas Harding's *An answere to Maister Juelles Challenge* (Leuven: 1564) STC 12758; see Ayre, ed. *The Works of John Jewel*, p. 776, where there is part of a quotation from Vigilius. In Jewel, in a related section, parts of Quotations 67, 70 and 71 are all found together. (Cf. Jelf, Richard William, ed., *The Works of John Jewel, D.D., Bishop of Salisbury*, vol. 3 (Oxford: Oxford University Press, 1848), pp. 443–5. The dialogue between Cranmer and Gardiner also covers a lot of similar ground to a number of these later quotations in SA. Cranmer first published *An Aunswere ... unto a craftie and Sophisticall cavillation, devised by Stephen Gardiner* in 1551, but few copies were made. If Stephyn knew it, then it was probably

Augustine is meditating on John 11:57 and how anyone might imagine they could 'take hold' of Jesus: 'How shall I hold what is not here? How shall my hand reach into heaven, to hold the one sitting there? Reach with faith and you have already taken hold. Your forefathers held in a fleshly way, you hold with the heart: but the "absent" Christ is still present.'[284] Note that he says *parentes* and not *Iudei* as in SA.

Stephyn (or his source) is therefore paraphrasing. These are afterthoughts to his doxology, as he perhaps senses the whole argument turns on this point. For Stephyn Christ is 'still present', although it is by faith that we know he is 'with us always'.

Quotation 71. SA 66v.11–14 (Latin) 66v.14–18 (Cornish)

Weston, paraphrasing St Augustine of Hippo, *In Joannis evangelium tractatus* 50, 4.[285]
Secundum maiestatem Christum tenemus ...
(We take hold of Christ according to his majesty)
[Foxe, TAMO, 1576, p. 1414 [1389]; (T&C vi, 512-13)—Harpsfield's Disputation]

Because so much of this final brief Quotation has been damaged, it is difficult to be sure of its original nature. (See Notes on 66v.33–5.) Incorrectly cited in SA, it is not from Theophylact but seems to be adapted from a continuation of Quotation 70.[286] Augustine is explaining that although Christ has—in one sense—departed (*abiit*), in another sense he is still here (*hic est*), because his majesty has never left the world (*maiestatem non abstulit mundo*).

Taking up this extrapolation of Matthew 28:20, Weston goes on: 'St Augustine saith, that these words *Ergo ero etc.*, 'I will be with you even to the end of the

---

the second edition (London: John Daye, 1580) that he used. Jewel is particularly drawn to Vigilius when he discusses whether Christ can be present simultaneously in heaven and earth (Vigilius of Thapsus, *Contra Eutychetem*, 4, 14 [PL 62, 98D]) or whether humanity is assumed into the divine (*Contra Eutychetem*, 4, 4 [PL 62, 121A]). The passage most frequently quoted in controversy, however, is *Contra Eutychetem*, 1, 6 [PL 62, 98D]: *Dei Filius secundum humanitatem suam recessit a nobis; secundum divinitatem suam semper est nobiscum* (The Son of God has left us according to his humanity; according to his Godhead, he is always with us).

284 *Quomodo tenebam absentem; quomodo in cælum manum mittam, ut ibi sedentem teneam. Fidem mitte et tenuisti. Parentes tui tenuerunt carne, tu tene corde: quoniam Christus absens etiam praesens est.* Cf. also Jelf, ed., *The Works of John Jewel*, vol. 3, p. 444, and Cox, ed., *The Writings and Disputations of Thomas Cranmer*, p. 49 in the Latin appendix.

285 Willems, ed., *In Iohannis evangelium tractatus* [CCSL 36], pp. 434–5 [PL 35, 1759–60].

286 Continuing the passage from *In Joannis evangelium tractatus* 50, 4 above: *Nisi praesens esset, a nobis ipsis teneri non poset. Sed quoniam verum est, quod ait: 'Ecce ego vobiscum sum usque ad consummationem saeculi; et abiit, et hic est; et rediit, et nos non deserit; corpus erit suum intulit cælo, maiestatem non abstulit mundo.*

world' are accomplished *secundum majestatem*, "according to his majesty" ... The church hath him not in flesh, but by belief.'[287]

Because the folio is so damaged, we are again in the realms of conjecture for Stephyn's final words. Nance wondered if they were *dir faith e thesan s[awyes]*—'we are saved by faith'—but surely Stephyn would have said 'saved by grace through faith' (Eph 2:8) if he had wanted to broach that subject.

But there is no need to assume he did. We are probably on stronger ground conjecturally piecing together what is left of the Latin and Cornish into something like *Secundum maiestatem Christum tenemus f[irmiter, per fidem ...]* and *Dir faith, eth esan s[ensy fast Christ, herwyth e majesty ...]*. Such words would form a fitting summary of Stephyn's work: 'Through faith we hold fast to Christ, according to his majesty.' Or, expanded slightly and reflecting his emphases and choices throughout: 'We have and hold Christ firmly, in all the majesty of his presence, through our faith in the sacrifice and sacrament of the altar.'

---

287 T&C vi, 512.

CHAPTER TEN

Notes

on the text and language of SA

These notes have two elements: (a) General Notes on overarching features of Stephyn's Cornish that may reflect the development of the language in its later phases, and (b) Textual Notes for specific passages in SA, including possible reconstructions in the case of damage. Citations follow the diplomatic edition above, in their MS form.

A limited Apparatus of divergences from other readings is provided in the Textual Notes. Readings cited are: N for Nance's first draft (N1 and N2 where his two transcriptions differ); C for Nance and Smith's final joint typescript and T for Nance's translation; B for Bice's cyclostyled reading, S for Syed's electronic version; H for Hawke's electronic version; F for my earlier transcription and E for the edited text below the diplomatic edition. (For more detail on these see p. 80, *Notes (& Apparatus)*.) None of them (except perhaps C) should be seen as representing the finished, settled view of its authors. All would no doubt have been revised further with opportunity for further study. I wish here to reaffirm my debt to these scholars, without whom I would have achieved nothing.

While the purpose of the Textual Notes is to comment on the Cornish, occasionally the Latin also features, if it is not wholly clear from the transcription, translation or Foxe. Unpacking the biblical and patristic references of the marginalia (and any theological issues) is left to the Commentary.

Simple (and largely contextual) translations are given, for the benefit of those who have not studied Cornish (or Latin), without intending this to represent a detailed analysis (which may, however, follow in the notes). Occasionally the difference in word order or construction compared with English makes a simple translation of isolated words unhelpful. In these cases readers are referred to the translation of the whole sentence in the edition.

Where there is a need to cite Cornish words more generally, forms found in SA (or, failing that, in TH) are preferred wherever possible. Occasionally the word divisions given in the 'Corrected, Edited Text' (E) are given where this might help understanding, but only in addition to the MS form. Grammatical abbreviations are explained in the introduction to the Glossary.

General Notes

& = an: 'the'—at 60r.6, 60r.19 and throughout SA the symbol & is used as a scribal shorthand for the Cornish definite article *an*, perhaps because of the partial similarity of sound with English 'and'. It does not usually represent the Cornish conjunction *ha*, 'and' (although there are exceptions such as *An Sacrament a corf & gois* 61v.1).

3 pl. ending: *inans y* 59v.27 'in them' is an example of the late 3 pl. ending *-ans* replacing the earlier *-a*. It is analysed by the writer as *in an sy*—or just possibly—since the word spacing is erratic—as *in ansy*.[1] This may or may not already have been pronounced with [dʒ] for the *s*, but either way illustrates the pathway developing in Stephyn's time by which the pers. pron. 3 pl. *y*, 'they', is replaced with a form closer to Lhuyd's *an dzhei* (or Boson's *an chei*).[2] Tregear has both forms: *inna y* TH 3r.27 but *innans* TH 38v.25. Another example of a 3 pl. ending taking on its late form in SA is *intrethans* 65r.16, 'amongst them'.

an > a: 'the'—there is some evidence of the definite article *an* occasionally taking the form *a* in SA: for example, at 61r.19 where we find *a keth deane ma*, for *an keth deane ma*, 'this same man'. (See also 63r.7, 63r.36, 64r.29—though these examples can be otherwise explained, as is the case with Stephyn's *a note* TH 55r.27m/*an note* TH 55v.1.)

auxiliaries: Cornish of all periods makes considerable use of auxiliary verbs, particularly *bos* 'to be', *gule* 'to do', *gallas* 'to be able', *dos* to come', *mennas* 'to wish', *gasa* 'to let', *gothvas* 'to know'. This is especially true of TH and SA, our primary sources for Cornish prose (as opposed to verse). For most verbs, only a few key tenses seem to have been commonly employed in ordinary prose: periphrasis with auxiliaries is generally preferred to inflexion of the verb itself.[3] Particular uses will be commented on as they arise, but it is perhaps worth highlighting one that parallels modern Welsh usage. This is the use of the periphrastic present, with *bos*, 'to be' (*bod* in Welsh) and the present participle (formed in Cornish by placing the particle *ow* before the verbal noun) together forming the present tense. So, 'I ask' in Cornish prose can be *eth esa' ve ow covyn* SA 64v.27 (lit. 'I am asking'). This is obviously comparable to older Welsh *ydd ydwyf fi yn gofyn* (contracting to *dwy'n gofyn* or *rwy'n gofyn* in modern use).

---

1   See Nicholas Williams, *Desky Kernowek: A Complete Guide to Cornish* (Cathair na Mart/Westport: Evertype, 2012), pp. 31 and 79, 81. This language revival work has wider usefulness for its many examples and explanations of unusual forms, with citations in manuscript spelling.
2   For Boson's usage, in *John of Chyanhor* (JCH 14), see Oliver J. Padel, ed., *The Cornish Writings of the Boson Family* (Redruth: Institute of Cornish Studies, 1975), pp. 16–17.
3   Williams, *Desky Kernowek*, p. 348.

bos + personal suffixes: In late Cornish, the verbal noun *bos*, 'to be, can be marked for person with an enclitic pronoun, and preceded by a verbal particle, *y* or *e*, perhaps by analogy with the use of *y(th)* in indirect speech.[4] It is lenited as *e vosama* at SA 62v.33, though not in the catchword *y bosama* at the foot of TH 43v. Tregear then goes on to write a different form, *ow bos ve*, on the next folio, revealing the complexity of *bos* at this stage of the language. See also *an vosan ny* SA 66v.15, *pan vosta* SA 63v.34.

bus: 'but', is a characteristically late replacement for *mes* or *saw*, as at 60r.21 (also conjecturally restored at 59r.34 where the original word is missing).

clerical Cornish: It has often been suggested (following Nance) that Tregear's Cornish was analogous to *brezhoneg beleg* ('clerical Breton'), which could drift into French idiom and syntax, while borrowing French and Latin vocabulary. It is perhaps harder to level the accusation of the latter at Stephyn than at Tregear, but many examples do occur in SA of lapses into English (*not* 59v.16, *openly* 60r.21, *expounding* 65r.20). These are found alongside borrowings that might have been attempts to stay close to the precise theological language of the originals (*participation* 65r.15, *consecration* 61v.32, *oblation* 64r.21, *satisfaction* 64r.26), although some borrowings have a more integrated form (*signifia* 65r.15). All of these introductions could be viewed as the Cornish of an inexpert or no longer habitual user (possibly even a learner—OP) intending to improve the translation later. On the other hand, they may simply reflect, in the context of bilingualism and the reformation controversies, a tendency to stay close to the source (see note on *an quantite a'n oblation* 64r.21). There might also have been a specific intent to enrich the language with more Classically resonant vocabulary (albeit mediated through English). A similar enrichment was under way in Welsh at the same period.[5]

conditional: In later Cornish the inflected conditional tense is increasingly replaced with the periphrastic use of an auxiliary verb, for example, *dos*, 'to come', and this is evident in both SA and TH after *mar*. (Cf. *mar tema disquethas theugh*, 'if I should show you' SA 60r.7; *mar te why demandea*, 'if you should ask', SA 64r.7; *mar tewgh why ha cowse*, 'if you should speak', TH 22v.11; *mar tewgh why gylwall*, 'if you should call', TH 36r.13.) The construction is particularly useful with unreal conditions in past time.[6]

---

4   Williams, *Desky Kernowek*, p. 87.
5   Bowen, *Welsh Recusant Writings*, pp. 2–4.
6   Williams, *Desky Kernowek*, pp. 112–13, 119.

contractions: *nena* 62r.20 and *nona* 66v.7, 'then', are typically late forms of *ena*, either with accreted *n* as George suggests, or possibly affected by earlier forms such as *yn vrna*, PA 12.5—lit. 'in that hour', *y'n ur-na*, as Nance believed.[7] (Compare North Welsh *rwan*, 'now' from *yr awr hon*.) Other attestations are *nenna nyns egow why* TH 16v.14-15 and *nenna an dzhei a varginiaz*, JCH 4 (Lluyd). For another late contraction see *may hallo* > *may halla* > *malla* below.

dictation?: There is some weak evidence in Tregear that the scribe may have been working from a translator's dictation. For example, we find: *pedyr arug thotha narracion* TH 45r.2-3 (= *Pedyr a rug thotha an arracion*, where *an arracion* represents 'the oration' not 'a narration'—RE). In SA, there is even less evidence of this, and Stephyn's autograph signature seems close to the hand used throughout. With examples such as *an nethewan* 61r.14, 17 for *an Ethewan* at 61r.14, it should be remembered that words are not always analysed as they were at an earlier stage of the language. But see Notes on 59v.22, 60v.26, 61r.21, 62v.34, 64r.22, 64v.13, 65v.16 and 66r.8.

dre > der/dir: 'through'—the earlier form *dre* (e.g. PA 3.1) is often replaced by *der* (e.g. BK 8, SA 59v.17) by this period, with *dir* also appearing in SA as at 61r.33. This tendency in pronunciation appears also to be at work in the alternation between *hedre vo* OM 1464, BK 1536 and *hader vo* BK 1528 or *dirr vo* SA 60v.27.

ema > oma: '(there) is' or 3 sg. pres. of *bos* 'to be' used as an auxiliary. It may be that Stephyn pronounced this something like [ə'maː], given his *o ma* for *e ma* at 61r.23. Interestingly, even in a stressed syllable, he can write *a thoskas* at 63r.15 (rather than *a thyscas* TH 38r.2, *a theskas* TH 21v.21, *diskys* SA 63r.26). Perhaps there was an influence on him from *y mae* and *dysgu* in Welsh.

enaf > ena: 'soul', is written as *ena* at 60v.26, as *enaf* at 60v.27 and *nenaf* at 60v.32 (with intruded *n* from the definite article *an* before it). It is interesting to see the fluidity around this final *f*, again reminiscent of Welsh. See also *(esoff > esa)*. (It can occur in earlier Cornish, as OM 1645 and 1649 show.)

English influence: Vocabulary is the obvious area in which Cornish has been considerably influenced by English, not only in the late period but throughout its recorded history (as English itself was affected by Norman French). A glance at

---

7   Ken George, ed., *An Gerlyver Meur*, 3rd edn (Kesva an Taves Kernewek, 2020), p. 477 (under *nena*) and p. 187 (under *ena*), [henceforth cited as *Gerlyver Meur*]; Robert Morton Nance, *A New Cornish-English Dictionary* (St Ives: Federation of Old Cornwall Societies, 1938), reprinted as *Gerlyver Noweth Kernewek-Sawsnek ha Sawsnek-Kernewek* (Redruth: Dyllansow Truran, 1989), [henceforth cited as *Gerlyver Noweth*], p. 52 (under *ena*).

the glossary will make this immediately clear. In SA we also find many examples of English syntax and expressions, such as *hy a dowlas in* 64r.24 'she cast in', and *derag dorn* 62r.28 'before hand'. The latter is a typical example of a late assimilation to English usage, in place of the older *kyns/kens* (cognate with Welsh *gynt*) still used at 62v.17. (Another example would be the apparently unnecessary use of *an*, as at *An Sacrament an aulter* 61r.1, 'the sacrament of the altar' and *an girreow an Sacramentys* 62r.13-14, 'the sacramental words'. These examples may be explained away as *an* followed by *a'n = a + an*, not unlike *An Sacrament a corf & gois agen savior Iesus* 61v.1. But see also *an skavall e drys eff/ow thrys ve* 64v.27, 29.) Contemporary English spelling continues to further influence the Cornish of SA, just as it did the older texts. Words such as *feyth* PC 1469, *offren* CW 1237, *trobles* CW1458, *remembrans* TH 30v.1, *tochya* TH 46r.11, *vndyrstondia* TH 1v.7 (*wondyrstondya* TH 1v.18) and *crowwelder* Bodewryd 67,[8] are given in SA as *faith* 59v.16, *offering[ys]* 64r.24, *troublis* 66v.7, *remembrance* 66v.10, *touchia* 60v.7, *vnderstandya* 65v.15 and *cruelte* SA 65v.14. Occasionally, though, there are instances where the introduction of one form from English, such as *Greciens*, is thought better of, and corrected to one thought more traditional, as with *Grekys* 63v.30.

esoff > esa: 'I am'—the usage at 60r.35, 64r.31, 64v.27,29 of the 1 sg. of the long form of the present tense of *bos*, 'to be', as an auxiliary, echoes the form *eth esoff ve* at TH 17r.16 (and *innaff ve* at SA 61r.36-37). However, Stephyn never writes the final *ff* for the pres. 1 sg. even when *esa* is followed by a vowel—see especially *e thesa ow trylya* SA 64v.29. It was evidently silent and may even have been so in Tregear's pronunciation, despite his traditional spelling. Nonetheless, to help readers to recognize this usage and distinguish between pres. 1 sg. and imperf. 3 sg., the absent final *ff* is indicated—in the edited text (E) only—by an apostrophe: *esa'*. See also (*enaf > ena*).

ewa: In Tudor and later Cornish, *ewa* (e.g. CW 2079, TH 1r.5, SA 64r.19, BK 3040) becomes a common contraction of *ew ef* 'he is/it is'.

g > k: There are a number of unusual hardenings of consonants (and the converse) in SA, difficult to explain. A good example is *haker*, 'ugly, disfigured, frightful, bad', at 60v.25. The usual form of this word throughout the history of the language is *hager* (e.g. PA 47.6, OM 1080, PC 1530, RD 1984, BK 84, CW 421 and even JCH 26)—although the comparative does harden the 'g' as at *hakere* RD 350, 2071. See also 63v.10-11, where *th'agen sawya ny*, 'to preserve us', is written *thaken sawya ny*; and 60v.35, where *megys*, 'fattened, fed' is written

---

8 See Andrew Hawke, 'A Rediscovered Cornish-English Vocabulary' [NLW Bodewryd MS 5], in Philip Payton, ed., *Cornish Studies*, 2nd series, 9 (Exeter: University of Exeter Press, 2001), line 67, p. 99. Though Bodewryd is later than SA, the form suggests more than a simple borrowing.

mekys. A hardening of *b* > *p* occurs at 62r.19, where we find *bopell* (lenited from *popell*, 'people', cf. 66r.36) where we would have expected *bobell* (e.g. CW 2383, 1516). We also see *v* > *f* at 66v.18, where *evelap*, 'likeness', is emended to *efelap*. This tendency is interesting, as while Stephyn can spell words conventionally, he often spells to reflect significant contemporary pronunciation (as with *esoff* > *esa* above). For a reverse change of *p* > *b*, *c* > *g*, see General Notes *(kepar > pecar)*.

gerryow/gyrryw > gerrow/gyrrow: 'words'—this plural appears to be simplifying, with two forms becoming evident, one with—and one without—the *y* as part of the plural. At 59r.12 the second *y* is written over the *o* of an earlier *gyrrow* (and again at 59r.15), which may be a correction by another hand, or an immediate correction by Stephyn—see greis gwreis at 63r.34.

gule > gwell/gwiel/gwiell/gweill/gwyell: 'to do'. The forms with *w* are characteristically late spellings, all found in SA, for example, at 59r.35 *(gwell)*.

ha/hag: 'and'—the final *g* before vowels is dropped in SA. The conjunction *ha* usually changed before vowels in earlier Cornish to *hag* (as in Welsh *a/ac*), cf. *hag ef* PA 53.8, OM 612, PC 637, RD 225. This persisted to a considerable degree in early modern use—*hag ef* BK 2264, *hag eff* TH 1r.8—although in TH there are instances of the *g* being dropped altogether, for example, *ha eff* TH 15r.14. In SA *hag* is no longer found. Compare other late sources such as *ha an* Gwavas Collection f. 110r (in *Pader an Arloth*, the Lord's Prayer), from the early eighteenth century, or *ha agaz* in *Delkiow Sevi*, the traditional song printed by Pryce in 1790 (ACB 224).

kepar > pecar: 'like, as'—the metathesis of the first two consonants is a late feature found at *pecar* 61r.17 and possibly in an original *begar* 59r.37, corrected to *kepare*, the usual written form in SA. (Both *pagar* and *pacar* are used in the Cornish version of the Lord's Prayer given by John Davies.)[9] The usage *kepar dell* (before verbs) and *kepar ha* (before nouns) is also becoming more fluid in SA. While we have *kepar dell wruck* 60v.10 we have *kepar a rug* 61r.14. There is no *ha* in *kepare e lell ha meer inheritance* 60r.3, although a silent *h* could be postulated (so no *ha* is introduced in E for the reconstruction *k[epare e gerryow]* 59r.1).

lavirta ge: 'you (will) say', 2 sg. pres./fut. of *levar/lavar* (see below). The 2 sg. originally ended in *-yth*, but this form existed in older Cornish, too, as at *leuerta* PC 2017. For good measure, the pronoun itself—*sy/ge*—is sometimes added, as here and in *y thosta ge* CW 822, 'you are'.[10]

---

9   John Davies, ed. & tr., *Llyfr y Resolucion* (London: Beale, 1632), reprinted 1684.
10 For an interesting discussion of these points, see Williams, *Desky Kernowek*, p. 117.

lever > lavar: 'say'—later texts tend increasingly towards spelling *lavar* with *a*, just as there is a tendency to move from *leverel > leverall > laveral* or even to *laull*. However, both *e* and *a* are found throughout the history of the language, for example *leuer* PA 135.7, BK 2092; *laver* PC 71, BK 753; *lavar* PA 93.2, BK 224; *leuerel* OM 499; *leverel* TH 51v.10; *leverall* SA 59r.3; *laveral* JCH 6. The form *ny lavar* may come about analogically by loss of *i*-affection, as in Breton (NW).[11]

ll & lh: The late Albert Bock made a careful study (using my draft transcription, F) of instances of the orthographic representation of /l/ versus /ll/ in SA where these followed a stressed vowel and preceded an unstressed one (excepting spontaneous English loanwords). He argued that Stephyn was remarkably consistent in his use of both *l* and *ll/lh* in this position, despite his flexibility with regard to earlier scribal tradition, suggesting a possible distinction in pronunciation persisted in Tudor Cornish.[12]

ls > sl > s > r: 2 pl. imperative *golsowowh* CW 114 appears to have the form *gosoweth* at SA 62v.18 and *gosough* at SA 63r.6, with final *th* for *gh* in the first example (if this is not an unusual 2 sg. form) and the loss of *l*. (There was always fluidity between *sl* and *ls* in writing. Examples of the range of forms possible for this word alone—not all of the imperative—include *golsoug* CF 1; *golsowens* PA 2.2; *gosloweugh* PC 3217; *golsowowh* CW 114; *goslow* CW 637; *golsowogh* CW 1429; *golsow* BK 235; *golsowas* TH 19v.1; *gosough* SA 63r.6; *gosowhog* SA 65r.6, *kozowo* James Jenkins. In late Cornish, even the residual *s* can become *r* in forms such as *gorowas*.)[13] It is interesting to see the termination *-g* for *-gh* in the 2 pl. can occur in both CF and SA, so far separated in age.

may hallo > may halla > malla: 'so that'—after *may*, the subjunctive of *gallas*, 'to be able', often has the sense of 'in order that, so that'.[14] The earlier *may hallo* OM 545, as C notes, became *may halla*, SA 60v.30, 31, TH 7v.22, BK 1220, BM 13, and then could be further contracted (as at SA 60v. 32, 60v.34–5, 61r.24 and 65r.13) to *malla*.

---

11   Nicholas Williams, '*I*-Affection in Breton and Cornish', in Philip Payton, ed., *Cornish Studies*, 2nd series, 14 (Exeter: University of Exeter Press, 2006), pp. 24–43.
12   Albert Bock, 'Representation of intervocalic single /l/ and geminate /ll/ in *Sacrament an Alter*' (University of Vienna: 2010), https://homepage.univie.ac.at/albert.bock/archive/l_ll_lh_SA.pdf, accessed 3 September 2018. But see Nicholas Williams *Cornish Today, Third Edition* (Cathair na Mart/Westport: Evertype, 2006-1st edn 1995), pp. 56–57, and Nicholas Williams, *Towards Authentic Cornish* (Cathair na Mart/Westport: Evertype, 2006), Chapter 6, 'The gemination of consonants', pp. 42–50, for another view.
13   Nance, *Gerlyver Noweth*, p. 68.
14   Williams, *Desky Kernowek*, p. 131.

mutations: These are characteristic of Celtic languages, but are erratic in SA. Stephyn shows little rigour with regard to lenition, perhaps even an opposite tendency. We have *y wely* 59r.13 changed to *e gwely* (though it is just possible the original form was *y gwely*) and *the gwlas neff* 60r.11—though lenition is still observed in cases such as *y errow* 59r.19–20. We have *tha gweil* 62v.15, where we might expect *tha weil* (cf. *the wul* RD 1832) and *tha gonys* 62v.16, where we might expect *tha wonys* (cf. *the wonys* TH 5v.3). Tregear seems more traditional than Stephyn in this regard: within the space of a few lines at TH 5v.2–4 he correctly provects and lenites the forms *ha'w conys* and *the wonys*, as well as using the radical form of the verbal noun, *gonys*. Of course, the same verb is also correctly provected by Stephyn, at 62r.27—see *(o/ow)* below. Provection after *mar*, 'if', is also still punctiliously observed, as at TH 38r.13, TH 22v.11, SA 64r.7. It is not always easy to determine, however, whether the spoken use of mutations was becoming erratic or whether they were no longer written systematically. The same scribe can write *a Thew* at SA 59r.16, with the expected lenition, but then *the Dew* at SA 60v.28. (Compare *the thew* at TH 1r.19.) At times in SA, we see mutation very much alive, as in the lines 64v.27–33. At 64v.31 the radical *dore*, 'earth' (cognate with Welsh *daear*) lenites as *a thore*, 'of earth' (Welsh *o ddaear*). We also see it nasalized in *an nore* 64v.33, 'the earth'. Similarly with *trys*, 'feet' (cf. PC 835), lenited in *e drys ef* 64v.27, 'his feet' and spirantized in *ow thrys ve* 64v.29, 'my feet' (64v.29).

na: 'nor' or 'no' [?]—the most likely translation of *na* at 59r.14 (SA *na neg ew ef*; Foxe: 'and he is not') is the ordinary usage for 'nor'. It is just possible, however, that here we have evidence for a late usage of *na* as 'no', echoing English usage (and sometimes found in Welsh).

neg ew: 'it is not'—the form *neg ew* (e.g. at 59r.14) appears to represent a shift under way from earlier Cornish *nyns yw* (e.g. RD 2234) in a sequence *nyns > nyng > nyg/neg*, with *g* having its 'soft' sound (i.e. /dʒ/, as in modern English *j*). Of course, while the spelling *nyns yw, nyns o* is common in the Ordinalia, the pronunciation *nyng* is not exclusively 'late' and is found, for example, throughout PA (*c*. 1400) in forms such as *nyng ew, nynj o* (MS readings *nyn gew* PA 123.4, *nyn io* PA 214.8). Later writers, equally, can still freely use both *nyns* (*nynso* BK 166, TH 4v.5) and *nyng* (*nyn gegas* BK 168, *nyn gew* BK 737, SA 63r.24). We also have *nyn go=nyng o* SA 62v.36, *ne geran*, SA 59r.17, 59v.20, 63v.9, and *ne gesee* SA 59a.9 (q.v.). Traditional spelling may persist alongside developed or more recent pronunciation, with sound changes occurring earlier than is widely reflected in orthography. It could, of course, be argued that *neg ew/neg esee* represents a shift to *nag ew/nag usy* (previously only used in negative answers), which appears in some very late writings and is paralleled in some dialects of Welsh and Breton. But this seems unlikely: even the *nag* in Bodinar's *nag es* is ambiguous, and while it could represent [nædʒ] in the light of his *pager* (presumably [ˈpædʒər]) shortly afterwards, it could alternatively represent [næg] (WB letter).¹⁵

o/ow: The present verbal particle usually forms the present participle along with the following verbal noun, which it provects (as with *o tisquethas* 61r.21, *o conys* 62r.27). Along with other late texts, however, SA sometimes omits the particle while retaining provection if applicable (as with *tibbry* 61r.23, *kelwall* 63v.30), although *gonis* is not provected at 63r.18. (N.B. Both spellings of *ow* are widely used in SA, *ow* twice as frequently as *o*.)

orth > worth: At 59r.38 an original *orth* (or, less likely, *erth*) is altered to ʷ*orth* (also found at 64v.32) but see the specific note. (In this instance the word is acting as a verbal particle.) But we also find the forms *vrth (urth)* 59r.22 and *owrth* 64r.10, and many examples of *worth* (60v.35, 61r.31, 63r.4, etc.) This may indicate a growing preference for *worth* over *orth*, but both forms are found together throughout the history of the language (OP)—for instance, *orth* PA 80.4, 117.1, OM 800, TH 7v.26, BM 4487, BK 341, CW 70; *worth* PA 180.2, 242.8, OM 805, TH 35v.18. It is true that *orth* is more common in earlier texts and there are distinct preferences among texts: BK and BM are both strongly for *orth* but Tregear and Stephyn seem to prefer *worth*. (Jordan's tendency in CW towards the former may indicate his reliance on earlier texts.)

possessives: The absence of the possessive pronoun *agan* at 63r.35, before *sawya* in the phrase *rag sawya ny*, 'to save us', may be an indication of a later move to form possessives with the following pronoun alone (in this case *ny*). But see also 63v.10, where the traditional use continues.

pre-occlusion?: In later Cornish, in some stressed, short syllables, *m* could be pronounced with an intrusive but unexploded *b* before the *m*, and *n* with a similar unexploded *d*. So *mam*, 'mother', could be pronounced as [maᵇm], and *pen*, 'head', as [peᵈn]. While this is not shown in spelling at all in TH, which could have local features distinct from SA, there may or may not be an attempt to show it in SA in the word *mamb*, 'mother', at SA 59r.34. This could, of course, be simply an anglicism in spelling, as in the English word 'lamb' (OP).

preterite: The 3 sg. preterite of regular verbs often ends in *-as*, but there are cases where there is an overlap in form with the past participle and we find *-ys*. For example, the pret. of *sevall*, 'to stand', can be *sevys* (PA 81.2) or *savaz*

---

15   Iwan Wmffre, *Late Cornish*, Languages of the World/Materials 135 (Munich/Newcastle: Lincom, 1998), p. 72.

(JCH 33); of *leverall*, 'to say', both *leverys* (RD 4) and *lavarraz* (WR, Genesis 3:4).[16] A similar situation obtains with some other verbs such as *cowse* 'to speak', but the tendency to *-as/-az* increases in the later language.[17] The existence of forms with *-ys/-is*, however, is particularly relevant to instances where there is doubt, however small, in SA about whether a form was originally 3 sg. preterite or the past participle—for example, *[y] cowsis > [y$^{e\,vos}$] cowsis* 62r.14 (cf. TH 43r.25 *eff a cowsys*; TH 32r.1 *a cowsys*), and the case of *[ha'n] hynwis* 61v.33 or of *wensys* 64v.5.

res/rys ew > a res/rys [thyn]: 'we ought to, we should'. The earlier idiom was *rys/res yv [thyn]*, 'we must' (lit. 'a necessity it is [to us]', perhaps sometimes even understood as 'given it is [to us]). This led to constructions such as *a vea res thotha bos* SA 66r.10,' it should be' (see Notes on that passage) or *a vea res thetha receva* TH 16r.4, 'they should receive'. In due course *res* underwent further development and began to be personalized (NW) as in *ny a rys/ny a res*, 'we should, must', eventually almost becoming a quasi-verb in its own right. Compare *rys yv thyso* OM 1800, *res yv thyso* PC 2619, *rys ew theso* BK 1112, 'you (s.) should', with *ny a rys* SA 59r.39, 'we should'.

ryp > reb: 'beside'—a typically later form, as at 60r.22 where the inflected 3 sg. *rebta* 'beside him' is also later in form.

rth > r and rgh > rh > rth: By Stephyn's time *th* was silent in the combination *-rth*, which may have been reduced to something like /ɹ./. Tregear sometimes writes it, sometimes not. (A good example is the verb *gortheby* BM 3532, which Tregear has as *gurryby* TH 44r.1, but he also has *gurthebys* TH 44r.3 and *gorrybys* TH 20v.8). The pres./fut. 3 sg. was traditionally written *gorthyb* BK 2094, the lenited form being *worthyb* BK 52. These become *gorryb* CW 1196, and *worryb* SA 61v.34. (See also Stephyn's *e ker* 65v.22 for Tregear's *in kerth* TH 6v.24.) Underlining this, we sometimes see the erroneous introduction of silent *th* into words traditionally ending with simple *r*, such as at SA 59r.33, 59v.26 where the spelling *lowarth* is used for the word *lowar*, 'many', cf. TH 1v.15. See also SA 59v.26, 61r.19 & 64r.34. The word *lowarth* itself meant 'garden' as in the Passion Poem: PA 140.2, 233.1, but, if still in use, it would have been pronounced with a silent *th* by the period of SA).[18] Other, related back formations occur

---

[16] William (or Wella) Rowe (or Kerew), of Hendra in Sancreed, made a number of translations of biblical passages towards the end of the seventeenth century. See Rod Lyon, *An Kernewek a Wella Rowe* (Hellys [Helston]: Kesva an Taves Kernewek, 1998), p. 1.

[17] Williams, *Desky Kernowek*, pp. 118–19.

[18] In fact, it does not seem to have survived. Tregear and Jordan use forms of *jardin* like modern Breton: *Jardyn* TH 2r.24; *iarden* CW 1801. For more on final *rth* see Williams, *Desky Kernowek*, p. xxxiii, section 0.3.5 (by Michael Everson).

at this period: words such as *Werghes* (lenited from *gwerghes*, 'virgin') can be spelled *worthias* SA59r.22 or *worthyas* BK 159.

s > j: As at 62r.18, the letter *i*, when consonantal in SA, can represent the sound of modern English *j* (i.e. /dʒ/) rather than modern English *y* (i.e. /j/).[19] Both *pesadow* TH 39v.16 and *peiadow* (SA 62r.18, BK 2775) are found, and perhaps both were pronounced *pejadow* (as *I* and *J* are still interchangeable at this point— see also *peIadow* SA 63r.36, BK 731, BK 1177m and *peIadaw* BK 763). Perhaps Stephyn's pronunciation of *Iesus/Iesu* was similarly with an initial /dʒ/ (as in Lhuyd's later *dzeziu̯* AB 67b).

s > r: As noted above *s* can become *r* in late Cornish (see General Notes *(ls > sl > s > r)* for the example of *golsowas > gorowas*). This is most evident in late forms such as *theara vee* WB 1 (for *y thesave* TH 33r.5) or *ne geran ny* SA 63v.9 (for *ny gesan ny* TH 9v.7-10). Tregear consistently writes *esan ny* in the 1550s (TH 10v.7, 11r.16, 56r.14, 57r.23), but Stephyn uses both forms: *erany* 65r.13 and *e thesan ny* 61r.32.

simplification: Prepositions usually combine in Cornish with personal pronouns in 'conjugated' forms, for example *inna* TH 2v.17 (earlier *inno* BM 995), 'in it'; *gansa eff* TH 21v.3 (earlier *ganso ef* PA 163.3, RD 556), 'with him'; *theso ge* TH 44r.5, 6 (earlier *thyso gy* BM 573). In later Cornish these were increasingly simplified to the radical forms and personal pronoun, evidently beginning in SA with forms such as *in ef* 61r.37, *gans ef* 59v.16, *the gee* 62r.38 (which cannot all be due to elision). Note, though, some simplified forms at an early date, for instance, *the gy* RD 1091, 2037, and conjugated forms at a late date, such as *thyso* CW 871 (although perhaps influenced by earlier sources).

theffa: The phrase *nep ne theffa regardya*, 'who does not take account of' 59r.15, is one example among several of *dos* being used as an auxiliary, often (as in this case) in the subjunctive. See also 64v.35, 66r.25-6, 66r.27 and General Notes *(conditional)*. The present and past subjunctive had largely fallen together in later Cornish in most verbs, because the reduction of *-o* to *-a* in the 3 sg. meant that they often could not be distinguished (NW). As with *a theffan ry* 66r.27, the subjunctive of *dos* is particularly useful in clauses that have a future context.[20]

the vos: Stephyn regularly uses the infinitive of *bos* in idioms such as *kyns an girryow benegas the vos leveris*, 'before those holy words are said' (lit. 'before the blessed words to be spoken') 61v.31-2. See also 62r.13-14, 62v.7, etc. The roots

---

19   Williams, *Desky Kernowek*, pp. 20, 24-25.
20   Richard R.M. Gendall, *A Student's Grammar of Modern Cornish* (Menheniot: The Cornish Language Council, 1991), p. 82.

of this construction existed in Middle Cornish (e.g. *kynsys y the tremene an mor ruyth*, 'before they cross the Red Sea, OM 1634) but became standardized later, as here (OP).

thi'th: lit. 'to your', a 'prepositional pronoun' combining the preposition *the/ tha/thi* ('to') with the possessive pronoun *tha* ('thy', 'your' 2 sg.) in the enclitic form *'th*. A good example of its traditional use can be found at 60v.9—*kee tha'th tre*, 'go to your home'. At 64r.2–3, however, *Corf thith Dew*, 'the Body of your God', shows how in later Cornish *theth/thath/thith* can at times replace *tha* (or *a'th*, 'of your', as at 63v.36) with the simple sense of 'your'.

thotho > thetha: lit. 'to it'—at 64r.19 we find a later form of the 3 sg. m. prepositional pronoun *thetha* superseding the *thotho* of the *Ordinalia* (e.g. OM 191 and passim). In Tregear *ow ionya nessa thotha* TH 25v.19 already occurs for Bonner's 'adioynynge to it'. Interestingly he can also still use the earlier 3 pl. *thetha* TH 25r.3, TH 25v.2 (cf. also BK 2722) alongside the later *thethans* TH 16r.26, TH 36v.10 (*thothans* CW 401). Both final *a* and final *o* for 3 sg. m. are found in *Beunans Meriasek* (BM 466 *dotha*, BM 453 *dotho eff*). In SA we have *thotheff* 66v.24 and *th[e]theffe* 59r.36–37.

wosa > osa > udzha: 'after'—the form *wosa/wose* is widespread in the earlier period right up to Tregear: *wose* OM 280, PC 1315, RD 226, *wosa* TH 4r.26 and passim, CW 1936. The form *osa* SA 61v.32, 62r.38 looks like a transitional form on the way to late *ouga/ugge/udzha*, and may indeed have been pronounced in a way closer to them. (For example, the *ugge hedda* of Nicholas Boson, on page 5 of his *Nebbaz Gerriau dro tho Cornoack*,[21] would have been written by Stephyn *osa henna*, but we cannot be sure where on the spectrum between [ˈɔːzə] and [ˈʊdʒə] his pronunciation would have fallen.) Lhuyd spells this word *udzha* AB 124b.

y > e: 'his'—for the 3 sg. poss. pron. 'his', for example, 59r.13 *e gwely*: where *e* overwrites the original *y*.

y > hy: 'they'—the 3 sg. pers. pron. is sometimes written with an *h* in SA, for example, at 61r.16, 61v.23, perhaps because the initial *h* was not being pronounced clearly in many words by this period, leading to this sort of back-formation. Similarly, at 60r.10, *hef* is written for *ef*.

y^e: 'to'—this contraction should be expanded as *the* as in English, but in Cornish it is not the definite article (which is *an*) but the preposition *the*, meaning 'to' (or *the* in words beginning *the-*).

---

21 Padel, *Cornish Writings*, p. 29.

yndan > dan: 'under'—the form *dan* is paralleled in Welsh from an early date, but in Cornish is prefixed with *yn* in most earlier texts: *yn dan* OM 2807, PC 2259, RD 661. The use of *yn/in* continues into the Tudor period with *in dan* BK 1041, TH 13r.16, CW 75; *indan* TH 54r.24 and beyond with *yn dan* (LLR—*Credo* in endpapers). It would be interesting to find the use of *dan* beginning in SA, although see the caveat in the Textual Note on 60r.37.

ynweth > y weth > aụêdh: 'also, as well'—many early texts show the division *yn weth* (e.g. PA 97.4, OM 990, PC 714, RD 162) for *ynweth*, but the word is also found widely as *ynweth* (e.g. CW 1339, TH 10v.19). A progression that anticipates later usage may be under way in SA: 'the *n* is not sounded in Late Cor[nish] and is not [found] in B[reton] *ivez*.'[22] This appears to be reflected in the forms *y weth* at 59r.18–19 and *e weth* at 59v.17 (although it remains possible that there once was an *n* at the right of line 59r.18, now completely lost). Lhuyd (in 1706) offers both *aụêdh* and *enụêdh* (e.g. AB 113, 223), where his *ụ* and *dh* represent the *w* and *th* in English 'weather'.

Textual Notes and Apparatus

59r.1	**59:** the folio number inserted in pencil near the top right of each throughout the manuscript after SA was bound together with TH.
59r.1–2	**Christ ny rug vsya trope:** 'Christ did not use a trope' (MS continues *Christ ny rug vsya trope k[..............] / dewetha, kepare del vg[e] S. A[ust]*, H *Crist ny rug v[.. ..... / deweth kepar [... .. ...]*, omitted from B). Possibly intended as an augmented introduction and therefore inserted at the head of this page, where the folio is damaged. Thus *I ma S. Austen ow leverall*, 'St Augustine says' could have been replaced when read out (for example) by something like *Christ ny rug usya trope [kepare e gerryow] dewetha, kepare del uge S. Austen ...* 'Christ did not use a trope as his last words, as St Augustine says ...'
59r.3	**ow:** verbal particle forming the present participle. It appears as both *o* and *ow* in SA.
59r.5m	**Dist:** occurs throughout the marginalia of SA and its source, probably as an abbreviation of *Distinctio* and therefore a reference to an extract of the passage in Gratian, Ivo of Chartres or Peter Lombard—although it may also stand for *Disputatio*. N2 and C have 'chapter'. (Unlikely to be for *[Donat]ist[as]*.)

---

22 Nance, *Gerlyver Noweth*, p. 186.

59r.5	**ituri ad inferos:** 'on his way to the next world, descending to the dead', lit. 'going to the underworld/lower place'. (The Apostles' Creed also properly has *inferos*, rather than *infernos/inferna/infernum*).
59r.6	**no*n* iudicatur hæres:** 'is not counted an heir'. St Augustine appears to have said something slightly different, that is, 'that heir would be counted impious' (or 'disrespectful'). Textual or scribal errors may account for a confusion between *impius* and *illius*, which then necessitated further minor changes to preserve the sense.
59r.10	**quis no*n* obseruet:** 'who <u>does not</u> keep'. The Cornish translation ignores the *non*, giving *pew vge ow despisea ha gwetha y erriow*, 'who despises and who <u>keeps</u> his words' (59r.19-20). In fact this *non* is not present in all sources, though it is in Foxe—see Commentary, Quotation 2, note 9.
59r.11	**y^e:** 'to'—'Scribe's contraction for *the (dhe)*'—Nance's pencil note on C.
59r.12	**me agispys:** 'I ask you', H *me agispys*, N, B *me agis pys* (cf. *me agis pys* PA 182:5), with verbal particle *a*, infixed 2 pl. poss. pron. *gis* as object, and 3 sg. *pys* from the verb *pysy* (e.g. at OM 1608, PC 37), 'to pray, ask'. (E *me a'gis pys*.)
	gyrryw: 'words'—the second *y* is written over the *o* of an earlier *gyrrow* (and again at 59r.15), for example, *gyrrow > gyrry[o]w*. See General Notes (*gerryow*).
59r.12–13	**vo:** 3 sg. (pres.) subjunctive of *bos*, 'to be', lenited from *bo*.
59r.13	**e gwely:** 'his bed', MS *^ey ^gwely*, N, C, H *y gwely*—the 3 sg. (m.) poss. pron. *e* before *gwely* overwrites the original *y* and the initial *g* also seems also have been inserted later (incorrectly, according to earlier usage) before the existing *w*. See General Notes (*mutations*) and (*y > e*). This could be seen as evidence of correction by another scribe, or later correction by Stephyn, taking contemporary usage more into account, or an immediate action (cf. 63r.34).
59r.14	**vos:** the end of the word is obscured: it is possible it was originally *vose*.
	den veith ny lavar a vos gow gansa: 'no one says he is lying', lit. 'no man at all speaks of there being a lie with him'. Original *e* in *laver* appears to have been altered to the *a* in *lavar*. See General Notes (*laver*).
	na negew ef: 'nor is he', N, H *ena neg ew ef*, B *ena. negew ef*, Foxe 'and he is not'. See General Notes (*na*).
59r.14–15	**compti[s] y e heare:** 'counted (as) his heir', N, B, C *ow ki[ll] e heare*, H *ow ki[ll] ey heare*. Here again the *e* replaces an older *y*, which has

	initially been overwritten (unclearly) with an *e*, then a further *e* has been added. The resulting blot is hard to construe as *vel*, but this may be missing from the previous line (giving *comptis vel e heare*, more clearly 'counted <u>as</u> his heir') although Foxe has simply 'accompted his heire'. The *t* in *compti[s]* is fairly clear given other examples such as in *poyntma* (59v.28). The *[s]* is admittedly conjectural. See General Notes (*y > e*).
59r.15	**nepne theffa regardya:** 'who does not take account of'—the overwriting of a *p* here over *b* (in original *neb ne*?) may indicate Stephyn revising, or someone else he asked to look over the manuscript (compare the *p* in *pew* four lines below). See also General Notes (*theffa*). For *regardia*, see 59r.17.
59r.16	**fatla wrene ny:** lit. 'how do we', MS *fatla wrere^{ne} ny*, N, C, B, H *fatla wrene ny*—a possible original *fatla wrere ny avoydaya* appears to have been altered to *fatla wrene ny avoydaya*, 'how shall we ... escape'—using the 3 pl. pres./fut. of the auxiliary *gule*, 'to do' (cf. *a wren ny* RD 1471) as an auxiliary. If we read *fatla wre neny*, it is also possible that emphasis may be indicated, that is, *fatla wre[n] neny avoydaya*, 'how shall *we* avoid'. (It is hard to explain the original *wrere* except perhaps as unlikely forms of the 1. pl. conditional or subjunctive. But what may appear to modern eyes as a *c*, *l* or *i* written under the *n* may be better explained as a continuation of the downstroke of the *p* above or the final portion of the later *n*.)
59r.16–17	**ne geran cregy:** 'we do not believe', MS, N, C, B, H *ne geran cregy*. Nance notes in N2 that *ne geran cregy* = *neg eran cregy* = *nyns eson ow crysy*, and, in C, even more plainly: '*neg* for *nynj*'. (In fact, the form *nyng* does occur in SA, at 59v.2, but the usual form is *neg*: hence E, *neg eran cregy*.) See General Notes (*neg ew*).
59r.18	**han:** may be a slip, echoing the English: in the original, 'and' occurs here. Alternatively, *han* could possibly represent *ha'gan*—'and our' (RE), or just possibly *an*, 'the', leading into the next clause.
59r.18–19	**y weth:** 'also'—see General Notes (*ynweth > y weth > auêdh*)—the word is split over two lines so perhaps *yweth* is intended, but see *e weth* at 59v.17. Stephen invariably writes *in* for 'in', so it is unlikely the unusual *y* represents a contraction for *yn*. (If so, he misses opportunities to use it above at *agyn* and below at *vyn*.)
59r.20	**ha ef:** 'and he', instead of *hag ef*. See General Notes (*ha/hag*).
59r.22	**worthias:** 'Virgin', for older *werghes* (e.g. RD 403 a lenited form of *gwerghes*, 'virgin'). Cf. also *worthyas* (BK 159). See General Notes (*rth > r*). Comparison of the *or* in *corf* (59r.37) with the *er* in *gerryow* (59r.17) makes the *or* definite.

59r.23	**in mentem:** 'in mind, to mind', first correctly read by RE. N, B *mementum*, H *mementem*.
59r.24	**hon[o]ratus:** 'honoured'. The *-ratus* is clear, though Nance read the word as *honorauis*.
	fruaris: 'you may enjoy'. This appears to read *frnaris*, but there are sufficient examples of a badly formed *n* in the text to make *fruaris* certain, given the source text.
59r.25	**gas ve y^e remmembra:** 'let me remind you', Foxe: 'Let it come into thy remembraunce'. While we have *y^e* here, that is, *the*, I have emended to *gas ve th[a] remmembra* in E to show this is the 2 sg. poss. pron. and not the def. art.
59r.26	**arave:** MS *arave* = *ara ve*, most likely representing *a wraf ve*, 'I do' (NW), rather than the late *ora vee*, 'I know'. The initial *a* is in any case clear. The final *f* or *ff* of the 1 sg. ending is not present and was clearly disappearing: Ton writes *a raff* at BM 1393, *ny raff* at 1257, 1390; Jordan has *ny wraf* at CW 1440 but *ny wra* at CW 2508; Tregear has *fatell rave* TH 43r.14, 19. See General Notes (*esoff*>*esa*).
59r.27	**owsetha:** 'sitting'. The *w* is blotted, but its initial downstroke is clear.
	e thony: 'we are' = *eth on ny*. See note on 59r.30.
	gans an kethsam tra: lit. 'with the selfsame thing'. Nance's phrase in T, 'by that selfsame substance', has been used in the translation.
59r.28	**abell:** 'able'—note the use of this anglicized construction instead of *gallas* here.
59r.30	**y thony:** 'we are' = *yth on ny*. See note on 59r.27.
	vn: 'one'—what appears to be an original *on* has been altered to *vn* (E *un*).
59r.31	**agen:** either the simple 2. pl. poss. pron. 'our' or *a'gen*—that is, 'of our' with infixed poss. pron. (KS) as in E.
	lavar: Again a possible original *laver* may have been altered to *lavar*, as at 59r.14, q.v.
59r.32	**dclarya:** 'declare'—N, B, H, E *declarya*.
59r.33	**lowarth:** for *lowar*, 'many' as at TH 1v.15. See General Notes (*rth* > *r*).
59r.34	**mamb:** 'mother'—see General Notes (*pre-occlusion?*).
	wore: lit. 'puts', 3rd pers. sg. pres. from *gora*, 'to put, place' [cf. TH 46v.4]. The lenition implies the usual preceding particle *a*, which is not written.
	ye vaga: lit. 'to feed' (here, 'to be fed').
	[bus]: N1 [mes?], N2 [bus], C, B [mas]—for *ma's/marnas*, perhaps because it appears at line 35. The form *bus*, 'but' is entirely conjectural in E by analogy with 60r.21. See General Notes (*bus*).

59r.35	**arluth:** 'lord', spelled with a secretary hand descending *r*, rather than the usual small *r*.
	gwell: 'to do'. See General Notes *(gule > gwell)*.
59r.36-7	**th[e]/theffe:** for *thetheffe* 'to him', N, B *thotheffe*, H *th[o]/theffe*. Either *thetheffe* or *thotheffe* is plausible, given earlier *thotho ef* OM 1328, but the remains of the letter look more like *e*. See General Notes *(thotho > thetha)*.
59r.37	**[kepare] a ra:** 'as (does)', MS *b*ᵏ*eg*ᵖ*are a ra*, N, H *be[ni]ell a ra*, B *be ell a ra*—although from the outset we might have expected *kepare*, 'as, like', the word appears originally to have been *begar*. (On this same folio, 59r, the *b* is very similar to that in *bugell* at line 32, and in *trembla* at line 28; it contrasts considerably with the *k* in *kigg* in line 30 and in *kethsam* in line 27. It seems that the original *b* may have been modified by the addition of the central line that is often found in k, the final *e* is added just below the arch of the *r*, and the clear, original *g* may be overwritten by a *p*—now unclear—but cumulatively creating *kepare* as at 59r.2.) See General Notes *(g > k)* and *(kepar > pecar)*. Nance himself clearly thought the initial letter here was *b*, not *k*, wondering if the word was not *bonyl* (i.e. from *bo an eyll*, 'or else') perhaps in the form *be[ni]ell*, but this does not explain the remains of the *g*.
59r.38	ʷ**orth agyn maga ny:** 'feeds us', N, C, B *vrth agyn maga ny*, H *vrth agyn magany*. Again the word ʷ*orth* has been clearly altered, probably from an original *orth* (or just possibly *erth*) by the overwriting of a *w*, or a *v* partially altered to a *w* (or possibly *vo*). The effect of the inserted letter over the original *o* gives the appearance of *e*. It is arguable therefore whether it is now intended to read *worth* (as given here) or *vorth, verth, werth* or *vrth*. The form *worth* is supported by 64v.32. See General Notes *(orth > worth)*.
	e may: appears to represent *e ma*, as suggested in E. See General Notes *(ema > oma)* and 59v.12. In traditional Cornish orthography, however, a final -*y* could indicate lengthening of a vowel. (The temptation to suggest the influence of Welsh *y mae* here, from Stephyn's surmised travels, should probably be resisted.)
59r.38-9	**gans e [gor]f** ᵃʸ **gos[e]f:** 'with his Body and his Blood', C, B *gans e / gorf kiyg ha gosef*, H *gans e / gorf kiug ha gos*. Originally the word was *gorf* (lenited from *corf*, 'body'). At some point it was overwritten by *gos*, 'blood' (or even *go*ᵒ*s* or *go*ᵉ*s*, though the intruded letter is faint and debatable). Part of the remaining *rf* may have been intended or adapted to read *gosef*, 'his blood', while *ay* or *hay*, 'and his', was inserted before and above. The *h* of *hay* is, however, unlikely, an *f*

| | later lengthened below being a better explanation. This *f* appears to be the final letter of a word of which little else survives, but a new *gorf* seems likely. In summary, an original *e gorf*, 'body', was probably altered to *e gorf ay gos (ef)*, 'his body and his blood', departing from Foxe. |

59r.39 **ny a rys recevya:** 'we should receive', MS *ny a rys recevya* or *ny a rys e recevya*, N2 *ny a rys (ef) vya*, C *ny a rys(che)vya*, B *ny a rys (ef)*, H *ny a rysche vya*—the manuscript is severely damaged and extremely difficult to read at this point, with confusion due to the tail of the *y* above crossing the word—compare the clear *recevya* at 59v.22. The 'we should receive' is implicit in Weston's phrase in Foxe's account—he is responding to Cranmer who uses exactly these words just before. See General Notes *(res/rys ew > ny a res/rys)*.

59v.1 **[Erubesc]it:** 'blushes'. Most of the word is no longer visible in the MS, but it is reconstructed on the basis of Foxe and the Cornish translation.

nutrix: one could read *matrix* (N, B, H) here for *nutrix*, although it is the latter in Foxe. The sense is the same in each case—a 'nursing mother'.

59v.4 **nobis propinabit:** 'he will offer/pledge/supply to us'.

59v.8 **treweythow:** 'sometimes', N, B, H *trewythyow*—the *y* seems partly modified or overwritten, perhaps to form an unusual *e*. So *trewethow* (or possibly *treweythow*) may have been the final intention. There is no *y* in the plural ending as Nance thought—see General Notes *(gerryow/gyrryow)*.

59v.8–9 **rag boos mammath:** lit. 'to be a nurse' (i.e. a 'nursing mother'—or a wet-nurse).[23] N, B, H *rag boos mammeth*. The spelling is definitely *mammath* here (cf. *mamaid* VC 148). The word is also found in Lhuyd (*mammath* AB 101c) and BM 1675 (*mammethov* pl.)

59v.9 **ne gesee o gwell in della genan:** lit. 'he is not doing so with us', N, C, B *ne gesa o gwell indella genan*, H *ne gesa, o gwell indella genan*, lit. 'he was not doing so with us'. It is very hard to read the *ee* as an *a*. The *esee* probably represents *usy/uge/egy* (E *neg esee o gwell indella genan*). SA does use *ee* for *y* in *Tee* 61v.5, *gee* 62r.37, *thees* 62v.35, and *e* for *u* in *nyng egy* 65v.9, *nyng egy* 66r.25, so a further spelling of *esee* would at least be possible (KS). Additionally, *esee* could represent *neg ese e o gwell indella genan* where *ese e = usy e[f]* (NW).

---

23 Nicholas Williams, *Clappya Kernowek* (Portreath: Agan Tavas, 1997), p. 152, translates idiomatically 'to be breastfeeding'.

59v.10	**boos:** 'food', reflecting a progression in the pronunciation of this noun from *buit* VC 881 > *boys* PA 10.8 > *bos* OM 378 > *boos* CW 1032 > *bûz* AB 47c. But the later pronunciations are rooted in the earlier, and perhaps local uses retained elements of earlier forms, for example, *bois* TH 52r.23.
59v.12	**e may:** here *e may* represent *ema [e]* (as adopted in E, with *ef* losing its final *f*). Simple *ema* could also be intended (as with the instance at 59r.38 q.v.) as just above at 59v.10 we have *e ma ef*.
59v.13	**chapte*r* [a] Mathew:** the large *a* is blotted, during the overwriting of a previous error. Part of an *f* seems visible: the error might have been an English *of*, in view of *not* at 59v.16 below, and *only* at 59v.17.
	levera[..]: 'says', N, B, H *leverall*—a fairly certain reading, though in fact only a small mark remains after the *a*, but it looks more like the remains of a letter than of a comma. See notes on *levera* 63r.22.
59v.14	**the vose mab dene:** lit. 'to be a human being, part of mankind'; 'to become man' (Foxe) in the sense of taking on human nature.
59v.16	**gans ef:** 'with him', see General Notes *(simplification)*.
	ha gvle ny: 'and make us', an example of the tendency in late modern Cornish to simplify such constructions by omitting the poss. pron. before the verb. See General Notes *(possessives)*.
59v.17	**der:** a later form of *dre*, 'through'. See General Notes *(dre > der)*.
	in very deed: in this and the adjacent lines Stephyn has drifted into using a number of English words (*in very deed, [n]ot*), as well as words derived from English (*whippys*) or spelt in an English way (*faith*), clearly confirming the source in Foxe and raising questions about the nature of his bilingualism.
59v.18 (&m)	**gans ganow:** lit. 'by mouth', perhaps a customary name for this passage (because of its subject matter); or (with Nance in C) an idiomatic phrase for 'with his own mouth'; or simply a reference to 2 Co 13:1.
59v.20	**i.:** representing *id est*, 'that is', as throughout SA.
	nyn gew: 'it is not'. The fact that we can have *nyn gew* for *nyng ew* in SA underlines the likelihood that *ne gew* (cf. 59r.14, 17 & passim) represents the same words and a similar pronunciation. See General Notes *(neg ew)*.
	nebas: the word often means 'little, few', not simply 'some',[24] and not only with plural nouns, as we see here. T gives 'slight'.

---

24 Ray Edwards, *Notennow Kernewek 4* (Sutton Coldfield: Kernewek Dre Lyther/Kesva an Taves Kernewek, 1997), pp. 64–5, argues it usually means the former in earlier texts.

59v.21 **recevya:** 'receive'—the word is cut short by the page and therefore repeated at the beginning of the next line.

59v.22 **corf:** 'body' is probably written in error here for *ganow*, 'mouth'. The edited version is so emended. If dictated, it is possible that *an gor'-na* was heard for a late pronunciation of *an ganow*, with the *f* in *corf* elided, but a simple error is more likely—see General Notes (dictation?).

59v.26 **lowarth onyn:** 'many a one' (*lowarth* for *lowar*). See General Notes (*rth > r*).

fatla: here *fatla*, normally 'how', introduces a simple indirect statement, and is perhaps best translated 'that'.

59v.27 **in an sy:** 'in them'. This is a late form, analysed in E as *inans y*, but it is possible the author was beginning to analyse differently, heralding the later usage *an dzhei*. See General Notes (*3 pl. ending*) and *ens sy* in the same line.

59v.28 **Chrisostom**[em][a] **in [k]eth keth poyntma ow leverall:** 'Chrysostom says, on this same point', N, C, B *Chrisostom e ma then keth poynt ma ow leverall*, H *Chrisost[om e ma then] keth poyntma ow leverall*. Probably an unclear, blotted *keth* was written, then repeated for clarity (as elsewhere in SA, for example, 59v.21). The *ema* above right of Chrisostom is small, damaged, unclear and seems added as a correction or an afterthought. I have emended in E to *[ema] Chrisostom in keth poynt-ma ow leverall*. (Foxe 1570 has 'point', 1576 has 'poynt'.)

59v.29 **Antiochenum:** N1 *Antiochem*, N2 *Antiochennm*, B *Antiocheuum*, H *antiocheum*.

59v.30 **melotem:** 'sheep skin'—the final letter is an expanded contraction; although Foxe has final *m* here, final *n* would be supported by the Greek.

veré: 'truly'. There is a short line like an acute accent over the final *e*, where the edge of the folio is damaged. It may be nothing to do with *vere* but, interestingly, the final *e* in *verè* is also accented in Foxe (with a grave accent).

59v.31 **fuit:** not *suis* as in N and B.

prætiosior: not *pretiosor* as in N and B.

59v.33 **iustum:** 'just man'—N, B, H *intum*.

59v.34 **[vel]letis:** 'you would want'. This word is damaged but *[...]letis* can be made out. N, B, *[]eus*, H *[...]eus*.

59v.35 **misterijs:** as in Foxe, or *misteriis*, as in N, H—either are possible readings. (B *misterii*).

59v.36 **[H]elias:** not *[]dia* as in N, B or *[..]dias* as in H. The [H] is only partly visible.

59v.38	**[qu]idem exvt[us C]hristus autem:** 'indeed cast it off: but Christ'—the MS is damaged and/or trimmed.
60r.1	**et nobis carnem reliquit, et ipsam habens ascendit:** 'both left his flesh for us and yet ascended with it'—not *carne* as in N, H. Stephyn reinforces the meaning by adding the *carnem* not present in Foxe. (Note *ipsam* is missing from the computer transcription S.)
60r.3	**rag e tho:** 'for it was' (i.e. imperf. 3 sg. of *bos*); N, C, H *rag e tho*, B *rage e tho*.
	e gwryonath: 'in truth'; N, B, H, F *e gwreonath*, but the *y*, though faint, is clear. For *e*, 'in', compare *e weth* 59v.17 (for *ynweth*).[25]
60r.4	**deow:** 'two', clarified by the superscription of *ii* or *ij*.
60r.5	**a wartha:** 'above'. This is written with the secretary hand descending *r*, easily confused by the modern eye with a *z*. It appears to be a scribal variant, without phonetic significance. In later Cornish the word can often be spelled *awarra* (RG), see General Notes *(rth > r)*, although the pronunciation of the *th* can also reappear (as possibly in Boson's epitaph of 1716 for Keigwin, where we find *noadgez e wortha*, 'flown above').[26]
60r.6	**tha bedery:** 'to think', N, C, B, H *the bredery*. The idiomatic phrase *tha bedery tha vos* means 'to wish to be'.
	benegas: 'happy', lit. 'blessed'. Frequently, *benegas* is used in SA to translate 'holy/sacred/blessed' (e.g. at 63v.36, 65v.22), but here it translates Foxe's 'happy' (OP).
	&: here '&' is used as a shorthand for the Cornish def. art. *an*. See General Notes *(& > an)*.
60r.7	**pan drevynnough leverall:** 'what will you say' (2 pl. pres./fut. of *mennas*, rather than 2 pl. subjunctive) confirmed by Foxe.
	mar tema disquethas theugh: 'if I show you' is perhaps better than the 'if I should show you' of T, with the protasis of a real condition (NW).[27]
60r.8	**mere moy agis helma:** 'much greater than these', lit. 'much more than this'.
	pan vo ny: 'when we are', N, C, B *pan veny*, H *pan ve ny*. Compare the *o* of *me a wor* in line 5, and the *e* of *e mantall* in line 9, or of *the gwlas neff* in line 10. The present subjunctive is normal after *pan* when referring to an event in the indefinite future.[28]

---

25 T translates 'for it was <u>his</u> truth'—but one might expect lenition if so. In any case, *e gwryonath* clearly stands for the 'in deede' of Foxe.
26 Gendall, *Tavas a Ragadazow*, p. 165.
27 See General Notes *(conditional)* for more on this usage.
28 Williams, *Desky Kernowek*, p. 133.

60r.9 **Helias asas:** 'Elijah left', 3 sg. pret. (*gasas* BK 851) of the verb *gasa* 'to leave', lenited by the verbal particle *a*, so corresponding to *a asas* TH 40r.26. The same usage as in *hef a sas* in the next line. In both cases there is elision, possibly in different ways, as suggested by Nance in N2 and C. Read, as in E, *[a] asas/a [a]sas*.

60r.10 **Mab Dew:** 'Son of God', N, B *mas Dew*.
the*n* **neff:** 'to the heavens', lit. 'to the heaven'.
hef a sas: 'he left'. In E *ef a [a]sas* is seen as the most likely interpretation, Another possibility is *h[a] ef a [a]sas*, with further elision. The *h* is clear, but may be silent—see General Notes (*y > hy*). While the *f* looks a little like a *b*, compare the second *f* of *neff*, the previous word, and—more importantly—the *f* in *ef a woras* in the line below. The text could also be a copy and *hef asas* written for *neb asas*, 'who left', by scribal error (NW). See *Helias asas* 60r.9 above.

60r.11 **the gwlas neff:** 'into the kingdom of heaven', lit. 'to the land of heaven'. See General Notes (*mutations*).
60: the folio number is repeated again here.

60r.15 **tradit volentibus:** 'he gives [himself] to those willing'—N, H *traditur dentibus*.

60r.16 **complecti:** 'embrace', N1, N2 *complecti*, C, B, H *compleati*.
præstigii: the manuscript, correctly read by Nance, has *præstigii* for Foxe's *præstigiis*, 'in a hidden way/by illusion'. B, H *præstigi*.

60r.17 **y^e:** so N1 but N2 *the*.

60r.18 **markell:** 'miracle', N, C, B, H *mirkell*.
blonogath: 'will', a variant of, for example, *bolungeth* OM 873 (the *g* is soft, as English *j*), cf. *blonogeth/blonogath* TH 22v.17/18, *bolnogeth* BM 310, but note also *bolenegoth* PC 1139.
the ny: 'to us'—as above at 60r.11—or *theny* (as in N, C, B, H) representing *the[n] ny*, represented in E as *the' ny*.

60r.19 **^intyr dowla tuse & beis:** 'in human hands', that is, E *intyr dowla tuse an beis*, lit. 'between the hands of men of the world'. See General Notes (*&=an*).

60r.20 **Canevar den gwyrria*n*:** 'every righteous man'—T.[29]
e gowis: 'to get, receive him', from *cawas* CW 1219 a variant of *cafus* TH 51v.7, 'to get, have'. Correctly mutated, though in later Cornish the word had this mutation permanently.

60r.21–2 **tha keneve[.] a whelha:** lit. 'to as many as see'—N, B, H, E *tha kenever a whelha*—with conjunction, particle and subjunctive 3

---

29 And Williams, *Clappya Kernowek*, p. 55; alternatively 'every honest man', Williams, *Desky Kernowek*, p. 216.

NOTES 243

60r.22 **rebta:** 'beside him'—*reb*, here in an inflected 3 sg. form, is the same word as *ryp* PA 208.1, RD 266. See General Notes *(ryp > reb)*. The adverbial use of *der/dre* with an abstract noun is also common at this stage.

60r.23 **war^e an ^{nore} b^vys:** 'on the earth, in the world'; originally perhaps *war an bys*, with *b*. At some point Stephyn or an editor makes this emendation (which reflects common usage for this phrase from medieval to late Cornish) correctly leniting *bys*, 'world', to *vys* after *nore* (itself mutated from *dor*, 'earth'). It is possible, however, that the *e* in *ware* is original.

60r.24 **squardis:** 'torn'—this might appear to be *sqwardis* or even *sqvwardis* to modern eyes, but careful comparison with other instances of secretary hand *qu* in the text, suggest it is in fact *squardis*, with an irregular upstroke in the *u*. The letter *w* is quite different to its modern form (see *ware* in the line above) and in this hand *ar* is often written in this way (see *arluth* at 59v.25).

60r.25 **summo:** 'greatest'—N, H *summus*.

60r.26 **Nam:** 'for'—N, H *Non*.

60r.27 **regiis:** from *regia, -ae* 'court, palace'—N, H *regus* (but Nance in his translation, *regnus*). The *regum* [*sic*] later in the line is presumably for *regium*, 'royal', agreeing with *corpus* (correct in 60r.29).

60r.30 **cælos cælorum:** 'heaven of heavens'—it is arguable whether we have *æ* or *œ* here (H giving the latter) but compare *œ* in *præstantissimum* (and *cœlis*) at 60r.28.

60r.33-4 **Absterg[e] igitur:** 'wipe clean therefore'—N, H *Abstergitur*.

60r.35 **thesa ve o disquethas these:** 'I show you, I will show you'—see General Notes *(esoff > esa)*. Analysed in E as *[e]th esa' ve o disquethas these*, where *esa'* is for *esaff*. The use of *these*, 'to you', 2 sg., reflects the personal tone of the original—although there is a tendency to use 2 pl. more widely at this stage in the language, as at 60v.4. 60v.3.

waren nore: 'on the earth'—this could represent a contraction *ware'n nore* or *en* for *an* as in E, *war en nor*.

60r.35-6 **ew worthy [y^e] vos an moygha honoris:** 'the one who is worthy to be the most highly honoured' (NW). The folio is damaged and any *y^e* is now lost.

60r.37 **[d]an:** 'under', N2 *[..]dan*, N1, C *in [d]an*, H *[in] / [d]an*—enough of the 'd' survives to be sure of the reading: compare with the 'd' of *dew* at 60r.39, which is well aligned with *dan*. (There is no evidence of *[in]* on line 36, but the folio is heavily damaged so it may once have been present.)

60r.38	**arluth:** the *r* in *arluth* here is the secretary hand descending *r* found also at 60r.5. It appears to have no significance as the word is written with the usual *r* in most other instances.
60r.39	**sittis [lemmyn]:** 'set now', N, S *sittis [?lemmyn]*, B *sittis lemmyn*, H *sittis*. Foxe's English suggests an original (now missing) *lemmyn* translating the 'now', following *sittis*, restored in E.
60r.40	**nore vise:** 'world, earth', MS, H *nore vise*, N, B *nore vese*, S *nors vese*.
60v.1	**Sacrame[n]t:** 'Sacrament', MS *Sacramet*, N *Sacrament*, H *Sacrament*. Damage here makes any faded remnant of the abbreviation mark for *n* difficult to distinguish from random markings of the MS. But the intended form is clear from other occurrences, such as 61r.1.
60v.2	**dew:** 'God'—can be read *dew* or *Dew* (as N, H)—sometimes Stephyn uses a larger lower case *d* for the capital letter.
	in ^{gl}gwlas: 'in the land', N *in gwlas*, H *in <gl> gwlas*, F *in gwolas*. An original *gw* in *gwlas* seems to have been overwritten at some point with *gl*.[30] (An attempt may then have been made to turn this back into *gw*.) Whatever the case, the intention was surely to write *in gwlas neff*, as in E, but it is fascinating to see the various attempts to correct and recorrect the forms.
60v.3	**ne gesa:** N2 correctly glosses this as *nyns esof*, 'I am not', as part of the long present,[31] so the form *neg esa'* is used in E. See 60r.35 and General Notes (*esoff > esa*).
60v.5	**Tee:** the Cornish now switches back from the 2 pl. of *theugh*, 'to you', adopted in the previous line, to the 2 sg. of *tee/te*, 'thou'.
	pavanar: 'how, in what manner'—since *fatel* increasingly takes on the meaning 'that', *pa[n] vanar* is often used in Tudor Cornish for 'how' (NW)—cf. *yn pan vaner ym bema*—'how I got it' CW 757.
60v.6	**esta o qvelas:** 'you [not only] see' is understood—and so T—but 'not only' is omitted from the Cornish here (although supplied— strangely in English—in the next clause).
60v.7	**war[e]:** 'on', N, B, H *war*.
60v.8	**[a]n nor:** 'the earth', N, B, H, F *[a]n nore*.
	vova: 'he is' (subj.)—this has the appearance of a lenited form of *bo*, the 3 sg. pres. subj. of *bos*, with enclitic 3 sg. pers. pron. -*va* for *eff* is analogous to *fe* for *ef* in Welsh. It could, however, represent *bue/beu*, the 3 sg. preterite, given the source text, 'when thou hast

---

30 The reading *in gwolas* offered in F, p. 19, seems unlikely: it would involve an enlarged and modern-shaped new *w* partly overwriting the original *gw*, leaving part of the original *w* to be read as an *o*.

31 See Williams, *Desky Kernowek*, p. 15.

	receaued'. For another *vova* see 63r.11; for other instances of *vo* see 60r.8, 60v.27, 61r.21, 62r.18 & 19, 64r.27.
60v.9	**thaworth:** 'from'—N, C *tha worth*, B, H, F *the worth* (*worth* is a little higher than *tha*). The *r* is another secretary hand descending *r*.
60v.11	**ara:** 'do', B, H *ara*, N, *a ra*, with 3 sg. pres. of *gul* used as an auxiliary in the usual way: E *ny a ra touchia*, 'we (do) touch'.
60v.13	**keveris:** 'together', for *keffrys* (as in TH 16r.7). The spelling suggests it was stressed on the first syllable.
	De carnis: the *D* is clear, but appears to be written over an *n*, possibly from an original *in*.
60v.15	**frivolæ:** 'trifling, paltry'—N1, C, H *frivolæ*, N2, B *frivola*.
60v.18	**crederit [sic]:** N1, C, H *crederit*, N2, B *rederit*—as so often Bice seems to follow Nance's pencil fair copy, N2, rather than Nance and Smith's corrected final typescript, C. In any case, the form is probably meant for *crediderit* as in Foxe (see Commentary, Quotation 16).
60v.19	**[ca]rdo:** 'hinge'—N, H *illo*.
60v.19/20	**effici[t] [u]t anima:** 'makes it possible that the soul …' N, H *efficit anima*.
60v.21	**inugitur:** from *inungo/inunguo*, a variant of *ungo/unguo* and meaning therefore 'is anointed'. I have corrected the edited text (E *inu[n]gitur*) from the MS *inugitur*, in the light of Foxe. N, H *mingitur*.
	consecretur: 'may be consecrated'—N, H *consecratur*.
60v.24	**vescitur:** 'is nourished' as also at 61r.23. The *s* of *spiritu* above runs down to the *c*. N, H *vestitur*.
60v.25	**haker:** 'ugly, disfigured, frightful, bad, evil'. The form *hager* would have been expected. See General Notes *(g > k)*.
60v.26	**derag dew & neff:** 'before the God of heaven' with & for *an* as usual (or for *in* ('in'); or for *a*, 'of', with the intruded *n* as below).
	ena/enaf/nenaf: 'soul', written as *ena* here, as *enaf* in line 27 and *nenaf* in line 32 (with intruded *n* from the def. art. *an* before it.) See General Notes *(enaf > ena)*.
	neffra: '[was] never'—*neffra o*, if dictated, might have sounded very similar to *neffra*, 'never', on its own. The *[o]* has therefore been supplied at this point in E, even though the verb might have been placed elsewhere, or have been *ew* or *e ma*.
60v.27	**dirr vo an enaf:** 'as long as the soul is', N, B, H *dirr vo an enef*—the contraction is already under way in BK: see *ha der vo* BK 1528 (though see also *hedre vo* BK 1536 as in *hedre vo* OM 1464, RD 1865). This could be evidence that *hedre* was stressed on the second syllable (NW). The *a* in *enaf* is clear in the MS.

60v.28	**yᵉ dew & neff:** 'to the God of heaven', H *yᵉ dew & neff*, N, C, B, *the dew an neff*, E *the dew an neff*—see note for 60v.26 above and General Notes *(mutations)*.
60v.29	**glanhis:** a final long *s* is written over the normal, σ-like form of *s*.
60v.30	**consecratis:** 'consecrated'; there were several words for this, each with slightly different emphases, for example, *benegys* 65v.23, *sacrys* BM 531.
60v.32–3	**rag malla an nenaf [bo]s golowis:** lit. 'so that the soul can be enlightened', *malla* being a contraction of *may halla*—see General Notes *(may hallo > may halla > malla)*. The intruded *n* of *nenaf* (correctly written *enaf* at 60v.27) is removed in E, as at 60v.29, 30, 31.
60v.33	**spiris sans:** 'Holy Spirit', N, C, B, H *spirissans*. Either reading is possible.
60v.35	**mekys:** Nance notes in C *mekys = megys* = 'fattened, fed' (from the verb *maga*—for which see 59r.33–8). See General Notes *(g > k)*.
	Dew golosake: 'Almighty God', as at *the thu golosek* TH 5 and *Du galosek* BM 1975. Note also *arluth gallosek* RD 118 and *dev gallosek* RD 2394. Yet we also have CW 12 *dew an tase ol gollosacke*. (This last form may reflect a form in use in parishes for the Apostles' Creed: cf. *Me a greas in dew taz oll golosack*, 'I believe in God the Father Almighty', LLR endpapers.)
60v.35–6	**hae vab ras:** 'and his beloved Son', lit. 'and his Son of Grace'. Nance suggests the idiomatic translation '(dearly) beloved Son' in C. The contraction *hae/hay* is found elsewhere, such as at 61r.16, and is of longstanding (e.g. *hay* PA 91.4).
60v.37	**An sac:** catchword only, for *An sacrament* on the next folio.
61r.2	**ganaw:** 'mouth'—N *ganow*, H *ganaw*.
61r.3	**gyrreow:** MS *geyrreow*, N *gyrreow*, H *gyrrow*—the *y* overwrites an earlier *e* (or vice versa) and *-ew* or *-ow* is altered at the same time to *-eow*. See General Notes *(gerryow/gyrryw > gerrow/gyrrow)*.
61r.4	**quod:** the lower part of the *d* is visible—N, H *quo[.]*.
61r.4m	**Reus erit:** 'will be guilty'—N *Deus erit*. The 'R' is confirmed by the main text, Foxe and the sources.
61r.6	**insaniebant:** 'they were insane, incensed'—N, H *infamebant*.
61r.7	**corpus:** A repetition of the cramped *corpus* of the previous line. Similarly with *tenent* at the end of the line (the final *t* also being given under the marginal note), and with *simplex* at 61r.10.
61r.8	**execrabili ore:** '[with] an impure mouth'—possibly altered from *execrabile*. N, B, H have *erre* for *ore*.
61r.8–9	**menti[o] / [n]em:** N *menti[?]ec*, H *menti[ ]/[ ]emc*. Both are correct to draw attention to a mark following the word, very like a

	modern *c*, but it lacks the horizontal stroke of the scribe's *c* as in *recipiunt* in the previous line. Possibly an anomalous comma or a partially blotted colon.
61r.11	**henna ye leverall:** 'that is to say', The *ew* is implicit here (see 60r.34 and passim) but omitted in the text (though supplied in E).
61r.14	**kepar a rug Iudas betraya:** 'as Judas betrayed'—note here that Stephyn uses *kepar a*, rather than *kepar del*, and his usage is retained in E. (Also note S *bctraya*, N, B, H *betraya*.)
	dew: N, B, H *Dew*. See note for 60v.2.
	an nethewan: the traditional Cornish word *Ethewan* for the Jews is used by SA, rather than *Iewes/Iewys* as might be expected from Foxe and Tregear. The initial *n* (here and at 61r.17) is intruded from the def. art. *an*, as with *nenaf* at 60v.29, 30.
61r.15–16	**e movns h^ly dishonora Christ:** 'they dishonour Christ', N1 *e mowns hy dishonora Christ*, N2 *e mowns y [ow] dishonora Christ*, C *e mowns hy [o] dishonora Christ*, B *e mowns y [o] dishonora Christ*, H *e mowns y y dishonora Christ*. The particle *ow* is omitted, as noted by Nance in N2. Either the *y* of an original *hy* has been overwritten by an *I*, or an irregular contraction for *hy* has been overwritten, then repeated in the margin. (For the *h* in *hy* see *hynvis* 61v.32, *vrth* 61v.27.) But it is clear from the 3 pl. pres. of *bos*, 'to be'—*e movns*—that the pers. pron. intended is 3 pl. *y*, and not 3 sg. *hy*, as in *vons y* on the next line—see General Notes (*y > hy*). Though the *v* in *emovns* could be a contracted *w*, the letter here looks more like the *v* of *vge* 61r.19 than the *w* of *dowla* 61r.17 and *ganaw* 61r.18. So E gives *emouns y dishonora Christ*.
61r.17	**pecar:** 'as'; see General Notes (*kepar > pecar*).
61r.19	**dall:** N, B *dell*, H *dall* or *dell*, with *maga pell dall* meaning 'in so far as'.
	a keth deane ma Phoceus: 'this same man Photius', E *a' keth deane-ma, Phoceus* to indicate *a'* represents the def. art., usually *an*. As H notes, Nance also took the *a* to represent *an* (N, B, H *a*, C *a[n]*.) See General Notes (*an > a*).
	lowarth gwyeth: 'often'—with *lowar*, 'many', see General Notes (*rth > r*), and *gwyeth* 'time, occasion'. This latter word may have contained a diphthong as in modern dictionaries, for example, *gweyth*,[32] *gweith*,[33] and not a short *y* as in Unified Cornish.[34]

---

[32] Williams, *English-Cornish Dictionary*, pp. 381–82.
[33] Gendall, *Tavaz a Ragadazow*, p. 178.
[34] Nance, *Gerlyver Noweth*, p. 77, but see George, *Gerlyver Meur*, 3rd edn, p. 270.

61r.20	**arluth:** the *r* here is again the descending form of the letter—see 60r.5.
61r.21	**o tisquethas:** 'showing'—see General Notes *(o/ow)*. The original *o* was small and may have looked like an *a*, so has been rewritten.
	ny*n* go ef only deane ew^{vo} **sacrificed:** Foxe, 'it is not simply man that is sacrificed'. Stephyn changes the tense here from 'is' to 'was' (unless we consider *nyn go ef* to be an erratic spelling for *nyng ew ef*, 'it is not', especially if dictated). Further along, *ew* has been altered to read *evo*—the 3 sg. pres. subj.—as representing an indefinite future, with *vo* being written over the *w*, and the initial *e* being left to stand as an irregular form of the particle *a* (see *a vo offrys* 64r.27). Interestingly 'sacrificed' is left in English here, although Stephyn uses *benygys gans prontyrryan* at SA 65v.23 to translate *a sacerdotibus sacrificatum* 'sacrificed of the priestes'. (He translates *tempore sacrificij*, 'sacrifice tyme', as *termyn an sacrafice* at 60r.14, and uses the word again at 64r.19 and 66r.16. Tregear uses *sacrifice* at TH 56r.17.)
61r.23	**an corf o ma tibbry:** 'the body eats', N *an corf o [e] ma tibbry[s]*, H *an corf o ma tibbry*, C, B *an corf e ma tibbry*. T has 'is eaten', but no *s* at the end of *tibbry* is visible, which the positioning of the comma confirms. Nance realized this when checking C, and corrected *tibbry[s]* to *tibbry*. With the provection of initial *d* to *t* in *tibbry*, it is certain that we are dealing with *an corf oma [o] tibbry*, with *ema* spelt irregularly in this instance and the particle *o* or *ow* omitted, as often in SA. See General Notes *(o/ow)* and *(ema > oma)*.
61r.24	**enaf:** N, C, B *enef*, H *enaf* or *enef*.
	malla: 'in order that'—see General Notes *(may hallo > may halla > malla)*.
61r.29	**coniungit:** 'joins together', N, H *commingit*.
	gobe[.]: N, B *gober*, H, E *gobe[r]*, 'wages, reward for work', E *gober*.
61r.30	**an ober warbarth:** translating 'one work ... together', N, C, B *an ober warbarth*, H *an ober war barth*. Of course, *an* here may simply be the def. art. (as assumed in E and the translation) but the fact that 'one' is used in Foxe raises the faint possibility that Stephyn may have used it to represent *un* (at 59r.30 he first spells this *on*). Although *warbarth* could be transcribed as one word or two, the *r* and *b* are no further apart than the *r* and *a* in *seperatis* in the line above.
	John 17.21 & 14.10–11: the reference to John 14 is written just below that for John 17.
61r.33	**dîr henna:** lit. 'through that', *dîr* for *der*, see General Notes *(dre > der)*. The appearance of something like a circumflex over

	the *i* could be the result of a blot or other mark and appears to have no significance.
61r.33m	**trinitate:** The final *-te* of *trinitate* in the margin lies between lines 61r.33 and 61r.34.
61r.34	**verel[.]:** N, B, H, E *verel[y]*, 'truly', as at 61r.35.
	dib[...]: N, B, H, E *dib[bry]*, 'eats'—Foxe 'eateth'.
61r.36	**innaff:** 'in me'—N, C *in noff*, B *in neff*, H *innaff*.
61r.37	**in ef:** 'in him'—see General Notes (*simplification*).
	h[an]: or *h[a]*—N, H *h[a]*—only the *h* is in fact visible now. The edited text considers the context of the phrase: E *a'n kig ha'n Gois*.
61r.38	**tella:** lit. 'place', N1 *tellar*, N2, C, B *tella[r]*, H *tella*—for 'room' in Foxe. E *tella[r]* in light of *tillar* 65v.25.
61r.39	**distvny:** lit. 'testimony, witness'—N, C, B *distuny*, H *distvny*. The word is found as early as *tistuni* VC 428, and is widespread in the texts of Middle Cornish: for instance, *dustuny* PA 82.4, PC 1272, RD 1053; *dustyny* PC 1312; *destiny* PC 2023.
61r.40	**ha e weth:** 'and also', N, B, H *ha e weth*—the 'h' is visible in the MS but difficult to see in copies.
61r.41	**[ag]e*n* [a]rl[.]th Ies[..]** ^{Christ}: 'our Lord Jesus Christ'—these words are still half visible under the conservation tape of the MS, though effectively lost in copies. The final word *Christ* is clearer, as added to the line above. E *agen Arluth Jesus Christ*. (The form *Jesus/Iesus* is more common in the Cornish of this MS, although there is an instance of *Jesu/Iesu* at 66v.18.)
61v.2	**Ambros o leverall:** 'Ambrose says', for *[ema] Ambros o leverall*.
61v.3	**tocius:** 'whole', N, C, H *totus(?)*, B *tactus*. (The spelling *tocius* is a variant for *totius*: at this period, when *c* and *t* could be pronounced similarly as /ts/ before *i* and *e*, they were interchangeable, as already seen with *concio/contio*.)
61v.5	**ea:** 'those things', N, B, H *ea*, C *eo* (altered).
61v.6–7	**nouas:** 'new', *nou[as]* on line 6 (N, H *non*) is repeated owing to lack of space on the next line as the full word *nouas* (N, C, H *[natur]as*, B *naturas*).
61v.7	**vtim[ur]:** 'use', is confirmed by the source text. N, H *vtinam*.
61v.9	**Nunquid:** that is, *numquid*, 'is it the case (that)', N *Numquid*, H *Nunquid*.
61v.10	**vsus:** 'use/course'—the initial italic *v* here, as in the lines above and below, could be seen as lower or upper case.
61v.11	**consueuit:** 'tends', N, H *conseuit*.
61v.13	**cum:** 'when, since', MS *cum*, N, H *tum*.
61v.23	**hy a ve gwris:** 'they were made', MS, H *hy a ve gwris*, B *ny a ve gwris*—H points out that this *hy* represents *y*, 3 pl. and not *hy*, 3 sg.

	f. (Hence E, *[y] a ve gwris*.) A similar phrase occurs in the next line with *y* unambiguously spelled: *y a ve creatis*, 'they were created'. See General Notes (*y > hy*).
61v.24	**Gear Christ ill changia:** lit. 'the word of Christ can change'—the negative of the question has been omitted here in error, but is restored in E as *na ill* in line with Stephyn's usage: *Gear Christ, [na] ill changia*, 'Can the word of Christ (not) change'. See *Na illans y bos seperatis* at 61r.29 and *na illen denaha* at 66r.14.
61v.25	**Na esyn vsya:** 'Let us not use'—see note on 65v.19–20.
61v.26	**ha e negegath:** 'and his birth'; *negegath* represents *(g)enesygeth* in the spelling of BM 4387 (*ay genesygeth* Stokes; *aygenesygeth* MS).[35] The initial *g* is omitted, as it is properly lenited, and the first *e* elided.
61v.28	**goris:** MS *goris* or *goriis*, N, B *goris*, H *goriis*—the context is *goris in crows*, 'crucified', lit. 'put on the cross'. An argument could be made for a truncated *ii* and therefore *goriis*, as the letter is dotted twice.
61v.29–30	**ay corf ha e gois benegas:** 'of his holy Body and Blood'.
61v.32	**lever^{is}benegis:** 'said', C *lever^{is}benegis*, N, H *leverbeneg is*, B *leveris*. Stephyn, or a later scribe, corrects the phrasing 'before the holy words were blessed (*benegis*)', to 'before the holy words were said' (*leveris*). At first the final *-is* of *benegis* is left to stand fore the *-is* of *leveris*, then a superscript *-is* is added.
	hy*n*vis: 'called', MS *hynvis*: emended to *hyn[w]is* in E (to agree with *hynwis* in the next line and the usual *hynwys* as at PA 214.1, OM 80, PC 1951, RD 197, BK 1513, TH 29r.5 etc.)
	osa: 'after'—see General Notes (*wosa > osa > udzha*).
61v.33	**e tho gwris:** 'it is made'—*e tho* here may represent *eth ew* (pres. 3 sg. of *bos*) rather than *eth o* (imperf. 3 sg. of *bos*)—Foxe '<u>is</u> signified'—nonetheless E retains *eth o gwris*.
	han hynwis e gois: 'and he called it his Blood'. The translation and edited text (E *a'n hynwis e Gois*, following Nance) interpret *han* as representing *ha a'n*, including an infixed pronoun, with *hynwis* as preterite—see General Notes (*preterite*). This would match Foxe, where we have 'He calleth <u>it</u> hys bloud …'
61v.34	**worryb:** 'answer'—another illustration of how the 'th' in 'rth' was silent in Stephyn's Cornish. See General Notes (*rth > r*).
61v.35	**achy:** 'within'—more traditionally written *agy* (e.g. *a gy* at BK 2353). Foxe, 'inward'.

---

35 Whitley Stokes, ed. *Beunans Meriasek: The Life of St Meriasek, Bishop and Confessor, a Cornish Drama* (BM) (London: Trübner & Co., 1872), p. 254; see also https://www.library.wales/discover/digital-gallery/manuscripts/the-middle-ages/beunans-meriasek [f. 171, for which enter 178 of 211], National Library of Wales, Aberystwyth (2018). Accessed 25 May 2018.

	a whrella: the 3 sg. subj. of *gule*, 'to make or do' (*a rella*, TH 19v.9, *a wrello* OM 231).
61v.37	**chpter:** MS *chpter*, N, C, H *ch[a]pter*, B *chapter*, S *chopter*.
61v.38–9	**Sacramentorum:** 'of the sacraments', C *sacramentorium*.
61v.41	**consecratione:** 'by consecration'. This additional word is not found in the best editions of Ambrose's original. I have therefore taken it as standing alone in E, as a feature of the dialogue.
62r.1–2	**[....] ha gwyn d[i]r girreow dew trilys [y^e] corf ha [....] y thew:** reconstructed in E as *[Bara] ha gwyn dir girreow Dew trilys [the] Corf ha [Gois] y thew*: 'Bread and wine through God's words are changed to Body and Blood'. (It is also possible we have *th'y/th'e*, so 'to his Body and Blood'.) This heading is easier to read beneath the MS conservation tape than copies suggest and the headings of the following folios also give some help. A few words remain open to interpretation: *girreow* or *gerreow*—N, H *gerriow*; *trilys*—N, H *trelys*. The *gois* has been lost owing to damage. The *y thew* is on the line below, partly boxed off. Nance, in T, speculates that this phrase may have had an English precursor—perhaps (despite, as he says, the weak rhyme) 'Bread and Wine by the word of God / Is made to be Christ's Body and Blood'.
62r.3	**Nam ad reliqua omnia quædicuntur:** the next phrase in Ambrose's original—*in superioribus, a sacerdote dicuntur*—is here omitted (but restored in E): see Commentary, Quotation 23.
62r.3–4	**[defer]tur:** 'offered', restored in E from Foxe—the MS is torn or damaged at the right, for the next few lines.
62r.4	**cæ[teris]:** 'others', restored in E—N2, B *co[]*, N1, C *ce[teribus]*, H *ce[teribus]*.
62r.5	**[iam non]:** restored in E—N, H *[non]*.
62r.6m	**Exodi 20.11:** the 11 is written below the 20.
62r.7	**nimpe:** that is, *nempe*, 'surely'—N, H *incipe*.
62r.8	**ommia:** restored to *omnia* in E.
62r.10	**ergo:** N *ergo*, B *erg*.
62r.13	**An keth bara ma ew bara:** 'This same bread is bread', N, C, B *An keth bara ma ew bara*, H *An keth bara ma bara*.
62r.13–14	**an girreow an Sacramentys:** 'the sacramental words', Foxe has *verba Sacramentorum*, 'the words of the Sacrament'. See General Notes (*English influence*).
62r.14	**y$^{e\ vos}$ cowsis:** 'are spoken', lit. 'to be spoken', N, C, B *the vos cowsis*, H *y$^{e\ vos}$ cowsis*. The *vos* is inserted as a correction above and to the right of *y^e*. See General Notes (*the vos*).
	pan O: probably for *pan vo* as at 59r.12, 60r.8 etc. See note on 62r.18.

62r.15	**&:** that is, *an*, 'the'—see General Notes *(& = an)*.
	kig: Nance in T translates *kig*, 'flesh, meat', figuratively as 'feast'.
62r.16	**confirnia:** 'confirm', MS possibly *confirma*, but the dot over the final stroke of the 'm' suggests *confirmia* or *comfirmia* was intended), H *confirmia*, N, C, B *confirmia*. Emended to *confir[m]ia* in E.
62r.17	**&:** see above at 62r.15
62r.18	**a vo:** the subjunctive used to express an indefinite future, but here translated by the present. This is also normal use after *pan* as in 62r.19 below and 62r.14 above.
	peiadow: 'prayers', MS *ger*^*pe* *peiadow*, N, C, B, H *gere peiadow*, with the *i* probably pronounced as /dʒ/. The MS could be read as having *ger* (or Nance's *gere*) before *peiadow*, but it is more likely that a form of *gerryow/girreow*, 'words', was begun (in an instance of dittography) then overwritten with *pe* for *peiadow*, 'prayer', before being crossed out as unclear, with the word *peiadow* begun again. (A less likely explanation is that *gwreis*—compare 62r.34—was begun, corresponding to Foxe's 'made', but then overwritten.) See General Notes *(s > j)*.
62r.19	**bopell:** 'people'—the *p* is unexpected (see *bobell* CW 2383, and SA 59r.20, 63v.26, 65v.23) but also found in the unlenited form *popell* at 66r.36. See General Notes *(g > k)*.
	meternath: 'kings' translating Foxe's 'kinges', with a pronunciation closer to the *myterneth* of BM 2428 than the *myghterneth* of PC 785.
62r.20	**reverent:** 'revered, sacred', or—in this context—perhaps 'most holy'.
	nena: 'then'—see General Notes *(contractions)* and note on *nona* 66v.7.
62r.23	**ma:** N *na*, C, B, H *ma*.
62r.24,26	**& arluth:** that is, *an Arluth*, 'the Lord'—see General Notes *(& = an)*.
62r.24	**an nore:** 'and the earth'—probably for *han nore*, as in the other clauses. Part of the final *e* of *nore* is visible beneath the conservation tape.
62r.27	**te a wele:** 'you see' (sg.)—a good example of the use of the 'monoform', that is, the 2 sg. pron. being used with the 3 sg. pres./fut. form. The final *e* is silent.
	g Crefder: 'strength'; Stephyn almost writes *grefder* as f., but corrects to m.
	o conys: 'working'—that is, *o[w] conys* is the pres. participle of *gonys*, later written *gunnes*, 'to labour, work', and here correctly provected. (The form *gunit(h)iat ereu* VC 340, 'agricultural labourer', raises the question of whether the pronunciation with 'u' was a longstanding one.) See General Notes *(mutations)*.

62r.28	**derag dorn:** 'before hand'—see General Notes *(English influence)*.
62r.31	**ergo tibi respondeam:** N2 has *ergo tibi respondeam* but this is erased in N1. C, H *ergo tibi respondeo*, B *erg tibi respondeo*, Foxe *ergo tibi vt respondeam—[ut]* is restored in E.
62r.34	**Nefna ve gwreis, more na ve gwreis, nore na ve:** 'Heaven was not [made], sea was not [made], earth was not'. Stephyn himself or a later editor has struck out *gwreis* twice, perhaps for reasons of euphony as *na ve*, 'was/were not', can stand alone here (as at BK 380, 470. See Glossary under **na³**.
62r.35	**o cowse:** 'speaking'—the normal form in older texts was *keusel*—cf. *ov keusel* OM 2794, *ow keusel* RD 1392. By Tregear's time the form *cowse* was common, both for the present participle and the infinitive (cf. *ow cowse* TH 7v.9). It is unsurprising to find the same form used in Stephyn. (Note, however, that both forms still occur in Jordan—*ow cowse* CW 156; *a wrug cowsall thagye* CW 2350.) By the early seventeenth century *cowza* can be found, as in the phrase *meea nauiduacowzasawznack* (=*meea na vidna cowza Sawznack*), 'I will not speak English' (unless this represents *cowz a(n) Sawznack*).³⁶
	ef causis: 'he spoke', omitting both the usual particle *a* (cf. TH 43r.25 *eff a cowsys*; TH 32r.1 *a cowsys*) and the lenition (cf. TH 43r.15 *eff a gowsys*; TH 23r.2 *a gowsis*). As the above examples show, spelling *causis* with *ow* rather than *au* would have been more traditional.
62r.36	**commandias:** N, C, *commaundias*, B *commandias*, H *commaundias*—*an*, *aun* or *am* are all arguably possible readings. Stephyn elsewhere uses *commandias*, so this is given in E. The *d* is obscured by the base of the *s* from *cowse* above.
62r.37	**tha orybe gee:** 'to answer you' (sg.)—note the usual loss of *th* as described in General Notes *(rth > r)* and the complete loss of initial *g* rather than mutation to *w*. The final *e* of *orybe* is sounded: compare *the worthyby*, PC 206 & 2009. Here *tha* is probably the preposition *the*, 'to', rather than the possessive pronoun *tha*. Stephyn spells it both as *the* and *tha*—as in *tha vos consecratis* and *the vos consecratis* in this and the following line.
62r.38	**osa:** 'after', for earlier *wosa*—see General Notes *(wosa > osa > udzha)*.
	the gee: 'to you' (sg.)—see General Notes *(simplification)*.
62r.41	**i.:** as at 59v.20.
62r.42	**consecrᵃetis:** 'consecrated'—the *e* is overwritten with an *a*.

---

36 Richard Carew, *The Survey of Cornwall* (London: John Jaggard, 1602), [reprinted in facsimile in DCRS, n.s. vol. 47, John Chynoweth, Nicholas Orme and Alexandra Walsham, eds, *The Survey of Cornwall by Richard Carew* (Exeter: DCRS, 2004), f. 56r.

	ith thew: 'it is', N, B, H *ith thew*, C *eth thew*. Compare *e thew* 62r.39 or earlier *yth yv* RD 2567. (E *ith ew*.)
62r.42–3	**ruge ... dos:** preterite with *gule* as auxiliary lit. 'when the words of our Saviour Christ did come upon it'—treated more freely (as present tense) in the translation.
62v.1	**[....] han gwyn:** 'and wine' (lit. 'and the wine')—N, H therefore reconstruct the missing words as *An bara*, but *Bara* seems more likely in the light of 63r.1. The *h* of *han* is partly visible.
62v.5	**vini:** 'of wine', N, H *vini*; B *vino*.
	operata fu[erint]: 'will have operated/done their work', N, H *operata s[unt]*.
62v.6	**efficitur:** it is difficult to translate words with theological significance such as *efficitur* (derived from *ex* and *facio*). Technical terms such as 'confected' are no longer properly understood. I have preferred a paraphrase—'is made really present'—which expresses the sense. Thompson & Srawley give 'when the words of Christ have operated, then and there it is made to be the blood of Christ'.[37]
	henna ew: the colon following *henna ew* is partly obscured by the extended tail of the 's' from *chalys* on the line below.
62v.7	**kyns an girreow Christ tha vos leveris:** 'before the words of Christ are said'—lit. 'before the words of Christ to be said'. See General Notes *(the vos)*.
	len[...]: N, C, B, H *len(wys)*, 'filled'. Although conjectural, Nance's suggestion seems a reliable one, and accords with the source text. (E [*lenwis*].)
62v.8	**en[a]:** 'there', N, *ena*, H *en[a]*. This interpretation reflects the 'there' in Foxe, although the word could possibly be a first attempt to write *ema*, 'it is', repeated at the beginning of the next line.
62v.12	**tant[a] vis:** 'such force', N, H *tant[um] vis*. The *a* is partly visible.
62v.14	**mar see¹s:** 'if there is' (= *mars us*, e.g. *marsus* PC 2978, *mar sus* BM 1203). N, H *mar sees*—this occurrence could be either *mar sees*, altered from *mar seis*, or vice versa. I have opted for the latter after comparing with *pa seil* below.
62v.15	**tha gwiel:** lit. 'to make'—not the expected *tha wiel*, with lenition. See, similarly, *tha gonys* on the line below, and General Notes *(mutations)*.
62v.16	**pa seil:** 'how much/many'—cf. *Py sul yv sum an flehys* BM 1604, 'how many is the sum of the children', and *py suel a vynnyth* PC 592, 'however much you want'. Welsh *pa sawl* also means 'how

---

37 Thompson and Srawley, eds, *St Ambrose on the Mysteries*, p. 114.

many'. Tregear spells the words *py sell* in *Pysell defferans a bewnans* TH 27r.19 for 'Howe great dyfference of life' in Bonner. The letters *sei* appear to have been overwritten or re-inked.

tha gonys ha changya: lit. 'to work and change'. This may represent a tendency for some verbs in SA to attract *ha* in idiomatic use by analogy with the construction *dos ha*.

62v.17 **kep*ar* del ve:** 'as was'. Above the comma which follows *ve*, just to the right of the 'e', there are two marks side by side. The first like a grave accent, the second, following it, like a thin comma.

62v.18 **Gosoweth:** 'listen'. This might at first sight be thought to represent *gos[l]ow [w]orth* (cf. *gosleuw orthyf* PC 496) but it is probably a form of the 2 pl. imper. (rather than 2 sg. attested as *goslow* at OM 1365) like *gosough* 63r.6, with *-th* for *-gh*. See General Notes *(ls > sl > s > r)*.

62v.20m **cap. 1:** or *cap. 2*—marks on the MS make the reading unclear. The text confirms that 'Chapter 1' was intended.

62v.22 **et:** N *etiam*, H *et[iam]*.

62v.23 **co*n*uertere:** 'change, alter', N, H *connotere*.

Deinde: 'then'—perhaps corrected from an original *Deende*.

62v.25 **manducaturi:** a difference from Foxe, who has *manducari* (restored in E)—'to be eaten' is intended in both cases.

62v.27 **habes:** 'you have'—N1 *habis* or *habes*, N2, C, B, H *habes*.

62v.28 **hoc dicerent:** lit. 'might say this', but since that could refer to Peter's words, when it in fact refers to the those of the disciples who went away, a freer translation seems desirable—'might speak as they did'.

veluti: 'as if', N, H *velliti*.

62v.29 **horror cruoris:** that is, repugnance at a carnal interpretation of the words 'drinking of blood'—lit. a 'horror of gore'.

62v.30 **redemtionis:** N *redemptionis*, H *redemtionis*.

62v.33 **fattellans bos gwyer:** possibly *fatell ellans bos gwyer?*—'how can they be true?', or *fatell ans bos gwyer?*—'how are they true?' Either way this corresponds to 'how be they true?' in Foxe.

e vosama ow gwel[as an] shap: 'I see the form', N, C, B, *e vosama ow gwel[es] an shap*, H *e vosama ow gwel[es an] shap*—using a (somewhat muddled) late, inflected form of *bos*, 'to be', as an alternative to the more traditional *eth esa' ve*. See General Notes *(bos + personal suffixes)*. The MS is cut, but *gwelas* seems likely by analogy with 59r.19, 59r.28 etc.

62v.34 **an not:** N, B, H *an not*, C *ha not*—the *an* here seems to be English 'and', followed also by English 'not'—as Nance suggests. (It is perhaps also theoretically possible that the *n* is doubled as a result of dictation and we have Cornish *ha*, 'and', followed by English 'not'.)

	ky[n]s[a]: 'first', N Kensa, H k[ensa].
62v.36–7	**nyn go abe[.] perthy gyrreow:** 'were not able to take (the) words', N, H *nyn go abel thy gyrreow*. The *p* of *perthy* (cf. BM 2635) is marked for a contraction, representing *per-/par-* before *-thy*. (E *nyng o abel perthy gyrreow*.) See General Notes *(neg ew)*.
	arluth: with a descending 'r'.
62v.37–8	**th[e v]oes dibbrys:** 'to be eaten' (N, H *th[a] vos dibbrys*) giving *pan ruga ry e corf the voes dibbrys, ha e gois the vos evys*, 'when he gave his Body to be eaten, and his Blood to be drunk'. While the MS appears to have *ves* (or even *-wes*) rather than *vos*, careful comparison with the letters *voe* in *the voese* 59v.15, and *tha voese* in 59v.15–16, confirms *[v]oes* as the most likely reading—although a different 's' is used, and the final 'e' omitted.
62v.38–9	**[…]wort[.] age arluth Christ:** 'from Christ their Lord', E *[tha] worth age arluth Christ*. (The earlier suggestions of *corf* were a misreading of *worth*: N2 *[ha …] corf agen arluth Christ*, B *[ha gois ha] corf agen arluth Christ*, C, H *[ha gois ha] corf agen arluth Christ*, F *[tha] [worth] corf age arluth Christ*.) The *age* refers back to the disciples who went away (agreeing with *age* in line 62v.37). The form *thaworth* rather than *theworth* has been chosen for the reconstruction on the basis of the forms at 60v.9, 63r.3 and 63v.29.
63r.1a	**Christ:** this lies to the right hand side of the folio, between lines 63r.1 and 63r.2, just above *bewn[a]n[s]*.
63r.2	**bewn[a]n[s] heb dewath:** 'eternal life' (lit. 'life without end'), N, B *bewnans heb dewath*, H *bewnan[s] heb dewath*.
63r.3	**pe tha ve mos tha worthas:** 'where shall I go from you', N, B *petha ve mos the worthas*, H *pe tha ve mos the worthas*. The word for 'where' here (*peth/pith*, 'what') is fairly common as an alternative for *ple/py le*. Adam says *ny won vyth pethaf lemyn* 'I do not know at all where I shall go now' OM 355 (contrasting with *py le ytheth*, 'where are you going' RD 851). In C Nance has a note (in Unified Cornish) plausibly suggesting *pyth af-vy ha mos adhyworthys*, with *ha* unwritten, missed or elided by the scribe (as in a similar construction at 64r.7). Another good contender would of course be *peth [of] ve [ow] mos thaworthas*, with the 1 sg. pres. as an auxiliary, followed by the pres. participle, its particle omitted. The edited text sits on the fence here, with *peth a' ve mos thaworthas*, allowing either interpretation in the context of Stephyn's flexible spelling. See General Notes *(o/ow)*, *(esoff > esa)*.
63r.4	**kepare a vo ceartaine abhorria worth gois:** 'as though there should be a certain horror of blood' (Foxe). The verbal noun *abhorria* may be used here either as a noun ('abhorrence') or as a

NOTES 257

	pres. participle (*abhorria*=*ow abhorria*). If the latter is the case note, as elsewhere in SA, *owth* is not introduced before vowels.
63r.5a	**e ma remaynea y^e redemya: / a redemtion:** lit. 'the redemption remains [to redeem]', N, B *ema remaynea the redemya an redemtion*, H *e ma remaynea y^e redemya / a redemption*. The words *a redemtion* lie to the right-hand side of the folio, between lines 63r.5 and 63r.6, and exactly beneath the words *ye redemya*, as if in correction of them (as Nance remarks, in C). The word *remaynea* may originally have been *remayn*, with the tail of the *n* crossed through and -*ea* added. Despite all this confusion, it seems likely the scribe finally intended *wath dir grace Christ ema remaynea a[n] redemtion*, 'yet through Christ's grace the redemption remains' rather than *wath, dir grace, Christ ema remaynea the redemya*, 'yet, through grace, Christ remains to redeem'. The original in Foxe has 'and yet the grace of redemption should remayne'.
63r.6	**te a recevest … te a obtaynest:** N, B, H *te a receves … te a obtaynes*—probably Stephyn or his scribe has simply slipped into English spelling here while following the Foxe text closely, despite knowing perfectly well (as most commentators have presumed) what would be appropriate forms of *recevya* SA 59v.21 and *obtaynia* TH 51r.28 in Cornish. Examples like *te a recevias* 63r.22 underline this (as does the long history of forms like *recevys* OM 2160).
63r.7	**grace han gallus a nature a Christ:** 'the grace and power of the nature of Christ'—*a nature* here could represent *a'n nature*, 'of the nature'. See General Notes (*an* > *a*).
	Gosough pan dresy S. Ambros […]: 'Hear what St Ambrose [says]'. Since this parallels the form at 62v.18, it reinforces the idea that what we have there (and certainly here) is **gos(ow)ough*, imper. 2 pl., 'hear'. For *esy/uge* see General Notes (*s* > *j*). The conjectured [*o leverall*] is omitted after *S. Ambros* but restored in E.
63r.8	**operar^tus:** 'worked', corrected (possibly from *operarus*) by the overwriting of a bold *t*.
63r.10	**mittitur:** 'put', C, H *mittitur*, N, B *mutatur*.
63r.11	**sangui^snis:** 'Blood'—*sanguinis* has been corrected to *sanguis* by the overwriting of the final -*nis*.
	dices: 'you say', N, C, H *dices*, B *dicis* (the *e* looks like an undotted *i* in N2).
63r.11m	**4:** C has '6' for this marginal reference.
63r.12	**speciem:** 'species, outward appearance', C, H *speciem*, B *specim*.
63r.13	**mortis similitudinem sumsisti:** 'you took on the form of death', N *magis similitudine scisisti*, H *mortis similitudine scisisti*.
63r.14	**63:** the folio number '63' has been added to the right of *pretium*.

	horror cruoris: see 62v.29 and note.
63r.18	**e ma gonis:** lit. 'it works', for *ema o conis* (the pres. participle, as at 62r.27). In the same sentence *gonis* is used with two different auxiliaries, *bos* and *gule* (with *crvg* correctly mutated after *mar*). See General Notes *(mutations)* and *(o/ow)*.
63r.19	**a thoskas:** 'have learnt', N, H *a theskas*, 3 sg. pret. of *dysky*, 'to teach, learn' (cf. TH 38r.2 *a thyscas*, TH 21v.21 *a theskas*). See General Notes *(ema > oma)*.
	gwrys: *gwrys* here has been corrected—probably straightaway— from *gwrs*.
	cosʳf: *corf* is intended, though *cosrf* is written, or perhaps *cof* was begun, then altered to *corf*, with the partly formed *f* still visible.
63r.20-1	**geir benegas:** 'holy word', N, C, B, H *geir dew benegas*. There are some marks to the right of *geir*, at the edge of the paper, which could represent -*ow* (see especially the *ow* at 63v.22), -*ew*, or just be blots. The sense does not require the plural or *Dew*, 'God', and the word is singular in Foxe. The marks look nothing like *nef*, '(of) heaven', which might have reflected Foxe's 'heavenly'.
63r.21	**Matesyn:** 'perhaps', N, C, B, H *ma[r]tesyn*. The *r* is omitted, as possibly unpronounced, but the word *martesyn* (cf. TH 4r.14) is clearly intended.
63r.22	**shap a gois:** 'the likeness of blood'—T has 'a shape of blood', but this seems over-literal.
	recevias: 'have received', N, C, B, H *recevas*. While Tregear is clear that the verb is *receva* (TH 16r.4, 12; cf. also *receve*, the earlier spelling of the same form in PA 233.3), Stephyn always uses *recevia* (SA 61r.16, 18, 32).
63r.24	**abhorris:** lit. 'abhorred'.
	what: 'yet'—no doubt *whath* is intended as just above at 63r.21. N, C, B, H *what[h]*.
63r.24-5	**ow conys an prys:** lit. 'works the price'—what at first sight seems to be a Cornish idiom for 'pays the price' (Nance translated it 'performs the price') may simply reflect Chedsey's 'worketh the price' in Foxe.
63r.26-7	**henna ew girrew Justin:** 'that is, [in] the words of Justin', N2 *henna ew / girrew Iustin*, C, B, H *henna ew [in] girre[o]w Justin*.
63r.31	**nutriuntur:** N, C, B *mitriuntur*, MS, H *nutriuntur*.
	Iesu: here a plainer capital italic *I* is used, rather than the usual italic capital found in *Iesus* below at 63r.34, which is similar to a modern *J*.
63r.34	**hagen:** 'our', probably representing *agen* here rather than *ha'gen*, 'and our'.
	ew: lit. 'is'—translated 'was' to help the sense.

	greis gwreis: 'made', C *greis gwreis* B *greis gwreis* H *gweis gwreis*. The scribe appears initially to have written *greis*. Then, perhaps after trying to correct it to *gwreis*, resulting in a blot, he decides to rewrite the word altogether. This demonstrates that some corrections that look later were almost immediate.
63r.35	**rag sawya ny:** 'to save us'—see General Notes (*possessives*). The punctuation shown in the diplomatic edition—;—faithfully represents the appearance of the MS but is not a modern semicolon. Above the comma, there appears to be a point/inkmark below the 'C' of *Christ* in the previous line, in addition to the internal point indicating that it is a capital.
	disquethis: 'revealed', lit. 'shown'.
	thyn[y]: 'to us'. There is a downward tail to the right of *thyn*, curving to the right—probably a final -*y*. N, C, B, H *thyn*.
63r.36	**bois:** 'the food', N, C, B, H *[an] bois*. The MS is damaged here and *an* is no longer visible, but seems likely from 'the meate' in Foxe.
	peIadow: N, C, B, H *pesadow*—this word may or may not have originally been *pesadow* (or *peiadow*), but it has been corrected as *peIadow/peJadow* with a capital I/J (these being interchangeable at this period). It is therefore represented as *pejadow* in E, as best indicating the likely pronunciation of /dʒ/ (as at *peiadow*, SA 62r.18). This is of interest as attestation of the use of English *i* or *j* for this sound in the evolving traditional orthography. See General Notes (*s > j*). Note also *a* after *geir* may be def. art.
63v.1	**[...] g[..]reow dew:** 'through God's words', N, C, B *dir gyrryow Dew*, H *[dir gyrry]ow Dew*, E *[dir] girreow dew*. The final *r* of *dir* can be seen faintly, the tail of the initial *g* and the second *r* of *girreow* more definitely.
	gwris eth ew: 'are made'—these words lie to the right of the folio, between lines 63v.1 and 63v.2, below *gois Christ* and above *sumimus*, boxed off.
63v.2	**ver[o, hae]c:** 'indeed this'. The initial *ver-* is fairly clear, though faded, in the MS, but *haec* is very unclear. I have reconstructed it on the evidence of Foxe, supported by the survival of parts of the second downward stroke of the initial *h* and—less clearly—the *æ*, comparing closely other instances of *haec*, especially at 65v.26. N, C *[v.......o]*, H *v[.......]*.
	pro pane potuue communi: 'for common bread or drink', with the enclitic -*ve* following *potu* (and an anomalous point over the first stroke of the final *n*), N2 ..*to pane potune communi*, C *[..o] pane potune communi*, B *[v.........] pane ...* (much of this line is blank in B), H *pro pane potune communi* (E *pro pane potuve communi*).

63v.3	**Imo:** 'rather, on the contrary', N1 & 2 *Imo*, [missing from B], C *Immo*, H <u>*Immo*</u>? What appears to be an abbreviation mark over the *m* is a continuation of the abbreviation of *-que* in *Neque* above.
63v.4	**[et]:** this *et* is now lost, through damage to the right side of the folio, but confirmed by Foxe.
63v.5	**consecratu[m]:** the final 'm' is lost through damage.
63v.6–7	**per mutacione*m* etriuntur:** E *per [im]mutationem e[nu]triuntur*, 'nourished by alteration' following Foxe; in the MS *im-* may have been lost at the margin. N1 *etriuntur*, N2 *etriuutur?*, C, B *esuriuntur* (this runs counter to the surmise that Bice used mainly N1).
63v.9	**Ne geranny:** E *Neg eran ny*, lit. 'we are not', but used as an auxiliary here. See General Notes *(s > j), (s > r)*.
	bara ha dewas: 'food and drink', lit. 'bread and drink'.
63v.10–11	**thaken sawya ny:** 'to save us'—compare with *rag sawya ny* in 63r.35, showing the use of both *the* and *rag* in this context. The form *thaken* (for the contraction *th'agen*) is interesting, see General Notes *(g > k)*. Nance translates 'heal' rather than 'save'—perhaps sensitive to potential theological controversy.
63v.11	**vova:** here we do have the 3 sg. pres. subj. of *bos*, with enclitic 3 sg. pers. pron. *-va* for *eff*. See note on SA 60v.8.
63v.12	**Eu*m*:** acc. m. sg. of determinative pron. *is*, translated by Foxe as 'the same'. N, C, H *Eumm*, B *Eum*.
63v.14	**fractus:** while SA faithfully follows Foxe's *fractus* here (referring to 'broken' bread) other sources give *factus* (referring to 'made' bread), following the original Greek, and this alteration is made in E to better reflect Irenaeus (see Commentary, Quotation 33).
	Eucharest[ia]: 'Eucharist', N *Eucharest[ ]*, B *Eucharest?*, H *Euchares[t]*.
63v.17	**keith:** 'same', N, C, H *keith*, B *kith*.
63v.18	**cressya:** 'give increase', N, C, B, H *creffya*. Nance presumably believed this **creffya* to be a variant of *creffe* 63v.21, 'to strengthen' (see note below). However, the 'ss' is clear and *cressya* CW 1255 would be much closer to the 'encreaseth' of Foxe (as to the Latin verb *augeo* used here).
63v.21	**creffe:** here we do have *creffe/crefhe*, 'strengthen' (see note above). Foxe still has 'increased' so the different verb in Cornish is interesting, and may reflect the addition of *consisto* to *augeo*, although in general Stephyn's translation simply follows Foxe's English. (See note on 63v.18 above and *crefhe*, NG 1).[38]

---

[38] Padel, *Cornish Writings*, p. 25. The use of the suffix, *-he*, to make a verbal noun from an adjective, in this case *cref*, 'strong', had persisted into Late Cornish. See also Wmffre, *Late Cornish*, p. 60.

63v.21–2	**Irenæus pelha ow levera:** 'Irenaeus further says', N1, N2, C, H *Irenæus pelha ow levera*, B, *Ireneus pelha ow levera(ll)*. Nance in N2 notes that *ow levera* could represent either *(yma) ow levera(ll)* or possibly *a levere*. His first suggestion is the one accepted in E, that is, that the final *-ll* of *leverall* has been dropped. (This is unexpected, however, when even late forms like *lauall* retain the *-l*.) With regard to his second suggestion, while *pelha a lever* would indeed be another way of saying this, the *ow* is clear and the final *-a* of *levera* is unmistakeable. (Among other possibilities, the 3 sg. imperf. would be *a levery* TH 32r.20; 3 sg. subj. *lavarra* TH 17.1, *lauarra* TH 20r.2; see also *a lavare, a lâre* in Breton.)
63v.25	**fatla:** N1 & 2, C *fatla*, B, H *farla* (but N1 could easily be misread as *farla*).
63v.27	**megis gans:** 'fed by'—note use of *gans*, 'with/by' alongside this verb.
63v.29	**ij folen tha worth an dallath:** directly translating Weston's '2 leaves from the beginning'—a confirmation of the source.
63v.30	**An Greciens**[kys]**:** 'the Greeks', MS, H *Greciens* [kys], N, B *An Greciens*—a correction of *Greciens* to *Grekys*, with the original conclusion of the word overwritten by *-kys* above. The final form may represent a desire to use the accepted Cornish, *Grekys* TH 26v.18 (although Foxe also has 'Greekes' at this point, and both forms are from English in any case). **e ma:** MS *e ma* or *ema*—N *e ma*, H *ema*. **kelwall:** note the provection even though the particle *o(w)* is absent. **Eucharistia:** the first *i* has possibly been corrected from an *e*—see 63v.14. **grasce:** this may represent an initial *grace*, corrected to *gras* by the insertion of *s*, without deleting the underlying *-ce*. Alternatively it could be an attempt to show a distinctive pronunciation of this word (perhaps similar to other borrowings like *spas, fas* and *plas*). (Less likely, it may be an attempt to represent *grasse* CW 1310, 'to thank'.)
63v.31	**altare cibi [s ....] / tualibus:** 'to the altar [to be filled] with spiritual food', N, B *altarem tibi [... ri?...]tualibus*, H *altarem tibi [spiri]tualibus*, Foxe, E *altare cibis spiritualibus*. (The tail of the initial *g-* of *grasce* above is easily mistaken for a contraction mark over the *-e* of *altare*; the *-s* of *cibis* is visible but separated from *cibi*, and the very top of the later *s* of *spiri-* is arguably also present.
63v.32	**saciandus:** E *satiandus*, 'satisfied, filled', in which the second *a* may have been altered from an original *e*. N, H *faciendus*.

63v.34,37 **gwra marvgian:** 'marvel at' (T 'make marvel'.) The verbal usage *gull marthussyan* (TH 38v.21 translating Bonner's 'to merueyle') is the Cornish equivalent of Latin *miror*. Tregear also has *dre wondres marthugian* TH 2v.3 (lit. 'by wondrous marvels') for the 'in a most merueluous sort' of Bonner, perhaps indicating that he may have pronounced both -*g*- and -*ssy*- here as /dʒ/ (see also *marthuggian* TH 37v.24). Again, while he still writes *rth* in both his forms, he may not have been pronouncing the *th* by this point, cf. *marvgian* SA 63v.34, 37 *marrudgyan* CW 1764 and General Notes *(rth > r)*. The word literally means 'marvels', although (as at CW 1764) it can have a singular sense.

63v.35 **imban:** 'up', N, B *inban*, H *imban*—while the 'm' may be a slip, it could also be an indication of development in the pronunciation of *in ban* at this point and is therefore retained in E. Nance (in C) notes that 'Tregear has *in man* and *yn ban* ... later still this became *a man.*' This *imban* may therefore represent an assimilation, halfway between the other two forms Nance cites (OP). An overview of the range of forms, not in date order, would be: *yn ban* TH 46v.15, *in ban* BK 9, TH 11v.14, CW 1560 (*in badn* CW 2203), *imban* SA 63v.35, *in man* TH 42v.7, *am'àn* AB 252/JCH 33.

63v.36 **faith ... the:** lit. 'faith to' reflecting Foxe's 'looke in faith to'.
Bara: a catchword for the next page.

63v.37 **honor:** 'honour' (& so T), C *honor*, N1 & 2 [.....], B *[l .....]*, H *hanow*. (E *gwra marugian a'y honor*—Foxe 'maruell at his honour').
gwra worthel[y e Do ... ia]: 'worthily touch him', [with either *Do ... ia* or *Dou..ia* in the MS], N1, C *gwra worthia*, N2, B *gwra wo ...*, H *gwra worthea [.........]*. (E *gwra worthely e douchia*, Foxe 'worthely touch him'.)

64r.1 **Corf ha gois C[.................]:** 'are made the Body and Blood of Christ', E *Corf ha Gois C[hrist gwris eth ew]*. The reconstruction (also found in N, C, B, H) seems certain (by analogy with 63v.1)—as does the *dir* on the same line.

64r.3 **thith:** lit. 'to your', here simply 'your', 2 sg., see General Notes *(thi'th)*.
si quæras: 'if you ask' (2 sg. subj.)—so N, C but B, H *quæris* (N2 clear but N1 harder to read).
voluit Ecclesia eligere: 'the Church opted for'—lit. 'the Church wished to choose'.

64r.6 **apparentiam:** 'appearance', N, C *apparentiam*: but B *appaentiam*, H *appæntiam*.
et cæt[era]: N, H *et cet[era]* here and 64r.10.

64r.7	**Mar tewhy demandea:** 'if you (pl.) should ask'. *Mar tewhy* represents *mar tewgh why ha* as at TH 39v.11, and is another example of *dos*, 'to come', used as an auxiliary to form a conditional. It is often (but not exclusively) used with *ha*, which is perhaps implicit here. See General Notes *(conditional)*, *(mutations)*.
64r.8	**Vnderstandyng:** 'understanding', N, C *Vnderstandyng*, H *Vnde rstandyng*. From this point in the copy of H that I have, there are occasional gaps in the electronic file lasting until just before *pro quibus offertur* at 64r.17. While I have noted key differences, they may be the result of electronic transmission and not necessarily in the original file.
	Arickell: 'article', corrected in E because of *artickell*, 64r.10.
64r.9	**girryow an scripture** [a] **yll:** 'the words of Scripture can'—the particle *a* has been inserted later, slightly above the line.
64r.9–10	**kepare dell vgy apperia:** lit. 'as it appears' (T 'as is made plain', Foxe 'as appeareth'). Again, the particle *o/ow* before *apperia* is omitted.
64r.10	**owrth:** MS, N, B, H *owrth*, C *towrth*—the latter possibly from a misreading of N1 or of the sign for the insertion of the particle *a* (previous note). See General Notes *(orth > worth)*.
64r.11	**vim satisfactiu[a]m:** 'power of satisfaction', N, H *vim satifacti[o]nem* (N1 originally had *satifactiu..*).
64r.13	**apud:** here 'in', as 'in [the Gospel of] Luke'. H puts *apud* at the beginning of the next line.
64r.15	**quamuis:** 'although, however, as much as', N1, N2, C, H *quamuis*, B *quamis*, S *quanis*. (E *quamvis*.)
	ex sui quantitate: lit. 'of the quantity of itself' [Foxe], N, H *ex sui quantitate*, B *ex siu quantitate*.
64r.16	**satisfactoriaillis:** 'satisfactory for those', MS *ad satifaciendum pro omni pœna: tamen fit satisfactoriaillis*—and so N (except *satisfactiendum* for *satifaciendum*) but H *ad satisfactoria_illis* for this whole line.
64r.18–19	**magape[ll] del ewa sacrafice:** lit. 'as far as it is a sacrifice', T 'as long as it is a sacrifice', N, C, B *maga pe[ll] dell ewa sacrifice*, H *magapel dell ewa sacrifice*. Probably originally *ll* as in *maga pell* TH 19v.1 and *Maga pell* TH 33r.7. See General Notes *(ewa)*.
64r.19	**e ma thetha:** 'it has'—lit. there is to it', 3 sg. m. Here the later form *thetha* has superseded the earlier *thotho* of the *Ordinalia* etc.—see General Notes *(thotho > thetha)*.
64r.19–20	**neb a vge offra an affection:** 'whoever offers from the heart', lit. 'whoever offers the affection'.

64r.21	**an quantite an oblation:** 'the quantity of the oblation' (= *an quantite a'n oblation*; see *ex sui quantitate* under 64r.15 above). As with *satisfaction* and *affection*, we see the Cornish here shadowing as closely as possible the technical, doctrinal terminology of Aquinas. George has raised the interesting question of whether Stephyn knew the ordinary Cornish word for 'quantity', *myns*.[39] (Tregear certainly did, see TH 7r.26. He also knew the word for 'gift' yet happily uses *gyftes* TH 2v.8 as well as *royow* TH 4v.4). Given the translation choices of the rest of the passage it is perhaps unsurprising that here Stephyn stays close to the language of the *Summa Theologica*. See General Notes *(clerical Cornish)*.
64r.22	**e ma:** seemingly added as an afterthought, out of normal word order, which should be *[ema] an Arluth Dew ow leverall*, as restored in E.
	in nawaile: 'in the Gospel'. The *in* represents *i'n*, 'in the', and an additional *n* has been intruded before *awaile* as commonly in SA. The emendation is made in E *i'n Awaile*.
64r.23	**rag an wethvas:** 'of the widow', lit. 'for the widow' (cf. *gwethfas*, TH 40v.13).
64r.24	**hy a dowlas in:** 'she cast in'; Tregear has *tewlell* as the verb. A late form, *toula*, is found in Price. See General Notes *(English influence)*.
	offeringys a Dew: 'divine offerings', lit. 'offerings of God', N, C, B, H *offering*, with the usual contraction for *-ys* perhaps confused with the sign for the insertion of *a Dew* above *moy*.
	y: the 3 sg. pers. pron is still clearly understood as *y* despite late analysis such as *in an sy*. See General Notes *(3 pl. ending)*.
64r.28	**& not:** 'and not'—left in English—N, B *ha not*, H *& not*.
64r.29	**Vigilius a martyr:** the indefinite article is present in Foxe (and T) and *a* may merely represent a slip into English (see '& not' just above). However, it could also represent the definite article in Cornish which occasionally has this form: see General Notes *(an > a)*. The ordinary Cornish word for 'martyr' in TH and SA is *martyr* (but see also *mertheryys* PC 3220, 'martyred').
64r.30	**[...]th:** 'by'—H, E *[wor]th*, N1 *[dywor]th*, N2 *[thywor]th*, B *thyworth*. See Appendix A under TH 54v.18–28m, where we probably have *y^e [w]orth* rather than *worth*.
64r.31	**e thesa ve ow menya:** 'I mean'—see General Notes *(esoff > esa)*.
64r.33	**[.]i[.]ilius:** N, H *Aurelius* (perhaps thinking of Augustine's first name). E *[Vig]ilius*, as in Foxe 64r.34.
	Fulgentius: N1 *Fulninius?* N2 *Eulo..*, C, B, H *Eu* .....

---

39 George, ed., *Gerlyver Meur*, 3rd edn, p. 549.

64r.34	**lowarth:** for *lowar*, 'many'—see General Notes *(rth > r)*.
erall: 'other/s'—MS *erall*, N1 *erell*, N2, C, B, H *erall*. (For possible alternative readings *eroll*, *erill*, see the *i* and *o* in *Hierom* in the line above; for *erell*, the *e* in *egglos*, three lines up; but *erall* is the usual form in SA.)
64v.1	**[................] gyrryow dew:** E *[Bara ha gwyn dir] gyrryow Dew*, 'Bread and wine through the words of God'. The corner is severely damaged, but the headings of the preceding folios enable reconstruction.
64v.3	**ow thesyre:** 'my desire'. It seems unlikely that Stephyn is aspirating a conjectural **tesyre* here: a theoretical **desyre* is implied at *my^{e}r a thesyre* 64v.10 (q.v.), but perhaps it had acquired a semi-permanent lenition in his usage, and see also note on 64v.12.
64v.3–5	**Pask onn:** 'Passover', lit. 'Passover of lamb, paschal lamb'. This phrase appears twice in SA within a few lines, translating Ward's 'Paschall'. (We might have expected the reverse word order, *onn pask*, or Tregear's version—TH 52r.25 *paschal one*, TH 52v.2 *paschall oyen*.) By extension, it refers to the Passover meal and Christ's Last Supper. *Pask* itself is used in Cornish for both Passover/ the Paschal sacrifice and Easter, though predominantly for the former. (For Passover see PC 618, 623, 672, 720, 2035, 2038, 2369; SA 64v.3, 64v.4; *pasch* at PA 124.6, 229.3 and—lenited as *e bask*—SA 64v.10. For Easter see RD 1108.) This usage is not to be confused with the form *pascon* (as in *pascon agan arluth ker*, PA 228.4) which means 'passion' and was presumably pronounced similarly to the English word. (See *passyon* OM 2840, PC 3223, RD 1082, 2556, BK 37, 1445—as well as BK 131, 3141 with a more general sense of 'suffering'—*pascyon* RD 505, and *pascion* TH 12v.23, 15r.20, 15v.8, 16r.1, 16r.5, 16r.16, 16v.1, 16v.5, 16v.23, 30v.20, 51v.2.)
64v.5	**ow Christ wensys:** 'was it, [that] Christ desired'—N1 *ow Christ wensys*, N2 *ow=o Christ wensys*, C *usy Christ wensys*, B *ow? Christ wensys*, H *ew Christ wensys*. This form at first looks like the past participle of *whanse* (TH 16v.11), but it seems more likely that the construction is intended as the preterite, that is, *pana Pask Onn [o], Christ [a] wensys tha thibbry gans e Apostelath?*—'what sort of Passover was it, that Christ desired to eat with his Apostles?' (Nance in N1 notes '*whansys* not *whansus*' and in N2 that *ow = o* [3 sg. imperf], but in C tries to see *vsy* or *ew*. Only the second *l* of Tertullian below, and the comma before *ow*, make this confusion possible.)
64v.8	**distribut[um]:** N, H *distribut[um]*, B *distribuil[ ]*. Foxe *distributum*, 'distributyng'.

64v.10 **a ruge protestia:** lit. 'protested'. Foxe, 'protestyng'.
my^e r a thesyre: 'much desire/longing', N, B, H *myr a thesyre*, S *myre a thesyre*. The *my^e r* of the diplomatic edition was originally written *myr*, but an *e* has been inserted above the *y*, possibly intending to correct the spelling of the word to *mer* as in *mer gras* BK 3073, or even to spell the word as *myer* as at BK 2971, although the latter may be a simple error. Historically spelt *mur* (and cognate with Welsh *mawr*) it is thought that the *u* represented /ø:/ in Middle Cornish, moving later to /ɛ:/—cf. *meare* at CW 206 and *meer* at BK 2923, SA 60r.3 and CW 204. It is interesting, therefore, that *myr* is altered to *mer/myer*, while *meer* is left untouched. (For other treatment of *desyre/deserya* see note on 64v.3 and 64v.12.)

64v.12 **ye deserya:** 'to desire'. This *y^e* appears to be crossed through by a long line from the top of the *f* to the left to the bottom right of the *y*; surely accidental, as the *the* is needed here. Here we would expect *the theserya*, but there is no mutation (unless Stephyn sometimes perceives *desyre/deserya* with an initial *d*, sometimes with a *t*).
ha e ruk e distributia: 'and distributed it'. The second *e* (inserted later) is the poss. pron. 3 sg., for 'it' in English. The first, originally a different placing of the same poss. pron., is perhaps intended to stand for *a*, the verbal particle *Christ* being the subject (or—less likely—for the alternative particle *y* as in *y ruk pesy* BM 4425).

64v.13 **ef a ruk e corf:** 'he made [it] his Body'—N, B, H *ef a ruk e corf*, S *efe a ruk e corf*. Perhaps *ef a ruk [e] e Corf* is intended, although only one *e* is found, and this has been suggested in E. See General Notes (dictation?).

64v.14 **ow lever[...]:** N, B, H (and E) *ow lever[all]* (but see *ow levera* 63v.22).

64v.15 **gwrēgh honar^no r[a]:** 'honour', N *gwregh honora*, H *gwregh hona^no r[a]*. Interestingly, *gwregh* has an abbreviation mark above the *e*. The next word appears to have been originally written as *honarr[a]* but then corrected to *honor[a]*, with the *-no-* inked over the *-nar-*. Finally, another *no* is then inserted above, to remove all doubt that the final intention is *gwregh honora* ('honour, worship', cf. 64v.31).
eius: 'his', N *ejus* (and so throughout this passage), H *eius*.
.i.: for *id est*, 'that is', as above at 59v.20 and throughout this passage.

64v.16 **dry^s es:** 'feet', with an original *dryes* corrected to *drys*.
Quæro: 'I ask', N *Quaere*, H *Quæro*.
quid: 'what', N, H *quid*, B *quia*.

64v.17 **psalm 96. Adorate ...:** 'Psalm 96. Worship ...'—the incorrect reference in the text reflects Foxe 1570 and 1576: it is correct in

1563 and 1583). The marginal reference is correct in all editions and SA. See Commentary, Quotation 43 for further detail and comment on the *Adorare/Adorate* discrepancy between Foxe and Stephyn.

Scriptura: 'Scripture', H *Scriptura*, B *Scripturae*.

64v.17–18 **Terra scabellum pedum eius meorum:** 'the earth is my footstool'—an additional *eius* has been deleted after *pedum* at the beginning of line 18, having been misread from the previous *pedum eius*, lines 16–17.

64v.18 **conuerto:** 'I turn', N, H *conuerto*, B *couerto*.

64v.19 **sine impietate:** 'without impiety'. Because repetition of key words has caused confusion, a whole section is missing here, both from Foxe and SA. The full text is restored in E: see Commentary, Quotation 43.

64v.19–20 **adoretur:** 'may be worshipped', split over the two lines. A new -*ur* has been written over the previous letters, which may have seemed unclear or blotted.

64v.26m **Act. 7.40:** in the MS the '0' appears bisected by the vertical line turning slightly at its end, but the reading 7.40 is clear. These figures lie just below the abbreviation *Act.* in the margin of line 26. For Stephyn's use of verses as well as chapters in biblical citations see Appendix A.

64v.27 **E thesa ve:** so N, or as H *Ethesa ve*. Nance notes (in C) *e thesa* = *yth esof*—see General Notes (*esoff > esa*).

an skavall e drys eff: 'his footstool', N *an skavall e drys eff*, B, H *an scavall e drys eff*. See General Notes (mutations), (English influence).

64v.28 **& Scripture:** N, H, B *an Scripture*. As noted above (e.g. 60r.6) & can represent the def. art. *an* in SA, but here perhaps both *ha*, 'and', and the def. art. combined together as *ha'n Scripture*: Foxe 'and the Scripture'.

thym: '(to) me' N, B *thyn*, C, H *thyn*. While the sign for a contraction over the *y* could technically represent either -*n* or -*m*, it should be read -*m* here—that is, *thym*, '(to) me', rather than *thyn*, '(to) us'. Augustine has *dicit mihi*, and Ward, in Foxe, 'telleth me'.

64v.29 **ow thrys ve:** '[of] my feet', see General Notes (mutations).

& scripture: with & as *an*, the definite article.

e thesa ow trylya: 'I turn'—see General Notes (*esoff > esa*).

64v.30 **tho:** 'to', N, C, H *then*, B *then*. There is no *n* here. The perceived 'abbreviation mark' for the *n* of Nance's expected *the'n*, 'to the', was either the base of the *v* of *ve* above, or the serif of the capital A of *Arluth*.

	war a[......]: N, C, B, H *war a [nore]*, 'on the earth'. Almost certainly this was *war a nore* (= *war an nore*) as at 64v.33 below. The spacing is similar. In E I have used *a'* to indicate *an*—see General Notes *(an > a)*.
64v.31	**dore a thore:** 'earth from earth'—see General Notes *(mutations)*.
64v.32	**kigg & nore:** 'flesh of the earth', H *kigg & nore*, N, B *kigg an nore*, C *kigg* an *nore*. See General Notes *(& = an)*. E *kigg [a'n] nore* to emphasize 'of'.
64v.33	**w₀rthias:** 'Virgin'—as at 59r.22, 61r.31, 61v.27—probably corrected from a first-written *wrthias*. N, H *werthias*. Cf. *worthyas* BK 159, note on 59r.22 and General Notes *(rth > r)*. The older form was *werghes* PC 403 (unlenited plural *gwerhesow* at BK 1308, 1717).
64v.34	**thⁱebbry:** 'eat'; *thibbry*, possibly altered from an earlier *thebbry*.
64v.35	**[den] vith:** 'no one', N1 & 2 *denvyth*, C *[den]vith*, H, B *[den]vyth* (cf. *den veith* 59r.14, 59v.24).
	arr ne theffa [..................]: N, C, B, H *arr ne theffa [ha e worthia]*, with *arr ne* representing the *erna* of BM 3985. Nance, in C, glosses *erna dheffo ha'y wordhya* in Unified Cornish, 'until he come to worship'—see General Notes *(theffa)*. Foxe has 'except he haue worshypped before'. Perhaps *[ha e] honora* would have been more likely than Nance's conjectural *[ha e] worthia* (see Stephyn's usage at 64v.31, 65r.5) or, more simply, *honora derag dorn* as suggested in E. (There are no lost words to the right of this line before the catchword, so we must presume some omitted from a line below, where the folio is damaged.)
	Bara: catchword, as usual, for the next folio.
65r.1	**gyrryow:** 'words', and so N, C, B, H—probably not *gyrryew* (as in F).
65r.2–3	**[....................] Panem et calicem Cererem [.............................]:** 'Bread and cup/chalice ....Ceres', N1 *Panem et carnem ..erem*, N2 *Panem et carnem C..xeren[ ]*, C *Panem et carnem G[.]ere[ ]*, B *Panem et carnem ..xere..*, H *Panem et carnem C[.]rece[ ]*. The portions in square brackets are completely lost, but can be reconstructed from the Latin original in Foxe: E *[.13 Non nulli propter] Panem et calicem Cererem [& Bacchum nos colere existimabant]*, lit. 'Some considered [our] Bread and Cup to be the cult of Ceres and Bacchus'.
65r.4	**e ma ran ow pedery:** 'there are some who were thinking', MS *e ma ran ow pedery*, N1 *[henna] ew pedery*, N2, C, B *henna ew, pederro*, H *ew [= henna ew], pederro*.
	fatla e[... y ....]: reconstructed in E as *fatla e[ran ny insted a bara]*, lit. 'how [we are instead of bread]', N, C, B, H *fatla [.....]*. The text can only be conjecturally reconstructed. The tail of a *y* is visible

on the right—not quite in the place we would expect for *esyn ny* 65v.19 but exactly right for *erany* 65r.13.) Another possibility would be *wreny insted a bara*, which would fit better with *honora*, given the absence of *ow/owth*, but what survives of the initial letter points more to an *e* than a *w*. Another possibility would be the simpler *erany in bara*.) Either way, Stephyn should have used a word for 'chalice' or 'cup', rather than simply for 'wine', here. See Commentary, Quotation 44.

65r.5 **honora dew a bara ha dew a [g..n]e:** N1 *honora der a bara*, N2, C, B *honores der an bara*, S *honeres ce na*, H *honora der an bara ha Dew a*. Reconstructed—fairly certainly—in E as *honora dew a bara ha dew a gwyne*, 'worship/honour a god of bread and a god of wine': part of the tail of the *y* in *gwyne* is just visible below, as is the final *e*. The conjectural *gwyne* is not lenited after *a*, 'of', in line with the unlenited *bara*. (It is possible, however, that *a* is the definite article here.) Either way, Stephyn alludes to Ceres and Bacchus, rather than making a definite reference. Between *honora* and *dew a bara* there is a kind of bracket.

65r.6 **Gosowhog pandregy Chrisostom ow leverall whar an keth place na:** 'Listen [to] what Chrysostom says, upon that same place', and so N, B, H, but whole phrase missing from S. *Gosowhog* represents a form of *golsowogh*, for example CW 1429, 2 pl. imper., its termination reminiscent of CE—see General Notes *(ls > sl > s > r)*. Note also the spelling of *place*, and compare *grasce* at 63v.30. This may be a simple anglicism, or may distinguish the pronunciation of the final *-s* in this loan word.

65r.8 **participatio:** 'participation'—see the Commentary, Quotation 45, for the point being made by Chrysostom in Greek.

65r.9 **multam:** 'greater', N1 & 2, B *multa*, C, H *multam* (suggesting B might not have used C but see 65r.12).

65r.10 **participatio[n]e:** 'by participation'—the *n* has partly faded. N, H *participatio*.
tantum: lit. 'such', N, B, H *Christum*.

65r.12 **hunc:** 'this', N1 & 2 *huc*, C, B, H *hac* (suggesting B might also take into account C but see 65r.9).

65r.13 **coniungimur:** 'are joined together', N *conjugimur*.
erany: 'we are'—C notes *erany* = *eson ny* (i.e. long pres. 1 pl. of *bos*, 'to be', cf. *eson* RD 1291). See General Notes *(s > r)*.

65r.15 **parti^{ci}pation:** 'participation', with the letters *ci* inserted above, in correction of *partipation*. See General Notes *(clerical Cornish)*.
malla: 'in order that'. See General Notes *(may hallo > may halla > malla)*.

	signifia: 'signify, represent'. This seems to have been in Cornish usage (*signifia* TH 28r.23, *signifya* TH 53v.4) as was the loan word *sign* SA 66v.28, *signn* TH 28r.24, *signe* TH 28v.13, 'sign'. (The expected *arweth has not so far been found in the traditional language, despite Breton *arouez* and Welsh *arwydd*.)
65r.16	**intrethans:** 'between them, amongst them'—translating Watson's 'betwixt the same'. See General Notes *(3 pl. ending)*.
	kepare: 'as'—Nance (in C) conjectures a missing *dell* (cf. *kepare del* 59r.2, *kepare dell* 64r.9–10; *kepar del ew* BK 1151) which is supplied in E. The folio is badly damaged on the left.
65r.19	**Me a thro:** 'I will bring'—3 sg. pres./fut. of *dry* 59v.15 'to bring'—lenited by the particle *a*. Nance suggested 'adduce' as the translation here. Cf. *me a doro* BM 3981. For 'dr' leniting to 'thr' see *a ʒroppye* = *a throppye* PA 173.6), although the form here is a slight contraction, see *a thora* TH 16v.7–8, *a thoro* PC 192).
65r.20	**expoundyng:** by contrast with usage such as *signifia* 65r.15, this is an example of the naked use of an English word—see General Notes *(clerical Cornish)*.
65r.21	**i. regum:** '1 Kings' in the Septuagint. 1 Samuel 21:13 in Hebrew and modern Bibles. See Commentary, Quotation 46.
65r.22	**quis intelligat:** 'who may understand', N1 *quis intellig[atur]*, N2, C, B *quis intelligatur*, H *quis intellig[...]*.
65r.23	**i[n]telliga[tur]:** 'is it understood', N, H *[.......]*.—reconstructed from Foxe.
65r.24	**d:** N1 & 2, C *d*.—there is no visible *-e* after the *d* here, but *d[e]* seems intended.
	aut[e]m: 'himself', N, H *a[ ]*.
65r.25	**in manibu[s .....]:** N *manibus*, H *manibu[ ]*. The folio is damaged to the right, on and below this line. Reconstructed in E on the basis of Foxe as *manibu[s suis]*, 'in his hands'.
65r.26	**[.....] Corpus:** E *[illud] Corpus*, 'that Body', reconstructed on the basis of Foxe.
65r.27	**fat[......] hemma bos vnderstandis:** 'how [can] this be understood', N, B, H *fat[la ill] hemma bos vnderstandis*. The edited text follows Nance's suggestion, which accords well with Foxe's 'How this may be understood'.
65r.28	**ye vos gwrys [i..d ....]:** lit. 'to be done [in man]', N, B, H *ye vos gwrys[..........]*. The reconstruction in E—*the vos gwrys [in deane]*—is based on Foxe's 'in man' and the possible remains of the *i* and *d*. Other possibilities might have been *[in den]*, *[in dean]* or—less likely—*[ye then]*, *[ye thean]*, *[ye theane]*, 'to a man'.

65r.28–30	**[.......] veith ny*n* gew [..] cafas:** and so N, B, H. Reconstructed in E as *[Rag den] veith nyng ew [degys inter e thowla e honyn. Na wrene ny] cafas*: '[for] no [man] is [carried in his own hands. We do not [find]', This reconstruction, though based on Stephyn's usage, is purely conjectural. We cannot know to what extent he rearranged or summarized Smith's 'For no man is caryed in his own hands ... we do not finde'. *Ne wrene ny* could equally have been *nyn geran ny/ne gesan ny*. (For *den veith* see 59v.14, 24.)
65r.31	**an prophet be[...........]:** N, B, H *an prophet be[negas ....]*. Reconstructed in E as *an prophet be[negas David]*. Nance is probably correct about *benegas*, and the name David seems likely, based on Foxe's 'of David'. The contraction in *prophet* is expanded as *pro-* in light of Tregear's consistent use of *profet/profett*, for example, TH 1r.1, 4; 7r.8 etc. (Compare *an profus a nazare*, PC 2197.)
65r.32–3	**tha worth [...........................] hony*n* [..............]:** as also N, B, H. Again, the suggested reconstruction—*thaworth [an lether, mas a Christ / e] honyn [eth eran ny e gafas]*: 'from [the letter, but of Christ] himself [we find it]', is purely conjectural, but based on Foxe: 'after the letter ... Of Christ we finde it'. (Of course, *eran* could have been *esan*. For *lether* see BK 1820.)
65r.34	**rag [.................................]:** as also N, B, H. Any reconstruction of the final section at the base of this folio is in the realms of complete conjecture. The edited text offers *rag [Christ o degys inter e thowla e honyn]*, 'for Foxe's [Christ was borne in hys own hands]'. A possible continuation could then have been *pan ruk e leverall: Hem ew ow Corff ve, rag eff a ruke degy an kethsam Corff inter e thowla e honyn etc*, translating 'when he sayth: This is my body, for he caryed that same body in hys owne handes. &c.' But it is equally possible that Stephyn's version was much truncated or divergent from Foxe.
65v.1	**[....................]ryow dew Corf ha gois Christ ew:** N *[Bara ha gwyn] dir gyrryow dew kyg ha gois Christ ew*, C, B *[Bara ha gwyn] dir gyrryow dew kyg ha gois Christ ew (gwris)*, H *[Bara ha gwyn dir gyr]ryow dew kyg ha gois Christ ew/*. The diagonal line noted in H is in the MS, and continues down through the references below. There is little space for the *gwris* suggested in C. *Corf*, 'Body', is fairly clear—not *kigg*, 'flesh', as in F, or *kyg* as in N etc. No tail of a *y* from *kyg* is visible here, and the lower part of the word *Corf* can be read. (Compare the lower part of *Corf* at 65v.11.) Hence the reconstruction in E *[Bara ha gwyn dir girr]yow Dew Corf ha Gois Christ*

	ew: 'Bread and wine, through God's words, are the Body and Blood of Christ'.
65v.2	**[......................C]orf Christ ew, ᵉma warre an alter:** or, as in N1, C, H *corf Christ ew yna (> ena) war an alter*, N2, B *corf Christ ew yna war an alter*. Reconstructed in E as *[Rag henna an gwyr ha naturall] Corf Christ ew ema warre an alter*, on the basis of Tresham's 'Ergo, the true and naturall body of Christe is on the aultar'. With no tail of a 'y' visible (Nance may have mistaken the comma after *ew* for one) we appear to have the suffix form *ma*, corrected to the unusually spelled *ema* (for *umma, omma*), 'here', by the addition of an *e* just to the left and above the original word. (Despite the comma before, it seems unlikely the verb is being restarted.) In the reconstruction, *naturall* is used for 'natural', as *natur/nature* is the usual Cornish word for 'nature' from the early texts (*natur* PA 211.5, RD 458) through to Tregear and Stephyn (*nature* TH 1v.25 and passim, SA 62v.36, 63r.7). Tregear also invariably uses *naturall* as the adjective, as at TH 7r.21, 13v.15, 25r.27–8, 41v.1 (*naturall corfe*), 54v.7 and also uses *an gwyr* several times (although normally to mean 'the truth').
	14: possibly a reference to Mk 14:17–21 before the MS was damaged. The diagonal line is in the MS.
65v.2–3	**Luk 22:** this reference to Lk 22:21 lies below the '14' and between the lines as a gloss.
65v. 3	**[.......................S.] Austen:** E *[Me a bref henna thaworth S.] Austen*: '[I prove that from St] Augustine' is a completely speculative reconstruction, given the available space and Tresham's original 'I proue the contrary by S. Austen', noting that the words 'the contrary' would probably have been omitted following the previous phrase. *Me a bref* occurs at BK 263.
65v.3–4	**Joan. 13:** 'John 13'. This and the following references are inserted between lines 3 and 4: I have not counted them as constituting a line but as part of the marginalia after the diagonal line. The reference is to Jn 13: 21–30 (especially v. 26, singled out to the right). For the marginal references see Commentary.
65v.4	**buccellam:** 'morsel', N, H *[....]ellam*, B *[scab]ellam*. Foxe—in all editions—has *buccellulam*—a diminutive form of the Vulgate's *buccellam*. The change perhaps indicates a familiarity with the biblical text on the part of Stephyn.
65v.4–5	**non malum accip[...../......... acci]piendo Pec[c]auit:** N *non mal[.......]endo per ault.*, B *non ma[......]endo per ault*, H *non maln ... / [......]endo per ault*. Restored in E to *non malum accip[iendo] / [sed male] accipiendo peccavit*, 'sinned, not by taking something evil,

65v.5–6	[but by the evil way] he took it'. The spacing of the words here could indicate damage to the folio even before Stephyn's use. **kepare a ruk [..........]ysya:** 'just as ......', N1 &2, B *kepare a ruk [Judas a thebbras heb] yfya*, C *kepare a ruk [Judas a thebbras heb glor]yfya*, H *kepare a ruk [..... / glor]yfya*. Nance was right to suspect *Judas* here, as the passage echoes Tresham's 'Lyke as Iudas, [to whom the Lorde gaue the morsel] dyd offend', with the central clause left untranslated, and the sense of 'offend' changed. Conjectural reconstruction in E has been kept to a minimum—*kepare a ruk [Judas desp]ysya*, 'just as Judas despised'—since Stephyn has clearly shortened and rearranged the original. See Glossary, *despisea*.
65v.6	**not:** English 'not', N, H *[...]* (N1 alone has *oft/ost*). The *not* is somewhat unclear, but visible, with the appearance of an *s* in the middle being due to damage above, allowing part of the *[c]* of *Pec[c]auit* to come close to the *o*. English 'not' (used elsewhere—e.g. SA 60r.21) offers the best sense, although *not ef the recevia* is admittedly bizarre Cornish.
65v.7	**[...26 21...]:** This may represent one of the references later rewritten to the right after damage. The upper parts of the references may be lost: *Joan 13* from above *26*, and *Luk 22* from above *21*. But it might also read *20 21* with only *Joan 13* lost above, perhaps referring to Jn 13: 20–21. See Appendix A. **[........] recevias:** '[but he] received', N *[rag / ....]*, C *[... / rag eff a] recevias*. Maintaining the simplified translation, E suggests *[mas ef a] recevias*, 'but that he received' for Tresham's 'but in receiuyng'. (Either *mas* or *bus* could have been used.) To the left of the word *recevias* are the remains of a marginal reference, the lower part of which can just be read. **badd:** 'bad, evil'. Cornish uses both *bad* and *drok/drog* throughout most periods of the language. In the earlier texts, *bad* can have a distinct meaning of 'careless' or 'carelessly' (PC 2284, RD 1774, 1886) while the native *drok* (PA 21.4, OM 221, RD 2576) or *drog* (OM 417) holds the primary meaning and remains dominant in the saints' plays (*drok* BM 3204 etc., BK 228, *drog* BM 457, BK 10 etc.). Tregear, however, uses both words widely and indiscriminately (*bad* TH 21v.16, 24v.14, 34r.12, 34r.15; *drog* TH 2v.2, 3v.9, 6v.12 etc.) with, in one place, *vel bad*, 'or bad', inserted explicitly above *drog* TH 34r.13. SA only has *badd* (pronounced as in English *bad*), as here (but Stephyn uses *drocolath*, 'evil [behaviour]', at TH 55v.1.) CW only has *drog* (CW 2212) *droge* (CW 2399) and *droke* (CW 335 etc.) but it is adapted from an earlier text. Late Cornish still uses both forms: N. Boson has *bad-ober* (JCH 31, 32) and T. Boson

	droage in his Lord's Prayer, Gwavas Collection, f. 107r. (Most other translators of this prayer also prefer *drok, drog, droge* or *droag*, although they were perhaps influenced by earlier translations.) **e[..]:** N, H *[...]*, E *Ema*—the suggestion seems reliable, given the context. E *Ema S. Austen ow cowse nebas moy*, 'St Augustine says a little more'.
65v.8	**manduc[at]:** 'eat', N1 & 2 *manduc[ ]*, C, H *manduc[ant]*, B *manduc[at]*.
65v.10	**ha rag henna nyn gew:** 'and therefore it is not'. As discussed in the Commentary, Quotation 48, the Cornish paraphrase here is a serious distortion of the English original, giving almost the opposite sense to the one intended by Tresham. I have reflected this by enclosing *{nyng}*, the negative particle, in curly brackets in E. Tresham's double negative no doubt caused the trouble. The intended meaning would have been clearer if *rag henna nyng ew* had been replaced by something like *bus whath eth ew*.
65v.11	**Theophelact:** N, in the body of the text, *Theophelas 7* (*Theophilus 7* in T). In fact, as H recognizes, *Theophilact* is first inserted as a marginal reference, but then used as part of the text. **ruke:** 'did'—N, B *ruk*, H *ruke*.
65v.14	**a thisquethas an cruelte:** 'showed the cruelty', N, C, B, H *a thysquethas an cruelte*. While *cruelte* could simply be the English word, *crowwelder* is found at line 67 in NLW Bodewryd MS 5, possibly underlining Stephyn's tendency to anglicize spellings.[40] See General Notes *(English influence)*.
65v.16	**hemma ew ᵍⁱʳʳʸᵒʷ kvsell an Nice:** Foxe: 'The wordes of the Councel be these'. The Cornish translation reads a little awkwardly and we might have expected Stephyn to say *[An] rema ew girryow Kusell a Nice*—cf. *rema ew e irrow* 59v.19. This could be an indication that a scribe was at work and misheard—see General Notes *(dictation?)* and next note. The *girryow*, 'words', is a correction, inserted above *ew*, with an insertion mark below. (See also note on 65v.26.) **humiliter:** perhaps distracted by the capital *N* and final *e* of Nice, Stephyn has failed to begin the quotation with *Ne*. This runs counter to the suggestion of dictation made above, as the mistake would be more likely if Stephyn was writing himself, his eyes moving rapidly between the two pages. **spec[te]mus:** 'let us look', N, H *petimus*.
65v.19–20	**Na esyn ny meras war:** N1, C *Na esyn [n]y meras wor*, N2, B, *Na esyn [n]y miras wor*, H *Na esyn ny meras wor*, translating 'Let vs not looke ... vppon' in Foxe and echoing *Na esyn vsya* at 61v.25. In both

---

40 Hawke, 'A Rediscovered Cornish-English Vocabulary', line 67, p. 99.

	places *na esyn ny* means 'let us not'. This is a good instance of the verb *gasa*, 'to allow, let' being used periphrastically to form the 1 pl. imper., with the negative *na* leniting *gesyn* to *esyn*.[41] There are parallels with *gas ve the remmembra* 59r.25, *gas an mynd confessia* 61v.34 and *gas an golan percyvia da* 61v.36. (Here, the original abbreviation mark in *esyn* has been altered to give the full word *esyn*. Nance read *wor'* for 'upon', perhaps expecting *meras worth* here, but it seems more likely we have *war* rather than *wor'*. Admittedly Stephyn's practice with silent *th* is not consistent: he writes it unnecessarily in *lowarth* 59r.33, but not at all in *e ker* at 65v.22—see General Notes (*rth > r*).
65v.20	**an bara** ^{han} **dewas:** 'the bread and the drink'—*han* is inserted above the line as a correction between *bara* and *dewas*, with an insertion mark.
	derevall: for Watson's 'lyfting'; here for the present participle *[ow] derevall*.
65v.20,21	**mas:** 'but'—the second *mas* (65v.21), in erroneous repetition, would have been better as *ow* (as suggested in E).
65v.22	**e ker:** 'away' representing the earlier *in kerth* TH 6v.24. The phrase here suggests how Stephyn might translate *Agnus Dei, qui tollis peccata [mundi]*, 'Lamb of God, you take away the sins of the [world]': *Onne Dew/Onne a Thew....vge ow kemeras e ker pegh/pehosow an [beys]*. See General Notes (*rth > r*).
65v.23	**benegys:** 'consecrated'—lit. 'blessed' but here translating 'sacrificed'.
65v.24	**hewwall:** 'high'—this is the *vhell* of Tregear (TH 11r.6 etc.). Cf. also *ughell* PA 16.2, *vhell* BM 4, *ughall* CW 231.
65v.26	**Cucell an Nice:** 'the Council of Nicaea', N, B, H *Cucell a Nice*, but *an* is certainly written here for *a*, as above at 65v.16. Not *Cu[n]tell*—see note on 66r.32.
65v.29	**[.......s] onyn an apostelath:** '[not] one of the Apostles', N, B *[ne gus] onyn an apoisteleth*, H *[ne gus] onyn an apostelath*. Nance seems correct in his reconstruction, though this might be more likely in the form *nyn gvs* as at 61r.38, 64v.34, reflected in E *nyng us*.
	a lev[................] ew: N1, S *a le[veris bemma] ew*, N2, C, B *a le[veris hemma] ew*, H *a le[veris hemma e]w*, 'said [this] is', Another very plausible reconstruction by Nance, who noticed the still partly visible *e* of *ew*.
65v.30	**[................................] leveris:** N, B, H *leveris*—conjecturally reconstructed in E as *[Arluth Jesus Christ. Nyng us onyn an reverent*

---

41 Williams, *Clappya Kernowek*, p. 119; Williams, *Desky Kernowek*, pp. 150, 152.

prontyrryan a] leveris: '[Lord Jesus Christ. Not one of the reverend priests] said'. This part of the MS is completely lost except *leveris* (cf. 62r.18, 62v.7, 17.)

65v.31 **[............................ o]rf ef**: N, B, H ... *co]rf ef*, conjecturally reconstructed in E as *[sacrafice an alter tha vos figur e go]rf ef*, '[the sacrifice of the altar (was) a figure of his] Body'. Another large portion of the MS is lost here, but *e [go]rf ef* seems most likely in context. In the suggested reconstruction, I have avoided translating 'unbloody' mainly because there is no attested Cornish word. In middle Cornish, *gosys* is attested for 'bloodied' (PA 219.6). In BK a pres./fut. 3 sg. verbal form, *dywoys*, 'bleed' (in the sense of remove blood) is attested (BK 2731). In late Cornish *gooshak* is found for 'bloody' (in Pryce's vocabulary, from T. Tonkin), and this might have been *goisake* in Stephyn's spelling. In turn this could suggest forms like **dywoisake, *anwoisake* for 'bloodless, unbloody', but they are so far removed from anything actually found in the traditional Cornish of the period that they fail to meet the criteria for these suggested reconstructions. Something like *sacrafice heb gois* or even *unbloudy sacrafice* would have been more likely.

65v.32 **[1]383**: of great significance as a possible page reference to Foxe—see Introduction 2:6.

66r.1 **[...]a ha gwyn dir ger[...............................]**: E *[Bara]a ha gwyn dir ger[ryow Dew corf ha gois Christ gwris e thew]*, 'Bread and wine through God's words are made the Body and Blood of Christ'. This reconstruction on the basis of previous folios differs in the *e* clearly present in *ger[ryow]* as at 59r.17, by contrast with the more usual *girreow, gyrryow* in these headings.

66r.2 **N[............................]**: though almost entirely missing, it is possible to attempt a reconstruction based on the reference mentioned in the next note and Foxe. So E has *N[on solum homines, etc. Id est, Nyng ew]*: 'It is not only men, etc. That is, It is not' (In the MS form it would have been *Nyn gew* or *Ne gew*.

66r.3 **tvs only angwra**: 'men only that make it', N1, B *bus only an owriek*, N2 *lus only an owriek*, C, H *Avs only an owriek*. This was for many years thought to represent *an owriek*—an allusion to the 'golden mouthed' St John Chrysostom. On close examination of the MS, however, it is *angwra*, followed by a full stop, and confirmed by the reference to the original in Foxe (see Commentary, Quotation 53). With only minimal reconstruction, the whole phrase becomes E *[Nyng ew] tus only a'n gwra*, '[It is not] only men that make it' (referring to making their voice known in prayer).

NOTES 277

	CeChrisostom [..............]: N1 & 2, B *Chrisostom*, C, H *CChrisostom*. The name here is preceded by an additional capital *C* (not a lower case *k*) overwriting an *e* (from an intended *ema*?) and then discarded to begin again. The following reconstruction in E *[yweth, whar an]* (which could also have been *e weth* in the MS) reflects Foxe's 'againe, vpon the'. There is hardly space for anything else.
66r.4	**Acts Apostelath:** MS *Apostelath*, N, B *Apostolis*, H *Apostoli[s..]th*. The damage to the MS here led to two small surviving fragments to the top right of the folio becoming detached. When refixed, one was wrongly placed slightly below and to the right of its original position, leading to the erroneous reading *Acts Apostolis*, instead of the correct *Acts Apostelath*. (This first portion has *th:Qu* surviving on the first line, and *[l]avirta ge* on the second line.) The second detached portion, to the right of the first, was placed three lines two high and therefore, also, too far to the right. (This second portion has *host* on the first line, *e ma* on the second and *temere ab Apostolis* on the third.) Correctly positioned, *host* should therefore properly follow *ge*; then *ema* slots in neatly after *pronter*; and *temere ab Apostolis* after *Non*. See diplomatic edition and Appendix B to understand these readjustments.
	Qu[......................]: N, B *[..........]*, H *l[......]nere*, reconstructed in E as *Qu[id dicis? Hostia in]*, 'What [do you say? The Host is in]' (leading to *manibus sacerdotis*, 'the hands of the priest'). Once the incorrect positioning of the fragments described above is understood, the conjectural reconstruction is clear, given Foxe's text. (The *[.....]nere* in H should be understood in the context of *temerė* 66r.7 described below.)
66r.5	**Pan[...] lavirta ge[....] host:** 'What do you say[? The] host', N1 *p ... ge*, N2 *... ge*, C *[p ... aro]ge*, B *[..........]*, H *P .... ge[..........]*. A suggested reconstruction of the whole phrase is given in E—*Pand[ra] lavirta ge[? An] host benegas e ma inter dowla an pronter*, 'What do you say? The Blessed Host is in the hands of the priest'. (*An host benegas* could equally be 'the sacred Host', or perhaps even 'the Host that is consecrated/offered': in the original Greek there is a sense of a sacrifice/sacrificial victim.) The whole reconstruction thus requires very little speculation—much can be seen, although the damage to the folio and incorrect placing of two fragments explain the loss of part of some letters. The full phrase neatly translates *Quid dicis? Hostia in manibus sacerdotis* in Foxe. See General Notes *(lavirta ge)*.
66r.6–7	**e ma Chrisostom:** the second separated fragment alluded to above also resulted in the erroneous placing of MS *e ma* above and to the right, here correctly reassigned to follow *pronter [........]*.

It seems likely that *[etc.]* followed *pronter*, and that *[Ha]*, 'and', may have introduced *e ma*—once again, part of the manuscript is lost here. (The folio number '66' was pencilled in between lines 5 and 6 at a much later point.)

66r.7 **Non temerė ab Apostolis est institutum:** 'It was not rashly instituted by the Apostles', see notes on misplaced fragments above under 66r.4 and the arrangement in the diplomatic edition. (The *temere ab Apostolis* has been wrongly affixed to the right of *Qu* three lines above.) N, B *Non [...............] Apostolis est institutum* (although, in his MS translation, Nance suggests *prosperantur*), H *Non [prosperantur] Apostolis est institutum*. (Incidentally, in the 1570, 1576 and 1583 editions of Foxe, there is a grave accent over the final *è* in *temerè*. Since there is a small point above the *e* in the same place in SA, we may have the remnant of a copied accent, though the MS is damaged and the mark may be insignificant.)

66r.8 **nyn gew:** = *nyng ew* 'it is not' but probably written in error for *nyng o*, 'it was not', as in Foxe. The edited text is emended to reflect this—see General Notes *(dictation?)*.

dir hastenab: 'rashly, in haste'. The ending of *hastenab* is noteworthy and appears to contain a suffix of abstraction, *-enab*. Tregear has *hevelep* TH 1v.1, *heveleb* TH 1v.17 but also *heveleneps* [sic] TH 1v.24 for 'likeness', in close proximity (which has led some to suggestions of a derivation from *eneb*, 'face' VC 754 and Late Cornish, cf. Welsh *wyneb*). TH 16v.18 has *methewnep* for 'drunkenness' and *cotheneb* TH 34v.7 for Bonner's 'antiquity'. Nance (in his article on *The Tregear Manuscript*, Old Cornwall, vol. 4, no. 11) says: '*Hastenab (hastenep)*, m., hastiness, haste; suffix *-enep, -ness*.' This would parallel the Welsh suffix *-ineb* in *claerineb, doethineb, gwylltineb*. The discovery of *Bewnans Ke* has given further corroboration, notably in the words *folneb*, 'foolishness' (cf. Welsh *ffolineb*) and *rowndenab*, 'roundness' at BK 281, 283.[42]

apoyntis yᵉ worth: E *apoyntis theworth*, 'appointed/instituted by'.

66r.8m **[...]8:** this reference has suffered damage. It may be to Augustine (or Ambrose—see Commentary, Quotation 59) on Psalm 38, but equally the missing characters may be *[..13]8* or *[..1 3]8*, possibly for (Chrysostom on Philippians) *homil 3*, where this passage is found in some old editions. The folio in Foxe, 1576, is also intriguingly 1388 here, but a second 8 is not present. (The 8 is in the wrong place to refer to the *De octo dulcitii quaestionibus*—see Commentary, Quotation 56.)

---

42 Thomas and Williams, *Bewnans Ke*, p. 28 [f. 2v, stanza 38].

66r.9	**ow scrifa:** '[is] writing, writes', N, B *ow scryfa*, C, H *ow scrifa*.
	thanphilippians**:** 'to the Philippians'—N, B *than philipians*, C, H *thanphilippians*.
66r.10	**A remembrance a vea res thotha bos:** lit. 'of remembrance that it should be' (T: 'of a remembrance that they should have', 3 pl., but *thotha* here is a late form of *thotho*, 3 sg.). This passage is a simple continuation of the previous passage, *Non temere ab Apostolis est institutum*, completed in Cornish (and Foxe's English) but not in Latin. *A vea* is the conditional (also pluperfect) of *bos*, 'to be'—cf. *vya* BM 582, 3180, 4180. Here *a vea res thotha bos* is best translated 'that it should be, that it needs to be'. We have a similar construction in Tregear: *a vea res thetha* TH 16r.4 'them, that should' or 'those who need to' (here *thetha* is 3 pl.). See also *dell vea res thyn* TH 9v.9—'as we should'.[43] See also General Notes (*res/rys ew > a res/rys*).
66r.11	**E[.....]id[.o]n:** E *Enchiridion*, confirmed by Foxe.
66r.12	**& 110 chap**te**r:** The usual & for *an*, 'the'.
	suorum**:** lit. 'of them', N2, C, H *fami[liaribus]*, N1, B *familiar*.
66r.13	**viuentiu**m**m:** for *viventium*, 'liuyng' (Foxe); H *viuentinum*, N *viuentium*. Possibly an unclear *viuentium* was first written, then an abbreviation mark added, leaving the original half-formed *-m* unchanged.
66r.14	**tha vos:** MS *tha vos*, N, B, H *tha vos y*. There is no *y* following here. What has previously been mistaken for one is the upper part of the *s* below.
	an nenevow: E *an Enevow*, lit. 'the Souls'—the plural of *enaf* 60v.27. The Cornish expression for the souls of the departed is even more economical than the English ('the Holy Souls'). The initial *n* is a common intrusion after *an* in SA. See 66r.16.
66r.15	**aga hvnthmans:** 'their friends', N, B, H *hvthmans*: note both the expected spirantization of *c* to *h* here and the unexpected abbreviation mark over the *v* (= *u*), which would normally represent *n* or *m*, exactly as it does over the second syllable of the word). This may be an error but is left in E in case it is a clue to pronunciation.
	pan **vo offrys:** 'when we offer', lit. 'when is offered'.
66r.16	**[a]n sacrafice:** 'the Sacrifice', N, B *an sacrafice*, H *& [= an] sacrifice*—the damage to the folio below *n* does give the appearance of Stephyn's abbreviation for 'and' in copies.

---

43 See Williams, *Clappya Kernowek*, pp. 64–6, *Desky Kernowek*, p. 70, and Gendall, *Tavaz a Ragadazow*, pp. 75–6.

pege rag: 'pray for'—in Cornish the preposition with this verb can be either *rag*, 'for', or *gans*, 'with'. Compare *peys ragovy* BM 2115, *peys ragoen* BM 2742, and *peys rag* BM 3868 with *ov pesy gena* BM 707. Neither preposition is used in praying for forgiveness: *pesy gevyans* BM 3359. At first it appears we have *pege* written in error for *pejadow*, 'prayer' (cf. 62r.18, 63r.36), or possibly a contraction of *[ny a] pege* (where *pege* represents *peys*) or an implicit *[eth esan ny o] pege* (where *pege* represents *pesy*)—both meaning 'we pray [for]'. But, studying Foxe's version, the most likely explanation for this slip is that Stephyn simply omitted to translate part of the original, 'of the Mediator ... for them. Where he proueth the verity of Christes body'. Then *[ow] pege* could simply an attempt to render Foxe's 'praying' which follows just afterwards (OP). Reflecting this insight I suggest in E a possible conjectural form of the phrase Stephyn omits: *[a'n Mean ragthans. Omma ema ef ow prevy an gweronath]*, '[of the Mediator for them. Here he is proving the truth]'. The word *mean* for 'mediator' is attested at the period: *Eff ew an mean vs intra du ha den* TH 11r.11, translating 'He is the mediatoure betwene God and man' and *ragthans* is found at TH 23r.8. Alternatively, we could replace *a'n Mean* with *a Corf Christ*, which might explain the confusion and omission better.

an nene^w vow: for *an Enevow*, 'the Souls' as above at 66r.14. Possibly altered from an original *an nenevow* (and so N, B, H) with the *v* overwritten as *w*: if so, the resulting *enewow* may indicate a changing pronunciation.

66r.17 **leveris a feran:** 'said Mass', N, B, H *leveris a seran*. The expression *leverall aferan* is the exact equivalent of the still-used Catholic expression 'to say Mass', meaning 'to celebrate the Eucharist' (also found as *Y leferys offeren* at BM 4419). In SA it was for many years misread as *leveris a *seran*, following Nance. In his manuscript English translation, Nance has: 'This same Augustine said a "*seran*" for his mother Monica'. Above the word *seran* he has inserted the gloss 'prayer for rest for her soul.' The word thus made its way into subsequent dictionaries, and was supposed to relate to Latin *serenare*. On closer inspection, however, it is clear that the '*s*' is not an *s* at all, but an *f*, and that MS *a feran* represents *aferan*, a late spelling of *offeren* CE 37, *oferen* PC 764, BK 1212, 'Mass'.

Monaca: 'Monica', N, B, H *Monica*.

66r.18 **h[...]:** E *h[abitat]*, Foxe 'dwelleth', N, H *s[istet]*. We can reconstruct this not only from Foxe but also from Stephyn's insertion of the same quotation into the margin of Tregear's homilies (TH 57r.13–16m). Nance's conjectural *sistet* arose because—at the damaged edge of the page—the *h* could easily be read as *si*.

66r.19	**Commun[...]**: for 'Communion', N, B, *Communion*, C, H *Commun[ion]*. Nance plausibly reconstructed this as *Communion* although I have preferred *y* in E on the basis of *communyon* (or, arguably but less obviously *communyan*) at TH 39r.8 and *comminyan* in the Cornish creed on the concluding folio of LLR.
66r.20	**in[...]**: N, B *in(nan)*, E *in[nan ny]* (or simply *in[nan]*) 'in us'. Nance's conjectural reconstruction is very likely: both *innan* and *innan ny* are found in Tregear (e.g. TH 5r.13, 10r.19). (We also find *innaff* at SA 61r.36, and *in an sy* at SA 59v.27, so the original spelling might possibly have been *innany/in an ny*.)
66r.21	**principem sacerd[otem]**: the source shows us this does indeed represent *principem sacerdotem* (acc. sg. 'the Prince-Priest', or High/Chief Priest) not *principem sacerdotum* (gen. pl. 'the Prince of Priests', as in N, C, B, H). The half-detached fragment recorded above as *[otem]* seems correctly placed. Though unclear, parts of letters can be identified.
66r.21m	**[De]**: a likely reconstruction of the beginning of the marginal reference, given what follows, but now completely missing.
66r.22	**e[w]**: 'is'—only the smallest part of the *w* now survives, but it is in exactly the right place and the reconstruction is likely.
66r.23	**then [...]**: N, B, H, E *then [ny ha]*. The reconstruction could equally have been *then [ha]* or *then[y ha]* (cf. *thyn[y]* SA 63r.35). Nance's suggestion has been adopted in E.
66r.24	**ema an doctors [...]**: the conjectural restoration in E is *ema an doctors [ow hagrya]*, 'the theologians agree', referring to the 'Doctors of the Church', the early Fathers. Tregear has *ow hagrya* at TH 34v.16 and 52v.20, and Harpsfield uses 'do agree' in Foxe's version. Other solutions are, however, possible. N, H both plausibly conjecture *ow leverall* following here, or we might suggest something like *ow(th) assentya* (not attested in this spelling but as *assentye* PC 2037, RD 583 and in the conjugated form *assentyas* CW 248, showing it survived as a verb). Stephyn does not use *owth*, however, though it is found at BK 24 in *owth ola hag owth owtya*—MS *ow thola hag owthowtya*.
66r.25	**deow habblys**: 'Maundy Thursday', here standing for *De [Y]ow Habblys*, Harpsfield's 'the supper of the Lord'. The form *de-/du-* is a shorter form of *deth/dyth/dith*, 'day' (see PC 746, 1760, TH 53r.21) and *-ow* of *Yow*, 'Thursday', which appears in this same context at *deyow hablys* PA 41.5 and *duyow hamlos* PC 654. Breton and Welsh both have cognates of the Cornish word *cablys* PC 2434. In the latter it seems to mean 'betrayal' at first sight, but the GPC looks rather in the direction of Old Irish *caplat* and therefore

ultimately to Late Latin *capitilavium* 'head-washing' (or *capillatio* 'hair cutting or shaving'). In modern Irish *Déardaoin Caplaide* is still used alongside *Déardaoin Mandála* (NW).

66r.25-6   **arna theffe[.../...]eᵃn keth geyr ma:** which, before damage to the MS, might have been *arna theffe[ns y th]en keth geyr ma*, lit. 'until they come to this same word' Foxe 'before they come vnto Panis' etc. The *[th]en* appears to have been altered to *[th]an*: the overwritten *a* has been preferred in E. N1 & N2, B *arr na theffa [leverall] an keth geyr ma*, C *ar na theff[a leverall] an keth geyr ma*, (= *erna dheffa*) *an keth geyr ma*, H *arna theffe [leverall] an keth geyr ma*.

66r.27   **a theffan ry:** 'that I shall give', see General Notes (*theffa*).
Rag [...] / diᵉbbry: N, C, B *Rag [res ew] dibbry*, H, RE *Rag [dir] dibbry*— but the earlier *dibbry* has been amended to *debbry*. E reconstructs as *Rag [eff neb uge o] debbry*, 'for he who eats', following *neb vge o recivia corf dew* SA 61r.25-6. An alternative reconstruction, *Rag [eff neb a ra] debbry*, could be based on *rag eff a ra* TH 22r.6 and *rag neb a rug* TH 40r.24.) Nance's suggestion of *res ew dibbry* could also have been *thetheffe res ew debbry* in the light of SA 66r.28 and *rys ew thotha* BK 2257, 2370. Or we could offer *ef a rys debbry*, based on one of Stephyn's own idioms at SA 59r.39—but Harpsfield only says 'that he who eateth'.

66r.28   **yᵉ theff[.......]:** N, C, B *the theff[...]*, H *yᵉ theff[a ...]*, F *yᵉ theff[...]*, RE *y theff[a]...* It would be puzzling if we had *theffa* here—see General Notes (*theffa*)—we would not expect *the* before it or other conjugated forms of *dos* like *deffa*, *deffry*.⁴⁴ At first sight, as Nance summarizes in C, 'no known Cor. seems to fit here'.⁴⁵ Nonetheless, the following is a possible solution: first we have *thetheff* or *thetheff[e]*, 'to him' (as representing *thotheff* at 66a.24, *th[e]theffe* or *th[o]theffe* at SA 59r.36, *thotha eff* TH 23r.9, 57r.19 and *thotheff* TH 23r.10). Then some lost words might follow, meaning 'will come/should be/will be' or even 'is'. (In Stephyn's Cornish these might be, respectively, *a ra dos/a vea res bos/a ra bos* or *a veth* or even *ew*.) Finally we have

---

44   For instance, National Library of Wales Bodewryd MS 5 has *pan deffry*, 'when thou comst'—see Hawke, 'A Rediscovered Cornish-English Vocabulary', line 85, p. 99. But in our context this only reinforces how out of place *the* is before the conjugated form of *dos*. To get around this, the use of an antiquated form of the verbal noun could be postulated. Forms like *ow tevones/deuones* are certainly found in the older texts, for example, at PA 61.5, 93.7; RD 1350, 2302. See Nance, *Gerlyver Noweth*, p. 41, under *dos*, where he notes 'the longer inf. forms are used for euphony or slight emphasis'. But *the *theffos/*theffones the* does not really sound like Stephyn.
45   His suggested reconstruction (in Unified Cornish) is *dhe dheservya*, but—as he notes—the MS actually has *ff* rather than *ss* or *s*.

bewnans heb dewath, 'life without end').[46] So Harpsfield's 'that he who eateth Christ's fleshe (&c, after a certaine manner) should liue for euer' could become, as reconstructed in E, *Rag [eff neb uge o] dibbry worthely kigg agen Saviour Christ, theth'eff [a ra dos] bewnans heb dewath*. A brief list of alternative explanations should also be given. (a) 'Truly', *theffry* (cf. *defry* OM 271, lenited as *theffry* OM 1264) although it does not seem to fit the syntax or sense. (b) The idea of 'waking to eternal life' is possible, but we would have to postulate an otherwise unattested verb **deffry*, cognate with Welsh *deffro, deffroi*, 'to awake'. (c) A strange spelling of *thyuvne* (= *thyvuna*) BM 1785, *dysvna* (= *dyfuna*) BK 349.[47] (d) *Rag [henna] dibbry worthely kigg agen Saviour Christ, yth yw eff bewnans heb dewath* has also been suggested (NW, private communication). This makes good sense, but does not match well with *yᵉ theff* as found.

66r.29 **effunditur:** the underlining below this word in the diplomatic text represents a heavy black line in the MS.

66r.31 **remissione:** the 'ss' here is in combined italic form β.

66r.32 **speciems:** N, H *species*. (The sign for a contraction over the *e* is definitely present, but is probably the result of Stephyn starting to write *speciem* by mistake, correcting modestly to *species*, then finally adding a decisive and partly overwritten large *s*.)

66r.33 **præciosum:** N, H *prætiosum*, B *pretiosum*. The likely reading here is *c*: Nance's *t* may be in part due to the overlap with downstroke of the *q* above, though Stephyn can write *c* very like *t* (as at 65v.26).

66r.34 **nowᵗʰ:** 'new'—often spelled *nowyth* in the texts, for example, OM 806, PC 2124, BK 1921, TH 27r.20, CW 2283. N *now[eth]*, B *noweth*, H *nowth*, The letters *th* lie above and slightly to the right of *now*. There is no *e* or *y*, and although there appears to have been damage to the text, there seems to be little room for either. At this period *wᵗʰ* was a common way of writing English 'with' (OP), which suggests that this word should be read as *nowith*, as shown in E, and at TH 18v.9, 14; 27v.13, 19; 31r.2; 53v.6.

ew: although *ew* follows a colon in the original, this is simply another case of the erratic punctuation so common in SA.

---

46 Since the first letters of the illegible remnants resemble either an *a*, followed (just possibly) by *r*, the reconstruction in E adopts *a ra dos*, although *a ra bos* is also possible. The tempting *a vea res thotha bos* SA 66r.10, rearranged, has too many letters for the space.

47 This verb seems to end with -*a*/-*e*. Forms with final *y*, like *dyfuny*, 'to awake', in Robert Williams, *Lexicon Cornu-Britannicum* (Llandovery: Roderic and London: Trubner, 1865), p. 122, and *difuny, difyny* 'to awake', in William Pryce, *Archæologia Cornu-Britannica, or an Essay to Preserve the Ancient Cornish Language* (Sherborne: Cruttwell, 1790), p. 91, may be less reliable, as drawn mostly from Tonkin and Gwavas. The cognates are Welsh *dihuno*; Breton *dihuna*.

66r.35 **e thew:** 'it is', MS can be read either as *e thew* or *ethew*, N, B, H *ethew*.

agyn: 'our', MS *a gyn* or *agyn*, N, B, H *agyn*.

66r.36 **ragan [..]:** N, H *ragan [ny,]*, B *ragan ny*—the MS is torn but *ny* is a very likely conjectural reconstruction. There are possible remains of the upper right of a *y*, and Nance may be right about the following comma though very little is left.

popell: 'people', N, B, H *pobell*. The word is usually spelled with a *b*, and is cognate with *pobl*, *pobol* in Welsh: for example, *pobel* VC 182, OM 1543, *pobell* CW 1516, *poble* WB. See General Notes (*g* > *k*).

66v.1 **[...] panis:** In E a completely conjectural reconstruction—*[Panis quia dicitur] panis*—is offered, based on the words which follow, *Corpus quia dicitur Corpus*, and the Cornish translation: '*Panis ew henwis bara, Corpus ew henwis Cor[ff]*', '[the] Bread is called *Panis*, [the] Body is called *Corpus*'. See note on 66r.6 and Appendix B to understand the displaced fragments at this point: importantly, the *Panis ew* needs to move back from just above line 4 in the MS to the beginning of line 6, before *henwis bara*.

dicitur: 'is said'—the usual abbreviation for *-ur*, like an inverted 3, is inserted slightly above the end of the word.

66v.2 **[...]monem de Tempore:** probably for *[in Ser]monem de Tempore*, a reference to a 'Discourse [Sermon] on the Seasons of the Year'. See Commentary, Quotation 65.

66v.3 **[..o]mnia infidelitatis suspicio:** the repositioned correct fragment here (from just below) supplies the *[o]mnia in-* to reunite with the *-fidelitatis suspicio* corresponding to *oll thiscrygians*. (N, H *Panis a*, B *Panis A* at the beginning of this line: however, as explained under 66r.4 and 66v.6, the folio has been carefully but incorrectly repaired when some damaged areas became detached.)

66v.4 **[....]iuet:** MS *[....]iuet* or possibly *[....]inet*, N, H *[...]uet*—this looks a little, as Nance thought, like *-uet*, eg. as in Luther's *quod me mouet* (= *movet*) at TH 50r.1. The *i* is partly visible, however, and *-inet* is also just possible, with the sense then pointing perhaps to a word like *pertinet*.

66v.6 **Panis ew henwis bara:** 'bread is called *panis*', N, B, H *[Panis ew] henwis bara*. The misplaced fragment *Panis ew* (often misread in the past as *Panis A*) is still positioned in the MS at the BL just above the beginning of 66v.4 (at the time of writing). However, it is wrongly placed, as the analysis of the opposite side of this folio has demonstrated (requiring a similar readjustment here). The words have therefore been moved in the diplomatic edition from

	just above the beginning of line 66v.4 to the beginning of line 66v.6. Our gain in understanding is minimal—Nance had already guessed '*Panis ew*' from the Latin above (or suspected the correct placing as a possibility, or even seen the manuscript before it was repaired). Bice gives *panis* in both positions.
66v.7	**[g]as oll thiscrygians:** 'leave all disbelief', corresponding with the *[o]mnia infidelitatis suspicio* above. Before *oll*, certainly an *s* and possibly an *a* before it can just about be made out, suggesting *[g]as*, 'leave' (imper. 2 sg.)—though Stephyn often uses the word in the sense 'let' 59r.25, 61r.17, 61v.34, 61v.36. (See also *gas ve*, 'let me', at CW 523, 742.) Nance, in N2 and C, conjectured *gesugh*, the 2 pl. form. **nona navethi[...] troublis:** 'then you will not be troubled', N, B, H *nenna naveth[ogh]*. Nance conjectured this might have lost a 2 pl. ending -*ogh*, but the *i* of a 2 sg. form, -*ith*, is just visible. The phrase can be reconstructed as *nona na vethith troublis*, 'then you will not be troubled', cf. *nefre ny vethyth* OM 1465; *yn nef ny vythyth trygys* PC 858 and General Notes *(contractions)*. In the case of *nona* for *nena* 62r.20, Stephyn does sometimes write *o* for *e*: see General Notes *(ema > oma)*. The word *troublis* is found as *trobles* at CW 1458.
66v.8	**gans Accidens na substans v[e]tholl:** 'by accidents nor substance at all'. The *e* in *v[e]tholl* is partly visible. **manum mittam:** MS *manum mittam*—& so N2,—C, H *manum-mittam*, B *manummittam*.
66v.9m	✠**infra:** the sign of the cross and word *infra*, 'below', link this line with a fuller quotation, similarly marked with a cross, below at line 66v.29. Line 9—although I have numbered it in the ordinary sequence—has been inserted in slightly smaller script between the lines above and below it, in Stephyn's italic hand (as found in the marginal notes and his notes on the last two homilies of TH).
66v.10	**Crig ge:** 'believe', imper. 2 sg. of the verb *crysy*, 'to believe', with the 2 sg. pers. pron. These two words represent *crys* RD 965, and *sy* OM 315. While it is commonly said that forms with *g* like *thege* BK 1784, 2633 supplanted forms with *s* like *the sy* OM 315 as the language developed, the picture is actually more complex. The use of *s*, often perceived as 'older' (e.g. *crys* RD 1691, *crysy* OM 1508), is frequently found in later texts (e.g. *crys* BK 1852, CW 1615, *crysy* TH 38r.15, 54v.22, *cresy* BM 971, *creys* CW 172). Equally, the supposedly 'later' use of *g* = /dʒ/—as here in *crig* (or as in *cregyans*, 'belief', TH 18r.23)—can be found in much earlier ones (cf. *cregyans* PA 44.7). It is likely that the missing words preceding *Crig ge* were *Henna ew*, as offered conjecturally in E.

	ha e thesta [...]: the missing present participle (presumably *tibbry* as at 61r.23, for *o tibbry*) is conjectured in E on the basis of the Latin Crede *et edisti*, 'Believe and you have eaten'. However *eth esta* is not the preterite of the auxiliary *bos*, but either the 2 sg. pres. or imperf., so the translation is simplified to 'believe and you eat'. Also note *ha* not *hag*, and the interesting introduction of *edisti* for *manducasti* in Foxe.
66v.13	**huius:** Foxe has *maximè hominis carnem*, 'especially the flesh of man', not *maximè huius carnem* as apparently here (with *huius* meaning 'of this'). Although no *m* is visible, there appears to be the remains of a sign for a contraction, so perhaps an abbreviation for *hominis* (as in the original) was intended, but not written.
66v.14–15	**yᵉ worth [...] elyment the gela:** presumably 'from [one] element to another', though the right of the folio after *yᵉ worth* is lost. N *theworth [...] elyment the gela* C, B *theworth [an neyl] elyment the gela*, H *theworth [vn] elyment the gela*. Hawke's suggestion of *vn* is very plausible—there is little space for more. Despite this, Nance's suggestion of *an neyl* (for *an eyl*) has been taken up in E as more idiomatic (and with more precedent in TH: cf. *an neyl thy gela* TH 16v.12-13). Here *the* represents *th'e* (for older *th'y*). See also *an mor the gela cowal* BK 1199.
66v.15	**an vosan ny:** this is a late, personalized form, with the infinitive of *bos* taking on a personal ending. The word *an* may represent *agan*: in older Cornish the expression would merely have been *agan bos ny*, and the lenition here is hard to explain. It is found elsewhere in SA as in *e vosama* at 62v.33. Tregear does not lenite in similar circumstances, such as the catchword *y bosama* at the foot of TH 43v. See General Notes *(bos + personal suffixes)*.
	gwa[n ...]: 'weak [and]', N, B, H *gwa[n]*—the final -*n* of *gwan* is supplied confidently, given the first three letters and the English, but the *ha*, 'and', that follows in E—reflecting the original Latin and English—is conjectural.
66v.15–16	**kemeras skrvth:** N, B, H *ow kemeras skrvth*. Nance's *ow* is preferred in the reconstruction because it is possible that the *ow* or *ew* at the beginning of line 24 is a wrongly attached fragment from this line (see note on 66v.24). See also PA 254.7 (262 in the MS)—*scruth own mur askemeras*—suggesting that *kemeras scruth* means 'to shiver with horror, to be deeply shocked'. In Welsh *ysgryd*, *sgryd*—'trembling, horror' is related to *cryd* (GPC); Breton *skrija* is related to *krid[ienn]*; Old Irish *crith*.[48]

---

[48] Victor Henry, *Lexique Etymologique du Breton Moderne* (Rennes: Plihon & Hervé, 1900), pp. 82, 244. Henry also points out Greek *kradaw*, 'shake'.

66v.16	**kref[f ...]:** C *kreff[ha]*, B *kreffha*, H *kref[fha]*. Part of the downward stroke of the second *f* may be visible. This is a useful confirmation of *krîv* (AB 52) 'raw, fresh' which survived in dialect as 'creeved'.[49] The *ha*, now lost, is conjectural.
66v.17	**rag henn[a ...]:** N, B, H *rag hem[ma]*. Surely *rag henna*—'therefore, for that reason'—and not *rag hemma* as in N. (Nance in his own translation has 'therefore'.) The folio is damaged here, but *gwris ew* or *ew* (the latter in N) or perhaps even more likely *e thew/eth ew* (as in the next line and supplied in E) may have followed.
66v.18	**[h]e^f velap:** N, B, H *hevelep*. An original *v* appears to have been at least partly overwritten by an *f*—interestingly, since Tregear and Ton both write *hevelep* (TH 55v.2; BM 2150). There is no certainty over the initial *h* that Nance reported—we may have either *efelap* or *hefelap*: the marginal line introduces confusion and the faint markings be due to the damaged edge of the folio. See General Notes (*g > k*). **a bara:** the def. art. *an* sometimes becomes *a* in later Cornish, but here may be *a*, 'of', without the usual lenition following it. Nance in C suggests *hemma gwelys ew in hevelep a bara*. **arluth:** with the *r* a secretary hand 'descending r'.
66v.23–5	**[ow] or [ew]:** N, B, F *[osa]*, H *[...]*. There is a small, detached and reattached fragment to the left of, and between, lines 24 and 25, reading *ow* (or possibly *ew*). This may properly belong to the right of line 15, where *ow* has already been conjectured, or to the right of line 17, where *ew* has already been conjectured. The almost non-existent remains of what might be the upper part of a *d* at the end of line 23 might suggest *dir*, as conjectured in E. Formerly it was argued (N, F) that the fragment was in the right place and represented *osa/wosa*, 'after' (see 62.38 and note on 61v.32)—possibly spelled as *ow[sa]* or *ow[ga]*, in line with *secundum benedictionem*, 'after the blessing'. Other suggestions, such as the fragment being part of an instance of *w[orth]* (e.g. SA 60v.35) or *w[osa]* (e.g. TH 4r.26) seem unconvincing.
66v.24	**beniiicter (or bennicter):** N, B *benigicter*, H *benicter*—it is possible to read the letters after the *e* (which has the contraction for *n* or *m* above it) as either *iii* or *ni* (slight wear explaining the fact that there is one or more *i* without a surviving dot). So we have either *beniiicter* or *bennicter*. In E *benijicter* has seemed the more reasonable interpretation of *beniiicter*, on the basis of *benegicter/ benegitter* at TH 4r.9/TH 31r.15.

---

49 Nance, *Gerlyver Noweth*, p. 31, under *cryf*.

	spvrissans: 'Holy Spirit'—the *v* is inserted over what appears to have been an *i* in an original *spirissans*. (E *Spuris Sans*.)
66v.24–25	**rebo oll honor ha glory:** 'be all honour and glory'. This so-called jussive use of the subj. 3 sg, with the particle *re*, is usual in doxologies, and this phrase is found in exactly the same form at TH 16r.26.
66v.25	**in gwlas heb deweth:** 'in the eternal land', lit. in the land without end'. 'by introducing the doxology here Stephyn probably intended to bring his work to a close, only later interpolating Quotation 71, and its reference above. Nance suggests, in T, the translation 'world without end'.
66v.27	**scryfys a vea res bos a laha:** 'should be written down'? When we compare the whole phrase word by word with the Latin original, at first it appears that *supra*, 'above', is the only word in the phrase not translated. But if Stephyn's phrase means 'should be written down by this sign ✠' it is fine as it is. Pryce, borrowing from Lhuyd, gives this very expression, *skrefa alêr*, 'write down'.[50] On this analysis, *a laha* represents *alaha* (compare *a feran* for *aferan* 66r.17) which would be an attempt to spell the word later spelt *alêr*. With regard to its origin, we might be dealing with a member of the family of words that refer to place/path/way, which show variability of spelling such as: *war aga lyrth* TH 36r.6, 'behind them'; *warlerth* TH 18r.11, 'after'; *a thellar* TH 19r.3 'behind' (*a theller* in Drake).[51] It could represent a word in its own right, *alaha/alêr*, with the meaning 'down here, in place' (or just possibly be a free spelling of *holergh* itself, obliquely representing *supra* with the meaning 'behind, previously'). Because of the absence of an *r*, however, this explanation might well be felt to be unsatisfactory, in which case there are others. The word *laha* itself occurs many times throughout the Cornish texts, always for 'law', usually spelt this way, although we can discern a progression, *lagha* > *laha* > *la*. Some examples would be: 'law'—*lagha* RD 11, *laha* OM 2644, *la* TH 14r.23, 4; 'by law'—note that Tregear always uses *la*, not *laha*. Expressions include *dre lagha* PC 2383, RD 1981, *dre laha* PA 99.5, PC 1827, 'in the law'—rendered *in la* TH 20v.7. The exact words *a laha* occur in *a aswon mur a laha* PC 1457, 'who knows much about law'. We also have *erbyn alaha* PC 572, 'against the law', with the *a* here apparently representing *an*, the def. art. (A false lead is *thy laha* BK 866, an instance where *h* is written for *w* in

---

50 George, ed., *Gerlyver Meur*, 2nd edn, p. 52; 3rd edn, p. 51.
51 Cf. Pryce, *Archæologia Cornu-Britannica*, p. 248.

the common expression for 'praise him!'—*thy lawe* OM 1169.) It is possible therefore that, in SA, *a laha* means 'by law, by rights', with an extended meaning of 'applicable to' (KS). Nance conjectured something similar, giving the meaning 'by rights' (although we might have expected *dre laha* as in the examples above). A completely different suggestion (RE) that the MS reads *a latha* (and is thus related to *lathye* OM 2473, 2480, *lathys* OM 2446 and *laʒijs* PA 179.7) seems less likely.[52]

66v.28 **signma, signma** or **signna:** N, B *sign ma*, H *signma*. The possible abbreviation mark over the 'g' in *sign* is uncharacteristic (and could be an unusually extended tail of the 'g' in *gyrryow* above). Either way, the Latin *hoc signa* suggests *sign-ma*, 'this sign'.

66v.34–5 **e thesan s[.........]:** 'we [hold]?', N, B, H *e thesan s[.....]*. The completely missing section can hardly be reconstructed now, but the simplified suggestion of *eth esan sensy fast Christ herwyth e majesty*, 'we hold Christ fast according to his majesty', is employed in E: *braster* could have been used for 'majesty', but the *majesty* seems more likely. The expression *sensy fast* has a parallel in the (admittedly early) Charter Endorsement/Interlude (*sense fast indella* CE 41). Another possibility instead of *herwyth e majesty* might be *in gorrians*, 'in glory', but what remains beneath the conservation tape is almost illegible. (Nance in C conjectured *s[awyes]*, 'saved'.)

---

52 For *lathye*, 'to lay or place', see Williams, *Lexicon Cornu-Britannicum*, p. 230.

APPENDIX A

Thomas Stephyn's Contributions to TH

The patristic references made in Stephyn's hand in TH 51v–58r, mostly corresponding to references in SA (see Commentary at Quotation number (Q) given below), are listed here. In a few cases he has merely added a more specific reference to one already made by Tregear. No attempt is made to list here all the marginal biblical references he also added (probably from the Geneva Bible printed in England from 1576—see below): these will be the subject of discussion in Bruch's forthcoming edition of TH, which will also comment on Tregear's main patristic and biblical references from Bonner and Stephyn's purpose in adding further marginalia. Three passages in Cornish by Stephyn in TH are additionally referenced in this list and included in the scope of the Glossary. Note that Bruch's line numbers do not include headings and marginalia.

TH 51v.9–14m 'Oecumenius of Tricca' ['Photius'] *Commentarius in Epistolam I ad Corinthios*, on 1 Cor 11:27: Q 17

TH 51v.16–18m Tertullian *De Resurrectione [Mortuorum]* 8, 2: Q 16, 18, 20

TH 51v.18–20m Hilary *De Trinitate* 8, 13: Q 3, 21

TH 52r.11–12m Chrysostom, *Homiliae in primum ad Corinthios*, 24, 8 [not '34']: Q 14

TH 52r.15–18m Ambrose, *De Mysteriis [De Iis]*, 1, 9, 52: Q 22

TH 52r.19–22m 'Ambrose', *De Sacramentis*, 4, 4: Q 23, 24, 28, 30

TH 52r.22–23m 'Ambrose', *De Sacramentis*, 4, 5: Q 25, 26, 63

TH 52v.1–3m Eusebius 'Gallicanus' ['Emissenus'], *Collectio Homilarum*, 17, 3: Q 36

TH 52v.11–14m 'Ambrose', *De Sacramentis*, 6, 1: Q 29

TH 52v.15–16m Justin Martyr, *Apologiae*, 1, 66: Q 31, 32, 35

TH 52v.17–18m Irenaeus, *Adversus Haereses*, 5, 2, 2–3: Q 33, 34

TH 53r.1–3m Tertullian, *[Adversus] Marcionem*, 4, 40: Q 41, 42

TH 53v.17–20m Augustine of Hippo, *De Baptismo (contra Donatistas)*, 5, 8, (9): Q 48

TH 53v.20–24m ('Oecumenius' as at TH 51v.9–14m): Q 17

TH 54r.8–9m Chrysostom ['Augustine'], *Homiliae in Acta Apostolorum*, 21, 4; Q 54

TH 54r.10–14m (Chrysostom as at TH 52r.11–12m) [reference given as both Homily 24 and Homily 34]: Q 14

TH 54r.14–16m Augustine of Hippo, *Enarrationes in Psalmos*, 33, 1, 10: Q 46

TH 54r.16–17m Augustine of Hippo, *Enarrationes in Psalmos*, 98, 9: Q 43

TH 54r.24–25m, 25+ Augustine of Hippo, *Contra Faustum Manichaeum*, 20, 13: Q 44

TH 54r.26m+ (Ambrose as at TH 52r.15–18m): Q 22

TH 54r.26m+ ('Ambrose' ref. as at TH 52r.19–22m): Q 23, 24, 28, 30

TH 54v.10–17m 'Chrysostom', *Expositio in Psalmos*, 50, 1, 6: Q 6

TH 54v.11–13m Chrysostom, *Homiliae in Matthæum*, 82, 5: Q 4, 7, 13

TH 54v.18–28m Ridley in, Foxe, TAMO, 1576, p. 1398 [1373]; (T&C vi, 474): Q 40 *onyn an catholik egglos ew Vigilius, a ve diskis y^e [w]orth an Abosteleth a Christ. An Catholik egglos ew rema* ... 'one of the Catholic Church is Vigilius, who was taught by the Apostles of Christ. The Catholic church is these ...' (The list of Fathers follows.)

TH 55r.8–16m ('Ambrose' ref. as at TH 52r.19–22m): Q 23

TH 55r.17–20m Chrysostom, *Homiliae ad populum Antiocheum* 2, 26: Q 11

TH 55r.26, 27+ [28–30] Stephyn, in paraphrase of note from Geneva Bible (**not in SA**): *The Bible and Holy Scriptvres, conteyned in the Olde and Newe Testament* (Geneva: Rowland Hall, 1560), f. 7v (Gen 18:8n): [first printed in England in 1576, the first full English Bible with chapter and verse numbering] note (e) for verse 8: 'For as God gaue them bodies for a time, so he gaue them ye faculties thereof, to walke, to eat and drincke, & suche like'—*a[n] note verse 8 redewgh ... kepare a rvke Dew ry theniij ell corfow rag tyrmyn, endella Dew a ros thethan̄s an̄ vse age corfow, henna ew, the walkea, ye dibbry, ha eva, ha tacclennow erall, kepa[re]...* 'the note verse 8 read ... as God gave to the 3 angels bodies for a time, so God gave to them the use of their bodies, that is, to walk, eat, drink and other things, as ...'

TH 55v.1+ Stephyn, in paraphrase of note from Geneva Bible (**not in SA**): *The Bible and Holy Scriptvres, conteyned in the Olde and Newe Testament* (Geneva: Rowland Hall, 1560), f. 25r (Ex 3:2n) note (c) on verse 2: 'This signifieth that the Church is not consumed by ye fier of afflictions, because God is in the middes thereof'—*an note war Exodi. 3 vers. 2. kithew an Egglos ponishes grevously, whath grace Dew, ow qvetha [y^e]worth drocolath ...* 'the note on Exodus 3 verse 2. Although the Church is punished grievously, yet the grace of God [is] protecting [it] from evil [behaviour].

TH 55v:7–20m (Ambrose ref. as at TH 52v.11–14m): Q 29

TH 55v.26–32 (Augustine ref. as at TH 54r.16–17m): Q 43

TH 56r.1–3m (Chrysostom ref. as at TH 52r.11–12m): Q 14

TH 56r.4–7m (Chrysostom ref. as at TH 54r.10–14m): Q 54 (**not Q 53**)

TH 56r.14–19m (Eusebius 'Gallicanus' ref. as at TH 52v.1–3m): Q 36

TH 56r.26+ [27–29] (Justin Martyr ref. as at TH 52v.15–16m): Q 31, 32

TH 56v.1–5m ('Ambrose' ref. as at TH 52r.22–23m): Q 25

TH 57r.1–5m ('Ambrose' ref. as at TH 52r.19–22m): Q 23

TH 57r.8–9m (Justin Martyr ref. as at TH 52v.15–16): Q 31, 32

TH 57r.11–15m Cyril of Alexandria, *In Joannis Evangelium* 10, 2: Q 58

TH 57r.20–21 Chrysostom *Homiliae in Joannem*, 46, 3: Q 13

TH 57r.25+ [26–28] (Eusebius 'Gallicanus' ref. as at TH 52v.1–3m): Q 36

TH 57v.1+ (**not in SA**) Augustine of Hippo, *Sermo* 123, 5 (*on Jn 2:1–11*): [PL 38, 686]: this sermon was cited as *De Verbis Domini* 42 or 43 in older *catenae*. The final phrase *[Secundo] nomine panis spiritualem panem petimus* is not in Augustine but is found in Johannes Herolt, *Liber discipuli de eruditio christifidelium* (Reutlingen: Michael Greyff, 1481), XXI, *De Oratione Dominica*, 4, where the whole text is a much closer match for the text in TH. (Note that some later editions of this work, e.g. 1506 and 1530 do not contain the phrase.)

TH 57v.1–3m (**not in SA**) Hugh de Folieto (Fouilloi), *De Claustro Animae*, 3, 10 [PL 176, 1108D]: includes *quod est robor animae (et alimonia spiritualis)* but without the preceding *Dem sacrum Corpus Christi*.

TH 57v.11–14m (**not in SA**) 'Aquinas', quoted in *In hoc libello continentur tres tractatuli* (Cologne: Heinrich Quentell, 1490), f. 19v. This work, as its opening words suggests, contains three short treatises, named on the title page as: Aquinas's *De Mirabili Quidditate et Efficacia Venerabilis Sacramenti Eucharistie*; Nicolaus de Lyra's *De Idoneo Ministrante idem sacramentum (Dicta de Sacramento)*, and a *catena* of quotations, *De Expositione Dominice Orationis*, where the relevant passage is found.

TH 57v.14–18m (Tertullian ref. as at TH 51v.16–18m) 8, 2: Q 16, 18, 20

TH 57v.22–26m (**not in SA**) Cyprian of Carthage ['Chrysostom'] *Liber de Oratione Dominica*, 4, 18 [PL4, 531A].

TH 57v.27+ [28–30] ('Ambrose' ref. as at TH 52r.19–22m): Q 30, 63

TH 57v.27+ [31–33] Chrysostom, *Homiliae in primum Corinthios*, 24, 4: Q 45

TH 58r.1+ (Augustine ref. as at TH 54r.14–16m): Q 46

TH 58r.1–6m (Ambrose ref. as at TH 52r.15–18m): Q 22

TH 58r.11m (Augustine ref. as at TH 54r.16–17m): Q 43

TH 58r.11–13m (**not in SA**) John of Damascus, *De Fide Orthodoxa*, 4, 3 [PG 94, 1106B], also quoted in Aquinas, *Summa Theologica*, III, Q. 25, Art. 2, and cf. Foxe 1576, bk 10, 1415 [1390] where Smith alludes to another relevant passage in *De Fide Orthodoxa*, 4, 13 [PG 94, 1146A].

TH 58r.14–19m (Augustine ref. as at TH 54r.16–17m): Q 43

TH 58r.20 (Eusebius 'Gallicanus' ref. as at TH 52v.1–3m): Q 36

APPENDIX B

Images to Support Notes on 66r.1–9 and 66v.1–8

© British Library Board (BL Add. MS. 46397) reproduced with kind permission.

f. 66r.1–9, showing fragments as repositioned during conservation

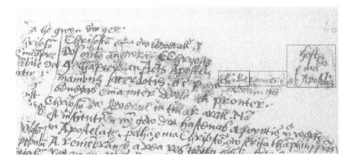

f. 66r.1–9, showing fragments in their original locations

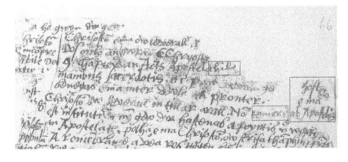

f. 66v.1–8, showing fragments as repositioned during conservation

f. 66v.1–8, showing fragments in their original locations

Glossary

This glossary aims to contain all the words found in SA, with sufficient references to enable readers to understand the range of uses. No attempt is made to reference every instance of every common word. Generally, most of these are only given citations for their first few appearances. (Words and forms from two short passages of Cornish in Thomas Stephyn's hand in TH are also included, where they do not also occur in SA: these references have TS after them—see Appendix A.)

Bold type is used for words and forms actually found in SA. Regular type is used where the radical form of an occurring mutated or conjugated word is given from another text. In most cases these forms are found in TH. (Occasionally a form from BK, BM, CW, AB or Bodewryd is cited if a form from TH is wanting, and in three exceptional cases OM and PC are given as the authority.) No purely conjectural reconstructions are included, but occasionally a conjectural radical form backed by mutated forms or other texts is included in regular type, preceded by an asterisk.

Initial mutation of words is a feature of Cornish (as of the other Celtic languages) and can pose problems when looking up words in glossaries and dictionaries. To assist the reader, mutated forms are included, with a redirection to the radical forms, under which the various instances are grouped. (With immediately adjacent potential entries such as *corf/corfow*, *decevya/decevis* it is assumed that it is sufficient to list under the radical.) Also grouped are very similar adjacent forms (e.g. *martesyn/matesyn*, 'perhaps'). Given the interchangeability of *i/j* and *v/u* at this period, both possible transcriptions are offered where this could aid understanding. (Superscript numbers to the right of words do not indicate mutations, but simply distinguish different words with the same spelling.) Where mention is made of the Notes, the section concerned will be found under the reference given immediately before, unless otherwise specified.

The gender of Cornish nouns is not always certain. I have generally followed Nance, Williams and George where they agree, without undertaking an exhaustive study for each word. Where uncertainty remains, because there is less evidence from lenition to go on, a provisional status as masculine is given. Future research may revise those judgements, although it should be remembered that the gender of words in Breton and Welsh is not necessarily a guide to that of the cognate words in Cornish, and that lenition of following adjectives—which can be helpful in identifying feminine nouns—is not always regularly observed. For these reasons even long-accepted genders can be unreliable. (The word *dorn*, 'hand', for example, is masculine in some dictionaries and feminine in others. Yet Tregear lenites it after the definite article—*an thorne vhella* TH 34r.9.)

There are multiple forms within the tenses of the verb *bos*, 'to be'—far more than commonly appreciated—and different scholars categorize them differently. Here I simply group the varieties of forms by tense/function without finer distinctions, acknowledging that readers will go to other works for more analysis.

With regard to vocabulary, there had been extensive borrowing from English into Cornish for hundreds of years when SA was written, and it felt natural to Tudor speakers of the language to continue that process, not least perhaps because the Renaissance saw many borrowings into English and Welsh. Nonetheless, it is difficult to avoid feeling that some new English borrowings, rather than being enrichments, were unnecessary—which has led some to question the fluency of Stephyn and Tregear. Certainly, reading their translations, one sometimes has the sense of a great vessel shipping water, half unknowingly, as bilingualism became the order of the day. The compromises involved (e.g. *walkias* SA 64v.33, 'walked'—and Tregear prefers the same verb—rather than *kerras* WR Gen 3:8, 'walked') perhaps show a language becoming careless about the extent and necessity of borrowing from its dominant neighbour. It may be that this later proved to be a factor in its demise: in adapting to the needs of the early modern world the written language showed such deference to English as to seem to undermine the case for its own usefulness. (Bodinar's letter, however, reminds us that the vibrancy and distinctiveness of the spoken language persisted for some while longer in its traditional strongholds.)

The question sometimes arises, therefore, as to which words in the glossary should be considered English and which were 'naturalized' as Cornish words. There is no easy answer to this, and I have not resolved the question systematically. *Sacrificed*, *entitled* seem obviously English, but *soundis* and *defendis* have Cornish endings and relate to verbal nouns also found in Tregear or elsewhere. I have generally made the decision by looking at form, frequency and occurrence in other texts, and how the words are used and adapted in both TH and SA. In addition to new coinages, the increasingly anglicized spelling of Stephyn compared with Tregear is discussed in General Notes *(English influence)*.

Such questions also have a bearing on the debate about whether there was a scribal tradition surviving in Tudor Cornish writing, or whether those concerned were just writing words as they sounded, according to English (or sometimes Latin) conventions. Some of Stephyn's spellings (including of very common words, such as *ger, kig* and *bos*) suggest complete fluidity. Others (such as *benegas, Dew* and *kemeras*) show much more consistency. Others again have both traditional and newer spellings (see *gule/gwiell, enaf/ena*). Personally, my judgement is that there is a measure of continuity with the spelling of the plays, though I realize not all will agree. One has the sense—with words such as *gos/gois* or *bos/bois*—of an awareness of a tradition, even if Stephyn is clearly changing spellings to suit new pronunciations or displaying great variety with the simplest words.

Grammatical Abbreviations

adj. adjective; **adv.** adverb; **art.** article; **comp.** comparative; **conj.** conjunction; **def.** definite; **dem.** demonstrative; **f.** feminine; **fut.** future; **imper.** imperative; **imperf.** imperfect; **indef.** indefinite; **int.** interjection; **interrog.** interrogative; **lit.** literally; **m.** masculine; **n.** noun; **neg.** negative; **num.** numeral; **part.** particle; **p. pt.** past participle; **pers.** personal; **pl.** plural; **poss.** possessive; **pron.** pronoun; **prop.** proper; **prep.** preposition; **pres.** present; **pret.** preterite (past); **rel.** relative; **sg.** singular; **subj.** subjunctive; **vb.** verb (verbal noun).

&, [see *an¹* or *ha*]

a¹, def. art. *the* 61r.19, 63r.5, 63r.36 [see *an¹*; 64r.29 could be Eng. indef. art.]

a², prep. *from, of* 59r.13, 14, 16; 59v.27; with def. art. **an** [=*a'n*] 61v.22; with poss. pron. 2 sg. **ath** [=*a'th*] 63v.36; with poss. pron. 3 sg. **ay** [=*a'y*] 61r.33, 61v.29, 63v.37

a³, verbal part., affirmative rel. pron. 59r.13, 21, 25, 26, 31, 32, 37, 39; **e** 61r.21, 64v.13; with inf. object pron. 2 pl. **agis** [=*a'gis*] 59r.12

abel/abell, adj. *able* 62v.36/59r.28

abhorria, vb. *(to) be horrified (by), abhor* 63r.4; p. pt. **abhorris** 63r.24

abolstolath, see *apostelath*

accidens, pl. *accidents* (theological term) 66v.8

achy, prep. *within, inside* 61v.35

accordyng, Eng. *according* 64r.27

Acts Apostelath, prop. n. *Acts of the Apostles* 66r.4 [see *apostelath*]

aferan, [*a feran*] m. *Mass* 66r.17

affection, Eng. *affection, (the) affections, feelings, heart* 64r.20

affirmya, vb. *(to) affirm* 59r.40

aga, poss. pron. 3 pl. *their* 66r.15; [in *th'aga*] 65v.10; **age** 62v.37, 64r.27; **a ge** 61r.29

agan, poss. pron. 1 pl. *our* 59r.35, 66r.24, 65r.17, 18 [*th'agan*]; **agen** 59r.30, 31; 60r.38, 60v.34; **agyn** 59r.18, 38; 59v.22, 63r.20; **a gyn** 66r.35; with conj. *ha*; **han** [*ha+agan*] 59r.36

age/a ge, see *aga*

agen, see *agan*

agis¹, conj. *than* 60r.4, 6, 8; 64r.24

agis², [=*a'gis*] see *a³* poss. pron. 2 pl.

agyn, [see *agan*]

alaha, [*a laha*] prep. *down* as in *write down?* 66v.27—see Notes [i.e. on 66v.27] and *laha*

alter, m. *altar* 60v.1, 63v.35, 65v.2, 22; **aulter** 61r.1

Ambros, prop. n. *Ambrose* 61v.37

Amen, int. *Amen* 61v.34, 66v.25

an¹, def. art. *the* 59r.12, 15, 20, 21, 22, 27, 28, 29, 31, 37; **a** 61r.9; **&** [=*an*] 60r.19, 60v.26, 28, 33; 64v.29; & [*a'n=a²+an¹*] 64v.32; **an** [=*a'n*] *and the*, see *ha+an¹* 61r.1, 12; 61v.22

an², [*han=h'an* and in *an vosan ny*?] see *agan*

an³, 61r.30 either *an¹* or possibly for *un*—see Notes [i.e. on 61r.30]

an not, Eng. *and not* 62v.34

anger, m. *anger* 59r.16

angwra, [=*a'n gwra*] see *gule*

anoyntis, p. pt. *anointed* 60v.30 [from vb. *anoyntya?]

ansy/an sy, ~ 3 pl. ending and pers. pron.; **illansy** 61r.29; **in an sy** [=*inans y/in ansy*] 59v.27

apostelath, m./pl. *apostolate/apostles* 64v.5, 65v.29, 66r.9; **abostolath** 64r.30; **abosteleth** TH 54v.20mTS

apperia, vb. *(to) appear* 64r.10

appoyntya, vb. *(to) institute, appoint* [TH 30v.20]; p. pt. **appoyntis** 63r.36, **apoyntis** 66r.8

ara, [=*a ra*] see *gule*

arall, adj. *another, other,* 60r.8 [or for pl.]; pl. **erall** 59r.34, 62r.18, 63r.17, 64r.34

arave, see *gule*

argumentys, pl. *arguments* 61v.25

arickell, see *artickell*

Arluth, m. *Lord* 59r.18, 30, 35; 59v.22; 60r.38, 60v.34

arr ne, see *arna*

arna/arr ne, conj. *till, until, except, unless* 66r.25/64v.35

arthelath, m. pl. *archangels* 59r.28

artickell, m. *article [of faith]* 64r.10; **arickell** 64r.8

asas, see *gasa*

ascendias, see *assendia*

ascendis, see *assendia*

assendia, vb. *(to) ascend* [TH 33v.3]; p. pt. **ascendis** 59r.18; pret. 3 sg. **ascendias** 60r.10

ath, see *a²*

Athanasius, prop. n. *Athanasius* 64r.32

Augustine, prop. n. *Augustine* 64r.33 [see *Austen*]

aulter, see *alter*

Austen, prop. n. *Augustine* 59r.3 [see *Augustine*]

a[v], [in *pe tha ve=peth a[v] ve*] where *a[v]* = pres./fut. 1 sg. of *bos* or *mos* (q.v.)

ave, [=*a³ ve*] see *bos*

avoydaya, vb. *(to) avoid* 59r.16

avyn, [*a vyn*] see *a³*, *mennas*

awaile, m. *gospel* 64r.22 [in *nawaile=i'n awaile*]

awartha/a wartha, adv. *above* 60r.5

awolas/a wolas, adv. *below* 60r.5

ay, see *a²*

badd, adj. *evil, bad* 65v.6, 7 [see Notes for *badd* v. *drog*]

bara, m. *bread* 62r.13, 15, 16, 41; 66r.27, 66v.14, 22

bedery, see *pedery*

begar, [bᵏegᵖare] = *pecar?* < *kepare* q.v.

beys, m. *world* 66r.36; **beis** 60r.19; **vys** 60r.23; **vise** 60r.40 **ves** 60v.3 see *norvys*

benega, vb. *(to) bless, sanctify, consecrate, sacrifice (liturgically)* [TH 13r.4]; p. pt. **benegys** 65v.23

benegas, adj. *holy, blessed, sacred, happy* 59r.20, 60r.6, 61r.16–17, 33; 61v.30

benijicter/beniiicter, m. *benediction, blessing* 66v.24;

[*benegicter/benegitter* TH 4r.9/TH 31r.15]
benyn, f. *woman* [TH 22v.11]; pl. **benenas** 59r.34
betraya, vb. *(to) betray* 61r.14
bew, adj. *alive* 66r.15
bewnans, m. *life* 63v.27, 63r.2, 66r.29; [*bewnans heb dewath/deweth=eternal life*]
bith, adv. *ever, whatever, any* [TH 7v.28]; **vith** 64v.35, 66r.25; **veth** 61r.38; **veith** 59r.14, 60r.4; **v[e]tholl** 66v.8 *at all*
bithquat*h*, adj. *ever* 59r.32 [from *bith, gwyeth*]
blonogath, m. *will* 60r.18
bobell, see *popell*
bois/boos, see *bos²*
bos¹, vb. *(to) be* 60v.30, 31; 66r.10; **boos** 59v.8; **vos** 59r.14, 60r.35, 61v.31; **vose** 59v.14, 64r.21; **vois** 63r.37; **[v]oes** 62v.38; **voese** 59v.15; with suff. pron. 1 sg. **vosama** 62v.34—see Gen. Notes (*bos + pers. suffixes*); 2 sg. **vosta** 63v.34—see Gen. Notes (*bos + pers. suffixes*); short pres. 1 sg. **a'** [*pe tha ve=peth o' ve?*] 63r.3?—see Notes and *mos*; 2 sg. **os** 63r.25 [*e thos=eth os*]; with suff. pron. **esta** 59r.26; 60v.6; **esta** 63r.23, 66v.10 [*e thesta=eth esta*]; 3 sg. **ew** 59r.11, 12, 14 [*ne gew=neg ew*], 18, 25; 66v.22 [*nyngew=nyng ew*]; 61r.40, 64r.20, 26 [*e thew=eth ew*]; with suff. pron. **ewa** 64r.19; **o** [*nyn go=nyng ew*] 61r.21?—see Notes; [*e tho=eth ew*] 61r.33?—see Notes]; 1 pl. **on** [*e thony=eth on ny*] 59r.27, 30; 61r.33, 65r.17; 3 pl. **yns** 59r.28 [*negyns= neg yns*]; **ens** 59v.27; **yns** 59r.28 [*neg yns*]; **ans** 62v.33 [=*fattell yns?* or =*fattel ellans?*—see Notes]; long pres. 1 sg. **esa** [*(e) thesa=eth esaf)*] 59r.16; 64r.31 [*e thesa ve*], 64v.27 [*ethesa ve*]; 3 sg. **e ma** [with *e³*] 59r.22, 59v.22; **e may** 59r.38; **yma** 60v.27; **o ma** 61r.23; **ima/i ma** 59r.3, 59v.25; 1 pl. **esan** [*e thesan (ny)*] 61r.32, 66v.34; **eran/erany** 59r.16; 63v.9 [*ne geranny=neg eran ny*]/65r.13; 3 pl. **e mouns** [*e movns*] 61r.15; with indef. subjects **us/vs** 60v.7, 61r.38 [*nyn gvs=nyng us*]; **ees** or **eis** [in *mar sees/seis=mars ees/eis*] 62v.14; with def. subjects **uge/vge** 59r.1, 19; 61r.19; **ugy/vgy** 59r.27, 40; 59v.26; 60r.18, 62v.13, 63v.25; **use/vse** 59r.29; **egy** 65v.9; **esy** [*pan dresy=pandr'esy*] 63r.7; **esee** [*ne gesee*] 59v.9; fut. 2 sg. **vethi[th]** 66v.7 [*nona navethi[..]=nona na vethi[th]?*]; 3 sg. **veth** 60v.29; impf. 3 sg. **o** 60r.3 [*e tho=eth o*]; 61r.21, 61v.32; 62v.17 [*na go=nag o*]; **ow** 64v.5—see Notes; 62r.37, 62v.15, 36 [*nyn go=nyng o*]—see Notes for 61r.21; long imperf. 3 sg. **esa** 60r.4 [*e thesa=eth esa*] 60v.3 [*ne gesa=neg esa*]; pret. 3 sg. **ve** 61r.31; 62r.23-6; 62v.17, 64r.29, 65r.21; with 3 sg. pers. pron. **vova** 63v.11, 60v.8—see Notes; subj. 3 sg. **vo** 59r.12, 13; 60.8, 20; 60r.22, 61r.21, 61v.36; **o** 62r.14? subj. 3 sg. **bo** 66v.24 used as jussive **rebo** [*re² bo*] *may (it/there) be*; 3 pl. **vons** [*vonsy=vons y*] 61r.16, 30; pluperfect (or conditional) 3 sg. **vea** 66r.10, 66v.27
bos², m. *food, meat* 61r.35; **boos** 59v.10; **bois** 63r.36, 63v.36
bostia, vb. *(to) boast* 59v.26

bug*ell*, m. *shepherd* 59r.32
bras, adj. *great* [TH 1v.5]; comp. **brassa** 65r.16; **brossa** 65r.15
brassa/brossa, see *bras*
bus, conj. *but* 60r.21, 60v.6, 7; 61v.32, 62r.38 [see also *mas*]
but, Eng. *but* [see also *bus*]

cafas, vb. *(to) have, get possess* 65r.30 [see *kafus*; TH 19r.12]; also in form **cowis* [see *cawas* CW 1219]; **gowis** 60r.20
calys, adj. *hard, difficult* [TH 53r.13, 17]; **galys** 64r.8
canevar, see *keneve[r]*
Catholik, adj. *Catholic* TH 54v.18mTS, 22mTS
causya, vb. *(to) cause* 60v.28
ceartaine, see *certyn*
certyn, adj. *certain* 60r.7; **ceartaine** 63r.4
chalys, m. *chalice* 62v.7, 63v.17, 66r.34; **chalis** 63r.20
changia/changya, vb. *(to) change* 62r.27, 35/62v.16
chapter, m. *chapter* 59r.4, 62v.19; **chpter** 61v.37
chieffly, Eng. *chiefly* 66v.17 [*chyfly* TH 43r.26]
chpter, see *chapter*
Chrisostom, prop. n. *[John] Chrysostom* 59r.40, 60r.12, 64r.33; **Chrisostome** 59r.22
Christ, prop. n. *Christ* 59r.21, 31, 35; 60r.22, 60v.34; **Crist** 59r.1
clowas, vb. *(to) hear, perceive* 62r.35; p. pt. **clowis** 59r.13; pres./fut. 3 sg. **glow**
clowis, see *clowas*
colan, f. *heart* 65v.21; **golan** 61v.36; **holan** 64v.3
coeth, see *coth*

common, adj. *common* 63v.9 [cf. *commyn* TH 57v.3, 16]
commondya, vb. *(to) command* [TH 1r.13]; pret. 3 sg. **commandias** 61v.23, 62r.24–6; [cf. *recommaundias* Bodewryd 93]
communication, m. *communion, communication* 65r.13
comptis, see *contya*
contya vb. *(to) count* [TH 23r.25]; p. pt. **comptis** 59r.14
concernya, vb. *(to) touch (on), concern* 61r.37
confessia, vb. *(to) profess, confess* 61v.35
confirmia, vb. *(to) confirm* 63v.17; **confirnia** or **confirma** 62r.16—see Notes
conjunction, [*coniunction*] Eng. *conjunction* 65r.16
consecration, Eng. *consecration* 61v.32, 62r.16, 63r.20
consecratis, p. pt. *consecrated* 60v.30, 62r.38, 42; 63v.11 [from vb. **consecratya?*]
consydra, vb. *(to) consider* [TH 21r.17]; p. pt. **consideris** 64r.21
conys, see *gonis*
corf, m. *body* 59r.22; 60r.38; **gorf** 59r.36, 38; **gorfe** 59r.39; **corff** 62v.4; pl. **corfow** 63v.18, 21
corporally, Eng. *corporally* 66r.20
cosrf, [=*corf*, q.v.] 63r.19
coth, adj. *old* 59v.26; **coeth** 64r.34
cothman, m. *friend* [TH 21v.16]; pl. **hvnthmans** 66r.15
covyn, see *govyn*
cows/cowse, vb. *(to) speak* 61v.35/62r.35, 65v.8; [as a noun **cowse** *speech, entreaty, mention* 66r.25]; pret. 3 sg. **cowsas** 61v.23;

GLOSSARY 303

causis 62r.35; **gowsys** 61r.34;
  p. pt. **cowsis** 62r.14; **cowsys** 62v.8
creature, Eng. *creature* 62r.26, 63v.17
creatya, vb. (to) create [TH 1r.25];
  p. pt. **creatis** 61v.24, 62r.36
crefder, m. *strength* 62r.27
creffe, vb. *(to) strengthen, increase*
  63r.21
cregy, vb. *(to) believe* 59r.17, 65v.21;
  imper. 2 sg. **crig ge** 66v.10
cressya, vb. *(to) increase* 63r.18
criggyans, m. *belief, faith* 60v.27
Crist, see *Christ*
cruelte, m. *cruelty* 65v.14 [cf.
  crowwelder Bodewryd 67]
crug/crvg, see *gule*
crya, vb. *(to) cry (out)* [TH 9v.1]; pret.
  3 sg. **cryas** 61v.30
cryas, see *crya*
cucell, f. *council, counsel* 65v.26;
  kvsell, 65v.16; [*cusel da* BM 3297]
C[yr]ill, prop. n. *Cyril* 64r.32

da[1], adj. *good* 60r.18, 60v.27, 61r.40,
  63v.36, 65v.21
da[2], see *inta*
dall, see *dell*
dallath, m. *beginning* 63v.29
dan, prep. *under* 61r.32
davas, m. *sheep* [TH 23r.15]; pl. **devas**
  [TH 9r.5]; **thevas** 59r.33
dclarya, see *declarya*
dean/deane, see *den*
debbry, see *dibbry*
decevya, vb. *(to) deceive* [TH 46v.14];
  p. pt. **decevis** 59v.27
declarya, [**dclarya**] vb. *(to) declare*
  [TH 1r.26] 59r.32
defendya, vb. *(to) defend* [TH 25r.4];
  p. pt. **defendis** 60v.31
degy, vb. *(to) carry* [PC 2313]; p. pt.
  degys 65r.21

dell, conj. *as* 59r.40; **del** 59r.2; **dall**
  61r.19; [both *kepare dell* and *kepare
  a* before verbs in SA]
demandea, vb. *(to) demand* 64r.7
den, m. *man, human being* 59r.14;
  60r.20, 60v.26; **dean** 60r.6; **deane**
  60v.13, 61r.19, 21; supp. pl. **tvs/
  tus** 66r.3; **tuse** 60r.19
den veith, *no man, no one, any man*
  59r.14, 59v.24
denaha, vb. *(to) deny* 66r.14
dene, see *den* and *mab den*
dens, pl. *teeth* 60r.24
deow, num. *two* 60r.4
Deow Habblys, m. *Maundy Thursday,*
  [by extension *The Last Supper*]
  66r.25; [=*De (Y)ow Habblys*; cf.
  deyow hablys PA 41.5]
departia, vb. *(to) depart* [TH 50v.12];
  pret. 3 sg. **departias** 62v.38
der, see *dir*
derag, prep. *before, in front of, in the
  presence of* 60v.26 [see *derag dorn*];
  with poss. pron. 1 pl. **deragan**
  60r.40; **deragen** 60v.3, 65v.20
derag dorn, adv. *beforehand* 61v.25,
  62r.28; **derag dorne** 62v.15–16, 17
deragan/deragen, see *derag*
derevall, vb. *(to) raise, lift up* 65v.20
deserya, vb. *(to) desire, long for* 64v.12
desyre, m. *desire, longing* [TH 2v.17];
  thesyre 64v.3—see Notes, 64v.11
desyrius, adj. *desirous, willing* 60r.20
despisea, vb. *(to) despise* 59r.19;
  possibly [*desp*]*ysya* at 65v.6?
desquethas, see *disquethas*
deth, m. *day* 60r.23
devethis, see *dos*
devotion, Eng. *devotion* 64r.28, 66r.15
Dew, m. *God* 59r.17, 31; 60v.13,
  60v.26, 35; 62r.1, 65v.6, 7, 10, 14,

16, 22; **Thew** 59r.16, 60r.18, 39; 65v.24

dewas, m. *drink* 61r.35, 36; 63v.9, 65v.20; **thewas** 59v.11

deweth, m. *end, limit* 66v.25; **dewath** 63r.3, 63v.27, 66r.29

dewetha, adj. *last* 59r.2, 12

dewys, vb. *(to) choose* 64r.8

dibbris, see *dibbry*

dibbry, vb. *(to) eat* 64v.3; 61r.35, 64v.3, **debbry** [<dibbry] 66r.28; **tibbry** 60v.33, 61r.23; **tybbry** 64v.35, 65v.9; **thibbry** 60v.7; **thybbry** 64v.11, 66v.16; p. pt. **dibbris** 61r.2; **dibbrys** 62v.38; imper. 2 pl. **debbrog[h]** 62v.3

dir, prep. *through, by means of* 60r.21, 60v.27, 61r.33, 39; 62r.16, 17; **der** 59v.17

dirr, conj. *while* 60v.27

*****discipel** m. *disciple* [*desgibl* AB 55a]; pl. **discipels** 62v.36, 64v.13

dishonora, vb. *(to) dishonour* 61r.16

discrigians, m. *unbelief* [TH 57r.22]; **thiscrygians** 66v.7

disquethas, vb. *(to) show* 60r.7, 35; **desquethas** 60v.3; **tisquethas** 61r.13, 21; p. pt. **disquethis** 60r.18, 63r.35; pret. 3 sg. **thisquethas** 65v.14

distributia, vb. *(to) distribute, share out* 64v.13

distuny/distvny, m. *testimony* 61r.39

dochya, see *touchia*

doctor, m. *Doctor of the Church, Father* [TH 40r.1]; pl. **doctors** 66r.24

dore, m. *earth, ground* 64v.31 [see *nore*]; **thore** 64v.31

dorn, f. [*an thorne* TH 34r.9] *hand* 61r.25; **dorne** 62v.16 [see *derag dorn*]

dos, vb. *(to) come* 59r.20, 62r.43; **tos** 59r.29, **tose** 66r.23; pres./fut. 1 sg. contracted with suff. pron. **tema** 60r.7—see Notes; 2pl. **tewhy** 64r.7—see Notes; subj. pres./fut. 3 sg. **theffa** 59r.15, 61r.35; 1 pl. **theffan** 66r.27; 3 pl. **theffe[*ns y*]** 66r.25; p. pt. **devethis** 60r.21, 62r.14, 20 **davethis** 63v.35

dowt, m. *doubt* [TH 52v.24]; pl. **doubtys** 61r.39

doutya, *(to) doubt* [BK 1669; *dowtya* TH 9v.7]; pres./fut. 3 sg. **dout** 59v.23

dowla, dual *hands* 60r.19, 60v.32, 66r.6; [cf. *dule* BK 2991, 3035 = **deow**+*luff* BK 4431]; **thowla** 65r.21

dowlas, see *tewlell*

dowr, m. *water* 62v.8, 63r.20

drevynnough, [in *pandre vynnough*] see *pandra, mennas*

dresy, [in *pan dresy=pandra+esy* see *pandra, bos*]

drocolath, f. *evil, evil behaviour* TH 55v.1+TS

druge/drvge, [in *pan drvge=pandra+uge* see *pandra, bos*]

dry, vb. *(to) bring* 59v.15; pres./fut. 3 sg. **thro** 65r.19

dysky, vb. *(to) teach, learn* [TH 8v.23]; p. pt. **diskys** 63r.26, 64r.29; **diskis** TH 54v.20mTS; pret. 3 sg. **thoskas** 63r.19

e ma/e may, see *e³/eth, bos*

e tho/e thony, see *e³/eth, bos*

e¹, [=*y*] poss. pron. 3 sg. m. *his, its* 59r.13, 15, 32, 33, 34, 36, 37, 38, 39; y 59r.3, 4, 19

e², see *hy¹*

e³/eth, [=*y³/yth*] affirmative & rel. part. 59r.22, 38; 59v.10/59r.27,

60r.3, 4 [see *bos*]; **o** 61r.23; **yth** 59r.30 [*y thony=yth on ny*] 62r.2 [*y thew=yth ew*]

e⁴, sometimes for *in* q.v., see also *y weth/e weth, e ker, e mes*]

e⁵, sometimes for *a³*, q.v.

e⁶, sometimes for *ef*, q.v.

e ker, adv. *away* 65v.22; [cf. *in kerth* TH 6v.24]

e mes, adv. *out, out of, from* 65v.25; [cf. *in mes* TH 2r.5]

eaisy, adj. *easy* 64v.9 [or possibly for Eng. *easily*, as in Foxe]

ef, pers. pron. 3 sg. *he, him* 59r.14, 20, 21, 32, 35, 39; **effe** 59r.37; **hef** 60r.10; **eff** 60r.23, 64v.27; **e** 60r.3, 59v.9?

efelap/[h]efelap, [*efvelap*] < *evelap*, m. *likeness, resemblance* 66v.17 [see Notes and *hevelep* BM 2150, TH 1v.1]

eff/effe, see *ef*

egglos/egglys, f. *church* 64r.7, 29, 31; 64v.7/59v.27

ell, m. *angel* TH 55r.28TS, pl. **elath** 59r.28

elyment, m. *element* 66v.15

Elias, prop. n. *Elijah* 60r.6, **Helias** 60r.4

Eliseus, prop. n. *Elisha* 60r.2

ema¹/e ma, see *bos*

ema², [*ᵉma*] see *umma*

Emisene, prop. n. *Emissenus* 64r.32 [for Eusebius 'Gallicanus', not of Emesa]

en[a], adv. *there* 62v.8

enaf/enaff, m. *soul* 60v.27, 61r.24/60v.9; **ena** 60v.26, 28; [*an nenaf = an¹ enaf*] 60v.29, 30, 31, 32, 35; pl. **enevow** [*an nenevow = an¹ enevow*] 66r.14; pl. **enewow** 66r.16

endella, see *indella*

endewis, p. pt. *endued, filled* 60r.8 [from **endewya*?]

ens, see *bos*

entituled, Eng. *entitled*

entra, vb. *(to) enter* 59v.24

Epiphanius, prop. n. *Epiphanius* 64r.33

erall, see *arall*

eran/erany, see *bos*

errow, see *ger*

esta, see *bos*

esyn, see *gasa—na esyn=let us not* 61v.25, 65v.19 [see Notes at 65v.19–20]

eth, see *e³/eth*

ethesa, [*=eth esa'*] see *bos*

Ethewan, pl. *Jews* 61r.14, 17 [*an nethewan=an Ethewan*; cf. *ȝethov* sg. BM 3535]

Eusebius, prop. n. *Eusebius* 64r.32

Eucharistia, term quoted as Greek for *thanksgiving, eucharist* 63v.30

eva, vb. *(to) drink* 60v.34, 61r.36, 63r.23; p. pt. **evys** 62v.38

ew/ewa, see *bos*

eweth/e weth, see *y weth*

exampill, m. *example* [TH 6v.25]; pl. **exampels** 61v.26

excellent, Eng. *excellent*

expoundyng, Eng. *expounding*

faith, f. *faith* 59v.16, 26; 61r.40, 63v.36, 66v.34

faithfully, Eng. *faithfully* 65v.21

fattell/fatla, interrog. adv. *how* 62v.33/59r.16, 26, 59v.26, 62r.16, 62v.13, 65v.21

fattellans, [=*fattell ellans* or *fattell ans*] see Notes on 62v.33 and *gallas, bos*

feran, see *aferan*

figur, m. *figure, symbol* 65v.29; **figure** 66v.22
flehis, see *flogh*
flogh, m. or f. *child* 59r.37; pl. **flehis** 59r.34
folen, m. *page, sheet* 63v.29
Fulgentius, prop. n. *Fulgentius* 64r.33

gallas, vb. *(to) be able* [BK 1393]; pres./fut. 3 sg. **ill** 60v.5, 61v.24, 62v.9, 63v.26; **yll** 64v.9; 1 pl. **illen** 66r.14; 3 pl. **illans** [*illansy=illans y²/ill ansy*] 61r.29; **ellans** 62v.33; subj. pres./fut. 3 sg. **halla** 60v.30, 31, 34; **malla** [=*may halla*] 60v.32, 61r.24, 65r.15
gallus, m. *power, might, ability* 59r.31, 62v.13, 14, 16; 63r.7, 64r.19
galys, see *calys*
ganow, m. *mouth* 59r.39, 59v.18, 21, 22; 61v.35; **ganaw** 61r.2, 18; [cf. *ganaw* Bodewryd 11]
gans, prep. *with, by* 59r.27, 30, 33, 36, 37, 38, 39; with pers. pron. 2 sg. **genas** 63r.2, 60v.9; 3 sg. m. **gansa** 59r.14, 60r.11; 1 pl. **genan** 59v.10; 2 pl. **genogh** 64v.4
gasa, vb. *(to) let, leave* [TH 19r.2]; imper. 2 sg. **gas** 59r.25, 61v.34, 36; 66v.7; 1 pl. **gesen** 62r.16; neg. **esyn** [*na esyn*] 61v.25, 65v.19—see Notes; pret. 3 sg. **asas** 60r.9, **a sas** 60r.10—see Notes; p. pt. **gesis** 61r.38
ge, [in *a ge*] see *age*
ge/gee, suff. pron. 2 sg. *you* 63r.2, 66r.5/62r.37, 38 [see *te*]
geer, see *ger*
geir/geyr, see *ger*
gela, see *the gela*
gemeras, see *kemeras*
gen, see *thagen* [*the+agan*]

genas, see *gans*
*****genegegath,** f. *birth, nativity* [=*genesegeth* TH 6v.21, following *geneges*]; **enegegath** [*ha e negegath=ha'e enegegath*] 61v.26
genis/genys, adj. *born* 61v.27/61r.31
genogh, see *gans*
ger, m. *word* 61v.23; **geer** 61v.36; **gere** 62r.27; **gear** 61v.24; **geir** 62r.20, 23, 35; **geyr** 62v.35, 66r.26; pl. **gerryow** 59r.17; **girryow** 61v.31; **gyrriow** 64r.1; **gyrryow** 59r.12, 15; **gyrreow** 61r.3; **girreow** 62r.1, 13, 42; 62v.7; **girrew** 63r.27; **errow** 59r.20; **irrow** 59v.19
geran/geranny, [*ne geran/ne geranny=neg eran/neg eran ny*; see *ne, bos*]
gere, see *ger*
gerryow, see *ger*
gesa, [=*neg esa*; see *ne, bos*]
gesee, [=*neg esee*; see *ne, bos*]
gesen, see *gasa*
gesis, see *gasa*
gew, [in *nyn gew, ne gew*; see *ne, bos*]
gifte, m. *gift* 63v.26 [Tregear uses *gyftes* TH 2v.8 as well as *royow* TH 4v.4]
gilty, m. *guilty* 61r.12
gilwis, see *gylwall*
glanhe, vb. *(to) wash, clean* [TH 8r.22]; p. pt. **glanhis** 60v.29
glory, m. *glory* 66v.25
glow, see *clowas*
glwlas, see *gwlas*
go, [in *nyn go*; see *ne, bos*]
gobe[r], m. *reward, pay, wages* 61r.29
gois, see *gos*
golan, see *colan*
golhe, vb. *(to) wash* 60v.9; p. pt. **gulhis** 60v.29

golosake, adj. *mighty, powerful, Almighty* 60v.35

golowder, m. *brightness, glory* 59r.29

*****golowy,** vb. *(to) illuminate* [*ov colowhy* BM 3614]; p. pt. **golowis** 60v.3

gonis, vb. *(to) work, labour* 63r.17; **gonys** 62v.16, 63r.18; **conis** 62r.27; **conys** 62v.14, 63r.25

gorf/gorfe, see *corf*

gora, vb. *to put, place* [TH 46v.4]; pres./fut. 3 sg. **wore** 59r.34; pret. 3 sg. **woras** 60r.11; p. pt. **goris** 61v.28, 63r.20

gos, m. *blood* 60r.25, 61r.20, 59r.39 [altered to **go°s** or **go°ˢs**?]; **gose** 60v.34; **gois** 61r.35, 38, 41; 63r.21-4; **woos** 59v.12

gosough, see *golsowes*

go[l]sowes vb. *(to) listen* [TH 33v.8]; imper. 2 pl. **gosough** 63r.7; **gosoweth** 62v.18—see Notes; **gosowhog** 65r.6

gothvas, vb. *(to) know* [TH 20r.16]; pres./fut. 3 sg. **wor** 60r.5

govyn vb. *(to) ask* [TH 24v.12]; **covyn** 64v.27

gow, m. *lie, falsehood* 59r.14

gowis, see *cafas*

gras[ce], m. *grace, gratitude, thanks* 63v.30—see Notes; **ras** 60v.36; **grace** 63r.5, 7, TH 55v.1+TS

grond, m. *ground, earth* 64v.28

Grecians, see *Grekys*

Grekys, pl. *Greeks* 63v.30 [corrected from *Grecians*]

grevously, Eng. *grievously* TH 55v.1+TS

gule/gvle, vb. *(to) do* 59v.15; **gwyell** 61r.20; **gwiell** 61r.30, 62r.20; **gwiel** 62v.15; **gwell** 59r.35; **gweill** 62r.29; pres./fut. 1 sg. **rav** 59r.25; 3 sg. **gwra** 62r.35, 65v.3 [*a'n gwra*, with infixed pron. 3 sg]; **ra** 59r.37, 62r.21, 60v.11 [*ara*]; 1 pl. **wrene** 59r.16; imper. 2 sg. **gwra** 60v.9; 63v.34, 37; 2 pl. **gwregh** 64v.15; pret. 3 sg. **rug** 59r.1, 60r.2; **ruge** 59r.21, 32; 62r.42 **rugg** 59v.24; **wruck** 60v.10; **ruk** 61r.17, 64v.13; **ruke** 64r.7; **crug** [*crvg*] 63r.17; contracted with pers. pron. 3 sg. **ruga** 62v.37; subj. 2 sg. **whrella** 61v.35; p. pt. **gwrys** 62v.9, 64r.26; **gwris** 61v.23, 62r.17, 64v.1; **gwryes** 63r.20; **gwres** 59r.30, 62r.15; **gwreis** 62r.23-6, 34-6

gule honora *(to) honour*; imper. 2 sg. **gwra honora** 64r.2; 2 pl. **gwregh honora** 64v.15

gule marugian *(to) marvel* [cf. *gull marthussyan* TH 38v.21]; imper. 2 sg. **gwra marvgian** 63v.34, 37

gurryby, vb. *(to) answer* [TH 44r.1]; **orybe** 62r.37; pres./fut. 3 sg. **worryb**

gus/gvs, [in *nyng us*; see *ne, bos*]

gulhis, see *golhe*

gvle, see *gule*

gwa[n], adj. *weak* 66v.15

gweill, see *gule*

gwelas, vb. *(to) see* 59r.19, 28; **welas** 59r.29; **quelas** 60v.6; pres./fut 3 sg. **wele** 62r.27; **welle** 62v.13; pret. 3 sg. **welas** 66r.23; subj. 3 sg. **whelha** 60r.22; p. pt. **gwelis** 63r.22; **gwelys** 60r.23

gwell, see *gule*

gwely, m. *bed* 59r.13 [altered from originally lenited *wely*]

gweranath, see *gwryonath*

gwetha, vb. *(to) keep* 59r.19; **quetha** TH 55v.1+TS

gwethfas f. widow [TH 40v.13];
    wethvas 64r.23
gwiel/gwiell, see *gule*
gwlas, m. *land* 60r.11, 39; 66v.25;
    glwlas 60v.2
gwlas neff, m. *heaven, the kingdom of heaven* 60r.11, 39
*Gworthias f. *Virgin* [guerheys BK 3836]; Worthias 59r.22, 61r.31, 61v.27
gwra, see *gule, marugian*
Gwrerer, m. *Creator* 61r.22
gwres/gwreis, see *gule*
gwris/gwryes, see *gule*
gwyer, adj. *true* 62v.33, 34
gwyn/gwyne, m. *wine* 62r.1, 62v.1, 63r.20/65r.5
gwryonath, m. *truth, reality* 60r.3, 61v.34; gweranath 61r.37
gwyeth, f. *occasion, time* 61r.19
gwyrryan, adj. *just, righteous* 60r.6; gwyrrian 60r.20
gylwall, vb. *(to) call* 65r.15; kelwall 63v.30; p. pt. gilwis 64r.29
gyn, see *agan*
gyrreow/gyrriow/gyrryow, see *ger*

ha, conj. *and* 59r.13, 17, 18, 19, 20, 26, 28; & 64r.27 [or Eng. *and*]; with def. art. han 60r.12, 61r.20, 63r.19, 20 [and 59r.18? or Eng *and*]; with possess. adj. 3 sg. hay 59r.38, hae 60v.35, 61r.16; 1 pl. hagen 63r.34; NB hef 60r.10—either [*ha+ef*] or [*ef*] q.v., with Notes on 60r.10
hae, [=*ha'e*; see *ha, e¹*]
hagen, [=*ha'gan*; see *ha, agan*]
haker, adj. *foul, ugly* 60v.25
halla, see *gallas*
han, [=*ha'gan*? see *agan*] 59r.18, 36
han, [=*ha'n* with def. art.; see *ha*] 60r.12, 61r.20, 62r.25, 62v.1

han, [=*ha'n* with infixed pronoun; see Notes on 61v.33
hastenab, m. *rashness, haste* 66r.8
hay, [=*ha'y*; see *ha, e¹*]
heare, m. *heir* 59r.15
heb/hebb, prep. *without* 59r.29 [*hebb*], 63r.3, 63v.27, 66r.29
hef, see *ha, ef*
hefelap, see *efelap*
Helias, see *Elias*
helma, see *hemma*
hem, see *hemma*
hemma, dem. pron. *this* 59r.12, 64v.14; helma 60r.8; hem 62v.4
hen, see *henna*
henna, dem. pron. *that* 59r.25; 59v.7, 10; 60r.2, 34; 61r.33; hen 59r.11
henwis, see *hynwall*
hewwall, adj. *high, exalted* 65v.24; [*vhell* TH 11r.6; *uhall* BK 2371]
Hierom, prop. n. *Jerome* 64r.33
holan, see *colan*
homeli, m. *homily* 59v.13; homili 59v.18; homele 60r.25
honor/honour, m. *honour* 66v.25/59r.32, 59v.21
honora, vb. *(to) honour* 59r.26, 64v.31, 65r.5; p. pt. honoris 60r.36
honyn, m. *self* 59r.33, 36, 37; 61r.22; e honyn 61v.30 *himself*
host, m. *(eucharistic) host, victim* 66r.5
hvnthmans, see **cothman*
hy¹, pers. pron. 3 sg. f. *she, her* 64r.24; e 59r.37
hy², [=*y*] see *y²*
hynwall, vb. *(to) name* [TH 29r.3]; p. pt. hynwis 61v.33; hynvis 61v.32; henwis 66v.6;

Iesus/Iesu, see *Jesus/Iesus*
ill/illansy/illen, see *gallas*
ima, see *bos*

imban, adv. *up, upward* 63v.35
in, prep. *in* 59r.3, 4, 13; 60r.18,19;
  e 60r.3 [see also in *e weth*];
  with pers. pron. 1 sg. **innaff ve**
  61r.36-7; 3 pl. **in an sy** [*inans y/
  in ansy*] 59v.27; **in,** [=*i'n; in+an¹*]
  60r.40, 60v.3, 66r.10; **in grows**
  [=*i'n grows*] 61v.28 *on the Cross*
in an sy, see *in*
in ded, Eng. *indeed* 60r.9, 63r.6
in very deed, Eng. *in truth, in reality*
  [but see *very*]
*****inclithias**, vb. *(to) bury* [*anclethias*
  BM 1323; *anclithias* CW 2080];
  p. pt. **inclithis** 61v.29
indella/in della, adv. *so, likewise,
  similarly* 59r.35, 59v.9, 60r.38
  indelma 61r.13; **in delma** 61v.38;
  endella TH 55r.29TS
inheritance, Eng. *inheritance*
innaff, see *in*
insted/in sted, Eng. *instead [of]*
  59v.10, 11
inta, adv. *well* 59r.26, 60r.5; **da** [used
  adverbially] 61v.35, 36
inter/intyr, prep. *between, among*
  65r.21, 66r.6/60r.19; with pers.
  pron. 3 pl. **intrethans** [*in trethans*]
  65r.16
Irenae/Irenaeus, prop. n. *Irenaeus*
  64r.32/63v.21

Judas/Iudas, prop. n. *Judas* 61r.13
ith, see *e³/eth*
Iudas, see *Judas*
iudgia, see *judgia*
Ivnyas/Ivnys, see **junya*
Iustin/Iustine, see *Justin*
Jesus/Iesus, prop. n. *Jesus* 60v.8, 34,
  36; 61v.1, 26, 30; *Jesu/Iesu* 66v.18
Judas/Iudas, prop. n. *Judas* 61r.13,
  65v.11, 15

judgia/iudgia, vb. *(to) judge* 59r.20
*****junya/*iunya** vb. *(to) join* [*dzhunia*
  AB 74b]; pret. 3 sg. **junyas** [*Ivnyas*]
  59r.36; p. pt. **junys** [*Ivnys*] 60v.28,
  63r.19, 65r.17
Justin/Iustin, prop. n. *Justin* 63r.27;
  Iustine 64r.31

kee, see *mos*
kegg, see *kig*
keith, see *keth*
*****kela**, m. *companion, mate* [cf. BK *the
  gela* 1199] only in the phrase **the
  gela** 66v.15 [=*th'e¹ gela*] *to another,
  to its mate*
kelwall, see *gylwall*
kemeras, vb. *(to) take, receive*
  59r.21-2; 63v.9, 66v.16; pres./fut. 3
  sg. **gemar** [*agemar*] 59v.8; imper. 2
  sg. **kemer** 63v.36; 2 pl. **kemerogh**
  62v.3; pret. 3 sg. **kemeras** 64v.31,
  65v.22; **gemeras** 61r.31, 64v.12
keneve[r], adj. *whoever, as many, all
  (those)* 60r.21 **canevar** 60r.20
kepar, see *kepare*
kepare, conj. *as* 59r.2, 37, 60r.3;
  65r.16 **pecar** 61r.17; ~~begar~~
  >**kepare** 59r.37; **kepare ha** 60r.36;
  65v.5 **kepar a** 61r.14, 27; 63r.3;
  kepare dell 64v.9; **kepar dell**
  60v.10; **kepar del** 62v.17;
ker, see *e ker*
keth, adj. *same* 59r.15, 59v.28; 61r.3,
  62r.13, 29; 64v.8 **keith** 59r.21,
  63r.17
kethsam, adj. *same, selfsame* 59r.27,
  64v.34
keveris, adv. *also, likewise* 60v.12
  [*keveris Dew ha deane*=both God and
  man]
kig/kigg, m. *flesh* 60r.10,
  61r.36/59r.30, 61r.31; **kigge**

59r.21; **kyg** 61r.34, 41; **kygg** 66v.16; **kegg** 59v.11;
kith, [*kithew=kith ew*]
kref[f], adj. *raw* 66v.16
kusell/kvsell, see *cucell*
kyn, adj. *other, different, another* 61v.32
kyn, [TH 40v.6] conj. *though, although*; before vowels **kith** TH 55v.1+TS [where *kithew=kith ew*, see TH 14r.1 *kynthew*]
kynde, m. *kind, form, nature* [TH 2r.25]; pl. **kyndes** 62v.36
kyns, prep. *before* 61v.31, 62r.13, 37, 41; 62v.7
ky[n]s[a], adj. *first* 62v.34

laha, f. *law, right* 66v.27? *a laha* = *by rights?* [but see *alaha* and Notes on 66v.27. NB Tregear has *la* rather than *laha* for 'law': *an la a nature* TH 14r.23]
lavar/laver/lavirta, [(l)*avirta*] see *leverall*
leath, m. *milk* 59r.38
lell, adj. *true, proper* 60r.3, 61r.32, 61v.27
lemmyn, adv. *now* 60v.3; **lemmen** 62r.26; **lymmyn** 61r.18, 39; **lymmen** 62r.39
len[wis], p. pt. *filled* 62v.7 [*lynwys* TH 33r.20; **lynwall* is only found as *colynwall* in TH
lever, m. *book* 59r.3, 61v.37, 62v.19, 63v.29
leverall, vb. *(to) say, tell* 59r.3, 11, 23, 25 **levera[l]** 59v.13; **levera** 63v.22; pres./fut. 2 sg. **[l]avirta ge** 66r.5; 3 sg. **lavar** 59r.14, 31; 62v.33; **laver** 62r.38, 64v.11; pret. 3 sg. **leveris** 62v.35, 63r.2, 64v.13, 65v.30; p. pt. **leveris** 61v.32, 62r.18, 62v.7

lowar[th], [=*lowar*] adj. *many, much* 59r.33, 59v.26, 64r.34; **lowar[th] gwyeth** 61r.19 *often*
lowr, adj. *enough* 59v.13
lymmen/lymmyn, see *lemmyn*

ma^1, [= -*ma*] dem. pron. (suff.) *this* 59r.15, 61r.3, 62r.13m 64r.30
ma^2, pers. pron. (suff.) *I, me* 62v.33 [*vosama*]
ma^3, in *e^3 ma*; see *bos*
mab, m. *son* 59r.17; **vab** 60v.36
mab den, m. *mankind, man, human* 60v.26; **mab dene** 59v.14; **mab deane** 60v.27
Mab Dew, m. *Son of God* 59r.17, 60r.10
Mab Ras, m. *Beloved Son* 60v.36 [lit. *Son of Grace*]
maga^1, vb. *(to) feed, nourish* 59r.33, 37, 38; **vaga** 59r.34; pret. 3 sg. **magas** 59r.36; p. pt. **megis** 63v.27, 35; **megys** 59r.27, 61r.24; **mekys** 60v.35
maga^2, conj. *as, so* 60r.6, 61r.19
magape[ll] dell, conj. *in so far as, in as much as, whereas* 64r.18–19; **magapell dall** 61r.19 [see *maga^2, pell, dell*]
malla, see *gallas*
mam, f. *mother* 59r.37, 59v.8; **mamb** 59r.34; **vam** 59v.27, 64r.31, 66r.17
mamb, see *mam*
mammath, f. *nursing mother, wet-nurse,* 59v.8
maner, f. *way, manner* 65v.7
mantall, f. *mantle, cloak* 60r.2, 9
mar^1, conj. *if* 60r.7; 63r.17, 64r.7; before vowels **mars** 62v.14
mar^2, adv. *so, as, such a* 62v.14, 64r.8
mar sees/seis, [=*mars ees*; see *mar^1, bos*]

markell, m. *miracle* 60r.18
marnance, see *myrnans*
marow, adj. *dead* 61v.28, 66r.11
martesyn, adv. *perhaps* 62v.32; **matesyn** 63r.21
martyr, m. *martyr* 64r.29
Marya, prop. n. *Mary* 59r.22, 64v.33; **Maria** 61r.32, 61v.27
marugian/marvgian, pl. marvels, wonders 63v.34 [see *gule marugian*]
mas, conj. *but* 59r.35; 60v.4; 61r.21, 63r.6, 66v.22; **mase** 60v.26 [see also *bus*]
master, m. *master* 60v.5
mater, m. *matter, enterprise* 65r.16
may, conj. *so that* 60v.30
may, [in *e may*; see *bos*]
me, pers. pron. 1 sg. *I, me* 59r.12, 60r.4, 61r.37, 64v.11, 65r.19
megis/megys/mekys, see *maga¹*
members, Eng. *limbs, members* 59r.33
mennas, vb. *(to) will* [*mennas* PC 378; *the vynnas* TH 34v.1]; pres./fut. 3 sg. **vyn** 63r.21, 59r.20 [*avyn*]; 2 pl. **vynnough** 60r.7; pret. 3 sg. **vennas** 59r.35
mention, Eng. *mention*
menya, vb. *(to) mean* 64r.31
mer, adj. *great, much* 63r.18; **meer** 60r.3; **myᵉr** 64v.10 [*myr>mer* or *myer*]; **ver** 62v.14; comp. **moy** 60r.4, 8; 62v.16; superl. **moygha** 60r.36, 60v.7; **moigha** 60r.37; **mere a** [*=mer+a²*] adj. *much, many* 59r.29; **myᵉr a** [*myr a >mer a* or *myer a*] 64v.10; **mer voy/mere moy** *much more, much greater* 63r.18/60r.8
meras, vb. *(to) look, observe, behold* 65v.20
mere a/moy/voy, see *mer*

merwell, vb. *(to) die* [TH 3v.7]; **verwall** 59r.13
meternath, see *mytearne*
met, adj. *meet, suitable, fitting* 64v.12
meth, f. *shame* 59v.8
*****mithas**, vb. *(to) speak, say* [cf. *methes* OM 159]; pres./fut. 3 sg. **mith** 64v.27
mittes, pl. *mites, small coins* 64r.23
Monaca, prop. n. *Monica* 66r.17
more, m. *sea* 62r.25
mos, vb. *(to) go* 59v.23; imper. 2 sg. **kee** 60v.9; pres./fut. 1 sg. **a[v]** in *pe tha ve=peth a[v] ve* 63r.3—see Notes and *bos*
mouns/movns, see *bos*
moy, adj. comp. *more* 60r.8, 62v.9, 64r.20, 65v.8; **voy** 63r.18 [see *mer*]
moygha/moigha, adj. superl. *most, greatest* 60r.36, 37; 60v.7 [see *mer*]
mustethas, [*mvstethas*] m. *filth, defilement* 60v.10; used adjectivally by position at 61r.17, 18
mynd, m. *mind* 61v.35, 65v.21, 24
myrnans, m. *death* 63r.23; **marnance** 59r.13
myᵉr, [*myr* corrected to *mer* or *myer*, by *e* written above *y*] see *mer*
mystery, m. *mystery* 61r.33; pl. **mysteris** 60r.8
mytearne, m. *king* 60r.36; pl. **meternath** 62r.19

na¹, [= *-na*] dem. pron. (suff.) *that* 59r.21, 59v.24, 64v.33, 34; 65r.17
na², conj. *nor* 59r.14, 66v.8
na³, neg. part. 59r.35, 61r.29, 65v.15 [see *ne*]; **na ve** 62r.34 *was/were (it) not*—see Notes; dependent neg. part. 61v.29, 62v.17, 63v.26, 65r.14; before vowels **nag** 62v.17 [*na*

go=nag o]; imper. neg. part. 61v.25, 65v.19, 66r.14

na ve/navethi, [see *na³, bos*]

nanyle, conj. *neither, nor* 59r.17; 60v.4

nappith, [=*neb+pith*] m. *something, anything* 61v.25

nature, m. *nature* 63r.7

nawaile, see *awaile*

ne, neg. part. 59r.15, 62r.20; **ny** 59r.1, 14; 62r.28; **na** [q.v.] 59r.35, 61r.29, 65v.15; before vowels **neg** 59r.14, 16, 28; **ny*n*g** 61r.21, 62r.37 [=*nyns* TH 13v.10]

neb, rel. pron. *who(ever), someone, anyone* 61r.25, 35; 64r.19; **nep** 59r.15

nebas, adj. *small, slight, minor* 59v.20, 65v.8

nef/neff, m. or f. *heaven* 59r.18, 62r.24/60r.10, 60v.26

neffra, adv. *ever, (not) ever, forever* 60v.26

nefna, see *nef, na³*

neg, see *ne*

negegath, see *genegegath**

negew, [=*neg ew*; see *ne, bos*]

negyns, [=*neg yns*; see *ne, bos*]

nena, adv. *then* 62r.20; **nona** 66v.7 [see Gen. Notes (contractions)]

nenaf/nenevow/nenewow, see *enaf*

nep, see *neb*

nethewan, see *Ethewan*

Nice, prop. n. *Nicaea* 65v.16, 26

nona, see *nena*

nor, m. *earth, world* 60v.8; **nore** 60r.23, 62r.24 [mutation of *dore*]; **waren nore**, 60r.35 [*war an nore*=on the earth]

norvys/nor vys, m. *earth, world* 60r.23, 61v.22; **nore vyse** 60r.40 **nore ves** 60v.3 [see *nor, beys*]

not, Eng. *not* 59v.16, 60r.21, 60v.6, 64r.27

note, m. *note* TH 55v.1+TS

now^(th)/nowith, adj. *new* 66r.34 [*w^(th)* like abbreviation for *with* in Eng.? (OP)]

ny¹, see *ne*

ny², pers. pron. 1 pl. *we, us* 59r.16, 36, 38, 39; **nyy** 59v.9

ny*n*, [=*nyng*, as in **ny*n* gew** 66v.22; see *ne, bos*]

o¹, see *ow¹*

o², see *bos*

o³, see *e³*

o⁴, int. *O* 60r.18 [here as vocative]

o⁵, [=*vo?*—see *bos* and Notes on 62r.14]

ober, m. *work* 61r.30; pl. **oberow** 61v.22

oblation, Eng. *oblation, offering* 64r.21, 25

obtaynia, vb. *(to) obtain* [TH 51r.28]; pres./fut. 2 sg. **obtaynest** 63r.6 [for *obtaynes—see Notes

offeryngys, pl. *offerings* 64r.24

offra, vb. *(to) offer* 64r.20, 66r.24; p. pt. **offrys** 64r.27, 66r.15

offrennia, vb. *(to) offer, make offering of* 64r.23

oll, adj. *all, every* 59r.20; 60r.8; 60v.5, 7, 10; 61r.22, 61v.22; 64r.24, 66r.7

omma, see *umma*

onen, see *onyn²*

only, adv. *only* 59v.17, 60v.6, 61r.21, 63r.2, 66r.3

onn, m. *lamb* 64v.4, 5; **onne** 65v.21, 25 [see *Pask*]

onyn¹, num. *one* 60r.5, 64r.29, 34

onyn², m., f. *one, a (single) person* 59v.16, 26; 61r.34; **onen** 59r.13

openly, Eng. *openly* 60r.21

GLOSSARY 313

*ordayna vb. *(to) ordain* [ordaynas TH 31v.3]; p. pt. **ordaynes** 62v.36
orybe, see *gurryby*
Origene, prop. n. *Origen* 64r.32
orth, [>*worth*] see *worth*
osa, prep. *after* 61v.32, 62r.38
ow¹, pres. verbal part. 59r.3, 19, 23, 27, 28, 29; **o** 59v.9, 23; 60r.22, 61r.30
ow², poss. pron. *my* 61r.34, 35, 36
ow³, [= *o*] see *bos*
own, m. *fear, awe* 59r.29
owr, m. *gold* 60r.4
owrth, see *worth*

pa, [see *pavanar, paseil, pith*]
paseil, interrog. pron. *how much*, 62v.16
pavanar, interrog. pron. *what kind, what sort, what manner* 60v.5
pan, conj. *when* [used relatively] 59r.12, 60r.7, 8; 60v.8, 61r.12, 30; 62v.37
pana, interrog. pron. *what, what sort of* 59r.26, 32; 64v.5
pandra, pron. *what* 62v.9, **pan dre** 60r.7; **panadra** 59r.12; **pan dresy** 63r.7; **pan dregy** 65r.6; **pan drvge** 62v.18 [=*pandra+uge*; see *bos*] *what (is)*; **pandrew** 64v.27 [=*pandra+ew*; see *bos*] *what is*
paris, adj. *ready* 59r.13
parti^ci pation, Eng. *participation* 65r.14
Pask, m. *Passover, (& Easter)* 64v.11; **Bask** 64v.11; **Pask Onn** 64v.3-4, 4-5 *paschal lamb*
Paule, prop. n. *Paul* 66r.29
payn, m. *pain, penalty, torment* 64r.26, 28
pe, [in *pe tha ve*; see *pe(th)/pith*]

pecar, conj. *as* 61r.17 [metathesis from *kepare*, q.v.]
Peder, prop. n. *Peter* 63r.2
pedery, vb. *(to) think, consider* 65r.4; **bedery** 60r.6
peiadow/peIadow, see *pejadow*
pejadow, [*peiadow/peIadow*] m. *prayer* 62r.18, 63r.36
percyvia, vb. *(to) perceive, discern* 61v.36
pege, vb. *(to) pray, entreat* 66r.16 [cf. *pesy/pegy* TH 9v.8/BK 133]; pres./ fut. 3 sg. **pys** 59r.12
pegh, m. *sin* 65v.22; pl. **pehosow** 60v.10
pell, adj. *far* 61r.19; comp. **pelha** 62v.10, 63v.22, 66r.9
pensevik/pensevike, m. *prince* 66r.23/60v.5 [*Pensevik Pronter* = *High Priest*]
percevia, vb. *(to) perceive* 60v.5
perthy, vb. *(to) bear, abide, tolerate* 62v.36
pe(th), adv. *where* 63r.3. See *pith*.
pew, interrog. pron. *who* 59r.19, 31
Philippians, prop. n. *Philippians* 66r.9
Phoceus, prop. n. *Photius* 61r.2, 19
pith, [interrog. or rel.] pron. *what, that* 62r.28, 62v.15, 63r.26, 65v.6; also *where* as in **peth** [*pe tha ve*] 63r.3—see Notes; **(an) pith**, m. *(the) thing* 61v.35, 62r.17, 65v.23
place, m. *place* 65r.6
playn, adj. *plain* 62r.29, 62v.10
popell, f. *people* 66r.36; **bopell** 62r.19; **bobell** 59r.20, 63r.26, 65v.23
poynt, m. *point* 59v.28
praga, interrog. adv. *why, wherefore* 64r.7
presius/presivs, adj. *precious* 60r.4, 63r.23, 66r.35

prys, m. *price* 63r.25
pronter, m. *priest* 62r.21, 66r.6, 23; pl. **prontyrryan** 65v.23
prophet, m. *prophet* 65r.31
protestia, vb. *(to) protest, declare, express* 64r.10
pub, adj. *each, every* 60r.23, 37; 60v.7, 62r.26; **pup** 61r.22
punyssya, [TH 38v.5, 8] vb. *(to) punish* ~ p. pt. **ponishes** TH 55v.1+TS]

quantite/quantyte, m. *quantity* 64r.21, 25/28—see Notes
queth, m. *cloth, royal canopy* 60r.37

ra, see *gule*
rag, prep. *for, in order to* 59r.16, 22, 27, 28, 29, 30
rag henna, adv. *therefore,* 59v.10, 61v.29, 62r.15, 36; 62v.14
ran, f. *part, portion, some (people)* 65r.4, 65v.9
ras, see *gras, Mab Ras*
rav, [*arave*] see *gule*
re¹, [in *rema* q.v.] pron. *some people, some things* **rema** *these* 59v.19
re², perfective/optative part. see *rebo, bos*
reb, prep. *beside, by, close to* [*reb* WR Mt 4:18; *ryb* TH 46v.7]; with pers. pron. 3 sg. **rebta** 60r.22
rebo, see *re², bos*
rebta, see **reb*
rebukya, vb. *(to) rebuke* 65v.15
recevia, vb. *(to) receive* 60r.2, 61r.16, 18, 32; 63r.26, 65v.6; **recivia** 61r.25; **recevya** 59r.39, 59v.21, 22; pres./fut. 2 sg. **recevest** 63r.6 [for **receves*]—see Notes pret. 3 sg. **recevias** 63r.22, 65v.7; p. pt. **recevis** 60v.8
redemya, vb. *(to) redeem* 63r.5, 25

redemtion, m. *redemption* 63r.5
redya, [TH 2r.7] vb. *(to) read* ~ pret. 3 sg. **redias** 61v.22; p. pt. **redys** 63v.29 [imper. 2 pl. **redewgh** TH 55r.27mTS]
regardia/regardya, vb. *(to) regard* 59r.17/59r.15
relevis, [(r)elevis] p. pt. *relieved* 66r.15 [from vb. **relevya?*]
rema, [=*an¹ re¹-ma¹*] *these* 59v.19
remaynea, vb. *(to) remain* 63r.5
remembrance, m. *memory, commemoration, remembrance* 66r.10; [cf. *remembrans* TH 30v.1]
remmembra, vb. *remember, recall* 59r.25
remnant, m. *remainder, rest, remnant* 62r.1
res, m. *need, necessity, 'must'* [with *bos, the*] 66r.10, 66v.27; quasi-verbal, personalized form, pres./fut. 3 sg. **rys** 59r.39; see General Notes (*res/rys yv > a res/rys*)]
reverent, adj. *reverend, revered, sacred* 62r.20, 63v.35
reys, see *ry*
ros, see *ry*
rug/ruga/ruge/rugg/ruk/ruke, see *gule*
ruth, adj. *red* 60r.24
ry, vb. *(to) give* 62v.37, 66r.27; 59r.21; pret. 3 sg. **ros** 64v.34; p. pt. **reys**
rys, see *res*

S., [=Sen], m. *Saint* 59r.3
sacrament, m. *sacrament* 60v.1, 12; 61r.1, 61v.1, 61v.37, 66r.10; pl. **sacramentys** 62r.14, **sacramentes** 63r.18; **Sacrament an Alter/Aulter** *The Blessed Sacrament* 60v.1/61r.1

GLOSSARY

sacrafice/sacrifice, m. *sacrifice* 64r.19, 66r.16/60r.20
sacrificed, Eng. *sacrificed* 61r.21
sans, adj. *holy* 60v.33, 64r.29
sarchia, vb. *(to) search, investigate* 64v.29
sas, see *gasa*
satisfaction, Eng. *satisfaction* 64r.19, 26
Saviour, m. *Saviour* 59r.18, 60v.6, 8, 36; 61r.12; **Savior** 61v.1
sawya, vb. *(to) save, heal, preserve* 63r.35, 63v.11, 65v.10; p. pt. **sawis** 60v.26
scavall/skavall, m. *stool, bench* 64v.31/28; [*scavall e drys=his footstool*, cf. *skavall droose* CW 20]
scholar, m. *disciple, scholar, student* 60r.8
scrifa, vb. *(to) write* 66r.9; p. pt. **scryfys** 66v.27
Scripture, m. *Scripture* 64r.9, 64v.28, 29
sees/seis, see *bos*
selis, p. pt. *signed, sealed* 60v.31 [cf. *ov sel pryve* OM 2600, *my privy seal*]
sensy, vb. *(to) hold* 61r.18
sentence, m. *sentence* 62r.29 [*sentens* TH 51v.9]
seperatya, vb. *(to) separate* [TH 30v.26]; p. pt. **seperatis** 61r.29
setha, vb. *(to) sit* 59r.27; 60r.19, 36
settia, vb. *(to) set, place, lay* [BM 2478]; p. pt. **sittis** 60r.39, 65v.21, 25; **sittys** 65v.20
sevall, vb. *(to) stand* 60r.22
shap, m. *shape, form* 63r.22
sign, m. *sign* 66v.28 [*an keth signma=this same sign*]
signifia, vb. *(to) signify* 65r.15
sittis/sittys, see **settia*

skollya, vb. *spill, pour out* [TH 7v.17]; p. pt. **skullys/skvllys** 66r.34; **skulliys/skvlliys** 66r.36
skruth/skrvth, m. *horror, abhorrence* 66v.16; in **kemeras skrvth** 66v.16 *be horrified by, abhor to*
skvllys/skvlliys, see *skollya*
sort, m. *sort, kind* 60v.6
sowndya, vb. *(to) sound* [TH 53r.6]; p. pt. **soundis** 61v.36
Spiris Sans, prop. n. *Holy Spirit* 60v.3; **Spvrissans** 66v.24
spirituall, Eng. *spiritual* 63v.35
spitfull, Eng. *spiteful* 61r.15
Spurissans/Spvrissans, see *Spiris Sans*
squerdya, vb. *(to) tear, break* [BM 3915]; p. pt. **squardis** 60r.24
stat, m. *state, estate, royal status* 60r.37
subtelnath, m. *subtlety* 60r.21
substans, m. *substance* 66v.8; **substance** 60v.25
sufficient, Eng. *sufficient* 64r.25
sy, see *ansy*

tabell, m. *table* 59r.26
tacclow, pl. *things* 60r.8 [see *tra*]
takclennow, pl. things 61v.24; **taglenno** 63r.17; **tacclennow** TH 55r.30TS [see *tra*]
tas, m. *father* 63r.17; pl. **tasow** 59v.26, 64r.31; **tasaw** 64r.34
tastia, vb. *(to) taste* 65v.11; pret. 3 sg. **tastyas** 65v.15
tavas, m. *tongue* 60r.24
te, pers. pron. 2 sg. *you* 61v.22, 34; 62r.27, 62v.32, 63r.18; **tee** 60v.5 [see *ge/gee*]
tella, see *tillar*
tema, see *dos*

Tertullia*n*, prop. n. *Tertullian* 64r.32
testament, prop. n. *testament, covenant* 66r.34; **Testament Now**[th] *New Testament*
tewhy, see *dos*
tewlell vb. *(to) throw, cast, fling* [TH 24v.16]; pret. 3 sg. **dowlas** 64r.24
tha¹, see *the*
tha², poss. pron. 2 sg. *your* 59r.26; **y**[e] [= *the*] 59r.25 [but *tha* 62r.37 = def. art. see Notes & *the¹*]
tha ve/thave, [in *pe tha ve=peth a[v] ve*] see *a[v], bos, mos*
thaga, [=*the+aga*] see *the*
thagen/thagy*n*/thaken, see *the*
tha*n*, [=the'n] see *the, an¹*
thath, see *the*
thavos, [=*tha¹ vos*] see *the, bos*
tha worta/thaworta, see *thaworth*
thaworth/tha worth, prep. *from* 60v.9, 63v.29; **y**[e] **worth** 66r.8, 66v.14; with pers. pron. 2 sg. **tha worthas** 63r.3; 3 sg. pl. **thaworta** 59r.30
the¹, [and *y*[e]=the] prep. *to* 59r.11, 13, 20, 25, 28, 34; **tha** 59v.15, 24; 60r.20, 21; 65v.24; **tho** 64v.29; **than/then** [*the'n=the+an¹*] *to the* 66r.9/59r.18, 21, 60r.10, 62r.15; with pers. pron 1 sg. **thy*m*** 64v.28; 2 sg. **these** 60r.35; **thees** 62v.35; 3 sg. **thetha** 64r.19; **thotha** 66r.10; **thotheff** 66v.24; **th[*e*th]effe** [=*theth(a)/thoth(a) effe*] 59r.36-7; **y**[e] **theff** 66r.28; 1 pl. **then** 64v.34, 66r.23; **thyn** 63r.35; **the ny** 60r.11, **theny** 60r.18; 2 pl. **theugh** 60r.7; 60v.4; 3 pl. **thethans** 64r.26-7; 65v.10; with poss. pron. 2 sg. **thath/theth** [*'th = infixed form of tha¹*] 60v.9; 3 sg. [**y**[e]] *for th'e?* 62r.1; 1 pl. [=*the+agan*] **thagyn** 59v.15;

tha gen 59v.21; **thaken** 63v.10; 3 pl. **thaga** [=*the+aga*] 65v.10
the², = *tha²* q.v.
thees, see *the*
theffa/theffan/theffe[ns], see *dos*
then, [=the'n] see *the, an¹*
then/theny, [=*then/thyn, then ny*] see *the*
Theophelact, prop. n. *Theophylact (of Ohrid)* 65v.11
thesa, [*e thesa=eth esa*] see *bos*; NB can be both pres. 3 sg. and imperf. 1 sg.
thesan, [*e thesan=eth esan*] see *bos*
these, see *the*
thesta, [*e thestsa=eth esta*] see *bos*
theth, see *the*
thetha/thethans, see *the*
thetheffe, see *the*
theugh, see *the*
thevas, see *davas*
thew, [*e thew=eth ew*] see *bos*
Thew, see *Dew*
thewas, see *dewas*
thibbry, see *dibbry*
thisquethas, see *disquethas*
thiscrygians, see *discrigians*
tho¹, see *the¹*
tho², [*e tho=eth o; see bos*]
thony, [*e thony/y thony=eth on ny; see e³, bos*]
thore, see *dore*
thos, [*e thos=eth os; see bos*]
thotha/thotheff, see *the*
thro, see *dry*
thybbry, see *dibbry*
thy*m*, see *the*
thyny, see *the*
tibbry, see *dibbry*
tillar, m. *place* 66r.7; **tella[r]** 61r.38 [*tella veth=no place at all*]
tirmyn, m. *time* 60r.19

tisquethas, see *disquethas*
tose, see *dos*
touchia, vb. *(to) touch* 60v.7 11; **dochya** 60v.6, 63v.37 [?]; p. pt. **touchis** 60r.23, 60v.12, 32
tra, m. *thing* 59r.27, 60v.7, 61r.22; 61v.32; supp. pl. **tacclow** 60r.8; **takclennow** 61v.24
transfurmys/transfvrmys, p. pt. *transformed* 66v.22; [*transformys* CW 2113, vb. not found in texts]
travith, [=*tra+bith*] f. *nothing, anything* [in neg. phrases] 61v.25
tre, f. *homestead, home* 60v.9
trega, vb. *(to) dwell, live/abide (in)* 61r.36, 66r.20
trembla, vb. *tremble* 59r.28
trethans, [*in trethans*] see *inter*
treweythow, adv. *sometimes* 59v.8
trope, m. *trope, figure of speech* 59r.1
tros, m. *foot* [CW 355]; pl. **treys** [TH 21v.9] **drys** 64v.16 (altered from *dryes*), 27, 31; **thrys** 64v.29
*****trobla,** vb. *(to) trouble* [cf. *ow throbla* BM 949]; p. pt. **troublis** 66v.8
trylya, vb. *(to) turn, turn/change into* 64v.29; p. pt. **trylis** 62r.1, 62v.1, 66v.14
tuse/tvs, see *den*
tybbry, see *dibbry*
tyrmyn, m. *time, term* 64r.30
tyrry, vb. *(to) break* 65r.14

uge/vge, see *bos*
ugy/vgy, see *bos*
umma/vmma, adv. *here* 60r.10, 22, 23; 64v.30, 65r.19; **omma** 64v.33; **ema** 65v.2
un/vn, num. *one* 59r.30 (altered from *on*), **an** 61r.30?—see Notes

understandya/vnderstandya, vb. *(to) understand* 65v.15; p. pt. **vnderstandis** 64r.9, 65r.28, 65v.15
understandyng/vnderstandyng, Eng. *understanding* 64r.8
urth/vrth, see *worth*
use/vse¹, see *bos*
use/vse², m. *use*
usya/vsya, vb. *(to) use* 59r.1, 61v.25, 26

vab, see *mab*
vaga, see *maga*
vam, see *mam*
ve¹, [<*me*] 59r.25, 26; 60r.35, 61r.37 *I, me, (of) me, my*
ve², see *bos*
vea, see *bos*
vegwreis, [=*ve² gwreis*]
veith, see *bith*
vennas, see *mennas*
ver, see *meer*
verely, Eng. *verily, truly* 61r.34, 40, 41
verwall, see *merwell*
very, adj. *true, very* 60v.4
ves, see *beys*
veth¹, see *bos*
veth²/v[e]tholl, see *bith*
vge/uge/ugy/vgy, see *bos*
Vigilius, prop. n. *Vigilius* 64r.29
vise, see *beys*
vith, see *bith*
vmma, see *umma*
vn/vn-, see *un/un-*
vo, see *bos*
voes/voese, see *bos*
vois, see *bos*
vonsy, [=*vons y*; see *bos, y²*]
vos/vose, see *bos*
vosama, see *bos*
vosta, see *bos*
vova, see *bos*

voy, see *moy, mer voy*
vrth/urth, see *worth*
vs/us, see *bos*
vse/use, see *bos*
vsya, see *usya*
vyn, see *mennas*
vys, see *beys*

walkea, vb. *(to) walk* TH 55r.30TS; pret. 3 sg. **walkias** 64v.33
war, prep. *on, upon* 64v.30; **ware** 60r.23, 60v.7; **whar** 61r.3, 65r.6; **warre** 65v.2; with pers. pron. 3 sg. m. **warnotha** 62r.43
war byn/warbyn, prep. *against* 61r.15
warbarth, adv. *together* 61r.30, 63v.19
ware/warre, see *war*
waren, see *war, an*
warlerth, prep. *after, in* 65v.7
warnotha, see *war*
wartha, see *awartha*
wath, see *whath*
welas, see *gwelas*
wele/welle, see *gwelas*
welha, see *gwelas*
wely, see *gwely*
weth, [*e weth*] see *y weth*
wethvas, see **gwethfas*
whanse, vb. *(to) desire, want, long for* [TH 16v.11]; pret. 3 sg. **wensys** 64v.5
whar, see *war*
whath, adv. *yet, still, furthermore* 62v.2, 64r.26, 65v.15; **what** 63r.24; **wath** 63r.5
whelas, vb. *(to) seek, search for* 64v.30

whrella, see *gule*
why, pers. pron. 2 pl. *you* 60r.5, 22; 62v.13
whyppya, vb. *(to) whip* [BK 360]; p.pt. **whyppys** 59v.15
woos, see *gos*
wor, see *gothvas*
woras, see *gora*
wore, see *gora*
worryb, see *gurryby*
worth, prep. *at, by, from* 60v.35, 61r.31, 63r.4, 64v.32; ʷ**orth** 59r.38
worth, ~ **owrth** 64r.10; **urth** [*vrth*] 59r.22, 61r.27
worthely, Eng. *worthily* 63v.37, 66r.28
Worthias, see **Gworthias*
worthy, adj. *worthy, deserving* 60r.35
wrene, see *gule*
wruck, see *gule*

y¹, [=*e¹* q.v.]
y², [see also *ansy*] pers. pron. *they, them* 62v.38, 64r.24, 59v.27 [*ens sy=ens y*], 61r.16, 30 [*vonsy=vons y*]; **hy** 61v.23; **h¹y** 61r.16
y³, [=*e³* q.v.]
y weth, [or *yweth=ynweth*] adv. *also, likewise* 59r.18-19; **e weth** 59v.11, 13; 60r.11, 61r.32
yᵉ/yᵉ theff, see *the*
yᵉ worth, see *thaworth*
yll, [=*ill*] see *gallas*
yma, [=*ema*; see *bos*]
yns, see *bos*
ysya, [partial word] see *despisea*
yth, see *e³/eth*
yweth, see *y weth*

Bibliography

Primary Sources

Manuscripts

Archives and Cornish Studies Service, Kresen Kernow, Redruth [formerly the Cornwall Record Office, Truro] (CRO)
Parish Registers of Newlyn East—*Volume 1: Baptisms from 1560 and Marriages and Burials from 1559.*
FS/3/1254 Extracts from parish registers, Newlyn East.

British Library (BL)
Add. MS 46397—Tregear, John, *Homelies xiij in cornysch*, Puleston Papers.
MS Harley 422, articles 53, 60, 68.—Ridley's notes for the Oxford Disputations of 1554.
MS Harley 3642—Report from Weston to Bonner of the Oxford Disputations of 1554.

Cambridge University Library (CUL)
Kk.5.14, folios 13–29—Notary's Report of the Oxford Disputations of 1554.
MS Add. 3041 (C)—Nicholas Roscarrock (attr.) *A Briefe Regester or Alphabeticall Catalogue [...]* ('Lives of the Saints'), c. 1610–20.

Cornwall Record Office (CRO) *see* **Archives and Cornish Studies Service**

Courtney Library of the Royal Institution of Cornwall (at the Royal Cornwall Museum), Truro
Bassett Collection, HB/1/1 (Henderson Calendar 5, page 145, no. 587)—Conveyance involving Ralph Trelobys.
Nance Bequest. The surviving papers and manuscripts of Robert Morton Nance, with A.S.D. Smith. (The papers are cited by box then folder, with the thematic renumbering of P.A.S. Pool in brackets, e.g. 7: 22 (46), representing Box 7, Folder 22—i.e. renumbered by Pool as Folder 46.)

St Aubyn Collection, HA/14/7 (Henderson Calendar 16, page 106, no. 225)—Conveyance involving Ralph Trelobys.

Henderson, Charles, *Materials for a History of the Parish of Newlyn, Part II: Subsidies*, in MS form (dated approximately 1924).

Devon Record Office/Devon Heritage Centre (DRO), Exeter

Chanter 12 II—*Episcopal Registers of Richard Fox*.
Chanter 13—*Episcopal Registers of Hugh Oldham*.
Chanter 14—*Episcopal Registers of John Veysey* (institutions and ordinations).
Chanter 15—*Episcopal Registers of John Veysey* (includes copy of *Valor* 86r–99v).
Chanter 18—*Episcopal Registers of James Turberville*.
Chanter 20—*Episcopal Registers of William Bradbridge*.
Chanter 21—*Episcopal Registers of John Woolton*.
Z19/10/1a: f. 44—Photostats of William Alley's list of clergy for Exeter Diocese, *c*. 1561.
Z19/10/1b: f. 54—transcript of William Alley's list of clergy for Exeter Diocese, *c*. 1561 (see Parker Library)—probably made by A.J. Watson of the British Museum in 1927.

Durham University Library (Chapter Library)

DUL MS Cosin V.IV.2, ff. 161r–165r.—A late fifteenth-century collection of patristic and other quotations and *sententiae*, probably by Thomas Olyphant.

Exeter Cathedral Archive, Exeter (Dean & Chapter Manuscripts)

D&C Exeter MS 3688 (D&C 3688)—'Bishop Veysey's *Valor*'—a manuscript 'further list' of clerical subsidy information for Exeter, submitted to the crown on 3 November 1536. (See also DRO, Chanter 15.)

Kresen Kernow *see* Archives and Cornish Studies Service

Parker Library, Corpus Christi College, Cambridge

MS 97—William Alley's list of clergy for Exeter Diocese, *c*. 1561.
MS 340, 11, ff. 247–64—Notes on Ridley's arguments in the Oxford Disputations of 1554—*Disputatio habita Oxonii 2 Aprilis, 1554, de reali presentia corporis Christi in eucharistia, respondente D. Ridley episcopo Londiniensi*.
MS 340, 13, ff. 271–80—Notes on Cranmer's arguments in the Oxford Disputations of 1554—*Disputatio Oxoniae habita 16 Aprilis, 1554, de reali presentia respondente Thoma Cranmer, opponente D. Chedsey*.

The National Archives (TNA), Kew

TNA E 36/64—Subscriptions to renunciation of papal supremacy. Province of Canterbury. With signatures.

TNA E 25/58/3—Glasney by Penryn, Corn; provost and college of the Collegiate Church (Acknowledgement of supremacy, with signatures).
TNA PROB/11/25—Will of Richard Hilley, clerk, of St Dunstan in the East, London, 1534.
TNO PROB 11/30/240—Prerogative Court of Canterbury, Will Registers—the will of Thomas [Chard] Solubrie [of Solubria] bishop, of Saint Mary Oterey [Ottery], Devon (4 November 1544).
TNA, PROB/11/47/298—Prerogative Court of Canterbury, Will Registers—will of Lawrence Godfrey, clerk, vicar of St Piran in Zandes [Perranzabuloe], Cornwall (7 October 1564).
TNA, SP (Hen. VIII) 1/123, pp. 40–1—State Papers, Henry VIII.
TNA, SP (Hen. VIII) 1/127, p. 183 (not p. 193 as in the TNA/PRO calendar)—State Papers, Henry VIII.

National Library of Wales/Llyfrgell Genedlaethol Cymru, Aberystwyth
Peniarth MS 105B—*Beunans Meriasek*, 'The Life of St Meriasek/Meriadoc', a saint's play in Cornish copied in the early sixteenth century. Digital images are on the National Library's website: https://www.library.wales/discover/digital-gallery/manuscripts/the-middle-ages/beunans-meriasek/. National Library of Wales, Aberystwyth (2018). Accessed 25 May 2018.
NLW MS 23849D—*Beunans Ke*, 'The Life of St Kea', an incomplete copy of a saint's play in Cornish copied in the sixteenth century and recently discovered. Digital images are on the National Library's website: https://www.library.wales/discover/digital-gallery/manuscripts/early-modern-period/beunans-ke/. National Library of Wales, Aberystwyth (2018). Accessed 25 May 2018.

Oxford University Library
MS Bodl. 791—The Cornish *Ordinalia*, three plays on the Creation of the World (*Origo Mundi*), the Passion of Christ (*Passio Christi*) and the Resurrection (*Resurrection Domini*), in Cornish verse, with Latin stage directions. Digital images are on the Bodleian website: https://digital.bodleian.ox.ac.uk/inquire/p/7ee6264a-64fb-4455-8f87-dff7c56e0d46. Accessed 25 May 2018.
MS Bodl. 219—*The Creacion of the World* (*Gwreans an Bys*), a play based on *Origo Mundi* completed in 1611 by William Jordan. Digital images are on the Bodleian website: https://digital.bodleian.ox.ac.uk/inquire/p/a9a0261a-0a22-4728-85b3-224880379c69. Accessed 25 May 2018. (Other manuscripts of this play exist, but this is the earliest.)

Somerset Record Office (SRO)
D/D/breg/10—*Episcopal Registers of Cardinal Hadrian de Castello*, bishop of Bath and Wells.

West Country Studies Library (now at the Devon Heritage Centre), Exeter
Hennessy's Incumbents—a record of beneficed clergy abstracted from the MS registers of the bishops of Exeter by the Rev. G.L. Hennessy, rector of Monkokehampton.

Wiltshire and Swindon Record Office (WRO), Salisbury
WRO, D1, 2/14—*Episcopal Registers of Edmund Audley*.
WRO, D1, 2/15—*Episcopal Registers of Cardinal Campeggio*.

Early Printed Books

Bonner, Edmund, *A Profitable and Necessarye Doctryne [...] for the instruction and enformation of the people beynge within his diocese of London [...]* (London: John Cawood, 1554).

Bonner, Edmund, *Articles to be inquired of in the general visitation [...]* (London: John Cawood, 1554).

Bonner, Edmund, ed. *Homelies sette forthe by the righte reuerende father in God, Edmunde Byshop of London [...]* (London: John Cawood, 1555). A printing of this work very similar to the printing likely to have been used by Tregear himself can be found in the British Library, shelfmark 1026.e.14 (STC 3285.4).

Bonner, Edmund (or John Harpsfield), 'Aunswere made to certayne common obiections against the presence of Chryste's bodye and bloud in the Sacramente of the Aultare', in Bonner, *Homelies*, ff. 61–73.

Bonner, Edmund, *An Honest Godly Instruction, and information for the tradying, and bringinge up of Children, set furth by the Bishoppe of London [...]* (London: John Cawood, 1556).

Carew, Richard, *The Survey of Cornwall* (London: John Jaggard, 1602) [reprinted in facsimile in DCRS, n.s. vol. 47, John Chynoweth, Nicholas Orme and Alexandra Walsham, eds, *The Survey of Cornwall by Richard Carew* (Exeter: DCRS, 2004)].

Cranmer, Thomas, *A defence of the true and catholike doctrine of the sacrament of the body and bloud of our sauiour Christ [...] approued by ye consent of the moste auncient doctors of the Churche* (London: Reginald Wolfe, 1550).

Cranmer, Thomas, *An Aunswere ... unto a craftie and Sophisticall cavillation, devised by Stephen Gardiner* (London: John Daye, 1580) [1st edn was published in 1551].

Davies, John, ed. and tr., *Llyfr y Resolucion* (LLR) (London: Beale, 1632), reprinted 1684. [This is largely a Welsh translation and adaption of Robert Person's *Book of Christian Exercise*, 1585, with a small amount of additional material in the Cornish language.]

Foxe, John, *Rerum in Ecclesia Gestarum, quæ postremis & pericolis his temporibus euanerunt [...]* (Basle: Nicolaus Brylinger, 1559).

Foxe, John, *Actes and Monuments of matters most special and memorable [...]* (London: John Day, 1576).

[Geneva Bible] *The Bible and Holy Scriptvres, conteyned in the Olde and Newe Testament* ... (Geneva: Rowland Hall, 1560), first printed in England in 1576. An online facsimile may be found on the Internet Archive at https://archive.org/details/TheGenevaBible1560/. Accessed 27 October 2018.

[Great Bible] *The Byble in Englyshe that is to saye the content of al the holy scripture* ... (London: Richard Grafton and Edward Whitchurch, 1540). An online facsimile may be found on the Internet Archive at https://archive.org/details/GreatBible1540/. Accessed 27 October 2018.

Harding, Thomas, *An answere to Maister Juelles Challenge* (Leuven/Louvain: 1564), STC 12758.

Hervet, Gentian, *D. Ioannis Chrysostomi Archiepiscopi Constantinopolitani Opera etc.* (Venice: Ad Signum Spei (Speranza), 1549), vol. 1.

Morgan, William, tr., *Y Beibl Cyssegr-lan, sef yr Hen Destament, a'r Newydd* (London: Christopher Barker, 1588).

Persons [Parsons], Robert, *A Treatise of Three Conversions of England from Paganism to Christian Religion* (London: Henry Hills, 1603), reprinted 1688.

Plunket, Francis, *Heroum Speculum: De vita DD. Francisci Tregeon cuius corpus septendecim post annos in aede D. Rochi integrum inventum est [...]* (Lisbon: Officina Craesbeeckiana, 1655). Printed edition in *Miscellanea, 15*, Catholic Record Society (CRS) Record Series 32 (London: CRS, 1932).

Sander, Nicholas, *The Supper of our Lord set foorth according to the truth of the Gospel & Catholike faith* (Leuven/Louvain: Joannes Foulerus, 1566).

Trapezontius, George, trans., *Opervm Divi Ioannis Chrysostomi Archiepiscopi Constantinopoli etc.* (Basle: Ex Officina Hervagiana, 1539), vol. 2. (The copy at the College of St Cuthbert, Ushaw, Durham, was once owned by Dom Stephen Morley, a monk of Durham Abbey.)

Tunstall, Cuthbert, *De ueritate corporis et sanguinis domini nostri Jesu Christi in eucharistia*, 2nd edn (Paris: Michel de Vascosan, 1554).

[Vermigli, Pietro Martire], *A discourse or traictise of Petur Martyr Vermilla Flore[n]tine, the publyque reader of diuinitee in the Vniuersitee of Oxford ... wherein he openly declared his whole and determinate iudgemente concernynge the sacrament of the Lordes supper in the sayde Vniuersitee* (London: Robert Stoughton [i.e. E. Whitchurch] for Nicholas Udall, 1550).

Early Printed Books Consulted through Google Books

Affelmann, John, *Censura Censuræ Lampadianæ Theologica et Scholastica: seu, Invicta Adsertio Doctrinæ Catholicæ de omnipræsentia Christi secundum naturam ejus humanam et dea ea libellorum beati D. Philippi Nicolai ... Adversus vanissimas M. Joannis Lampadii ...* (Rostock: Typis Reusnerianis, 1610), f. 106, Google Books, https://books.google.co.uk/books?id=XxNlAAAAcAAJ. Accessed 23 December 2018.

D[ivi] Aurelii Augustini Hipponensis Episcopi Operum, vol. 10 (Paris; Cum Privilegio Regis, 1586). Google Books, https://books.google.co.uk/books?id=AQtNwydFMPIC. Accessed 20 December 2018.

Divi Cyrilli Archiepiscopi Alexandrini Opera Omnium ... Tomus Primus [vol. 1] (Cologne: Melchior Novesian, 1546), f. 283v. Google Books, https://books.google.co.uk/books?id=0RURAAAAYAAJ. Accessed 29 December 2018.

[Duns Scotus] *Reportata super primum Sententiarum fratris Johannes duns Scoti ...* (Paris: Jean Granion [apud Clausum Brunellum], 1517–1518). Google Books, https://books.google.co.uk/books?id=goxKAAAAcAAJ. Accessed 18 August 2018.

[Fisher, John], *De Veritate Corporis Christi in Eucharistia*, 1st edn (Cologne: Ex Officina Quenteliana, 1527). Google Books, https://books.google.co.uk/books?id=gZlkAAAAcAAJ. Accessed 20 December 2018.

Garet, Jean, *Omnium Ætatum Nationum ac Provinciarum in Veritate Corporis Christi in Eucharistia*, 3rd edn (Antwerp: [house of] Philip Nutius, 1569). Google Books, https://books.google.co.uk/books?id=PM87AAAAcAAJ. Accessed 1 August 2018.

[Oecumenius], *Commentaria in hosce Novi Testamenti tractatus* (Paris: apud Carolum Morellum, 1630): volume 1 of *Oecumenii Operum et Arethae in Apocalypsin*. Google Books, https://books.google.co.uk/books?id=VPZh9KO8ko8C. Accessed 1 August 2018.

[Oecumenius], *Expositiones antiquae ac valde utiles brevitatem: una cum perpicuitate habentes mirabilem ... ab Oecumenio & Aretha collectae* (Verona: 1532). Google Books, https://books.google.co.uk/books?id=2dKwgxqg950C. Accessed 1 August 2018.

Tavernier, Jean, *De veritate corporis et sanguinis Christi in sacramento altaris*, 1st edn (Paris: Vivant Gaultherot, 1548), 2nd edn (Paris: Claude Fremy, 1556). References are to the 2nd edn. Google Books, https://books.google.co.uk/books?id=l92KcH6qFckC. Accessed 1 October 2018.

Theophylacti Archiepiscopi Bulgariae In Quatuor Domini Nostri Iesu Christi Euangelia ... (Paris: Charles Guillard, 1546). Google Books, https://books.google.co.uk/books?id=dHa2sDC8ujYC. Accessed 18 October 2018.

Printed and Online Editions and Records

Cornish-Language Texts

Archæologia Brittanica (AB), Edward Lhuyd (Oxford: Lhuyd [printed at the Sheldonian Theatre], 1707).

Archæologia Cornu-Brittanica, or an Essay to Preserve the Ancient Cornish Language (ACB), William Pryce (Sherborne: Cruttwell, 1790).

Beunans Meriasek: The Life of St Meriasek, Bishop and Confessor, a Cornish Drama (BM), Whitley Stokes, ed. (London: Trübner & Co., 1872) is the published edition but Myrna [May] Combellack [Harris], 'A Critical Edition of *Beunans*

Meriasek' (PhD dissertation, 1985, University of Exeter) has generally been preferred for citation. Where uncertainties remain, the online images of NLW, Peniarth MS 105B (see above under Manuscripts: National Library of Wales) have been consulted.

Bewnans Ke: The Life of St Kea, a Critical Edition with Translation (BK), Graham Thomas and Nicholas Williams, eds, Exeter Medieval Texts & Studies (Exeter: UEP/National Library of Wales (NLW), 2007). For uncertain portions of the text the online images of NLW MS 23849D have been consulted (see above under Manuscripts: National Library of Wales, there listed as *Beunans Ke*).

Bodewryd MS 5 (NLW) (Bodewryd), Andrew Hawke, 'A Rediscovered Cornish-English Vocabulary', in Philip Payton, ed., *Cornish Studies*, 2nd series, 9 (Exeter: UEP, 2001), pp. 83–104.

The Cornish Writings of the Boson Family (Boson), Oliver J. Padel, ed. (Redruth: Institute of Cornish Studies, 1975). This edition (pp. 14–23) is also the source of citations from Nicholas Boson's *Jooan Chei a Horr* (JCH) and *Nebbaz Gerriau dro tho Carnoack* (NG).

Gwreans an Bys: The Creation of the World, a Cornish Mystery (CW), Whitley Stokes, ed. (London/Edinburgh, Williams & Norgate, 1864). Paula Neuss, ed., *The Creacion of the World: A Critical Edition and Translation*, Garland Medieval Texts, 3 (New York and London: Garland, 1983) has generally been preferred for citation. For uncertain portions of the text the online images of BL MS Bodl. 219 (see above under Manuscripts: Bodleian Library) have been consulted.

The Ordinalia—in three plays: *Origo Mundi* (OM), *Passio Christi* (PC) and *Resurrexio Domini* (RD)—Edwin Norris, ed., *The Ancient Cornish Drama* (Oxford: OUP, 1859) for Citation. For uncertain portions of the text the online images of BL MS Bodl. 791 (see above under Manuscripts: Bodleian Library) have been consulted. Use has also been made of Nance and Smith's work, noted under Graham Sandercock (and Ray Chubb) in Secondary Sources.

Passyon agan Arluth (PA), Goulven Pennaod, ed., *Passyon Agan Arluth/Pasion Hon Aotrou: Barzhoneg kernevek eus ar 15t kantved* (Quimper: Preder, 1978) [based on the edition of R. Morton Nance and A.S.D. Smith published between 1933-35, in the cyclostyled magazine *Kernow* (1-14)] for citation. For uncertain portions of the text the black and white images in Harry Woodhouse, ed., *The Cornish Passion Poem in facsimile* (Penryn: Gorseth Kernow, 2002) have been consulted. (After completion but before publication of this edition of SA, a new edition has become available which includes colour reproductions of MS Harley 1782: Nicholas Williams, ed., with Michael Everson and Alan M. Kent, *The Charter Fragment and Pascon agan Arluth* [Corpus Textuum Cornicorum, vol. 1] (Dundee: Evertype, 2020).)

Sacrament an Altar (SA), BL Add. MS 46397, ff. 59r–66v (see above, under Manuscripts, British Library); citation is from this edition of SA. (The edition by Ray Edwards noted below under TH was based on my draft, unpublished readings (see under Privately Circulated/Unpublished Works.)

The Tregear Homilies (TH), BL Add. MS 46397, ff. 1r–58v (see above, under Manuscripts, British Library); Benjamin Bruch, ed., unpublished edition (privately circulated, 2008—updated by a privately circulated reading of TH 11–12 by D.H. Frost, 2009) for citation. Also invaluable were: the unpublished reading by Andrew Hawke, ed., *Homelyes xiij in cornysche* [privately circulated computer file, 1978–98]; Christopher Bice, ed., *Homelyes xiij in cornysch* [based on Nance's transcription and privately circulated, 1969], republished by Ray Edwards, ed., *The Tregear Homilies* (Sutton Coldfield: Kernewek Dre Lyther, 1994); and Ray Edwards, ed., *The Tregear Homilies with The Sacrament of the Altar [converted to Kernewek Kemmyn by Keith Syed]* (Sutton Coldfield: Kernewek Dre Lyther, 2004). See also the MA thesis of Talat Chaudhri under Secondary Sources.

Vocabularium Cornicum (VC) [Old Cornish Vocabulary], Enrico Campanile, ed., in *Annali della Scuola Normale Superiore di Pisa*, 2nd series, 30 (Pisa: Scuola Normale Superiore, 1961), from BL MS Cotton Vespasian A xiv 001–105 [s. xii] ff. 7r–10, *Vocabularium Cornicum* (The Old Cornish Vocabulary) in *Vitae sanctorum Wallensium*. A tabular summary may be found online at https://wikisource.org/wiki/Vocabularium_Cornicum. Accessed 25 May 2018. use has also been made of E.V.T. Graves, 'The Old Cornish vocabulary', PhD dissertation: Columbia University, 1962.

'William Bodinar's Letter, 1776' (WB), P.A.S. Pool and O.J. Padel, eds, in *Journal of the Royal Institution of Cornwall* (Truro: RIC, 1975–6), pp. 231–6. (After completion but before publication of this edition of SA, a new examination has become available: Joseph F. Eska and Benjamin Bruch, 'The Late Cornish Syntax of William Bodinar', *Études Celtiques* 47 (2021), pp. 197–218.)

[William Rowe] (WR) Robert Morton Nance, 'The Cornish of William Rowe' [Kerew], *Old Cornwall* II (11), 1936, pp. 32–6; II (12) 1936, pp. 25–7; III (1), 1937, pp. 41–4); *An Kernewek a Wella Rowe*, Rod Lyon, ed. (Hellys [Helston]: Kesva an Taves Kernewek, 1998), from BL Add. MS 28554, the transcription by Rev. Henry Ustick around 169 (WR); J. Loth, ed., 'Textes inédits en cornique moderne', *Revue Celtique*, 23, 173–200.

It is beyond the scope of this bibliography to list versions in the various respellings of Cornish produced by language revivalists, although particularly helpful examples are given above, and the work of the late Ray Edwards under the auspices of Kernewek Dre Lyther deserves special mention.

There are, of course, many other sources of traditional Cornish, some fragmentary. Some useful lists of the latter are provided by George, ed., *Gerlyver Meur*, 2nd edn, pp. 12–17; 3rd edn, pp. 12–14.

Other Primary Sources and Records
NB translations of patristic texts will be found under secondary sources

Acts of the Privy Council of England (APC), vols 7, 9, 13, ed. John Roche Dasent (London: HMSO, 1893-6). Also available in facsimile through *British History Online*. http://www.british-history.ac.uk/acts-privy-council/vol7. Accessed 13 May 2016.

Alberigo, Giuseppe, ed., *Conciliorum Oecumenicorum Decreta*, 3rd edn (Bologna: Istituto per la Scienze Religiose, 1973).

Ayre, John, ed., *The Works of John Jewel, Bishop of Salisbury*, parts 2 and 3 (Cambridge: CUP and The Parker Society], 1847-1848).

Bateson, Mary, ed., 'A Collection of Original Letters from the Bishops to the Privy Council, 1564', *The Camden Miscellany*, 9 (London: Camden Society, 1893).

Biblia Hebraica Stuttgartensia, Karl Elliger, Willhelm Rudolph et al., eds, *editio funditus renovata* (Stuttgart: Deutsche Bibelstiftung, 1977).

Biblia Sacra Vulgata, R. Gryson, R. Weber, B. Fischer et al., eds, 4th edn (Stuttgart: Deutsche Bibelgesellschaft, 1994). All quotations from the Vulgate are from this edition unless otherwise specified.

Bray, Gerald, ed., *The Books of Homilies: A Critical Edition* (Cambridge: James Clarke & Co., 2016). https://doi.org/10.2307/j.ctt1hfr2n0

Calendar of Patent Rolls; Philip and Mary, 1554-5, vol. 2 (London: HMSO, 1936-9); *Elizabeth I, 1558-1603* (London: HMSO, 1939).

Calendar of State Papers Domestic—Elizabeth I, Addenda, 1547-1565, ed. Mary Anne Everett Green (London: Longmans, Green & Co., 1870).

Calendar of Wills, Administrations and Accounts relating to the Counties of Cornwall and Devon, proved in the Connotorial Archidiaconal Court of Cornwall, part I, 1569-1699, ed. R.M. Glencross (London: British Record Society, 1929).

Calendar of Wills and Administrations relating to the Counties of Devon and Cornwall, proved in the Consistory Court of the Bishop of Exeter, 1532-1800, vol. 2, ed. Edward Alexander Fry (Plymouth: William Brendon & Son, 1914).

Calendar of Wills and Administrations relating to the Counties of Devon and Cornwall, proved in the Court of the Principal Registry of the Bishop of Exeter, 1559-1799 and, of Devon only, proved in the court of the Archdeaconry of Exeter 1540-1799, vol. 1, ed. Edward Alexander Fry (Plymouth: William Brendon & Son, 1908).

Caley, John and Hunter, Joseph, eds, *Valor Ecclesiasticus, tempore Regis Henrici Octavi* (London: British Record Commission, 1810-34), 6 vols.

Campion, Edmund, *Ten Reasons [Rationes Decem]* (London: Manresa Press, 1914), Latin Text pp. 30-87, English Translation pp. 89-145.

Catechism of the Catholic Church [CCC] (London: Catholic Truth Society, 2016), revised edn.

Chadwick, Henry, ed., *De Sacramentis. Saint Ambrose on the Sacraments—The Latin text* (London: A.R. Mowbray & Co., 1960). This edition is an abstract of the text from Otto Faller, *Ambrosius: Explanatio symboli, De sacramentis, De mysteriis, De paenitentia, De excessu fratris Satyri, De obitu Valentiniani, De obitu Theodosii*, Corpus Scriptorum Ecclesiasticorum Latinorum (CSEL) vol. 73 (Vienna: Hoelder-Pichler-Tempsky, 1955), issued as part of the series Studies in Eucharistic Faith and Practice, no. 5.

Christmas, Henry, ed., *The Works of Nicholas Ridley, DD, sometime Bishop of London* (Cambridge: CUP, 1841). [Appendix 1, pp. 433–85, is based on Foxe's Latin account of Ridley's Disputation, *Rerum in Ecclesia Gestarum [...]* (Basle: Nicolaus Brylinger, 1559).] Google Books, https://books.google.co.uk/books?id=bZnNnPJUn7MC. Accessed 9 November 2018.

Clauis Patrum Graecorum, M. Geerard, J. Noret, F. Glorie, eds. (Turnhout: Brepols, 1974–2018).

Corpus Thomisticum [Opera Omnia S. Thomae de Aquino], http://www.corpusthomisticum.org/iopera.html. Universidad de Navarra, Pamplona (2000). Accessed 17 April 2015.

Cox, John Edmund, ed., *The Writings and Disputations of Thomas Cranmer ... Relative to the Sacrament of the Lord's Supper*, Parker Society (Cambridge: CUP, 1844).

Cox, John Edmund, ed., *Miscellaneous Writings and Letters of Thomas Cranmer, Archbishop of Canterbury*, Parker Society (Cambridge: CUP, 1846).

Daniélou, Jean, Anne-Marie Malingrey, Robert Flacelière, eds, *Jean Chrysostome: Sur l'incompréhensibilité de Dieu* [Sources Chrétiennes 28 bis, CPG 4318] (Paris: Editions du Cerf, 1970).

Decretum Gratiani (Concordia discordantia canonum) digital edition, Gratian (c. 1150), http://geschichte.digitale-sammlungen.de/decretum-gratiani/online/angebot. Bayerische StaatsBibliothek (2009). Accessed 16 February 2015.

Dekkers, Eligius, Jean Fraipont et al., eds, *Sancti Aurelii Augustini: Enarrationes in Psalmos I-L* [CCSL 38] (Turnhout: Brepols, 1956) [reprinted 1990].

Dekkers, Eligius, Jean Fraipont et al., eds, *Sancti Aurelii Augustini: Enarrationes in Psalmos LI-C* [CCSL 39] (Turnhout: Brepols, 1956) [2nd edn 1990].

Douch, H.L., ed., *The Cornwall Muster Roll for 1569* (Bristol: T.L. Stoate, 1984).

Erbermann, Vitus, ed., *Disputationum Roberti Bellarmini Politiani S.J., S.R.E. Cardinalis De Controversiis Christianæ Fidei ... 4 vols* (Venice: Malachinus, 1721). Google Books, https://books.google.co.uk/books?id=wlJ5HeirAfYC. Accessed 18 October 2018.

Evans, Ernest, ed., *Q. Septimii Florentis Tertulliani De Resurrectione Carnis Liber/Tertullian's Treatise on the Resurrection* (London: SPCK, 1972), online version at http://www.tertullian.org/articles/evans_res/evans_res_01title.htm. Accessed 18 October 2018.

Evans, Ernest, ed., *Tertullian: Adversus Marcionem* (Oxford, OUP, 1972), online version at http://www.tertullian.org/articles/evans_marc/evans_marc_00index.htm. Accessed 18 October 2018.

Field, Frederick, ed., *Ioannis Chrysostomi Archiepiscopi Constantinopolitani Interpretatio Omnium Epistolarum Paulinarum* ... (Oxford: J.H. Parker, 1847).

Field, Frederick, ed. *[Joannis] Chrysostomi homiliae in Matthaeum*, 3 vols (Cambridge: CUP, 1838–1839).

Gay, S.E., H. Fox, S. Fox and H. Tapley-Soper, *The Register of Marriages, Baptisms and Burials of the Parish of Camborne, Co. Cornwall, A.D. 1538 to 1837* (Exeter: Devon and Cornwall Record Society, 1945) ed., 2 vols.

Gerlo, A., et al., eds, *Tertulliani Opera II: Opera montanistica* (CCSL 2) [19, J.G.P. Borleffs, ed., *De resurrectione mortuorum*, pp. 921–1012] (Turnhout: Brepols, 1954), reprinted 1996.

Gildersleeve, Basil Lanneau, *The Apologies of Justin Martyr, to which is appended the Epistle to Diagnotus* (New York: Harper & Brothers, 1877).

Glorie, F. (after J. Leroy), *Eusebius 'Gallicanus', Collectio Homilarum*, vol. 1 (CCSL 101) (Turnhout: Brepols, 1970).

Hansen, Günther Christian, ed., *Anonyme Kirchengeschichte (Gelasius Cyzicenus, CPG 6034)* (Berlin: Walter de Gruyter, 2002). https://doi.org/10.1515/9783110889482

Harrison, Douglas, ed., *The First and Second Prayer Books of Edward VI* (London: Dent, 1968).

Harvey, John H., ed., *William Worcestre: Itineraries* (Oxford: Clarendon, 1969).

Isaacson, R.F., and R. Arthur, *The Episcopal Registers of the Diocese of St David's, 1397–1518*, Roberts, Cymmrodorion Record Series (London: The Honourable Society of Cymmrodorion, 1917), 3 vols.

Jelf, Richard William, ed., *The Works of John Jewel, D.D., Bishop of Salisbury*, vol. 3 (Oxford: OUP, 1848).

Jenkyns, Henry, *The Remains of Thomas Cranmer, D.D., Archbishop of Canterbury*, 4 vols (Oxford: OUP, 1833).

John Paul II (Pope) [Karol Woytyła], Apostolic Letter, *Dominicae Cenae* (24 February 1980), https://www.vatican.va/content/john-paul-ii/en/letters/1980/documents/hf_jp-ii_let_19800224_dominicae-cenae.html. Accessed 1 November 2018.

Knöll, Pius, ed., *S. Aureli Augustini: Confessionum libri XIII* [CSEL 33] (Vienna: Tempsky, 1896).

Kokkinakis, Athenagoras [Archbishop of Thyateira and Great Britain], *Η Λειτουγία της Ορθοδόξου Εκκλησίας/The Liturgy of the Orthodox Church* (London and Oxford: Mowbrays, 1979).

Kristensson, G., ed., *John Mirk's Instructions for parish priests*, Lund Studies in English 49 (London: Lund, 1974).

Labbé, Philippe and Gabriel Cossart, eds, *Sacrosancta Concilia ad Regiam Editionem Exacta* ... (Paris: Societas Typocraphica Librorum Ecclesiasticorum, 1671), 17 vols.

Le Neve, John, *Fasti Ecclesiae Anglicanae 1300-1541, IX, Exeter Diocese*, compiled and revised by Horn, Joyce M. (London: Athlone Press, University of London Institute of Historical Research, 1964).

Legg, John Wickham, ed., *Missale as Usum Ecclesie Westmonasteriensis* (London: Harrison & Sons, 1891) reprinted for The Henry Bradshaw Society (Woodbridge, Suffolk: Boydell & Brewer, 1999), vol. 1, pp. 393-4.

Lewis, E.A., ed., *Welsh Port Books, 1550-1603: with an Analysis of the Customs Revenue Accounts of Wales for the Same Period*, Cymmrodorion Record Series XII (London: The Honourable Society of Cymmrodorion, 1927).

Letters and Papers, Foreign & Domestic, Henry VIII, Volumes 7-12, ed. James Gairdner (London: HMSO, 1883-1890).

Libri Quattuor Sententiarum, digital transcription of Magistri Petri Lombardi [Peter Lombard], *Sententiae in IV libros distinctae*, Abbey of Grottaferrata (Rome: Quaracchi, 1971), http://www.hs-augsburg.de/~harsch/Chronologia/Lspost12/PetrusLombardus/pet_s100.html, Hochschule Augsburg, Bibliotheca Augustana. Accessed 16 February 2015.

McLelland, Joseph C., tr. and ed., *Peter Martyr Vermigli: The Oxford Treatise and Disputation on the Eucharist, 1549* (Kirksville: Thomas Jefferson University Press, 1994).

Mansi, Giovanni Domenico, *Sacrorum Conciliorum Nova et Amplissima Collectio* (Florence: Antonio Zatta, 1768), vol. 13, Documenta Catholica Omnia online, http://www.documentacatholicaomnia.eu/04z/z_1692-1769__Mansi_JD__Sacrorum_Conciliorum_Nova_Amplissima_Collectio_Vol_013__LT.pdf.html. Accessed 5 November 2018.

Military Survey (1522), see Stoate, T.L., ed., *Cornwall Military Survey 1522*.

Minns, Dennis and Paul Parvis, eds, *Justin, Philosopher and Martyr: Apologies* [Oxford Early Christian Texts] (Oxford: OUP, 2009).

Mirk's Festial: A Collection of Homilies by Johannes Mirkus (John Mirk), edited from Bodl. MS. Gough Eccl. Top. 4, with variant readings from other MSS., ed. Theodor Erbe (London: Kegan, Paul, Trench, Trübner & Co. for the Early English Texts Society, 1905). Internet Archive, https://archive.org/details/mirksfestialcoll01mirkuoft/page/n1. Accessed 23 December 2018.

Morris, J., *The Troubles of our Catholic Forefathers, related by themselves* (London: Burns & Oates, 1877).

Muller, J.A., ed., *The Letters of Stephen Gardiner* (Cambridge: CUP, 1933).

Munier, Charles, ed. *Saint Justin: Apologie pour le Chretiens* [Sources Chrétiennes 507] (Paris: Éditions du Cerf, 2006).

Muster Roll (1569), see Douch, H.L., ed., *The Cornwall Muster Roll for 1569*.

Nairn, J. Arbuthnot, ed., Περι Ἱερωσυνης *(De Sacerdotio) of St John Chrysostom* (Cambridge: CUP, 1906). https://doi.org/10.1093/jts/os-VII.28.575

New Oxford Annotated Bible: New Revised Standard Version with the Apocrypha, Fifth Edition, ed. Michael D. Coogan (Oxford: OUP, 2018).

Nova Vulgata: Bibliorum Sacrorum Editio, iuxta editionem typicam alteram (Vatican City: Libreria Editrice Vaticana, 1998).

Orme, Nicholas, ed., *Nicholas Roscarrock's Lives of the Saints, Cornwall and Devon* (Exeter: Devon and Cornwall Record Society, 1992). [Devon and Cornwall Record Society, new series, 35] edited from Cambridge University Library, MS Add. 3041 (C).

Paul VI (Pope) [Giovanni Battista Montini], *Mysterium Fidei*, tr. Rev. A. Garvey (London, Catholic Truth Society, 1965).

Paul VI (Pope) [Giovanni Battista Montini], *The 'Credo' of the People of God* (London: Catholic Truth Society, 1968).

Peel, Albert, ed., *The Seconde Parte of a Register, being a calendar of Manuscripts under that title intended for publication by the Puritans about 1593, and now in Dr Williams' Library, London* (Cambridge: CUP, 1915), 2 vols.

Petschenig, Michael, ed., *S. Aureli Augustini Operi 7: Psalmus contra partem Donati, Contra epistulam Parmeniani, De baptismo* [CSEL 51/1] (Vienna: Tempsky, 1908).

Petschenig, Michael, ed. *S. Aureli Augustini: Contra litteras Petiliani, Epistula ad catholicos de secta Donatistarum, Contra Cresconium grammaticum et Donatistam* [CSEL 52] (Vienna: Tempsky, 1909).

Petschenig, Michael, ed. (editio altera, rev. Michaela Zelzer), *Sancti Ambrosi Opera 6: Explanatio psalmorum XII* [CSEL 64] (Vienna: Verlag der Österreichischen Akademie der Wissenschaften, 1999).

Phillimore, W.P.W. and Thomas Taylor, et al. [inc. William J. Stephens for later volumes], eds, *Cornwall Parish Registers: Marriages* (London: Phillimore & Co., 1900–10), vols 1 (1900), 5 (1903), 16 (1909), 18 (1910).

Proctor, Francis and Christopher Wordsworth, eds, *Breviarum ad Usum Insignis Ecclesiae Sarum*, vol. 1, *Kalendarium et Temporale* (Cambridge, CUP, 1882).

Reports from Commissioners etc. 1846: Seventh Report of the Deputy Keeper of the Public Records (London: William Clowes/HMSO, 1846).

Rousseau, Adelin, et al., eds, *Irénée de Lyon, Contre les hérésies: Dénonciation et refutation de la gnose au nom menteur*, nouvelle edition (Paris: Éditions du Cerf, 2001).

Sandon, Nick, ed., *The Use of Salisbury: The Ordinary of the Mass*, 2nd edn (Newton Abbot, Antico Church Music, 1990).

Schmitz, Josef, ed. *De Sacramentis. De Mysteriis/Über die Sakramente. Über die Mysterien* (Freiburg: Herder, 1990)—part of the series of critical editions, *Fontes Christiani*.

The Second Report of the Royal Commission on Historical Manuscripts, Appendix (London: Eyre & Spottiswoode, 1874).

Septuaginta, Alfred Rahlfs, ed., 2 vols (Stuttgart: Deutsche Bibelstiftung, 1935).
Smulders, P., *Sancti Hilarii Pictaviensis Episcopi: De Trinitate, Libri VIII-XII* [CCSL 62A] (Turnhout: Brepols, 1980).
Snell, Lawrence S., *Documents towards a History of the Reformation in Cornwall: 1. The Chantry Certificates for Cornwall* (Exeter: James Townsend & Sons, 1953).
Stoate, T.L., ed., *Cornwall Military Survey 1522, with the Loan Books and a Tinners Muster Roll c. 1535* (Bristol: T.L. Stoate, 1987).
Stoate, T.L., ed., *Cornwall Subsidies in the reign of Henry VIII, 1524 and 1543 and the Benevolence of 1545* (Bristol: T.L. Stoate, 1985).
Stubbs, William, ed., *Registrum Sacrum Anglicanum*, 2nd edn (Oxford: OUP, 1897).
The Survey of Cornwall by Richard Carew (facsimile edition), ed. John Chynoweth, Nicholas Orme and Alexandra Walsham (Exeter: DCRS, 2004).
A Survey of London, written in the year 1598 by John Stow, ed. Antonia Fraser (Stroud: Sutton, 2005).
Talbot, Clare, ed., *Miscellanea: Recusant Records*, Catholic Record Society, 53 (London: Catholic Record Society, 1961).
TAMO (1563, 1570, 1576, 1583), Foxe, John, *Actes and Monuments*—from *The Acts and Monuments Online* or *TAMO* (1563, 1570, 1576 and 1583 editions) (The Digital Humanities Institute, Sheffield, 2011). Available from: https://www.dhi.ac.uk/foxe/, accessed 1 December 2019. (Online variorum edition from the John Foxe Book of Martyrs Project, a collaboration between the University of Sheffield, the British Academy and the Arts and Humanities Research Council.) Used with permission in this edition.
[Sancti] Thomae de Aquino, *Summa Theologiae* (Roma, Editiones Paolinae, 1962).
Thomas, R.J., Gareth A. Bevan, Patrick Donovan, eds, *Geiriadur Prifysgol Cymru/A Dictionary of the Welsh Language* (Aberystwyth: University of Wales Press, 1967–2002); and Gareth A. Bevan, Patrick Donovan, Andrew Hawke, eds, *Geiriadur Prifysgol Cymru/A Dictionary of the Welsh Language*, 2nd edn (Aberystwyth: University of Wales Press, 2002–present) and GPC Online, http://geiriadur.ac.uk/gpc/gpc.html. Accessed 5 May 2015.
Toulmin Smith, Lucy, ed., *The Itinerary of John Leland*, 5 vols (London: George Bell & Sons, 1907).
Townsend, George and Stephen Reed Cattley (T&C), eds, *The Acts and Monuments of John Foxe* (London: Seeley and Birnside, 1838).
Valor Ecclesiasticus, see Caley, John and Hunter, Joseph, eds, *Valor Ecclesiasticus*.
van den Hout, M.P.J., M. Evans et al., eds, *Sancti Aurelii Augustini: De fide rerum invisibilium; Enchiridion ad Laurentium de fide et spe et caritate etc.* [CCSL 46] (Turnhout: Brepols, 1969).
Verheijen, Lucas, ed., *Sancti Augustini: Confessionum libri XIII* [CCSL 27] (Turnhout: Brepols, 1981).
Vivian, J.L. and Drake, Henry H., eds, *The Visitation of the County of Cornwall in the year 1620* (Harleian Society, 1st series, 9) (London: Harleian Society, 1874).

Vivian, J.L., *The Visitations of Cornwall, comprising the Heralds' Visitations of 1530, 1573 & 1620* (Exeter: W. Pollard, 1887). Although the print version was used throughout, the Visitations are now online: http://www.uk-genealogy.org.uk/england/Cornwall/visitations/imgs/p469.jpg. Accessed 1 November 2015.

Willems, Radbod, ed., *Sancti Aurelii Augustini: In Iohannis evangelium tractatus CXXIV, 59, 1* [CCSL 36] (Turnhout: Brepols, 1954).

Zycha, Josef, ed., *S. Aureli Augustini Operum 6: De utilitate credendi, De duabus animabus, Contra Fortunatum Manichaeum, Contra Adimantum, Contra epistulam fundamenti, Contra Faustum Manichaeum* [CSEL 25/1] (Vienna: Tempsky, 1891).

Secondary Sources

Published Works

Ackroyd, Peter R., *The First Book of Samuel* (Cambridge: CUP, 1971).

Allen, Amanda Wrenn, *The Eucharistic Debate in Tudor England: Thomas Cranmer, Stephen Gardiner and the English Reformation* (London and New York: Lexington, 2018).

Allen, Pauline ed., *John Chrysostom, Homilies on Paul's Letter to the Philippians* (Atlanta: Society of Biblical Literature, 2013).

Bailey, Lisa [Kaaren], 'Monks and Lay Communities in Late Antique Gaul: The Evidence of the Eusebius Gallicanus Sermons', *Journal of Medieval History*, 32, 4 (December 2006), pp. 315–332. https://doi.org/10.1016/j.jmedhist.2006.09.001

Bailey, Lisa Kaaren, *Christianity's Quiet Success: The Eusebius Gallicanus Sermon Collection and the Power of the Church in Late Antique Gaul* (Notre Dame: University of Notre Dame Press, 2010). https://doi.org/10.2307/j.ctvpj7d4d

Bainbridge, William S., ed., *The Westminster Hymnal* (London: Burns & Oates, 1956).

Bernard, G.W., *The King's Reformation* (New Haven and London: Yale University Press, 2005).

Besamusca, Bart, Gareth Griffith, Matthias Meyer, Hannah Morcos, 'Author Attributions in Medieval Text Collections: An Exploration', in *Amsterdamer Beiträge zur älteren Germanistik* 76 (Leiden: Brill, 2016).

Bettenson, Henry, ed. and tr., *The Early Christian Fathers* (Oxford: OUP, 1974).

Bettenson, Henry, ed. and tr., *The Later Christian Fathers* (Oxford: OUP, 1978).

Betty, J.H., *Wessex from AD 1000: A Regional History of England* (London: Longman, 1986).

Bock, Albert, 'Representation of Intervocalic Single /l/ and Geminate /ll/ in Sacrament an Alter' (University of Vienna: 2010) https://homepage.univie.ac.at/albert.bock/archive/l_ll_lh_SA.pdf. Accessed 3 September 2018.

Boggis, R.J.E., *A History of the Diocese of Exeter* (Exeter: William Pollard & Co., 1922).
Bossy, John, *The English Catholic Community, 1570-1850* (London: Dalton, Longman & Todd, 1975).
Boulding, Maria, tr., *Expositions of the Psalms, vol. 2, 33–50* [The Works of St Augustine: A translation for the 21st century] (New York: New City Press, 2000). Google Books, https://books.google.co.uk/books?id=uKE0rsMmmR4C&lpg=PA1. Accessed 26 October 2018.
Bourke, Vernon J., ed., *Saint Augustine: Confessions* [The Fathers of the Church, 21] (New York, Catholic University of America, 1953).
Bowen, Geraint, *Welsh Recusant Writings* (Cardiff: University of Wales, 1999).
Boyan, ed. 'Life of Francis Tregian, Written in the Seventeenth Century by Francis Plunkett, Cistercian Monk', in *Miscellanea*, Catholic Record Society, 32 (London: Catholic Record Society, 1932).
Boyan, P.A. and G.R. Lamb, *Francis Tregian: Cornish Recusant* (London: Sheed & Ward, 1955).
Brigden, S., *London and the Reformation* (Oxford: Clarendon Press, 1989).
Bruch, Benjamin. 'Medieval Cornish Versification: An Overview'. *Keltische Forschungen*, 4: 55–126 (2009). https://benjaminbruch.com/wp-content/uploads/2019/12/Bruch_Medieval_Cornish_Versification.pdf. Accessed 30 August 2022.
Bruch, Benjamin. 'Word and Music in Middle Cornish Drama'. *Ars Lyrica* 17: *Ars Lyrica Celtica; In Memoriam Bernard Le Nail*, 45–74 (2008 [2010]). https://benjaminbruch.com/wp-content/uploads/2019/12/Bruch_Word_and_Music.pdf. Accessed 30 August 2022.
Burr, David, 'Eucharistic Presence and Conversion in Late Thirteenth-Century Franciscan Thought', in *Transactions of the American Philosophical Society*, 74, 3 (Philadelphia: American Philosophical Society, 1984), Google Books, https://books.google.co.uk/books?id=3z4LAAAAIAAJ&lpg=PP1. Accessed 18 October 2018.
Caball, Marc, 'Gaelic and Protestant: A Case Study in Early Modern Self-Fashioning, 1567–1608', *Proceedings of the Royal Irish Academy: Archaeology, Culture, History, Literature*, vol. 110C (Dublin: Royal Irish Academy, 2010), pp. 194–5. https://doi.org/10.3318/PRIAC.2010.110.191
Caraman, Philip, *The Western Rising, 1549* (Tiverton: Westcountry Books, 1994).
Carleton, Kenneth, 'Thomas Watson (1513–1584)', in *Oxford Dictionary of National Biography* online. https://doi.org/10.1093/ref:odnb/28865
Chadwick, Henry, *The Early Church* (London: Pelican, 1967) [reprinted Penguin, 1990].
Chaudhri, Talat, 'A Description of the Middle Cornish Tregear Manuscript', MA thesis, 2001, Aberystwyth University. http://cadair.aber.ac.uk/dspace/handle/2160/377. Accessed 8 February 2016.

Chubb, Ray, Richard Jenkin and Graham Sandercock, eds, *The Cornish Ordinalia, first play: Origo Mundi* (Portreath: Agan Tavas, 2001)—based on the MS edition of R. Morton Nance and A.S.D. Smith.
Chynoweth, John, *Tudor Cornwall* (Stroud: Tempus Publishing, 2002).
Clark, Francis, *Eucharistic Sacrifice and the Reformation* (Chulmleigh: Augustine Publishing Company, 1980).
Clark, Margaret, 'Owen Oglethorpe (1502/3–1559)', in *Oxford Dictionary of National Biography* online. https://doi.org/10.1093/ref:odnb/20617
Coffey, John, *Persecution and Toleration in Protestant England, 1558-1689* (Harlow, Essex: Longman/Pearson, 2000).
Collinson, Patrick and John Craig, eds, *The Reformation in English Towns, 1500-1640* (Basingstoke: Macmillan, 1998). https://doi.org/10.1007/978-1-349-26832-0
Collinson, Patrick, 'Truth and Legend: The Veracity of John Foxe's Book of Martyrs', in *Elizabethans* (London and New York: A&C Black, 2003), pp. 151-69.
Collinson, P. and P. Ha, eds, *The Reception of Continental Reformation in Britain and Ireland* [Proceedings of the British Academy 164] (Oxford: OUP for the British Academy, 2010).
Collinson, Patrick, *John Foxe as Historian*—Essay 3 in the introductory material for *The Unabridged Acts and Monuments Online* or *TAMO*, https://www.dhi.ac.uk/foxe/index.php?realm=more&gototype=&type=essay&book=essay3 (The Digital Humanities Institute, Sheffield, 2011). Accessed 10 June 2014.
Combellack, Myrna, *The Camborne Play: A Verse Translation of* Beunans Meriasek (Redruth: Dyllansow Truran, 1988).
Craig, John, 'Erasmus or Calvin? The Politics of Book Purchase in the Early Modern English Parish', in P. Collinson and P. Ha, eds, *The Reception of Continental Reformation in Britain and Ireland* [Proceedings of the British Academy 164] (Oxford: OUP for the British Academy, 2010), pp. 39-62. https://doi.org/10.5871/bacad/9780197264683.003.0003
Cross, Claire, 'Religion in Doncaster from the Reformation to the Civil War', in Patrick Collinson and John Craig, eds, *The Reformation in English Towns, 1500-1640* (Basingstoke: Macmillan, 1998). https://doi.org/10.1007/978-1-349-26832-0_3
Deacon, Bernard, *The Cornish Family* (Fowey: Cornwall Editions, 2004).
Deacon, Bernard, *The Surnames of Cornwall* (Redruth: CoSerg, 2019).
Deferrari, Roy J., ed., *St Ambrose: Theological and Dogmatic Works* (Washington: Catholic University of America, 1963).
Dickens, A.G., *The English Reformation*, revised edn (London: Fontana, 1967).
Douglas, Brian, *A Companion to Anglican Eucharistic Theology, Volume 1: The Reformation to the 19th Century* (Leiden/Boston: Brill, 2012). https://doi.org/10.1163/9789004221321
Dugmore, C.W., *The Mass and the English Reformers* (London: Macmillan, 1958).

Duffy, Eamon, *The Stripping of the Altars: Traditional Religion in England 1400-1580*, 1st edn (New Haven and London: Yale University Press, 1992) and 2nd edn (New Haven and London: Yale University Press, 2005).

Duffy, Eamon, *The Voices of Morebath: Reformation & Rebellion in an English Village* (New Haven and London: Yale University Press, 2001).

Duffy, Eamon and David Loades, eds, *The Church of Mary Tudor* (Aldershot and Burlington: Ashgate, 2006).

Duffy, Eamon, *Fires of Faith: Catholic England under Mary Tudor* (New Haven and London: Yale University Press, 2009).

Duffy, Eamon, *Reformation Divided: Catholics, Protestants and the Conversion of England* (London: Bloomsbury, 2007).

Edwards, Ray, *Notennow Kernewek 4 [Peswara Dyllans 2000]* (Sutton Coldfield, Kernewek Dre Lyther/Kesva an Taves Kernewek, 1997).

Ellis, Peter Berresford, *The Cornish Language and its Literature* (London: Routledge, Kegan & Paul, 1974).

Emden, A.B., *A Biographical Register of the University of Oxford, A.D. 1501 to 1540* (Oxford: Clarendon Press, 1970).

Eska, Joseph F. and Benjamin Bruch, 'The Late Cornish Syntax of William Bodinar', *Études Celtiques* 47 (2021), pp. 197-218.

Evenden, Elizabeth and Thomas S. Freeman, *Religion and the Book in Early Modern England: The Making of Foxe's 'Book of Martyrs'* (Cambridge: CUP, 2011).

Fathers of the English Dominican Province, tr., *The Summa Theologica of St Thomas Aquinas* (London: Burns Oates & Washbourne, 1920-35).

Fox, H.S.A, and Oliver J. Padel, eds (2000), *The Cornish Lands of the Arundells of Lanherne, Fourteenth to Sixteenth Centuries*, Devon and Cornwall Record Society (DCRS), new series, 21 (Exeter: Devon and Cornwall Record Society, 2000).

Freeman, Thomas S., 'Notes on a Source for John Foxe's Account of the Marian Persecution in Kent and Sussex', *Historical Research*, 67 (1994). https://doi.org/10.1111/j.1468-2281.1994.tb01825.x

Freeman, Thomas S., 'Fate, Faction, and Fiction in Foxe's Book of Martyrs', *Historical Journal*, 43 (2000). https://doi.org/10.1017/S0018246X99001296

Frost, D.H., 'Sacrament an Alter—a Tudor Cornish patristic *catena* drawn from Foxe's account of the Oxford disputations of 1554', in Philip Payton, ed., *Cornish Studies*, 2nd series, 11 (Exeter: UEP, 2003), pp. 291-307.

Frost, D.H., 'Glasney's Parish Clergy and the Tregear Manuscript', in Philip Payton, ed., *Cornish Studies*, 2nd series, 15 (Exeter: UEP, 2007), pp. 27-89. https://doi.org/10.1386/corn.15.1.27_1

Frost, D.H., 'Interpreting a Medieval Church through Liturgy', in the Proceedings of the National History Museum of Wales Conference 'The Welsh Medieval Church and its Context' (15 Nov. 2008), http://www.museumwales.ac.uk/teilo/conference/. Accessed 10 June 2014.

Frost, D.H., 'Glasney's Parish Clergy and the Tregear Manuscript' (revised and updated version) in Payton, Philip, ed., *Cornwall in the Age of Rebellion, 1490-1690* (Exeter: UEP, 2021), ch. 7, pp. 162–328.

Fryde, E.B., D.E. Greenway, S. Porter and I. Roy, eds, *Handbook of British Chronology*, 3rd edn (Cambridge: CUP, 1986).

Fuidge, N.M., *Michell, John (d. c. 1588), of Truro, Cornw.*, History of Parliament Online, http://www.historyofparliamentonline.org/volume/1558-1603/member/michell-john-1588. Accessed 25 May 2016.

Fuidge, N.M., *Meyrick (Merrick) Gelly (c. 1556-1601), of Gellyswick, Hascard, Pemb.; Wigmore Castle, Herefs; Gladestry, Rad. And Essex House, London.* History of Parliament Online, http://www.historyofparliamentonline.org/volume/1558-1603/member/meyrick-(merrick)-gelly-1556-1601. Accessed 25 May 2016.

Fulton, Helen, ed. *Medieval Celtic Literature and Society* (Dublin: Four Courts Press, 2005), pp. 95–116.

Gendall, Richard R.M., *A Student's Grammar of Modern Cornish* (Menheniot: The Cornish Language Council, 1991).

Gendall, Richard R.M., *Tavas a Ragadazow* (Menheniot: Teer ha Tavaz, 2000).

George, Ken, ed., *An Gerlyver Meur*, 2nd edn (Bodmin: Kesva an Taves Kernewek, 2009); 3rd edn (Kesva an Taves Kernewek, 2020).

Gibbs, Gary G., 'William Tresham, 1495–1569', in *Oxford Dictionary of National Biography* online. https://doi.org/10.1093/ref:odnb/27714

Gregory, Brad S., *Salvation at Stake: Christian Martyrdom in Early Modern Europe* (Cambridge, MA: Harvard University Press, 1999).

Gwyn, Peter, *The King's Cardinal: The Rise and Fall of Thomas Wolsey* (London: Pimlico, 2002).

Haigh, Christopher, 'The Continuity of Catholicism in the English Reformation', in *Past and Present*, 93, 1 (November 1981), pp. 33–69. https://doi.org/10.1093/past/93.1.37

Haigh, Christopher, 'The English Reformation: A Premature Birth, A Difficult Labour and a Sickly Child', *The Historical Journal*, 33: 2 (1990), pp. 449–59. https://doi.org/10.1017/S0018246X0001342X

Haigh, Christopher, *English Reformations: Religion, Politics and Society under the Tudors* (Oxford: Clarendon Press, 1993).

Haigh, Christopher, 'Catholicism in Early Modern England and Beyond' (review article) in *The Historical Journal*, 45: 2 (Cambridge: CUP, 2002), pp. 481–94. https://doi.org/10.1017/S0018246X02002479

Hamrick, Stephen, *The Catholic Imaginary and the Cults of Elizabeth, 1558-1582* (Farnham: Ashgate, 2009).

Handford, S.A., tr., *Caesar: The Conquest of Gaul*, 1.1 (Harmondsworth: Penguin, 1951).

Harkins, Paul W., tr., *On the Incomprehensible Nature of God by St John Chrysostom* (Washington: Catholic University of America, 1982).

Hasler, P.W., *The History of Parliament: The House of Commons, 1558-1603*, 3 vols (London: The Stationery Office/Boydell & Brewer, 1981).

Hawke, Andrew, *The Cornish Dictionary Project: First Progress Report* (Redruth: Institute of Cornish Studies, 1981).

Hawke, Andrew, 'A Rediscovered Cornish-English Vocabulary' [NLW Bodewryd MS 5], in Philip Payton, ed., *Cornish Studies*, 2nd series, 9 (Exeter: UEP, 2001), pp. 83-104.

Heal, Felicity, *Reformation in Britain and Ireland* [Oxford History of the Christian Church] (Oxford: OUP, 2003). https://doi.org/10.1093/0198269242.001.0001

Heal, Felicity, 'Mediating the Word: Language and Dialects in the British and Irish Reformations', *Journal of Ecclesiastical History*, 56: 2 (Cambridge: CUP, April 2005), pp. 261-86. https://doi.org/10.1017/S0022046904003161

Henderson, Charles, 'The 109 Ancient Parishes of the Four Western Hundreds of Cornwall', in the *Journal of the Royal Institution of Cornwall (JRIC)* [written 1923-1924, posthumously published], new series, 2, 3 (1955), pp. 1-104; 2, 4 (1956), pp. 105-210; 3, 2 (1958), pp. 211-382; 3, 4 (1960), pp. 383-497.

Henry, Victor, *Lexique Etymologique [des termes les plus usuels] du Breton Moderne* (Rennes: Plihon & Hervé, 1900).

Highley, Christopher and John N. King, eds, *John Foxe and his World* (Oxford: Routledge, 2017) [first published in 2002]. https://doi.org/10.4324/9781315251486

Hill, Robert Charles, *St John Chrystostom: Commentary on the Psalms* (Massachusetts: Holy Cross Press, 1998), 2 vols.

Holmes, Julyan, 'On the track of Cornish in a bilingual country', in Philip Payton, ed., *Cornish Studies*, 2nd series, 11 (Exeter: UEP, 2003), pp. 270-90.

Hooper, E.G.R., ed., *Passyon agan Arluth* (Camborne, Kesva an Tavas Kernewek, 1972)—based on the MS edition of R. Morton Nance and A.S.D. Smith.

Hutton, Ronald, *The Rise and Fall of Merry England, the Ritual Year 1400-1700* (Oxford: OUP, 1994). https://doi.org/10.1093/acprof:oso/9780198203636.001.0001

Jenkins, Robert Thomas, ed., *Dictionary of Welsh Biography* (down to 1940) (London: The Honourable Society of Cymmrodorion, 1959).

Jenner, Henry (1904), *A Handbook of the Cornish Language, chiefly in its later stages with some account of its history and literature* (London: David Nutt, 1904).

Jenner, Henry, 'A Cornish Oration in Spain in the Year 1600', in the 90th *Annual Report of the Royal Cornwall Polytechnic Society* (1923) cited from Peter Berresford Ellis, *The Cornish Language and its Literature* (London: Routledge, Kegan & Paul, 1974), p. 70.

Jeremias, Joachim, *The Eucharistic Words of Jesus* (London, SCM, 1966).

Juhász, Gergely M., *Translating Resurrection: The Debate between William Tyndale and George Joye in its Historical and Theological Context* (Leiden: Brill, 2014). https://doi.org/10.1163/9789004259522

Jungmann, Joseph A., *The Mass of the Roman Rite: its Origins and Development*, vols 1 and 2, trans. by Francis A. Brunner from the German edition *Missarum Sollemnia* of 1949 (New York: Benziger, 1951), reprinted (Notre Dame: Ave Maria Press, 2012).

Keble, John, ed., *The Homilies of St John Chrysostom, Archbishop of Constantinople, on the First Epistle of St Paul the Apostle to the Corinthians*, Part I, Homilies i–xxiv (Oxford: John Henry Parker, 1839).

Kelly, J.N.D., *Early Christian Creeds*, 3rd edn (London: Longman, 1972).

Kelly, J.N.D., *Early Christian Doctrines*, 5th edn (London: Adam & Charles Black, 1977).

Kennedy, Thomas, 'The Edwards Family of Plas Newydd in Chirkland', in *Trafodion Cymdeithas Hanes Sir Ddinbych/Denbighshire Historical Society Transactions*, 60, 41 (1992), pp. 71–85.

Knighton, C.S., 'Hugh Weston (1510–1558), dean of Windsor', in *Oxford Dictionary of National Biography* online. https://doi.org/10.1093/ref:odnb/29122

Knox, Ronald A., tr., *The Holy Bible: a translation from the Latin Vulgate in the light of the Hebrew and Greek originals* (London: Burns & Oates, 1961).

Lewis, Charlton D., *An Elementary Latin Dictionary* (Oxford: OUP, 1981) (1st edn 1891).

Loades, David, *Mary Tudor: A Life* (Oxford: Blackwell, 1992).

Loades, David (D.M.), ed., *John Foxe: An Historical Perspective* (Aldershot: Ashgate, 1999).

Loades, David, *Mary Tudor: The Tragical History of the First Queen of England* (Kew: The National Archives, 2006).

Loades, David, 'The Marian Episcopate', in Eamon Duffy and David Loades, eds, *The Church of Mary Tudor* (Aldershot: Ashgate, 2006), pp. 33–56.

Lord, Peter (with John Morgan-Guy), *The Visual Culture of Wales: Medieval Vision* (part of the University of Wales Centre for Advanced Welsh and Celtic Studies Project, 'The Visual Culture of Wales' (Cardiff: University of Wales Press, 2003).

Lossky, Vladimir, *The Mystical Theology of the Eastern Church* (Cambridge and London: James Clark & Co., 1957; reprinted 1973).

Löwe, J. Andreas, 'Richard Smyth [Smith] (1499/1500–1563)', in *Oxford Dictionary of National Biography* online. https://doi.org/10.1093/ref:odnb/25885

MacCulloch, Diarmuid, 'The Myth of the English Reformation', *Journal of British Studies*, 30: 1 (1991), pp. 1–19.

MacCulloch, Diarmaid, *Thomas Cranmer: A Life* (New Haven and London: Yale University Press, 1996).

MacCulloch, Diarmaid, *Tudor Church Militant: Edward VI and the Protestant Reformation* (London: Allen Lane/Penguin, 1999).
McGrath, Patrick and Joy Rowe, 'The Marian Priests under Elizabeth I', *Recusant History*, 17: 2 (1984), pp. 103–20.
MacMahon, Luke, 'William Chedsey (1510/11–1577), Roman Catholic priest', in *Oxford Dictionary of National Biography* online. https://doi.org/10.1093/ref:odnb/5204
Matthews, John Hobson, *A History of the Parishes if Saint Ives, Lelant, Towednack and Zennor in the County of Cornwall* (London: Elliott Stock, 1892).
Mattingly, Joanna, 'The Helston Shoemakers' Guild and a Possible Connection with the 1549 Rebellion', in Philip Payton, ed., *Cornish Studies*, 2nd series, 6 (Exeter: UEP, 1998), pp. 23–45.
Mayer, Thomas F., 'The Success of Cardinal Pole's Final Legation', in Eamon Duffy and David Loades, eds, *The Church of Mary Tudor* (Aldershot and Burlington: Ashgate, 2006), pp. 149–75.
Mayer, Wendy, *The Homilies of St John Chrysostom—Provenance: Reshaping the Foundations*, Orientalia Christiana Analecta 273 (Rome: Pontificio Istituto Orientale, 2005).
Mayer, Wendy, 'The Biography of John Chrysostom and the Chronology of his Works', from the proceedings of the conference Chrysostomika II, Augustianum, Rome, 2007; updated 2014 and uploaded to Academia.edu, https://www.academia.edu/6448810/The_Biography_of_John_Chrysostom_and_the_Chronology_of_his_Works. Accessed 1 November 2018.
Miles Brown, H., *What to look for in Cornish Churches* (Newton Abbot: David & Charles, 1973).
Morini, Massimiliano, *Tudor Translation in Theory and Practice* (London: Routledge, 2017), first published 2006. https://doi.org/10.4324/9781315235547
Mozley, James Frederic, *John Foxe and his Book* (London: SPCK, 1940).
Murdoch, Brian, *Cornish Literature* (Cambridge: D.S. Brewer, 1993).
Nance, Robert Morton, *Gerlyver Noweth Kernewek ha Sowsnek: A New Cornish-English Dictionary* (St Ives: Federation of Old Cornwall Societies, 1938), reprinted in *Gerlyver Noweth Kernewek-Sawsnek ha Sawsnek-Kernewek* (Redruth: Dyllansow Truran, 1989).
Nance, Robert Morton, 'The Tregear Manuscript', in *Old Cornwall*, IV (1950), pp. 429–34.
Nance, Robert Morton, 'More about the Tregear Manuscript', in *Old Cornwall*, V (1951), pp. 21–27; 61–67.
Nance, Robert Morton, 'Something New in Cornish', in the *Journal of the Royal Institution of Cornwall*, new series, 1 (1952), pp. 119–21.
Nance, Robert Morton, 'Cornish Words in the Tregear MS', in *Zeitschrift für Celtische Philologie*, 24 (1954), pp. 1–5. https://doi.org/10.1515/zcph.1954.24.1.1

Nash, Gerallt D., ed., *Saving St Teilo's: Bringing a medieval church to life* (Cardiff: National Museum of Wales, 2009).

Neville, Graham, tr., *Saint John Chrysostom: Six Books on the Priesthood* (London: SPCK, 1977).

Newcomb, Mark Anthony, *The Ark, the Covenant, and the Poor Men's Chest: Edmund Bonner and Nicholas Ridley on Church and Scripture in Sixteenth-Century England* (South Bend: St Augustine's Press, 2016).

Newman, John Henry, ed., *Catena Aurea: Commentary on the Four Gospels collected out of the Works of the Fathers by St Thomas Aquinas*, 4 vols (Oxford: John Henry Parker, 1841). Reprinted in facsimile (London: St Austin Press, 1997).

Oliver, George, *Lives of the Bishops of Exeter* (Exeter: William Roberts, 1861).

Olson, Lynette, 'Tyranny in *Beunans Meriasek*', in Philip Payton, ed., *Cornish Studies: Five* (Exeter: UEP, 2002), pp. 52-9, updated as 'Beunans Meriasek—A Political Play?', in Philip Payton, ed., *Cornwall in the Age of Rebellion, 1490-1690* (Exeter: UEP, 2021), pp. 118-34.

Onions, C.T., ed., *The Shorter Oxford English Dictionary*, 3rd edn (Oxford: Clarendon, 1965).

Orme, Nicholas, *The Minor Clergy of Exeter Cathedral 1300-1548* (Exeter: University of Exeter, 1980).

Orme, Nicholas, *English Church Dedications*, Exeter (Exeter: University of Exeter, 1996).

Orme, Nicholas, *Medieval Children* (New Haven and London: Yale University Press, 2001).

Orme, Nicholas, *Medieval Schools, from Roman Britain to Renaissance England* (New Haven and London: Yale University Press, 2006).

Orme, Nicholas, *Cornwall and the Cross: Christianity 500-1560* (Chichester: Phillimore and Victoria County History, 2007).

Orme, Nicholas, 'The Cornish at Oxford, 1180-1540', *Journal of the Royal Institution of Cornwall* (2010), pp. 43-82.

Orme, Nicholas (with a contribution from Oliver Padel), *A History of the County of Cornwall, Volume II, Religious History to 1560* (Woodbridge: Boydell & Brewer for the University of London Institute of Historical Research, 2010) [Victoria County History].

Orme, Nicholas, *The Church in Devon 400-1560* (Exeter: Impress, 2013), pp. 97-8.

Orme, Nicholas, *Going to Church in Medieval England* (New York and London: Yale University Press, 2021).

Padel, Oliver J., ed., *The Cornish Writings of the Boson Family* (Redruth: Institute of Cornish Studies, 1975).

Padel, O.J., *Cornish Place-Name Elements*, English Place-Name Society vols 56/57 (Nottingham: English Place-Name Society, 1985).

Padel, O.J., 'Cornish Surnames in 1327', *Nomina*, 9 (1985), pp. 81-7.

Padel, O.J., *A Popular Dictionary of Cornish Place-Names* (Penzance: Alison Hodge, 1988).
Padel, Oliver, 'Oral and literary culture in medieval Cornwall', in Helen Fulton, ed., *Medieval Celtic Literature and Society* (Dublin: Four Courts Press, 2005), pp. 95–116.
Padel, O.J., 'Where was Middle Cornish Spoken?' *Cambrian Medieval Celtic Studies*, 74 (Winter 2017) (Aberystwyth: CMCS, 2017), pp. 4–5, 14–15.
Payton, Philip, ed., *Cornish Studies*, 2nd series, 9, 11 (Exeter: UEP, 2001, 2003).
Payton, Philip, *Cornwall: A History*, 2nd edn (Fowey: Cornwall Editions, 2004).
Payton, Philip, ed., *Cornish Studies*, 2nd series, 14, 15 (Exeter: UEP, 2006, 2007). https://doi.org/10.1386/corn.14.1.1_2
Payton, Philip, ed., *Cornwall in the Age of Rebellion, 1490-1690* (Exeter: UEP, 2021). https://doi.org/10.47788/LZGH4973
Peacock, E. and Rev. F.J. Furnivall, eds, *Instructions for parish priests by John Mirc*, EETS 31 (London: Early English Texts Society, 1868, rev. edn. 1902).
Peers, Chris, *Offa and the Mercian Wars* (Barnsley: Pen & Sword, 2017).
Penglase, Charles, 'The Future Indicative in the Early Modern Cornish of Tregear', *Etudes Celtiques*, 34 (2000), pp. 215–31. https://doi.org/10.3406/ecelt.1998.2139
Peter, Thurstan C., *The History of Glasney Collegiate Church, Cornwall* (Camborne: Camborne Printing and Stationary Company, 1903).
Redworth, Glyn, *In Defence of the Church Catholic: The Life of Stephen Gardiner* (Oxford: Basil Blackwell, 1990).
Redworth, Glyn, 'John Seton (1508/9–1572), Roman Catholic priest and writer on logic', in *Oxford Dictionary of National Biography* online. https://doi.org/10.1093/ref:odnb/25124
Roberts, Glyn (2004), 'William Glyn (1504–1558), bishop', in the National Library of Wales' *Y Bywgraffiadur Cymreig/Dictionary of Welsh Biography* online. https://biography.wales/article/s-GLYN-WIL-1504
Rogerson, J.W. and J.W. McKay, *Psalms 51-100* (Cambridge: CUP, 1977).
Rose-Troup, Frances, *The Western Rebellion of 1549: An Account of the Insurrections in Devonshire and Cornwall against Religious Innovations in the Reign of Edward VI* (London: Smith, Elder & Co., 1913).
Rose-Troup, Frances, 'Lists Relating to Persons Ejected from Religious Houses', *Devon & Cornwall Notes & Queries*, 17 (January 1932–October 1933), pp. 81–96, 143–4, 191–2, 238–40, 285–88, 334, 337, 381; and 18 (1934–1935), p. 45).
Rowse, A.L., *Tudor Cornwall* (London: Jonathan Cape, 1941). If cited in the revised edition (1969) the date is always given.
Rubin, Miri, *Corpus Christi: The Eucharist in Late Medieval Culture* (Cambridge: CUP, 1991).

Saak, Eric Leland, *High Way to Heaven: the Augustinian platform between reform and Reformation, 1292-1524* (Leiden: Brill, 2002). https://doi.org/10.1163/9789004474598

Saak, Eric Leland, *Creating Augustine: Interpreting Augustine and Augustinianism in the Later Middle Ages* (Oxford: OUP, 2012). https://doi.org/10.1093/acprof:oso/9780199646388.001.0001

Sandercock, Graham, ed., *The Cornish Ordinalia, second play: Christ's Passion* (Saltash: The Cornish Language Board, 1982)—based on the MS edition of R. Morton Nance and A.S.D. Smith.

Sandercock, Graham, ed., *The Cornish Ordinalia, third play: Resurrection* (Saltash: Kesva an Tavas Kernewek/The Cornish Language Board, 1984)—based on the MS edition of R. Morton Nance and A.S.D. Smith.

Schaff, Philip, ed., *St Augustine: the Writings against the Manichaeans, and Against the Donatists*, Nicene and Post-Nicene Fathers, First Series (originally published 1887) (New York: Cosimo, 2007).

Srawley, James Herbert, ed., *The Catechetical Oration of Gregory of Nyssa* (Cambridge: CUP, 1903).

Snell, Lawrence S., *The Suppression of the Religious Foundations of Devon and Cornwall* (Marazion: Wordens of Cornwall, 1967).

Spriggs, Matthew, 'Where Cornish was Spoken and When: A Provisional Synthesis', in Philip Payton, ed., *Cornish Studies*, 2nd series, 11 (Exeter: UEP, 2003), pp. 228-69 and (updated) in Philip Payton, ed., *Cornwall in the Age of Rebellion, 1490-1690* (Exeter: UEP, 2021), pp. 40-105.

Spriggs, Matthew, 'Additional Thoughts on the Medieval Cornish Bible', in Philip Payton, ed., *Cornish Studies*, 2nd series, 14 (Exeter: UEP, 2006), pp. 44-55. https://doi.org/10.1386/corn.14.1.1_2

Stephenson, J., ed., *Creeds, Councils and Controversies* (London: SPCK, 1973).

Stoyle, Mark, *West Britons: Cornish Identities and the Early Modern British State* (Exeter: UEP, 2002).

Stoyle, Mark, 'Rediscovering Difference: The Recent Historiography of Early Modern Cornwall' [2002] in Philip Payton, ed., *Cornish Studies: Ten* (Exeter: UEP, 2002), pp. 104-15 and reprinted in Philip Payton, ed. *Cornwall in the Age of Rebellion, 1490-1690* (Exeter: UEP, 2021), pp. 377-90.

Stoyle, Mark, 'Fully Bent to Fighte Oute the Matter: Reconsidering Cornwall's Role in the Western Rebellion of 1549', *The English Historical Review*, 129, 538 (Oxford: OUP, 2014), pp. 549-77.

Stoyle, Mark, 'A Hanging at St Keverne: The Execution of Two Cornish priests in 1549', *Devon and Cornwall Notes and Queries*, 42: 1 (2017), pp. 1-4.

Stoyle, Mark, *A Murderous Midsummer: The Western Rising of 1549* (New Haven, CT, and London: Yale University Press, 2022).

Styles, Philip, *A History of the County of Warwick, Volume 3: Barlichway Hundred* (London: Victoria County History, 1945).

Thebridge, Stella, ed., *Holy Trinity, Sutton Coldfield: The Story of a Parish Church and its People, 1250-2020* (Cheltenham: The History Press, 2020), especially chapter 2, 'John Vesey', pp. 40–59.

Thomas, Charles, *The Christian Antiquities of Camborne* (St Austell: Warne, 1967).

Thompson, Hamilton A., *The English Clergy (Ford Lectures for 1933)* (Oxford: OUP, 1947).

Thompson, T. and J.H. Srawley, eds, *St Ambrose on the Mysteries and the Treatise on The Sacraments by an unknown author*, Translations of Christian Literature, Series III, Liturgical Texts (New York, Macmillan, 1919).

Van de Weyer, Robert, *The First English Prayer Book* (Winchester: John Hunt, 2008).

Vincent, John A.C., trans., *Abstract of Glasney Cartulary, a Quarto MS ... in the Library of Jonathan Rashleigh, Esq. of Menabilly* (Truro: Lake & Lake, 1879).

Wabuda, Susan, 'Henry Bull, Miles Coverdale, and the making of Foxe's Book of Martyrs', in Diana Wood, ed., *Martyrs and Martyrologies*, Studies in Church History 30 (Oxford: Blackwell, 1993), pp. 255–6. https://doi.org/10.1017/S0424208400011736

Wabuda, Susan, *Preaching During the English Reformation* (Cambridge: CUP, 2002).

Walsham, Alexandra, *Church Papists: Catholicism, Conformity and Confessional Polemic in Early Modern England* (Woodbridge: The Boydell Press, 1993) [reprinted 1999].

Walsham, Alexandra, 'Yielding to the Extremity of the Time': Conformity, Orthodoxy and the Post-Reformation Catholic Community', in Peter Lake and Michael Questier, eds, *Conformity and Orthodoxy in the English Church, c. 1560-1660* [Studies in Modern British Religious History series] (Woodbridge: The Boydell Press, 2000).

Walsham, Alexandra, '"Domme preachers"? Post-reformation English Catholicism and the culture of print', *Past and Present*, 168: 1 (August 2000), pp. 72–123. https://doi.org/10.1093/past/168.1.72

Walsham, Alexandra, *Charitable Hatred: Tolerance and Intolerance in England, 1500-1700* (Manchester and New York: Manchester University Press, 2006).

Walsham, Alexandra, 'History, Memory and the English Reformation', *The Historical Journal*, 55: 4 (Cambridge: CUP, December 2012), pp. 899–938. https://doi.org/10.1017/S0018246X12000362

Walsham, Alexandra, *Catholic Reformation in Protestant Britain* [Catholic Christendom 1300–1700] (Aldershot: Ashgate, 2014).

Ware, Archimandrite Kallistos [Metropolitan Kallistos of Diokleia] and Mother Mary, tr., *The Lenten Triodion* (London: Faber & Faber, 1978).

Ware, Timothy [Metropolitan Kallistos of Diokleia], *The Orthodox Church* (Harmondsworth: Penguin Books, 1963) reprinted 1978, pp. 290–4.

Whetter, James, *The History of Glasney College* (Padstow: Tabb House, 1988).

Williams, Glanmor, *Wales and the Reformation* (Cardiff: University of Wales Press, 1999).
Williams, Nicholas, *Clappya Kernowek* (Portreath: Agan Tavas, 1997).
Williams, Nicholas, *English-Cornish Dictionary/Gerlyver Sawsnek-Kernowek* (Dublin/Redruth: Everson Gunn Teoranta/Agan Tavas, 2000).
Williams, Nicholas, *Cornish Today, Third Edition* (Cathair na Mart/Westport: Evertype, 2006–1st edn published 1995).
Williams, Nicholas, *Towards Authentic Cornish* (Cathair na Mart/Westport: Evertype, 2006).
Williams, Nicholas J.A., 'I-Affection in Breton and Cornish', in Philip Payton, ed., *Cornish Studies*, 2nd series, 14 (Exeter: UEP, 2006), pp. 24–43. https://doi.org/10.1386/corn.14.1.24_1
Williams, Nicholas, *Desky Kernowek: A Complete Guide to Cornish* (Cathair na Mart/Westport: Evertype, 2012).
Williams, Robert, *Lexicon Cornu-Britannicum* (Llandovery: Roderic and London: Trubner, 1865).
Wizeman, William, SJ, *The Theology and Spirituality of Mary Tudor's Church* [Catholic Christendom 1300–1700] (Aldershot: Ashgate, 2006).
Wizeman, William, SJ, 'John Harpsfield (1516–1578), religious writer and Roman Catholic priest', in *Oxford Dictionary of National Biography* online. https://doi.org/10.1093/ref:odnb/12368
Wizeman, William, SJ, 'The Theology and Spirituality of a Marian Bishop: the Pastoral and Polemical Sermons of Thomas Watson', in Eamon Duffy and David Loades, eds, *The Church of Mary Tudor* (Aldershot and Burlington: Ashgate, 2006), pp. 258–80.
Wmffre, Iwan, *Late Cornish* (Languages of the World/Materials 135) (Munich/Newcastle: Lincom, 1998).
Wood, Diana, ed., *Martyrs and Martyrologies*, Studies in Church History 30 (Oxford: Blackwell, 1993), pp. 255–6.
Wooding, Lucy E.C., *Rethinking Catholicism in Reformation England* (Oxford: Clarendon Press, 2000).
Wooding, Lucy [E.C.], 'The Marian Restoration and the Mass', in Eamon Duffy and David Loades, eds, *The Church of Mary Tudor* (Aldershot and Burlington: Ashgate, 2006), pp. 227–57.
Wooding, Lucy, 'Erasmus and the Politics of Translation in Tudor England', *Studies in Church History*, 53 (Cambridge: CUP, 2017), pp. 132–45. https://doi.org/10.1017/stc.2016.9
Wooding, L.E.C., 'Thomas Harding (1516–1572), theologian and religious controversialist', in *Oxford Dictionary of National Biography* online. https://doi.org/10.1093/ref:odnb/12264

Privately Circulated/Unpublished Works

Bice, Christopher, ed., *Homelyes xiij in cornysch* (based on Nance's transcriptions and privately circulated in cyclostyled form, 1969).

Bruch, Benjamin, 'Analysis and Classification of Twelve Copies of Bishop Edmund Bonner's Homilies (1555)', Canolfan Uwchefrydiau Cymreig a Cheltaidd Prifysgol Cymru [University of Wales Centre for Advanced Welsh and Celtic Studies], 29 June 2007. (Privately circulated, 2007.)

Bruch, Benjamin, 'Towards a Critical Edition of the Tregear Homilies', 27th Annual Harvard Celtic Colloquium, Barker Centre, Harvard University, 5 October 2007. (Privately circulated, 2007.)

Bruch, Benjamin, *The Tregear Homilies*, unpublished edn (Privately circulated, 2008.) Updated with the privately circulated readings of TH 11-12 and SA by D.H. Frost, 2009.

Field, C.W., *Exeter Diocese in 1563: Alley's Survey* (Robertsbridge, Sussex: privately published typescript, 1994).

Field, C.W., *The Province of Canterbury and the Elizabethan Settlement of Religion* (Robertsbridge, Sussex: privately published typescript, 1972).

Frost, D.H., *Sacrament an Alter*, draft unpublished reading (privately circulated, 2003), revised unpublished reading (privately circulated, 2009).

Frost, D.H., *The Tregear Homilies 11-12*, unpublished reading (privately circulated, 2009).

Gunn, H.S., *History of the Old Manor House of Wood Bevington* (privately printed, 1911).

Hawke, Andrew, *Homelyes xiij in cornysche*, electronic file of unpublished reading [privately circulated, 1977-1998].

Mullins, Daniel J., '*St Francis Xavier College*' [unpublished lecture given to the Wales and Marches Catholic History Society at St David's Catholic College, Cardiff, in June 2006].

Syed, R. Keith R., *Homelyes xiij in cornysch* (privately circulated, 2003), an electronic copy of Christopher Bice's cyclostyled transcription of the Tregear Homilies.

Index

abbreviations   19n, 77, 221
   Cornish language texts   ix
   general   ix–x
   grammatical   299
   notes   x–xi
Abimelech   192
accidents (in philosophy and theology).
      See under Eucharistic theology
Achish of Gath   192
Act of Supremacy   44, 50, 71
Actes and Monuments. See under Foxe, John
Advent (parish)   47
aferan (Mass)   138, 204, 280, 288, 299.
      See also Eucharistic theology; Mass
aken, for *agan* (our)   118, 225, 260, 316
alaha. See *laha*
Allen, Pauline   202
Alley, William, bishop of Exeter   33, 57
Ambrose of Milan, (St)   167, 185
   De Mysteriis (De Iis)   167–8
   De Sacramentis   169–72, 212
   Ennarationes in 12 Psalmos Davidicos
      207–8
an, a (the)   222
an dzhei (in later usage, for 3 pl.)   222, 240
Anomoeanism (Eunomianism). See under
      Arianism
Anthropomorphism (heresy)   181
Antioch   157, 202
anti-semitism   163–4
Aquinas, Thomas, (St)   14, 160, 171, 196, 294
   Catena Aurea   17, 196
   Summa Theologica   183–4
Arianism   166, 167, 169
   Anomoeanism (Eunomianism)   200
Armada, Spanish   29
Arundell family of Lanherne   24, 29, 53
Ascham, Roger   26
Augustine of Hippo, (St)   150, 185, 187, 195
   Ad Fratres in Eremo   209
   Confessiones   204–5
   Contra Donatistas   194–5

   Contra Faustum   189–90
   De Cena Domini   209
   De Unitate Ecclesiae   150
   Enarrationes in Psalmos   187–9, 191–3
   Enchiridion   203–4
   In Joannis Evangelium Tractatus   209n,
      214–15, 217–19
   Pseudo-Augustine   212–13
   Sermones   209, 212–13
auxiliary verbs   222

Babington plot   29
Bacchus   189
badd (bad)   134, 273–4, 300
Baddesley Clinton, Warks.   51–2
Bailey, Lisa Kaaren   180
Barrett, Richard, merchant   46
Bartholomew, John, seaman   47
Basil the Great, (St)   185
begar(?) for *kepar* (as)   84, 226, 237, 300
beniiicter [benijicter?] (blessing)   144, 287,
      300
Beunans Ke   15n, 78, 278, 321, 325
Beunans Meriasek   59–61, 232, 321, 324–5
Bible, Welsh   27
Bice, Christopher   x, 12, 13
bilingualism   34n, 41, 223, 239, 298
Bilney, Thomas, preacher   64
bishops, required to report to Privy Council
      51
Bishops' Registers. See Registers
Black Rubric   156
Blaxton, John, treasurer of Exeter cathedral
      49
Bock, Albert   227
Bodewryd MS   225, 274, 282n, 297
Bodinar, William, of Mousehole   228, 298
Bodmin (priory)   49
Bonaventure   14
Bonner, Edmund, bishop of London   4,
      9–10, 15, 36, 68
   A Profitable and Necessarye Doctrine   9

An Honest Godly Instruction 10
Aunswere to certayne obiections 5, 13
Homelies 4, 5, 9–11, 13, 16, 18, 68
Book of Martyrs (*Actes and Monuments*).
  See under Foxe, John
Borlase family of Treluddra 53–4
bos (to be), late usages 223
  classification of forms 298
Boson, Nicholas, of Newlyn 222
Bossy, John 67
Bradbridge, William, bishop of Exeter 30
Brittany 45, 47, 50, 53, 72
  Bretons in Cornwall 46
  brezhoneg beleg (clerical Breton) 223
Brixiano, Bernardo, translator 157
Bronescombe, Walter, bishop of Exeter 58
Bruch, Benjamin xi, 10, 11, 16, 78, 291
buccellam 194, 272
Budock (parish) 33
Bull, Henry, rector of Courteenhall 63
bus (but) 92, 94, 104, 108, 223, 302, 311
Butler, Simon, vicar of St Clement 44

Camborne (parish) 35, 72
Campion, Edmund, (St) 29, 53, 69
Canon, Roman (Eucharistic prayer) 172, 210–11
  pre-Gelasian 169, 199n
Carew, George, archdeacon of Totnes 43
Carew, Sir Peter 53
Carselyk, William, pilgrim 46
Carvanell, Alexander, 'searcher' 45
Castello, Hadrian de, cardinal, bishop of Bath and Wells 36n
Castro, Fray Alfonso de 21
catenae 13, 17, 68, 163, 168, 173
Catholics
  safe houses and centres 22, 52, 73
  See also Counter-Reformation; Mary I; recusants
Ceres 189
chained libraries 26
chantries 57, 58, 205. See also priests
chaplains. See under priests
Chard, Thomas, bishop of Solubria 36, 49
Chaudhri, Talat 5, 10
Chedsey (Chidgey), William, archdeacon of Middlesex 51, 149n, 258; and constantly through the source text 95–121 and commentary 149–80
Chepstow (Cas-gwent) 72
Christ 65; and constantly through the edition 82–145 and the commentary 149–219

Chrysostom, John, (St) 152, 185, 276
  De Incomprehensibili Dei Natura 200
  De Sacerdotio 158
  De Statuis 157–8, 202
  Hom. in Act. Apost. 201
  Hom. in Jn 159
  Hom. in Mt 152, 154, 159
  Hom. in 1 Cor. 160, 190–1, 210
  Hom. in 2 Cor. 155
  In epistolam ad Phil. 202–3
  Pseudo-Chrysostom *Expositio in Psalmos* 153, 292
Church of England 37
church papism 37–9, 71
churchwardens' accounts 23
Cicero, Marcus Tullius 26
Clement IV, pope 183
Cock, Alexander, seaman 47
Coken, John 53
Colan (parish) 33
Cole, Henry, dean of St Paul's 51
Colmer, Christopher, vicar of St Allen 32
Colyton (parish in Devon) 49
Combellack, Myrna 60, 61n, 80
communion. See under Eucharistic theology
conditional 223
consecration. See under Eucharistic theology
Constantinople 152, 160, 163, 195, 199n, 200n, 202
contractions 224
Convocation (of 1553) 196–7
Cornish Catholics 38
  gentry 29, 38
Cornish language 3–4, 6–7, 9, 12, 14–16, 17, 18
  Celtic language 27
  clerical Cornish 223
  Cranmer's attitude to 11, 27
  English influence 224–5, 298
  geminate *ll* 227
  gender of nouns 297–8
  late features 18, 20, 221
  medieval drama 59
  Middle Cornish 28
  Tudor Cornish 28
corporaliter 140–1, 205, 206
Corpus Christi (feast) 14, 17
Corpus Dei 181
councils, Lateran IV 193
  Nicaea I 166, 196–8
  Nicaea II 161, 197–9
Counter-Reformation 13, 42, 67, 68–9
Coverdale, Miles, bishop of Exeter 59, 63

INDEX 349

cows(e), for *keusel* (to speak)   253
 (especially) and   104, 134, 140, 223,
   230, 274, 302
Craig, John   23
Crane, Henry, rector of Withiel   42
Cranmer, Thomas, archbishop of Canterbury
   9, 11, 14, 17, 18, 22, 147, 208
 choice of texts   26
 dialogues with Gardiner   217
 Disputation   26, 89, 91, 93
 views on Cornish language   11, 27
 views on Eucharist   148n, 149–56,
   158–85, 160, 162, 164, 168–9,
   170–3, 178–9, 194, 197, 206,
   207–11, 213, 217–18, 238
Creed (parish)   50
Creed (summary of faith)   167, 170, 203, 246
Crespin, Jean, reformer   65
Cromwell, Thomas, Lord Privy Seal   45
cross, sign (marked in MS)   214, 285
Crowan (parish)   35, 36, 48, 57, 72
crypto-papists   65. *See also* church papism
Cullompton (parish in Devon)   49
Cyprian of Carthage, (St)   185, 194
Cyril of Alexandria, (St)   185, 205–6
 In Jn Evang.   205–6

Damascus, John of, (St)   294
 De Fide Orthodoxa   294
David, King   192
Davies, John, translator, *Llyfr y Resolucion*
   226
Day, George, bishop of Chichester   9
Day, John, printer   64
Decretum (Decrees). *See* Gratian
definite article   222
deow habblys (Maundy Thursday)   140, 281,
   303
departed, prayer for   201–5
deprivations. *See under* Elizabeth I
der, dir(r) for *dre* (through)   86, 92, 96, 224,
   248
derag dorn(e) (beforehand)   104, 108, 110,
   253, 268, 303
destruction of images   58–9
Dickens, A.G.   67
dictation   224
dir(r). *See der*
disciplina arcani   167, 188
Disputations, Cambridge and Oxford (1549)
   21
 Heidelberg (1518)   21
 Leipzig (1519)   21

 Oxford (1554)   14, 16, 19, 20–2, 25
   (Eucharistic procession), 63, 66,
   68, 210
 Regensburg (1541)   21
 Zurich (1523)   21
 'disputing for his form'   21, 208
 textbooks   21
Dom(inus) (as title for priests)   33n, 60
Donatism   150–1
Douai (Douay)   38n, 71, 72n, 156n
Duffy, Eamon   29n, 37, 64, 67, 68
Duns Scotus, John (Bl.)   14, 182
 In Sententiarum   182–3

e ker, for *in kerth* (away)   136, 230, 275, 305
Easter initiation rites   167, 169
editorial method   77–81
Edward VI   11, 21, 22, 29, 37, 42, 57, 165, 205
Edwards, Ray   xi, 78, 81, 154
Edwards family of Plas Newydd, Chirk   3
Elijah (and Elisha)   157–8
Elizabeth I   22, 29, 37, 42, 73, 165
 accession   49, 51
 resignations and deprivations   50
 'settlement' of religion   50
Emissenus. *See* Eusebius 'Gallicanus'
Epiphanios, deacon   199
Epiphanius of Salamis, (St)   185
Erasmus, Desiderius, priest   23, 26
eternal life   174, 179, 210, 214, 256, 283
Eucharistic theology   149–219
 accidents and substance   213
 'by mouth'   153–6, 159
 communion and participation   190, 206
 consecration   168–70, 175, 177, 189, 210
 discerning the Body   152, 163
 figurative language   149, 172, 187–8,
   196, 199
 incarnational   161–2, 166, 176, 177, 187,
   195, 197, 206
 linking heaven and earth   156–60, 176,
   178, 192, 200
 Mass for the departed   201–5
 mixing of the chalice   175, 212
 'pledge'   178
 power of the Word of God   168, 171–5
 preparatory prayers   207
 propitiatory   201, 205
 real presence   151, 166, 171, 186, 188,
   197, 199, 208
 receptionism   171, 194
 sacramental principle   165–6, 169, 171,
   193, 195
 sacred species   174

sacrifice of the Mass   184, 198–9, 200–3, 206
'similitude'   173–5
touching Christ   159–62, 181
transelementation   215
transforming and satisfactory power   170, 184
transubstantiation   21, 24, 68, 149n, 182–3, 190, 193, 196–7, 200
unbloody sacrifice (*incruentem sacrificium*)   198–9, 276
unworthy reception   164, 165, 194, 196, 208–10
whole Christ   178
words of institution   168, 170, 172, 211
See also Cranmer, views on Eucharist
eulogia   206n
Eunomianism. *See under* Arianism
Eusebius 'Gallicanus' ('Emissenus')   180, 185
   Hom. de Corpore et Sanguine Christi   180–2
Eusebius of Caesarea   66, 185
Exeter (cathedral)   26, 36, 49, 50
   chapter   49
   St John's Priory   36

faith and works   215, 219
Fathers of the Church   157, 206, 281
fattellans ('how be they')   112, 255, 301, 305
Faustus of Milevum   189
Fécamp, Jean de   207
Feock (parish)   33
figura   187–8, 196, 216
final 'f'   224, 225
final (and medial) 'rth'   230–1, 250
fines for recusancy   38
Fisher, John, cardinal, bishop of Rochester   21
Flint (Fflint)   72–3
Folieto, Hugh de   294
Fowey   72
Foxe, John, historian   13, 22, 63–9
   Actes and Monuments   5, 14, 19, 20, 23–5, 64–5, 67, 79, 147
   Rerum (in Ecclesia) Gestarum   19n, 189n, 192n, 213n, 217
   notes quoted in SA   95
   use of Latin   20, 25, 63
Fulgentius of Ruspe, (St)   185, 211n, 264

gans ganow (by mouth)   86, 153, 156, 162, 239
   ganaw   246
   See also Eucharistic theology, 'by mouth'

Gardiner, Stephen, bishop of Winchester   9, 51, 217n
Gelasius of Cyzicus   196–8
Gendall, Richard   xi, 78
gender of Cornish nouns. *See under* Cornish language
Geneva Bible   179, 291–3
gentry, Cornish. *See* Cornish Catholics
George, Ken   224, 264, 297, 326
Gethsemane   194
Gladestry, Radnor   51–2
Glasney College (of Our Lady and St Thomas of Canterbury), Penryn   28, 34, 48, 57, 72
   canons (prebendaries)   28, 57
   dissolution   57
   parishes   33, 48
   school   57
Gluvias (parish)   33
Glyn (Glynn), William, bishop of Bangor   131, 190
Gnosticism   162, 177, 186, 195
Godfrey, Lawrence, vicar of Perranzabuloe   34
Godolphin, Sir William   47
grace through faith   219
grasce, for *gras* (thanks)   120, 179, 261, 269
Gratian   14, 17, 173, 181
Gregory the Great, (St), pope, *Regula Pastoralis*   158
Grisling, Peter, 'searcher'   45
gule (to do), late forms   226, 237, 299, 307
Gwavas, William, of Penzance   226
gwra marugian (be amazed)   120, 181, 262
gwyne (wine) for *chalys* (chalice)   130, 190

ha (and), before vowels   226, 235
Hadton. *See* Ton, Richard
Haigh, Christopher   67
haker, for *hager* (ugly)   96, 225, 245, 308
hardening of consonants   225, 245, 246, 250, 252, 260
Harding, Thomas, prebendary of Winchester   22, 71, 143, 207, 217
Harpsfield, John, archdeacon of London   4, 9, 51, 141, 147, 208–10, 281, 282, 283
Harpsfield, Nicholas, archdeacon of Canterbury   66
Hatcher, C.W.H.   xi, 78
Hawke, Andrew   xi, 10, 12, 81, 282n
Heath, Nicholas, archbishop of York   71
helma, for *hemma* (this, these)   90, 241, 308
Helston   72
Hendye, Humphrey (Humphridus)   38

INDEX

Hennessy's Incumbents   32
Henry VIII   29, 37, 43, 66, 211
Hereford (cathedral)   26
   bishop   50
   recusant enclave   50
hermeneutical method   147–8
Herolt, Johann, preacher and writer   294
Hervet, Gentian, canon of Rheims   154
Hewitt, John, Breton pilgrim   46
Heynes, Simon, dean of Exeter   58
Hilary of Poitiers, (St)   215
   De Trinitate   151, 166
Holy Souls   201, 205
Holy Spirit   216
horror cruoris   112, 113, 114, 115, 174, 216, 255, 258
Hoskin, John, of Truro   46
humanism   68
Humphrey, Lawrence, dean of Winchester   26
hypostatic union   206

i-affection   227
icons   65, 161, 199
imban, for *in ban* (up)   120, 262, 309
incarnation. *See* Eucharistic theology, incarnational
incruentem sacrificium. *See* Eucharistic theology, unbloody sacrifice
Ireland   30, 72
   Irish language   27, 282
   Old Irish   281, 286
Irenaeus, (St)   177, 179
   Adversus Haereses   177–9
Ivo of Chartres, (St)   14, 17

James family of Newlyn East   53
James II   53
Jenkins, Thomas   53
Jenner, Henry   15
Jerome, (St)   158
Jesuits   29, 37, 38
Jewel, John, bishop of Salisbury   22, 207, 217
Jews   163–4
John Chrysostom, (St). *See* Chrysostom, John
Jordan, William   236
Judas   155, 165, 194–6
Justin Martyr, (St)   26, 175
   Apologiae   175–7, 179, 291

Kea and Kenwyn (parish)   33
Kenall, John, vicar of Wendron   43
Kerrier (Kirrier), northern   72

Kilkhampton (parish)   38

laha, in *a laha*   144, 288–9, 299, 310
Lamb of God (*Agnus Dei*)   197
Lanherne. *See* Arundell family
Lantregar (Tréguier)   45
Last Supper   165, 185
Lateran. *See* councils
Latimer, Hugh, bishop of Worcester   14, 64, 66, 143, 147, 201–7, 211, 215
   views on Eucharist   200, 202–4
Latin, liturgical   170
   influence on Celtic languages   223
   and throughout the notes   233–89
Launceston Priory   36
lavar, for *lever* (say)   227, 234, 310
lavirta ge (you say)   226, 277, 310
lectus. *See tectum*
Lee, Rowland, bishop of Coventry and Lichfield   43
Lent and Holy Week   167
Leuven (Louvain)   22, 71
Lhuyd, Edward, naturalist and linguist   222, 224
Lincoln family of Newlyn East   53
liturgy   5, 14, 16, 27, 161–2, 170, 200–1, 211
   Divine Liturgy   161, 201, 206n, 208n
ll and *lh* in Cornish   227
Llandeilo-Talybont (St Teilo's)   16 and note
Logan, Richard   8
Lombard, Peter, bishop of Paris, *Libri Quatuor Sententiarum*   14, 17
Loo, John, Breton pilgrim   46
Louvain. *See* Leuven
lowarth, for *lowar* (many)   84, 88, 98, 124, 230, 236, 275, 310
Lyra, Nicolaus de   294

Mabe (parish)   48
MacCulloch, Diarmaid   68
Mackechnie, John   3, 12, 15
Magdalen [*Maudelyn*], ship   45
Maker (parish)   43
malla, from *may hallo* (so that)   96, 100, 130, 224, 227, 246, 248, 306, 310
mamb, for *mam* (mother)   84, 229, 236, 310
Manaccan (parish)   33, 36, 50
Manichaeism   189, 195
Marcion and Marcionism   186, 189
Martin, Gregory, priest   27n
Martyn, Richard, vicar of Newlyn East   42, 48, 50n, 72
Mary, Blessed Virgin   151, 170, 197
   title *Theotokos* (Mother of God)   181, 206

Mary, Queen of Scots 71
Mary I 4, 9, 22, 29, 33, 42, 67, 71, 72, 165, 197
   Church priorities 9–10, 13, 42, 67, 68–9
   Marian priests. *See under* priests
   persecution of heretics 66
Mass iv, 30, 38, 42, 68, 149n, 180, 184,
      199–207, 211, 280
   clandestine celebration of 30, 38
   See also Eucharistic theology; liturgy
Matthew, William, pilgrim 46
Mayer, Wendy 154n, 157n, 158n, 221n
Mayne, Cuthbert, (St) 38
mekys, for *megys* (fed) 96, 245–6, 310–11
mensa (altar table) 198
merito continge 181
Mevagissey (parish) 33
Michell, John, merchant and sailor 46
Milan 167
Milford Haven (Aberdaugleddau) 72
Military Survey (1522) 35, 46, 48
mirare 180
missal 207, 210
Monica, (St) 204
Monophysitism 197
Montacute, Priory of St Peter and St Paul 36
Montanism 162
Morebath (parish in Devon) 38
Morgan, William, bishop of St Asaph 27
mutations 228, 234, 267–8, 297
Mylor (parish) 33, 48–9, 72
mystical theology 208

Nablus (Neapolis) 175
Nadton. *See* Ton, Richard
Nance, Robert Morton x, 3, 8, 12, 13, 15, 25,
      31, 61, 80, 81, 194n, 202, 224, 278, 297;
      and throughout the notes
Nazianzen, Gregory, (St), *De Fuga* 158
ne gesee (he is not) 86, 228, 238, 301
ne gew [neg ew] (is not), for *nyns ew* 86, 130, 228, 301
Neath (Castell-nedd) 72
neophytes 167, 169
Nestorius 206
New Testament, Irish 27
Newlyn East (parish) 24, 36, 41, 44–5, 48, 50, 57, 72, 73
   recusant centre 53–4
Newport (Casnewydd) 72
Nicaea (Nice). *See under* councils
Northern Rebellion 71
not (Eng.) used in Cornish text 112, 124, 255, 273, 312

Nutcombe, Thomas, sub-dean of Exeter 49

O'Domhnuill, Uilliam (William Daniel), archbishop of Tuam 27
obtaynest (you obtain) 20, 114, 257, 312
Ockham, William of, friar 14
Oecumenius 'of Tricca', *Comm. in epistolam 1 Cor.* 163, 164–5
   confusion with Photius 163n, 164
Offa's dyke 52
Oglethorpe, Owen, bishop of Carlisle 83, 145, 149
Oldon, Ralph, vicar of Perranzabuloe 43
Oliver family of Newlyn East 53
Orme, Nicholas 43n, 45n
osa (after) 104, 108, 232, 250, 253, 287, 313
Otes, Richard, of Feock 46–7
owriek (false reading) 276
Owry, Amy and John 35
Oxford Disputations. *See under* Disputations
Oxford Movement 68

Padel, Oliver xi, 34n, 35n, 41n, 78
papal authority 21, 44
Parker, Matthew, archbishop of Canterbury 33
Parsons, Robert. *See* Persons
Passio Christi 154
Passover 186, 194
   Pask Onn 265
patristic texts 13, 15, 19, 21, 25
Paul, (St) 165
pecar, for *kepar* (like, as) 98, 226, 237, 247, 309, 313
peiadow (pejadow) for *pesadow* (prayer) 106, 116, 231, 252, 259, 313
Pendleton, Henry, canon of St Paul's 4, 9
Penkevill, Michael, seminarian 72
Penryn 57, 58
Pentreth, Richard, seminarian 18, 72
Penwith, eastern 72
Perranarworthal (parish) 48
Perranzabuloe (parish) 34, 43, 47
personalized forms of *bos* 223, 230, 255, 286
Persons (Parsons), Robert, Jesuit priest 66
Peter Martyr. *See* Vermigli, Peter Martyr
Philip II of Spain 21
Philip III of Spain 18
Photius I, archbishop of Constantinople 197. *See also under* Oecumenius
Pie (Pye), William, dean of Chichester 171, 215
pilgrimages 42, 45

INDEX

Pius V, pope 22
   Regnans in Excelsis 71
plurals 222, 226
Pole, Reginald, cardinal, archbishop of Canterbury 10
Polycarp, (St) 66, 175
Pool, Peter A.S. 10, 80n, 319
popell (people) 140, 226, 252, 284, 313
possessives 229
Prayer Book 38
   Rebellion (Western Rising, 1549) 11, 29
Prayer of Humble Access 178
pre-occlusion 229
preterite 229
priests, chantry 28, 205
   chaplains 28, 30, 31
   from Brittany 46
   'Marian' 29, 38, 51
   mission/seminary 13, 37
   secular 28
   seminary 13
   traditional/conservative 37–9
Privy Council 52, 53
propitiatory sacrifice. *See under* Eucharistic theology
Protestantism 22, 25
   proto-Protestants 65
Pseudo-Chrysostom. *See under* Chrysostom
Puleston family of Emral 3
Pythagoras 175

Q[uo]d, abbreviation 6 and note
Quo Vadis legend 156

Rabus, Ludwig, dean of Ulm 65
Rad Ton. *See* Ton, Richard
real presence. *See under* Eucharistic theology
reb (beside) 230, 243, 314
   rebta 92
recevest (you receive) 114, 257, 314
recevia, for *receva* (to receive) 134, 258, 273, 314
recusants 4, 18, 29, 37, 49–51, 53–4, 68
Registers, Bishops' (Exeter)
   Veysey 32
   Woolton 32
Regnans in Excelsis. *See under* Pius V
Rerum (in Ecclesia) Gestarum. *See under* Foxe, John
res ew (ought to) 230, 279, 282
reus erit (1 Cor. 11:27) 163, 246
revelation 182
revisionist approach 66, 67
Reynolds, Thomas, dean of Exeter 49

rhetoric 21
Ridley, Nicholas, bishop of London 14, 26, 63, 66, 125, 145, 147, 156–8, 171, 176, 184–200, 213, 215–17, 292
   views on the Eucharist 156, 158, 171, 185–6, 188–90, 192–3, 196–9, 216–17
Roche (parish) 46, 50
Rokeby, John, rector of St Erme 50
Roman Canon. *See* Canon, Roman
Rome, exiles in 38
Roscarrock, Nicholas 42
Rose, John, vicar of Maker 43
Rowe, Alice, recusant 53
Royal Institution of Cornwall 12, 53n, 80

Saak, Eric Leland 209n, 213n
Sacrament an Alter authorship 16–18, 44–5
   damage 13, 18
   date 13, 18, 23–5, 48, 72
   fragments 202, 277–9, 295–6
   title 5, 244
sacrifice of the Mass. *See under* Eucharistic theology
Salpyn, William, pilgrim 46
Sampson, John, curate of Mabe 48
Sanders, Nicholas, priest 22
Sara, G.C., rector of St Dennis 31
Saul, King 192
scholastic theology 14, 121, 183
scribal tradition 298–9
searchers (customs officials/spies) 45
secundum majestatem 218
seminary priests. *See under* priests
Septuagint 192
seran (false reading). *See aferan*
Seton, John, priest 156, 211
Sir (as title for priests) 33n
Sithney (parish) 33, 35, 72
Six Articles 211
Smart, John, prebendary of Exeter 50
Smith (Smyth), Richard, canon of Christ Church 71, 89, 91, 133, 137, 141, 156
Smith, A.S.D. x, 12, 80
species. *See* Eucharistic theology, sacred species
St Agnes (chapel of ease) 47
St Allen (parish) 4, 24, 31, 33–4, 36, 41, 47, 50, 72, 73
St Clement (parish) 43
St Columb Major (parish) 38, 50
St Enoder (parish) 33
St Erme (parish) 43, 50
St Goran (parish) 33

St Ives (Corn.)   24n, 72
St Just in Penwith (parish)   33
St Mawgan   54. *See also* Arundell family
St Nectan (chapel)   42
St Teilo's, National History Museum of Wales. *See* Llandeilo-Talybont
Stephens, Thomas, priest in Warwickshire and the Welsh borders   51
Stephyn, Thomas, vicar of Newlyn East   5, 7, 8, 12, 15–17, 22, 28, 36, 41–54, 61, 68–9, 71, 72–3
 authorship of SA   7–8, 17, 44–5
 chaplain of Mylor   48
 curate of Newlyn   42–5
 made vicar   41
 pilgrimage to Brittany   45–7
 possible alias (Trebilcok)   46
 'recusancy'   49–51
 references added to TH   148, 291–4, 297
 signature (autograph) and hand   7, 43–4, 77, 148
 theological perspective (throughout commentary)   149–219
 use of Cornish   20
 use of Foxe   24, 26
Stevyn, Thomas, priest in Devon   48–9
Stithians (parish)   35, 47
Stoics   175
Stoyle, Mark   29n
substance (in philosophy and theology). *See* Eucharistic theology
suffix of abstraction (*-enab*)   278
Summe Sacerdos (prayer)   207
surnames   41, 47n, 55
Sutton Coldfield   9, 49n, 59
Syed, Keith   x, xi, 78, 80

TAMO (The Acts and Monuments Online)   5n, 15, 20, 23–5, 66n, 79, 292; and cited constantly through the edition and commentary
Tavernier, Jean   160n, 173
Taylor, John, rector of St Erme   43
tectum   160
temere ab Apostolis (fragments of MS)   202, 277–9, 295
Temple (Jerusalem)   189
Tertullian   162, 195
 Adversus Marcionem   185–7
 De Resurrectione Carnis   162, 164–5, 178
the gee (to you)   108, 253, 304, 306
theffa (auxiliary use of *dos*)   82, 100, 128, 231, 235, 268, 282, 304, 316

Theophylact of Ohrid, (St)   195–6, 216, 274
 Enarratio in Evangelium Jn   216–17
 Enarratio in Evangelium Mt   195–6, 215–16
Theotokos (Mother of God). *See under* Mary, Blessed Virgin
thetha (to him/her/it)   7, 122, 232, 237, 263, 279, 316
Thomas, Charles   60
Thomas, Graham   15, 78
Thomas Aquinas, (St). *See* Aquinas
thoskas (learnt)   114, 224, 258, 304
Throckmorton plot   29
tithes, appropriation of   28
Ton, Richard (Rad Ton?) curate of Crowan   60–1, 72, 236
 author of *Beunans Meriasek*   59–60
 burial at Camborne   61
Tonkin, Phillip, chaplain of St Agnes   46–7
Townsend and Cattley (edition of Foxe)   79
traditionalist clergy   17, 29, 51, 67, 68–9
Tradrack, John, Breton first mate   46
transelementation. *See under* Eucharistic theology
translation   26, 27
transubstantiation. *See under* Eucharistic theology
Trebilcock, Thomas, 'priest of Newlyn'   46
Tregear, John, vicar of St Allen   3, 4, 6, 8, 13, 15–17, 28, 31–9, 49, 61, 68–9, 71, 72–3, 148
 burial/death   31, 38, 39
 'church papist' views   29, 37–9
 possible family connections   35
 translation methodologies   25–8
 use of Cornish   20
 vicar   31–4
 will   31
Tregear Manuscript   3–6, 8, 72–3, 78, 278
Tregian family of Golden   30
 Sir Francis   38
Tregonwell. *See* Owry   35
Tréguier, Brittany   45, 47
Tregythyowe, John, vicar of Mylor   48
Trehar, Pascow, of Newlyn   46
Trelobys, Ralph, vicar of Crowan and Newlyn East   36, 44, 46, 48, 55–61, 72
 canon (prebendary) of Glasney   57–8, 72
Treluddra. *See* Borlase family
Treruffe, William, vicar of St Allen   32, 36
Trescothick (Trescowthick), Simon, recusant   53
Tresham, William, canon of Christ Church   135, 193–5, 215, 272–4

Tresteyn, John, vicar of Newlyn East   35–6, 48–9
trials (Oxford, 1555)   22
trope   149–50, 233, 317
Truro   45, 46, 72
Trychay, Christopher, vicar of Morebath, Devon   37
Tunstall, Cuthbert, bishop of Durham   14, 17–18, 157, 158
Turberville, James, bishop of Exeter   11n, 42

unbloody sacrifice. *See under* Eucharistic theology

Valor Ecclesiasticus   33n, 56
   Veysey's *Valor*. *See under* Veysey
van Haemstede, Adrian, reformer   65
Vermigli, Peter Martyr, abbot and reformer   21, 22
Veysey, John, bishop of Exeter   9, 42, 59
   death   59
   involvement in Sutton Coldfield   59
   Valor (D&C 3688)   43, 57, 61
vicars   28
Vigilius, bishop of Thapsus   217, 264, 292
   Contra Eutychetem (Adversus Nestorium et Eutychem)   217
Vyvyan, Thomas, bishop of Megara   49

Wales   4, 9, 16, 38, 72–3
   Welsh Catholics   3n, 9, 38
   Welsh Marches (borders)   50, 52, 73
   See also Welsh language
Walsham, Alexandra   37, 68
Ward ('Master Warde' in Ridley's Disputation)   26, 119, 127, 129, 176, 186–8, 265, 267
watchers (spies)   24
Watson, Thomas, bishop of Lincoln   10, 68, 131, 135, 137, 191, 196, 198, 270, 275
Wells (cathedral)   36
Welsh Catholics. *See under* Wales
Welsh language   12, 27, 52n, 73, 222–6, 228, 233, 237, 244, 254, 266, 270, 278, 281, 283–4, 286, 298
Welsh Marches. *See under* Wales
Wendron (parish)   43
Western Rising. *See* Prayer Book, Rebellion
Weston, Hugh, dean of Windsor   14, 150n, 238, 261; and constantly through the source text 83–145 and commentary 150–218
Widow's Mite (Lk 21:2)   184
Williams, Nicholas   xi, 15, 78, 227, 297
Wizeman, William   69
Wood Bevington, Warks.   51–2
Wooding, Lucy   26, 67–8
worryb (answer)   104, 230, 250, 307, 318
worth, for *orth*   229, 237, 318
worthias (virgin)   84, 100, 104, 170, 231, 235, 268, 308

y^e (with superscript *e*) for *the* (to)   232, 234
Yendall, Robert, vicar of Menheniot   50
Young, John, canon of Ely   103–11, 168–73
yweth, for *ynweth* (also)   82, 233, 235, 318
   e weth   86, 249, 318

Zennor (parish)   33
Zwingli, Ulrich, priest and reformer   21

Ingram Content Group UK Ltd.
Milton Keynes UK
UKHW041337190723
425434UK00005B/23